# Microsoft® POWERPOINT® 2010
## COMPREHENSIVE

Gary B. Shelly
Susan L. Sebok

COURSE TECHNOLOGY
CENGAGE Learning™

SHELLY
CASHMAN
SERIES®

Australia • Brazil • Japan • Korea • Mexico • Singapore • Spain • United Kingdom • United States

# COURSE TECHNOLOGY
## CENGAGE Learning

**Microsoft® PowerPoint® 2010: Comprehensive**
**Gary B. Shelly, Susan L. Sebok**

Vice President, Publisher: Nicole Pinard

Executive Editor: Kathleen McMahon

Product Manager: Jon Farnham

Associate Product Manager: Aimee Poirier

Editorial Assistant: Aimee Poirier

Director of Marketing: Cheryl Costantini

Marketing Manager: Tristen Kendall

Marketing Coordinator: Adrienne Fung

Print Buyer: Julio Esperas

Director of Production: Patty Stephan

Content Project Manager: Jill Braiewa

Development Editor: Deb Kaufmann

Copyeditor: Troy Lilly

Proofreader: Karen Annett

Indexer: Rich Carlson

QA Manuscript Reviewers: Chris Scriver,
John Freitas, Serge Palladino, Susan Pedicini,
Danielle Shaw

Art Director: Marissa Falco

Cover Designer: Lisa Kuhn, Curio Press, LLC

Cover Photo: Tom Kates Photography

Text Design: Joel Sadagursky

Compositor: PreMediaGlobal

Microsoft and the Office logo are either registered trademarks or trademarks of Microsoft Corporation in the United States and/or other countries. Course Technology, a part of Cengage Learning, is an independent entity from the Microsoft Corporation, and not affiliated with Microsoft in any manner.

Library of Congress Control Number: 2010942460

International Edition:
ISBN-13: 978-0-538-74885-8
ISBN-10: 0-538-74885-0

Cengage Learning International Offices

**Asia**
www.cengageasia.com
tel: (65) 6410 1200

**Australia/New Zealand**
www.cengage.com.au
tel: (61) 3 9685 4111

**Brazil**
www.cengage.com.br
tel: (55) 11 3665 9900

**India**
www.cengage.co.in
tel: (91) 11 4364 1111

**Latin America**
www.cengage.com.mx
tel: (52) 55 1500 6000

**UK/Europe/Middle East/Africa**
www.cengage.co.uk
tel: (44) 0 1264 332 424

**Represented in Canada by**
**Nelson Education, Ltd.**
tel: (416) 752 9100 / (800) 668 0671
www.nelson.com

Cengage Learning is a leading provider of customized learning solutions with office locations around the globe, including Singapore, the United Kingdom, Australia, Mexico, Brazil, and Japan. Locate your local office at:
**www.cengage.com/global**

For product information: **www.cengage.com/international**
Visit your local office: **www.cengage.com/global**
Visit our corporate Web site: **www.cengage.com**

AVAILABILITY OF RESOURCES MAY DIFFER BY REGION. Check with your local Cengage Learning representative for details.

*We dedicate this book to the memory of James S. Quasney (1940 – 2009), who for 18 years co-authored numerous books with Tom Cashman and Gary Shelly and provided extraordinary leadership to the Shelly Cashman Series editorial team. As series editor, Jim skillfully coordinated, organized, and managed the many aspects of our editorial development processes and provided unending direction, guidance, inspiration, support, and advice to the Shelly Cashman Series authors and support team members. He was a trusted, dependable, loyal, and well-respected leader, mentor, and friend. We are forever grateful to Jim for his faithful devotion to our team and eternal contributions to our series.*

*The Shelly Cashman Series Team*

Printed in the United States of America
1 2 3 4 5 6 7 17 16 15 14 13 12 11

05502776

# Microsoft
# POWERPOINT® 2010
## COMPREHENSIVE

# Contents

# Microsoft **PowerPoint 2010**

## Appendices

# Preface

The Shelly Cashman Series® offers the finest textbooks in computer education. We are proud that since Mircosoft Office 4.3, our series of Microsoft Office textbooks have been the most widely used books in education. With each new edition of our Office books, we make significant improvements based on the software and comments made by instructors and students. For this Microsoft PowerPoint 2010 text, the Shelly Cashman Series development team carefully reviewed our pedagogy and analyzed its effectiveness in teaching today's Office student. Students today read less, but need to retain more. They need not only to be able to perform skills, but to retain those skills and know how to apply them to different settings. Today's students need to be continually engaged and challenged to retain what they're learning.

With this Microsoft PowerPoint 2010 text, we continue our commitment to focusing on the user and how they learn best.

## Objectives of This Textbook

*Microsoft PowerPoint 2010: Comprehensive* is intended for a ten- to fifteen-week period in a course that teaches PowerPoint 2010 as the primary component. No experience with a computer is assumed, and no mathematics beyond the high school freshman level is required. The objectives of this book are:

- To offer a comprehensive presentation of Microsoft PowerPoint 2010
- To expose students to practical examples of the computer as a useful tool
- To acquaint students with the proper procedures to create presentations suitable for coursework, professional purposes, and personal use
- To help students discover the underlying functionality of PowerPoint 2010 so they can become more productive
- To develop an exercise-oriented approach that allows learning by doing

## New to this Edition

*Microsoft PowerPoint 2010: Comprehensive* offers a number of new features and approaches, which improve student understanding, retention, transference, and skill in using PowerPoint 2010. The following enhancements will enrich the learning experience:

- Office 2010 and Windows 7: Essential Concepts and Skills chapter presents basic Office 2010 and Windows 7 skills.

- Streamlined first chapter allows the ability to cover more advanced skills earlier.

- Chapter topic redistribution offers concise chapters that ensure complete skill coverage.

- New pedagogical elements enrich material, creating an accessible and user-friendly approach.

  - Break Points, a new boxed element, identify logical stopping points and give students instructions regarding what they should do before taking a break.

  - Within step instructions, Tab | Group Identifiers, such as (Home tab | Bold button), help students more easily locate elements in the groups and on the tabs on the Ribbon.

  - Modified step-by-step instructions tell the student what to do and provide the generic reason why they are completing a specific task, which helps students easily transfer given skills to different settings.

## The Shelly Cashman Approach

### A Proven Pedagogy with an Emphasis on Project Planning

Each chapter presents a practical problem to be solved, within a project planning framework. The project orientation is strengthened by the use of Plan Ahead boxes, which encourage critical thinking about how to proceed at various points in the project. Step-by-step instructions with supporting screens guide students through the steps. Instructional steps are supported by the Q&A, Experimental Step, and BTW features.

### A Visually Engaging Book that Maintains Student Interest

The step-by-step tasks, with supporting figures, provide a rich visual experience for the student. Call-outs on the screens that present both explanatory and navigational information provide students with information they need when they need to know it.

### Supporting Reference Materials (Appendices and Quick Reference)

The appendices provide additional information about the Application at hand and include such topics as project planning guidelines and certification. With the Quick Reference, students can quickly look up information about a single task, such as keyboard shortcuts, and find page references of where in the book the task is illustrated.

### Integration of the World Wide Web

The World Wide Web is integrated into the PowerPoint 2010 learning experience by (1) BTW annotations; (2) BTW, Q&A, and Quick Reference Summary Web pages; and (3) the Learn It Online section for each chapter.

**End-of-Chapter Student Activities**

Extensive end-of-chapter activities provide a variety of reinforcement opportunities for students where they can apply and expand their skills.

## Instructor Resources

The Instructor Resources include both teaching and testing aids and can be accessed via CD-ROM or at login.cengage.com.

**Instructor's Manual** Includes lecture notes summarizing the chapter sections, figures and boxed elements found in every chapter, teacher tips, classroom activities, lab activities, and quick quizzes in Microsoft Word files.

**Syllabus** Easily customizable sample syllabi that cover policies, assignments, exams, and other course information.

**Figure Files** Illustrations for every figure in the textbook in electronic form.

**PowerPoint Presentations** A multimedia lecture presentation system that provides slides for each chapter. Presentations are based on chapter objectives.

**Solutions to Exercises** Includes solutions for all end-of-chapter and chapter reinforcement exercises.

**Test Bank & Test Engine** Test Banks include 112 questions for every chapter, featuring objective-based and critical thinking question types, and including page number references and figure references, when appropriate. Also included is the test engine, ExamView, the ultimate tool for your objective-based testing needs.

**Data Files for Students** Includes all the files that are required by students to complete the exercises.

**Additional Activities for Students** Consists of Chapter Reinforcement Exercises, which are true/false, multiple-choice, and short answer questions that help students gain confidence in the material learned.

---

**Book Resources**

🔒 Additional Faculty Files
🔒 Blackboard Testbank
🔒 Data Files
🔒 Instructor's Manual
🔒 Lecture Success System
🔒 PowerPoint Presentations
🔒 Solutions to Exercises
🔒 Syllabus
🔒 Test Bank and Test Engine
🔒 WebCT Testbank

Chapter Reinforcement Exercises

Student Downloads

---

## SAM: Skills Assessment Manager

SAM 2010 is designed to help bring students from the classroom to the real world. It allows students to train on and test important computer skills in an active, hands-on environment.

SAM's easy-to-use system includes powerful interactive exams, training, and projects on the most commonly used Microsoft Office applications. SAM simulates the Microsoft Office 2010 application environment, allowing students to demonstrate their knowledge and think through the skills by performing real-world tasks such as bolding word text or setting up slide transitions. Add in live-in-the-application projects, and students are on their way to truly learning and applying skills to business-centric documents.

Designed to be used with the Shelly Cashman Series, SAM includes handy page references so that students can print helpful study guides that match the Shelly Cashman textbooks used in class. For instructors, SAM also includes robust scheduling and reporting features.

## Content for Online Learning

Course Technology has partnered with the leading distance learning solution providers and class-management platforms today. To access this material, instructors will visit our password-protected instructor resources available at login.cengage.com. Instructor resources include the following: additional case projects, sample syllabi, PowerPoint presentations per chapter, and more. For additional information or for an instructor user name and password, please contact your sales representative. For students to access this material, they must have purchased a WebTutor PIN-code specific to this title and your campus platform. The resources for students may include (based on instructor preferences), but are not limited to: topic review, review questions, and practice tests.

## CourseNotes

Course Technology's CourseNotes are six-panel quick reference cards that reinforce the most important and widely used features of a software application in a visual and user-friendly format. CourseNotes serve as a great reference tool during and after the student completes the  course. CourseNotes are available for software applications such as Microsoft Office 2010, Word 2010, Excel 2010, Access 2010, PowerPoint 2010, and Windows 7. Topic-based CourseNotes are available for Best Practices in Social Networking, Hot Topics in Technology, and Web 2.0. Visit www.cengagebrain.com to learn more!

## A Guided Tour

Add excitement and interactivity to your classroom with "*A Guided Tour*" product line. Play one of the brief mini-movies to spice up your lecture and spark classroom discussion. Or, assign a movie for homework and ask students to complete the correlated assignment that accompanies each topic. "*A Guided Tour*" product line takes the prep work out of providing your students with information about new technologies and applications and helps keep students engaged with content relevant to their lives; all in under an hour!

## About Our Covers

The Shelly Cashman Series is continually updating our approach and content to reflect the way today's students learn and experience new technology. This focus on student success is reflected on our covers, which feature real students from the University of Rhode Island using the Shelly Cashman Series in their courses, and reflect the varied ages and backgrounds of the students learning with our books. When you use the Shelly Cashman Series, you can be assured that you are learning computer skills using the most effective courseware available.

# Textbook Walk-Through

The Shelly Cashman Series Pedagogy: Project-Based — Step-by-Step — Variety of Assessments

**Plan Ahead** boxes prepare students to create successful projects by encouraging them to think strategically about what they are trying to accomplish before they begin working.

**Step-by-Step** instructions now provide a context beyond the point-and-click. Each step provides information on why students are performing each task, or what will occur as a result.

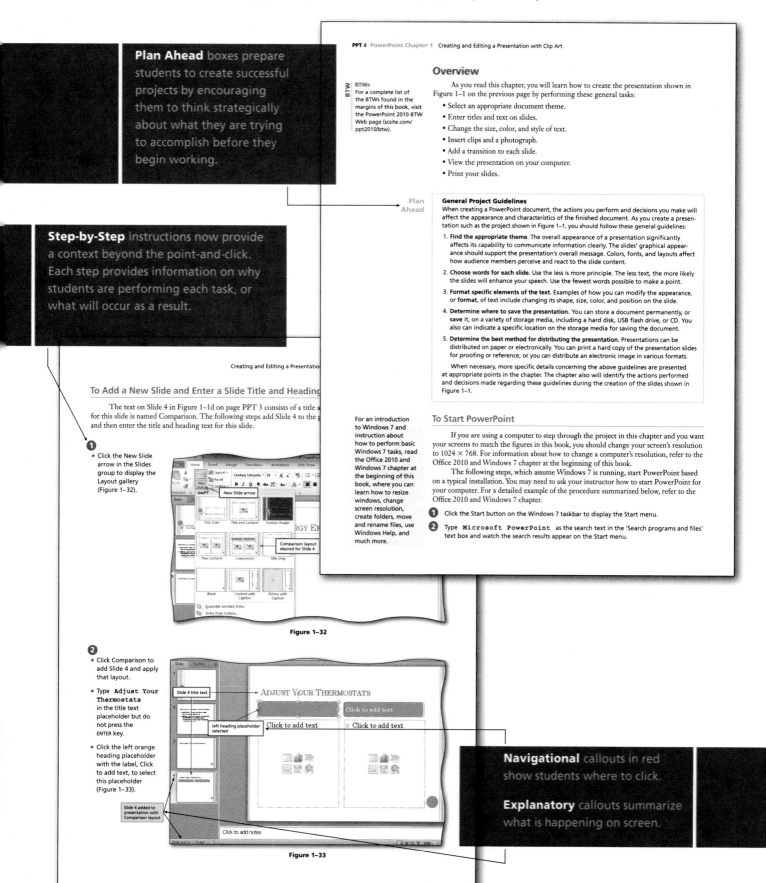

**BTW**
**BTWs**
For a complete list of the BTWs found in the margins of this book, visit the PowerPoint 2010 BTW Web page (scsite.com/ppt2010/btw).

## Overview

As you read this chapter, you will learn how to create the presentation shown in Figure 1–1 on the previous page by performing these general tasks:

- Select an appropriate document theme.
- Enter titles and text on slides.
- Change the size, color, and style of text.
- Insert clips and a photograph.
- Add a transition to each slide.
- View the presentation on your computer.
- Print your slides.

**Plan Ahead**

**General Project Guidelines**
When creating a PowerPoint document, the actions you perform and decisions you make will affect the appearance and characteristics of the finished document. As you create a presentation such as the project shown in Figure 1–1, you should follow these general guidelines:

1. **Find the appropriate theme.** The overall appearance of a presentation significantly affects its capability to communicate information clearly. The slides' graphical appearance should support the presentation's overall message. Colors, fonts, and layouts affect how audience members perceive and react to the slide content.

2. **Choose words for each slide.** Use the less is more principle. The less text, the more likely the slides will enhance your speech. Use the fewest words possible to make a point.

3. **Format specific elements of the text.** Examples of how you can modify the appearance, or **format**, of text include changing its shape, size, color, and position on the slide.

4. **Determine where to save the presentation.** You can store a document permanently, or **save** it, on a variety of storage media, including a hard disk, USB flash drive, or CD. You also can indicate a specific location on the storage media for saving the document.

5. **Determine the best method for distributing the presentation.** Presentations can be distributed on paper or electronically. You can print a hard copy of the presentation slides for proofing or reference, or you can distribute an electronic image in various formats.

When necessary, more specific details concerning the above guidelines are presented at appropriate points in the chapter. The chapter also will identify the actions performed and decisions made regarding these guidelines during the creation of the slides shown in Figure 1–1.

## To Start PowerPoint

If you are using a computer to step through the project in this chapter and you want your screens to match the figures in this book, you should change your screen's resolution to 1024 × 768. For information about how to change a computer's resolution, refer to the Office 2010 and Windows 7 chapter at the beginning of this book.

The following steps, which assume Windows 7 is running, start PowerPoint based on a typical installation. You may need to ask your instructor how to start PowerPoint for your computer. For a detailed example of the procedure summarized below, refer to the Office 2010 and Windows 7 chapter.

**1** Click the Start button on the Windows 7 taskbar to display the Start menu.

**2** Type **Microsoft PowerPoint** as the search text in the 'Search programs and files' text box and watch the search results appear on the Start menu.

For an introduction to Windows 7 and instruction about how to perform basic Windows 7 tasks, read the Office 2010 and Windows 7 chapter at the beginning of this book, where you can learn how to resize windows, change screen resolution, create folders, move and rename files, use Windows Help, and much more.

Creating and Editing a Presentation

### To Add a New Slide and Enter a Slide Title and Heading

The text on Slide 4 in Figure 1–1d on page PPT 3 consists of a title a for this slide is named Comparison. The following steps add Slide 4 to the p and then enter the title and heading text for this slide.

**1**
- Click the New Slide arrow in the Slides group to display the Layout gallery (Figure 1–32).

New Slide arrow

Comparison layout desired for Slide 4

**Figure 1–32**

**2**
- Click Comparison to add Slide 4 and apply that layout.

- Type **Adjust Your Thermostats** in the title text placeholder but do not press the ENTER key.

- Click the left orange heading placeholder with the label, Click to add text, to select this placeholder (Figure 1–33).

Slide 4 title text

ADJUST YOUR THERMOSTATS

left heading placeholder selected

Slide 4 added to presentation with Comparison layout

**Figure 1–33**

**Navigational** callouts in red show students where to click.

**Explanatory** callouts summarize what is happening on screen.

# Textbook Walk-Through

## To Move Manually through Slides in a Slide Show

After you begin Slide Show view, you can move forward or backward through the slides. PowerPoint allows you to advance through the slides manually or automatically. During a slide show, each slide in the presentation shows on the screen, one slide at a time. Each time you click the mouse button, the next slide appears. The following steps move manually through the slides.

**1**
- Click each slide until Slide 5 (Be Green) is displayed (Figure 1–73).

**Q&A** I see a small toolbar in the lower-left corner of my slide. What is this toolbar?
The Slide Show toolbar appears when you begin running a slide show and then move the mouse pointer. The buttons on this toolbar allow you to navigate to the next slide, the previous slide, to mark up the current slide, or to change the current display.

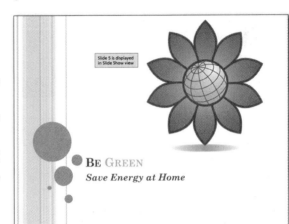

**Figure 1–73**

**2**
- Click the More button (Design tab | Themes group) to expand the gallery, which shows more Built-In theme gallery options (Figure 1–3).

**Experiment**
- Point to various document themes in the Themes gallery and watch the colors and fonts change on the title slide.

**Q&A** Are the themes displayed in a specific order?
Yes. They are arranged in alphabetical order running from left to right. If you point to a theme, a ScreenTip with the theme's name appears on the screen.

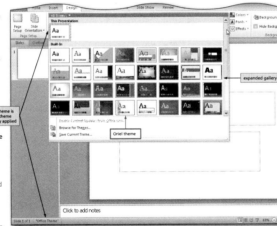

**Figure 1–3**

**Q&A** What if I change my mind and do not want to select a new theme?
Click anywhere outside the All Themes gallery to close the gallery.

**3**
- Click the Oriel theme to apply this theme to Slide 1 (Figure 1–4).

**Q&A** If I decide at some future time that this design does not fit the theme of my presentation, can I apply a different design?
Yes. You can repeat these steps at any time while creating your presentation.

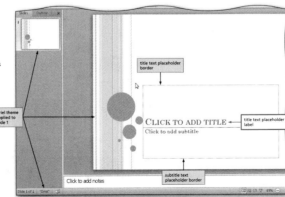

**Figure 1–4**

**Break Points** identify logical breaks in the chapter if students need to stop before completing the project.

**Break Point:** If you wish to take a break, this is a good place to do so. You can quit PowerPoint now (refer to page PPT 50 for instructions). To resume at a later time, start PowerPoint (refer to pages PPT 4 and PPT 5 for instructions), open the file called Saving Energy (refer to pages PPT 50 and PPT 51 for instructions), and continue following the steps from this location forward.

Resizing Clip Art and Photographs

**Chapter Summary** A concluding paragraph, followed by a listing of the tasks completed within a chapter together with the pages on which the step-by-step, screen-by-screen explanations appear.

## To Quit PowerPoint

The project now is complete. The following steps quit PowerPoint. For a detailed example of the procedure summarized below, refer to the Office 2010 and Windows 7 chapter at the beginning of this book.

**1** If you have one PowerPoint document open, click the Close button on the right side of the title bar to close the document and quit PowerPoint; or if you have multiple PowerPoint documents open, click File on the Ribbon to open the Backstage view and then click Exit in the Backstage view to close all open documents and quit PowerPoint.

**2** If a Microsoft Office PowerPoint dialog box appears, click the Save button to save any changes made to the document since the last save.

## Chapter Summary

In this chapter you have learned how to apply a document theme, create a title slide and text slides with a bulleted list, clip art, and a photograph, size and move clip art and a photograph, format and edit text, add a slide transition, ... and print slides as handouts. The items listed below include all the new ...chapter.

20. Insert a Clip from the Clip Organizer into the Title Slide (PPT 27)
...ph (PPT 9)
21. Insert a Clip from the Clip Organizer into a Content Placeholder (PPT 30)
22. Insert a Photograph from the Clip Organizer into a Slide without a Content Placeholder (PPT 32)
23. Resize Clip Art (PPT 33)
24. Move Clips (PPT 36)
25. Duplicate a Slide (PPT 38)
...ist
26. Arrange a Slide (PPT 39)
27. Delete Text in a Placeholder (PPT 41)
17)
28. Add a Transition between Slides (PPT 43)
29. Change Document Properties (PPT 46)
(PPT 21)
30. Save an Existing Presentation with the Same File Name (PPT 47)
...e and
31. Start Slide Show View (PPT 47)
32. Move Manually through Slides in a Slide Show (PPT 49)
(PPT 25)
33. Quit PowerPoint (PPT 50)
34. Open a Document from PowerPoint (PPT 50)
35. Print a Presentation (PPT 51)

## Learn It Online

Test your knowledge of chapter content and key terms.

*Instructions:* To complete the Learn It Online exercises, start your browser, click the Address bar, and then enter the Web address **scsite.com/ppt2010/learn**. When the PowerPoint 2010 Learn It Online page is displayed, click the link for the exercise you want to complete and then read the instructions.

**Chapter Reinforcement TF, MC, and SA**
A series of true/false, multiple choice, and short answer questions that test your knowledge of the chapter content.

**Flash Cards**
An interactive learning environment where you identify chapter key terms associated with displayed definitions.

**Practice Test**
A series of multiple choice questions that test your knowledge of chapter content and key terms.

**Who Wants To Be a Computer Genius?**
An interactive game that challenges your knowledge of chapter content in the style of a television quiz show.

**Wheel of Terms**
An interactive game that challenges your knowledge of chapter key terms in the style of the television show *Wheel of Fortune*.

**Crossword Puzzle Challenge**
A crossword puzzle that challenges your knowledge of key terms presented in the chapter.

## Apply Your Knowledge

Reinforce the skills and apply the concepts you learned in this chapter.

**Modifying Character Formats and Paragraph Levels and Moving a Clip**
*Note:* To complete this assignment, you will be required to use the Data Files for Students. See the inside back cover of this book for instructions on downloading the Data Files for Students, or contact your instructor for information about accessing the required files.

*Instructions:* Start PowerPoint. Open the presentation, Apply 1-1 Flu Season, from the Data Files for Students.
The two slides in the presentation discuss ways to avoid getting or spreading the flu. The document you open is an unformatted presentation. You are to modify the document theme, indent the paragraphs, resize and move the clip art, and format the text so the slides look like Figure 1–77 on the next page.

**Learn It Online** Every chapter features a Learn It Online section that is comprised of six exercises. These exercises include True/False, Multiple Choice, Short Answer, Flash Cards, Practice Test, and Learning Games.

**Apply Your Knowledge** This exercise usually requires students to open and manipulate a file from the Data Files that parallels the activities learned in the chapter. To obtain a copy of the Data Files for Students, follow the instructions on the inside back cover of this text.

*Continued >*

# Textbook Walk-Through

## Extend Your Knowledge

Extend the skills you learned in this chapter and experiment with new skills. You may need to use Help to complete the assignment.

Changing Slide Theme, Layout, and Text

*Note:*    To complete this assignment, you will be required to use the Data Files for Students. See the inside back cover of this book for instructions on downloading the Data Files for Students, or contact your instructor for information about accessing the required files.

*Instructions:*    Start PowerPoint. Open the presentation that you are going to prepare for your dental hygiene class, Extend 1–1 Winning Smile, from the Data Files for Students.
   You will choose a theme, format slides, and create a closing slide.

*Perform the following tasks:*
1. Apply an appropriate document theme.
2. On Slide 1, use your name in place of Student Name. Format the text on this slide using techniques you learned in this chapter, such as changing the font size and color and also bolding and italicizing words.
3. On Slide 2, change the slide layout and adjust the paragraph levels so that the lines of text are arranged under two headings: Discount Dental and Dental Insurance (Figure 1–78).
4. On Slide 3, create paragraphs and adjust the paragraph levels to create a bulleted list. Edit the text so that the slide meets the 7 × 7 rule, which states that each line should have a maximum of seven words,  and each slide should have  a maximum of seven lines.
5. Create an appropriate closing slide using the title slide as a guide.
6. The slides contain a variety of clips downloaded from the Microsoft Clip Organizer. Size and move them when necessary.
7. Apply an appropriate transition to all slides.
8. Change the document properties, as specified by your instructor. Save the presentation using the file name, Extend 1–1 Dental Plans.
9. Submit the revised document in the format specified by your instru

**Extend Your Knowledge** projects at the end of each chapter allow students to extend and expand on the skills learned within the chapter. Students use critical thinking to experiment with new skills to complete each project.

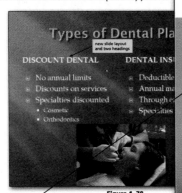

**Figure 1–78**

## Make It Right

Analyze a presentation and correct all errors and/or improve the design.

Correcting Formatting and List Levels

*Note:*    To complete this assignment, you will be required to use the Data Files for Students. See the inside back cover of this book for instructions on downloading the Data Files for Students, or contact your instructor for information about accessing the required files.

*Instructions:*    Start PowerPoint. Open the presentation, Make It Right 1–1 Air Ducts, from the Data Files for Students.
   Members of your homeowners' association are having their semiannual meeting, and each member of the board is required to give a short presentation on the subject of energy savings. You have decided to discuss the energy-saving benefits of maintaining the air ducts in your home. Correct the formatting problems and errors in the presentation while keeping in mind the guidelines presented in this chapter.

*Perform the following tasks:*
1. Change the document theme from Origin, shown in Figure 1–79, to Module.
2. On Slide 1, replace the words, Student Name, with your name. Format your name so that it displays prominently on the slide.
3. Increase the size of the clip on Slide 1 and move it to the upper-right corner.
4. Move Slide 2 to the end of the presentation so that it becomes the new Slide 3.
5. On Slide 2, correct the spelling errors and then increase the font size of the Slide 2 title text, Check Hidden Air Ducts, to 54 point. Increase the size of the clip and move it up to fill the white space on the right of the bulleted list.
6. On Slide 3, correct the spelling errors and then change the font size of the title text, Energy Savings, to 54 point. Increase the indent levels for paragraphs 2 and 4. Increase the size of the clips. Center the furnace clip at the bottom of the slide.
7. Change the document properties, as specified by your instructor. Save the presentation using the file name, Make It Right 1–1 Ducts Presentation.
8. Apply the same transition and duration to all slides.
9. Submit the revised document in the format specified by your instructor.

**Make It Right** projects call on students to analyze a file, discover errors in it, and fix them using the skills they learned in the chapter.

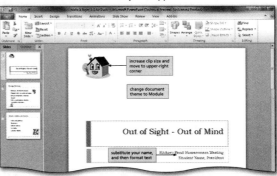

**Figure 1–79**

## In the Lab

Design and/or create a presentation using the guidelines, concepts, and skills presented in this chapter. Labs 1, 2, and 3 are listed in order of increasing difficulty.

**Lab1: Creating a Presentation with Bulleted Lists, a Closing Slide, and Clips**

*Problem:* You are working with upper-level students to host a freshmen orientation seminar. When you attended this seminar, you received some helpful tips on studying for exams. Your contribution to this year's seminar is to prepare a short presentation on study skills. You develop the outline shown in Figure 1–80 and then prepare the PowerPoint presentation shown in Figures 1–81a through 1–81d.

**Studying for an Exam**
Freshmen Orientation Seminar
Sarah Jones

**Prepare in Advance**
Location
    Quiet, well-lit
Timing
    15-minute breaks every hour
Material
    Quiz yourself

**Exam Time**
Day of Exam
    Rest properly
    Eat a good meal
    Wear comfy clothes
    Be early
    Be confident

*Perform the following tasks:*

1. Create a new presentation using the Aspect document theme.
2. Using the typed notes illustrated in Figure 1–80, create the title slide shown in Figure 1–81a, using your name in place of Sarah Jones. Italicize your name and increase the font size to 24 point. Increase the font size of the title text paragraph, Hit the Books, to 48 point. Increase the font size of the first paragraph of the subtitle text, Studying for an Exam, to 28 point.

**In the Lab** Three all new in-depth assignments per chapter require students to utilize the chapter concepts and techniques to solve problems on a computer.

**Cases & Places** exercises call on students to create open-ended projects that reflect academic, personal, and business settings.

---

## Cases and Places

Apply your creative thinking and problem-solving skills to design and implement a solution.

*Note:* To complete these assignments, you may be required to use the Data Files for Students. See the inside back cover of this book for instructions on downloading the Data Files for Students, or contact your instructor for information about accessing the required files.

As you design the presentations, remember to use the 7 × 7 rule: a maximum of seven words on a line and a maximum of seven lines on one slide.

**1: Design and Create a Presentation about Galileo**

**Academic**

Italian-born Galileo is said to be the father of modern science. After the invention of the telescope by a Dutch eyeglass maker named Hans Lippershey, Galileo made his own telescope and made many discoveries. You decide to prepare a PowerPoint presentation to accompany a speech that is required in your Astronomy class. You create the outline shown in Figure 1–88 about Galileo. Use this outline, along with the concepts and techniques presented in this chapter, to develop and format a slide show with a title slide and three text slides with bulleted lists. Add photographs and clip art from the Microsoft Clip Organizer and apply a transition. Submit your assignment in the format specified by your instructor.

**Galileo Galilei**
    Father of Modern Science
    Astronomy 201
    Sandy Wendt

**Major Role in Scientific Revolution**
February 15, 1564 - January 8, 1642
    Physicist
    Mathematician
    Astronomer
    Philosopher

**Galileo's Research Years**
    1581 - Studied medicine
    1589-1592 - Studied math and physics
    1592-1607 - Padua University
        Developed Law of Inertia
    1609 - Built telescope
        Earth's moon
        Jupiter's moons

**Galileo's Later Years**
    Dialogue - Two Chief World Systems
        Controversy develops
    1633 - Rome
        Heresy trial
        Imprisoned
    1642 - Dies

**Figure 1–88**

# Microsoft® POWERPOINT® 2010

COMPREHENSIVE

# Office 2010 and Windows 7: Essential Concepts and Skills

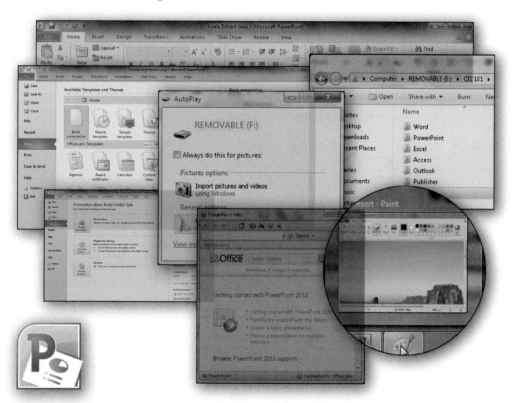

## Objectives

You will have mastered the material in this chapter when you can:

- Perform basic mouse operations
- Start Windows and log on to the computer
- Identify the objects on the Windows 7 desktop
- Identify the programs in and versions of Microsoft Office
- Start a program
- Identify the components of the Microsoft Office Ribbon

- Create folders
- Save files
- Change screen resolution
- Perform basic tasks in Microsoft Office programs
- Manage files
- Use Microsoft Office Help and Windows Help

# Office 2010 and Windows 7: Essential Concepts and Skills

## Office 2010 and Windows 7

This introductory chapter uses PowerPoint 2010 to cover features and functions common to Office 2010 programs, as well as the basics of Windows 7.

## Overview

As you read this chapter, you will learn how to perform basic tasks in Windows and PowerPoint by performing these general activities:

- Start programs using Windows.
- Use features in PowerPoint that are common across Office programs.
- Organize files and folders.
- Change screen resolution.
- Quit programs.

## Introduction to the Windows 7 Operating System

**Windows 7** is the newest version of Microsoft Windows, which is the most popular and widely used operating system. An **operating system** is a computer program (set of computer instructions) that coordinates all the activities of computer hardware such as memory, storage devices, and printers, and provides the capability for you to communicate with the computer.

The Windows 7 operating system simplifies the process of working with documents and programs by organizing the manner in which you interact with the computer. Windows 7 is used to run **application software**, which consists of programs designed to make users more productive and/or assist them with personal tasks, such as word processing.

Windows 7 has two interface variations, Windows 7 Basic and Windows 7 Aero. Computers with up to 1 GB of RAM display the Windows 7 Basic interface (Figure 1a). Computers with more than 1 GB of RAM also can display the Windows Aero interface (Figure 1b), which provides an enhanced visual appearance. The Windows 7 Professional, Windows 7 Enterprise, Windows 7 Home Premium, and Windows 7 Ultimate editions have the capability to use Windows Aero.

## Using a Mouse

Windows users work with a mouse that has at least two buttons. For a right-handed user, the left button usually is the primary mouse button, and the right mouse button is the secondary mouse button. Left-handed people, however, can reverse the function of these buttons.

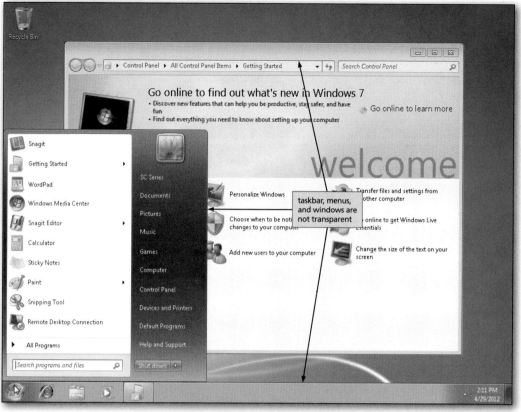

**(a) Windows 7 Basic Interface**

**(b) Windows 7 Aero Interface**

**Figure 1**

Table 1 explains how to perform a variety of mouse operations. Some programs also use keys in combination with the mouse to perform certain actions. For example, when you hold down the CTRL key while rolling the mouse wheel, text on the screen becomes larger or smaller based on the direction you roll the wheel. The function of the mouse buttons and the wheel varies depending on the program.

| Table 1 Mouse Operations | | |
| --- | --- | --- |
| **Operation** | **Mouse Action** | **Example*** |
| Point | Move the mouse until the pointer on the desktop is positioned on the item of choice. | Position the pointer on the screen. |
| Click | Press and release the primary mouse button, which usually is the left mouse button. | Select or deselect items on the screen or start a program or program feature. |
| Right-click | Press and release the secondary mouse button, which usually is the right mouse button. | Display a shortcut menu. |
| Double-click | Quickly press and release the left mouse button twice without moving the mouse. | Start a program or program feature. |
| Triple-click | Quickly press and release the left mouse button three times without moving the mouse. | Select a paragraph. |
| Drag | Point to an item, hold down the left mouse button, move the item to the desired location on the screen, and then release the left mouse button. | Move an object from one location to another or draw pictures. |
| Right-drag | Point to an item, hold down the right mouse button, move the item to the desired location on the screen, and then release the right mouse button. | Display a shortcut menu after moving an object from one location to another. |
| Rotate wheel | Roll the wheel forward or backward. | Scroll vertically (up and down). |
| Free-spin wheel | Whirl the wheel forward or backward so that it spins freely on its own. | Scroll through many pages in seconds. |
| Press wheel | Press the wheel button while moving the mouse. | Scroll continuously. |
| Tilt wheel | Press the wheel toward the right or left. | Scroll horizontally (left and right). |
| Press thumb button | Press the button on the side of the mouse with your thumb. | Move forward or backward through Web pages and/or control media, games, etc. |

*Note: The examples presented in this column are discussed as they are demonstrated in this chapter.

## Scrolling

A **scroll bar** is a horizontal or vertical bar that appears when the contents of an area may not be visible completely on the screen (Figure 2). A scroll bar contains **scroll arrows** and a **scroll box** that enable you to view areas that currently cannot be seen. Clicking the up and down scroll arrows moves the screen content up or down one line. You also can click above or below the scroll box to move up or down a section, or drag the scroll box up or down to move up or down to move to a specific location.

## Shortcut Keys

In many cases, you can use the keyboard instead of the mouse to accomplish a task. To perform tasks using the keyboard, you press one or more keyboard keys, sometimes identified as

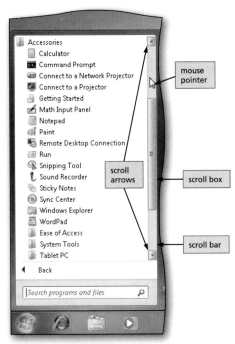

**Figure 2**

a **shortcut key** or **keyboard shortcut**. Some shortcut keys consist of a single key, such as the F1 key. For example, to obtain help about Windows 7, you can press the F1 key. Other shortcut keys consist of multiple keys, in which case a plus sign separates the key names, such as CTRL+ESC. This notation means to press and hold down the first key listed, press one or more additional keys, and then release all keys. For example, to display the Start menu, press CTRL+ESC, that is, hold down the CTRL key, press the ESC key, and then release both keys.

## Starting Windows 7

It is not unusual for multiple people to use the same computer in a work, educational, recreational, or home setting. Windows 7 enables each user to establish a **user account**, which identifies to Windows 7 the resources, such as programs and storage locations, a user can access when working with a computer.

Each user account has a user name and may have a password and an icon, as well. A **user name** is a unique combination of letters or numbers that identifies a specific user to Windows 7. A **password** is a private combination of letters, numbers, and special characters associated with the user name that allows access to a user's account resources. A **user icon** is a picture associated with a user name.

When you turn on a computer, an introductory screen consisting of the Windows logo and copyright messages is displayed. The Windows logo is animated and glows as the Windows 7 operating system is loaded. After the Windows logo appears, depending on your computer's settings, you may or may not be required to log on to the computer. **Logging on** to a computer opens your user account and makes the computer available for use. If you are required to log on to the computer, the **Welcome screen** is displayed, which shows the user names of users on the computer (Figure 3). Clicking the user name or picture begins the process of logging on to the computer.

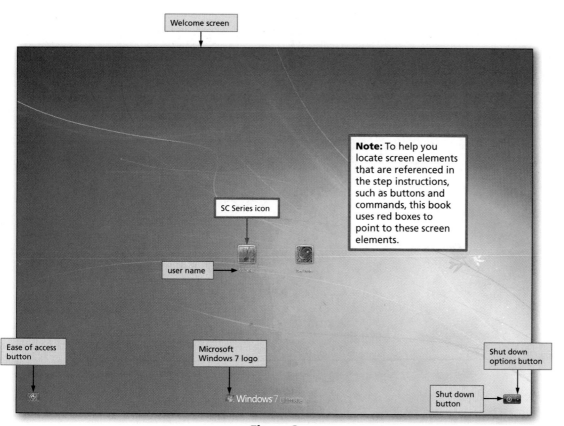

**Figure 3**

At the bottom of the Welcome screen is the 'Ease of access' button, the Windows 7 logo, a Shut down button, and a 'Shut down options' button. The following list identifies the functions of the buttons and commands that typically appear on the Welcome screen:

- Clicking the 'Ease of access' button displays the Ease of Access Center, which provides tools to optimize your computer to accommodate the needs of the mobility, hearing, and vision impaired users.
- Clicking the Shut down button shuts down Windows 7 and the computer.
- Clicking the 'Shut down options' button, located to the right of the Shut down button, provides access to a menu containing commands that perform actions such as restarting the computer, putting the computer in a low-powered state, and shutting down the computer. The commands available on your computer may differ.
  - The **Restart command** closes open programs, shuts down Windows 7, and then restarts Windows 7 and displays the Welcome screen.
  - The **Sleep command** waits for Windows 7 to save your work and then turns off the computer fans and hard disk. To wake the computer from the Sleep state, press the power button or lift a notebook computer's cover, and log on to the computer.
  - The **Shut down command** shuts down and turns off the computer.

## To Log On to the Computer

After starting Windows 7, you might need to log on to the computer. The following steps log on to the computer based on a typical installation. You may need to ask your instructor how to log on to your computer. This set of steps uses SC Series as the user name. The list of user names on your computer will be different.

- Click the user icon (SC Series, in this case) on the Welcome screen (shown in Figure 3 on the previous page); depending on settings, this either will display a password text box (Figure 4) or will log on to the computer and display the Windows 7 desktop.

**Q&A** Why do I not see a user icon?

Your computer may require you to type a user name instead of clicking an icon.

**Q&A** What is a text box?

A text box is a rectangular box in which you type text.

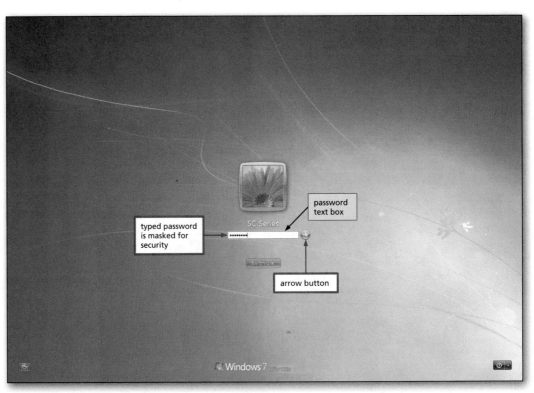

**Figure 4**

**Q&A** Why does my screen not show a password text box?

Your account does not require a password.

**2**

- If Windows 7 displays a password text box, type your password in the text box and then click the arrow button to log on to the computer and display the Windows 7 desktop (Figure 5).

**Q&A**

Why does my desktop look different from the one in Figure 5?

The Windows 7 desktop is customizable, and your school or employer may have modified the desktop to meet its needs. Also, your screen resolution, which affects the size of the elements on the screen, may differ from the screen resolution used in this book. Later in this chapter, you learn how to change screen resolution.

Figure 5

## The Windows 7 Desktop

The Windows 7 desktop (Figure 5) and the objects on the desktop emulate a work area in an office. Think of the Windows desktop as an electronic version of the top of your desk. You can perform tasks such as placing objects on the desktop, moving the objects around the desktop, and removing items from the desktop.

When you start a program in Windows 7, it appears on the desktop. Some icons also may be displayed on the desktop. For instance, the icon for the **Recycle Bin**, the location of files that have been deleted, appears on the desktop by default. A **file** is a named unit of storage. Files can contain text, images, audio, and video. You can customize your desktop so that icons representing programs and files you use often appear on your desktop.

## Introduction to Microsoft Office 2010

**Microsoft Office 2010** is the newest version of Microsoft Office, offering features that provide users with better functionality and easier ways to work with the various files they create. These features include enhanced design tools, such as improved picture formatting tools and new themes, shared notebooks for working in groups, mobile versions of Office programs, broadcast presentation for the Web, and a digital notebook for managing and sharing multimedia information.

# Microsoft Office 2010 Programs

Microsoft Office 2010 includes a wide variety of programs such as Word, PowerPoint, Excel, Access, Outlook, Publisher, OneNote, InfoPath, SharePoint Workspace, Communicator, and Web Apps:

- **Microsoft Word 2010**, or Word, is a full-featured word processing program that allows you to create professional-looking documents and revise them easily.
- **Microsoft PowerPoint 2010**, or PowerPoint, is a complete presentation program that allows you to produce professional-looking presentations.
- **Microsoft Excel 2010**, or Excel, is a powerful spreadsheet program that allows you to organize data, complete calculations, make decisions, graph data, develop professional-looking reports, publish organized data to the Web, and access real-time data from Web sites.
- **Microsoft Access 2010**, or Access, is a database management system that allows you to create a database; add, change, and delete data in the database; ask questions concerning the data in the database; and create forms and reports using the data in the database.
- **Microsoft Outlook 2010**, or Outlook, is a communications and scheduling program that allows you to manage e-mail accounts, calendars, contacts, and access to other Internet content.
- **Microsoft Publisher 2010**, or Publisher, is a desktop publishing program that helps you create professional-quality publications and marketing materials that can be shared easily.
- **Microsoft OneNote 2010**, or OneNote, is a note-taking program that allows you to store and share information in notebooks with other people.
- **Microsoft InfoPath 2010**, or InfoPath, is a form development program that helps you create forms for use on the Web and gather data from these forms.
- **Microsoft SharePoint Workspace 2010**, or SharePoint, is collaboration software that allows you to access and revise files stored on your computer from other locations.
- **Microsoft Communicator** is communications software that allows you to use different modes of communications such as instant messaging, videoconferencing, and sharing files and programs.
- **Microsoft Web Apps** is a Web application that allows you to edit and share files on the Web using the familiar Office interface.

# Microsoft Office 2010 Suites

A **suite** is a collection of individual programs available together as a unit. Microsoft offers a variety of Office suites. Table 2 lists the Office 2010 suites and their components.

Programs in a suite, such as Microsoft Office, typically use a similar interface and share features. In addition, Microsoft Office programs use **common dialog boxes** for performing actions such as opening and saving files. Once you are comfortable working with these elements and this interface and performing tasks in one program, the similarity can help you apply the knowledge and skills you have learned to other Office programs. For example, the process for saving a file in PowerPoint is the same in Word, Excel, and the other Office programs. While briefly showing how to use PowerPoint, this chapter illustrates some of the common functions across the Office programs and also identifies the characteristics unique to PowerPoint.

| Table 2 Microsoft Office 2010 Suites | | | | | |
|---|---|---|---|---|---|
| | Microsoft Office Professional Plus 2010 | Microsoft Office Professional 2010 | Microsoft Office Home and Business 2010 | Microsoft Office Standard 2010 | Microsoft Office Home and Student 2010 |
| Microsoft Word 2010 | ✔ | ✔ | ✔ | ✔ | ✔ |
| Microsoft PowerPoint 2010 | ✔ | ✔ | ✔ | ✔ | ✔ |
| Microsoft Excel 2010 | ✔ | ✔ | ✔ | ✔ | ✔ |
| Microsoft Access 2010 | ✔ | ✔ | ✗ | ✗ | ✗ |
| Microsoft Outlook 2010 | ✔ | ✔ | ✔ | ✔ | ✗ |
| Microsoft Publisher 2010 | ✔ | ✔ | ✗ | ✔ | ✗ |
| Microsoft OneNote 2010 | ✔ | ✔ | ✔ | ✔ | ✔ |
| Microsoft InfoPath 2010 | ✔ | ✗ | ✗ | ✗ | ✗ |
| Microsoft SharePoint Workspace 2010 | ✔ | ✗ | ✗ | ✗ | ✗ |
| Microsoft Communicator | ✔ | ✗ | ✗ | ✗ | ✗ |

# Starting and Using a Program

To use a program, such as PowerPoint, you must instruct the operating system to start the program. Windows 7 provides many different ways to start a program, one of which is presented in this section (other ways to start a program are presented throughout this chapter). After starting a program, you can use it to perform a variety of tasks. The following pages use PowerPoint to discuss some elements of the Office interface and to perform tasks that are common to other Office programs.

## PowerPoint

PowerPoint is a complete presentation program that allows you to produce professional-looking presentations. A PowerPoint **presentation** also is called a **slide show**. To make presentations more impressive, you can add charts, diagrams, tables, pictures, video, sound, and animation effects. Additional PowerPoint features include the following:

- **Word processing** — Create bulleted lists, combine words and images, find and replace text, import text from an outline, and use multiple fonts and font sizes.
- **Inserting multimedia** — Insert artwork and multimedia files into a slide show.
- **Saving to the Web** — You can publish your slide show to the Internet or to an intranet.
- **Collaborating** — Share a presentation with friends and coworkers. Ask them to review the slides and then insert comments to enhance the presentation.

## To Start a Program Using the Start Menu

Across the bottom of the Windows 7 desktop is the **taskbar**. The taskbar contains the **Start button**, which you use to access programs, files, folders, and settings on a computer. A **folder** is a named location on a storage medium that usually contains related documents. The taskbar also displays a button for each program currently running on a computer.

Clicking the Start button displays the Start menu. The **Start menu** allows you to access programs, folders, and files on the computer and contains commands that allow you to start programs, store and search for documents, customize the computer, and obtain help about thousands of topics. A **menu** is a list of related items, including folders, programs, and commands. Each **command** on a menu performs a specific action, such as saving a file or obtaining help.

The following steps, which assume Windows 7 is running, use the Start menu to start PowerPoint based on a typical installation. You may need to ask your instructor how to start PowerPoint for your computer. Although the steps illustrate starting the PowerPoint program, the steps to start any Office program are similar.

**1**

- Click the Start button on the Windows 7 taskbar to display the Start menu (Figure 6).

**Q&A** Why does my Start menu look different?

It may look different depending on your computer's configuration. The Start menu may be customized for several reasons, such as usage requirements or security restrictions.

**2**

- Click All Programs at the bottom of the left pane on the Start menu to display the All Programs list (Figure 7).

**Q&A** What is a pane?

A **pane** is an area of a window that displays related content. For example, the left pane on the Start menu contains a list of frequently used programs, as well as the All Programs command.

**Q&A** Why might my All Programs list look different?

Most likely, the programs installed on your computer will differ from those shown in Figure 7. Your All Programs list will show the programs that are installed on your computer.

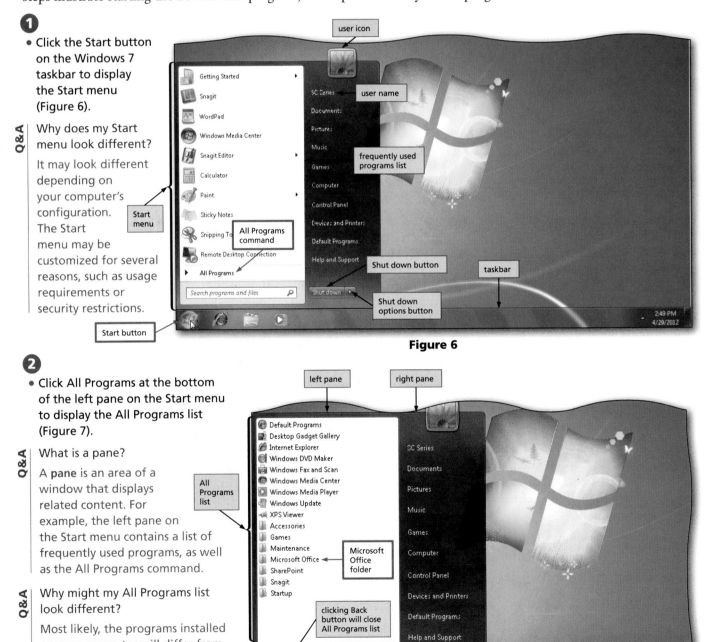

**Figure 6**

**Figure 7**

**3**

- If the program you wish to start is located in a folder, click or scroll to and then click the folder (Microsoft Office, in this case) in the All Programs list to display a list of the folder's contents (Figure 8).

**Q&A** | Why is the Microsoft Office folder on my computer?

During installation of Microsoft Office 2010, the Microsoft Office folder was added to the All Programs list.

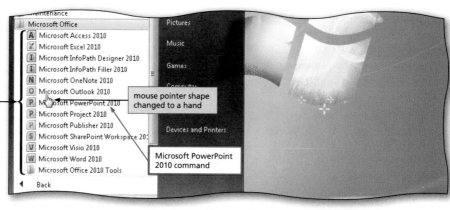

**Figure 8**

**4**

- Click, or scroll to and then click, the program name (Microsoft PowerPoint 2010, in this case) in the list to start the selected program (Figure 9).

**Q&A** | What happens when you start a program?

Many programs initially display a blank document in a program window, as shown in the PowerPoint window in Figure 9; others provide a means for you to create a blank document. A **window** is a rectangular area that displays data and information. The top of a window has a **title bar**, which is a horizontal space that contains the window's name.

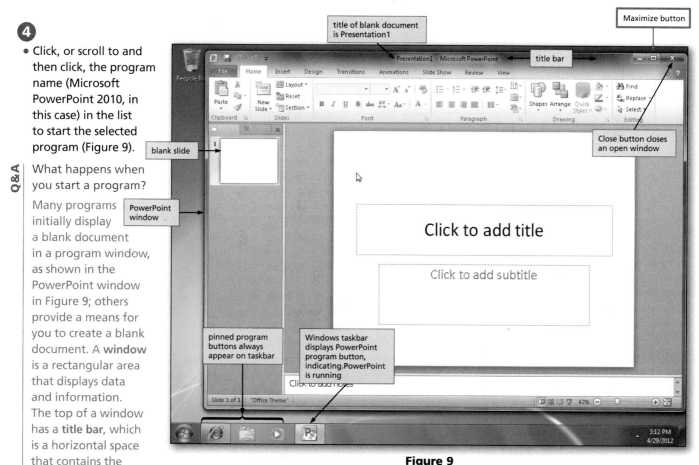

**Figure 9**

**Q&A** | Why is my program window a different size?

The PowerPoint window shown in Figure 9 is not maximized. Your PowerPoint window already may be maximized. The steps on the next page maximize a window.

| **Other Ways** | |
| --- | --- |
| 1. Double-click program icon on desktop, if one is present | 3. Display Start menu, type program name in search box, click program name |
| 2. Click program name in left pane of Start menu, if present | 4. Double-click file created using program you want to start |

## To Maximize a Window

Sometimes content is not visible completely in a window. One method of displaying the entire contents of a window is to **maximize** it, or enlarge the window so that it fills the entire screen. The following step maximizes the PowerPoint window; however, any Office program's window can be maximized using this step.

**1**

- If the program window is not maximized already, click the Maximize button (shown in Figure 9 on the previous page) next to the Close button on the window's title bar (the PowerPoint window title bar, in this case) to maximize the window (Figure 10).

**Q&A** What happened to the Maximize button?

It changed to a Restore Down button, which you can use to return a window to its size and location before you maximized it.

**Q&A** How do I know whether a window is maximized?

A window is maximized if it fills the entire display area and the Restore Down button is displayed on the title bar.

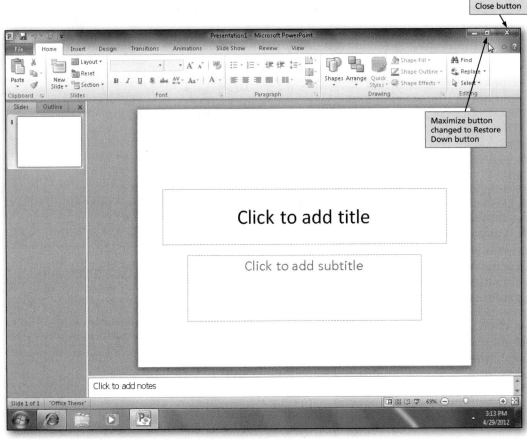

**Figure 10**

**Other Ways**

1. Double-click title bar
2. Drag title bar to top of screen

**BTW**

**Portrait Orientation**
If your slide content is dominantly vertical, such as a skyscraper or a person, consider changing the slide layout to a portrait orientation. To change the orientation to portrait, click the Slide Orientation button (Design tab | Page Setup group) and then click Portrait. You can use both landscape and portrait orientation in the same slide show.

## The PowerPoint Document Window, Ribbon, and Elements Common to Office Programs

The PowerPoint window consists of a variety of components to make your work more efficient and documents more professional: the window, Ribbon, Mini toolbar, shortcut menus, and Quick Access Toolbar. Many of these components are common to other Office programs and have been discussed earlier in this chapter. Other components, discussed in the following paragraphs and later in subsequent chapters, are unique to PowerPoint.

The basic unit of a PowerPoint presentation is a **slide**. A slide may contain text and objects, such as graphics, tables, charts, and drawings. **Layouts** are used to position this content on the slide. When you create a new presentation, the default **Title Slide** layout appears (Figure 11). The purpose of this layout is to introduce the presentation to the audience. PowerPoint includes eight other built-in standard layouts.

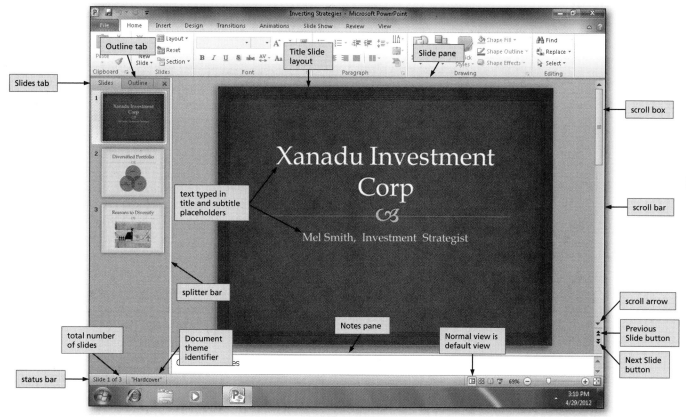

**Figure 11**

The default slide layouts are set up in **landscape orientation**, where the slide width is greater than its height. In landscape orientation, the slide size is preset to 10 inches wide and 7.5 inches high when printed on a standard sheet of paper measuring 11 inches wide and 8.5 inches high.

**Placeholders**   **Placeholders** are boxes with dotted or hatch-marked borders that are displayed when you create a new slide. All layouts except the Blank slide layout contain placeholders. Depending on the particular slide layout selected, placeholders are displayed for the slide title and subtitle; a content text placeholder is displayed for text, art, or a table, chart, picture, graphic, or movie. The title slide in Figure 11 has two text placeholders for the main heading, or title, of a new slide and the subtitle.

**Scroll Bars**   You use a scroll bar to display different portions of a document in the document window. At the right edge of the document window is a vertical scroll bar. If a document is too wide to fit in the document window, a horizontal scroll bar also appears at the bottom of the document window. On a scroll bar, the position of the scroll box reflects the location of the portion of the document that is displayed in the document window.

**Status Bar**   The **status bar**, located at the bottom of the document window above the Windows 7 taskbar, presents information about the document, the progress of current tasks, and the status of certain commands and keys; it also provides controls for viewing the document. As you type text or perform certain tasks, various indicators and buttons may appear on the status bar.

The left side of the status bar in Figure 11 shows the current slide followed by the total number of slides in the document and an icon to check spelling. The right side of the status bar includes buttons and controls you can use to change the view of a slide and adjust the size of the displayed document.

**Ribbon** The Ribbon, located near the top of the window below the title bar, is the control center in PowerPoint and other Office programs (Figure 12). The Ribbon provides easy, central access to the tasks you perform while creating a document. The Ribbon consists of tabs, groups, and commands. Each **tab** contains a collection of groups, and each **group** contains related functions. When you start an Office program, such as PowerPoint, it initially displays several main tabs, also called default tabs. All Office programs have a **Home tab**, which contains the more frequently used commands.

In addition to the main tabs, Office programs display **tool tabs**, also called contextual tabs (Figure 13), when you perform certain tasks or work with objects such as pictures or tables. If you insert a picture in a PowerPoint document, for example, the Picture Tools tab and its related subordinate Format tab appear, collectively referred to as the Picture Tools Format tab. When you are finished working with the picture, the Picture Tools Format tab disappears from the Ribbon. PowerPoint and other Office programs determine when tool tabs should appear and disappear based on tasks you perform. Some tool tabs, such as the Table Tools tab, have more than one related subordinate tab.

Items on the Ribbon include buttons, boxes (text boxes, check boxes, etc.), and galleries (Figure 12). A **gallery** is a set of choices, often graphical, arranged in a grid or in a list. You can scroll through choices in an in-Ribbon gallery by clicking the gallery's scroll arrows. Or, you can click a gallery's More button to view more gallery options on the screen at a time.

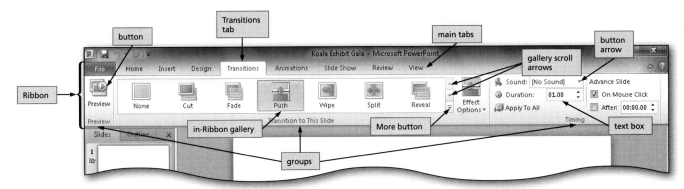

**Figure 12**

Some buttons and boxes have arrows that, when clicked, also display a gallery; others always cause a gallery to be displayed when clicked. Most galleries support **live preview**, which is a feature that allows you to point to a gallery choice and see its effect in the document — without actually selecting the choice (Figure 13).

Some commands on the Ribbon display an image to help you remember their function. When you point to a command on the Ribbon, all or part of the command glows in shades of yellow and orange, and an Enhanced ScreenTip appears on the screen. An **Enhanced ScreenTip** is an on-screen note that provides the name of the command, available keyboard shortcut(s), a description of the command, and sometimes instructions for how to obtain help about the command (Figure 14). Enhanced ScreenTips are more detailed than a typical ScreenTip, which usually displays only the name of the command.

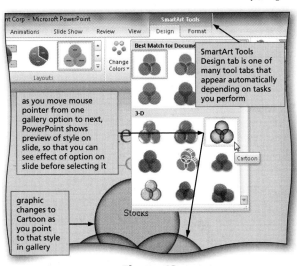
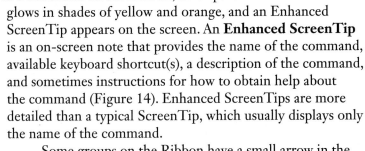

**Figure 13**

Some groups on the Ribbon have a small arrow in the lower-right corner, called a **Dialog Box Launcher**, that when clicked, displays a dialog box or a task pane with additional options for the group (Figure 15). When presented with a dialog box, you make selections and must close the dialog box before returning to the document. A **task pane**, in contrast to a dialog box, is a window that can remain open and visible while you work in the document.

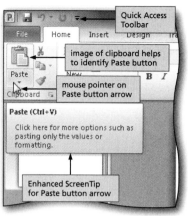

**Figure 14**

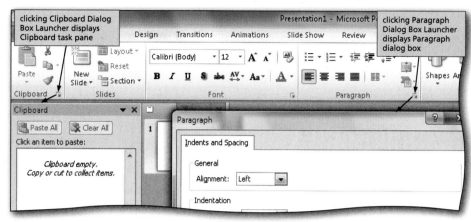

**Figure 15**

**Mini Toolbar**   The **Mini toolbar**, which appears automatically based on tasks you perform, contains commands related to changing the appearance of text in a document. All commands on the Mini toolbar also exist on the Ribbon. The purpose of the Mini toolbar is to minimize mouse movement.

When the Mini toolbar appears, it initially is transparent (Figure 16a). If you do not use the transparent Mini toolbar, it disappears from the screen. To use the Mini toolbar, move the mouse pointer into the toolbar, which causes the Mini toolbar to change from a transparent to bright appearance (Figure 16b). If you right-click an item in the document window, PowerPoint displays both the Mini toolbar and a shortcut menu, which is discussed in a later section in this chapter.

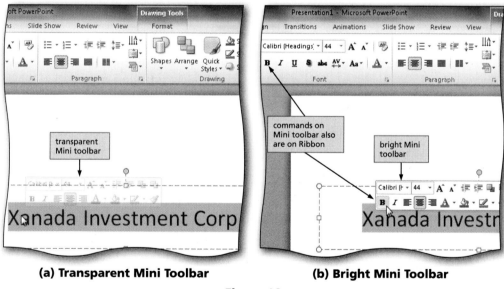

**(a) Transparent Mini Toolbar**          **(b) Bright Mini Toolbar**

**Figure 16**

**BTW**

**Turning Off the Mini Toolbar**
If you do not want the Mini toolbar to appear, click File on the Ribbon to open the Backstage view, click Options in the Backstage view, click General (Options dialog box), remove the check mark from the Show Mini Toolbar on selection check box, and then click the OK button.

**Quick Access Toolbar**   The **Quick Access Toolbar**, located initially (by default) above the Ribbon at the left edge of the title bar, provides convenient, one-click access to frequently used commands (Figure 14). The commands on the Quick Access Toolbar always are available, regardless of the task you are performing. The Quick Access Toolbar is discussed in more depth later in the chapter.

**KeyTips**   If you prefer using the keyboard instead of the mouse, you can press the ALT key on the keyboard to display **KeyTips**, or keyboard code icons, for certain commands

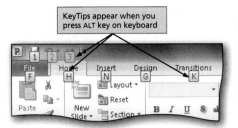

**Figure 17**

(Figure 17). To select a command using the keyboard, press the letter or number displayed in the KeyTip, which may cause additional KeyTips related to the selected command to appear. To remove KeyTips from the screen, press the ALT key or the ESC key until all KeyTips disappear, or click the mouse anywhere in the program window.

## To Display a Different Tab on the Ribbon

When you start PowerPoint, the Ribbon displays nine main tabs: File, Home, Insert, Design, Transitions, Animations, Slide Show, Review, and View. The tab currently displayed is called the **active tab**.

The following step displays the Insert tab and makes it the active tab.

**1**

- Click Insert on the Ribbon to display the Insert tab (Figure 18).

 **Experiment**

- Click the other tabs on the Ribbon to view their contents. When you are finished, click the Insert tab to redisplay the Insert tab.

**Q&A** If I am working in a different Office program, such as Word or Access, how do I display a different tab on the Ribbon?

Follow this same procedure; that is, click the desired tab on the Ribbon.

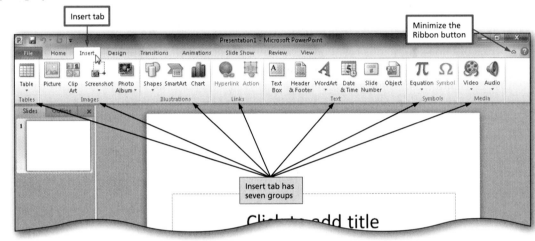

**Figure 18**

## To Minimize, Display, and Restore the Ribbon

To display more of a document or other item in the window of an Office program, some users prefer to minimize the Ribbon, which hides the groups on the Ribbon and displays only the main tabs. Each time you start an Office program, such as PowerPoint, the Ribbon appears the same way it did the last time you used that Office program. The chapters in this book, however, begin with the Ribbon appearing as it did at the initial installation of the PowerPoint program.

The following steps minimize, display, and restore the Ribbon in an Office program.

**1**

- Click the Minimize the Ribbon button on the Ribbon (shown in Figure 18) to minimize the Ribbon (Figure 19).

**Q&A** What happened to the groups on the Ribbon?

When you minimize the Ribbon, the groups disappear so that the Ribbon does not take up as much space on the screen.

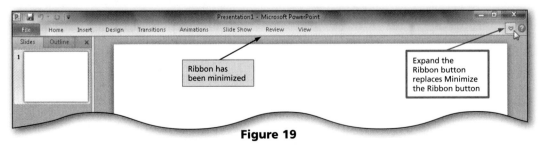

**Figure 19**

**Q&A** What happened to the Minimize the Ribbon button?

The Expand the Ribbon button replaces the Minimize the Ribbon button when the Ribbon is minimized.

- Click Home on the Ribbon to display the Home tab (Figure 20).

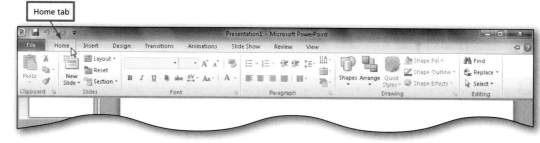

Home tab

**Figure 20**

**Q&A**

Why would I click the Home tab?

If you want to use a command on a minimized Ribbon, click the main tab to display the groups for that tab. After you select a command on the Ribbon, the groups will be hidden once again. If you decide not to use a command on the Ribbon, you can hide the groups by clicking the same main tab or clicking in the program window.

- Click Home on the Ribbon to hide the groups again (shown in Figure 19).

- Click the Expand the Ribbon button on the Ribbon (shown in Figure 19) to restore the Ribbon.

**Other Ways**

1. Double-click Home on the Ribbon
2. Press CTRL+F1

## To Display and Use a Shortcut Menu

When you right-click certain areas of the PowerPoint and other program windows, a shortcut menu will appear. A **shortcut menu** is a list of frequently used commands that relate to the right-clicked object. When you right-click a scroll bar, for example, a shortcut menu appears with commands related to the scroll bar. When you right-click the Quick Access Toolbar, a shortcut menu appears with commands related to the Quick Access Toolbar. You can use shortcut menus to access common commands quickly. The following steps use a shortcut menu to move the Quick Access Toolbar, which by default is located on the title bar.

- Right-click the Quick Access Toolbar to display a shortcut menu that presents a list of commands related to the Quick Access Toolbar (Figure 21).

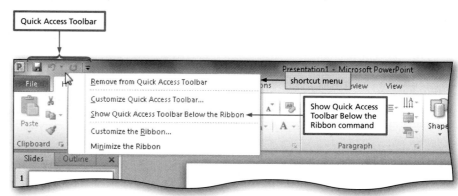

Quick Access Toolbar

**Figure 21**

- Click Show Quick Access Toolbar Below the Ribbon on the shortcut menu to display the Quick Access Toolbar below the Ribbon (Figure 22).

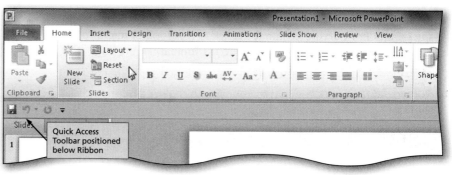

**Figure 22**

- Right-click the Quick Access Toolbar to display a shortcut menu (Figure 23).

- Click Show Quick Access Toolbar Above the Ribbon on the shortcut menu to return the Quick Access Toolbar to its original position (shown in Figure 21 on the previous page).

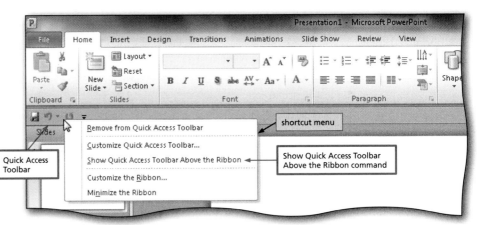

**Figure 23**

## To Customize the Quick Access Toolbar

The Quick Access Toolbar provides easy access to some of the more frequently used commands in Office programs. By default, the Quick Access Toolbar contains buttons for the Save, Undo, and Redo commands. You can customize the Quick Access Toolbar by changing its location in the window, as shown in the previous steps, and by adding more buttons to reflect commands you would like to access easily. The following steps add the Quick Print button to the Quick Access Toolbar in the PowerPoint window.

- Click the Customize Quick Access Toolbar button to display the Customize Quick Access Toolbar menu (Figure 24).

**Q&A** Which commands are listed on the Customize Quick Access Toolbar menu?

It lists commands that commonly are added to the Quick Access Toolbar.

**Q&A** What do the check marks next to some commands signify?

Check marks appear next to commands that already are on the Quick Access Toolbar. When you add a button to the Quick Access Toolbar, a check mark will be displayed next to its command name.

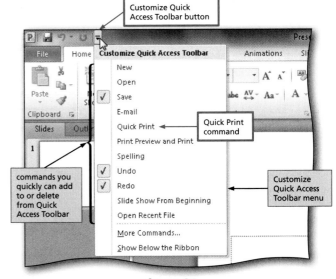

**Figure 24**

- Click Quick Print on the Customize Quick Access Toolbar menu to add the Quick Print button to the Quick Access Toolbar (Figure 25).

**Q&A** How would I remove a button from the Quick Access Toolbar?

You would right-click the button you wish to remove and then click Remove from Quick Access Toolbar on the shortcut menu. If you want your screens to match the screens in the remaining chapters in this book, you would remove the Quick Print button from the Quick Access Toolbar.

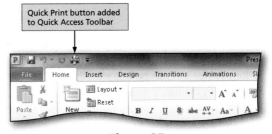

**Figure 25**

## To Enter Content in a Title Slide

With the exception of a blank slide and a slide with a picture and caption, PowerPoint assumes every new slide has a title. Many of PowerPoint's layouts have both a title text placeholder and at least one content placeholder. To make creating a presentation easier, any text you type after a new slide appears becomes title text in the title text placeholder. As you begin typing text in the title text placeholder, the title text also is displayed in the Slide 1 thumbnail in the Slides tab. The presentation title for this presentation is Xanada Investment Corp. The following steps enter a presentation title on the title slide.

**1**

• Click the label 'Click to add title' located inside the title text placeholder to select the placeholder (Figure 26).

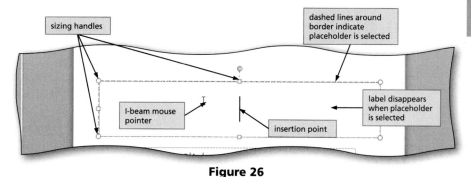

**Figure 26**

**2**

• Type **Xanada Investment Corp.** in the title text placeholder. Do not press the ENTER key because you do not want to create a new line of text (Figure 27).

**Q&A**

What are the white squares and circles that appear around the title text placeholder as I type the presentation title?

The white squares and circles are sizing handles, which you can drag to change the size of the title text placeholder. Sizing handles also can be found around other placeholders and objects within a presentation.

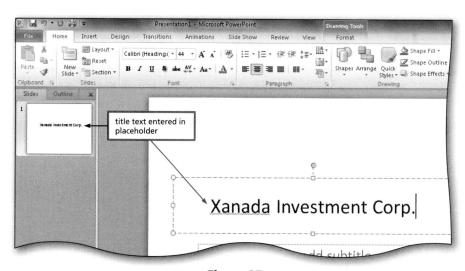

**Figure 27**

# Saving and Organizing Files

While you are creating a document, the computer stores it in memory. When you save a document, the computer places it on a storage medium such as a hard disk, USB flash drive, or optical disc. A saved document is referred to as a file. A **file name** is the name assigned to a file when it is saved. It is important to save a document frequently for the following reasons:

• The document in memory might be lost if the computer is turned off or you lose electrical power while a program is running.

• If you run out of time before completing a project, you may finish it at a future time without starting over.

When saving files, you should organize them so that you easily can find them later. Windows 7 provides tools to help you organize files.

## Organizing Files and Folders

A file contains data. This data can range from a research paper to an accounting spreadsheet to an electronic math quiz. You should organize and store these files in folders to avoid misplacing a file and to help you find a file quickly.

If you are a freshman taking an introductory computer class (CIS 101, for example), you may want to design a series of folders for the different subjects covered in the class. To accomplish this, you can arrange the folders in a hierarchy for the class, as shown in Figure 28.

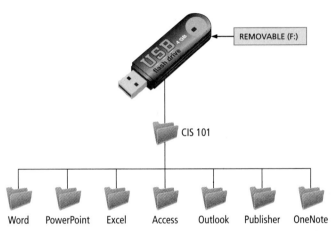

REMOVABLE (F:)

CIS 101

Word  PowerPoint  Excel  Access  Outlook  Publisher  OneNote

**Figure 28**

The hierarchy contains three levels. The first level contains the storage device, in this case a USB flash drive. Windows 7 identifies the storage device with a letter, and, in some cases, a name. In Figure 28, the USB flash drive is identified as REMOVABLE (F:). The second level contains the class folder (CIS 101, in this case), and the third level contains seven folders, one each for a different Office program that will be covered in the class (Word, PowerPoint, Excel, Access, Outlook, Publisher, and OneNote).

When the hierarchy in Figure 28 is created, the USB flash drive is said to contain the CIS 101 folder, and the CIS 101 folder is said to contain the separate Office folders (i.e., Word, PowerPoint, Excel, etc.). In addition, this hierarchy easily can be expanded to include folders from other classes taken during additional semesters.

The vertical and horizontal lines in Figure 28 form a pathway that allows you to navigate to a drive or folder on a computer or network. A **path** consists of a drive letter (preceded by a drive name when necessary) and colon, to identify the storage device, and one or more folder names. Each drive or folder in the hierarchy has a corresponding path.

Table 3 shows examples of paths and their corresponding drives and folders.

| Table 3 Paths and Corresponding Drives and Folders | |
| --- | --- |
| **Path** | **Drive and Folder** |
| Computer ▶ REMOVABLE (F:) | Drive F (REMOVABLE (F:)) |
| Computer ▶ REMOVABLE (F:) ▶ CIS 101 | CIS 101 folder on drive F |
| Computer ▶ REMOVABLE (F:) ▶ CIS 101 ▶ PowerPoint | PowerPoint folder in CIS 101 folder on drive F |

**BTW**

**Saving Online**
Instead of saving files on a USB flash drive, some people prefer to save them online so that they can access the files from any computer with an Internet connection. For more information, read Appendix C.

The following pages illustrate the steps to organize the folders for this class and save a file in one of those folders:

1. Create the folder identifying your class.
2. Create the PowerPoint folder in the folder identifying your class.
3. Save a file in the PowerPoint folder.
4. Verify the location of the saved file.

## To Create a Folder

When you create a folder, such as the CIS 101 folder shown in Figure 28, you must name the folder. A folder name should describe the folder and its contents. A folder name can contain spaces and any uppercase or lowercase characters, except a backslash (\), slash (/), colon (:), asterisk (*), question mark (?), quotation marks ("), less than symbol (<), greater than symbol (>), or vertical bar (I). Folder names cannot be CON, AUX, COM1, COM2, COM3, COM4, LPT1, LPT2, LPT3, PRN, or NUL. The same rules for naming folders also apply to naming files.

To store files and folders on a USB flash drive, you must connect the USB flash drive to an available USB port on a computer. The following steps create your class folder (CIS 101, in this case) on a USB flash drive.

**1**

- Connect the USB flash drive to an available USB port on the computer to open the AutoPlay window (Figure 29).

Q&A  Why does the AutoPlay window not open?

Some computers are not configured to open an AutoPlay window. Instead, they might display the contents of the USB flash drive automatically, or you might need to access contents of the USB flash drive using the Computer window. To use the Computer window to display the USB flash drive's contents, click the Start button, click Computer on the Start menu, click the icon representing the USB flash drive, and then proceed to Step 3 on the next page.

Q&A  Why does the AutoPlay window look different from the one in Figure 29?

The AutoPlay window that opens on your computer might display different options. The type of USB flash drive, its contents, and the next available drive letter on your computer all will determine which options are displayed in the AutoPlay window.

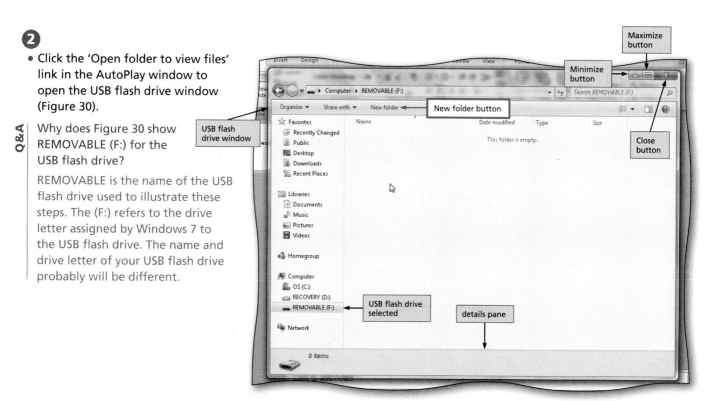

**Figure 29**

**2**

- Click the 'Open folder to view files' link in the AutoPlay window to open the USB flash drive window (Figure 30).

Q&A  Why does Figure 30 show REMOVABLE (F:) for the USB flash drive?

REMOVABLE is the name of the USB flash drive used to illustrate these steps. The (F:) refers to the drive letter assigned by Windows 7 to the USB flash drive. The name and drive letter of your USB flash drive probably will be different.

**Figure 30**

**3**

- Click the New folder button on the toolbar to display a new folder icon with the name, New folder, selected in a text box.

- Type CIS 101 (or your class code) in the text box to name the folder.

- Press the ENTER key to create a folder identifying your class on the selected drive (Figure 31). If the CIS 101 folder does not appear in the Navigation pane, double-click REMOVABLE (F:) in the Navigation pane to display the folder just added. If the CIS 101 folder does not appear in the Navigation pane, double-click REMOVABLE (F:) in the Navigation pane to display the folder just added.

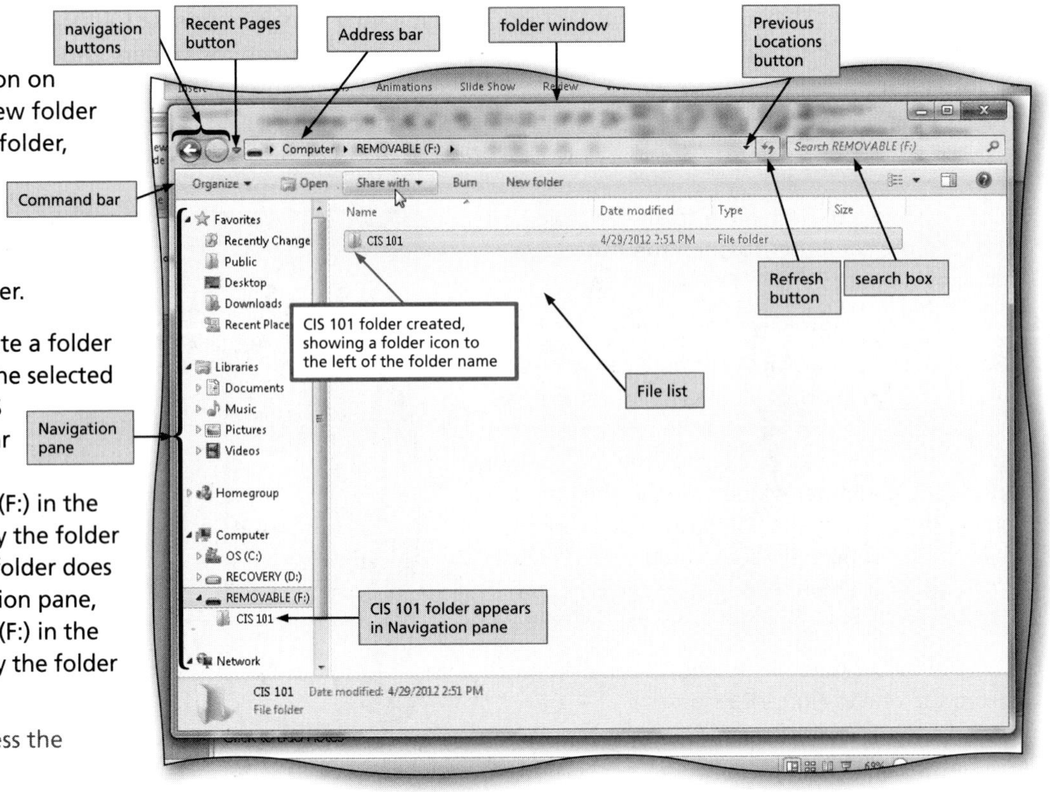

**Q&A** What happens when I press the ENTER key?

The class folder (CIS 101, in this case) is displayed in the File list, which contains the folder name, date modified, type, and size.

**Q&A** Why is the folder icon displayed differently on my computer?

Windows might be configured to display contents differently on your computer.

**Figure 31**

## Folder Windows

The USB flash drive window (shown in Figure 31) is called a folder window. Recall that a folder is a specific named location on a storage medium that contains related files. Most users rely on **folder windows** for finding, viewing, and managing information on their computer. Folder windows have common design elements, including the following (Figure 31).

- The **Address bar** provides quick navigation options. The arrows on the Address bar allow you to visit different locations on the computer.
- The buttons to the left of the Address bar allow you to navigate the contents of the left pane and view recent pages. Other buttons allow you to specify the size of the window.
- The **Previous Locations button** saves the locations you have visited and displays the locations when clicked.
- The **Refresh button** on the right side of the Address bar refreshes the contents of the right pane of the folder window.
- The **search box** to the right of the Address bar contains the dimmed word, Search. You can type a term in the search box for a list of files, folders, shortcuts, and elements containing that term within the location you are searching. A **shortcut** is an icon on the desktop that provides a user with immediate access to a program or file.
- The **Command bar** contains five buttons used to accomplish various tasks on the computer related to organizing and managing the contents of the open window.
- The **Navigation pane** on the left contains the Favorites area, Libraries area, Computer area, and Network area.

- The **Favorites area** contains links to your favorite locations. By default, this list contains only links to your Desktop, Downloads, and Recent Places.
- The **Libraries area** shows links to files and folders that have been included in a library.

A **library** helps you manage multiple folders and files stored in various locations on a computer. It does not store the files and folders; rather, it displays links to them so that you can access them quickly. For example, you can save pictures from a digital camera in any folder on any storage location on a computer. Normally, this would make organizing the different folders difficult; however, if you add the folders to a library, you can access all the pictures from one location regardless of where they are stored.

## To Create a Folder within a Folder

With the class folder created, you can create folders that will store the files you create using each Office program. The following steps create a PowerPoint folder in the CIS 101 folder (or the folder identifying your class).

- Double-click the icon or folder name for the CIS 101 folder (or the folder identifying your class) in the File list to open the folder (Figure 32).

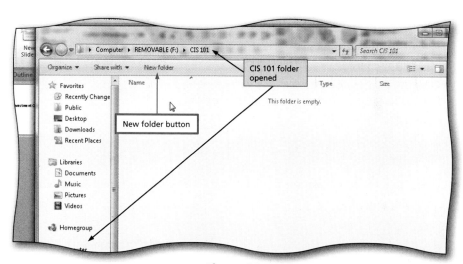

**Figure 32**

- Click the New folder button on the toolbar to display a new folder icon and text box for the folder.
- Type **PowerPoint** in the text box to name the folder.
- Press the ENTER key to create the folder (Figure 33).

**Figure 33**

## To Expand a Folder, Scroll through Folder Contents, and Collapse a Folder

Folder windows display the hierarchy of items and the contents of drives and folders in the right pane. You might want to expand a drive in the Navigation pane to view its contents, scroll through its contents, and collapse it when you are finished viewing its contents. When a folder is expanded, it lists all the folders it contains. By contrast, a collapsed folder does not list the folders it contains. These steps expand, scroll through, and then collapse the folder identifying your class (CIS 101, in this case).

● Double-click the folder identifying your class (CIS 101, in this case) in the Navigation pane, which expands the folder to display its contents and displays a black arrow to the left of the folder icon (Figure 34).

**Q&A** Why is the PowerPoint folder indented below the CIS 101 folder in the Navigation pane?

It shows that the folder is contained within the CIS 101 folder.

**Q&A** Why did a scroll bar appear in the Navigation pane?

When all contents cannot fit in a window or pane, a scroll bar appears. As described earlier, you can view areas currently not visible by (1) clicking the scroll arrows, (2) clicking above or below the scroll bar, and (3) dragging the scroll box.

**Experiment**

● Click the down scroll arrow on the vertical scroll bar to display additional content at the bottom of the Navigation pane.

● Click the scroll bar above the scroll box to move the scroll box to the top of the Navigation pane.

● Drag the scroll box down the scroll bar until the scroll box is halfway down the scroll bar.

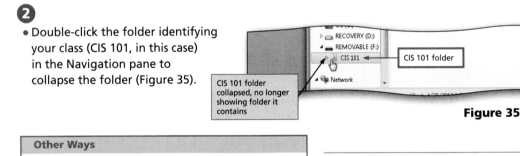

**Figure 34**

② 

● Double-click the folder identifying your class (CIS 101, in this case) in the Navigation pane to collapse the folder (Figure 35).

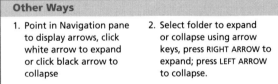

**Figure 35**

| Other Ways |  |
| --- | --- |
| 1. Point in Navigation pane to display arrows, click white arrow to expand or click black arrow to collapse | 2. Select folder to expand or collapse using arrow keys, press RIGHT ARROW to expand; press LEFT ARROW to collapse. |

## To Switch from One Program to Another

The next step is to save the PowerPoint file containing the slide title you typed earlier. PowerPoint, however, currently is not the active window. You can use the program button on the taskbar and live preview to switch to PowerPoint and then save the document in the PowerPoint document window.

If Windows Aero is active on your computer, Windows displays a live preview window whenever you move your mouse on a button or click a button on the taskbar. If Aero is not supported or enabled on your computer, you will see a window title instead of a live preview. These steps use the PowerPoint program; however, the steps are the same for any active Office program currently displayed as a program button on the taskbar.

The next steps switch to the PowerPoint window.

- Point to the PowerPoint program button on the taskbar to see a live preview of the open document(s) or the window title(s) of the open document(s), depending on your computer's configuration (Figure 36).

- Click the program button or the live preview to make the program associated with the program button the active window.

**Q&A**

What if multiple documents are open in a program?

If Aero is enabled on your computer, click the desired live preview. If Aero is not supported or not enabled, click the window title.

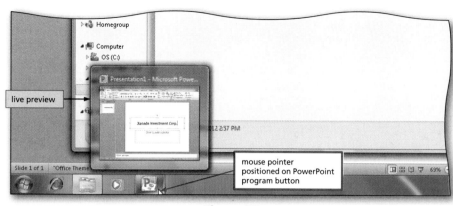

**Figure 36**

## To Save a File in a Folder

Now that you have created the folders for storing files, you can save the PowerPoint document. The following steps save a file on a USB flash drive in the PowerPoint folder contained in your class folder (CIS 101, in this case) using the file name, Investing Strategies.

- With a USB flash drive connected to one of the computer's USB ports, click the Save button on the Quick Access Toolbar to display the Save As dialog box (Figure 37).

**Q&A**

Why does a file name already appear in the File name text box?

PowerPoint automatically suggests a file name the first time you save a document. The file name normally consists of the first few words contained in the document. Because the suggested file name is selected, you do not need to delete it; as soon as you begin typing, the new file name replaces the selected text.

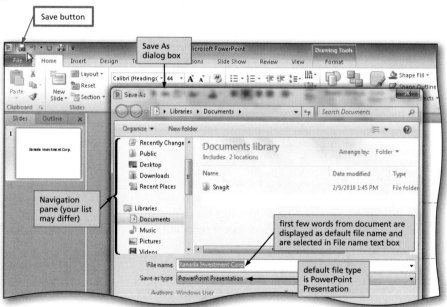

**Figure 37**

- Type **Investing Strategies** in the File name text box (Save As dialog box) to change the file name. Do not press the ENTER key after typing the file name because you do not want to close the dialog box at this time (Figure 38).

**Q&A**
What characters can I use in a file name?

The only invalid characters are the backslash (\), slash (/), colon (:), asterisk (*), question mark (?), quotation mark ("), less than symbol (<), greater than symbol (>), and vertical bar (|).

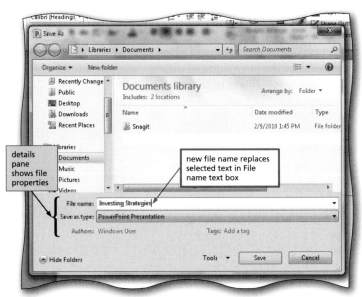

**Figure 38**

- Navigate to the desired save location (in this case, the PowerPoint folder in the CIS 101 folder [or your class folder] on the USB flash drive) by performing the tasks in Steps 3a, 3b, and 3c.

- If the Navigation pane is not displayed in the dialog box, click the Browse Folders button to expand the dialog box.

- If Computer is not displayed in the Navigation pane, drag the Navigation pane scroll bar until Computer appears.

- If Computer is not expanded in the Navigation pane, double-click Computer to display a list of available storage devices in the Navigation pane.

- If necessary, scroll through the dialog box until your USB flash drive appears in the list of available storage devices in the Navigation pane (Figure 39).

- If your USB flash drive is not expanded, double-click the USB flash drive in the list of available storage devices in the Navigation pane to select that drive as the new save location and display its contents in the right pane.

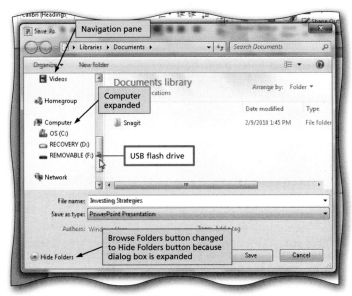

**Figure 39**

- If your class folder (CIS 101, in this case) is not expanded, double-click the CIS 101 folder to select the folder and display its contents in the right pane.

**Q&A**
What if I do not want to save in a folder?

Although storing files in folders is an effective technique for organizing files, some users prefer not to store files in folders. If you prefer not to save this file in a folder, skip all instructions in Step 3c and proceed to Step 4.

- Click the PowerPoint folder to select the folder and display its contents in the right pane (Figure 40).

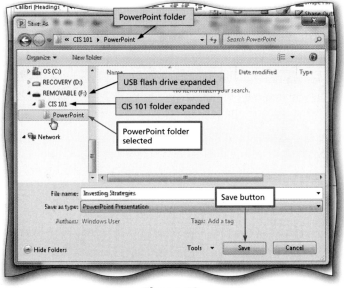

**Figure 40**

**4**

- Click the Save button (Save As dialog box) to save the document in the selected folder on the selected drive with the entered file name (Figure 41).

**Q&A**

How do I know that the file is saved?

While an Office program such as PowerPoint is saving a file, it briefly displays a message on the status bar indicating the amount of the file saved. In addition, the USB flash drive may have a light that flashes during the save process.

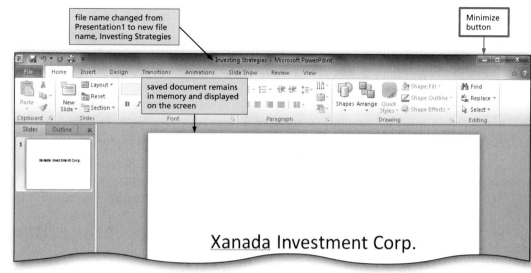

**Figure 41**

**Other Ways**

1. Click File on Ribbon, click Save, type file name, navigate to desired save location, click Save button

2. Press CTRL+S or press SHIFT+F12, type file name, navigate to desired save location, click Save button

## Navigating in Dialog Boxes

**Navigating** is the process of finding a location on a storage device. While saving the Investing Strategies file, for example, you navigated to the PowerPoint folder located in the CIS 101 folder. When performing certain functions in Windows programs, such as saving a file, opening a file, or inserting a picture in an existing document, you most likely will have to navigate to the location where you want to save the file or to the folder containing the file you want to open or insert. Most dialog boxes in Windows programs requiring navigation follow a similar procedure; that is, the way you navigate to a folder in one dialog box, such as the Save As dialog box, is similar to how you might navigate in another dialog box, such as the Open dialog box. If you chose to navigate to a specific location in a dialog box, you would follow the instructions in Steps 3a – 3c on the previous page.

**BTW**

**File Type**
Depending on your Windows 7 settings, the file type .ppt may be displayed immediately to the right of the file name after you save the file. The file type .ppt is a PowerPoint 2010 document.

## To Minimize and Restore a Window

Before continuing, you can verify that the PowerPoint file was saved properly. To do this, you will minimize the PowerPoint window and then open the USB flash drive window so that you can verify the file is stored on the USB flash drive. A **minimized window** is an open window hidden from view but that can be displayed quickly by clicking the window's program button on the taskbar.

In the following example, PowerPoint is used to illustrate minimizing and restoring windows; however, you would follow the same steps regardless of the Office program you are using.

The next steps minimize the PowerPoint window, verify that the file is saved, and then restore the minimized window.

**1**

- Click the Minimize button on the program's title bar (shown in Figure 41 on the previous page) to minimize the window (Figure 42).

**Q&A**

Is the minimized window still available?

The minimized window, PowerPoint in this case, remains available but no longer is the active window. It is minimized as a program button on the taskbar.

- If necessary, click the Windows Explorer program button on the taskbar to open the USB flash drive window.

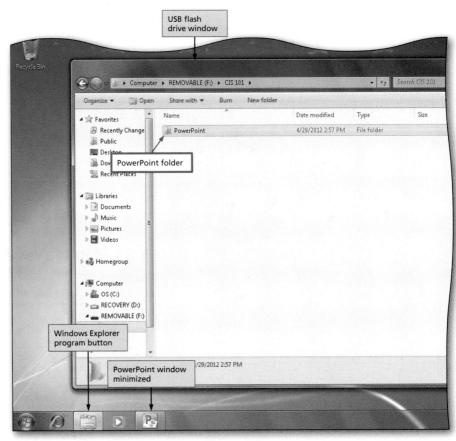

**Figure 42**

**2**

- Double-click the PowerPoint folder to select the folder and display its contents (Figure 43).

**Q&A**

Why does the Windows Explorer button on the taskbar change?

The button changes to reflect the status of the folder window (in this case, the USB flash drive window). A selected button indicates that the folder window is active on the screen. When the button is not selected, the window is open but not active.

**3**

- After viewing the contents of the selected folder, click the PowerPoint program button on the taskbar to restore the minimized window (as shown in Figure 41 on the previous page).

**Other Ways**

1. Right-click title bar, click Minimize on shortcut menu, click taskbar button in taskbar button area
2. Press WINDOWS+M, press WINDOWS+SHIFT+M

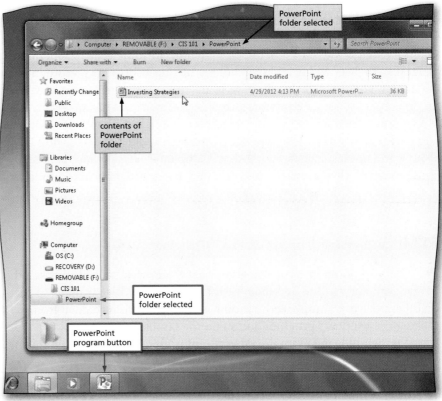

**Figure 43**

# Screen Resolution

**Screen resolution** indicates the number of pixels (dots) that the computer uses to display the letters, numbers, graphics, and background you see on the screen. When you increase the screen resolution, Windows displays more information on the screen, but the information decreases in size. The reverse also is true: as you decrease the screen resolution, Windows displays less information on the screen, but the information increases in size.

Screen resolution usually is stated as the product of two numbers, such as $1024 \times 768$ (pronounced "ten twenty-four by seven sixty-eight"). A $1024 \times 768$ screen resolution results in a display of 1,024 distinct pixels on each of 768 lines, or about 786,432 pixels. Changing the screen resolution affects how the Ribbon appears in Office programs. Figure 44 shows the PowerPoint Ribbon at screen resolutions of $1024 \times 768$ and $1280 \times 800$. All of the same commands are available regardless of screen resolution. PowerPoint, however, makes changes to the groups and the buttons within the groups to accommodate the various screen resolutions. The result is that certain commands may need to be accessed differently depending on the resolution chosen. A command that is visible on the Ribbon and available by clicking a button at one resolution may not be visible and may need to be accessed using its Dialog Box Launcher at a different resolution.

Comparing the two Ribbons in Figure 44, notice the changes in content and layout of the groups and galleries. In some cases, the content of a group is the same in each resolution, but the layout of the group differs. For example, the same gallery and buttons appear in the Drawing group in the two resolutions, but the layouts differ. In other cases, the content and layout are the same across the resolution, but the level of detail differs with the resolution. In the Clipboard group, when the resolution increases to $1280 \times 800$, the names of all the buttons in the group appear in addition to the buttons themselves. At the lower resolution, only the buttons appear.

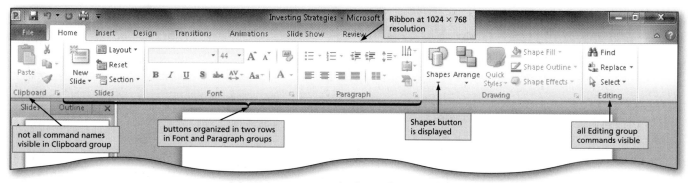

**(a) Ribbon at Resolution of 1024 × 768**

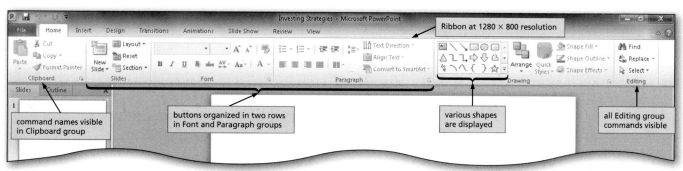

**(b) Ribbon at Resolution of 1280 × 800**

**Figure 44**

## To Change the Screen Resolution

If you are using a computer to step through the chapters in this book and you want your screen to match the figures, you may need to change your screen's resolution. The figures in this book use a screen resolution of 1024 × 768. The following steps change the screen resolution to 1024 × 768. Your computer already may be set to 1024 × 768 or some other resolution. Keep in mind that many computer labs prevent users from changing the screen resolution; in that case, read the following steps for illustration purposes.

- Click the Show desktop button on the taskbar to display the Windows 7 desktop.

- Right-click an empty area on the Windows 7 desktop to display a shortcut menu that displays a list of commands related to the desktop (Figure 45).

**Q&A**

Why does my shortcut menu display different commands?

Depending on your computer's hardware and configuration, different commands might appear on the shortcut menu.

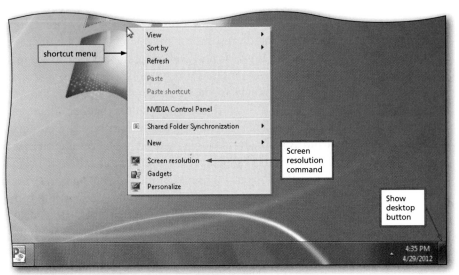

**Figure 45**

- Click Screen resolution on the shortcut menu to open the Screen Resolution window (Figure 46).

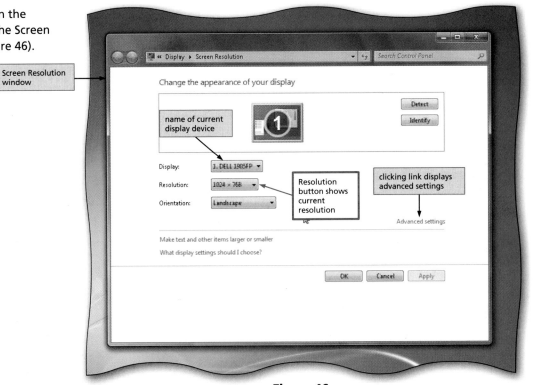

**Figure 46**

**3**

- Click the Resolution button in the Screen Resolution window to display the resolution slider.

**What is a slider?**

A **slider** is an object that allows users to choose from multiple predetermined options. In most cases, these options represent some type of numeric value. In most cases, one end of the slider (usually the left or bottom) represents the lowest of available values, and the opposite end (usually the right or top) represents the highest available value.

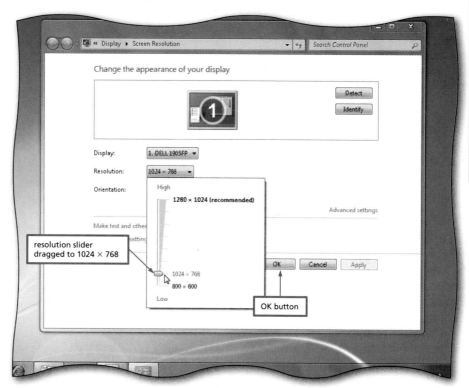

**4**

- If necessary, drag the resolution slider until the desired screen resolution (in this case, 1024 × 768) is selected (Figure 47).

**What if my computer does not support the 1024 × 768 resolution?**

Some computers do not support the 1024 × 768 resolution. In this case, select a resolution that is close to the 1024 × 768 resolution.

**Figure 47**

**5**

- Click an empty area of the Screen Resolution window to close the resolution slider.

- Click the OK button to change the screen resolution and display the Display Settings dialog box (Figure 48).

- Click the Keep changes button (Display Settings dialog box) to accept the new screen resolution.

**Why does a message display stating that the image quality can be improved?**

Some computer monitors are designed to display contents better at a certain screen resolution, sometimes referred to as an optimal resolution.

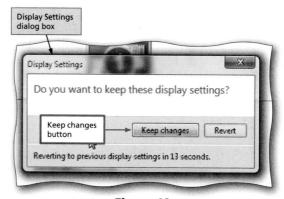

**Figure 48**

## To Quit a Program with One Document Open

When you quit an Office program, such as PowerPoint, if you have made changes to a file since the last time the file was saved, the Office program displays a dialog box asking if you want to save the changes you made to the file before it closes the program window. The dialog box contains three buttons with these resulting actions: the Save button saves the changes and then quits the Office program, the Don't Save button quits the Office program without saving changes, and the Cancel button closes the dialog box and redisplays the file without saving the changes.

If no changes have been made to an open document since the last time the file was saved, the Office program will close the window without displaying a dialog box.

The following steps quit PowerPoint. You would follow similar steps in other Office programs.

**1**

- If necessary, click the PowerPoint program button on the taskbar to display the PowerPoint window on the desktop.

- Point to the Close button on the right side of the program's title bar, PowerPoint in this case (Figure 49).

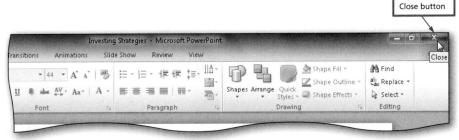

**Figure 49**

**2**

- Click the Close button to close the document and quit PowerPoint.

**Q&A** | What if I have more than one document open in PowerPoint?

You would click the Close button for each open document. When you click the last open document's Close button, PowerPoint also quits. As an alternative, you could click File on the Ribbon to open the Backstage view and then click Exit in the Backstage view to close all open documents and quit PowerPoint.

**Q&A** | What is the Backstage view?

The **Backstage view** contains a set of commands that enable you to manage documents and data about the documents. The Backstage view is discussed in more depth later in this chapter.

**3**

- If a Microsoft PowerPoint dialog box appears, click the Save button to save any changes made to the document since the last save.

| Other Ways |
|---|
| 1. Right-click the Office program button on Windows 7 taskbar, click    Close window or 'Close all windows' on shortcut menu<br>2. Press ALT+F4 |

**Break Point:** If you wish to take a break, this is a good place to do so. To resume at a later time, continue to follow the steps from this location forward.

# Additional Common Features of Office Programs

The previous section used PowerPoint to illustrate common features of Office and some basic elements unique to PowerPoint. The following sections continue to use PowerPoint to present additional common features of Office.

In the following pages, you will learn how to do the following:

1. Start an Office program (PowerPoint) using the search box.
2. Open a document in an Office program (PowerPoint).
3. Close the document.
4. Reopen the document just closed.
5. Create a blank Office document from Windows Explorer and then open the file.
6. Save the document with a new file name.

## To Start a Program Using the Search Box

The next steps, which assume Windows 7 is running, use the search box to start PowerPoint based on a typical installation; however, you would follow similar steps to start any program. You may need to ask your instructor how to start programs for your computer.

- Click the Start button on the Windows 7 taskbar to display the Start menu.

- Type **Microsoft PowerPoint** as the search text in the 'Search programs and files' text box and watch the search results appear on the Start menu (Figure 50).

**Q&A**

Do I need to type the complete program name or correct capitalization?

No, just enough of it for the program name to appear on the Start menu. For example, you may be able to type PowerPoint or powerpoint, instead of Microsoft PowerPoint.

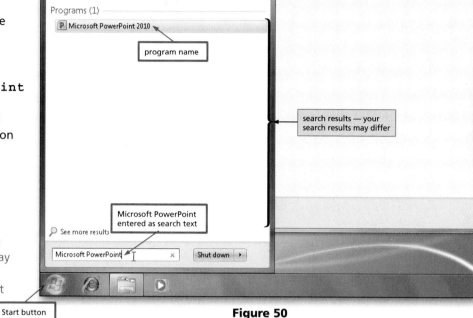

**Figure 50**

- Click the program name, Microsoft PowerPoint 2010 in this case, in the search results on the Start menu to start PowerPoint and display a new blank presentation in the PowerPoint window.

- If the program window is not maximized, click the Maximize button on its title bar to maximize the window (Figure 51).

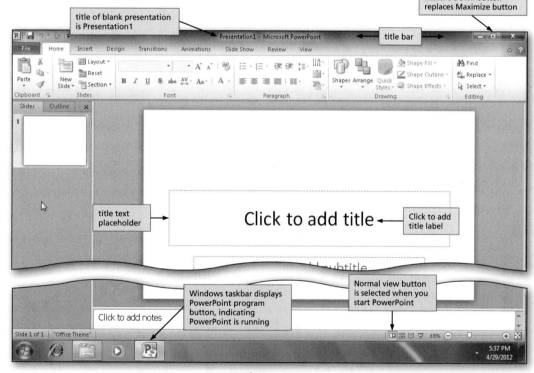

**Figure 51**

## To Open an Existing Office File from the Backstage View

As discussed earlier, the Backstage view contains a set of commands that enable you to manage documents and data about the documents. From the Backstage view in PowerPoint, for example, you can create, open, print, and save presentations. You also can share presentations, manage versions, set permissions, and modify document properties. In other Office 2010 programs, the Backstage view may contain features specific to those programs.

Assume you wish to continue working on an existing file, that is, a file you previously saved. The following steps use the Backstage view to open a saved file, specifically the Investing Strategies file, from the USB flash drive.

- With your USB flash drive connected to one of the computer's USB ports, if necessary, click File on the Ribbon to open the Backstage view (Figure 52).

**Q&A** What is the purpose of the File tab?

The File tab is used to display the Backstage view for each Office program.

**Figure 52**

- Click Open in the Backstage view to display the Open dialog box (Figure 53).

- Navigate to the location of the file to be opened (in this case, the USB flash drive, then to the CIS 101 folder [or your class folder], and then to the PowerPoint folder). For detailed steps about navigating, see Steps 3a – 3c on OFF 26.

**Q&A** What if I did not save my file in a folder?

If you did not save your file in a folder, the file you wish to open should be displayed in the Open dialog box before navigating to any folders.

**Figure 53**

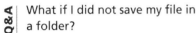

- Click the file to be opened, Investing Strategies in this case, to select the file (Figure 54).

- Click the Open button (Open dialog box) to open the selected file and display the opened file in the current program window.

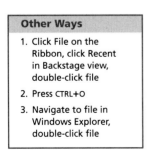

**Other Ways**

1. Click File on the Ribbon, click Recent in Backstage view, double-click file
2. Press CTRL+O
3. Navigate to file in Windows Explorer, double-click file

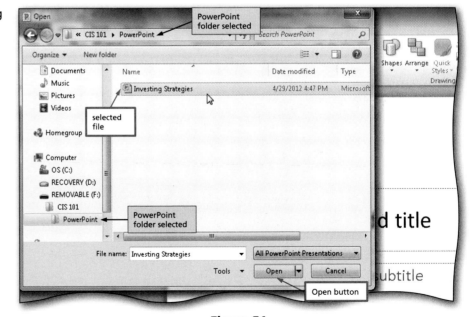

**Figure 54**

## To Create a New Document from the Backstage View

You can create multiple documents at the same time in an Office program, such as PowerPoint. The following steps create a file, a blank presentation in this case, from the Backstage view.

**1**

- Click File on the Ribbon to open the Backstage view.
- Click the New tab in the Backstage view to display the New gallery (Figure 55).

**Q&A**

Can I create documents through the Backstage view in other Office programs?

Yes. If the Office program has a New tab in the Backstage view, the New gallery displays various options for creating a new file.

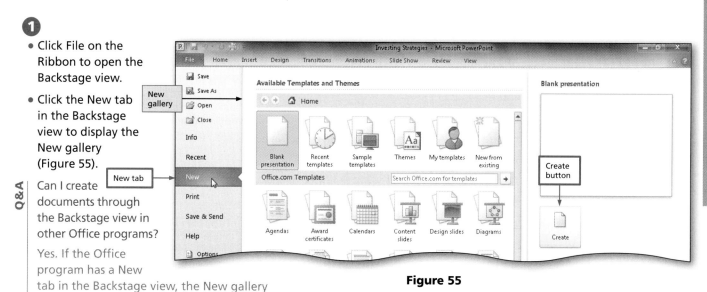

**Figure 55**

**2**

- Click the Create button in the New gallery to create a new presentation (Figure 56).

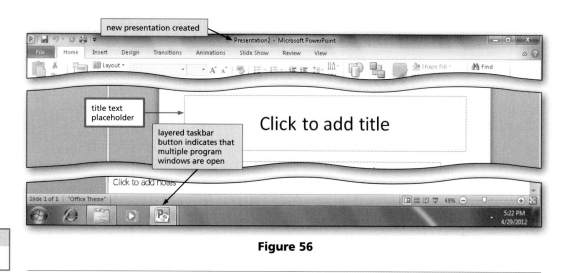

**Other Ways**

1. Press CTRL+N

**Figure 56**

## To Enter Content in a Title Slide of a Second PowerPoint Presentation

The presentation title for this presentation is Koala Exhibit Gala. The following steps enter a presentation title on the title slide.

**1** Click the title text placeholder (shown in Figure 56) to select it.

**2** Type **Koala Exhibit Gala** in the title text placeholder. Do not press the ENTER key (Figure 57).

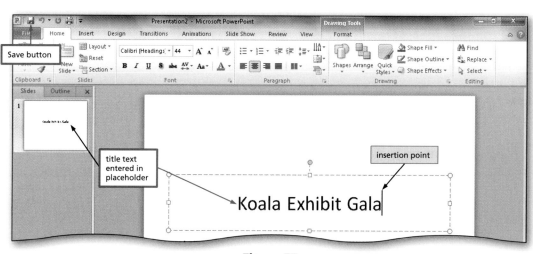

**Figure 57**

## To Save a File in a Folder

**BTW**

**Customizing the Ribbon**
In addition to customizing the Quick Access Toolbar, you can add items to and remove items from the Ribbon. To customize the Ribbon, click File on the Ribbon to open the Backstage view, click Options in the Backstage view, and then click Customize Ribbon in the left pane of the Options dialog box. More information about customizing the Ribbon is presented in a later chapter.

The following steps save the second presentation in the PowerPoint folder in the class folder (CIS 101, in this case) on a USB flash drive using the file name, Koala Exhibit Gala.

**1** With a USB flash drive connected to one of the computer's USB ports, click the Save button on the Quick Access Toolbar to display the Save As dialog box.

**2** If necessary, type `Koala Exhibit Gala` in the File name text box to change the file name. Do not press the ENTER key after typing the file name because you do not want to close the dialog box at this time.

**3** If necessary, navigate to the desired save location (in this case, the PowerPoint folder in the CIS 101 folder [or your class folder] on the USB flash drive).

**4** Click the Save button (Save As dialog box) to save the presentation in the selected folder on the selected drive with the entered file name.

## To Close a File Using the Backstage View

Sometimes, you may want to close an Office file, such as a PowerPoint presentation, entirely and start over with a new file. You also may want to close a file when you are finished working with it so that you can begin a new file. The following steps close the current active PowerPoint file (that is, the Koala Exhibit Gala presentation) without quitting the active program (PowerPoint in this case).

**1**
- Click File on the Ribbon to open the Backstage view (Figure 58).

**2**
- Click Close in the Backstage view to close the open file (Koala Exhibit Gala, in this case) without quitting the active program.

**Figure 58**

**Q&A** What if PowerPoint displays a dialog box about saving?

Click the Save button if you want to save the changes, click the Don't Save button if you want to ignore the changes since the last time you saved, and click the Cancel button if you do not want to close the document.

**Q&A** Can I use the Backstage view to close an open file in other Office programs, such as Word and Excel?

Yes.

## To Open a Recent Office File Using the Backstage View

You sometimes need to open a file that you recently modified. You may have more changes to make such as adding more content or correcting errors. The Backstage view allows you to access recent files easily. The next steps reopen the Koala Exhibit Gala file just closed.

**1**

- Click File on the Ribbon to open the Backstage view.

- Click the Recent tab in the Backstage view to display the Recent gallery (Figure 59).

**2**

- Click the desired file name in the Recent gallery, Koala Exhibit Gala in this case, to open the file (shown in Figure 57 on OFF 35).

**Q&A**

Can I use the Backstage view to open a recent file in other Office programs, such as Word and Excel?

Yes, as long as the file name appears in the list of recent files in the Recent gallery.

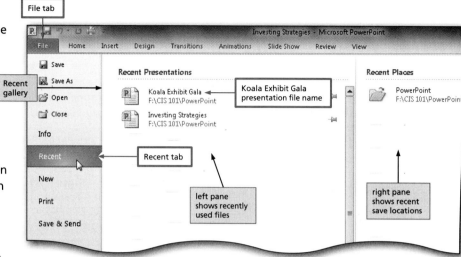

**Figure 59**

**Other Ways**

1. Click Start button, point to program name, click file name on submenu

2. Click File on Ribbon, click Open in Backstage view, navigate to file (Open dialog box), click Open button

## To Create a New Blank Office Document from Windows Explorer

Windows Explorer provides a means to create a blank Office document without ever starting an Office program. The following steps use Windows Explorer to create a blank PowerPoint document.

**1**

- Click the Windows Explorer program button on the taskbar to make the folder window the active window in Windows Explorer.

- If necessary, navigate to the desired location for the new file (in this case, the PowerPoint folder in the CIS 101 folder [or your class folder] on the USB flash drive).

- With the PowerPoint folder selected, right-click an open area in the right pane to display a shortcut menu.

- Point to New on the shortcut menu to display the New submenu (Figure 60).

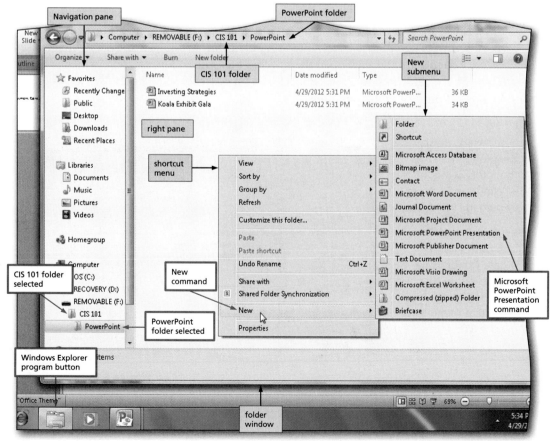

**Figure 60**

- Click Microsoft PowerPoint Presentation on the New submenu to display an icon and text box for a new file in the current folder window (Figure 61).

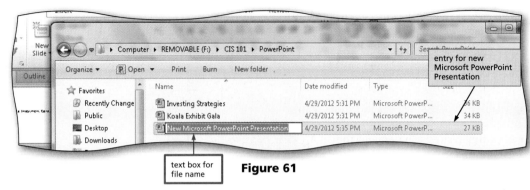

**Figure 61**

- Type **Koala Exhibit Gala Volunteers** in the text box and then press the ENTER key to assign a name to the new file in the current folder (Figure 62).

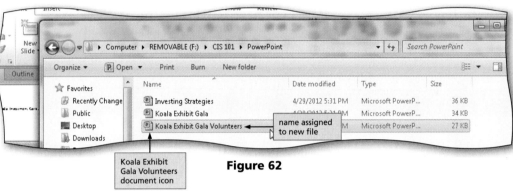

**Figure 62**

## To Start a Program from Windows Explorer and Open a File

Previously, you learned how to start an Office program using the Start menu and the search box. Another way to start an Office program is to open an existing file from Windows Explorer, which causes the program in which the file was created to start and then open the selected file. The following steps, which assume Windows 7 is running, use Windows Explorer to start PowerPoint based on a typical installation. You may need to ask your instructor how to start PowerPoint for your computer.

- If necessary, display the file to open in the folder window in Windows Explorer (shown in Figure 62).

- Right-click the file icon or file name (Koala Exhibit Gala Volunteers, in this case) to display a shortcut menu (Figure 63).

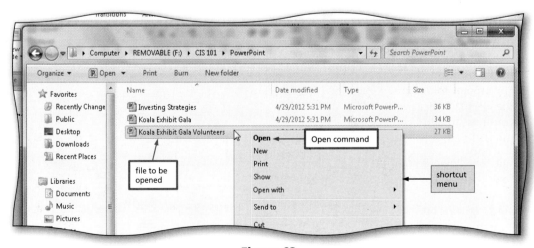

**Figure 63**

**②**

- Click Open on the shortcut menu to open the selected file in the program used to create the file, Microsoft PowerPoint in this case (Figure 64).

- If the program window is not maximized, click the Maximize button on the title bar to maximize the window.

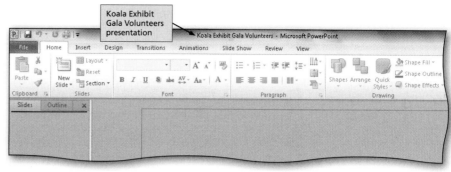

**Figure 64**

## To Enter Text in a Slide

The next steps enter text in a blank slide.

**1** Click the label, Click to add first slide, to display the title slide.

**2** Click the label, Click to add title, located inside the title text placeholder.

**3** Type `Koala Exhibit Staff and Volunteers` (shown in Figure 65).

## To Save an Existing Document with the Same File Name

Saving frequently cannot be overemphasized. You have made modifications to the file (presentation) since you created it. Thus, you should save again. Similarly, you should continue saving files frequently so that you do not lose your changes since the time you last saved the file. You can use the same file name, such as Koala Exhibit Gala Volunteers, to save the changes made to the document. The following step saves a file again.

**1**

- Click the Save button on the Quick Access Toolbar to overwrite the previously saved file (Koala Exhibit Gala Volunteers, in this case) on the USB flash drive (Figure 65).

**Q&A**

Why did the Save As dialog box not appear?

Office programs, including PowerPoint, overwrite the document using the setting specified the first time you saved the document.

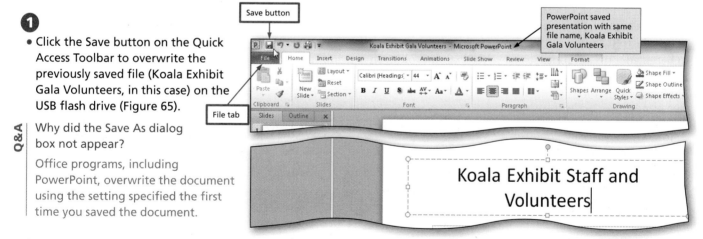

**Figure 65**

**Other Ways**

1. Press CTRL+S or press SHIFT+F12

## To Use Save As to Change the Name of a File

You might want to save a file with a different name and even to a different location. For example, you might start a homework assignment with a data file and then save it with a final file name for submitting to your instructor, saving it to a location designated by your instructor. The following steps save a file with a different file name.

**1** With your USB flash drive connected to one of the computer's USB ports, click File on the Ribbon to open the Backstage view.

**2** Click Save As in the Backstage view to display the Save As dialog box.

**3** Type `Koala Exhibit Staff and Volunteers` in the File name text box (Save As dialog box) to change the file name. Do not press the ENTER key after typing the file name because you do not want to close the dialog box at this time.

**4** Navigate to the desired save location (the PowerPoint folder in the CIS 101 folder [or your class folder] on the USB flash drive, in this case).

**5** Click the Save button (Save As dialog box) to save the file in the selected folder on the selected drive with the new file name.

**BTW**

**Multiple Open Files**
If the program button on the taskbar displays as a tiered stack, you have multiple files open in the program.

## To Quit an Office Program

You are finished using PowerPoint. The following steps quit PowerPoint.

**1** Because you have multiple PowerPoint documents open, click File on the Ribbon to open the Backstage view and then click Exit in the Backstage view to close all open documents and quit the PowerPoint program.

**2** If a dialog box appears, click the Save button to save any changes made to the file since the last save.

# Moving, Renaming, and Deleting Files

Earlier in this chapter, you learned how to organize files in folders, which is part of a process known as **file management**. The following sections cover additional file management topics including renaming, moving, and deleting files.

## To Rename a File

In some circumstances, you may want to change the name of, or rename, a file or a folder. For example, you may want to distinguish a file in one folder or drive from a copy of a similar file, or you may decide to rename a file to better identify its contents. The PowerPoint folder shown in Figure 66 contains the PowerPoint document, Koala Exhibit Gala. The following steps change the name of the Koala Exhibit Gala file in the PowerPoint folder to Koala Exhibit Presentation.

**1**

- If necessary, click the Windows Explorer program button on the taskbar to display the folder window in Windows Explorer.

- If necessary, navigate to the location of the file to be renamed (in this case, the PowerPoint folder in the CIS 101 folder [or your class folder] on the USB flash drive) to display the file(s) it contains in the right pane.

- Right-click the Koala Exhibit Gala icon or file name in the right pane to select the Koala Exhibit Gala file and display a shortcut menu that presents a list of commands related to files (Figure 66).

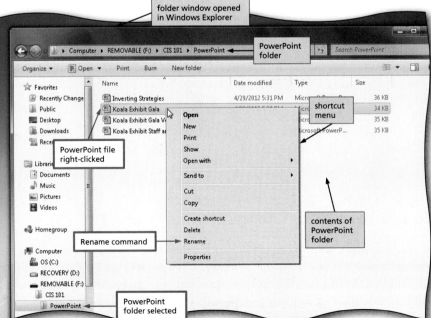

**Figure 66**

**2**

- Click Rename on the shortcut menu to place the current file name in a text box.

- Type **Koala Exhibit Presentation** in the text box and then press the ENTER key (Figure 67).

**Q&A** Are any risks involved in renaming files that are located on a hard disk?

If you inadvertently rename a file that is associated with certain programs, the programs may not be able to find the file and, therefore, may not execute properly. Always use caution when renaming files.

**Q&A** Can I rename a file when it is open?

No, a file must be closed to change the file name.

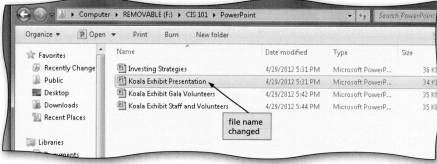

**Figure 67**

**Other Ways**

1. Select file, press F2, type new file name, press ENTER

## To Move a File

At some time, you may want to move a file from one folder, called the source folder, to another, called the destination. When you move a file, it no longer appears in the original folder. If the destination and the source folders are on the same disk drive, you can move a file by dragging it. If the folders are on different disk drives, then you will need to right-drag the file. The following step moves the Koala Exhibit Gala Volunteers file from the PowerPoint folder to the CIS 101 folder.

**1**

- In Windows Explorer, if necessary, navigate to the location of the file to be moved (in this case, the PowerPoint folder in the CIS 101 folder [or your class folder] on the USB flash drive).

- Click the PowerPoint folder in the Navigation pane to display the files it contains in the right pane (Figure 68).

- Drag the Koala Exhibit Gala Volunteers file in the right pane to the CIS 101 folder in the Navigation pane.

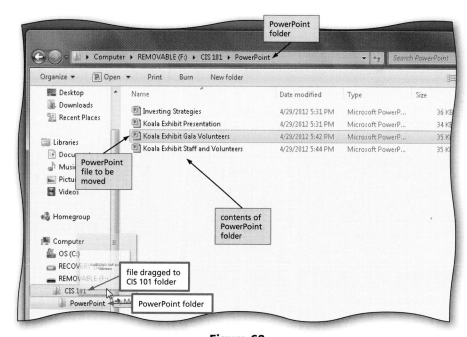

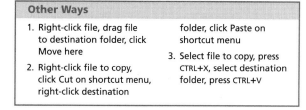

**Figure 68**

**Other Ways**

1. Right-click file, drag file to destination folder, click Move here

2. Right-click file to copy, click Cut on shortcut menu, right-click destination

folder, click Paste on shortcut menu

3. Select file to copy, press CTRL+X, select destination folder, press CTRL+V

## To Delete a File

A final task you may want to perform is to delete a file. Exercise extreme caution when deleting a file or files. When you delete a file from a hard disk, the deleted file is stored in the Recycle Bin where you can recover it until you empty the Recycle Bin. If you delete a file from removable media, such as a USB flash drive, the file is deleted permanently. The next steps delete the Koala Exhibit Gala Volunteers file from the CIS 101 folder.

- In Windows Explorer, navigate to the location of the file to be deleted (in this case, the CIS 101 folder [or your class folder] on the USB flash drive).

- If necessary, click the CIS 101 folder in the Navigation pane to display the files it contains in the right pane.

- Right-click the Koala Exhibit Gala Volunteers icon or file name in the right pane to select the file and display a shortcut menu (Figure 69).

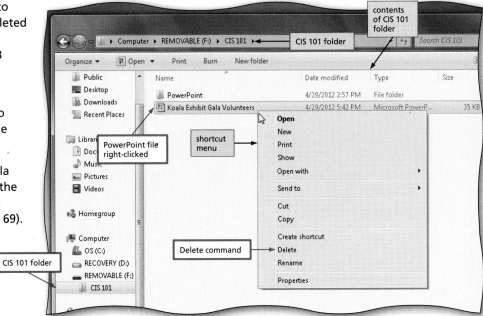

**Figure 69**

- Click Delete on the shortcut menu to display the Delete File dialog box (Figure 70).

- Click the Yes button (Delete File dialog box) to delete the selected file.

**Q&A** Can I use this same technique to delete a folder?

Yes. Right-click the folder and then click Delete on the shortcut menu. When you delete a folder, all of the files and folders contained in the folder you are deleting, together with any files and folders on lower hierarchical levels, are deleted as well.

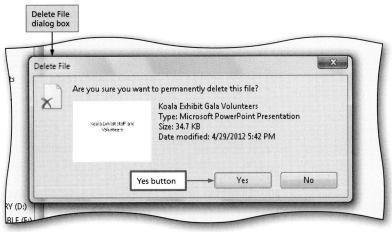

**Figure 70**

**Other Ways**

1. Select icon, press DELETE

# Microsoft Office and Windows Help

At any time while you are using one of the Microsoft Office 2010 programs, such as PowerPoint, you can use Office Help to display information about all topics associated with the program. This section illustrates the use of PowerPoint Help. Help in other Office 2010 programs operates in a similar fashion.

In Office 2010, Help is presented in a window that has Web-browser-style navigation buttons. Each Office 2010 program has its own Help home page, which is the starting Help page that is displayed in the Help window. If your computer is connected to the Internet, the contents of the Help page reflect both the local help files installed on the computer and material from Microsoft's Web site.

## To Open the Help Window in an Office Program

The following step opens the PowerPoint Help window. The step to open a Help window in other Office programs is similar.

**1**

- Start PowerPoint.

- Click the Microsoft PowerPoint Help button near the upper-right corner of the program window to open the PowerPoint Help window (Figure 71).

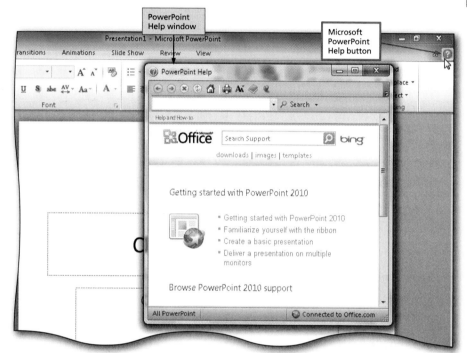

**Figure 71**

| Other Ways |
| --- |
| 1. Press F1 |

# Moving and Resizing Windows

Up to this point, this chapter has used minimized and maximized windows. At times, however, it is useful, or even necessary, to have more than one window open and visible on the screen at the same time. You can resize and move these open windows so that you can view different areas of and elements in the window. In the case of the Help window, for example, it could be covering slide elements in the PowerPoint window that you need to see.

## To Move a Window by Dragging

You can move any open window that is not maximized to another location on the desktop by dragging the title bar of the window. The following step drags the PowerPoint Help window to the top left of the desktop.

- Drag the window title bar (the PowerPoint Help window title bar, in this case) so that the window moves to the top left of the desktop, as shown in Figure 72.

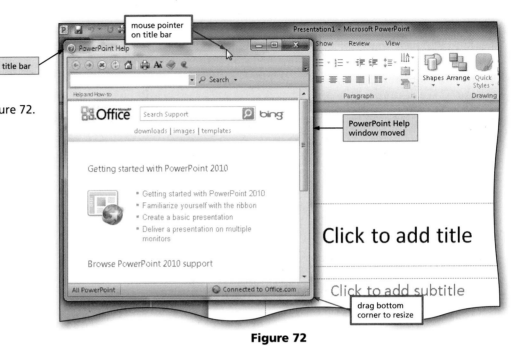

**Figure 72**

**Other Ways**

1. Right-click title bar, click Move on shortcut menu, drag window

## To Resize a Window by Dragging

Sometimes, information is not visible completely in a window. A method used to change the size of the window is to drag the window borders. The following step changes the size of the PowerPoint Help window by dragging its borders.

- Point to the lower-right corner of the window (the PowerPoint Help window, in this case) until the mouse pointer changes to a two-headed arrow.

- Drag the bottom border downward to display more of the active window (Figure 73).

**Q&A** Can I drag other borders on the window to enlarge or shrink the window?

Yes, you can drag the left, right, and top borders and any window corner to resize a window.

**Q&A** Will Windows 7 remember the new size of the window after I close it?

Yes. When you reopen the window, Windows 7 will display it at the same size it was when you closed it.

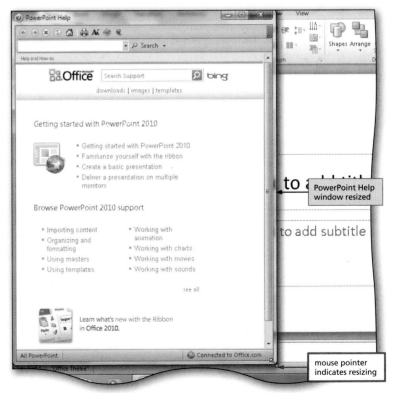

**Figure 73**

# Using Office Help

Once an Office program's Help window is open, several methods exist for navigating Help. You can search for help by using any of the three following methods from the Help window:

1. Enter search text in the 'Type words to search for' text box.
2. Click the links in the Help window.
3. Use the Table of Contents.

## To Obtain Help Using the 'Type words to search for' Text Box

Assume for the following example that you want to know more about the Backstage view. The following steps use the 'Type words to search for' text box to obtain useful information about the Backstage view by entering the word, Backstage, as search text.

**1**

- Type **Backstage** in the 'Type words to search for' text box at the top of the PowerPoint Help window to enter the search text.

- Click the Search button arrow to display the Search menu (Figure 74).

- If it is not selected already, click All PowerPoint on the Search menu, so that Help performs the most complete search of the current program (PowerPoint, in this case). If All PowerPoint already is selected, click the Search button arrow again to close the Search menu.

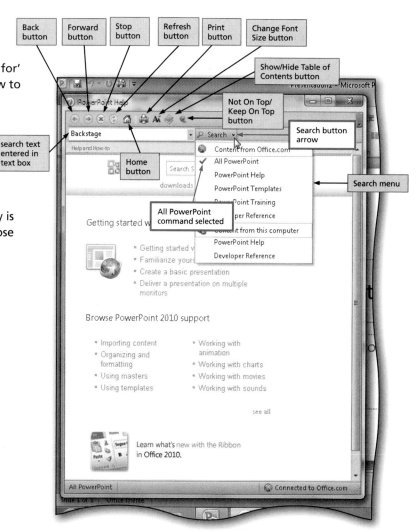

**Figure 74**

Why select All PowerPoint on the Search menu?

Selecting All PowerPoint on the Search menu ensures that PowerPoint Help will search all possible sources for information about your search term. It will produce the most complete search results.

**2**

- Click the Search button to display the search results (Figure 75).

**Q&A** Why do my search results differ?

If you do not have an Internet connection, your results will reflect only the content of the Help files on your computer. When searching for help online, results also can change as material is added, deleted, and updated on the online Help Web pages maintained by Microsoft.

**Q&A** Why were my search results not very helpful?

When initiating a search, be sure to check the spelling of the search text; also, keep your search specific, with fewer than seven words, to return the most accurate results.

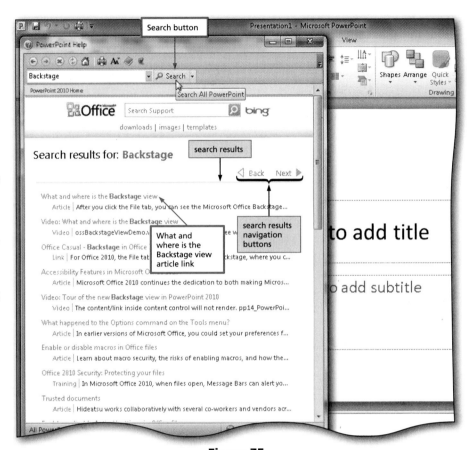

**Figure 75**

**3**

- Click the 'What and where is the Backstage view' link to open the Help document associated with the selected topic (Figure 76).

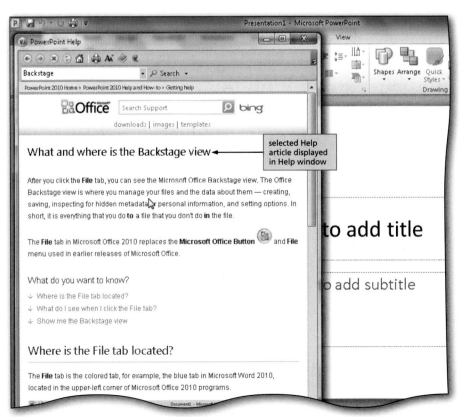

**Figure 76**

- Click the Home button on the toolbar to clear the search results and redisplay the Help home page (Figure 77).

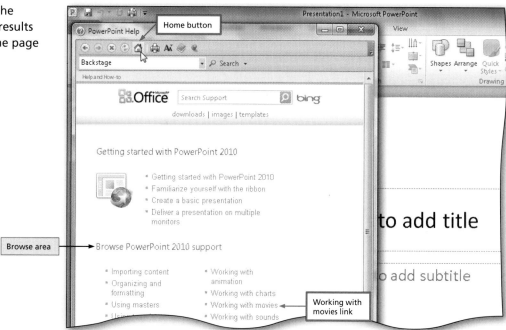

**Figure 77**

## To Obtain Help Using the Help Links

If your topic of interest is listed in the Browse area of the Help window, you can click the link to begin browsing the Help categories instead of entering search text. You browse Help just as you would browse a Web site. If you know which category contains your Help information, you may wish to use these links. The following step finds the Working with movies Help information using the category links from the PowerPoint Help home page.

- Click the 'Working with movies' link on the Help home page (shown in Figure 77) to display the 'Working with movies' page (Figure 78).

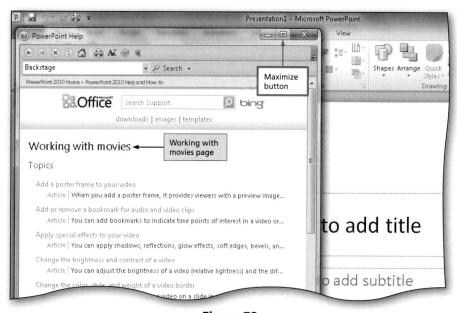

**Figure 78**

## To Obtain Help Using the Help Table of Contents

A third way to find Help in Office programs is through the Help Table of Contents. You can browse through the Table of Contents to display information about a particular topic or to familiarize yourself with an Office program. The following steps access the Help information about slide layouts by browsing through the Table of Contents.

**1**

• Click the Home button on the toolbar to display the Help home page.

• Click the Show Table of Contents button on the toolbar to display the Table of Contents pane on the left side of the Help window. If necessary, click the Maximize button on the Help title bar to maximize the window (Figure 79).

**Q&A**
Why does the appearance of the Show Table of Contents button change?

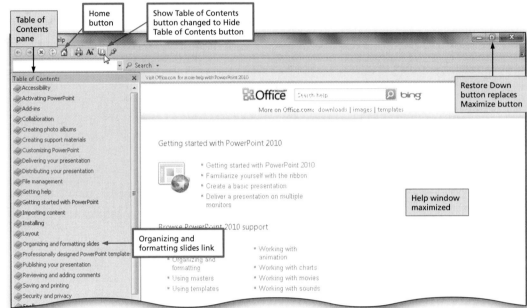

**Figure 79**

When the Table of Contents is displayed in the Help window, the Hide Table of Contents button replaces the Show Table of Contents button.

**2**

• Click the 'Organizing and formatting slides' link in the Table of Contents pane to view a list of Help subtopics.

• Click the 'Apply a layout to a slide' link in the Table of Contents pane to view the selected Help document in the right pane (Figure 80).

• After reviewing the page, click the Close button to quit Help.

• Click the PowerPoint Close button to quit the PowerPoint program.

**Figure 80**

**Q&A**
How do I remove the Table of Contents pane when I am finished with it?

The Show Table of Contents button acts as a toggle. When the Table of Contents pane is visible, the button changes to Hide Table of Contents. Clicking it hides the Table of Contents pane and changes the button to Show Table of Contents.

# Obtaining Help while Working in an Office Program

Help in Office programs, such as PowerPoint, provides you with the ability to obtain help directly, without the need to open the Help window and initiate a search. For example, you may be unsure about how a particular command works, or you may be presented with a dialog box that you are not sure how to use.

Figure 81 shows one option for obtaining help while working in PowerPoint. If you want to learn more about a command, point to the command button and wait for the Enhanced ScreenTip to appear. If the Help icon appears in the Enhanced ScreenTip, press the F1 key while pointing to the command to open the Help window associated with that command.

Figure 82 shows a dialog box that contains a Help button. Pressing the F1 key while the dialog box is displayed opens a Help window. The Help window contains help about that dialog box, if available. If no help file is available for that particular dialog box, then the main Help window opens.

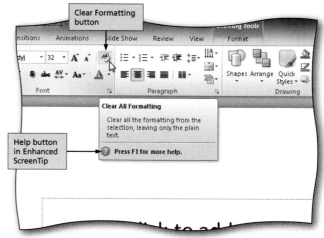

**Figure 81**

# Using Windows Help and Support

One of the more powerful Windows 7 features is Windows Help and Support. **Windows Help and Support** is available when using Windows 7 or when using any Microsoft program running under Windows 7. This feature is designed to assist you in using Windows 7 or the various programs. Table 4 describes the content found in the Help and Support Center. The same methods used for searching Microsoft Office Help can be used in Windows Help and Support. The difference is that Windows Help and Support displays help for Windows 7, instead of for Microsoft Office.

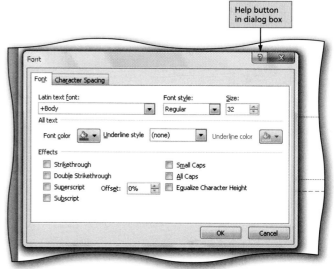

**Figure 82**

| Table 4 Windows Help and Support Center Content Areas | |
|---|---|
| **Area** | **Function** |
| Find an answer quickly | This area contains instructions about how to do a quick search using the search box. |
| Not sure where to start? | This area displays three topics to help guide a user: How to get started with your computer, Learn about Windows Basics, and Browse Help topics. Clicking one of the options navigates to corresponding Help and Support pages. |
| More on the Windows website | This area contains links to online content from the Windows Web site. Clicking the links navigates to the corresponding Web pages on the Web site. |

## To Start Windows Help and Support

The following steps start Windows Help and Support and display the Windows Help and Support window, containing links to more information about Windows 7.

**1**

- Click the Start button on the taskbar to display the Start menu (Figure 83).

**Q&A**

Why are the programs that are displayed on the Start menu different?

Windows adds the programs you have used recently to the left pane on the Start menu. You have started PowerPoint while performing the steps in this chapter, so that program now is displayed on the Start menu.

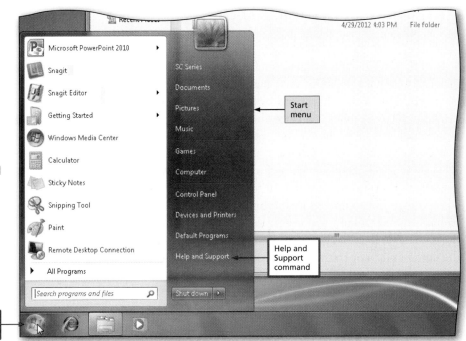

**Figure 83**

**2**

- Click Help and Support on the Start menu to open the Windows Help and Support window (Figure 84).

- After reviewing the Windows Help and Support window, click the Close button to quit Windows Help and Support.

**Other Ways**

1. Press CTRL+ESC, press RIGHT ARROW, press UP ARROW, press ENTER

2. Press WINDOWS+F1

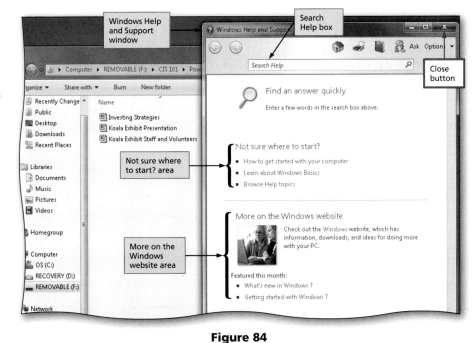

**Figure 84**

# Chapter Summary

In this chapter, you learned about the Windows 7 interface. You started Windows 7, were introduced to the components of the desktop, and learned several mouse operations. You opened, closed, moved, resized, minimized, maximized, and scrolled a window. You used folder windows to expand and collapse drives and folders, display drive and folder contents, create folders, and rename and then delete a file.

You also learned some basic features of Microsoft PowerPoint 2010. As part of this learning process, you discovered the common elements that exist among Microsoft Office programs.

Microsoft Office Help was demonstrated, and you learned how to use the PowerPoint Help window. You were introduced to the Windows 7 Help and Support Center and learned how to use it to obtain more information about Windows 7.

The items listed below include all of the new Windows 7 and Office 2010 skills you have learned in this chapter.

1. Log On to the Computer (OFF 6)
2. Start a Program Using the Start Menu (OFF 10)
3. Maximize a Window (OFF 12)
4. Display a Different Tab on the Ribbon (OFF 16)
5. Minimize, Display, and Restore the Ribbon (OFF 16)
6. Display and Use a Shortcut Menu (OFF 17)
7. Customize the Quick Access Toolbar (OFF 18)
8. Enter Content in a Title Slide (OFF 19)
9. Create a Folder (OFF 20)
10. Create a Folder within a Folder (OFF 23)
11. Expand a Folder, Scroll through Folder Contents, and Collapse a Folder (OFF 23)
12. Switch from One Program to Another (OFF 24)
13. Save a File in a Folder (OFF 25)
14. Minimize and Restore a Window (OFF 27)
15. Change the Screen Resolution (OFF 30)
16. Quit a Program with One Document Open (OFF 31)
17. Start a Program Using the Search Box (OFF 32)
18. Open an Existing Office File from the Backstage View (OFF 33)
19. Create a New Document from the Backstage View (OFF 34)
20. Close a File Using the Backstage View (OFF 36)
21. Open a Recent Office File Using the Backstage View (OFF 36)
22. Create a New Blank Office Document from Windows Explorer (OFF 37)
23. Start a Program from Windows Explorer and Open a File (OFF 38)
24. Save an Existing Document with the Same File Name (OFF 39)
25. Rename a File (OFF 40)
26. Move a File (OFF 41)
27. Delete a File (OFF 42)
28. Open the Help Window in an Office Program (OFF 43)
29. Move a Window by Dragging (OFF 43)
30. Resize a Window by Dragging (OFF 44)
31. Obtain Help Using the 'Type words to search for' Text Box (OFF 45)
32. Obtain Help Using the Help Links (OFF 47)
33. Obtain Help Using the Help Table of Contents (OFF 48)
34. Start Windows Help and Support (OFF 49)

 If you have a SAM 2010 user profile, your instructor may have assigned an autogradable version of this assignment. If so, log into the SAM 2010 Web site at www.cengage.com/sam2010 to download the instruction and start files.

## Learn It Online

Test your knowledge of chapter content and key terms.

*Instructions:* To complete the Learn It Online exercises, start your browser, click the Address bar, and then enter the Web address **scsite.com/office2010/learn**. When the Office 2010 Learn It Online page is displayed, click the link for the exercise you want to complete and then read the instructions.

### Chapter Reinforcement TF, MC, and SA
A series of true/false, multiple choice, and short answer questions that test your knowledge of the chapter content.

### Flash Cards
An interactive learning environment where you identify chapter key terms associated with displayed definitions.

### Practice Test
A series of multiple choice questions that test your knowledge of chapter content and key terms.

### Who Wants To Be a Computer Genius?
An interactive game that challenges your knowledge of chapter content in the style of a television quiz show.

### Wheel of Terms
An interactive game that challenges your knowledge of chapter key terms in the style of the television show *Wheel of Fortune*.

### Crossword Puzzle Challenge
A crossword puzzle that challenges your knowledge of key terms presented in the chapter.

## Apply Your Knowledge

Reinforce the skills and apply the concepts you learned in this chapter.

### Creating a Folder and a Document

*Instructions:* You will create a PowerPoint folder and then create a PowerPoint document and save it in the folder.

*Perform the following tasks:*

1. Connect a USB flash drive to an available USB port and then open the USB flash drive window.

2. Click the New folder button on the toolbar to display a new folder icon and text box for the folder name.

3. Type **PowerPoint** in the text box to name the folder. Press the ENTER key to create the folder on the USB flash drive.

4. Start PowerPoint.

5. Enter the text shown in Figure 85.

6. Click the Save button on the Quick Access Toolbar. Navigate to the PowerPoint folder on the USB flash drive and then save the document using the file name, Apply 1 Study Habits.

7. If your Quick Access Toolbar does not show the Quick Print button, add the Quick Print button to the Quick Access Toolbar. Print the document using the Quick Print button on the Quick Access Toolbar. When you are finished printing, remove the Quick Print button from the Quick Access Toolbar.

8. Submit the printout to your instructor.

9. Quit PowerPoint.

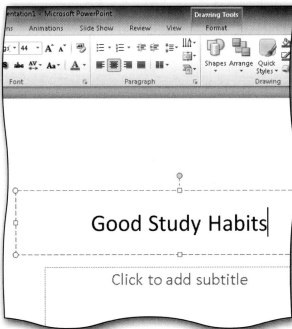

**Figure 85**

## Extend Your Knowledge

Extend the skills you learned in this chapter and experiment with new skills. You will use Help to complete the assignment.

### Using Help

*Instructions:* Use Office Help to perform the following tasks.

*Perform the following tasks:*

1. Start PowerPoint.

2. Click the Microsoft PowerPoint Help button to open the PowerPoint Help window (Figure 86).

**Figure 86**

3. Search PowerPoint Help to answer the following questions.

   a. What are three features new to PowerPoint 2010?

   b. What type of training courses are available through Help?

   c. What steps add a new group to the Ribbon?

   d. What are Quick Parts?

   e. What are document properties?

   f. What is SmartArt?

   g. How do you print slides as a handout?

   h. What type of graphics can you insert?

   i. How do you add transitions between slides?

   j. What is the purpose of the Navigation pane?

4. Submit the answers from your searches in the format specified by your instructor.

5. Quit PowerPoint.

## Make It Right

Analyze a file structure and correct all errors and/or improve the design.

*Note:* To complete this assignment, you will be required to use the Data Files for Students. See the inside back cover of this book for instructions on downloading the Data Files for Students, or contact your instructor for information about accessing the required files.

### Organizing Vacation Photos

*Instructions:* Traditionally, you have stored photos from past vacations together in one folder. The photos are becoming difficult to manage, and you now want to store them in appropriate folders. You will create the folder structure shown in Figure 87. You then will move the photos to the folders so that they will be organized properly.

1. Connect a USB flash drive to an available USB port to open the USB flash drive window.

2. Create the hierarchical folder structure shown in Figure 87.

3. Move one photo to each folder in the folder structure you created in Step 2. The five photos are located on the Data Files for Students.

4. Submit your work in the format specified by your instructor.

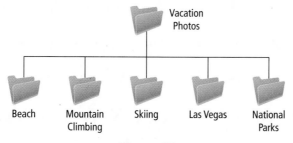

**Figure 87**

## In the Lab

Use the guidelines, concepts, and skills presented in this chapter to increase your knowledge of Windows 7 and PowerPoint 2010. Labs are listed in order of increasing difficulty.

### Lab 1: Using Windows Help and Support

*Problem:* You have a few questions about using Windows 7 and would like to answer these questions using Windows Help and Support.

*Instructions:* Use Windows Help and Support to perform the following tasks:

1. Display the Start menu and then click Help and Support to start Windows Help and Support.

2. Use the Help and Support Content page to answer the following questions.

   a. How do you reduce computer screen flicker?

   b. Which dialog box do you use to change the appearance of the mouse pointer?

   c. How do you minimize all windows?

   d. What is a VPN?

3. Use the Search Help text box in Windows Help and Support to answer the following questions.

   a. How can you minimize all open windows on the desktop?

   b. How do you start a program using the Run command?

   c. What are the steps to add a toolbar to the taskbar?

   d. What wizard do you use to remove unwanted desktop icons?

4. The tools to solve a problem while using Windows 7 are called **troubleshooters**. Use Windows Help and Support to find the list of troubleshooters (Figure 88), and answer the following questions.

   a. What problems does the HomeGroup troubleshooter allow you to resolve?

   b. List five Windows 7 troubleshooters that are not listed in Figure 88.

5. Use Windows Help and Support to obtain information about software licensing and product activation, and answer the following questions.

   a. What is genuine Windows?

   b. What is activation?

   c. What steps are required to activate Windows?

   d. What steps are required to read the Microsoft Software License Terms?

   e. Can you legally make a second copy of Windows 7 for use at home, work, or on a mobile computer or device?

   f. What is registration?

6. Close the Windows Help and Support window.

**Figure 88**

## In the Lab

### Lab 2: Creating Folders for a Pet Supply Store

*Problem:*  Your friend works for Pete's Pet Supplies. He would like to organize his files in relation to the types of pets available in the store. He has five main categories: dogs, cats, fish, birds, and exotic. You are to create a folder structure similar to Figure 89.

*Instructions:*  Perform the following tasks:

1. Connect a USB flash drive to an available USB port and then open the USB flash drive window.

2. Create the main folder for Pete's Pet Supplies.

3. Navigate to the Pete's Pet Supplies folder.

4. Within the Pete's Pet Supplies folder, create a folder for each of the following: Dogs, Cats, Fish, Birds, and Exotic.

5. Within the Exotic folder, create two additional folders, one for Primates and the second for Reptiles.

6. Submit the assignment in the format specified by your instructor.

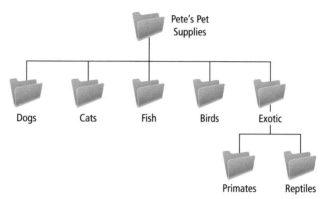

**Figure 89**

## In the Lab

### Lab 3: Creating PowerPoint Presentations and Saving Them in Appropriate Folders

*Problem:*  You are taking a class that requires you to complete three PowerPoint chapters. You will save the work completed in each chapter in a different folder (Figure 90).

*Instructions:*  Create the folders shown in Figure 90. Then, using PowerPoint, create a small file to save in each folder.

1. Connect a USB flash drive to an available USB port and then open the USB flash drive window.

2. Create the folder structure shown in Figure 90.

3. Navigate to the Chapter 1 folder.

4. Create a PowerPoint presentation containing the text, My Chapter 1 PowerPoint Document, and then save it in the Chapter 1 PowerPoint folder using the file name, PowerPoint Chapter 1 Document.

5. Navigate to the Chapter 2 folder.

6. Create another PowerPoint presentation containing the text, My Chapter 2 PowerPoint Document, and then save it in the Chapter 2 folder using the file name, PowerPoint Chapter 2 Document.

7. Navigate to the Chapter 3 folder.

8. Create another PowerPoint presentation containing the text, My Chapter 3 PowerPoint Document, and then save it in the Chapter 3 folder using the file name, PowerPoint Chapter 3 Document.

9. Quit PowerPoint.

10. Submit the assignment in the format specified by your instructor.

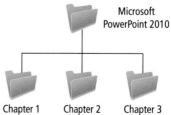

**Figure 90**

# Cases and Places

Apply your creative thinking and problem solving skills to design and implement a solution.

*Note:* To complete these assignments, you may be required to use the Data Files for Students. See the inside back cover of this book for instructions on downloading the Data Files for Students, or contact your instructor for information about accessing the required files.

## 1: Creating Beginning Files for Classes

### Academic

You are taking the following classes: Introduction to Engineering, Beginning Psychology, Introduction to Biology, and Accounting. Create folders for each of the classes. Use the following folder names: Engineering, Psychology, Biology, and Accounting, when creating the folder structure. In the Engineering folder, use PowerPoint to create a presentation with the name of the class and the class meeting location and time (MW 10:30 – 11:45, Room 317). In the Psychology folder, use PowerPoint to create your first lab presentation. It should begin with a title slide containing the text, Behavioral Observations. In the Biology folder, create another presentation with the title, Research. In the Accounting folder, create a PowerPoint presentation with the text, Tax Information. Use the concepts and techniques presented in this chapter to create the folders and files.

## 2: Using Help

### Personal

Your parents enjoy working and playing games on their home computers. Your mother uses a notebook computer downstairs, and your father uses a desktop computer upstairs. They expressed interest in sharing files between their computers and sharing a single printer, so you offered to research various home networking options. Start Windows Help and Support, and search Help using the keywords, home networking. Use the link for installing a printer on a home network. Start PowerPoint and then create a presentation describing the main steps for installing a printer. Use the link for setting up a HomeGroup and then type the main steps for creating a HomeGroup in the PowerPoint presentation. Use the concepts and techniques presented in this chapter to use Help and create the PowerPoint presentation.

## 3: Creating Folders

### Professional

Your boss at the bookstore where you work part-time has asked for help with organizing her files. After looking through the files, you decided upon a file structure for her to use, including the following folders: books, magazines, tapes, DVDs, and general merchandise. Within the books folder, create folders for hardback and paperback books. Within magazines, create folders for special issues and periodicals. In the tapes folder, create folders for celebrity and major release. In the DVDs folder, create a folder for book to DVD. In the general merchandise folder, create folders for novelties, posters, and games. Use the concepts and techniques presented in this chapter to create the folders.

# 1 | Creating and Editing a Presentation with Clip Art

## Objectives

You will have mastered the material in this chapter when you can:

- Select a document theme
- Create a title slide and a text slide with a multi-level bulleted list
- Add new slides and change slide layouts
- Insert clips and pictures into a slide with and without a content placeholder
- Move and size clip art

- Change font size and color
- Bold and italicize text
- Duplicate a slide
- Arrange slides
- Select slide transitions
- View a presentation in Slide Show view
- Print a presentation

# 1 | Creating and Editing a Presentation with Clip Art

## Introduction

A PowerPoint **presentation,** also called a **slide show,** can help you deliver a dynamic, professional-looking message to an audience. PowerPoint allows you to produce slides to use in an academic, business, or other environment. One of the more common uses of these slides is to enhance an oral presentation. A speaker may desire to convey information, such as urging students to volunteer at a fund-raising event, explaining changes in employee compensation packages, or describing a new laboratory procedure. The PowerPoint slides should reinforce the speaker's message and help the audience retain the information presented. Custom slides can fit your specific needs and contain diagrams, charts, tables, pictures, shapes, video, sound, and animation effects to make your presentation more effective. An accompanying handout gives audience members reference notes and review material for your presentation.

**Project Planning Guidelines**

The process of developing a presentation that communicates specific information requires careful analysis and planning. As a starting point, establish why the presentation is needed. Next, analyze the intended audience for the presentation and its unique needs. Then, gather information about the topic and decide what to include in the presentation. Finally, determine the presentation design and style that will be most successful at delivering the message. Details of these guidelines are provided in Appendix A. In addition, each project in this book provides practical applications of these planning considerations.

**BTW**

**Energy-Saving Information**
The U.S. Department of Energy's Web site has myriad information available on the topics of energy efficiency and renewable energy. These features can provide news and product research that you can share with audiences with the help of a PowerPoint presentation.

## Project — Presentation with Bulleted Lists and Clip Art

In this chapter's project, you will follow proper design guidelines and learn to use PowerPoint to create, save, and print the slides shown in Figures 1–1a through 1–1e. The objective is to produce a presentation, called It Is Easy Being Green, to help consumers understand basic steps they can take to save energy in their homes. This slide show has a variety of clip art and visual elements to add interest and illustrate energy-cutting measures. Some of the text has formatting and color enhancements. Transitions help one slide flow gracefully into the next during a slide show. In addition, you will print a handout of your slides to distribute to audience members.

**(a) Slide 1 (Title Slide with Clip Art)**

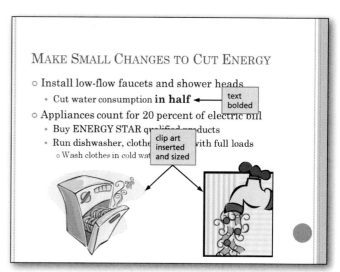

**(b) Slide 2 (Multi-Level Bulleted List with Clip Art)**

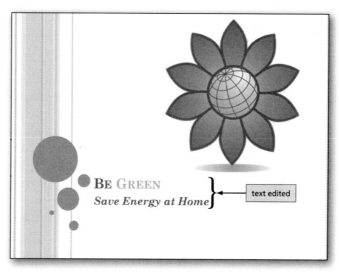

**(c) Slide 3 (Title and Photograph)**

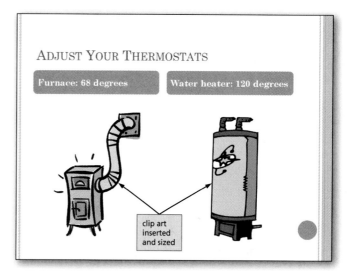

**(d) Slide 4 (Comparison Layout and Clip Art)**

**(e) Slide 5 (Closing Slide)**

**Figure 1–1**

# Overview

As you read this chapter, you will learn how to create the presentation shown in Figure 1–1 on the previous page by performing these general tasks:

- Select an appropriate document theme.
- Enter titles and text on slides.
- Change the size, color, and style of text.
- Insert clips and a photograph.
- Add a transition to each slide.
- View the presentation on your computer.
- Print your slides.

**Plan Ahead**

> **General Project Guidelines**
>
> When creating a PowerPoint document, the actions you perform and decisions you make will affect the appearance and characteristics of the finished document. As you create a presentation such as the project shown in Figure 1–1, you should follow these general guidelines:
>
> 1. **Find the appropriate theme.** The overall appearance of a presentation significantly affects its capability to communicate information clearly. The slides' graphical appearance should support the presentation's overall message. Colors, fonts, and layouts affect how audience members perceive and react to the slide content.
>
> 2. **Choose words for each slide.** Use the less is more principle. The less text, the more likely the slides will enhance your speech. Use the fewest words possible to make a point.
>
> 3. **Format specific elements of the text.** Examples of how you can modify the appearance, or **format**, of text include changing its shape, size, color, and position on the slide.
>
> 4. **Determine where to save the presentation.** You can store a document permanently, or **save** it, on a variety of storage media, including a hard disk, USB flash drive, or CD. You also can indicate a specific location on the storage media for saving the document.
>
> 5. **Determine the best method for distributing the presentation.** Presentations can be distributed on paper or electronically. You can print a hard copy of the presentation slides for proofing or reference, or you can distribute an electronic image in various formats.
>
> When necessary, more specific details concerning the above guidelines are presented at appropriate points in the chapter. The chapter also will identify the actions performed and decisions made regarding these guidelines during the creation of the slides shown in Figure 1–1.

## To Start PowerPoint

If you are using a computer to step through the project in this chapter and you want your screens to match the figures in this book, you should change your screen's resolution to 1024 × 768. For information about how to change a computer's resolution, refer to the Office 2010 and Windows 7 chapter at the beginning of this book.

The following steps, which assume Windows 7 is running, start PowerPoint based on a typical installation. You may need to ask your instructor how to start PowerPoint for your computer. For a detailed example of the procedure summarized below, refer to the Office 2010 and Windows 7 chapter.

**1** Click the Start button on the Windows 7 taskbar to display the Start menu.

**2** Type `Microsoft PowerPoint` as the search text in the 'Search programs and files' text box and watch the search results appear on the Start menu.

**3** Click Microsoft PowerPoint 2010 in the search results on the Start menu to start PowerPoint and display a new blank document in the PowerPoint window.

**4** If the PowerPoint window is not maximized, click the Maximize button next to the Close button on its title bar to maximize the window.

# Choosing a Document Theme

You can give a presentation a professional and integrated appearance easily by using a document theme. A **document theme** provides consistency in design and color throughout the entire presentation by setting the color scheme, font set, and layout of a presentation. This collection of formatting choices includes a set of colors (the Theme Colors group), a set of heading and content text fonts (the Theme Fonts group), and a set of lines and fill effects (the Theme Effects group). These groups allow you to choose and change the appearance of all the slides or individual slides in your presentation. The left edge of the status bar in Figure 1–2 shows the current slide number followed by the total number of slides in the document and a document theme identifier.

**Find the appropriate theme.**
In the initial steps of this project, you will select a document theme by locating a particular built-in theme in the Themes group. You could, however, apply a theme at any time while creating the presentation. Some PowerPoint slide show designers create presentations using the default Office Theme. This blank design allows them to concentrate on the words being used to convey the message and does not distract them with colors and various text attributes. Once the text is entered, the designers then select an appropriate document theme.

**Plan Ahead**

## To Choose a Document Theme

The document theme identifier shows the theme currently used in the slide show. PowerPoint initially uses the **Office Theme** until you select a different theme. The following steps change the theme for this presentation from the Office Theme to the Oriel document theme.

**1**

• Click Design on the Ribbon to display the Design tab (Figure 1–2).

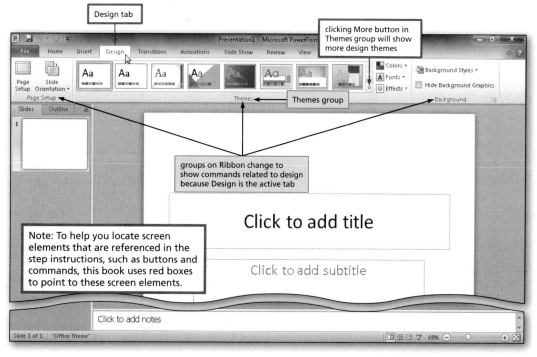

Figure 1–2

**2**

- Click the More button (Design tab | Themes group) to expand the gallery, which shows more Built-In theme gallery options (Figure 1–3).

**Experiment**

- Point to various document themes in the Themes gallery and watch the colors and fonts change on the title slide.

**Q&A** Are the themes displayed in a specific order?

Yes. They are arranged in alphabetical order running from left to right. If you point to a theme, a ScreenTip with the theme's name appears on the screen.

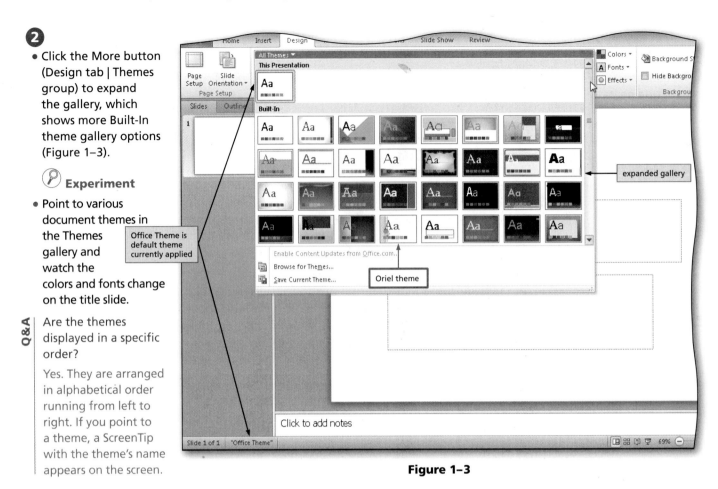

**Figure 1–3**

**Q&A** What if I change my mind and do not want to select a new theme?

Click anywhere outside the All Themes gallery to close the gallery.

**3**

- Click the Oriel theme to apply this theme to Slide 1 (Figure 1–4).

**Q&A** If I decide at some future time that this design does not fit the theme of my presentation, can I apply a different design?

Yes. You can repeat these steps at any time while creating your presentation.

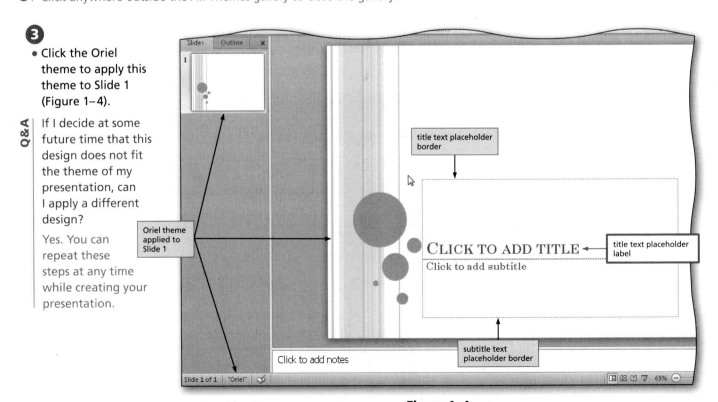

**Figure 1–4**

# Creating a Title Slide

When you open a new presentation, the default **Title Slide** layout appears. The purpose of this layout is to introduce the presentation to the audience. PowerPoint includes eight other built-in standard layouts. The default (preset) slide layouts are set up in **landscape orientation**, where the slide width is greater than its height. In landscape orientation, the slide size is preset to 10 inches wide and 7.5 inches high when printed on a standard sheet of paper measuring 11 inches wide and 8.5 inches high.

**Placeholders** are boxes with dotted or hatch-marked borders that are displayed when you create a new slide. Most layouts have both a title text placeholder and at least one content placeholder. Depending on the particular slide layout selected, title and subtitle placeholders are displayed for the slide title and subtitle; a content text placeholder is displayed for text, art, or a table, chart, picture, graphic, or movie. The title slide has two text placeholders where you can type the main heading, or title, of a new slide and the subtitle.

With the exception of a blank slide, PowerPoint assumes every new slide has a title. To make creating a presentation easier, any text you type after a new slide appears becomes title text in the title text placeholder. The following steps create the title slide for this presentation.

---

**Choose the words for the slide.**

No doubt you have heard the phrase, "You get only one chance to make a first impression." The same philosophy holds true for a PowerPoint presentation. The title slide gives your audience an initial sense of what they are about to see and hear. It is, therefore, extremely important to choose the text for this slide carefully. Avoid stating the obvious in the title. Instead, create interest and curiosity using key ideas from the presentation.

Some PowerPoint users create the title slide as their last step in the design process so that it reflects the tone of the presentation. They begin by planning the final slide in the presentation so that they know where and how they want to end the slide show. All the slides in the presentation should work toward meeting this final slide.

**Plan Ahead**

---

## To Enter the Presentation Title

The presentation title for Project 1 is It Is Easy Being Green. This title creates interest by introducing the concept of simple energy conservation tasks. The following step creates the slide show's title.

- Click the label, Click to add title, located inside the title text placeholder to select the placeholder (Figure 1–5).

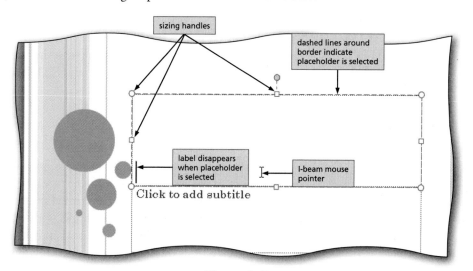

**Figure 1–5**

**2**

- Type **It Is Easy Being Green** in the title text placeholder. Do not press the ENTER key (Figure 1–6).

Q&A

Why does the text display with capital letters despite the fact I am typing uppercase and lowercase letters?

The Oriel theme uses the Small Caps effect for the title text. This effect converts lowercase letters to uppercase and reduces their size.

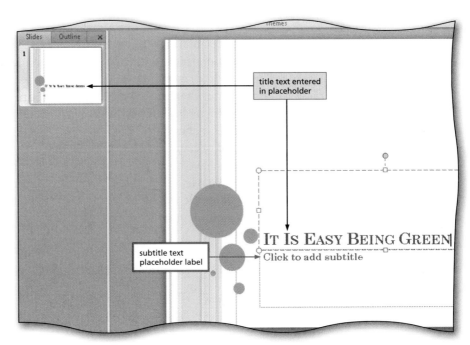

**Figure 1–6**

## Correcting a Mistake When Typing

If you type the wrong letter, press the BACKSPACE key to erase all the characters back to and including the one that is incorrect. If you mistakenly press the ENTER key after typing the title and the insertion point is on the new line, simply press the BACKSPACE key to return the insertion point to the right of the letter n in the word, Green.

When you install PowerPoint, the default setting allows you to reverse up to the last 20 changes by clicking the Undo button on the Quick Access Toolbar. The ScreenTip that appears when you point to the Undo button changes to indicate the type of change just made. For example, if you type text in the title text placeholder and then point to the Undo button, the ScreenTip that appears is Undo Typing. For clarity, when referencing the Undo button in this project, the name displaying in the ScreenTip is referenced. You can reapply a change that you reversed with the Undo button by clicking the Redo button on the Quick Access Toolbar. Clicking the Redo button reverses the last undo action. The ScreenTip name reflects the type of reversal last performed.

For an introduction to Office 2010 and instruction about how to perform basic tasks in Office 2010 programs, read the Office 2010 and Windows 7 chapter at the beginning of this book, where you can learn how to start a program, use the Ribbon, save a file, open a file, quit a program, use Help, and much more.

## Paragraphs

Text in the subtitle text placeholder supports the title text. It can appear on one or more lines in the placeholder. To create more than one subtitle line, you press the ENTER key after typing some words. PowerPoint creates a new line, which is the second paragraph in the placeholder. A **paragraph** is a segment of text with the same format that begins when you press the ENTER key and ends when you press the ENTER key again. This new paragraph is the same level as the previous paragraph. A **level** is a position within a structure, such as an outline, that indicates the magnitude of importance. PowerPoint allows for five paragraph levels.

## To Enter the Presentation Subtitle Paragraph

The first subtitle paragraph links to the title by giving further detail that the presentation will focus on energy-saving measures at home. The following steps enter the presentation subtitle.

**1**

● Click the label, Click to add subtitle, located inside the subtitle text placeholder to select the placeholder (Figure 1–7).

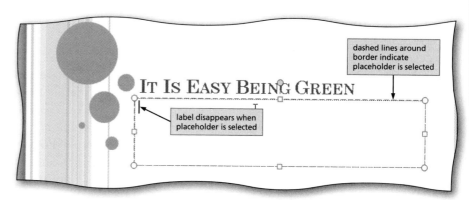

**Figure 1–7**

**2**

● Type `Saving Energy at Home` but do not press the ENTER key (Figure 1–8).

**Figure 1–8**

---

**Identify how to format specific elements of the text.**

Most of the time, you use the document theme's text attributes, color scheme, and layout. Occasionally, you may want to change the way a presentation looks, however, and still keep a particular document theme. PowerPoint gives you that flexibility.

Graphic designers use several rules when formatting text.

● Avoid all capital letters, if possible. Audiences have difficulty comprehending sentences typed in all capital letters, especially when the lines exceed seven words. All capital letters leaves no room for emphasis or inflection, so readers get confused about what material deserves particular attention. Some document themes, however, have a default title text style of all capital letters.

● Avoid text with a font size less than 30 point. Audience members generally will sit a maximum of 50 feet from a screen, and at this distance 30-point type is the smallest size text they can read comfortably without straining.

● Make careful color choices. Color evokes emotions, and a careless color choice may elicit the incorrect psychological response. PowerPoint provides a color gallery with hundreds of colors. The built-in document themes use complementary colors that work well together. If you stray from these themes and add your own color choices, without a good reason to make the changes, your presentation is apt to become ineffective.

# Formatting Characters in a Presentation

Recall that each document theme determines the color scheme, font set, and layout of a presentation. You can use a specific document theme and then change the characters' formats any time before, during, or after you type the text.

**BTW**

**Q&As**
For a complete list of the Q&As found in many of the step-by-step sequences in this book, visit the PowerPoint 2010 Q&A Web page (scsite.com/ppt2010/qa).

## Fonts and Font Styles

Characters that appear on the screen are a specific shape and size. Examples of how you can modify the appearance, or **format**, of these typed characters on the screen and in print include changing the font, style, size, and color. The **font**, or typeface, defines the appearance and shape of the letters, numbers, punctuation marks, and symbols. **Style** indicates how the characters are formatted. PowerPoint's text font styles include regular, italic, bold, and bold italic. **Size** specifies the height of the characters and is gauged by a measurement system that uses points. A **point** is 1/72 of an inch in height. Thus, a character with a font size of 36 is 36/72 (or 1/2) of an inch in height. **Color** defines the hue of the characters.

This presentation uses the Oriel document theme, which uses particular font styles and font sizes. The Oriel document theme default title text font is named Century Schoolbook. It has a bold style with no special effects, and its size is 30 point. The Oriel document theme default subtitle text font also is Century Schoolbook with a font size of 18 point.

## To Select a Paragraph

You can use many techniques to format characters. When you want to apply the same formats to multiple words or paragraphs, it is efficient to select the desired text and then make the desired changes to all the characters simultaneously. The first formatting change you will make will apply to the title slide subtitle. The following step selects this paragraph.

- Triple-click the paragraph, Saving Energy at Home, in the subtitle text placeholder to select the paragraph (Figure 1–9).

**Q&A**

Can I select the paragraph using a technique other than triple-clicking?

Yes. You can move your mouse pointer to the left of the first paragraph and then drag to the end of the line.

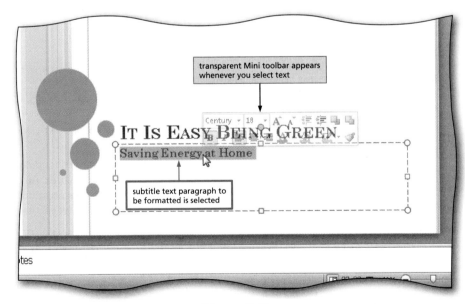

**Figure 1–9**

## To Italicize Text

Different font styles often are used on slides to make them more appealing to the reader and to emphasize particular text. **Italicized** text has a slanted appearance. Used sparingly, it draws the readers' eyes to these characters. The following step adds emphasis to the second line of the subtitle text by changing regular text to italic text.

- With the subtitle text still selected, click the Italic button on the Mini toolbar to italicize that text on the slide (Figure 1–10).

**Q&A**

If I change my mind and decide not to italicize the text, how can I remove this style?

Click the Italic button a second time or immediately click the Undo button on the Quick Access Toolbar or press CTRL+Z.

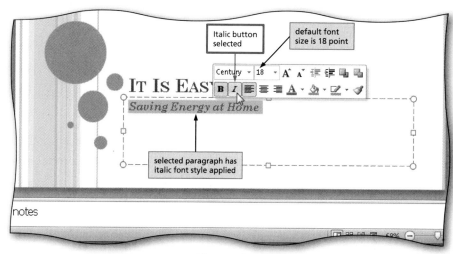

**Figure 1–10**

| Other Ways | | |
|---|---|---|
| 1. Right-click selected text, click Font on shortcut menu, click Font tab (Font dialog box), click Italic in Font style list, click OK button | 2. Select text, click Italic button (Home tab \| Font group) <br><br> 3. Click Font Dialog Box Launcher (Home tab \| Font | group), click Font tab (Font dialog box), click Italic in Font style list, click OK button <br><br> 4. Select text, press CTRL+I |

## To Increase Font Size

To add emphasis, you increase the font size for the subtitle text. The Increase Font Size button on the Mini toolbar increases the font size in preset increments. The following step uses this button to increase the font size.

- Click the Increase Font Size button on the Mini toolbar twice to increase the font size of the selected text from 18 to 24 point (Figure 1–11).

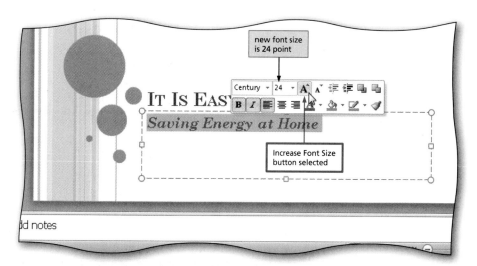

**Figure 1–11**

| Other Ways | | |
|---|---|---|
| 1. Click Font Size box arrow on Mini toolbar, click desired font size in Font Size gallery | 2. Click Increase Font Size button (Home tab \| Font group) <br><br> 3. Click Font Size box arrow (Home tab \| Font group), | click desired font size in Font size gallery <br><br> 4. Press CTRL+SHIFT+> |

## To Select a Word

PowerPoint designers use many techniques to emphasize words and characters on a slide. To add emphasis to the energy-saving concept of your slide show, you want to increase the font size and change the font color to green for the word, Green, in the title text. You could perform these actions separately, but it is more efficient to select the word and then change the font attributes. The following steps select a word.

- Position the mouse pointer somewhere in the word to be selected (in this case, in the word, Green) (Figure 1–12).

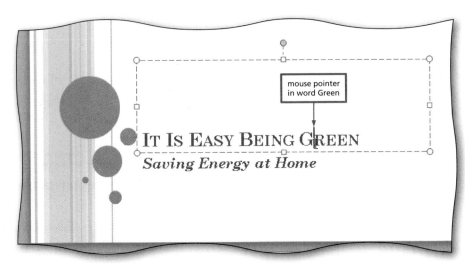

**Figure 1–12**

- Double-click the word to select it (Figure 1–13).

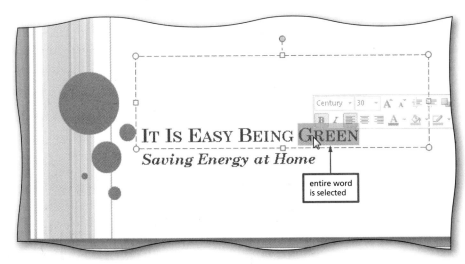

**Figure 1–13**

**Other Ways**

1. Position mouse pointer before first character, press CTRL+SHIFT+RIGHT ARROW

**Plan Ahead**

**Format text colors.**
When selecting text colors, try to limit using red. This color often is associated with dangerous or alarming situations. In addition, at least 15 percent of men have difficulty distinguishing varying shades of green or red. They also often see the color purple as blue and the color brown as green. This problem is more pronounced when the colors appear in small areas, such as slide paragraphs or line chart bars.

## To Change the Text Color

PowerPoint allows you to use one or more text colors in a presentation. To add more emphasis to the word, Green, in the title slide text, you decide to change the color. The following steps add emphasis to this word by changing the font color from black to green.

- With the word, Green, selected, click the Font Color arrow on the Mini toolbar to display the gallery of Theme Colors and Standard Colors (Figure 1–14).

**Q&A** If the Mini toolbar disappears from the screen, how can I display it once again?

Right-click the text, and the Mini toolbar should appear.

### 🔍 Experiment

- Point to various colors in the gallery and watch the word's font color change.

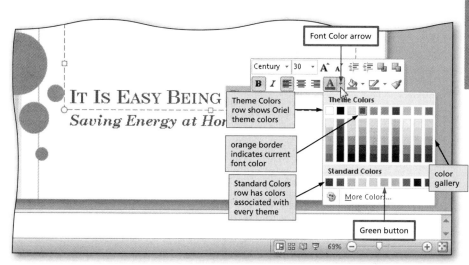

**Figure 1–14**

- Click the Green button in the Standard Colors row on the Mini toolbar (sixth color) to change the font color to green (Figure 1–15).

**Q&A** Why did I select the color Green?

Green is one of the 10 standard colors associated with every document theme, and it is a universal color to represent respecting natural resources. The color will emphasize the fact that the presentation focuses on green conservation measures.

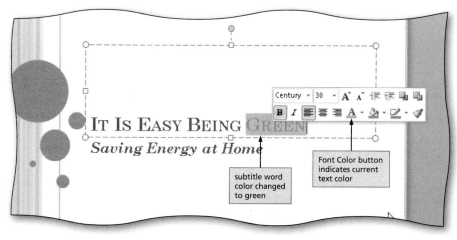

**Figure 1–15**

**Q&A** What is the difference between the colors shown in the Theme Colors area and the Standard Colors?

The 10 colors in the top row of the Theme Colors area are two text, two background, and six accent colors in the Oriel theme; the five colors in each column under the top row display different transparencies. These colors are available in every document theme.

- Click outside the selected area to deselect the word.

| Other Ways |
| --- |
| 1. Right-click selected text, click Font on shortcut menu, click Font Color button, click Green in Standard Colors row     2. Click Font Color arrow (Home tab | Font group), click Green in Standard Colors row |

**Organizing Files and Folders**
You should organize and store files in folders so that you easily can find the files later. For example, if you are taking an introductory computer class called CIS 101, a good practice would be to save all PowerPoint files in a PowerPoint folder in a CIS 101 folder. For a discussion of folders and detailed examples of creating folders, refer to the Office 2010 and Windows 7 chapter at the beginning of this book.

## To Save a Presentation

You have performed many tasks while creating this slide and do not want to risk losing work completed thus far. Accordingly, you should save the document.

The following steps assume you already have created folders for storing your files, for example, a CIS 101 folder (for your class) that contains a PowerPoint folder (for your assignments). Thus, these steps save the document in the PowerPoint folder in the CIS 101 folder on a USB flash drive using the file name, Saving Energy. For a detailed example of the procedure summarized below, refer to the Office 2010 and Windows 7 chapter at the beginning of this book.

**1** With a USB flash drive connected to one of the computer's USB ports, click the Save button on the Quick Access Toolbar to display the Save As dialog box.

**2** Type **Saving Energy** in the File name text box to change the file name. Do not press the ENTER key after typing the file name because you do not want to close the dialog box at this time.

**3** Navigate to the desired save location (in this case, the PowerPoint folder in the CIS 101 folder [or your class folder] on the USB flash drive).

**4** Click the Save button (Save As dialog box) to save the document in the selected folder on the selected drive with the entered file name.

# Adding a New Slide to a Presentation

With the text for the title slide for the presentation created, the next step is to add the first text slide immediately after the title slide. Usually, when you create a presentation, you add slides with text, clip art, graphics, or charts. Some placeholders allow you to double-click the placeholder and then access other objects, such as media clips, charts, diagrams, and organization charts. You can change the layout for a slide at any time during the creation of a presentation.

## To Add a New Text Slide with a Bulleted List

When you add a new slide, PowerPoint uses the Title and Content slide layout. This layout provides a title placeholder and a content area for text, art, charts, and other graphics. A vertical scroll bar appears in the Slide pane when you add the second slide so that you can move from slide to slide easily. A thumbnail of this slide also appears in the Slides tab. The following steps add a new slide with the Title and Content slide layout.

**1**
• Click Home on the Ribbon to display the Home tab (Figure 1–16).

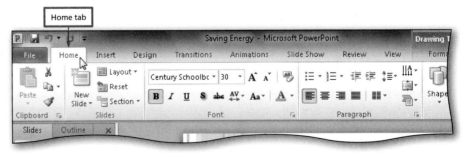

**Figure 1–16**

**2**

• Click the New Slide button (Home tab | Slides group) to insert a new slide with the Title and Content layout (Figure 1–17).

**Q&A** Why does the bullet character display an orange circle?

The Oriel document theme determines the bullet characters. Each paragraph level has an associated bullet character.

**Q&A** I clicked the New Slide arrow instead of the New Slide button. What should I do?

Click the Title and Content slide thumbnail in the layout gallery.

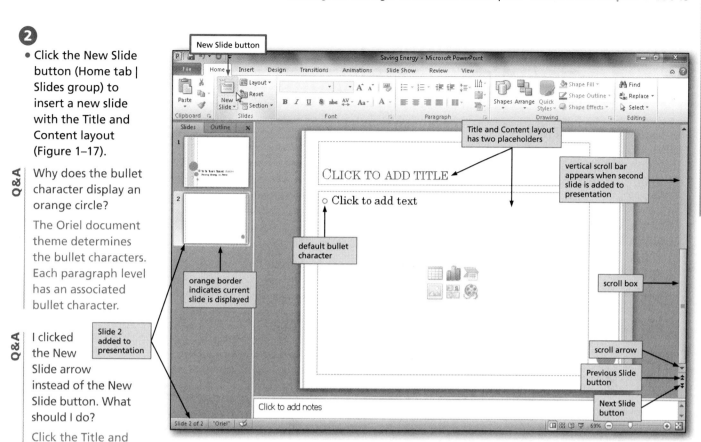

Figure 1–17

**Other Ways**

1. Press CTRL+M

**Choose the words for the slide.**
All presentations should follow the 7 × 7 rule, which states that each slide should have a maximum of seven lines, and each line should have a maximum of seven words. PowerPoint designers must choose their words carefully and, in turn, help viewers read the slides easily.
   Avoid line wraps. Your audience's eyes want to stop at the end of a line. Thus, you must plan your words carefully or adjust the font size so that each point displays on only one line.

**Plan Ahead**

# Creating a Text Slide with a Multi-Level Bulleted List

The information in the Slide 2 text placeholder is presented in a bulleted list with three levels. A **bulleted list** is a list of paragraphs, each of which is preceded by a bullet. A slide that consists of more than one level of bulleted text is called a **multi-level bulleted list slide**. In a multi-level bulleted list, a lower-level paragraph is a subset of a higher-level paragraph. It usually contains information that supports the topic in the paragraph immediately above it.

Two of the Slide 2 bullets appear at the same paragraph level, called the first level: Install low-flow faucets and shower heads, and Appliances count for 20 percent of electric bill. Beginning with the second level, each paragraph indents to the right of the preceding level and is pushed down to a lower level. For example, if you increase the indent of a first-level paragraph, it becomes a second-level paragraph. The second, fourth, and fifth paragraphs on Slide 2 are second-level paragraphs. The last paragraph, Wash clothes in cold water, is a third-level paragraph.

**BTW**

**The Ribbon and Screen Resolution**
PowerPoint may change how the groups and buttons within the groups appear on the Ribbon, depending on the computer's screen resolution. Thus, your Ribbon may look different from the ones in this book if you are using a screen resolution other than 1024 x 768.

Creating a text slide with a multi-level bulleted list requires several steps. Initially, you enter a slide title in the title text placeholder. Next, you select the content text placeholder. Then, you type the text for the multi-level bulleted list, increasing and decreasing the indents as needed. The next several sections add a slide with a multi-level bulleted list.

## To Enter a Slide Title

PowerPoint assumes every new slide has a title. The title for Slide 2 is Make Small Changes to Cut Energy. The following step enters this title.

**1**
- Click the label, Click to add title, to select it and then type **Make Small Changes to Cut Energy** in the placeholder. Do not press the ENTER key (Figure 1–18).

**Q&A** What are those six icons grouped in the middle of the slide?

You can click one of the icons to insert a specific type of content: table, chart, SmartArt graphic, picture, clip art, or media clip.

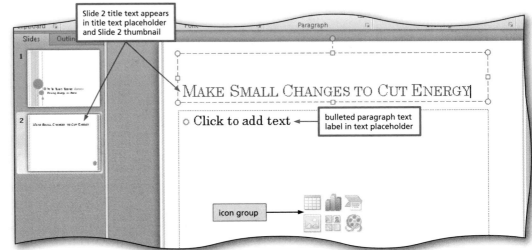

**Figure 1–18**

## To Select a Text Placeholder

Before you can type text into the text placeholder, you first must select it. The following step selects the text placeholder on Slide 2.

**1**
- Click the label, Click to add text, to select the text placeholder (Figure 1–19).

**Q&A** Why does my mouse pointer have a different shape?

If you move the mouse pointer away from the bullet, it will change shape.

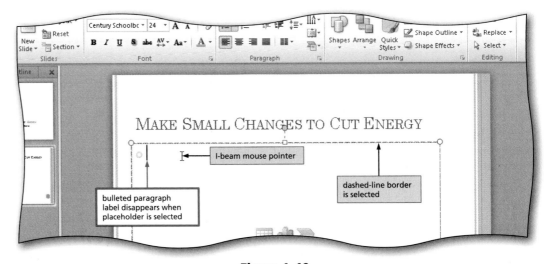

**Figure 1–19**

**Other Ways**

1. Press CTRL+ENTER

## To Type a Multi-Level Bulleted List

    The content placeholder provides an area for the text characters. When you click inside a placeholder, you then can type or paste text. As discussed previously, a bulleted list is a list of paragraphs, each of which is preceded by a bullet. A paragraph is a segment of text ended by pressing the ENTER key.

    The content text placeholder is selected, so the next step is to type the multi-level bulleted list that consists of six paragraphs, as shown in Figure 1–1b on page PPT 3. Creating a lower-level paragraph is called **demoting** text; creating a higher-level paragraph is called **promoting** text. The following steps create a multi-level bulleted list consisting of three levels.

 **1**
- Type `Install low-flow faucets and shower heads` and then press the ENTER key (Figure 1–20).

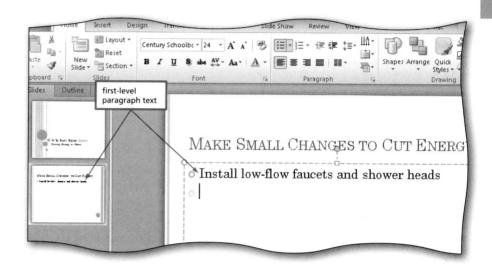

**Figure 1–20**

**2**
- Click the Increase List Level button (Home tab | Paragraph group) to indent the second paragraph below the first and create a second-level paragraph (Figure 1–21).

**Q&A** Why does the bullet for this paragraph have a different size and color?
A different bullet is assigned to each paragraph level.

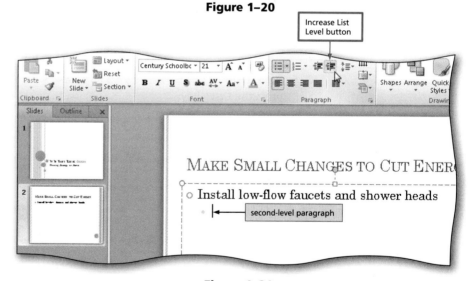

**Figure 1–21**

 **3**
- Type `Cut water consumption in half` and then press the ENTER key (Figure 1–22).

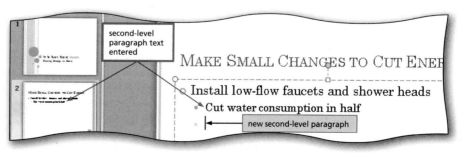

**Figure 1–22**

**4**

- Click the Decrease List Level button (Home tab | Paragraph group) so that the second-level paragraph becomes a first-level paragraph (Figure 1–23).

**Q&A** Can I delete bullets on a slide?

Yes. If you do not want bullets to display in a particular paragraph, click the Bullets button (Home tab | Paragraph group) or right-click the paragraph and then click the Bullets button on the shortcut menu.

**Other Ways**

1. Press TAB to promote paragraph; press SHIFT+TAB to demote paragraph

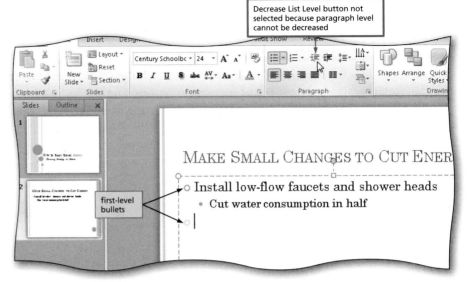

**Figure 1–23**

## To Type the Remaining Text for Slide 2

The following steps complete the text for Slide 2.

**1** Type `Appliances count for 20 percent of electric bill` and then press the ENTER key.

**2** Click the Increase List Level button (Home tab | Paragraph group) to demote the paragraph to the second level.

**3** Type `Buy ENERGY STAR qualified products` and then press the ENTER key to add a new paragraph at the same level as the previous paragraph.

**4** Type `Run dishwasher, clothes washer with full loads` and then press the ENTER key.

**5** Click the Increase List Level button (Home tab | Paragraph group) to demote the paragraph to the third level.

**6** Type `Wash clothes in cold water` but do not press the ENTER key (Figure 1–24).

**Q&A** I pressed the ENTER key in error, and now a new bullet appears after the last entry on this slide. How can I remove this extra bullet?

Press the BACKSPACE key twice.

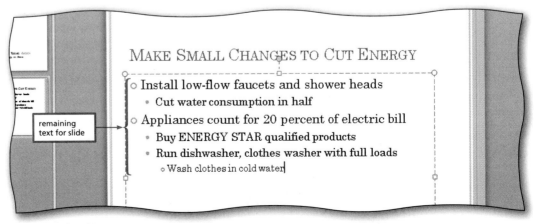

**Figure 1–24**

## To Select a Group of Words

PowerPoint designers use many techniques to emphasize words and characters on a slide. To add emphasis to your slide show's concept of saving natural resources, you want to bold and increase the font size of the words, in half, in the body text. You could perform these actions separately, but it is more efficient to select the words and then change the font attributes. The following steps select two words.

- Position the mouse pointer immediately to the left of the first character of the text to be selected (in this case, the i in the word, in) (Figure 1–25).

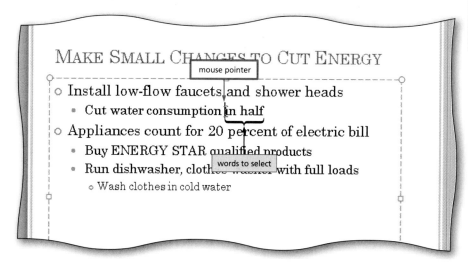

**Figure 1–25**

- Drag the mouse pointer through the last character of the text to be selected (in this case, the f in half) (Figure 1–26).

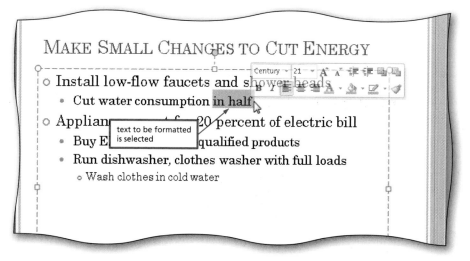

**Figure 1–26**

| Other Ways |
|---|
| 1. Press CTRL+SHIFT+RIGHT ARROW |

## To Bold Text

Bold characters display somewhat thicker and darker than those that display in a regular font style. Clicking the Bold button on the Mini toolbar is an efficient method of bolding text. To add more emphasis to the amount of water savings that can occur by installing low-flow faucets and shower heads, you want to bold the words, in half. The following step bolds this text.

**1**
- With the words, in half, selected, click the Bold button on the Mini toolbar to bold the two words (Figure 1–27).

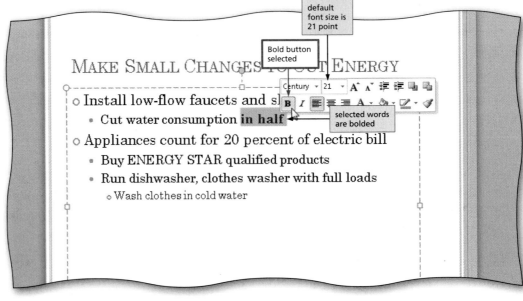

**Figure 1–27**

**Other Ways**

1. Click Bold button (Home tab | Font group)
2. Press CTRL+B

**Formatting Words**
To format one word, position the insertion point anywhere in the word. Then make the formatting changes you desire. The entire word does not need to be selected for the change to occur.

## To Increase Font Size

To add emphasis, you increase the font size for the words, in half. The following step increases the font size from 21 to 24 point.

**1** With the words, in half, still selected, click the Increase Font Size button on the Mini toolbar once (Figure 1–28).

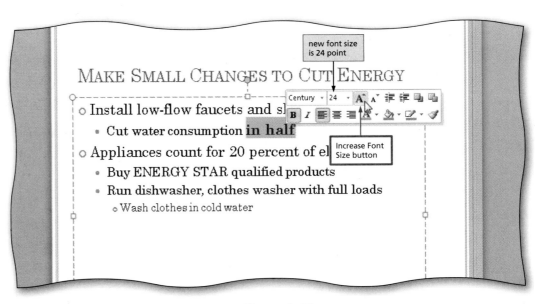

**Figure 1–28**

# Adding New Slides and Changing the Slide Layouts

Slide 3 in Figure 1–1c on page PPT 3 contains a photograph and does not contain a bulleted list. When you add a new slide, PowerPoint applies the Title and Content layout. This layout along with the Title Slide layout for Slide 1 are the default styles. A **layout** specifies the arrangement of placeholders on a slide. These placeholders are arranged in various configurations and can contain text, such as the slide title or a bulleted list, or they can contain content, such as SmartArt graphics, pictures, charts, tables, shapes, and clip art. The placement of the text, in relationship to content, depends on the slide layout. You can specify a particular slide layout when you add a new slide to a presentation or after you have created the slide.

Using the **Layout gallery**, you can choose a slide layout. The nine layouts in this gallery have a variety of placeholders to define text and content positioning and formatting. Three layouts are for text: Title Slide, Section Header, and Title Only. Five are for text and content: Title and Content, Two Content, Comparison, Content with Caption, and Picture with Caption. The Blank layout has no placeholders. If none of these standard layouts meets your design needs, you can create a **custom layout**. A custom layout specifies the number, size, and location of placeholders, background content, and optional slide and placeholder-level properties.

When you change the layout of a slide, PowerPoint retains the text and objects and repositions them into the appropriate placeholders. Using slide layouts eliminates the need to resize objects and the font size because PowerPoint automatically sizes the objects and text to fit the placeholders.

**BTW**

**Experimenting with Normal View**
As you learn to use PowerPoint's features, experiment with using the Outline tab and with closing the Tabs pane to maximize the slide area. To close the Tabs pane, click the x to the right of the Outline tab. To redisplay the Tabs pane, click the View tab on the Ribbon and then click Normal in the Presentation Views group.

## To Add a Slide with the Title Only Layout

The following steps add Slide 3 to the presentation with the Title Only slide layout style.

**1**
- If necessary, click Home on the Ribbon to display the Home tab.
- Click the New Slide arrow (Home tab | Slides group) to display the Layout gallery (Figure 1–29).

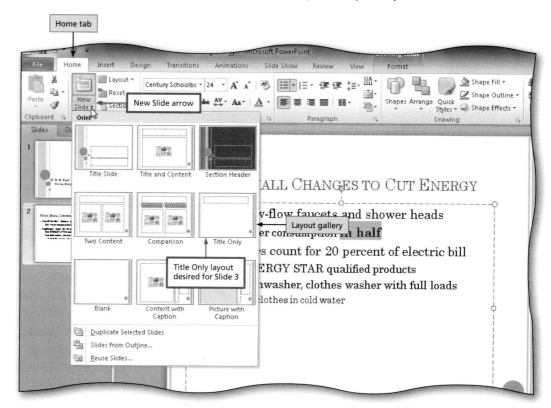

**Figure 1–29**

**2**

- Click Title Only to add a new slide and apply that layout to Slide 3 (Figure 1–30).

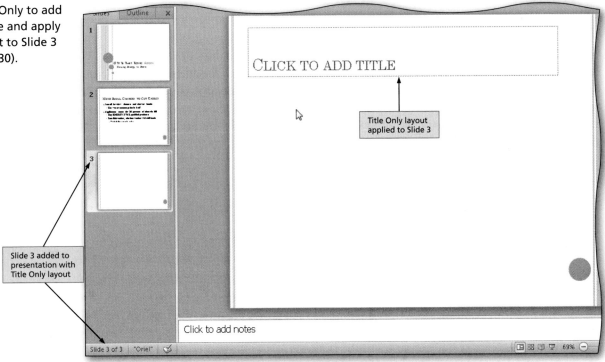

Title Only layout applied to Slide 3

Slide 3 added to presentation with Title Only layout

**Figure 1–30**

**Other Ways**

1. Press CTRL+M

## To Enter a Slide Title

The only text on Slide 3 is the title. The following step enters the title text for this slide.

**1** Type **Use Energy Efficient Lighting** as the title text but do not press the ENTER key (Figure 1–31).

BTW

**Portrait Page Orientation**
If your slide content is dominantly vertical, such as a skyscraper or a person, consider changing the slide layout to a portrait page orientation. To change the orientation, click the Slide Orientation button (Design tab | Page Setup group) and then click the desired orientation.

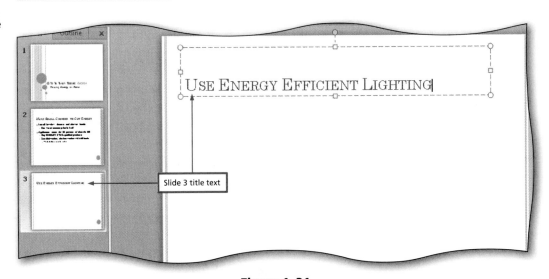

Slide 3 title text

**Figure 1–31**

## To Add a New Slide and Enter a Slide Title and Headings

The text on Slide 4 in Figure 1–1d on page PPT 3 consists of a title and two headings. The appropriate layout for this slide is named Comparison. The following steps add Slide 4 to the presentation with the Comparison layout and then enter the title and heading text for this slide.

- Click the New Slide arrow in the Slides group to display the Layout gallery (Figure 1–32).

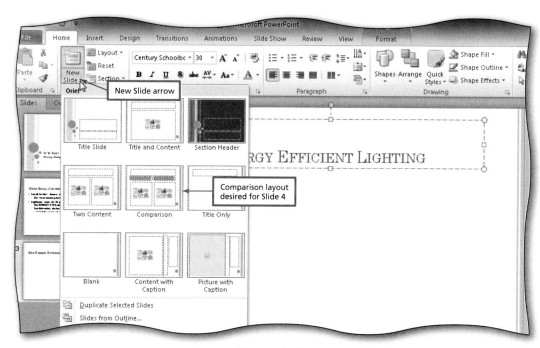

**Figure 1–32**

- Click Comparison to add Slide 4 and apply that layout.

- Type **Adjust Your Thermostats** in the title text placeholder but do not press the ENTER key.

- Click the left orange heading placeholder with the label, Click to add text, to select this placeholder (Figure 1–33).

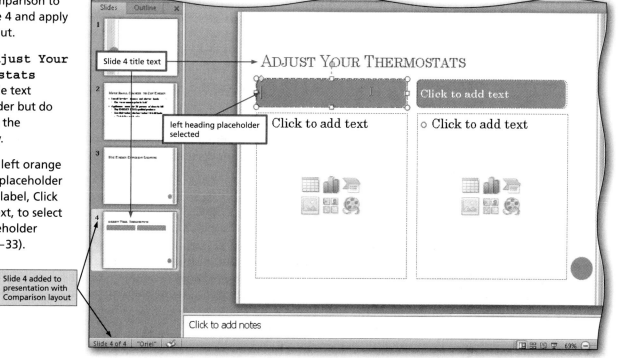

**Figure 1–33**

❸
- Type **Furnace: 68 degrees** but do not press the ENTER key.

- Click the right orange heading placeholder and then type **Water heater: 120 degrees** but do not press the ENTER key (Figure 1–34).

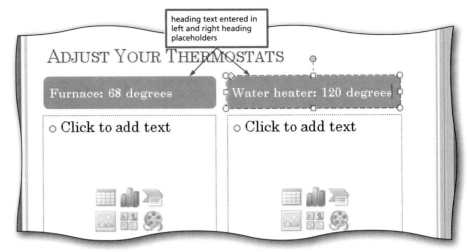

**Figure 1–34**

**Break Point:** If you wish to take a break, this is a good place to do so. You can quit PowerPoint now (refer to page PPT 50 for instructions). To resume at a later time, start PowerPoint (refer to pages PPT 4 and PPT 5 for instructions), open the file called Saving Energy (refer to pages PPT 50 and PPT 51 for instructions), and continue following the steps from this location forward.

## PowerPoint Views

The PowerPoint window display varies depending on the view. A **view** is the mode in which the presentation appears on the screen. PowerPoint has four main views: Normal, Slide Sorter, Reading, and Slide Show. It also has another view, called Notes Page view, used for entering information about a slide.

The default view is **Normal view**, which is composed of three working areas that allow you to work on various aspects of a presentation simultaneously. The left side of the screen has a Tabs pane that consists of a **Slides tab** and an **Outline tab**. These tabs alternate between views of the presentation in a thumbnail, or miniature, view of the slides and an outline of the slide text. You can type the text of the presentation on the Outline tab and easily rearrange bulleted lists, paragraphs, and individual slides. As you type, you can view this text in the **Slide pane**, which shows a large view of the current slide on the right side of the window. You also can enter text, graphics, animations, and hyperlinks directly in the Slide pane. The **Notes pane** at the bottom of the window is an area where you can type notes and additional information. This text can consist of notes to yourself or remarks to share with your audience. If you want to work with your notes in full page format, you can display them in **Notes Page view**.

In Normal view, you can adjust the width of the Slide pane by dragging the **splitter bar** and the height of the Notes pane by dragging the pane borders. After you have created at least two slides, a scroll bar containing **scroll arrows** and **scroll boxes** will appear on the right edge of the window.

**BTW**

**Using the Notes Pane**
As you create your presentation, type comments to yourself in the Notes pane. This material can be used as part of the spoken information you will share with your audience as you give your presentation. You can print these notes for yourself or to distribute to your audience.

## To Move to Another Slide in Normal View

When creating or editing a presentation in Normal view (the view you are currently using), you often want to display a slide other than the current one. Before continuing with developing this project, you want to display the title slide by dragging the scroll box on the vertical scroll bar. When you drag the scroll box, the **slide indicator** shows the number and title of the slide you are about to display. Releasing the mouse button shows the slide. The following steps move from Slide 4 to Slide 1 using the scroll box on the Slide pane.

- Position the mouse pointer on the scroll box.

- Press and hold down the mouse button so that Slide: 4 of 4 Adjust Your Thermostats appears in the slide indicator (Figure 1–35).

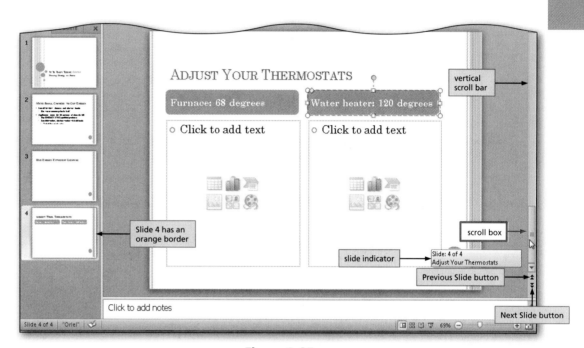

**Figure 1–35**

- Drag the scroll box up the vertical scroll bar until Slide: 1 of 4 It Is Easy Being Green appears in the slide indicator (Figure 1–36).

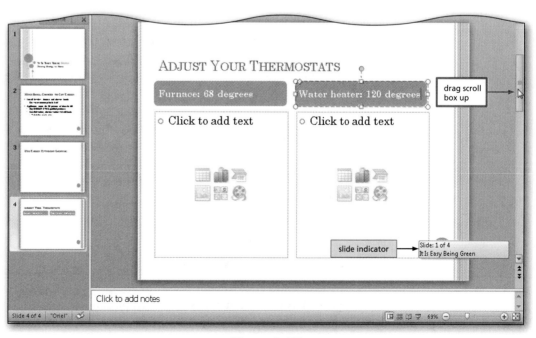

**Figure 1–36**

**3**
- Release the mouse button so that Slide 1 appears in the Slide pane and the Slide 1 thumbnail has an orange border in the Slides tab (Figure 1–37).

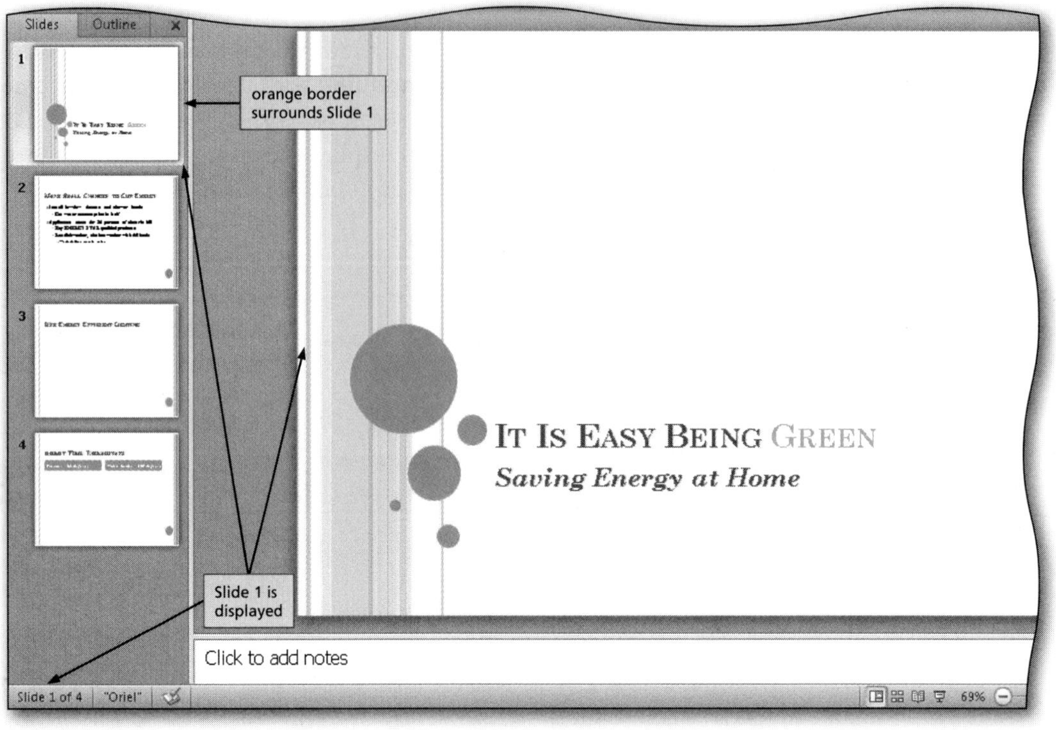

**Figure 1–37**

**Other Ways**

1. Click Next Slide button or Previous Slide button to move forward or back one slide
2. Click slide thumbnail on Slides tab
3. Press PAGE DOWN or PAGE UP to move forward or back one slide

**BTW**

**Today's Clip**
Each day, Microsoft features "today's clip," which reflects events or themes specific to this time. For example, the pictures, illustrations, and clip art have back-to-school images, winter scenes, and holiday characters.

# Inserting Clip Art and Photographs into Slides

A **clip** is a single media file that can include art, sound, animation, or movies. Adding a clip can help increase the visual appeal of many slides and can offer a quick way to add professional-looking graphic images and sounds to a presentation without creating these files yourself. This art is contained in the **Microsoft Clip Organizer**, a collection of drawings, photographs, sounds, videos, and other media files shared among Microsoft Office applications. The **Office Collections** contains all these media files included with Microsoft Office.

You also can add your own clips to slides. You can insert these files directly from a storage medium, such as a USB flash drive. In addition, you can add them to the other files in the Clip Organizer so that you can search for and reuse these images, sounds, animations, and movies. When you create these media files, they are stored on your hard disk in **My Collections**. The Clip Organizer will find these files and create a new collection with these files. Two other locations for clips are Shared Collections and Web Collections. Files in the **Shared Collections** typically reside on a shared network file server and are accessible to multiple users. The **Web Collections** clips reside on the Microsoft Clip Art and Media Home page on the Microsoft Office Online Web site. They are available only if you have an active Internet connection.

## The Clip Art Task Pane

You can add clips to your presentation in two ways. One way is by selecting one of the slide layouts that includes a content placeholder with a Clip Art button. A second method is by clicking the Clip Art button in the Images area on the Insert tab. Clicking the Clip Art button opens the Clip Art task pane. The **Clip Art task pane** allows you to search for clips by using descriptive keywords, file names, media file formats, and clip collections. Specific file formats could be for clip art, photographs, movies, and sounds.

Clips are organized in hierarchical **clip collections** that combine topic-related clips into categories, such as Academic, Business, and Technology.

Clips have one or more keywords associated with various entities, activities, labels, and emotions. In most instances, the keywords give the name of the clip and related categories. For example, an image of a cow in the Animals category has the keywords animals, cattle, cows, dairies, farms, and Holsteins. You can enter these keywords in the Search for text box to find clips when you know one of the words associated with the image. Otherwise, you might find it necessary to scroll through several categories to find an appropriate clip.

Depending on the installation of the Microsoft Clip Organizer on your computer, you might not have the clip art used in this chapter. Contact your instructor if you are missing clips used in the following steps. If you have an active connection to the Internet, clips from the Microsoft Office Online Web site will display automatically as the result of your search results.

**Adhere to copyright regulations.**

You have permission to use the clips from the Microsoft Clip Organizer. If you want to use a clip from another source, be certain you have the legal right to insert this file in your presentation. Read the copyright notices that may accompany the clip and may be posted on the Web site where you obtained the clip. The owners of these images and files often ask you to give them credit for using their work, which may be satisfied by stating where you obtained the images.

Plan
Ahead

## To Insert a Clip from the Clip Organizer into the Title Slide

Slide 1 uses the Title Slide layout, which has two placeholders for text but none for graphical content. You desire to place a graphic on Slide 1, so you will locate a clip art image of a green globe and flower and then insert it in this slide. Later in this chapter, you will size and position it in an appropriate location. The following steps add a clip to Slide 1.

**1**

- Click Insert on the Ribbon to display the Insert tab.

- Click the Clip Art button (Insert tab | Images group) to display the Clip Art task pane.

- Click the Search for text box in the Clip Art task pane, if necessary delete any letters that are present, and then type **green globe** in the Search for text box.

- If necessary, click the 'Include Office.com content' check box to select it (Figure 1–38).

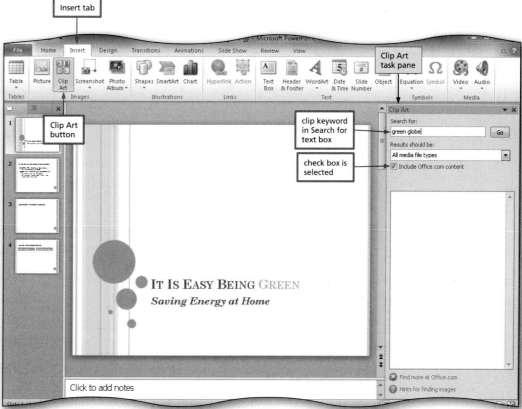

**Figure 1–38**

- Click the Go button so that the Microsoft Clip Organizer will search for and display all clips having the keywords, green globe.

- If necessary, click the Yes button if a Microsoft Clip Organizer dialog box appears asking if you want to include additional clip art images from Office.com.

- If necessary, scroll down the list to display the globe clip shown in Figure 1–39.

- Click the clip to insert it into the slide (Figure 1–39).

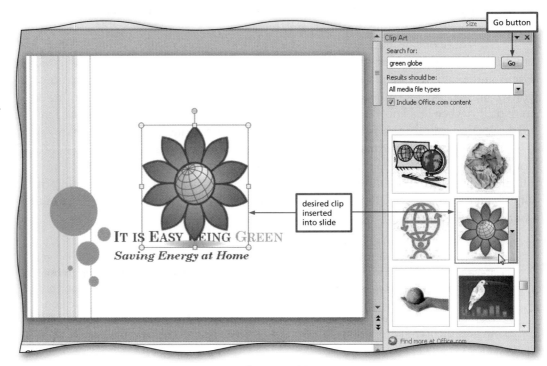

**Figure 1–39**

**Q&A** What if the globe image displayed in Figure 1–39 is not shown in my Clip Art task pane?

Select a similar clip. Your clips may be different depending on the clips installed on your computer and if you have an active connection to the Internet.

**Q&A** What is the yellow star image that displays in the lower-right corner of some clips in the Clip Art task pane?

The star indicates the image is animated and will move when the slide containing this clip is displayed during a slide show.

**Q&A** Why is this globe clip displayed in this location on the slide?

The slide layout does not have a content placeholder, so PowerPoint inserts the clip in the center of the slide.

## To Insert a Clip from the Clip Organizer into a Slide without a Content Placeholder

The next step is to add two clips to Slide 2. Slide 2 has a bulleted list in the text placeholder, so the icon group does not display in the center of the placeholder. Later in this chapter, you will resize the inserted clips. The Clip Art task pane is displayed and will remain open until you close it. The following steps add one clip to Slide 2.

**1** Click the Next Slide button to display Slide 2.

**2** Click the Search for text box in the Clip Art task pane and then delete the letters in the Search for text box.

**3** Type `faucets` and then click the Go button.

**4** If necessary, scroll down the list to display the faucet clip shown in Figure 1–40 and then click the clip to insert it into Slide 2 (Figure 1–40).

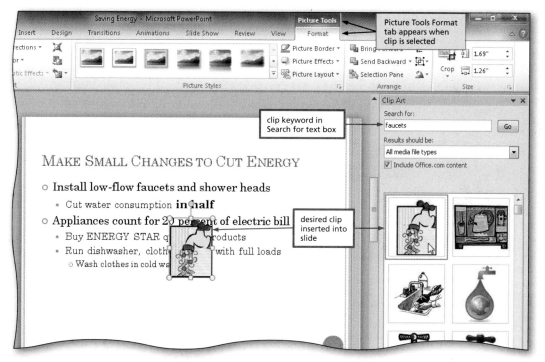

**Figure 1–40**

## To Insert a Second Clip from the Clip Organizer into a Slide without a Content Placeholder

The following steps add a second clip to Slide 2. PowerPoint inserts this clip on top of the faucet clip in the center of the slide. Both clips will be moved and resized later in this project.

**1** Click the Search for text box in the Clip Art task pane and then delete the letters in the text box.

**2** Type **dishwasher**, click the Go button, locate the clip shown in Figure 1–41, and then click the clip to insert it into Slide 2 (Figure 1–41).

**BTW**

**Clip Properties**
Each clip has properties that identify its characteristics. When you right-click a clip in the Microsoft Clip Organizer, you will see details of the clip's name, file type, size, dimensions, keywords, and creation date. You also can preview the clip and edit its assigned keywords.

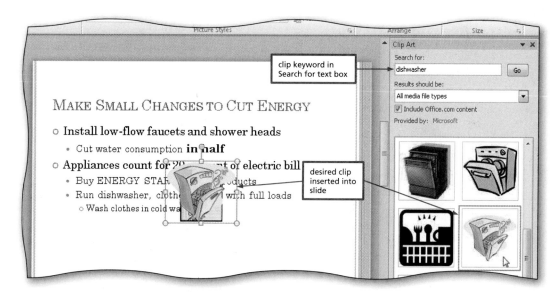

**Figure 1–41**

## To Insert a Clip from the Clip Organizer into a Content Placeholder

Slide 4 uses the Comparison layout, which has a content placeholder below each of the two headings. You desire to insert clip art into both content placeholders to reinforce the concept that consumers should adjust the heating temperatures of their furnace and water heater. The following steps insert clip art of a furnace into the left content placeholder and a water heater into the right content placeholder on Slide 4.

- Click the Close button in the Clip Art task pane so that it no longer is displayed.

- Click the Next Slide button twice to display Slide 4.

- Click the Clip Art icon in the left content placeholder to select that placeholder and to open the Clip Art task pane (Figure 1–42).

**Q&A**

Do I need to close the Clip Art task pane when I am finished inserting the two clips into Slide 2?

No. You can leave the Clip Art task pane open and then display Slide 4. It is often more convenient, however, to open this pane when you are working with a layout that has a content placeholder so that the clip is inserted in the desired location.

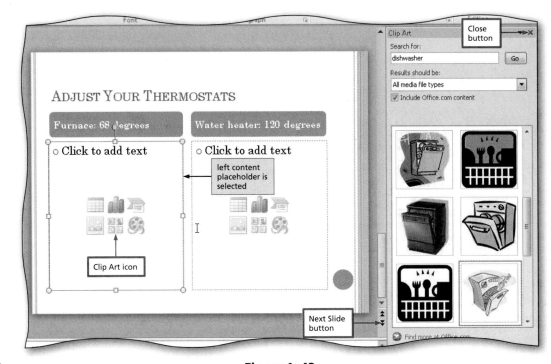

**Figure 1–42**

- Click the Search for text box in the Clip Art task pane, delete any letters that are present, type **furnace** in the Search for text box, and then click the Go button to search for and display all pictures having the keyword, furnace.

- If necessary, scroll down the list to display the furnace clip shown in Figure 1–43.

- Click the clip to insert it into the left content placeholder (Figure 1–43).

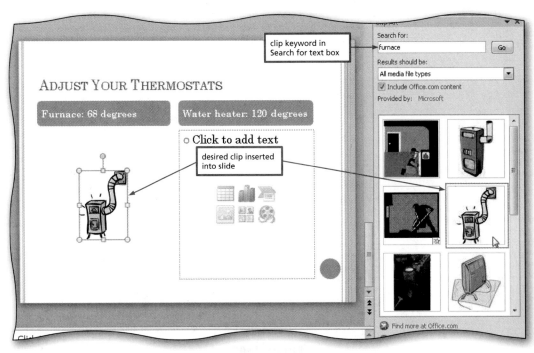

**Figure 1–43**

**3**

● Click anywhere in the right placeholder except one of the six icons to select the placeholder.

**Q&A**

I clicked the Clip Art icon by mistake, which closed the Clip Art task pane. How do I open it?

Click the Clip Art icon.

**4**

● Click the Search for text box in the Clip Art task pane, delete any letters that are present, type **water heater** in the Search for text box, and then click the Go button.

● If necessary, scroll down the list to display the water heater clip shown in Figure 1–44 and then click the clip to insert it into the right content placeholder (Figure 1–44).

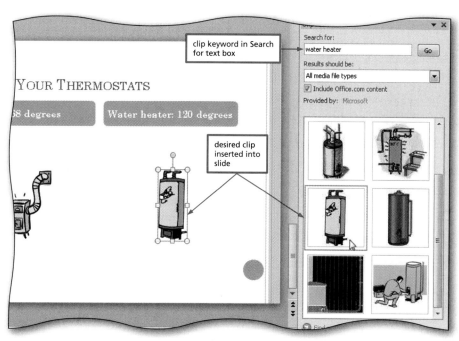

**Figure 1–44**

# Photographs and the Clip Organizer

In addition to clip art, you can insert pictures into a presentation. These may include scanned photographs, line art, and artwork from storage media, such as USB flash drives, hard disks, optical discs, and memory cards. To insert a picture into a presentation, the picture must be saved in a format that PowerPoint can recognize. Table 1–1 identifies some of the formats PowerPoint recognizes.

| Table 1–1 Primary File Formats PowerPoint Recognizes | |
| --- | --- |
| **Format** | **File Extension** |
| Computer Graphics Metafile | .cgm |
| CorelDRAW | .cdr, .cdt, .cmx, and .pat |
| Encapsulated PostScript | .eps |
| Enhanced Metafile | .emf |
| FlashPix | .fpx |
| Graphics Interchange Format | .gif |
| Hanako | .jsh, .jah, and .jbh |
| Joint Photographic Experts Group (JPEG) | .jpg |
| Kodak PhotoCD | .pcd |
| Macintosh PICT | .pct |
| PC Paintbrush | .pcx |
| Portable Network Graphics | .png |
| Tagged Image File Format | .tif |
| Windows Bitmap | .bmp, .rle, .dib |
| Microsoft Windows Metafile | .wmf |
| WordPerfect Graphics | .wpg |

**BTW**

**Compressing File Size**
When you add a picture to a presentation, PowerPoint automatically compresses this image. Even with this compression applied, a presentation that contains pictures usually has a large file size. To reduce this size, you can compress a picture further without affecting the quality of how it displays on the slide. To compress a picture, select the picture and then click the Compress Pictures button (Picture Tools Format tab | Adjust group). You can restore the picture's original settings by clicking the Reset Picture button (Picture Tools Format tab | Adjust group).

You can import files saved with the .emf, .gif, .jpg, .png, .bmp, .rle, .dib, and .wmf formats directly into PowerPoint presentations. All other file formats require separate filters that are shipped with the PowerPoint installation software and must be installed separately. You can download additional filters from the Microsoft Office Online Web site.

## To Insert a Photograph from the Clip Organizer into a Slide without a Content Placeholder

Next, you will add a photograph to Slide 3. You will not insert this picture into a content placeholder, so it will display in the center of the slide. Later in this chapter, you will resize this picture. To start the process of locating this photograph, you do not need to click the Clip Art button icon in the content placeholder because the Clip Art task pane already is displayed. The following steps add a photograph to Slide 3.

**1** Click the Previous Slide button to display Slide 3.

**2** Click the Search for text box in the Clip Art task pane, delete the letters in the text box, type **CFL,** and then click the Go button.

**3** If necessary, scroll down the list to display the picture of a light bulb shown in Figure 1–45, and then click the photograph to insert it into Slide 2 (Figure 1–45).

**Q&A** Why is my photograph a different size from the one shown in Figure 1–1c on page PPT 3?

The photograph was inserted into the slide and not into a content placeholder. You will resize the picture later in this chapter.

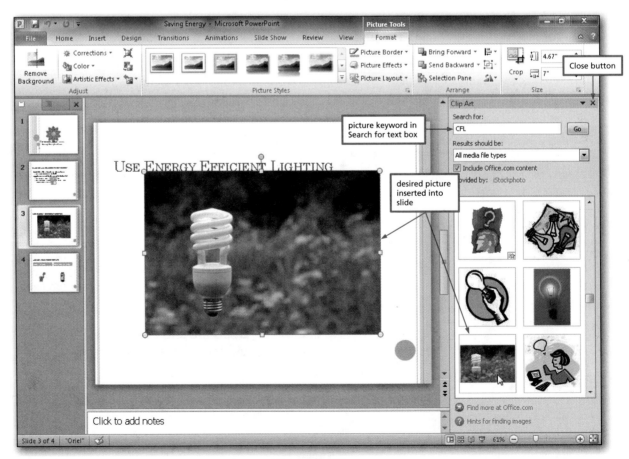

**Figure 1–45**

**Break Point:** If you wish to take a break, this is a good place to do so. You can quit PowerPoint now (refer to page PPT 50 for instructions). To resume at a later time, start PowerPoint (refer to pages PPT 4 and PPT 5 for instructions), open the file called Saving Energy (refer to pages PPT 50 and PPT 51 for instructions), and continue following the steps from this location forward.

# Resizing Clip Art and Photographs

Sometimes it is necessary to change the size of clip art. **Resizing** includes enlarging or reducing the size of a clip art graphic. You can resize clip art using a variety of techniques. One method involves changing the size of a clip by specifying exact dimensions in a dialog box. Another method involves dragging one of the graphic's sizing handles to the desired location. A selected graphic appears surrounded by a **selection rectangle**, which has small squares and circles, called **sizing handles** or move handles, at each corner and middle location.

## To Resize Clip Art

On Slides 1, 2, and 4, much space appears around the clips, so you can increase their sizes. Likewise, the photograph on Slide 3 can be enlarged to fill more of the space below the slide title. To change the size, drag the corner sizing handles to view how the clip will look on the slide. Using these corner handles maintains the graphic's original proportions. Dragging the square sizing handles alters the proportions so that the graphic's height and width become larger or smaller. The following steps increase the size of the Slide 1 clip using a corner sizing handle.

- Click the Close button in the Clip Art task pane so that it no longer is displayed.

- Click the Previous Slide button two times to display Slide 1.

- Click the globe clip to select it and display the selection rectangle.

- Point to the lower-left corner sizing handle on the clip so that the mouse pointer changes to a two-headed arrow (Figure 1–46).

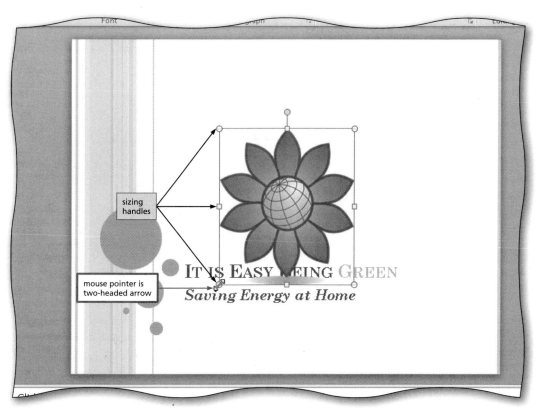

**Figure 1–46**

- Drag the sizing handle diagonally toward the lower-left corner of the slide until the mouse pointer is positioned approximately as shown in Figure 1–47.

**Q&A** What if the clip is not the same size as the one shown in Figure 1–47?

Repeat Steps 1 and 2.

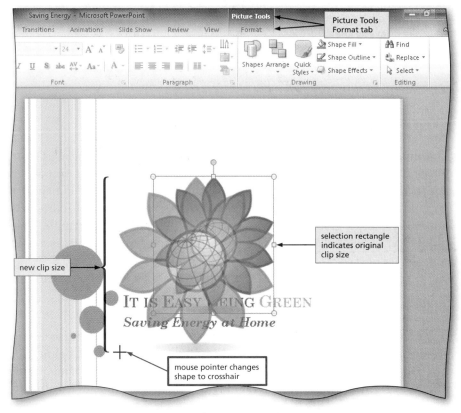

**Figure 1–47**

- Release the mouse button to resize the clip.
- Click outside the clip to deselect it (Figure 1–48).

**Q&A** What happened to the Picture Tools Format tab?

When you click outside the clip, PowerPoint deselects the clip and removes the Picture Tools Format tab from the screen.

**Q&A** What if I want to return the clip to its original size and start again?

With the graphic selected, click the Reset Picture button (Picture Tools Format tab | Adjust group).

**Figure 1–48**

## To Resize Clips on Slide 4

The two clip art images on Slide 4 also can be enlarged to fill much of the white space below the headings. You will reposition the clips in a later step. The following steps resize these clips using a sizing handle.

**1** Click the Next Slide button three times to display Slide 4.

**2** Click the furnace clip to select it.

**3** Drag the lower-left corner sizing handle on the clip diagonally outward until the clip is resized approximately as shown in Figure 1–49.

**4** Click the water heater clip to select it.

**5** Drag the lower-right corner sizing handle on the clip diagonally outward until the clip is resized approximately as shown in Figure 1–49.

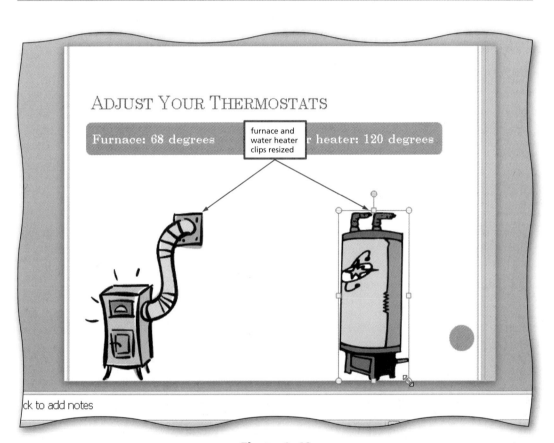

**Figure 1–49**

## To Resize a Photograph

The light bulb picture in Slide 3 can be enlarged slightly to fill much of the space below the slide title. You resize a photograph in the same manner that you resize clip art. The following steps resize this photograph using a sizing handle.

**1** Click the Previous Slide button to display Slide 3.

**2** Click the light bulb photograph to select it.

**BTW** | **Minimalist Design**
Resist the urge to fill your slides with clips from the Microsoft Clip Organizer. Minimalist style reduces clutter and allows the slide content to display prominently. This simple, yet effective design helps audience members with short attention spans to focus on the message.

**③** Drag the lower-left corner sizing handle on the photograph diagonally outward until the photograph is resized approximately as shown in Figure 1–50.

light bulb picture resized

**Figure 1–50**

## To Move Clips

After you insert clip art or a photograph on a slide, you might want to reposition it. The light bulb photograph on Slide 3 could be centered in the space between the slide title and the left and right edges of the slide. The clip on Slide 1 could be positioned in the upper-right corner of the slide. On Slide 4, the furnace and water heater clips could be centered under each heading. The following steps move these graphics.

**①**

- If necessary, click the light bulb photograph on Slide 3 to select it.

- Press and hold down the mouse button and then drag the photograph diagonally downward below the title text (Figure 1–51).

- If necessary, select the photograph and then use the ARROW keys to position it precisely as shown in Figure 1–51.

**Q&A**

The photograph still is not located exactly where I want it to display. What can I do to align the photograph?

Press the CTRL key while you press the ARROW keys. This key combination moves the clip in smaller increments than when you press only an ARROW key.

light bulb picture moved to desired location on Slide 3

**Figure 1–51**

- Click the Next Slide button to display Slide 4.

- Click the furnace clip to select it, press and hold down the mouse button, and then drag the clip to center it under the furnace heading.

- Click the water heater clip and then drag the clip to center it under the water heater heading (Figure 1–52).

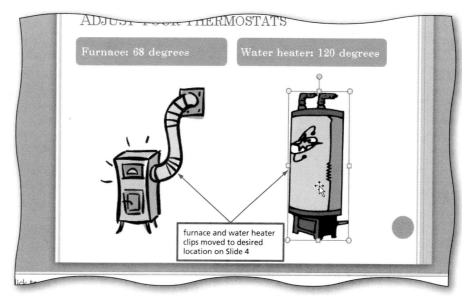

**Figure 1–52**

- Click the Previous Slide button twice to display Slide 2.

- Click the dishwasher clip, which is on top of the faucet clip, and then drag the clip to center it under the last bulleted paragraph, Wash clothes in cold water.

- Click the faucet clip and then drag the clip so that the faucet handle is centered under the words, full loads.

- Drag a corner sizing handle on the faucet clip diagonally outward until the clip is resized approximately as shown in Figure 1–53. You may need to drag the clip to position it in the desired location.

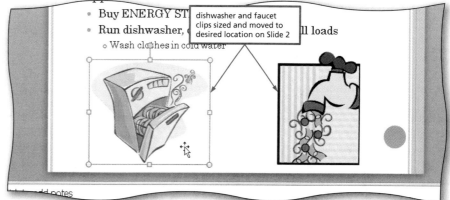

**Figure 1–53**

- Select the dishwasher clip and then resize and move it so that the clip displays approximately as shown in Figure 1–53.

- Click the Previous Slide button to display Slide 1.

- Click the globe clip and then drag it to the upper-right corner of the slide. You may want to adjust its size by selecting it and then dragging the corner sizing handles.

- Click outside the clip to deselect it (Figure 1–54).

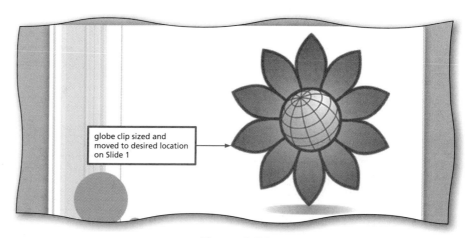

**Figure 1–54**

Plan
Ahead

**Choose a closing slide.**
After the last slide appears during a slide show, the default PowerPoint setting is to end the presentation with a **black slide**. This black slide appears only when the slide show is running and concludes the slide show, so your audience never sees the PowerPoint window. It is a good idea, however, to end the presentation with a final closing slide to display at the end of the presentation. This slide ends the presentation gracefully and should be an exact copy, or a very similar copy, of your title slide. The audience will recognize that the presentation is drawing to a close when this slide appears. It can remain on the screen when the audience asks questions, approaches the speaker for further information, or exits the room.

# Ending a Slide Show with a Closing Slide

All the text for the slides in the Saving Energy slide show has been entered. This presentation thus far consists of a title slide, one text slide with a multi-level bulleted list, a third slide for a photograph, and a fourth slide with a Comparison layout. A closing slide that resembles the title slide is the final slide to create.

## To Duplicate a Slide

When two slides contain similar information and have the same format, duplicating one slide and then making minor modifications to the new slide saves time and increases consistency.

Slide 5 will have the same layout and design as Slide 1. The most expedient method of creating this slide is to copy Slide 1 and then make minor modifications to the new slide. The following steps duplicate the title slide.

• With Slide 1 selected, click the New Slide arrow (Home tab | Slides group) to display the Oriel layout gallery (Figure 1–55).

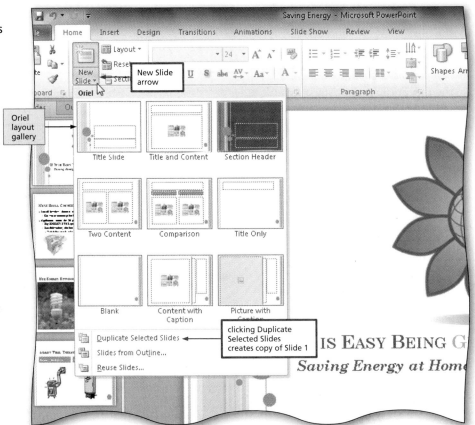

**Figure 1–55**

**2**

• Click Duplicate Selected Slides in the Oriel layout gallery to create a new Slide 2, which is a duplicate of Slide 1 (Figure 1–56).

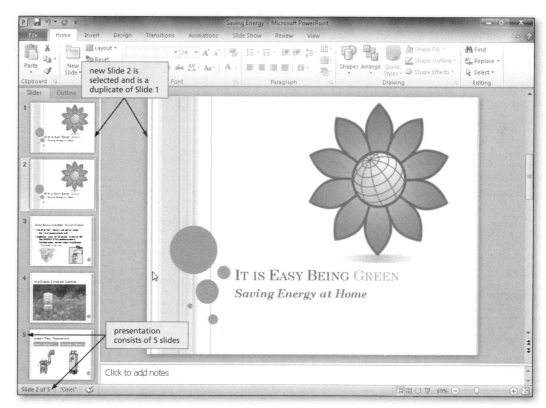

**Figure 1–56**

**Break Point:** If you wish to take a break, this is a good place to do so. You can quit PowerPoint now (refer to page PPT 50 for instructions). To resume at a later time, start PowerPoint (refer to pages PPT 4 and PPT 5 for instructions), open the file called Saving Energy (refer to pages PPT 50 and PPT 51 for instructions), and continue following the steps from this location forward.

## To Arrange a Slide

The new Slide 2 was inserted directly below Slide 1 because Slide 1 was the selected slide. This duplicate slide needs to display at the end of the presentation directly after the final title and content slide.

Changing slide order is an easy process and is best performed in the Slides pane. When you click the slide thumbnail and begin to drag it to a new location, a line indicates the new location of the selected slide. When you release the mouse button, the slide drops into the desired location. Hence, this process of dragging and then dropping the thumbnail in a new location is called **drag and drop**. You can use the drag-and-drop method to move any selected item, including text and graphics. The following step moves the new Slide 2 to the end of the presentation so that it becomes a closing slide.

**1**

- With Slide 2 selected, drag the Slide 2 slide thumbnail in the Slides pane below the last slide thumbnail (Figure 1–57).

**Q&A**

The Slide 2 thumbnail is not visible in the Slides pane when I am dragging the thumbnail downward. How do I know it will be positioned in the desired location?

A blue horizontal bar indicates where the slide will move.

cursor shape indicates drag-and-drop method

IT IS EASY BEING

*Saving Energy at Hon*

bar indicates new location of slide

Slide 2 of 5    "Oriel"

**Figure 1–57**

**Other Ways**

1. Click slide icon on Outline tab, drag icon to new location
2. Click Slide Sorter (View tab | Presentation Views group), click slide thumbnail, drag thumbnail to new location

# Making Changes to Slide Text Content

After creating slides in a presentation, you may find that you want to make changes to the text. Changes may be required because a slide contains an error, the scope of the presentation shifts, or the style is inconsistent. This section explains the types of changes that commonly occur when creating a presentation.

You generally make three types of changes to text in a presentation: additions, replacements, and deletions.

**BTW**

**Checking Spelling**
As you review your slides, you should examine the text for spelling errors. In Chapter 3, you will learn to use PowerPoint's built-in spelling checker to help you perform this task.

- Additions are necessary when you omit text from a slide and need to add it later. You may need to insert text in the form of a sentence, word, or single character. For example, you may want to add the presenter's middle name on the title slide.

- Replacements are needed when you want to revise the text in a presentation. For example, you may want to substitute the word *their* for the word *there*.

- Deletions are required when text on a slide is incorrect or no longer is relevant to the presentation. For example, a slide may look cluttered. Therefore, you may want to remove one of the bulleted paragraphs to add more space.

Editing text in PowerPoint basically is the same as editing text in a word processing program. The following sections illustrate the most common changes made to text in a presentation.

# Replacing Text in an Existing Slide

When you need to correct a word or phrase, you can replace the text by selecting the text to be replaced and then typing the new text. As soon as you press any key on the keyboard, the selected text is deleted and the new text is displayed.

PowerPoint inserts text to the left of the insertion point. The text to the right of the insertion point moves to the right (and shifts downward if necessary) to accommodate the added text.

# Deleting Text

You can delete text using one of three methods. One is to use the BACKSPACE key to remove text just typed. The second is to position the insertion point to the left of the text you want to delete and then press the DELETE key. The third method is to drag through the text you want to delete and then press the DELETE or BACKSPACE key. Use the third method when deleting large sections of text.

## To Delete Text in a Placeholder

To keep the ending slide clean and simple, you want to delete a few words in the slide show title and subtitle text. The following steps change It Is Easy Being Green to Be Green and then change Saving Energy at Home to Save Energy.

- With Slide 5 selected, position the mouse pointer immediately to the left of the first character of the text to be selected (in this case, the I in the word, It).

- Drag the mouse pointer through the last character of the text to be selected (in this case, the space after the y in Easy) (Figure 1–58).

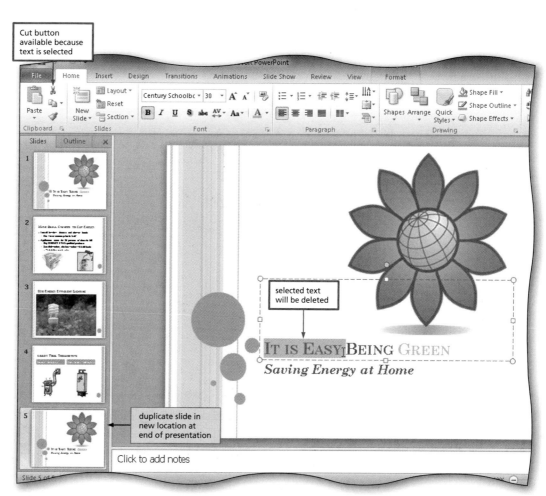

**Figure 1–58**

• Click the Cut button (Home tab | Clipboard group) to delete all the selected text (Figure 1–59).

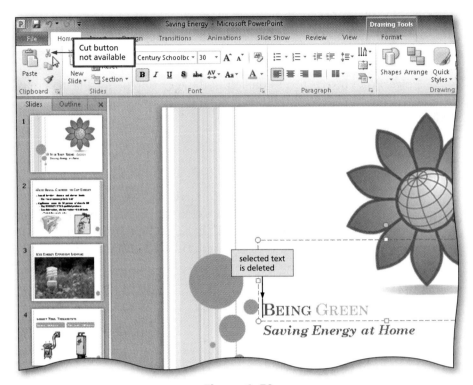

**Figure 1–59**

• Select the letters, ing, in the word, Being.

• Click the Cut button (Figure 1–60).

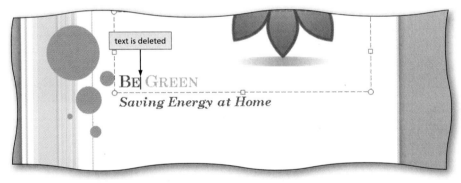

**Figure 1–60**

• Select the letters, ing, in the word, Saving, and then click the Cut button.

• Type  e  to change the word to Save (Figure 1–61).

**Other Ways**

1. Right-click selected text, click Cut on shortcut menu

2. Select text, press DELETE or BACKSPACE key

3. Select text, press CTRL+X

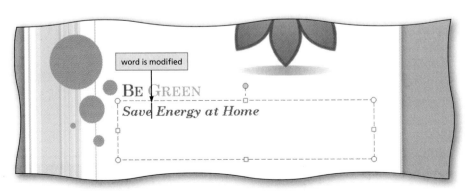

**Figure 1–61**

# Adding a Transition

PowerPoint provides many animation effects to add interest and make a slide show presentation look professional. **Animation** includes special visual and sound effects applied to text or content. A **slide transition** is a special animation effect used to progress from one slide to the next in a slide show. You can control the speed of the transition effect and add a sound.

PowerPoint provides a variety of transitions arranged into three categories that describe the types of effects: Subtle, Exciting, and Dynamic Content.

## To Add a Transition between Slides

In this presentation, you apply the Doors transition in the Exciting category to all slides and change the transition speed from 1.40 seconds to 2 seconds. The following steps apply this transition to the presentation.

**1**
- Click the Transitions tab on the Ribbon and then point to the More button (Transitions tab | Transition to This Slide group) (Figure 1–62).

**Q&A**

Is a transition applied now?

No. The first slide icon in the Transitions group has an orange border, which indicates no transition has been applied.

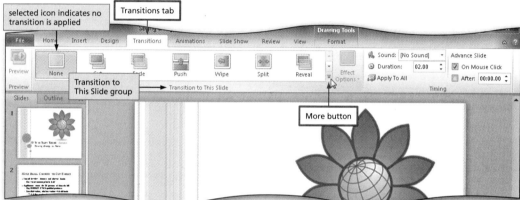

Figure 1–62

**2**
- Click the More button to expand the Transitions gallery.

- Point to the Doors transition in the Exciting category in the Transitions gallery (Figure 1–63).

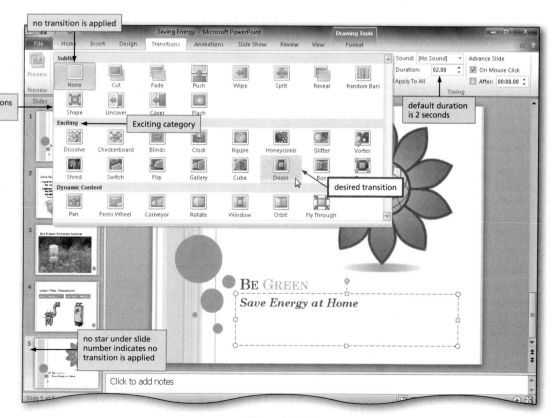

Figure 1–63

**3**

- Click Doors in the Exciting category in the Transitions gallery to apply this transition to the closing slide.

**Q&A** Why does a star appear next to Slide 5 in the Slides tab?

The star indicates that a transition animation effect is applied to that slide.

- Click the Duration up arrow (Transitions tab | Timing group) three times to change the transition speed from 01.40 seconds to 02.00 seconds (Figure 1–64).

**Q&A** Why did the time change?

Each transition has a default duration time. The Doors transition time is 1:40 seconds.

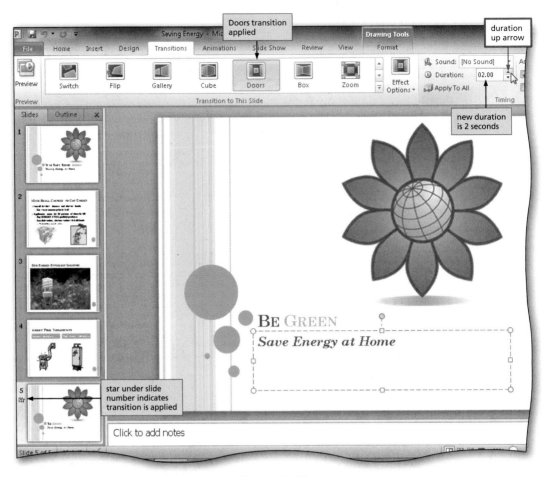

Figure 1–64

**4**

- Click the Preview Transitions button (Transitions tab | Preview area) to view the transition and the new transition time (Figure 1–65).

**Q&A** Can I adjust the duration time I just set?

Yes. Click the Duration up or down arrows or type a speed in the Duration text box and preview the transition until you find the time that best fits your presentation.

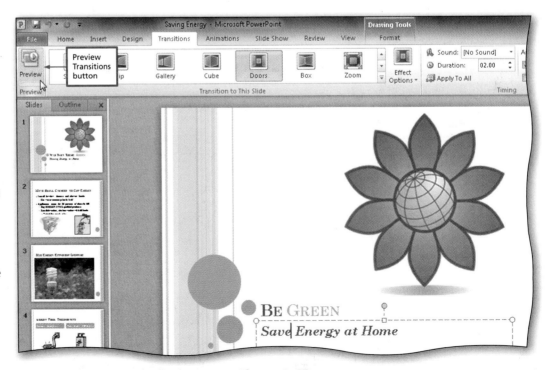

Figure 1–65

**5**

- Click the Apply To All button (Transitions tab | Timing group) to apply the Doors transition and the increased transition time to Slides 1 through 4 in the presentation (Figure 1–66).

**Q&A**

What if I want to apply a different transition and duration to each slide in the presentation?

Repeat Steps 2 and 3 for each slide individually.

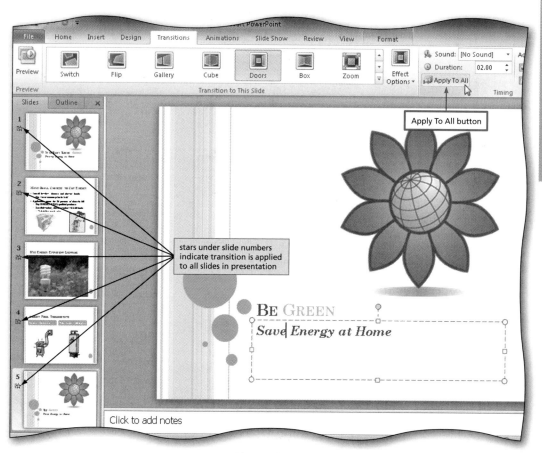

Figure 1–66

## Changing Document Properties

PowerPoint helps you organize and identify your files by using **document properties**, which are the details about a file. Document properties, also known as **metadata**, can include information such as the project author, title, subject, and keywords. A **keyword** is a word or phrase that further describes the document. For example, a class name or document topic can describe the file's purpose or content.

Document properties are valuable for a variety of reasons:

- Users can save time locating a particular file because they can view a document's properties without opening the document.

- By creating consistent properties for files having similar content, users can better organize their documents.

- Some organizations require PowerPoint users to add document properties so that other employees can view details about these files.

Five different types of document properties exist, but the more common ones used in this book are standard and automatically updated properties. **Standard properties** are associated with all Microsoft Office documents and include author, title, and subject. **Automatically updated properties** include file system properties, such as the date you create or change a file, and statistics, such as the file size.

## To Change Document Properties

The **Document Information Panel** contains areas where you can view and enter document properties. You can view and change information in this panel at any time while you are creating a document. Before saving the presentation again, you want to add your name and course information as document properties. The following steps use the Document Information Panel to change document properties.

- Click File on the Ribbon to open the Backstage view.

- If necessary, click the Info tab in the Backstage view to display the Info gallery (Figure 1–67).

**Q&A**

How do I close the Backstage view?

Click File on the Ribbon or click the preview of the document in the Info gallery to return to the PowerPoint document window.

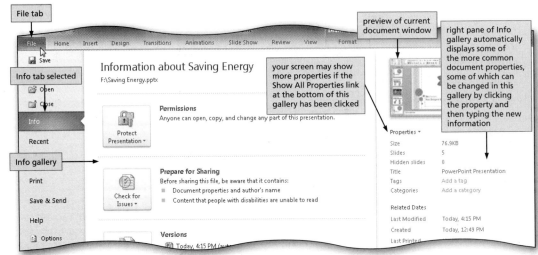

**Figure 1–67**

- Click the Properties button in the right pane of the Info gallery to display the Properties menu (Figure 1–68).

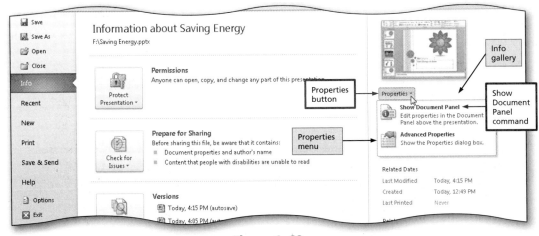

**Figure 1–68**

- Click Show Document Panel on the Properties menu to close the Backstage view and display the Document Information Panel in the PowerPoint document window (Figure 1–69).

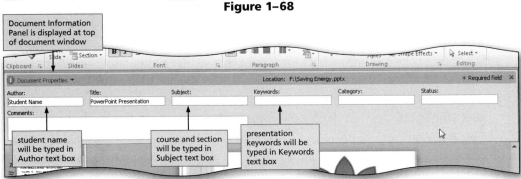

**Figure 1–69**

**Q&A**

Why are some of the document properties in my Document Information Panel already filled in?

The person who installed Microsoft Office 2010 on your computer or network may have set or customized the properties.

- Click the Author text box, if necessary, and then type your name as the Author property. If a name already is displayed in the Author text box, delete it before typing your name.

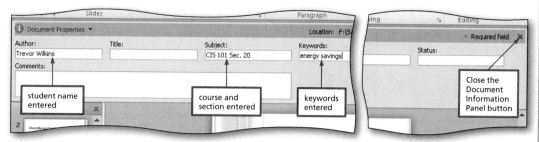

**Figure 1–70**

- Click the Subject text box, if necessary delete any existing text, and then type your course and section as the Subject property.

- If an AutoComplete dialog box appears, click its Yes button.

- Click the Keywords text box, if necessary delete any existing text, and then type **energy savings** as the Keywords property (Figure 1–70).

**Q&A**
What types of document properties does PowerPoint collect automatically?

PowerPoint records details such as time spent editing a document, the number of times a document has been revised, and the fonts and themes used in a document.

**⑤**

- Click the Close the Document Information Panel button so that the Document Information Panel no longer is displayed.

**Other Ways**

1. Click File on Ribbon, click Info in Backstage view, if necessary click Show All Properties link in Info gallery, click property to change and type new information, close Backstage view

## To Save an Existing Presentation with the Same File Name

You have made several modifications to the presentation since you last saved it. Thus, you should save it again. The following step saves the document again. For an example of the step listed below, refer to the Office 2010 and Windows 7 chapter at the beginning of this book.

**①** Click the Save button on the Quick Access Toolbar to overwrite the previously saved file.

**BTW**
**Saving in a Previous PowerPoint Format**
To ensure that your presentation will open in PowerPoint 2003 or older versions of this software, you must save your file in PowerPoint 97-2003 format. These files will have the .ppt extension.

# Viewing the Presentation in Slide Show View

The Slide Show button, located in the lower-right corner of the PowerPoint window above the status bar, allows you to show a presentation using a computer. The computer acts like a slide projector, displaying each slide on a full screen. The full-screen slide hides the toolbars, menus, and other PowerPoint window elements.

## To Start Slide Show View

When making a presentation, you use **Slide Show view**. You can start Slide Show view from Normal view or Slide Sorter view. Slide Show view begins when you click the Slide Show button in the lower-right corner of the PowerPoint window above the status bar. PowerPoint then shows the current slide on the full screen without any of the PowerPoint window objects, such as the menu bar or toolbars. The following steps start Slide Show view.

**1**

- Click the Slide 1 thumbnail in the Slides pane to select and display Slide 1.

- Point to the Slide Show button in the lower-right corner of the PowerPoint window on the status bar (Figure 1–71).

**Q&A** Why did I need to select Slide 1?

When you run a slide show, PowerPoint begins the show with the currently displayed slide. If you had not selected Slide 1, then only Slide 5 would have displayed in the slide show.

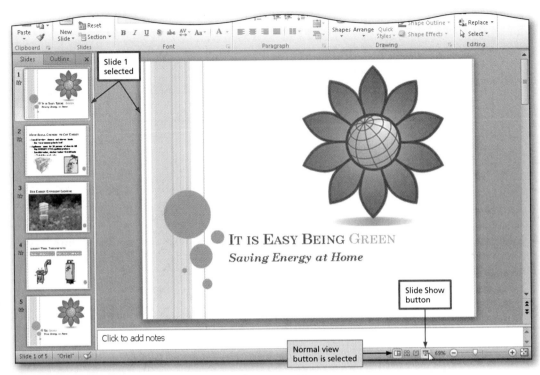

**Figure 1–71**

**2**

- Click the Slide Show button to display the title slide (Figure 1–72).

**Q&A** Where is the PowerPoint window?

When you run a slide show, the PowerPoint window is hidden. It will reappear once you end your slide show.

**Other Ways**

1. Click Slide Show From Beginning button (Slide Show tab | Start Slide Show group)

2. Press F5

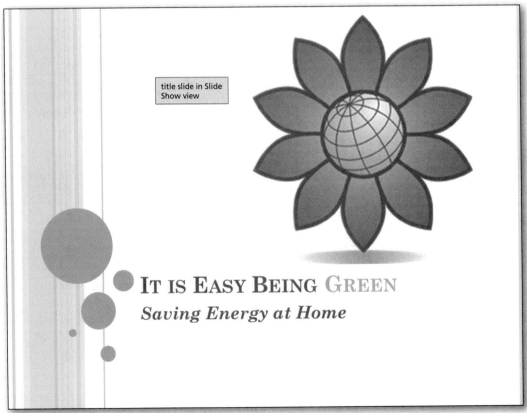

**Figure 1–72**

## To Move Manually through Slides in a Slide Show

After you begin Slide Show view, you can move forward or backward through the slides. PowerPoint allows you to advance through the slides manually or automatically. During a slide show, each slide in the presentation shows on the screen, one slide at a time. Each time you click the mouse button, the next slide appears. The following steps move manually through the slides.

**1**

- Click each slide until Slide 5 (Be Green) is displayed (Figure 1–73).

I see a small toolbar in the lower-left corner of my slide. What is this toolbar?

The Slide Show toolbar appears when you begin running a slide show and then move the mouse pointer. The buttons on this toolbar allow you to navigate to the next slide, the previous slide, to mark up the current slide, or to change the current display.

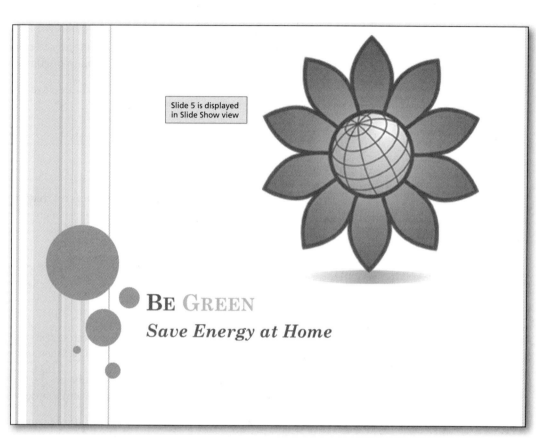

Slide 5 is displayed in Slide Show view

**BE GREEN**

*Save Energy at Home*

**Figure 1–73**

**2**

- Click Slide 5 so that the black slide appears with a message announcing the end of the slide show (Figure 1–74).

How can I end the presentation at this point?

Click the black slide to return to Normal view in the PowerPoint window or press the ESC key.

End of slide show, click to exit.

message announces end of slide show

**Figure 1–74**

| Other Ways |
|---|
| 1. Press PAGE DOWN to advance one slide at a time, or press PAGE UP to go back one slide at a time    2. Press RIGHT ARROW or DOWN ARROW to advance one slide at a time, or press LEFT ARROW or UP ARROW to go back one slide at a time    3. If Slide Show toolbar is displayed, click Next Slide or Previous Slide button on toolbar |

## To Quit PowerPoint

This project now is complete. The following steps quit PowerPoint. For a detailed example of the procedure summarized below, refer to the Office 2010 and Windows 7 chapter at the beginning of this book.

**1** If you have one PowerPoint presentation open, click the Close button on the right side of the title bar to close the document and quit PowerPoint; or if you have multiple PowerPoint presentations open, click File on the Ribbon to open the Backstage view and then click Exit in the Backstage view to close all open documents and quit PowerPoint.

**2** If a Microsoft PowerPoint dialog box appears, click the Save button to save any changes made to the document since the last save.

**BTW**

**Certification**
The Microsoft Office Specialist (MOS) program provides an opportunity for you to obtain a valuable industry credential — proof that you have the PowerPoint 2010 skills required by employers. For more information, visit the PowerPoint 2010 Certification Web page (scsite.com/ppt2010/cert).

## To Start PowerPoint

Once you have created and saved a document, you may need to retrieve it from your storage medium. For example, you might want to revise the presentation or print it. The following steps, which assume Windows 7 is running, start PowerPoint so that you can open and modify the presentation. You may need to ask your instructor how to start PowerPoint for your computer. For a detailed example of the procedure summarized below, refer to the Office 2010 and Windows 7 chapter at the beginning of this book.

**1** Click the Start button on the Windows 7 taskbar to display the Start menu.

**2** Type `Microsoft PowerPoint` as the search text in the 'Search programs and files' text box and watch the search results appear on the Start menu.

**3** Click Microsoft PowerPoint 2010 in the search results on the Start menu to start PowerPoint and display a new blank document in the PowerPoint window.

**4** If the PowerPoint window is not maximized, click the Maximize button next to the Close button on its title bar to maximize the window.

## To Open a Document from PowerPoint

Earlier in this chapter you saved your project on a USB flash drive using the file name, Saving Energy. The following steps open the Saving Energy file from the PowerPoint folder in the CIS 101 folder on the USB flash drive. For a detailed example of the procedure summarized below, refer to the Office 2010 and Windows 7 chapter at the beginning of this book.

**1** With your USB flash drive connected to one of the computer's USB ports, click File on the Ribbon to open the Backstage view.

**2** Click Open in the Backstage view to display the Open dialog box.

**3** Navigate to the location of the file to be opened (in this case, the USB flash drive, then to the CIS 101 folder [or your class folder], and then to the PowerPoint folder).

**4** Click Saving Energy to select the file to be opened.

**5** Click the Open button (Open dialog box) to open the selected file and display the opened document in the PowerPoint window.

# Printing a Presentation

After creating a presentation, you may want to print the slides. Printing a presentation enables you to distribute the document to others in a form that can be read or viewed but typically not edited. It is a good practice to save a presentation before printing it, in the event you experience difficulties printing.

---

**Determine the best method for distributing the presentation.**
The traditional method of distributing a presentation uses a printer to produce a hard copy. A **hardcopy** or **printout** is information that exists on a physical medium such as paper. For users who can receive fax documents, you can elect to print a hard copy on a remote fax machine. Hard copies can be useful for the following reasons:

* Many people prefer proofreading a hard copy of a document rather than viewing it on the screen to check for errors and readability.

* Hard copies can serve as reference material if your storage medium is lost or becomes corrupted and you need to recreate the document.

   Instead of distributing a hard copy of a presentation slides, users can choose to distribute the presentation as an electronic image that mirrors the original document's appearance. The electronic image of the document can be e-mailed, posted on a Web site, or copied to a portable storage medium such as a USB flash drive. Two popular electronic image formats, sometimes called fixed formats, are PDF by Adobe Systems and XPS by Microsoft. In PowerPoint, you can create electronic image files through the Print tab in the Backstage view, the Save & Send tab in the Backstage view, and the Save As dialog box. Electronic images of documents, such as PDF and XPS, can be useful for the following reasons.

* Users can view electronic images of documents without the software that created the original document (e.g., PowerPoint). Specifically, to view a PDF file, you use a program called Acrobat Reader, which can be downloaded free from Adobe's Web site. Similarly, to view an XPS file, you use a program called an XPS Viewer, which is included in the latest versions of Windows and Internet Explorer.

* Sending electronic documents saves paper and printer supplies. Society encourages users to contribute to **green computing**, which involves reducing the environmental waste generated when using a computer.

Plan
Ahead

---

## To Print a Presentation

With the completed presentation saved, you may want to print it. If copies of the presentation are being distributed to audience members, you will print a hard copy of each individual slide on a printer. The following steps print a hard copy of the contents of the saved Saving Energy presentation.

• Click File on the Ribbon to open the Backstage view.

• Click the Print tab in the Backstage view to display the Print gallery (Figure 1–75).

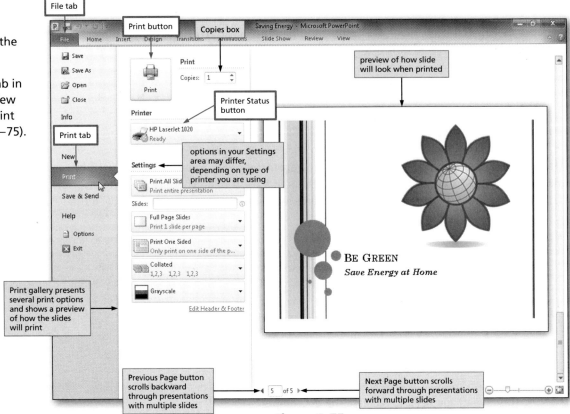

**Figure 1–75**

**Q&A**  How do I preview Slides 2 through 5?

Click the Next Page button in the Print gallery to scroll forward through pages in the document; similarly, click the Previous Page button to scroll backward through pages.

**Q&A**  How can I print multiple copies of my slides?

Increase the number in the Copies box in the Print gallery.

**Q&A**  What if I decide not to print the document at this time?

Click File on the Ribbon to close the Backstage view and return to the PowerPoint document window.

• Verify the printer name that appears on the Printer box Status button will print a hard copy of the document. If necessary, click the Printer Status button to display a list of available printer options and then click the desired printer to change the currently selected printer.

**BTW**

**Quick Reference**
For a table that lists how to complete the tasks covered in this book using the mouse, Ribbon, shortcut menu, and keyboard, see the Quick Reference Summary at the back of this book, or visit the PowerPoint 2010 Quick Reference Web page (scsite.com/ppt2010/qr).

• Click the Print button in the Print gallery to print the document on the currently selected printer.

• When the printer stops, retrieve the hard copy (Figure 1–76).

**Q&A** Do I have to wait until my document is complete to print it?

No, you can follow these steps to print a document at any time while you are creating it.

**Q&A** What if I want to print an electronic image of a document instead of a hard copy?

You would click the Printer Status button in the Print gallery and then select the desired electronic image option such as a Microsoft XPS Document Writer, which would create an XPS file.

**(a) Slide 1**

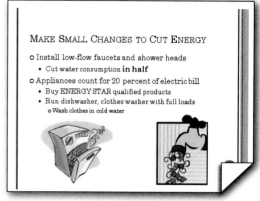

**(b) Slide 2**

**(c) Slide 3**

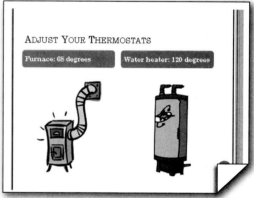

**(d) Slide 4**

**(e) Slide 5**

**Figure 1–76**

| Other Ways |
| --- |
| 1. Press CTRL+P, press ENTER |

## To Quit PowerPoint

The project now is complete. The following steps quit PowerPoint. For a detailed example of the procedure summarized below, refer to the Office 2010 and Windows 7 chapter at the beginning of this book.

**1** If you have one PowerPoint document open, click the Close button on the right side of the title bar to close the document and quit PowerPoint; or if you have multiple PowerPoint documents open, click File on the Ribbon to open the Backstage view and then click Exit in the Backstage view to close all open documents and quit PowerPoint.

**2** If a Microsoft Office PowerPoint dialog box appears, click the Save button to save any changes made to the document since the last save.

# Chapter Summary

In this chapter you have learned how to apply a document theme, create a title slide and text slides with a bulleted list, clip art, and a photograph, size and move clip art and a photograph, format and edit text, add a slide transition, view the presentation in Slide Show view, and print slides as handouts. The items listed below include all the new PowerPoint skills you have learned in this chapter.

1. Start PowerPoint (PPT 4)
2. Choose a Document Theme (PPT 5)
3. Enter the Presentation Title (PPT 7)
4. Enter the Presentation Subtitle Paragraph (PPT 9)
5. Select a Paragraph (PPT 10)
6. Italicize Text (PPT 11)
7. Increase Font Size (PPT 11)
8. Select a Word (PPT 12)
9. Change the Text Color (PPT 13)
10. Save a Presentation (PPT 14)
11. Add a New Text Slide with a Bulleted List (PPT 14)
12. Enter a Slide Title (PPT 16)
13. Select a Text Placeholder (PPT 16)
14. Type a Multi-Level Bulleted List (PPT 17)
15. Select a Group of Words (PPT 19)
16. Bold Text (PPT 19)
17. Add a Slide with the Title Only Layout (PPT 21)
18. Add a New Slide and Enter a Slide Title and Headings (PPT 23)
19. Move to Another Slide in Normal View (PPT 25)
20. Insert a Clip from the Clip Organizer into the Title Slide (PPT 27)
21. Insert a Clip from the Clip Organizer into a Content Placeholder (PPT 30)
22. Insert a Photograph from the Clip Organizer into a Slide without a Content Placeholder (PPT 32)
23. Resize Clip Art (PPT 33)
24. Move Clips (PPT 36)
25. Duplicate a Slide (PPT 38)
26. Arrange a Slide (PPT 39)
27. Delete Text in a Placeholder (PPT 41)
28. Add a Transition between Slides (PPT 43)
29. Change Document Properties (PPT 46)
30. Save an Existing Presentation with the Same File Name (PPT 47)
31. Start Slide Show View (PPT 47)
32. Move Manually through Slides in a Slide Show (PPT 49)
33. Quit PowerPoint (PPT 50)
34. Open a Document from PowerPoint (PPT 50)
35. Print a Presentation (PPT 51)

If you have a SAM 2010 user profile, your instructor may have assigned an autogradable version of this assignment. If so, log into the SAM 2010 Web site at www.cengage.com/sam2010 to download the instruction and start files.

# Learn It Online

Test your knowledge of chapter content and key terms.

*Instructions:* To complete the Learn It Online exercises, start your browser, click the Address bar, and then enter the Web address **scsite.com/ppt2010/learn**. When the PowerPoint 2010 Learn It Online page is displayed, click the link for the exercise you want to complete and then read the instructions.

### Chapter Reinforcement TF, MC, and SA

A series of true/false, multiple choice, and short answer questions that test your knowledge of the chapter content.

### Flash Cards

An interactive learning environment where you identify chapter key terms associated with displayed definitions.

### Practice Test

A series of multiple choice questions that test your knowledge of chapter content and key terms.

### Who Wants To Be a Computer Genius?

An interactive game that challenges your knowledge of chapter content in the style of a television quiz show.

### Wheel of Terms

An interactive game that challenges your knowledge of chapter key terms in the style of the television show *Wheel of Fortune*.

### Crossword Puzzle Challenge

A crossword puzzle that challenges your knowledge of key terms presented in the chapter.

# Apply Your Knowledge

Reinforce the skills and apply the concepts you learned in this chapter.

### Modifying Character Formats and Paragraph Levels and Moving a Clip

*Note:* To complete this assignment, you will be required to use the Data Files for Students. See the inside back cover of this book for instructions on downloading the Data Files for Students, or contact your instructor for information about accessing the required files.

*Instructions:* Start PowerPoint. Open the presentation, Apply 1-1 Flu Season, from the Data Files for Students.

The two slides in the presentation discuss ways to avoid getting or spreading the flu. The document you open is an unformatted presentation. You are to modify the document theme, indent the paragraphs, resize and move the clip art, and format the text so the slides look like Figure 1–77 on the next page.

*Continued >*

**Apply Your Knowledge** *continued*

*Perform the following tasks:*

1. Change the document theme to Urban. On the title slide, use your name in place of Student Name and bold and italicize your name. Increase the title text font size to 60 point. Resize and position the clip as shown in Figure 1–77a.

2. On Slide 2, increase the indent of the second, third, and fifth paragraphs (Cover mouth and nose with a tissue; No tissue? Use your elbow or sleeve; Use soap, warm water for 20 seconds) to second-level paragraphs. Then combine paragraphs six and seven (Drink fluids; Get plenty of rest) to read, Drink fluids and get plenty of rest, as shown in Figure 1–77b.

3. Change the document properties, as specified by your instructor. Save the presentation using the file name, Apply 1–1 Avoid the Flu. Submit the revised document in the format specified by your instructor.

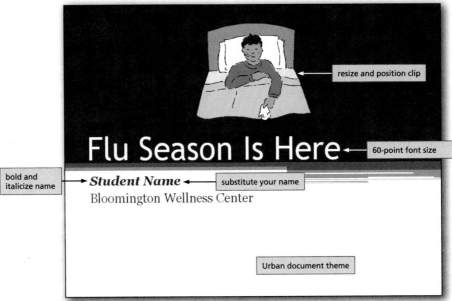

**(a) Slide 1 (Title Slide with Clip Art)**

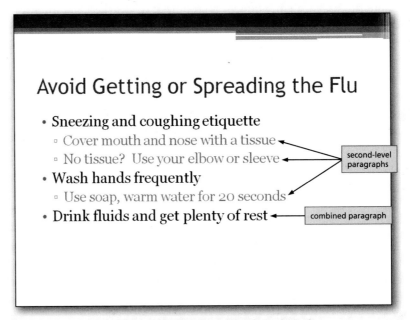

**(b) Slide 2 (Multi-Level Bulleted List)**

**Figure 1–77**

# Extend Your Knowledge

Extend the skills you learned in this chapter and experiment with new skills. You may need to use Help to complete the assignment.

### Changing Slide Theme, Layout, and Text

*Note:* To complete this assignment, you will be required to use the Data Files for Students. See the inside back cover of this book for instructions on downloading the Data Files for Students, or contact your instructor for information about accessing the required files.

*Instructions:* Start PowerPoint. Open the presentation that you are going to prepare for your dental hygiene class, Extend 1–1 Winning Smile, from the Data Files for Students.
 You will choose a theme, format slides, and create a closing slide.

*Perform the following tasks:*
1. Apply an appropriate document theme.
2. On Slide 1, use your name in place of Student Name. Format the text on this slide using techniques you learned in this chapter, such as changing the font size and color and also bolding and italicizing words.
3. On Slide 2, change the slide layout and adjust the paragraph levels so that the lines of text are arranged under two headings: Discount Dental and Dental Insurance (Figure 1–78).
4. On Slide 3, create paragraphs and adjust the paragraph levels to create a bulleted list. Edit the text so that the slide meets the 7 × 7 rule, which states that each line should have a maximum of seven words, and each slide should have a maximum of seven lines.
5. Create an appropriate closing slide using the title slide as a guide.
6. The slides contain a variety of clips downloaded from the Microsoft Clip Organizer. Size and move them when necessary.
7. Apply an appropriate transition to all slides.
8. Change the document properties, as specified by your instructor. Save the presentation using the file name, Extend 1–1 Dental Plans.
9. Submit the revised document in the format specified by your instructor.

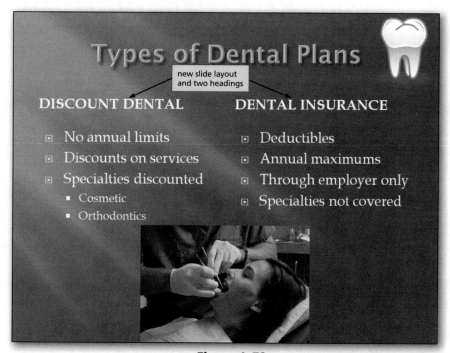

**Figure 1–78**

# Make It Right

Analyze a presentation and correct all errors and/or improve the design.

## Correcting Formatting and List Levels

*Note:* To complete this assignment, you will be required to use the Data Files for Students. See the inside back cover of this book for instructions on downloading the Data Files for Students, or contact your instructor for information about accessing the required files.

*Instructions:* Start PowerPoint. Open the presentation, Make It Right 1–1 Air Ducts, from the Data Files for Students.

Members of your homeowners' association are having their semiannual meeting, and each member of the board is required to give a short presentation on the subject of energy savings. You have decided to discuss the energy-saving benefits of maintaining the air ducts in your home. Correct the formatting problems and errors in the presentation while keeping in mind the guidelines presented in this chapter.

*Perform the following tasks:*
1. Change the document theme from Origin, shown in Figure 1–79, to Module.
2. On Slide 1, replace the words, Student Name, with your name. Format your name so that it displays prominently on the slide.
3. Increase the size of the clip on Slide 1 and move it to the upper-right corner.
4. Move Slide 2 to the end of the presentation so that it becomes the new Slide 3.
5. On Slide 2, correct the spelling errors and then increase the font size of the Slide 2 title text, Check Hidden Air Ducts, to 54 point. Increase the size of the clip and move it up to fill the white space on the right of the bulleted list.
6. On Slide 3, correct the spelling errors and then change the font size of the title text, Energy Savings, to 54 point. Increase the indent levels for paragraphs 2 and 4. Increase the size of the clips. Center the furnace clip at the bottom of the slide.
7. Change the document properties, as specified by your instructor. Save the presentation using the file name, Make It Right 1–1 Ducts Presentation.
8. Apply the same transition and duration to all slides.
9. Submit the revised document in the format specified by your instructor.

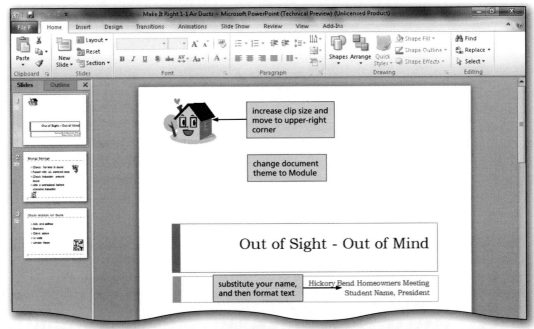

**Figure 1–79**

## In the Lab

Design and/or create a presentation using the guidelines, concepts, and skills presented in this chapter. Labs 1, 2, and 3 are listed in order of increasing difficulty.

### Lab 1: Creating a Presentation with Bulleted Lists, a Closing Slide, and Clips

*Problem:* You are working with upper-level students to host a freshmen orientation seminar. When you attended this seminar, you received some helpful tips on studying for exams. Your contribution to this year's seminar is to prepare a short presentation on study skills. You develop the outline shown in Figure 1–80 and then prepare the PowerPoint presentation shown in Figures 1–81a through 1–81d.

**Studying for an Exam**
Freshmen Orientation Seminar
Sarah Jones

**Prepare in Advance**
　Location
　　　Quiet, well-lit
　Timing
　　　15-minute breaks every hour
　Material
　　　Quiz yourself

**Exam Time**
　Day of Exam
　　　Rest properly
　　　Eat a good meal
　　　Wear comfy clothes
　　　Be early
　　　Be confident

**Figure 1–80**

*Perform the following tasks:*

1. Create a new presentation using the Aspect document theme.

2. Using the typed notes illustrated in Figure 1–80, create the title slide shown in Figure 1–81a, using your name in place of Sarah Jones. Italicize your name and increase the font size to 24 point. Increase the font size of the title text paragraph, Hit the Books, to 48 point. Increase the font size of the first paragraph of the subtitle text, Studying for an Exam, to 28 point.

**(a) Slide 1 (Title Slide)**
**Figure 1–81**

*Continued >*

**In the Lab** *continued*

3. Using the typed notes in Figure 1–80, create the two text slides with bulleted lists and find and insert clips from the Microsoft Clip Organizer, as shown in Figures 1–81b and 1–81c.

4. Create a closing slide by duplicating Slide 1, deleting your name, replacing the photograph with the photograph shown in Figure 1–81d, and moving the slide to the end of the presentation.

5. On Slide 3, change the font color of the words, Be confident, to Yellow (fourth color in the Standard Colors row).

6. Apply the Uncover transition in the Subtle category to all slides. Change the duration to 1.25 seconds.

7. Drag the scroll box to display Slide 1. Click the Slide Show button to start Slide Show view. Then click to display each slide.

8. Change the document properties, as specified by your instructor. Save the presentation using the file name, Lab 1–1 Study Skills.

9. Submit the document in the format specified by your instructor.

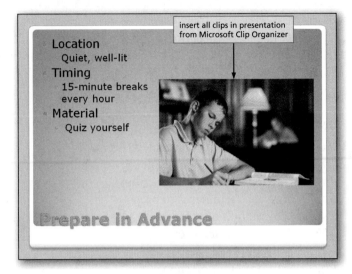

**(b) Slide 2**

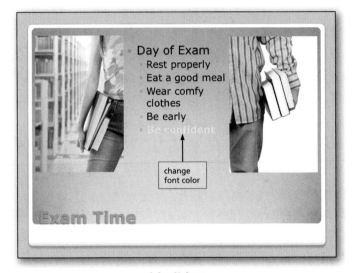

**(c) Slide 3**

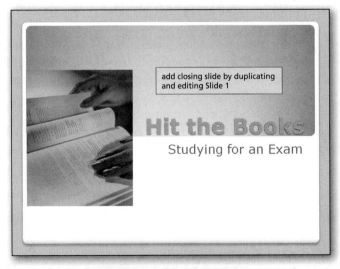

**(d) Slide 4 (Closing Slide)**

**Figure 1–81 (continued)**

# In the Lab

## Lab 2: Creating a Presentation with Bulleted Lists and Clips

*Problem:* Your health class instructor has assigned every student a different vitamin to research. She hands you the outline shown in Figure 1–82 and asks you to create the presentation about Vitamin D shown in Figures 1–83a through 1–83d on pages PPT 62 and PPT 63.

**Vitamin D**

**The Sunshine Vitamin**
Are You D-ficient?
Presented by Jim Warner

**Why Is Vitamin D Important?**
We need Vitamin D
Vital to our bodies
Promotes absorption of calcium and magnesium
For healthy teeth and bones
Maintains calcium and phosphorus in blood

Daily Requirements
How much do we need?
Child: 5 mcg (200 IU)
Adult: 10-20 mcg (400-600 IU)

**Vitamin D Sources**
Sunshine
Is our primary source
Vitamin manufactured by our body after exposure
Three times a week
For 10-15 minutes
Foods and Supplements
Contained in few foods
Some fish liver oils
Flesh of fatty fish
Fortified products
Milk and cereals
Available as supplement

**Vitamin D History**
Research began in 1924
Found to prevent rickets
United States and Canada
Instituted policy of fortifying foods with Vitamin D
Milk – food of choice
Other countries
Fortified cereal, bread, margarine

**Figure 1–82**

*Continued >*

**In the Lab** *continued*

*Perform the following tasks:*

1. Create a new presentation using the Solstice document theme.

2. Using the typed notes illustrated in Figure 1–82, create the title slide shown in Figure 1–83a, using your name in place of Jim Warner. Italicize the title, The Sunshine Vitamin, and increase the font size to 48 point. Change the font size of the first line of the subtitle text, Are You D-ficient?, to 36 point. Change the font color of the title text to Orange (third color in the Standard Colors row) and both lines of the subtitle text to Light Blue (seventh color in the Standard Colors row).

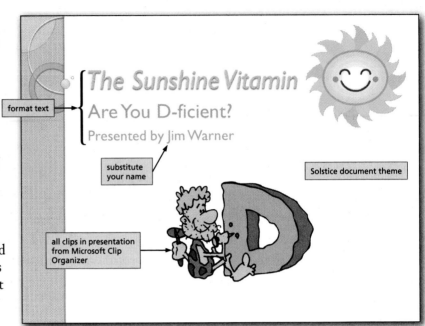

**(a) Slide 1 (Title Slide)**

3. Using the typed notes in Figure 1–82, create the three text slides with bulleted lists shown in Figures 1–83b through 1–83d. Change the color of the title text on all slides and the text above the bulleted lists on Slides 2 and 3 to Orange.

4. Add the photographs and clip art shown in Figures 1–83a through 1–83d from the Microsoft Clip Organizer. Adjust the clip sizes when necessary.

5. Apply the Ripple transition in the Exciting category to all slides. Change the duration to 2.00 seconds.

6. Drag the scroll box to display Slide 1. Click the Slide Show button to start Slide Show view. Then click to display each slide.

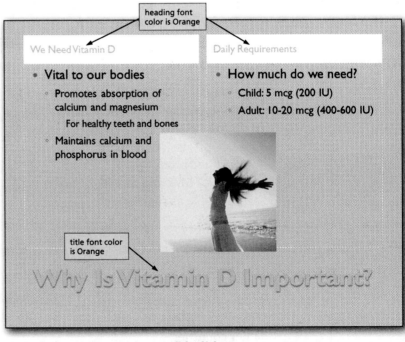

**(b) Slide 2**

**Figure 1–83**

7. Change the document properties, as specified by your instructor. Save the presentation using the file name, Lab 1–2 Vitamin D.

8. Submit the revised document in the format specified by your instructor.

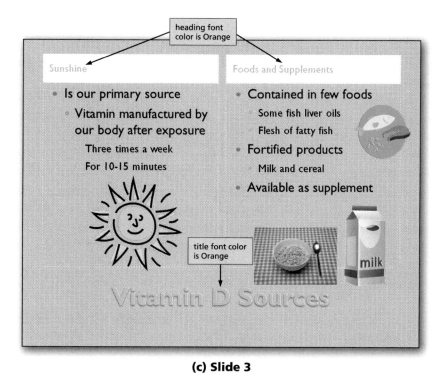

**(c) Slide 3**

**(d) Slide 4**

**Figure 1–83 (continued)**

# In the Lab

## Lab 3: Creating and Updating Presentations with Clip Art

*Problem:*  You are employed part time at your health club, and the Child Care Center director has asked you to put together a presentation for her to use at the next open house. The club has a large playroom that is perfect for children's parties.

*Instructions Part 1:*  Using the outline in Figure 1–84, create the presentation shown in Figure 1–85. Use the Office Theme document theme. On the title slide shown in Figure 1–85a, increase the font size of the title paragraph, Make It a Party!, to 48, change the font color to Red, and change the text font style to italic. Decrease the font size of the entire subtitle paragraph to 28, and change the font color to Blue.

**Make It a Party!**
> Host Your Child's
> Next Birthday Party
> At The Oaks Health Club

**We Do the Work**
**You Enjoy the Moment**
> Two-hour party
> Two chaperones
> Lunch & cake provided
> Game or craft activity available
> Decorations

**Two Party Packages**
> Package No. 1 - $8/child
>> Lunch
>>> Hot Dogs
>>> Pizza
> Package No. 2 - $12/child
>> Lunch including beverage
>>> Hot Dogs
>>> Pizza
>> Game
>> Craft (age appropriate)

**Reserve Your Party Date**
> Reserve 2 weeks in advance
> Deposit required
> Party room can hold 20 children
> Sign up in the Child Care Center

**Figure 1–84**

Create the three text slides with multi-level bulleted lists, photographs, and clip art shown in Figures 1–85b through 1–85d on the next page. Adjust the clip sizes when necessary. Apply the Vortex transition in the Exciting category to all slides and decrease the duration to 3.00 seconds. Change the document properties, as specified by your instructor. Save the presentation using the file name, Lab 1–3 Part One Child Party.

**(a) Slide 1 (Title Slide)**

**(b) Slide 2**
**Figure 1–85**

*Continued >*

**In the Lab** *continued*

## Two Party Packages

**Package No. 1 - $8/child**

- Lunch
  - Hot Dogs
  - Pizza

**Package No. 2 - $12/child**

- Lunch including beverage
  - Hot Dogs
  - Pizza
- Game
- Craft (age appropriate)

**(c) Slide 3**

## Reserve Your Party Date

- Reserve 2 weeks in advance
- Deposit required
- Party room can hold 20 children
- Sign up in the Child Care Center

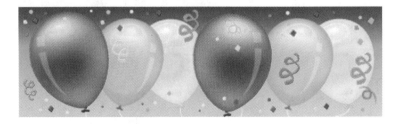

**(d) Slide 4**

**Figure 1–85 (continued)**

*Instructions Part 2:* The children's parties have proved to be a great perk for members of the health club. A large group of older adults work out at the club and also meet socially once a month. These members have asked about renting the playroom to hold a retirement party for some of their friends. You decide to modify the children's party presentation to promote retirement parties. Use the outline in Figure 1–86 to modify the presentation created in Part 1 to create the presentation shown in Figure 1–87 on the next page. Required changes are indicated by a yellow highlight.

   To begin, save the current presentation with the new file name, Lab 1–3 Part Two Retirement Party. Change the document theme to Flow. On Slide 3, change the pianist's name from Ms. Winn to your name. Apply the Fade transition in the Subtle category to all slides and change the duration speed to 2.25 seconds. View the slide show. Change the document properties, as specified by your instructor. Submit both Part One and Part Two documents in the format specified by your instructor.

**Make It a Party!**
   Host Your
   Retirement Party
   At The Oaks Health Club

**We Do the Work**
**You Enjoy the Moment**
   Two-hour party

   Lunch & cake provided

   Decorations
   Music

**Two Party Packages**
   Package No. 1 - $9/person
      Lunch
         Lasagna
         Salad & bread
   Package No. 2 - $20/person
      Lunch including beverage
         Lasagna
         Salad & bread
      Ms. Winn on piano
      Photo booth

**Reserve Your Party Date**
   Reserve 2 weeks in advance
   Deposit required
   Party room can hold 15 adults
   Sign up at the main desk

**Figure 1–86**

*Continued >*

**In the Lab** *continued*

**(a) Slide 1 (Title Slide)**

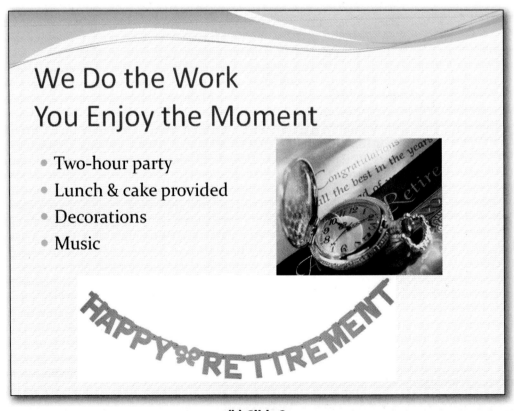

**(b) Slide 2**

**Figure 1–87**

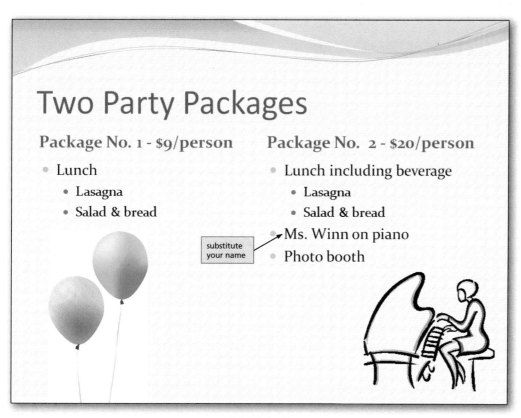

**(c) Slide 3**

**(d) Slide 4**
**Figure 1–87 (continued)**

# Cases and Places

Apply your creative thinking and problem-solving skills to design and implement a solution.

*Note:* To complete these assignments, you may be required to use the Data Files for Students. See the inside back cover of this book for instructions on downloading the Data Files for Students, or contact your instructor for information about accessing the required files.

As you design the presentations, remember to use the 7 × 7 rule: a maximum of seven words on a line and a maximum of seven lines on one slide.

## 1: Design and Create a Presentation about Galileo

### Academic

Italian-born Galileo is said to be the father of modern science. After the invention of the telescope by a Dutch eyeglass maker named Hans Lippershey, Galileo made his own telescope and made many discoveries. You decide to prepare a PowerPoint presentation to accompany a speech that is required in your Astronomy class. You create the outline shown in Figure 1–88 about Galileo. Use this outline, along with the concepts and techniques presented in this chapter, to develop and format a slide show with a title slide and three text slides with bulleted lists. Add photographs and clip art from the Microsoft Clip Organizer and apply a transition. Submit your assignment in the format specified by your instructor.

**Galileo Galilei**
    Father of Modern Science
    Astronomy 201
    Sandy Wendt

**Major Role in Scientific Revolution**
February 15, 1564 - January 8, 1642
    Physicist
    Mathematician
    Astronomer
    Philosopher

**Galileo's Research Years**
    1581 - Studied medicine
    1589-1592 - Studied math and physics
    1592-1607 - Padua University
        Developed Law of Inertia
    1609 - Built telescope
        Earth's moon
        Jupiter's moons

**Galileo's Later Years**
    Dialogue - Two Chief World Systems
        Controversy develops
    1633 - Rome
        Heresy trial
        Imprisoned
    1642 - Dies

**Figure 1–88**

## 2: Design and Create a Presentation Promoting Hiking for Family Fitness

**Personal**

A great way for the entire family to get exercise is by participating in a hiking adventure. Employees at the local forest preserve district near your home have remodeled the nature center, and you have volunteered to give a presentation at the open house to help families plan their hikes. Use the outline shown in Figure 1–89 and then create an accompanying PowerPoint presentation. Use the concepts and techniques presented in this chapter to develop and format this slide show with a title slide, three text slides with bulleted lists, and clip art. Add photographs and clip art from the Microsoft Clip Organizer and apply a transition. Submit your assignment in the format specified by your instructor.

**Take a Hike**
  An Adventure with Kids
  Presented by Joshua Lind
  Pines Nature Center

**Planning the Adventure**
  Trail length – varies by child's age
    Ages 2 to 4: 1 to 2 miles
    Ages 5 to 7: 3 to 4 miles
    Ages 8 to 12:  5 to 7 miles
  Backpack – limit to 20  percent of child's weight

**Packing Supplies**
  Snacks and Drinks
    Child's favorite healthy foods
      Fruit and nuts
    Water
  Miscellaneous
    Sunscreen
    Insect repellent
    First-aid kit

**Wearing the Right Clothes**
  Dress in layers
    Children get cold quicker than adults
  Wear long pants and long-sleeved shirt
    Protect against insects and cuts
  Wear a hat and comfortable shoes
    Keep body warm

**Figure 1–89**

*Continued >*

**Cases and Places** *continued*

### 3: Design and Create a Landscaping Service Presentation

**Professional**

The home and garden center where you work is hosting weekend clinics for customers. The owner asks you to give a presentation about the center's new landscaping division and hands you the outline shown in Figure 1–90. Use the concepts and techniques presented in this chapter to develop and format a PowerPoint presentation with a title slide, three text slides with bulleted lists, and clip art. Add photographs and clip art from the Microsoft Clip Organizer and apply a transition. Submit your assignment in the format specified by your instructor.

**Barry's Landscaping Service**
Bensenville, Indiana

**Full-Service Landscaping**
 Initial design
 Installation
 Maintenance

**Scope of Services**
 Landscape design
 Irrigation
 Lighting
 Lawn-care programs
 Tree/shrub maintenance
 Masonry, carpentry
 Water features

**Our Promise to You**
 Deliver on-time service
 Provide highest level of workmanship
 Give maximum value for your dollar
 Install high-quality plants and materials
 Respond quickly to your needs

**Figure 1–90**

# 2 | Enhancing a Presentation with Pictures, Shapes, and WordArt

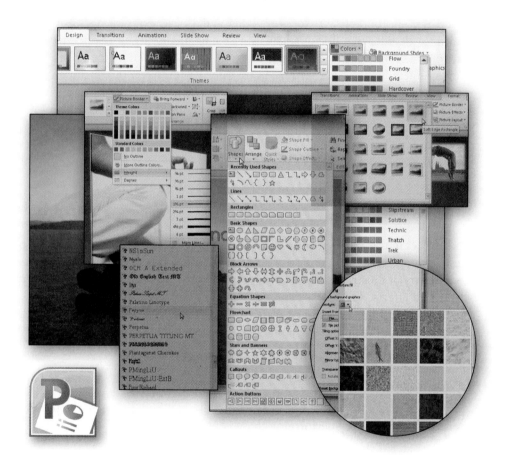

## Objectives

You will have mastered the material in this chapter when you can:

- Change theme colors
- Insert a picture to create a background
- Format slide backgrounds
- Insert and size a shape
- Add text to a shape

- Apply effects to a shape
- Change the font and add a shadow
- Format pictures
- Apply a WordArt style
- Format WordArt
- Format text using the Format Painter

# 2 | Enhancing a Presentation with Pictures, Shapes, and WordArt

## Introduction

In our visually oriented culture, audience members enjoy viewing effective graphics. Whether reading a document or viewing a PowerPoint presentation, people increasingly want to see photographs, artwork, graphics, and a variety of typefaces. Researchers have known for decades that documents with visual elements are more effective than those that consist of only text because the illustrations motivate audiences to study the material. People remember at least one-third more information when the document they are seeing or reading contains visual elements. These graphics help clarify and emphasize details, so they appeal to audience members with differing backgrounds, reading levels, attention spans, and motivations.

## Project — Presentation with Pictures, Shapes, and WordArt

**BTW**

**Yoga's Origins**
The term, yoga, is derived from the Sanskrit word yuj, meaning to join or unite. Yogis have been practicing this system of exercises and philosophy of mental control for more than 26,000 years.

The project in this chapter follows graphical guidelines and uses PowerPoint to create the presentation shown in Figure 2–1. This slide show, which discusses yoga and meditation, has a variety of illustrations and visual elements. For example, pictures have particular shapes and effects. The enhanced type has a style that blends well with the background and illustrations. Pictures and type are formatted using Quick Styles and WordArt, which give your presentation a professional look.

### Overview

As you read through this chapter, you will learn how to create the presentation shown in Figure 2–1 by performing these general tasks:

- Format slide backgrounds.
- Insert and format pictures by applying styles and effects.
- Insert and format shapes.
- Format text using WordArt.
- Print a handout of your slides.

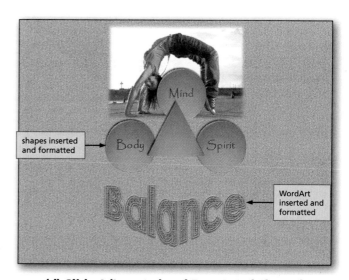

**(a) Slide 1 (Title Slide with Picture Background and Shapes)**

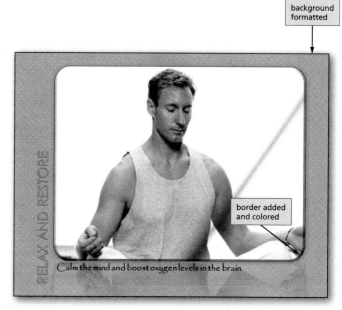

**(b) Slide 2 (Formatted Picture)**

**(c) Slide 3 (Formatted Picture)**

**(d) Slide 4 (Inserted and Formatted Shapes)**

**Figure 2–1**

Plan
Ahead

**General Project Guidelines**

When creating a PowerPoint presentation, the actions you perform and decisions you make will affect the appearance and characteristics of the finished document. As you create a presentation with illustrations, such as the project shown in Figure 2–1, you should follow these general guidelines:

1. **Focus on slide text content.** Give some careful thought to the words you choose. Some graphic designers advise starting with a blank screen so that the document theme does not distract from or influence the words.

2. **Apply style guidelines.** Many organizations and publishers establish guidelines for writing styles. These rules apply to capitalization, punctuation, word usage, and document formats. Ask your instructor or manager for a copy of these guidelines or use popular writing guides, such as the *The Chicago Manual of Style*, *The Associated Press Stylebook*, and *The Elements of Style*.

3. **Use color effectively.** Your audience's eyes are drawn to color on a slide. Used appropriately, color can create interest by emphasizing material and promoting understanding. Be aware of symbolic meanings attached to colors, such as red generally representing danger, electricity, and heat.

4. **Adhere to copyright regulations.** Copyright laws apply to printed and electronic materials. You can copy an existing photograph or artwork if it is in the public domain, if your company owns the graphic, or if you have obtained permission to use it. Be certain you have the legal right to use a desired graphic in your presentation.

5. **Consider graphics for multicultural audiences.** In today's intercultural society, your presentation might be viewed by people whose first language is different from yours. Some graphics have meanings specific to a culture, so be certain to learn about your intended audience and their views.

6. **Use WordArt in moderation.** Used correctly, the graphical nature of WordArt can add interest and set a tone. Format text with a WordArt style only when needed for special emphasis.

When necessary, more specific details concerning the above guidelines are presented at appropriate points in the chapter. The chapter also will identify the actions you perform and decisions made regarding these guidelines during the creation of the presentation shown in Figure 2–1.

# Starting PowerPoint

Chapter 1 introduced you to starting PowerPoint, selecting a document theme, creating slides with clip art and a bulleted list, and printing a presentation. The following steps, which assume Windows 7 is running, start PowerPoint. You may need to ask your instructor how to start PowerPoint for your computer. For a detailed example of the procedure summarized on the next page, refer to pages OFF 33 through OFF 35 in the Office 2010 and Windows 7 chapter.

For an introduction to Windows 7 and instruction about how to perform basic Windows 7 tasks, read the Office 2010 and Windows 7 chapter at the beginning of this book, where you can learn how to resize windows, change screen resolution, create folders, move and rename files, use Windows Help, and much more.

## To Start PowerPoint and Apply a Document Theme

**1** Click the Start button on the Windows 7 taskbar to display the Start menu.

**2** Type `Microsoft PowerPoint` as the search text in the 'Search programs and files' text box.

**3** Click Microsoft PowerPoint 2010 in the search results on the Start menu to start PowerPoint and display a new blank document.

**4** If the PowerPoint window is not maximized, click the Maximize button.

**5** Apply the Verve document theme.

---

Plan
Ahead

**Focus on slide text content.**
Once you have researched your presentation topic, many methods exist to begin developing slide content.

- Select a document theme and then enter text, illustration, and tables.

- Open an existing presentation and modify the slides and theme.

- Import an outline created in Microsoft Word.

- Start with a blank presentation that uses the default Office Theme. Consider this practice similar to an artist who begins creating a painting with a blank, white canvas.

  Experiment using different methods of developing the initial content for slides. Experienced PowerPoint users sometimes find one technique works better than another to stimulate creativity or help them organize their ideas in a particular circumstance.

For an introduction to Office 2010 and instruction about how to perform basic tasks in Office 2010 programs, read the Office 2010 and Windows 7 chapter at the beginning of this book, where you can learn how to start a program, use the Ribbon, save a file, open a file, quit a program, use Help, and much more.

# Creating Slides and Changing Font Colors and Background Style

In Chapter 1, you selected a document theme and then typed the content for the title and text slides. In this chapter, you will type the slide content for the title and text slides, select a background, insert and format pictures and shapes, and then insert and format WordArt. To begin creating the four slides in this presentation, you will enter text in four different layouts, change the theme colors, and then change the background style.

---

Plan
Ahead

**Apply style guidelines.**
A good stylebook is useful to decide when to use numerals or words to represent numbers, as in the sentence, More than 25 students are waiting for the bus to arrive. Stylebooks also offer rules on forming possessives, capitalizing titles, and using commas. Once you decide on a style to use in your presentation, apply it consistently throughout your presentation.

---

## To Create a Title Slide

Recall from Chapter 1 that the title slide introduces the presentation to the audience. In addition to introducing the presentation, this project uses the title slide to capture the audience's attention by using title text and a background picture. The following steps create the slide show's title slide.

**1** Type **Yoga and Meditation** in the title text placeholder.

**2** Type **Unify Your Mind,** in the subtitle text placeholder.

**3** Press the ENTER key and then type **Body,** as the second line in the subtitle text placeholder.

**4** Press the ENTER key and then type **and Spirit** as the third line in the subtitle text placeholder. Change the capital letter 'A' in the word, And, at the beginning of this line to a lowercase 'a' (Figure 2–2).

**Q&A**

Some stylebooks recommend using lowercase letters when using coordinating conjunctions (for, and, nor, but, or, yet, so) and also when using articles (a, an, the). Why is the case of the word, and, changed in the subtitle text?

By default, PowerPoint capitalizes the first word of each paragraph. For consistency, you can decide to lowercase this word to apply a particular style rule so that the word, and, is lowercase in both the title and subtitle text.

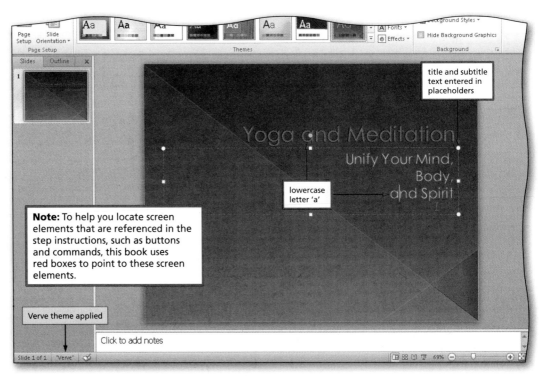

**Figure 2–2**

**BTW**

**Q&As**
For a complete list of the Q&As found in many of the step-by-step sequences in this book, visit the PowerPoint 2010 Q&A Web page (scsite.com/ppt2010/qa).

## To Create the First Text Slide

The first text slide you create in Chapter 2 emphasizes the relaxation and restoration benefits derived from practicing yoga and meditation. The following steps add a new slide (Slide 2) and then create a text slide using the Picture with Caption layout.

**1** Click Home on the Ribbon to display the Home tab, click the New Slide button arrow, and then click Picture with Caption in the Layout gallery to add a new slide with this layout.

**2** Type **Relax and Restore** in the title text placeholder.

**3** Press CTRL+ENTER to move to the caption placeholder and then type **Calm the mind and boost oxygen levels in the brain.** in this placeholder (Figure 2–3).

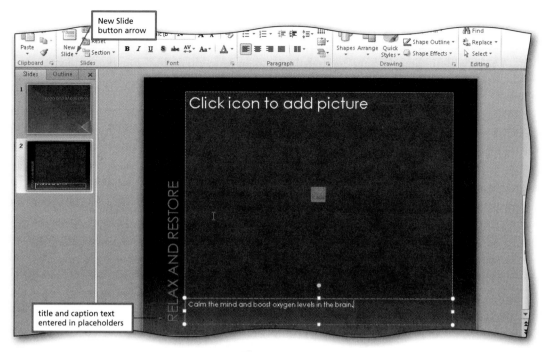

**Figure 2–3**

## To Create the Second Text Slide

The second text slide you create stresses the fact that yoga and meditation strengthen the body in multiple ways. The following steps add a new text slide (Slide 3) that uses the Content with Caption layout.

**1** Click the New Slide button arrow and then click Content with Caption in the Layout gallery to add a new slide with this layout.

**2** Type **Strengthen Body** in the title text placeholder.

**3** Press CTRL+ENTER and then type **Increase flexibility and tone muscles.** in the caption placeholder (Figure 2–4).

**Q&A** Why does the text display with capital letters despite the fact I am typing uppercase and lowercase letters?

The Verve theme uses the All Caps effect for the title text. This effect converts lowercase letters to uppercase.

**BTW**

**BTWs**
For a complete list of the BTWs found in the margins of this book, visit the PowerPoint 2010 BTW Web page (scsite.com/ppt2010/btw).

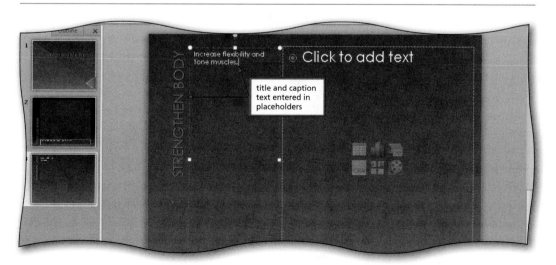

**Figure 2–4**

## To Create the Third Text Slide

Yoga and meditation help create balance in an individual's life. The last slide you create uses graphics to depict the connection among the mind, body, and spirit. You will insert symbols later in this project to create this visual element. For now, you want to create the basic slide. The following step adds a new text slide (Slide 4) that uses the Blank layout.

**1** Click the New Slide button arrow and then click Blank in the Layout gallery. (Figure 2–5).

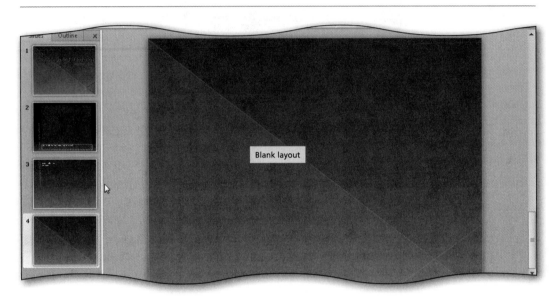

**Figure 2–5**

**BTW**

**The Ribbon and Screen Resolution**
PowerPoint may change how the groups and buttons within the groups appear on the Ribbon, depending on the computer's screen resolution. Thus, your Ribbon may look different from the ones in this book if you are using a screen resolution other than 1024 × 768.

# Presentation Template Color Scheme

Each presentation template has 12 complementary colors, which collectively are called the **color scheme**. You can apply these colors to all slides, an individual slide, notes pages, or audience handouts. A color scheme consists of four colors for a background and text, six accent colors, and two hyperlink colors. The Theme Colors button on the Design tab contains a square with four colors; the top two colors indicate the primary text and background colors, and the bottom two colors indicate the accent colors. You also can customize the theme colors to create your own set and give them a unique name. Table 2–1 explains the components of a color scheme.

**Table 2–1 Color Scheme Components**

| Component | Description |
| --- | --- |
| Background color | The background color is the fundamental color of a PowerPoint slide. For example, if the background color is black, you can place any other color on top of it, but the fundamental color remains black. The black background shows everywhere you do not add color or other objects. |
| Text color | The text color contrasts with the background color of the slide. As a default, the text border color is the same as the text color. Together with the background color, the text and border colors set the tone for a presentation. For example, a gray background with black text and border sets a dramatic tone. In contrast, a red background with yellow text and border sets a vibrant tone. |
| Accent colors | Accent colors are designed as colors for secondary features on a slide. They often are used as fill colors on graphs and as shadows. |
| Hyperlink colors | The default hyperlink color is set when you type the text. When you click the hyperlink text during a presentation, the color changes to the Followed Hyperlink color. |

## To Change the Presentation Theme Colors

The first modification to make is to change the color scheme throughout the presentation. The following steps change the color scheme for the template from a gray title slide background with pink text and accents to a blue background with pink and orange accents.

**1**

- Click Design on the Ribbon and then click the Theme Colors button (Design tab | Themes group) to display the Theme Colors gallery.

- Scroll down and then point to the Oriel built-in theme to display a live preview of this color scheme (Figure 2–6).

**Experiment**

- Point to various themes in the Theme Colors gallery and watch the colors change on Slide 4.

**Q&A** Why does a gold line surround the Verve color scheme in the Theme Colors gallery?

It shows the Verve document theme is applied, and those eight colors are associated with that theme.

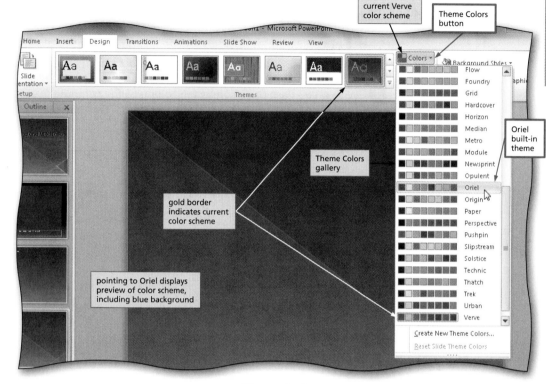

**Figure 2–6**

**2**

- Click Oriel in the Theme Colors gallery to change the presentation theme colors to Oriel (Figure 2–7).

**Q&A** What if I want to return to the original theme color?

You would click the Theme Colors button and then click Verve in the Theme Colors gallery.

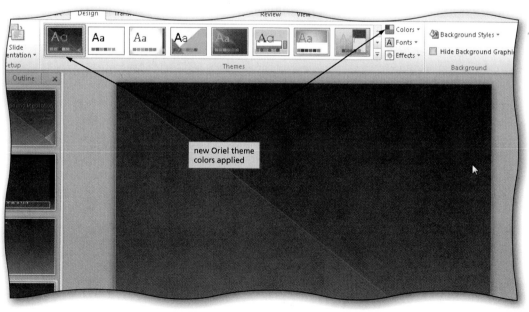

**Figure 2–7**

## To Save a Presentation

You have performed many tasks while creating this slide and do not want to risk losing work completed thus far. Accordingly, you should save the document.

The following steps assume you already have created folders for storing your files, for example, a CIS 101 folder (for your class) that contains a PowerPoint folder (for your assignments). Thus, these steps save the document in the PowerPoint folder in the CIS 101 folder on a USB flash drive using the file name, Yoga. For a detailed example of the procedure summarized below, refer to pages OFF 27 through OFF 29 in the Office 2010 and Windows 7 chapter at the beginning of this book.

**1** With a USB flash drive connected to one of the computer's USB ports, click the Save button on the Quick Access Toolbar to display the Save As dialog box.

**2** Type `Yoga` in the File name text box to change the file name. Do not press the ENTER key after typing the file name because you do not want to close the dialog box at this time.

**3** Navigate to the desired save location (in this case, the PowerPoint folder in the CIS 101 folder [or your class folder] on the USB flash drive).

**4** Click the Save button (Save As dialog box) to save the document in the selected folder on the selected drive with the entered file name.

# Inserting and Formatting Pictures in a Presentation

**BTW**

**Inserting Watermarks**
Checks, currency, business cards, and legal documents use watermarks to verify their authenticity. These semi-transparent images are visible when you hold this paper up to a light. You, likewise, can insert a clip art image or a picture as a watermark behind all or part of your slide to identify your unique PowerPoint presentation.

With the text entered and background formatted in the presentation, the next step is to insert digital pictures into the placeholders on Slides 2 and 3 and then format the pictures. These graphical images draw the viewers' eyes to the slides and help them retain the information presented.

In the following pages, you will perform these tasks:

1. Insert the first digital picture into Slide 3.
2. Insert the second digital picture into Slide 2.
3. Change the look of the first picture.
4. Change the look of the second picture.
5. Resize the second picture.
6. Insert a digital picture into the Slide 1 background.
7. Format slide backgrounds.

**Adhere to copyright regulations.**
You have permission to use the clips from the Microsoft Clip Organizer. If you want to use a clip from another source, be certain you have the legal right to insert this file in your presentation. Read the copyright notices that accompany the clip and are posted on the Web site. The owners of these images and files often ask you to give them credit for using their work, which may be satisfied by stating where you obtained the images.

Plan
Ahead

## To Insert a Picture

The next step in creating the presentation is to insert one of the digital yoga pictures in the picture placeholder in Slide 3. The picture is available on the Data Files for Students. See the inside back cover of this book for instructions on downloading the Data Files for Students, or contact your instructor for information about accessing the required files.

The following steps insert a picture, which, in this example, is located in the PowerPoint Chapter 02 folder on the same USB flash drive that contains the saved presentation, into Slide 3.

**1**
- With your USB flash drive connected to one of the computer's USB ports, click the Previous Slide button to display Slide 3.

- Click the Insert Picture from File icon in the content placeholder to display the Insert Picture dialog box.

**2**
- If Computer is not displayed in the navigation pane, drag the navigation pane scroll bar (Insert Picture dialog box) until Computer appears.

**Figure 2 – 8**

- Click Computer in the navigation pane to display a list of available storage devices in the Insert Picture dialog box. If necessary, scroll through the dialog box until your USB flash drive appears in the list of available storage devices.

- Double-click your USB flash drive in the list of available storage devices to display a list of files and folders on the selected USB flash drive. Double-click the Data Files for Students folder, double-click the PowerPoint folder, and then double-click the Chapter 02 folder to display a list of files in that folder.

- Scroll down and then click Hands Yoga to select the file name (Figure 2–8).

**Q&A** What if the picture is not on a USB flash drive?
Use the same process, but select the drive containing the picture.

**3**

- Click the Insert button (Insert Picture dialog box) to insert the picture into the content placeholder in Slide 3 (Figure 2–9).

**Q&A**

What are the symbols around the picture?

A selected graphic appears surrounded by a **selection rectangle**, which has small squares and circles, called **sizing handles**, at each corner and middle location.

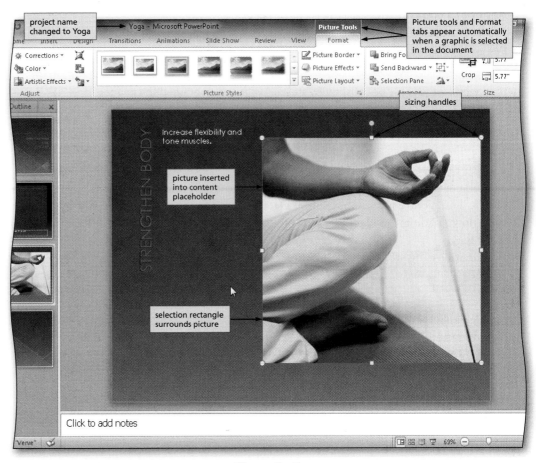

**Figure 2–9**

## To Insert Another Picture into a Content Placeholder

**BTW**

**Modernism's Effect on Graphic Design**
The modernist movement of the late nineteenth and twentieth centuries influenced the design principles in use today. Artists and architects of that era simplified the world in terms of legible fonts, abstract shapes, and balanced layouts. Modernists sought to create works independent of language so their message could reach people throughout the world.

The next step is to insert another digital yoga picture into the Slide 2 content placeholder. This second picture also is available on the Data Files for Students. See the inside back cover of this book for instructions on downloading the Data Files for Students, or contact your instructor for information about accessing the required files.

The following steps insert a picture into Slide 2.

**1** Click the Previous Slide button to display Slide 2.

**2** With your USB flash drive connected to one of the computer's USB ports, click the Insert Picture from File icon in the content placeholder to display the Insert Picture dialog box.

**3** If the list of files and folders on the selected USB flash drive are not displayed in the Insert Picture dialog box, double-click your USB flash drive to display them and then navigate to the PowerPoint Chapter 02 folder.

**4** Scroll down and then click Green Tank Meditation to select the file name.

**5** Click the Insert button (Insert Picture dialog box) to insert the picture into the Slide 2 content placeholder (Figure 2–10).

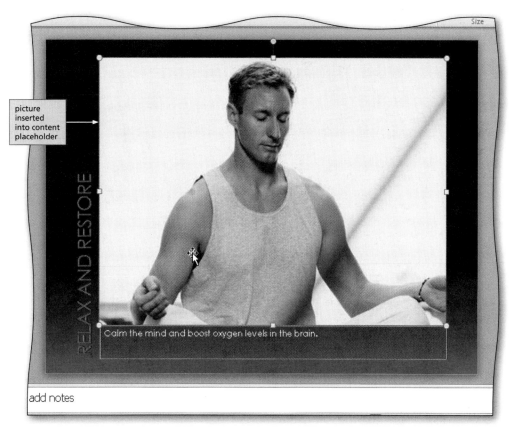

**Figure 2–10**

## To Insert a Picture into a Slide without a Content Placeholder

In Chapter 1, you inserted a clip into a slide without a content placeholder. You also can insert a picture into a slide that does not have a content placeholder. The picture for Slide 4 is available on the Data Files for Students. See the inside back cover of this book for instructions on downloading the Data Files for Students, or contact your instructor for information about accessing the required files. The following steps insert a picture into Slide 4.

**1**
- Click the Next Slide button two times to display Slide 4.

- With your USB flash drive connected to one of the computer's USB ports, click Insert on the Ribbon (Figure 2–11).

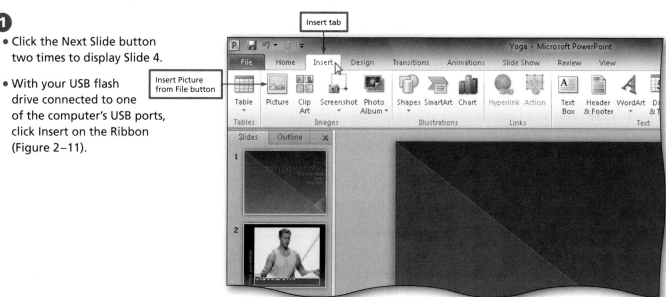

**Figure 2–11**

● Click Insert Picture from File
(Insert tab | Images group) to
display the Insert Picture dialog
box. If the list of files and folders
on the selected USB flash drive are
not displayed in the Insert Picture
dialog box, double-click your USB
flash drive to display them and
then navigate to the PowerPoint
Chapter 02 folder.

● Click Arch Yoga to select the file
name (Figure 2–12).

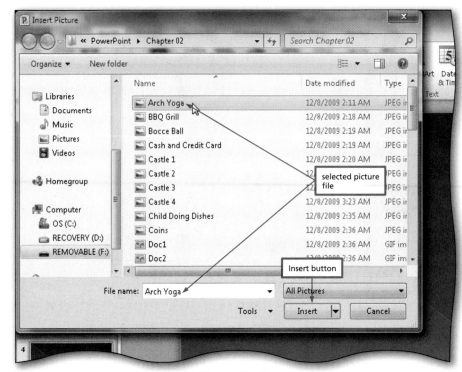

**Figure 2–12**

● Click the Insert button
(Insert Picture dialog box) to insert
the picture into the Slide 4 content
placeholder.

● Move the picture so that it
displays approximately as shown
in Figure 2–13.

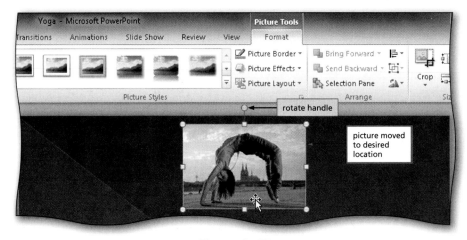

**Figure 2–13**

**Q&A**

What is the green circle attached to the selected graphic?

The green circle is a rotate handle. When you drag a graphic's rotate handle, the graphic
moves in either a clockwise or counter clockwise direction.

## To Correct a Picture

A photograph's color intensity can be modified by changing the brightness and contrast. **Brightness**
determines the overall lightness or darkness of the entire image, whereas **contrast** is the difference between
the darkest and lightest areas of the image. The brightness and contrast are changed in predefined percentage
increments. The following step increases the brightness and decreases the contrast to intensify the picture colors.

**1**

- With the Arch Yoga picture on Slide 4 still selected, click the Corrections button (Picture Tools Format tab | Adjust group) to display the Corrections gallery.

- Point to Brightness: +20% Contrast: −40% (fourth picture in first row of Brightness and Contrast area) to display a live preview of these corrections on the picture (Figure 2–14).

**Experiment**

- Point to various pictures in the Brightness and Contrast area and watch the brightness and contrast change on the picture in Slide 4.

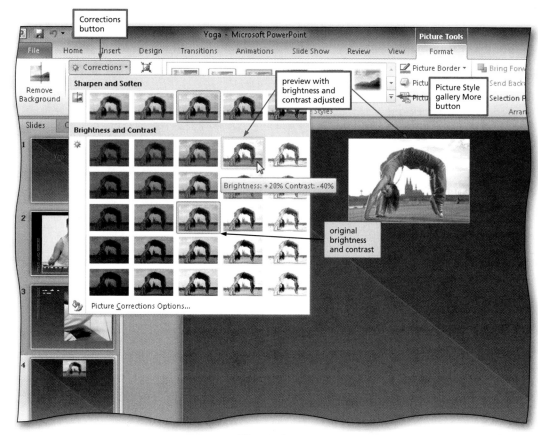

**Figure 2–14**

**Q&A** | Why is a yellow border surrounding the picture in the center of the gallery?
The image on Slide 4 currently has normal brightness and contrast (0%), which is represented by this center image in the gallery.

- Click Brightness: +20% Contrast: −40% to apply this correction to the yoga picture.

**Q&A** | How can I remove all effects from the picture?
Click the Reset Picture button (Picture Tools Format tab | Adjust group).

| **Other Ways** | |
|---|---|
| 1. Click Picture Corrections Options, move Brightness or Contrast sliders or enter | number in box next to slider (Format Picture dialog box) |

## To Apply a Picture Style

The pictures on Slides 2, 3, and 4 grasp the audience's attention, but you can increase their visual appeal by applying a style. A **style** is a named group of formatting characteristics. PowerPoint provides more than 25 picture styles that enable you easily to change a picture's look to a more visually appealing style, including a variety of shapes, angles, borders, and reflections. The photos in Slides 2, 3, and 4 in this chapter use styles that apply soft edges, reflections, or angled perspectives to the pictures. The following steps apply a picture style to the Slide 4 picture.

- With the Slide 4 picture selected, click the Picture Tools Format tab and then click the More button in the Picture Styles gallery (Picture Tools Format tab | Picture Styles group) (shown in Figure 2–14 on the previous page) to expand the gallery.

- Point to Soft Edge Rectangle in the Picture Styles gallery to display a live preview of that style applied to the picture in the document (Figure 2–15).

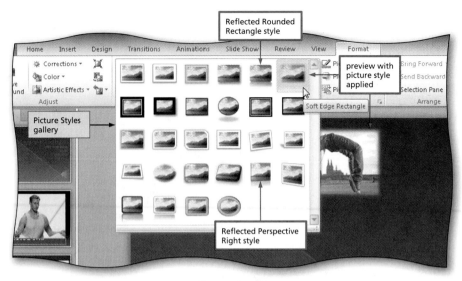

**Figure 2–15**

🔍 **Experiment**

- Point to various picture styles in the Picture Styles gallery and watch the style of the picture change in the document window.

- Click Soft Edge Rectangle in the Picture Styles gallery to apply the style to the selected picture (Figure 2–16).

**Figure 2–16**

## To Apply Other Picture Styles

The next step is to apply picture styles to the yoga pictures in Slides 3 and 2. To provide continuity, both of these styles will have a reflection. The following steps apply other picture styles to the Slide 3 and Slide 2 pictures.

**1** Click the Previous Slide button to display Slide 3.

**2** Click the Slide 3 picture to select it, click the Picture Tools Format tab, and then click the More button in the Picture Styles gallery to expand the gallery.

**3** Click Reflected Perspective Right in the Picture Styles gallery to apply this style to the picture in Slide 3.

**4** Click the Previous Slide button to display Slide 2.

**5** Click the Slide 2 picture to select it, click the Picture Tools Format tab, and then click the More button in the Picture Styles gallery to expand the gallery.

**6** Click Reflected Rounded Rectangle in the Picture Styles gallery to apply this style to the picture in Slide 2 (Figure 2–17).

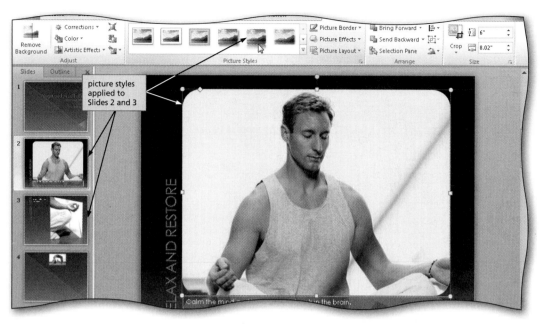

**Figure 2–17**

## To Apply Picture Effects

PowerPoint provides a variety of picture effects so that you can further customize a picture. Effects include shadows, reflections, glow, soft edges, bevel, and 3-D rotation. The difference between the effects and the styles is that each effect has several options, providing you with more control over the exact look of the image.

In this presentation, the photos on Slides 2 and 3 have an orange glow effect and have a bevel applied to their edges. The following steps apply picture effects to the selected picture.

**1**

- With the Slide 2 picture selected, click the Picture Effects button (Picture Tools Format tab | Picture Styles group) to display the Picture Effects menu.

**Q&A** What if the Picture Tools Format tab no longer is displayed on my Ribbon?

Double-click the picture to display the Picture Tools and Format tabs.

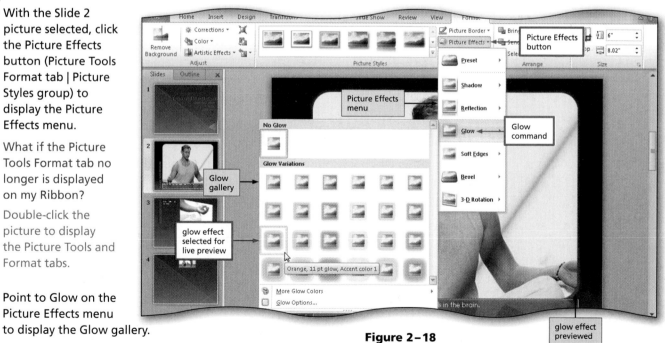

- Point to Glow on the Picture Effects menu to display the Glow gallery.

**Figure 2–18**

- Point to Orange, 11 pt glow, Accent color 1 in the Glow Variations area (leftmost glow in third row) to display a live preview of the selected glow effect applied to the picture in the document window (Figure 2–18).

### Experiment

- Point to various glow effects in the Glow gallery and watch the picture change in the document window.

- Click Orange, 11 pt glow, Accent color 1 in the Glow gallery to apply the selected picture effect.

- Click the Picture Effects button (Picture Tools Format tab | Picture Styles group) to display the Picture Effects menu again.

- Point to Bevel on the Picture Effects menu to display the Bevel gallery.

- Point to Angle (leftmost bevel in second row) to display a live preview of the selected bevel effect applied to the Slide 2 picture (Figure 2–19).

**Experiment**

- Point to various bevel effects in the Bevel gallery and watch the picture change in the slide.

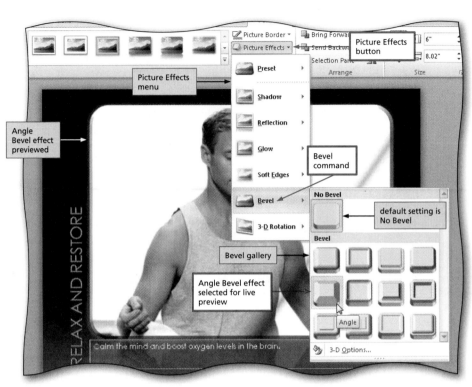

**Figure 2–19**

- Click Angle in the Bevel gallery to apply the selected picture effect.

| Other Ways |
|---|
| 1. Right-click picture, click Format Picture on shortcut menu, select desired options (Format Picture dialog box), click Close button Tools Format tab | Picture Styles group), select desired options (Format Picture dialog box), click Close button |
| 2. Click Format Shape dialog box launcher (Picture |

## To Apply a Picture Style and Effect to Another Picture

In this presentation, the Slide 3 picture also has orange glow and bevel effects. The following steps apply the picture style and picture effects to the picture.

1. Click the Next Slide button to display Slide 3 and then click the picture to select it.

2. Click the Picture Effects button (Picture Tools Format tab | Picture Styles group) to display the Picture Effects menu and then point to Glow on the Picture Effects menu to display the Glow gallery.

3. Click Orange, 11 pt glow, Accent color 1 (leftmost glow in third row) in the Glow gallery to apply the picture effect to the picture.

4. Click the Picture Effects button (Picture Tools Format tab | Picture Styles group) to display the Picture Effects menu again and then point to Bevel on the Picture Effects menu to display the Bevel gallery.

5. Click Convex (third bevel in second row) in the Bevel area to apply the picture effect to the selected picture (Figure 2–20).

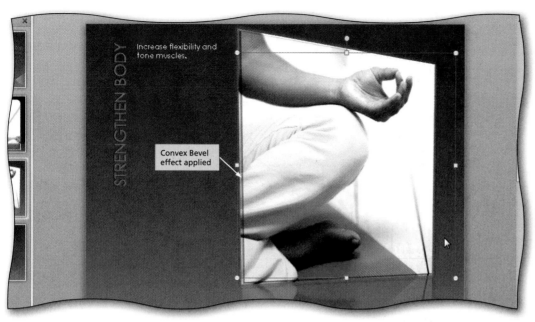

**Figure 2–20**

## To Add a Picture Border

The next step is to add a small border to the Slide 3 picture. Some picture styles provide a border, but the Reflected Rounded Rectangle style you applied to this picture does not. The following steps add a border to the Slide 3 picture.

**1**

- With the Slide 3 picture still selected, click the Picture Border button (Picture Tools Format tab | Picture Styles group) to display the Picture Border gallery.

**Q&A** What if the Picture Tools Format tab no longer is displayed on my Ribbon?

Double-click the picture to display the Picture Tools and Format tabs.

**2**

- Point to Weight on the Picture Border gallery to display the Weight list.

- Point to 1½ pt to display a live preview of this line weight on the picture (Figure 2–21).

 **Experiment**

- Point to various line weights in the Weight list and watch the line thickness change.

**Q&A** Can I make the line width more than 6 pt?

Yes. Click More Lines and then increase the amount in the Width box.

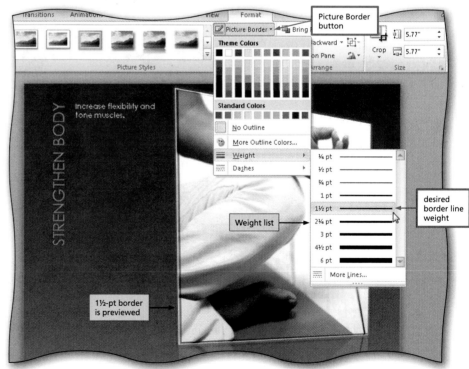

**Figure 2–21**

**3**

- Click 1½ pt to add this line weight to the picture.

## To Change a Picture Border Color

The default color for the border you added to the Slide 3 picture is White. Earlier in this chapter, you changed the color scheme to Oriel. To coordinate the border color with the title text color and other elements of this theme, you will use a shade of red in the Oriel color scheme. Any color galleries you display show colors defined in this current color scheme. The following steps change the Slide 3 picture border color.

- With the Slide 3 photo still selected, click the Picture Border button (Picture Tools Format tab | Picture Styles group) to display the Picture Border gallery.

**Q&A**

What if the Picture Tools Format tab no longer is displayed on my Ribbon?

Double-click the picture to display the Picture Tools and Format tabs.

- Point to Red, Accent 3 (seventh theme color from left in first row) in the Picture Border gallery to display a live preview of that border color on the picture (Figure 2–22).

### Experiment

- Point to various colors in the Picture Border gallery and watch the border on the picture change in the slide.

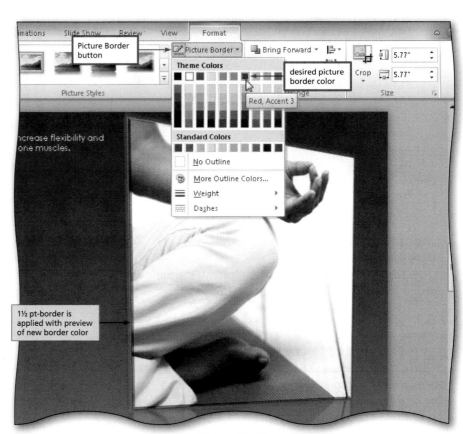

**Figure 2–22**

- Click Red, Accent 3 in the Picture Border gallery to change the picture border color.

## To Add a Picture Border and Color to Another Picture

In this presentation, the Slide 2 picture does not have a border as part of the Reflected Perspective Right picture style. The following steps add a border to Slide 2 and change the color.

1. Click the Previous Slide button to display Slide 2 and then click the picture to select it.

2. Click the Picture Border button (Picture Tools Format tab | Picture Styles group) to display the Picture Border gallery.

3. Point to Weight on the Picture Border gallery to display the Weight list and then point to 1½ pt to display a live preview of this line weight on the picture.

4. Click 1½ pt to add this line weight to the picture.

**5** Click the Picture Border button (Picture Tools Format tab | Picture Styles group) to display the Picture Border gallery again and then click Red, Accent 3 in the Picture Border gallery to change the picture border color (Figure 2–23).

1½ pt border is applied with new border color

**Figure 2–23**

## To Resize a Graphic by Entering Exact Measurements

The next step is to resize the Slide 3 picture so that it fills much of the empty space in the slide. In Chapter 1, you resized clips by dragging the sizing handles. This technique also applies to changing the size of photos. You also can resize graphics by specifying exact height and width measurements. The yoga picture can be enlarged so that its height and width measurements are 6.0". When a graphic is selected, its height and width measurements show in the Size group of the Picture Tools Format tab. The following steps resize the Slide 3 picture by entering its desired exact measurements.

**1**

• Click the Next Slide button to display Slide 3 and then select the picture. Click the Shape Height text box (Picture Tools Format tab | Size group) to select the contents in the text box and then type   6 as the height (Figure 2–24).

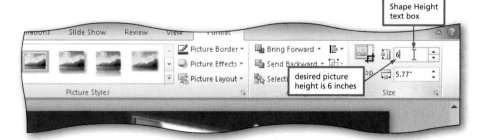

Shape Height text box

desired picture height is 6 inches

**Figure 2–24**

**Q&A** What if the contents of the Shape Height text box are not selected?

Triple-click the Shape Height text box.

**Q&A** Why did the width size also change?

PowerPoint kept the photo in proportion so that the width changed the same amount as the height changed.

**2**

- Click the Shape Width text box (Picture Tools Format tab | Size group) to select the contents in the text box and then type 6 as the width if this number does not display automatically.

- If necessary, move the photo to the location shown in Figure 2–25.

**Q&A** What if I want to return a graphic to its original size and start again?

With the graphic selected, click the Size and Position dialog box launcher (Picture Tools Format tab | Size group), if necessary click the Size tab (Format Picture dialog box), click the Reset button, and then click the Close button.

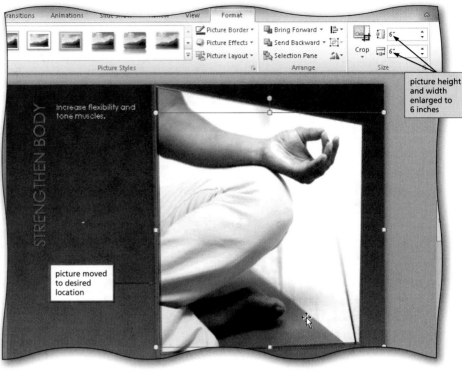

*picture height and width enlarged to 6 inches*

*picture moved to desired location*

**Figure 2–25**

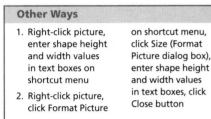

**Other Ways**

1. Right-click picture, enter shape height and width values in text boxes on shortcut menu
2. Right-click picture, click Format Picture
   on shortcut menu, click Size (Format Picture dialog box), enter shape height and width values in text boxes, click Close button

## To Resize Another Graphic Using Exact Measurements

The Arch Yoga picture on Slide 4 also can be enlarged to fill space at the top of the slide. The yoga picture can be enlarged so that its height and width measurements are 3" and 4.48", respectively. The following steps resize the Slide 4 picture.

**1** Click the Next Slide button to display Slide 4 and then select the picture. Click the Shape Height text box (Picture Tools Format tab | Size group) to select the contents in the text box and type 3 as the height.

**2** Move the photo to the location shown in Figure 2–26.

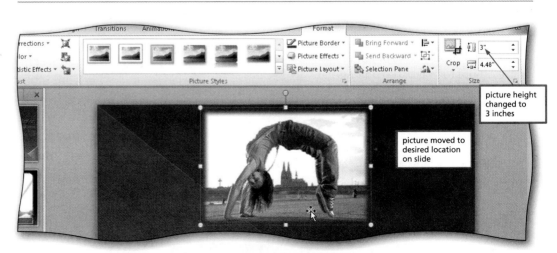

*picture height changed to 3 inches*

*picture moved to desired location on slide*

**Figure 2–26**

## To Save an Existing Document with the Same File Name

You have made several modifications to the document since you last saved it. Thus, you should save it again. The following step saves the document again. For an example of the step listed below, refer to page OFF 51 in the Office 2010 and Windows 7 chapter at the beginning of this book.

 Click the Save button on the Quick Access Toolbar to overwrite the previously saved file.

---

**Break Point:** If you wish to take a break, this is a good place to do so. You can quit PowerPoint now. To resume at a later time, start PowerPoint, open the file called Yoga, and continue following the steps from this location forward.

# Formatting Slide Backgrounds

A slide's background is an integral part of a presentation because it can generate audience interest. Every slide can have the same background, or different backgrounds can be used in a presentation. This background is considered **fill**, which is the content that makes up the interior of a shape, line, or character. Three fills are available: solid, gradient, and picture or texture. **Solid fill** is one color used throughout the entire slide. **Gradient fill** is one color shade gradually progressing to another shade of the same color or one color progressing to another color. **Picture or texture fill** uses a specific file or an image that simulates a material, such as cork, granite, marble, or canvas.

Once you add a fill, you can adjust its appearance. For example, you can adjust its **transparency**, which allows you to see through the background, so that any text on the slide is visible. You also can select a color that is part of the theme or a custom color. You can use **offsets**, another background feature, to move the background from the slide borders in varying distances by percentage. **Tiling options** repeat the background image many times vertically and horizontally on the slide; the smaller the tiling percentage, the greater the number of times the image is repeated.

**BTW**

**Resetting Backgrounds**
If you have made many changes to the background and want to start the process over, click the Reset Background button in the Format Background dialog box.

## To Insert a Texture Fill

A wide variety of texture fills are available to give your presentation a unique look. The 24 pictures in the Textures gallery give the appearance of a physical object, such as water drops, sand, tissue paper, and a paper bag. You also can use your own texture pictures for custom backgrounds. When you insert a fill, PowerPoint assumes you want this custom background on only the current slide displayed. To make this background appear on all slides in the presentation, click the Apply to All button in the Format Background dialog box. The following steps insert the Sand fill on Slide 4 in the presentation.

- Right-click anywhere on the Slide 4 blue background to display the shortcut menu (Figure 2–27).

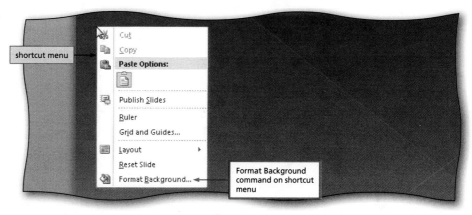

**Figure 2–27**

**2**

- Click Format Background on the shortcut menu to display the Format Background dialog box.

- With the Fill pane displaying, click 'Picture or texture fill' to expand the fill options (Figure 2–28).

 **Q&A** Why did the background change to a yellow texture?

This texture is the Papyrus background, which is the default texture fill.

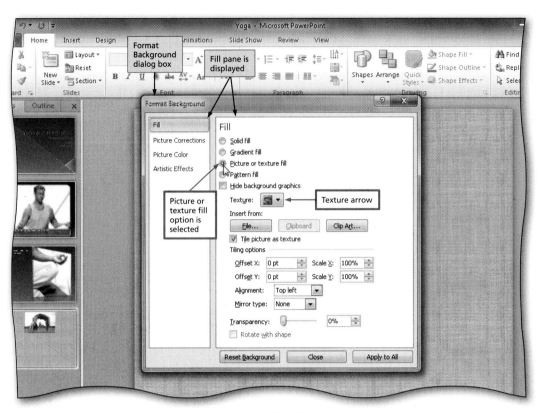

**Figure 2–28**

**3**

- Click the Texture arrow to display the Texture gallery (Figure 2–29).

**Q&A** Is a live preview available to see the various textures on this slide?

No. Live preview is not an option with the background textures and fills.

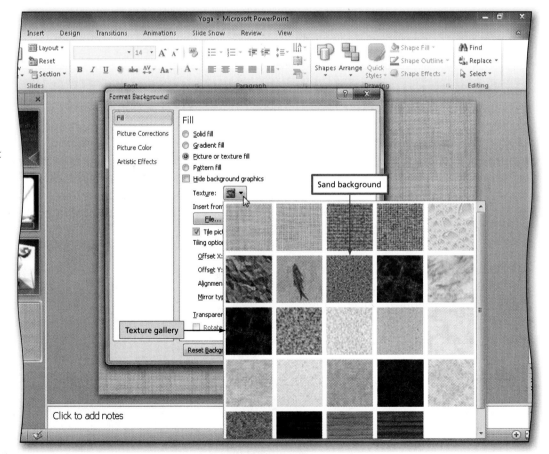

**Figure 2–29**

**4**

- Click the Sand background (third texture in second row) to insert this background on Slide 4 (Figure 2–30).

**Q&A** The Format Background dialog box is covering part of the slide. Can I move this box?

Yes. Click the dialog box title and drag it to a different location so that you can view the slide.

**Q&A** Could I insert this background on all four slides simultaneously?

Yes. You would click the Apply to All button to insert the Sand background on all slides.

**Other Ways**

1. Click Design tab, Background Styles, click Format Background (Design tab | Background group)

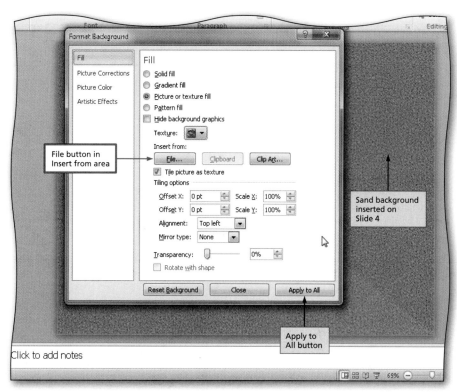

**Figure 2–30**

## To Insert a Picture to Create a Background

For variety and interest, you want to use another yoga picture as the Slide 1 background. This picture is stored on the Data Files for Students. PowerPoint will stretch the height and width of this picture to fill the slide area. The following steps insert the picture, Sunrise Yoga, on only Slide 1.

**1**

- Click the Previous Slide button three times to display Slide 1.

- With the Fill pane displaying (Format Background dialog box), click 'Picture or texture fill'.

- Click the File button in the Insert from area (shown in Figure 2–30) to display the Insert Picture dialog box.

- If necessary, double-click your USB flash drive in the list of available storage devices to display a list of files and folders on the selected USB flash drive and then navigate to the PowerPoint Chapter 02 folder.

- Scroll down and then click Sunrise Yoga to select the file name (Figure 2–31).

**Q&A** What if the picture is not on a USB flash drive?

Use the same process, but select the drive containing the picture.

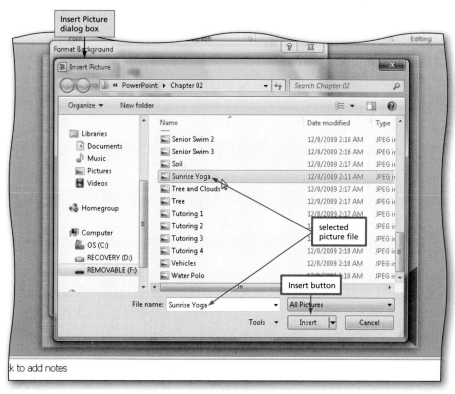

**Figure 2–31**

• Click the Insert button (Insert Picture dialog box) to insert the Sunrise Yoga picture as the Slide 1 background (Figure 2–32).

**Q&A** What if I do not want to use this picture?

Click the Undo button on the Quick Access Toolbar.

**Q&A** Why do the Left and Right offsets in the Stretch options area show a −6% value?

PowerPoint automatically reduced the photograph slightly so that it fills the entire slide.

**Q&A** Can I move the Format Background dialog box to the left so that I can see more of the subtitle text?

Yes. Click the dialog box title and then drag the box to the desired location on the slide.

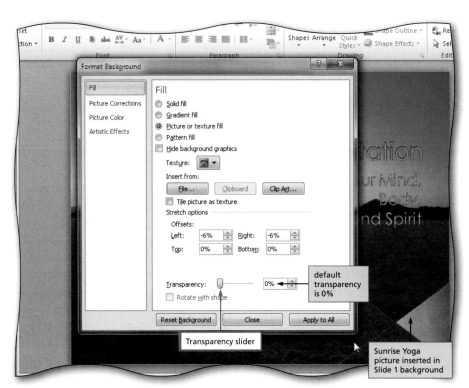

**Figure 2–32**

## To Format the Background Picture Fill Transparency

The Sunrise Yoga picture on Slide 1 is a rich color and conflicts with the title and subtitle text. One method of reducing this richness is to change the transparency. The **Transparency slider** indicates the amount of opaqueness. The default setting is 0, which is fully opaque. The opposite extreme is 100%, which is fully transparent. To change the transparency, you can move the Transparency slider or enter a number in the text box next to the slider. The following step adjusts the transparency to 10%.

• Click the Transparency slider and drag it to the right until 10% is displayed in the Transparency text box (Figure 2–33).

**Q&A** Can I move the slider in small increments so that I can get a precise percentage easily?

Yes. Press the RIGHT ARROW or LEFT ARROW key to move the slider in one-percent increments.

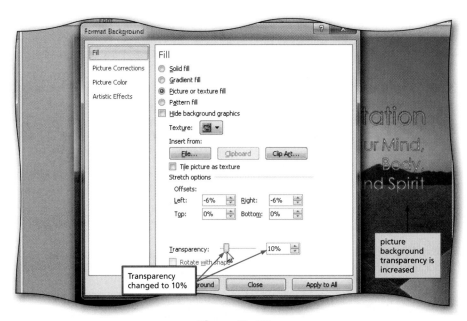

**Figure 2–33**

## To Format the Background Texture Fill Transparency

The Sand texture on Slide 4 is dark and may not offer sufficient contrast with the symbols and text you are going to insert on this slide. You can adjust the transparency of slide texture in the same manner that you change a picture transparency. The following steps adjust the texture transparency to 50%.

- Click the Next Slide button three times to display Slide 4.

- Click the Transparency slider and drag it to the right until 50% is displayed in the Transparency text box (Figure 2–34).

- Click the Close button (Format Background dialog box).

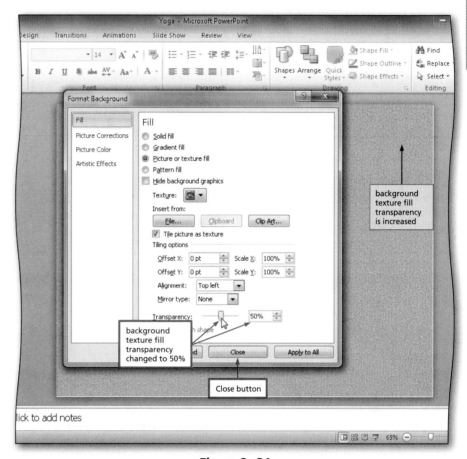

**Figure 2–34**

## To Choose a Background Style

Now that the backgrounds for Slides 1 and 4 are set, and the title and text paragraphs for the presentation have been entered, you need to make design decisions for Slides 2 and 3. In this project, you will choose a background for these slides. For each theme, PowerPoint provides 12 **background styles** with designs that may include color, shading, patterns, and textures. **Fill effects** add pattern and texture to a background, which add depth to a slide. The following steps add a background style to Slides 2 and 3 in the presentation.

**1**

- Click the Previous Slide button once to display Slide 3 and then click the Design tab on the Ribbon.

- Click the Background Styles button (Design tab | Background group) to display the Background Styles gallery.

- Right-click Style 11 (third style in third row) to display the shortcut menu (Figure 2–35).

**Experiment**

- Point to various styles themes in the Background Styles gallery and watch the backgrounds change on the slide.

**Q&A** Are the backgrounds displayed in a specific order?

Yes. They are arranged in order from light to dark running from left to right. The first row has solid backgrounds; the middle row has darker fills at the top and bottom; the bottom row has fill patterns. If you point to a background, a ScreenTip with the background's name appears on the screen.

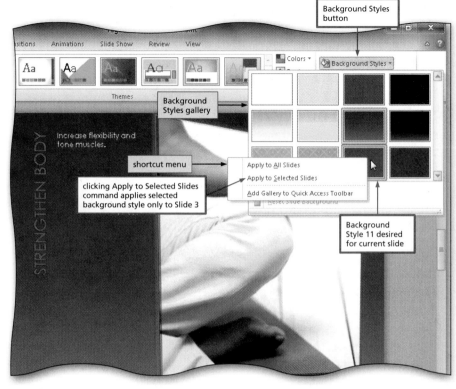

**Figure 2–35**

**2**

- Click Apply to Selected Slides to apply Style 11 to Slide 3 (Figure 2–36).

**Q&A** If I decide later that this background style does not fit the theme of my presentation, can I apply a different background?

Yes. You can repeat these steps at any time while creating your presentation.

**Q&A** What if I want to apply this background style to all slides in the presentation?

Click the desired style or click Apply to All Slides in the shortcut menu.

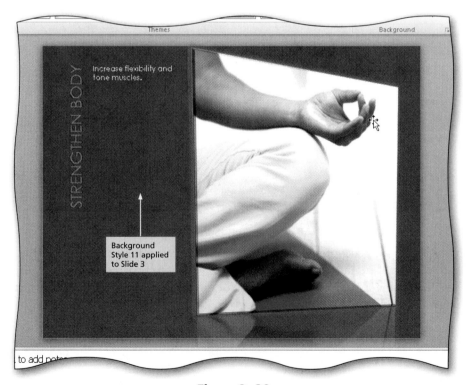

**Figure 2–36**

**Other Ways**

1. Click Background Styles, right-click desired background, press s

## To Choose Another Background Style

In this presentation, the Slide 2 background can have a coordinating background to complement the yoga picture. The following steps add a background to Slide 2.

**1** Click the Previous Slide button to display Slide 2. Click the Background Styles button (Design tab | Background group) and then right-click Style 10 (second style in third row) to display the shortcut menu.

**2** Click Apply to Selected Slides to apply this background style to Slide 2 (Figure 2–37).

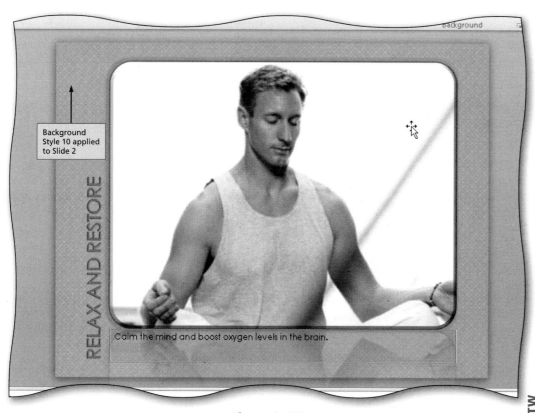

**Figure 2–37**

# Formatting Title and Content Text

Choosing well-coordinated colors and styles for text and objects in a presentation is possible. Once you select a particular Quick Style and make any other font changes, you then can copy these changes to other text using the **Format Painter**. The Format Painter allows you to copy all formatting changes from one object to another.

**BTW**

**Introducing the Presentation**
Before your audience enters the room, start the presentation and then display Slide 1. This slide should be visually appealing and provide general interest in the presentation. An effective title slide gives a good first impression.

## To Change the Subtitle and Caption Font

The default Verve theme heading, subtitle, and caption text font is Century Gothic. To draw more attention to subtitle and caption text and to help differentiate these slide elements from the title text, you want to change the font from Century Gothic to Papyrus. To change the font, you must select the letters you want to format. In Chapter 1, you selected a paragraph and then formatted the characters. To format the text in multiple paragraphs quickly and simultaneously, you can select all the paragraphs to be formatted and then apply formatting changes. The following steps change the subtitle and caption font.

**1**

- Click the Previous Slide button to display Slide 1. Move the mouse pointer to the left of the first subtitle paragraph, Unify Your Mind, until the mouse pointer changes to an I-beam (Figure 2–38).

**Figure 2–38**

**2**

- Drag downward to select all three subtitle lines that will be formatted (Figure 2–39).

**Figure 2–39**

**3**

- With the text selected, click Home on the Ribbon and then click the Font box arrow (Home tab | Font group) to display the Font gallery (Figure 2–40).

**Q&A**

Will the fonts in my Font gallery be the same as those shown in Figure 2–40?

Your list of available fonts may differ, depending on what fonts you have installed and the type of printer you are using.

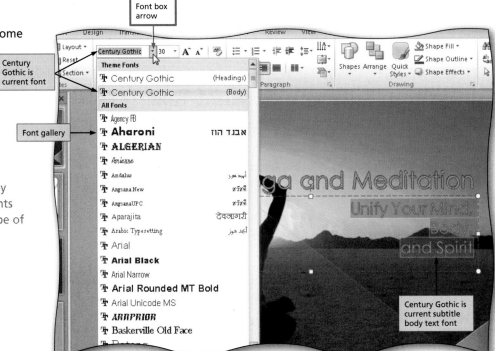

**Figure 2–40**

**4**

- Scroll through the Font gallery and then point to Papyrus (or a similar font) to display a live preview of the title text in the Papyrus font (Figure 2–41).

**Experiment**

- Point to various fonts in the Font gallery and watch the subtitle text font change in the slide.

- Click Papyrus (or a similar font) to change the font of the selected text to Papyrus.

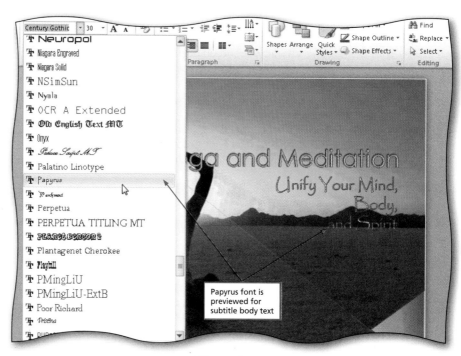

Figure 2–41

| Other Ways | | |
|---|---|---|
| 1. Click Font box arrow on Mini toolbar, click desired font in Font gallery<br><br>2. Right-click selected text, click Font on shortcut menu (Font dialog box), click | Font tab, select desired font in Font list, click OK button<br><br>3. Click Font dialog box launcher (Home tab \| Font group), click Font tab (Font dialog box), select | desired font in Font list, click OK button<br><br>4. Press CTRL+SHIFT+F, click Font tab (Font dialog box), select desired font in the Font list, click OK button |

## To Shadow Text

A **shadow** helps letters display prominently by adding a shadow behind the text. The following step adds a shadow to the selected subtitle text, Unify Your Mind, Body, and Spirit.

**1**

- With the subtitle text selected, click the Text Shadow button (Home tab \| Font group) to add a shadow to the selected text (Figure 2–42).

**Q&A**

How would I remove a shadow?

You would click the Shadow button a second time, or you immediately could click the Undo button on the Quick Access Toolbar.

Figure 2–42

## To Format the Subtitle Text

To increase readability, you can format the Slide 1 subtitle text by bolding the characters and changing the font color to yellow. The following steps format the Slide 1 subtitle text.

**1** With the subtitle text selected, click the Bold button (Home tab | Font group) to bold the text.

**2** Click the Font Color arrow and change the color to Light Yellow, Text 2 (fourth color in first row) (Figure 2–43).

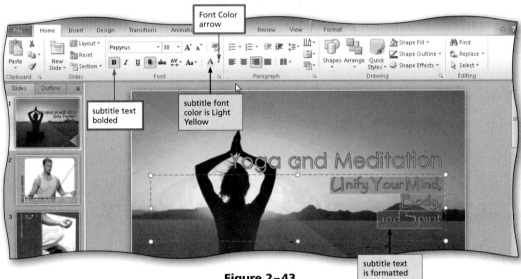

**Figure 2–43**

## To Format the Slide 2 Caption

The caption on a slide should be large enough for audience members to read easily and should coordinate with the font styles in other parts of the presentation. The caption on Slide 2 can be enhanced by changing the font, the font color, and the font size. The following steps format the Slide 2 caption text.

**1** Click the Next Slide button to display Slide 2. Triple-click the caption text to select all the characters, click the Font box arrow on the Mini toolbar, and then scroll down and click Papyrus.

**2** Click the Increase Font Size button on the Mini toolbar three times to increase the font size to 20 point.

**3** Click the Bold button on the Mini toolbar to bold the text (Figure 2–44).

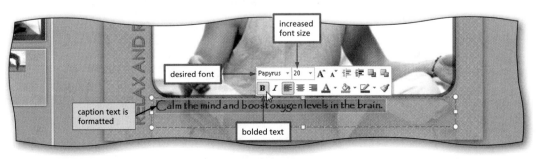

**Figure 2–44**

# Format Painter

To save time and avoid formatting errors, you can use the Format Painter to apply custom formatting to other places in your presentation quickly and easily. You can use this feature in three ways:

- To copy only character attributes, such as font and font effects, select text that has these qualities.
- To copy both paragraph attributes, such as alignment and indentation and character attributes, select the entire paragraph.
- To apply the same formatting to multiple words, phrases, or paragraphs, double-click the Format Painter button and then select each item you want to format. You then can press the ESC key or click the Format Painter button to turn off this feature.

## To Format Text Using the Format Painter

To save time and duplicated effort, you quickly can use the Format Painter to copy formatting attributes from the Slide 2 caption text and apply them to Slide 3. The following steps use the Format Painter to copy formatting features.

**1**

- With the Slide 2 caption text still selected, double-click the Format Painter button (Home tab | Clipboard group).

- Move the mouse pointer off the Ribbon (Figure 2–45).

**Q&A**   Why did my mouse pointer change shape?

The mouse pointer changed shape by adding a paintbrush to indicate that the Format Painter function is active.

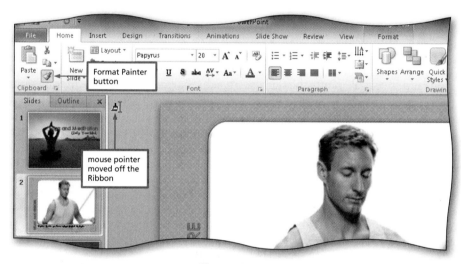

**Figure 2–45**

**2**

- Click the Next Slide button to display Slide 3. Triple-click the caption placeholder to apply the format to all the caption text (Figure 2–46).

- Press the ESC key to turn off the Format Painter feature.

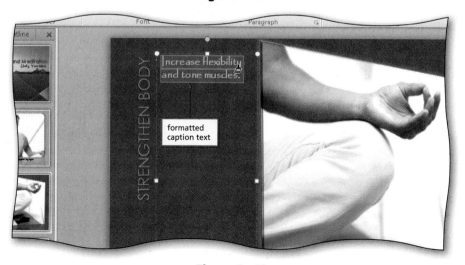

**Figure 2–46**

**Other Ways**

1. Click Format Painter button on Mini toolbar

**Break Point:** If you wish to take a break, this is a good place to do so. Be sure to save the Yoga file again and then you can quit PowerPoint. To resume at a later time, start PowerPoint, open the file called Yoga, and continue following the steps from this location forward.

**BTW**

*Sizing Shapes*
PowerPoint's Shapes gallery provides a wide variety of symbols that can help emphasize your major points on each slide. As you select the shapes and then size them, keep in mind that your audience will focus on the largest shapes first. The most important information, therefore, should be placed in or near the shapes with the most visual size.

# Adding and Formatting a Shape

One method of getting the audience's attention and reinforcing the major concepts being presented is to have graphical elements on the title slide. PowerPoint provides a wide variety of predefined shapes that can add visual interest to a slide. Shape elements include lines, basic geometrical shapes, arrows, equation shapes, flowchart symbols, stars, banners, and callouts. After adding a shape to a slide, you can change its default characteristics by adding text, bullets, numbers, and styles. You also can combine multiple shapes to create a more complex graphic.

Slides 1 and 4 in this presentation are enhanced in a variety of ways. First, a sun shape is added to the Slide 1 title text in place of the letter o. Then a circle shape is inserted on Slide 4 and copied twice, and text is added to each circle and then formatted. Finally, a triangle is inserted on top of the three circle shapes on Slide 4.

## To Add a Shape

Many of the shapes included in the Shapes gallery can direct the viewer to important aspects of the presentation. For example, the sun shape helps emphasize the presentation's theme of practicing yoga and meditation, and it complements the Sunrise Yoga background picture. The following steps add the Sun shape to Slide 1.

• Click the Previous Slide button two times to display Slide 1. Click the Shapes button (Home tab | Drawing group) to display the Shapes gallery (Figure 2–47).

**Figure 2–47**

**Q&A**

I do not see a Shapes button in the Drawing group. Instead, I have three rows of the shapes I have used recently in presentations. Why?

Monitor dimensions and resolution affect how buttons display on the Ribbon. Click the Shapes More button to display the entire Shapes gallery.

- Click the Sun shape in the Basic Shapes area of the Shapes gallery.

**Q&A** Why did my pointer change shape?

The pointer changed to a plus shape to indicate the Sun shape has been added to the Clipboard.

- Position the mouse pointer (a crosshair) above the person's hands in the picture, as shown in Figure 2–48.

crosshair mouse pointer

**Figure 2–48**

- Click Slide 1 to insert the Sun shape (Figure 2–49).

Sun shape inserted

**Figure 2–49**

| Other Ways |
| --- |
| 1. Click More button (Drawing Tools Format tab \| Insert Shapes group) |

## To Resize a Shape

The next step is to resize the Sun shape. The shape should be reduced so that it is approximately the same size as the letter o in the words Yoga and Meditation. The following steps resize the selected Sun shape.

- With the mouse pointer appearing as two-headed arrow, drag a corner sizing handle on the picture diagonally inward until the Sun shape is resized approximately as shown in Figure 2–50.

**Q&A** What if my shape is not selected?

To select a shape, click it.

**Q&A** What if the shape is the wrong size?

Repeat Steps 1 and 2.

smaller, lighter-shaded shape shows preview of resized Sun

**Figure 2–50**

**2**

- Release the mouse button to resize the shape.

- Drag the Sun shape on top of the letter o in the word, Yoga (Figure 2–51).

**Q&A**

What if I want to move the shape to a precise location on the slide?

With the shape selected, press the ARROW keys or the CTRL+ARROW keys to move the shape to the desired location.

Figure 2–51

**Other Ways**

1. Enter shape height and width in Height and Width text boxes (Drawing Tools Format tab | Size group)

2. Click Size and Position dialog box launcher

(Drawing Tools Format tab | Size group), click Size tab, enter desired height and width values in text boxes, click Close button

## To Copy and Paste a Shape

The next step is to copy the Sun shape. The duplicate shape will be placed over the letter 'o' in the word, Meditation. The following steps copy and move the identical second Sun shape.

**1**

- With the Sun shape still selected, click the Copy button (Home tab | Clipboard group) (Figure 2–52).

**Q&A**

What if my shape is not selected?

To select a shape, click it.

Figure 2–52

**2**

- Click the Paste button on the Home tab to insert a duplicate Sun shape on Slide 1.

- Drag the Sun shape on top of the letter o in the word, Meditation, and release the mouse button when a dashed line connects this Sun shape to the Sun shape that is displaying in the word, Yoga (Figure 2–53).

**Q&A** What does the dashed line represent?

PowerPoint displays this Smart Guide when two shapes are aligned precisely. In this case, the two Sun shapes are centered horizontally.

**Figure 2–53**

**Other Ways**

1. Right-click selected shape, click Copy on shortcut menu, right-click, click Paste on shortcut menu

2. Select shape, press CTRL+C, press CTRL+V

## To Add Other Shapes

Circles, squares, and triangles are among the geometric shapes included in the Shapes gallery. These shapes can be combined to show relationships among the elements, and they can help illustrate the basic concepts presented in your slide show. The following steps add the Oval and Isosceles Triangle shapes to Slide 4.

**1**

- Click the Next Slide button three times to display Slide 4 and then click the Shapes button (Home tab | Drawing group) to display the Shapes gallery (Figure 2–54).

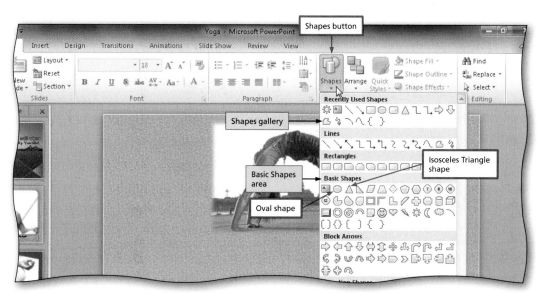

**Figure 2–54**

- Click the Oval shape in the Basic Shapes area of the Shapes gallery.

- Position the mouse pointer in the center of Slide 4 and then click to insert the Oval shape.

- Press and hold down the SHIFT key and then drag a corner sizing handle until the Oval shape forms a circle and is the size shown in Figure 2–55.

**Q&A**

Why did I need to press the SHIFT key while enlarging the shape?

Holding down the SHIFT key while dragging draws a perfect circle.

- Move the shape so it is positioned approximately as shown in the figure.

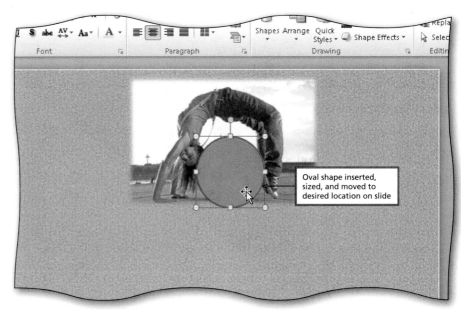

Oval shape inserted, sized, and moved to desired location on slide

**Figure 2–55**

- Click the Shapes button (Home tab | Drawing group) and then click the Isosceles Triangle shape in the Basic Shapes area of the Shapes gallery.

- Position the mouse pointer in the right side of Slide 4 and then click to insert the Isosceles Triangle shape.

- Resize the shape so that it displays approximately as shown in Figure 2–56.

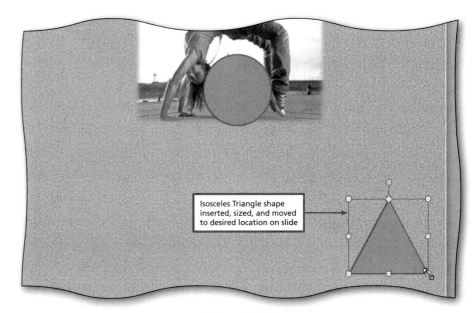

Isosceles Triangle shape inserted, sized, and moved to desired location on slide

**Figure 2–56**

## To Apply a Shape Style

Formatting text in a shape follows the same techniques as formatting text in a placeholder. You can change font, font color and size, and alignment. The next step is to apply a shape style to the oval so that it appears to have depth. The Shape Styles gallery has a variety of styles that change depending upon the theme applied to the presentation. The following steps apply a style to the Oval shape.

- Click the Oval shape to select it and then display the Drawing Tools Format tab (Figure 2–57).

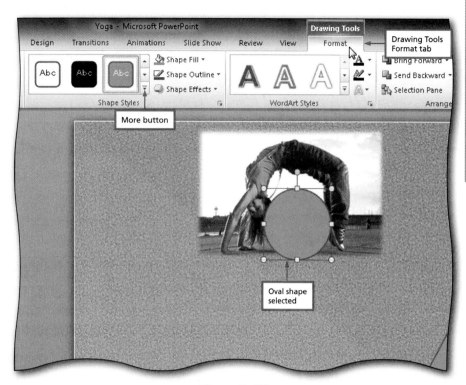

**Figure 2–57**

- Click the More button in the Shape Styles gallery (Drawing Tools Format tab | Shape Styles group) to expand the Shape Styles gallery.

- Point to Intense Effect – Orange, Accent 1 in the Shape Styles gallery (second shape in last row) to display a live preview of that style applied to the shape in the slide (Figure 2–58).

 **Experiment**

- Point to various styles in the Shape Styles gallery and watch the style of the shape change.

**3**

- Click Intense Effect – Orange, Accent 1 in the Shape Styles gallery to apply the selected style to the Oval shape.

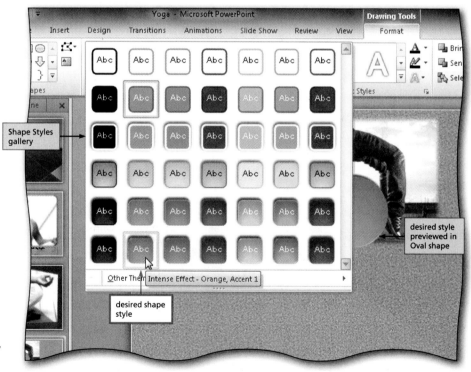

**Figure 2–58**

| Other Ways |
|---|
| 1. Click Format Shape dialog box launcher (Drawing Tools Format tab | Shape Styles group), select desired colors (Format Shape dialog box), click Close button    2. Right-click shape, click Format Shape on shortcut menu, select desired colors (Format Shape dialog box), click Close button |

## To Add Formatted Text to a Shape

Formatting text in a shape follows the same techniques as formatting text in a placeholder. You can change font, font color and size, and alignment. The next step is to add the word, Mind, to the shape, change the font to Papyrus and the font color to Blue-Gray, center and bold the text, and increase the font size to 24 point. The following step adds text to the Oval shape.

- With the Oval shape selected, type **Mind** in the shape.
- Change the font to Papyrus.
- Change the font color to Blue-Gray, Background 2 (third color in first Theme Colors row).
- Change the font size to 24 point and bold the text (Figure 2–59).

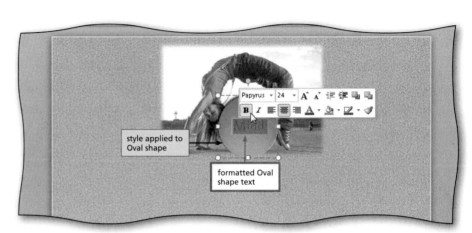

**Figure 2–59**

**Drawing a Square**
Holding down the SHIFT key while dragging a Rectangle shape draws a square.

## To Copy a Shape

Your presentation emphasizes that mind, body, and spirit are equal components in finding balance in life. Each of these elements can be represented by an oval. The following steps copy the Oval shape.

**1** Click Home on the Ribbon. Click the edge of the Oval shape so that it is a solid line.

**2** Click the Copy button (Home tab | Clipboard group).

**3** Click the Paste button (Home tab | Clipboard group) two times to insert two duplicate Oval shapes on Slide 4.

**4** Move the Oval shapes so they appear approximately as shown in Figure 2–60.

**5** In the left oval, select the word, Mind, and then type the word, **Body,** in the oval.

**6** In the right oval, select the word, Mind, and then type the word, **Spirit,** in the oval (Figure 2–60). You may need to enlarge the size of the oval shapes slightly so that each word is displayed on one line.

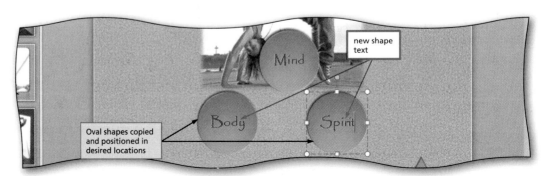

**Figure 2–60**

## To Apply Another Style

The triangle shape helps show the unity among body, mind, and spirit. You can apply a coordinating shape style to the isosceles triangle and then place it on top of the three ovals. The following steps apply a style to the Isosceles Triangle shape.

**1** Display the Drawing Tools Format tab. Click the Isosceles Triangle shape on Slide 4 to select it.

**2** Click the More button in the Shape Styles gallery (Drawing Tools Format tab | Shape Styles group) to expand the Shape Styles gallery and then click Intense Effect – Blue, Accent 2 (third style in last row) to apply that style to the triangle.

**3** Move the triangle shape to the center of the Ovals.

**4** Click the Bring Forward button twice (Drawing Tools Format tab | Arrange group) to display the triangle on top of the ovals. Resize the triangle if necessary so that it displays as shown in Figure 2–61.

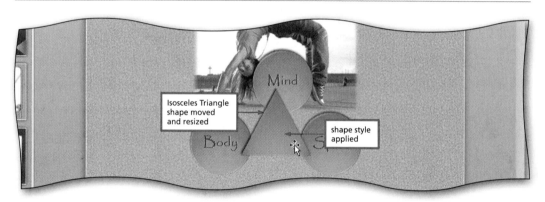

**Figure 2–61**

**Break Point:** If you wish to take a break, this is a good place to do so. Be sure to save the Yoga file again and then you can quit PowerPoint. To resume at a later time, start PowerPoint, open the file called Yoga, and continue following the steps from this location forward.

# Using WordArt

One method of adding appealing visual elements to a presentation is by using **WordArt** styles. This feature is found in other Microsoft Office applications, including Word and Excel. This gallery of decorative effects allows you to type new text or convert existing text to WordArt. You then can add elements such as fills, outlines, and effects.

As with slide backgrounds, WordArt fill in the interior of a letter can consist of a solid color, texture, picture, or gradient. The WordArt **outline** is the exterior border surrounding each letter or symbol. PowerPoint allows you to change the outline color, weight, and style. You also can add an **effect**, which helps add emphasis or depth to the characters. Some effects are shadows, reflections, glows, bevels, and 3-D rotations.

**BTW**

**Creating Logos**
Many companies without graphic arts departments create their logos using WordArt. The bevels, glows, and shadows allow corporate designers to develop unique images with 3-D effects that give depth to their companies' emblems.

**Use WordArt in moderation.**
Some WordArt styles are bold and detailed, and they can detract from the message you are trying to present if not used carefully. Select a WordArt style when needed for special emphasis, such as a title slide that audience members will see when they enter the room. WordArt can have a powerful effect, so do not overuse it.

**Plan Ahead**

## To Insert WordArt

Yoga and meditation can help individuals find balance among the mind, body, and spirit. The symbols on Slide 4 emphasize this relationship, and you want to call attention to the concept. You quickly can add a visual element to the slide by selecting a WordArt style from the WordArt Styles gallery and then applying it to a word. The following steps insert WordArt.

- With Slide 4 displaying, click Insert on the Ribbon.

- Click the WordArt button (Insert tab | Text group) to display the WordArt gallery (Figure 2–62).

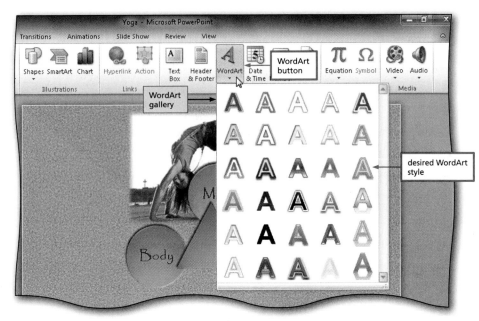

**Figure 2–62**

- Click Fill – Blue, Accent 2, Double Outline – Accent 2 (last letter A in third row) to display the WordArt text box (Figure 2–63).

**Q&A** What is a matte bevel style that is part of some of the styles in the gallery?

A matte finish gives a dull and rough effect. A bevel edge is angled or sloped and gives the effect of a three-dimensional object.

**Figure 2–63**

- Type **Balance** in the text box, as the WordArt text (Figure 2–64).

**Q&A** Why did the Format tab appear automatically in the Ribbon?

It appears when you select text to which you could add a WordArt style or other effect.

**Figure 2–64**

## To Change the WordArt Shape

The WordArt text is useful to emphasize the harmony among the mind, body, and spirit. You can further emphasize this word by changing its shape. PowerPoint provides a variety of graphical shapes that add interest to text. The following steps change the WordArt to Triangle Down shape.

**1**

- With the Slide 4 text still selected, click the Text Effects button (Drawing Tools Format tab | WordArt Styles group) to display the Text Effects menu (Figure 2–65).

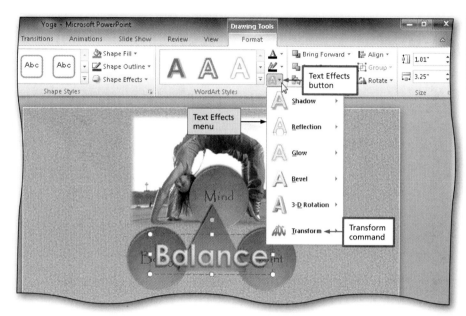

**Figure 2–65**

**2**

- Point to Transform in the Text Effects menu to display the WordArt Transform gallery (Figure 2–66).

 **Experiment**

- Point to various styles in the Transform gallery and watch the format of the text and borders change.

**Q&A** How can I see the preview of a Transform effect if the gallery is overlaying the WordArt letters?

Move the WordArt text box to the left or right side of the slide and then repeat Steps 1 and 2.

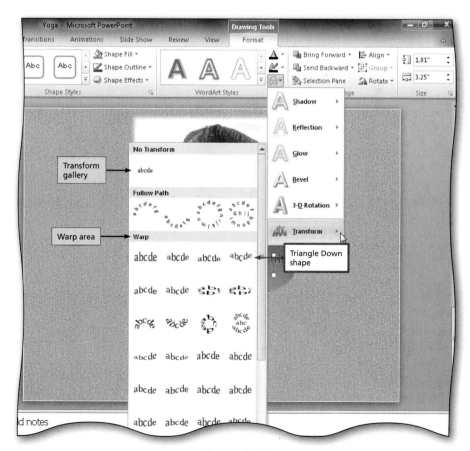

**Figure 2–66**

• Click the Triangle Down shape in the Warp area to apply the Triangle Down shape to the WordArt text (Figure 2–67).

**Q&A**  Can I change the shape I applied to the WordArt?

Yes. Position the insertion point in the text box and then repeat Steps 1 and 2.

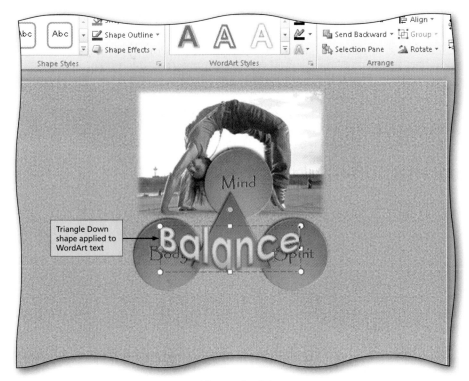

Triangle Down shape applied to WordArt text

**Figure 2–67**

• Drag the WordArt downward until it is positioned approximately as shown in Figure 2–68.

• Drag a corner sizing handle diagonally outward until the WordArt is resized approximately as shown in the figure.

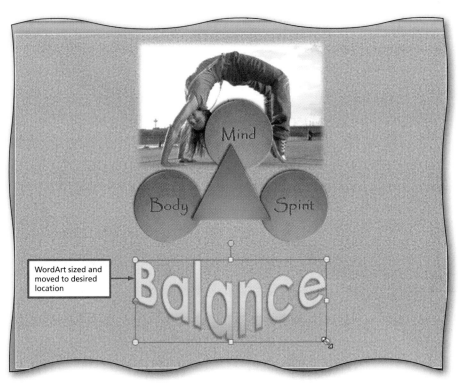

WordArt sized and moved to desired location

**Figure 2–68**

## To Apply a WordArt Text Fill

The Slide 4 background has a Sand texture for the background, and you want to coordinate the WordArt fill with a similar texture. The following steps add the Denim texture as a fill for the WordArt characters.

**1**

• With the WordArt text selected, click the Text Fill button arrow (Drawing Tools Format tab | WordArt Styles group) to display the Text Fill gallery.

**Q&A** The Text Fill gallery did not display. Why not?

Be sure you click the Text Fill button arrow, which is to the right of the Text Fill button. If you mistakenly click the Text Fill button, PowerPoint places the default fill in the WordArt instead of displaying the Text Fill gallery.

• Point to Texture in the Text Fill gallery to display the Texture gallery (Figure 2–69).

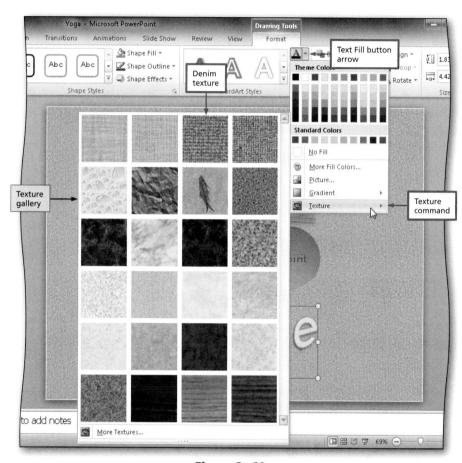

**Figure 2–69**

 **Experiment**

• Point to various styles in the Text Fill gallery and watch the fill change.

**Q&A** How can I see the preview of a fill if the gallery is overlaying the WordArt letters?

Move the WordArt text box to the left or right side of the slide and then repeat Step 1.

**2**

• Click the Denim texture (third texture in first row) to apply this texture as the fill for the WordArt.

**Q&A** Can I apply this texture simultaneously to text that appears in more than one place on my slide?

Yes. Select one area of text, press and then hold the CTRL key while you select the other text, and then apply the texture.

## To Change the Weight of the WordArt Outline

The letters in the WordArt style applied have a double outline around the edges. To emphasize this characteristic, you can increase the width of the lines. As with font size, lines also are measured in point size, and PowerPoint gives you the option to change the line **weight**, or thickness, starting with ¼ point (pt) and increasing in one-fourth–point increments. Other outline options include modifying the color and the line style, such as changing to dots or dashes or a combination of dots and dashes. The following steps change the WordArt outline weight to 6 pt.

 **1**

- With the WordArt still selected, click the Text Outline button arrow (Drawing Tools Format tab | WordArt Styles group) to display the Text Outline gallery.

- Point to Weight in the gallery to display the Weight list.

- Point to 6 pt to display a live preview of this line weight on the WordArt text outline (Figure 2–70).

**Experiment**

- Point to various line weights in the Weight list and watch the line thickness change.

**Q&A** Can I make the line width more than 6 pt?

Yes. Click More Lines and increase the amount in the Width box.

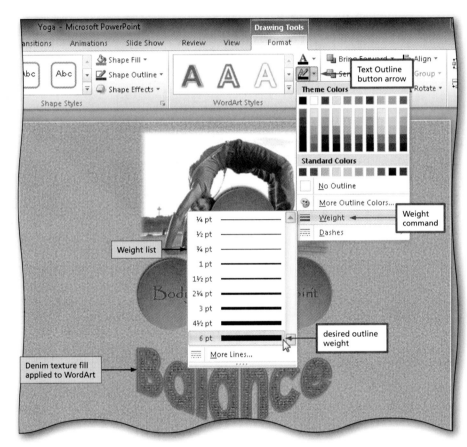

**Figure 2–70**

 **2**

- Click 6 pt to apply this line weight to the title text outline.

**Q&A** Must my text have an outline?

No. To delete the outline, click No Outline in the Text Outline gallery.

## To Change the Color of the WordArt Outline

The WordArt outline color is similar to the Denim fill color. To add variety, you can change the outline color. The following steps change the WordArt outline color.

**1**

- With the WordArt still selected, click the Text Outline button arrow (Drawing Tools Format tab | WordArt Styles group) to display the Text Outline gallery.

- Point to Orange, Accent 1 (fifth color in first row) to display a live preview of this outline color (Figure 2–71).

**Experiment**

- Point to various colors in the gallery and watch the outline colors change.

**2**

- Click Orange, Accent 1 to apply this color to the WordArt outline.

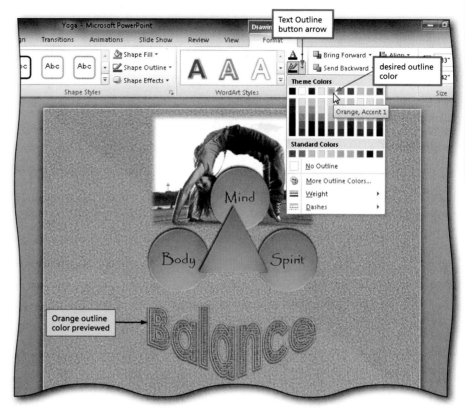

**Figure 2–71**

## To Add a Transition between Slides

A final enhancement you will make in this presentation is to apply the Rotate transition in the Dynamic Content category to all slides and change the transition speed to Slow. The following steps apply this transition to the presentation.

**1** Click Transitions on the Ribbon. Click the More button (Transitions tab | Transition to This Slide group) to expand the Transitions gallery.

**2** Click the Rotate transition in the Dynamic Content category to apply this transition to Slide 4.

**3** Click the Duration up arrow in the Timing group four times to change the transition speed from 02.00 to 03.00.

**4** Click the Preview Transitions button (Transitions tab | Preview area) to view the new transition time.

**5** Click the Apply To All button (Transitions tab | Timing group) to apply this transition and speed to all four slides in the presentation (Figure 2–72 on the next page).

**BTW**

**Selecting Effect Options**
Many PowerPoint transitions have options that you can customize to give your presentation a unique look. When you click the Effect Options button (Transitions tab | Transition to This Slide group), you can, for example, select the option to have a slide appear on the screen from the left or the right, or the screen can fade to black before the next slide is displayed.

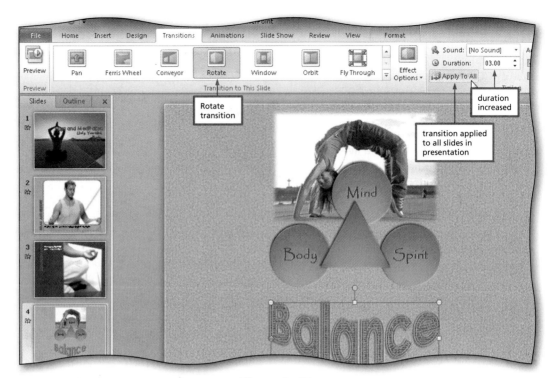

**Figure 2–72**

## To Change Document Properties

Before saving the presentation again, you want to add your name, class name, and some keywords as document properties. The following steps use the Document Information Panel to change document properties.

**1** Click File on the Ribbon to open the Backstage view. If necessary, click the Info tab.

**2** Click the Properties button in the right pane of the Info gallery.

**3** Click Show Document Panel on the Properties menu to close the Backstage view and display the Document Information Panel.

**4** Click the Author box, if necessary, and then type your name as the Author property.

**5** Click the Subject text box and then type your course and section as the Subject property.

**6** Click the Keywords text box and then type **yoga, meditation** as the Keywords property.

**7** Click the Close the Document Information Panel button so that the Document Information Panel no longer is displayed.

**BTW**

**Certification**
The Microsoft Office Specialist (MOS) program provides an opportunity for you to obtain a valuable industry credential — proof that you have the PowerPoint 2010 skills required by employers. For more information, visit the PowerPoint 2010 Certification Web page (scsite.com/ppt2010/cert).

## To Print a Presentation

With the completed presentation saved, you may want to print it. If copies of the presentation are being distributed to audience members, you will print a hard copy of each individual slide on a printer. The following steps print a hard copy of the contents of the saved Yoga presentation.

1 Click File on the Ribbon to open the Backstage view. Click the Print tab in the Backstage view to display the Print gallery.

2 Verify the printer name in the Printer box will print a hard copy of the document. If necessary, click the Printer box arrow to display a list of available Printer options and then click the desired printer to change the currently selected printer.

3 Click the Print button in the Print gallery to print the document on the currently selected printer. When the printer stops, retrieve the hard copy (Figure 2–73).

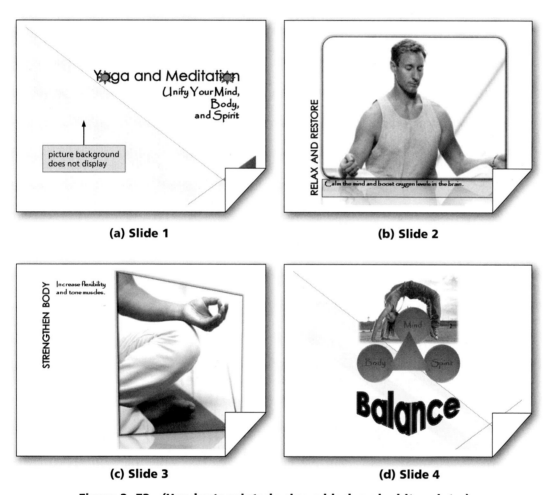

**(a) Slide 1**

**(b) Slide 2**

**(c) Slide 3**

**(d) Slide 4**

**Figure 2–73  (Handouts printed using a black-and-white printer)**

## To Save an Existing Presentation with the Same File Name

You have made several changes to the presentation since you last saved it. Thus, you should save it again. The following step saves the document again.

1 Click the Save button on the Quick Access Toolbar to overwrite the previously saved file.

**BTW**

**Quick Reference**
For a table that lists how to complete the tasks covered in this book using the mouse, Ribbon, shortcut menu, and keyboard, see the Quick Reference Summary at the back of this book, or visit the PowerPoint 2010 Quick Reference Web page (scsite.com/ppt2010/qr).

### To Run an Animated Slide Show

All changes are complete, and the presentation is saved. You now can view the Yoga presentation. The following steps start Slide Show view.

**1** Click the Slide 1 thumbnail in the Slides tab to select and display Slide 1.

**2** Click the Slide Show button to display the title slide and then click each slide to view the transition effect and slides.

### To Quit PowerPoint

This project is complete. The following steps quit PowerPoint.

**1** If you have one PowerPoint document open, click the Close Button on the right side of the title bar to close the document and then quit PowerPoint; or if you have multiple PowerPoint documents open, click File on the Ribbon to open the Backstage view and then click Exit in the Backstage view to close all open documents and quit PowerPoint.

**2** If a Microsoft PowerPoint dialog box appears, click the Save button to save any changes made to the presentation since the last save.

## Chapter Summary

In this chapter you have learned how to add a background style, insert and format pictures, add shapes, size graphic elements, apply styles, and insert WordArt. The items listed below include all the new PowerPoint skills you have learned in this chapter.

1. Change the Presentation Theme Colors (PPT 81)
2. Insert a Picture (PPT 83)
3. Insert a Picture into a Slide without a Content Placeholder (PPT 85)
4. Correct a Picture (PPT 86)
5. Apply a Picture Style (PPT 87)
6. Apply Picture Effects (PPT 89)
7. Add a Picture Border (PPT 91)
8. Change a Picture Border Color (PPT 92)
9. Resize a Graphic by Entering Exact Measurements (PPT 93)
10. Insert a Texture Fill (PPT 95)
11. Insert a Picture to Create a Background (PPT 97)
12. Format the Background Picture Fill Transparency (PPT 98)
13. Format the Background Texture Fill Transparency (PPT 99)
14. Choose a Background Style (PPT 99)
15. Change the Subtitle and Caption Font (PPT 101)
16. Shadow Text (PPT 103)
17. Format Caption Text Using the Format Painter (PPT 105)
18. Add a Shape (PPT 106)
19. Resize a Shape (PPT 107)
20. Copy and Paste a Shape (PPT 108)
21. Add Other Shapes (PPT 109)
22. Apply a Shape Style (PPT 110)
23. Add Formatted Text to a Shape (PPT 112)
24. Insert WordArt (PPT 114)
25. Change the WordArt Shape (PPT 115)
26. Apply a WordArt Text Fill (PPT 117)
27. Change the Weight of the WordArt Outline (PPT 118)
28. Change the Color of the WordArt Outline (PPT 118)

 If you have a SAM 2010 user profile, your instructor may have assigned an autogradable version of this assignment. If so, log into the SAM 2010 Web site at www.cengage.com/sam2010 to download the instruction and start files.

## Learn It Online

Test your knowledge of chapter content and key terms.

*Instructions:* To complete the Learn It Online exercises, start your browser, click the Address bar, and then enter the Web address **scsite.com/ppt2010/learn**. When the PowerPoint 2010 Learn It Online page is displayed, click the link for the exercise you want to complete and then read the instructions.

### Chapter Reinforcement TF, MC, and SA
A series of true/false, multiple choice, and short answer questions that test your knowledge of the chapter content.

### Flash Cards
An interactive learning environment where you identify chapter key terms associated with displayed definitions.

### Practice Test
A series of multiple choice questions that test your knowledge of chapter content and key terms.

### Who Wants To Be a Computer Genius?
An interactive game that challenges your knowledge of chapter content in the style of a television quiz show.

### Wheel of Terms
An interactive game that challenges your knowledge of chapter key terms in the style of the television show *Wheel of Fortune*.

### Crossword Puzzle Challenge
A crossword puzzle that challenges your knowledge of key terms presented in the chapter.

## Apply Your Knowledge

Reinforce the skills and apply the concepts you learned in this chapter.

### Changing the Background and Adding Photographs, WordArt, and a Shape Quick Style
*Note:* To complete this assignment, you will be required to use the Data Files for Students. See the inside back cover of this book for instructions on downloading the Data Files for Students, or contact your instructor for information about accessing the required files.

*Instructions:* Start PowerPoint. Open the presentation, Apply 2-1 Lab Procedures, from the Data Files for Students.

The four slides in the presentation present laboratory safety procedures for your chemistry class. The document you open is an unformatted presentation. You are to add pictures, which are available on the Data Files for Students. You also will change the background style, change slide layouts, apply a transition, and use the Format Painter so the slides look like Figure 2–74.

*Perform the following tasks:*
1. Change the background style to Style 5 (row 2, column 1).
2. On the title slide (Figure 2–74a), create a background by inserting the picture called Lab Assistant. Change the transparency to 30%.
3. Apply the WordArt style, Fill – Red, Accent 2, Matte Bevel (row 6, column 3) to the title text and increase the font size to 54 point. Also, apply the WordArt Transform text effect, Chevron Up (row 2, column 1 in the Warp area) to this text.
4. In the Slide 1 subtitle area, replace the words, Student Name, with your name. Bold and italicize your name and the words, Presented by, and then apply the WordArt style, Fill – Red, Accent 2, Warm Matte Bevel (row 5, column 3). Position this subtitle text and the title text as shown in Figure 2–74a.

*Continued >*

**Apply Your Knowledge** *continued*

5. On Slide 2, change the layout to Two Content and insert the pictures shown in Figure 2–74b called Female in Lab Coat and Female with Goggles. In the left placeholder, apply the Rotated, White picture style to the inserted picture. In the right placeholder, apply the Reflected Bevel, Black picture style to the inserted picture and then change the picture border color to Purple.

6. On Slide 3, change the layout to Two Content and insert the Fire Extinguisher picture shown in Figure 2–74c. Apply the Soft Edge Oval picture style and change the picture brightness to +20% (row 3, column 4 in the Brightness and Contrast area).

7. On Slide 4, change the layout to Picture with Caption and then insert the picture, Hand Washing shown in Figure 2–74d. Increase the subtitle text font size to 18 point. Change the title text font size to 28 point, add a shadow, change font to Algerian, and change the font color to Purple.

(a) Slide 1

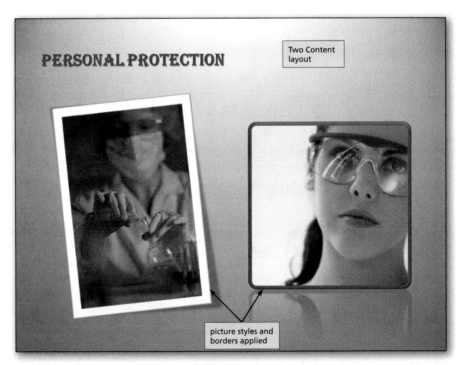

(b) Slide 2

Figure 2–74

8. Use the Format Painter to format the title text on Slides 2 and 3 with the same features as the title text on Slide 4.

9. Apply the Wipe transition in the Subtle category to all slides. Change the duration to 2.00 seconds.

10. Change the document properties, as specified by your instructor. Save the presentation using the file name, Apply 2-1 Chemistry Lab Safety. Submit the revised document in the format specified by your instructor.

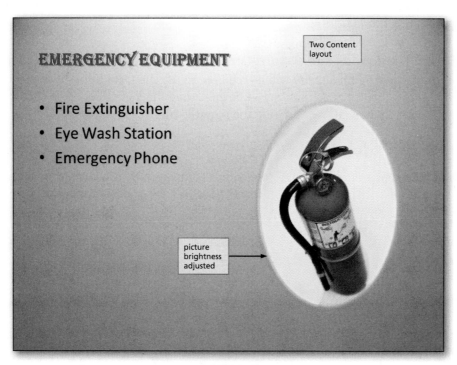

**(c) Slide 3**

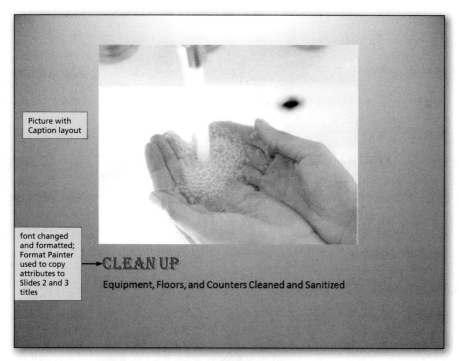

**(d) Slide 4**

**Figure 2 – 74 (Continued)**

# Extend Your Knowledge

Extend the skills you learned in this chapter and experiment with new skills. You may need to use Help to complete the assignment.

### Changing Slide Backgrounds and Picture Contrast, and Inserting Shapes and WordArt

*Note:* To complete this assignment, you will be required to use the Data Files for Students. See the inside back cover of this book for instructions on downloading the Data Files for Students, or contact your instructor for information about accessing the required files.

*Instructions:* Start PowerPoint. Open the presentation, Extend 2-1 Smith Family Reunion, from the Data Files for Students.

You will create backgrounds including inserting a picture to create a background, apply a WordArt Style and Effect, and add shapes to create the presentation shown in Figure 2–75.

*Perform the following tasks:*

1. Change the background style to Denim (row 1, column 3) and change the transparency to 48%. On Slides 2 through 5, change the title text to bold.

2. On the title slide (Figure 2–75a), create a background by inserting the picture called Tree, which is available on the Data Files for Students. Change the transparency to 40%.

3. Apply the WordArt style, Gradient Fill – Blue, Accent 1, to the title text and increase the font size to 66 point. Also, apply the WordArt Transform text effect, Arch Up (row 1, column 1 in the Follow Path area), to this text.

4. In the Slide 1 subtitle area, insert the Wave shape in the Stars and Banners area. Also, apply the Shape Style, Subtle Effect – Orange, Accent 6 to the Wave shape. Type **Highlights From Our Last Reunion** and increase the font size to 40 point, change the text to bold italic and change the color to Green. Position the shape as shown in Figure 2–75a.

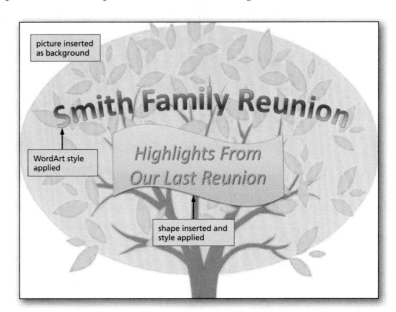

**(a) Slide 1**

**(b) Slide 2**

**Figure 2–75**

5. On Slide 2, change the layout to Two Content and insert the pictures shown in Figure 2–75b. The pictures to be inserted are called Bocce Ball and Frisbee Catcher and are available on the Data Files for Students. In the left placeholder, apply the Rotated White picture style to the inserted picture and change the picture border to Light Green. In the right placeholder, apply the Beveled Oval Black picture style to the inserted picture.

6. Insert the Plaque shape in the Basic Shapes area. Also, apply the Shape Style, Subtle Effect, Olive Green, Accent 3 and apply the Shape Effect, 3-D Rotation, Parallel, Off Axis 1 Right. Type **Cousin Tom & His Frisbee Moves** and increase the font size to 28 point. Move the shape as shown in Figure 2–75b.

**(c) Slide 3**

7. On Slide 3, change the layout to Picture with Caption and insert the picture shown in Figure 2–75c. The picture to be inserted is called BBQ Grill. Increase the title font size to 44 point. Also, increase the subtitle font size to 32 point, and then bold and italicize this text.

8. On Slide 4, change the layout to Two Content and insert the pictures shown in Figure 2–75d. The pictures to be inserted are called Reunion Boys and Reunion Toddler. In the left placeholder, apply the Rotated, White picture effect to the picture. In the right placeholder, apply the Bevel Perspective picture effect. Move the pictures as shown in Figure 2–75d.

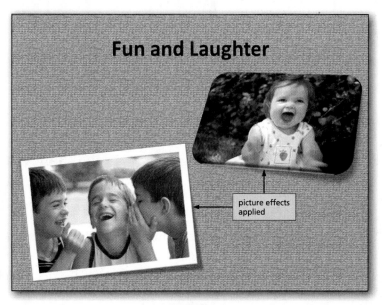

**(d) Slide 4**

**Figure 2–75 (Continued)**

*Continued >*

**Extend Your Knowledge** *continued*

9. On Slide 5, change the layout to Title and Content and insert the picture shown in Figure 2–75e. The picture to be inserted is called Reunion. Enlarge the picture as shown.

10. Insert the Oval Callout and Cloud Callout shapes in the Callouts area. In the Oval Callout shape, type **I hope Grandma makes cookies!** and change the font size to 24 point bold italic. Also add a Shape Style, Moderate Effect – Olive Green Accent 3 to this shape. In the Cloud Callout shape, type **I'm looking forward to our next reunion!** and change the font size to 24 point and the style to bold italic. Move the shapes as shown in Figure 2–75e. Use the adjustment handles (the yellow diamond below each shape) to move the callout arrows as shown in Figure 2–75e. You may need to use Help to learn how to move these arrows.

**(e) Slide 5**

11. On Slide 6, change the layout to Picture with Caption and insert the picture shown in Figure 2–75f and change the picture contrast to +20. The picture to be inserted is called Reunion Tree.

**(f) Slide 6**

**Figure 2–75 (Continued)**

12. Insert the Up Ribbon shape in the Stars and Banners area and type the words **Announcing Our Next Reunion**. Change the font color to Green, the font size to 32 point, and the style to bold italic. Also, apply the Shape Style, Subtle Effect – Orange Accent 6. In the title placeholder, type **Save the date – June 20, 2012** and change the font size to 28 point. Bold this text.

13. Add the Orbit transition under the Dynamic Content section to Slide 6 only. You may need to use Help to learn how to apply the transition to only one slide. Change the duration to 2.00 seconds.

14. Change the document properties, as specified by your instructor. Save the presentation using the file name, Extend 2-1 Smith Reunion.

15. Submit the revised document in the format specified by your instructor.

# Make It Right

Analyze a presentation and correct all errors and/or improve the design.

### Changing a Theme and Background Style

*Note:* To complete this assignment, you will be required to use the Data Files for Students. See the inside back cover of this book for instructions on downloading the Data Files for Students, or contact your instructor for information about accessing the required files.

*Instructions:* Start PowerPoint. Open the presentation, Make It Right 2-1 New Aerobics Classes, from the Data Files for Students.

Correct the formatting problems and errors in the presentation while keeping in mind the guidelines presented in this chapter.

*Perform the following tasks:*

1. Change the document theme from Flow, shown in Figure 2–76, to Waveform. Apply the Background Style 10 (row 3, column 2) to Slide 5 only.

2. On the title slide, change the title from New Aerobics Classes to New Pool Programs. Type your name in place of Northlake Fitness Center and change the font to bold italic.

3. Move Slide 2 to the end of the presentation so that it becomes the new Slide 5.

4. Adjust the picture sizes, font sizes, and shapes so they do not overlap text and are the appropriate dimensions for the slide content.

5. Apply the Ripple transition to all slides. Change the duration to 02.00.

6. Change the document properties, as specified by your instructor. Save the presentation using the file name, Make It Right 2-1 New Pool Programs.

7. Submit the revised document in the format specified by your instructor.

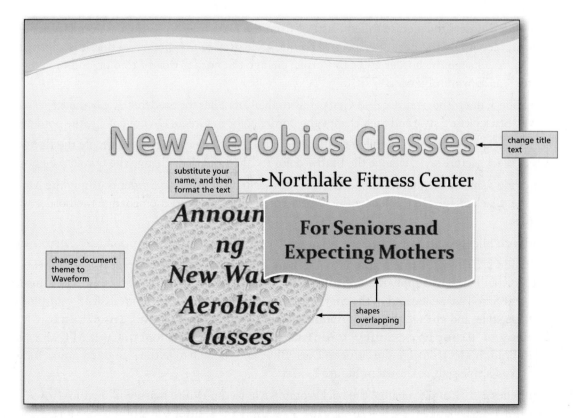

**Figure 2–76**

## In the Lab

Design and/or create a presentation using the guidelines, concepts, and skills presented in this chapter. Labs 1, 2, and 3 are listed in order of increasing difficulty.

### Lab 1: Creating a Presentation Inserting Pictures and Applying Picture Styles

*Problem:* You are studying German operas in your Music Appreciation class. Wilhelm Richard Wagner (pronounced 'va:gner') lived from 1813 to 1883 and was a composer, conductor, theatre director, and essayist known for his operas. Wagner wrote and composed many operas, and King Ludwig II of Bavaria was one of his biggest supporters. Because you recently visited southern Germany and toured King Ludwig's castles, you decide to create a PowerPoint presentation with some of your photos to accompany your class presentation. These pictures are available on the Data Files for Students. Create the slides shown in Figure 2–77 from a blank presentation using the Office Theme document theme.

*Note:* To complete this assignment, you will be required to use the Data Files for Students. See the inside back cover of this book for instructions on downloading the Data Files for Students, or contact your instructor for information about accessing the required files.

*Instructions:* Perform the following tasks:
1. On Slide 1, create a background by inserting the picture called Castle 1, which is available on the Data Files for Students.
2. Type **Fairy Tale Trip to Germany** as the Slide 1 title text. Apply the WordArt style, Fill – Tan, Text 2, Outline – Background 2, and increase the font size to 60 point. Change the text fill to the Papyrus texture, and then change the text outline weight to 1½ pt. Also, apply the Transform text effect, Arch Up (in the Follow Path area), to this text. Position this WordArt as shown in Figure 2–77a.
3. Type the title and content for the four text slides shown in Figure 2–77. Apply the Two Content layout to Slides 2 and 3 and the Picture with Caption layout to Slides 4 and 5.
4. On Slide 2, insert the picture called Castle 2 from the Data Files for Students in the right placeholder. Apply the Bevel Perspective picture style. Resize the picture so that it is approximately 4.5" × 6", change the border color to Purple, change the border weight to 6 pt, and then move the picture, as shown in Figure 2–77b.
5. On Slide 3, insert the picture called Castle 3 from the Data Files for Students. Apply the Reflected Bevel, Black picture style and then change the border color to Green. Do not change the border weight.
6. On Slide 4, insert the picture called Castle 4 from the Data Files for Students. Apply the Beveled Oval, Black picture style, change the border color to Blue, and then change the border weight to 6 pt.
7. On Slide 5, insert the picture called Castle 5 from the Data Files for Students. Apply the Moderate Frame, Black picture style, change the border color to Purple, and then change the border weight to 6 pt.
8. For both Slides 4 and 5, increase the title text size to 28 point and the caption text size to 24 point.
9. On Slide 2, change the title text font to Algerian, change the color to purple, and bold this text. Use the Format Painter to apply these formatting changes to the Slide 3 title text. In Slide 3, insert the Vertical Scroll shape located in the Stars and Banners area, apply the Subtle Effect – Purple, Accent 4 shape style, and change the shape outline weight to 3 pt. Type the text, **Inspiration for Disney's Sleeping Beauty Castle**, and then change the font to Curlz MT, or a similar font. Bold this text, change the color to Dark Blue, and then change the size to 28 point. Increase the scroll shape size, as shown in Figure 2–77c.
10. On Slides 2, 3, 4, and 5, change the background style to the White marble fill texture (row 2, column 5) and change the transparency to 35%. Apply the Glitter transition to all slides. Change the duration to 04.50.

11. Change the document properties, as specified by your instructor. Save the presentation using the file name, Lab 2-1 Trip to Germany.

12. Submit the revised document in the format specified by your instructor.

picture inserted as background

WordArt style, texture fill, and effect applied

**(a) Slide 1**

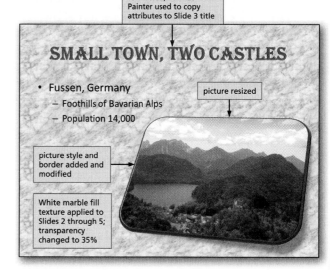

font changed and formatted; Format Painter used to copy attributes to Slide 3 title

picture resized

picture style and border added and modified

White marble fill texture applied to Slides 2 through 5; transparency changed to 35%

**(b) Slide 2**

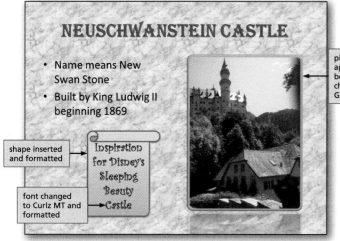

picture style applied and border color changed to Green

shape inserted and formatted

font changed to Curlz MT and formatted

**(c) Slide 3**

picture style applied and border color and weight changed

font size increased

**(d) Slide 4**

picture style applied and border color and weight changed

font size increased

**(e) Slide 5**

**Figure 2 – 77**

## In the Lab

### Lab 2: Creating a Presentation with a Shape and with WordArt

*Problem:*   With the economy showing some improvement, many small businesses are approaching lending institutions for loans to expand their businesses. You work part-time for Loans Are Us, and your manager asked you to prepare a PowerPoint presentation for the upcoming Small Business Fair in your community. The pictures for this presentation are available on the Data Files for Students.

*Note:*   To complete this assignment, you will be required to use the Data Files for Students. See the inside back cover of this book for instructions on downloading the Data Files for Students, or contact your instructor for information about accessing the required files.

*Instructions:*   Perform the following tasks:

1.  Create a new presentation using the Austin document theme.

2.  Type the title and content for the title slide and the three text slides shown in Figure 2–78a–d. Apply the Title Only layout to Slide 2, the Two Content layout to Slide 3, and the Picture with Caption layout to Slide 4.

3.  On both Slides 2 and 4, create a background by inserting the picture called Money. Change the transparency to 35%.

4.  On Slide 1, insert the picture called Meeting. Apply the Reflected Bevel, White picture style. Resize the picture so that it is approximately 3.76" × 4.7", change the border color to Dark Blue, change the border weight to 3 pt, and then move the picture, as shown in Figure 2–78a. Increase the title text font size to 60 point, and then apply the WordArt style, Fill – Orange, Accent 6, Warm Matte Bevel.

5.  Increase the subtitle text, Loans Are Us, font size to 28 point and then bold and italicize this text. Apply the WordArt style, Fill – Green, Accent 1, Metal Bevel, Reflection.

6.  On Slide 2, bold the title text. Insert the pictures called Doc1, Doc2, and Doc3. Resize these pictures so they are approximately 3" x 2.7" and then move them to the locations shown in Figure 2–78b. Insert the Flowchart: Decision shape located in the Flowchart area, apply the Subtle Effect – Orange, Accent 6 shape style, and then resize the shape so that it is approximately 1.5" × 5.83". Change the shape outline weight to 6 pt. Type **Assets, Liabilities & Sales Reports**  as the shape text, change the font to Aharoni, or a similar font, change the color to Dark Blue, and then change the size to 24 point.

7.  On Slide 3, bold the title text. Insert the picture called Presentation into the right placeholder, apply the Beveled Oval, Black shape picture style, resize the picture so that it is approximately 3.5" × 5.25", and then sharpen the picture 50%.

8.  On Slide 4, insert the picture called Cash and Credit Card. Change the title text font size to 36 point and bold this text. Change the subtitle text font size to 24 point and then bold and italicize these words.

9.  Apply the Shape transition to all slides. Change the duration to 01.25.

10. Change the document properties, as specified by your instructor. Save the presentation using the file name, Lab 2-2 Small Business Loans.

11. Submit the document in the format specified by your instructor.

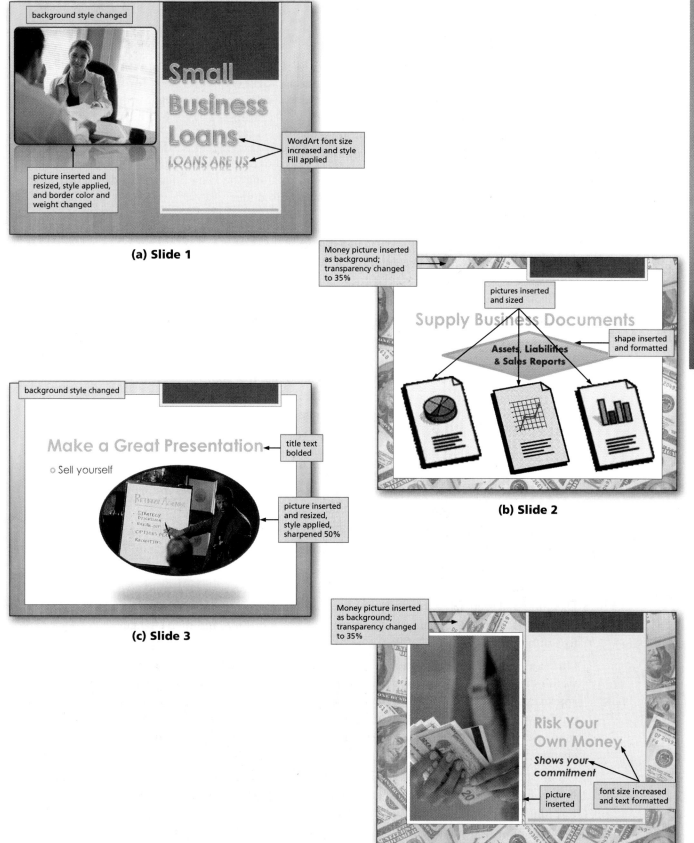

**Figure 2–78**

# In the Lab

## Lab 3: Creating a Presentation with Pictures and Shapes

*Problem:* One of your assignments in your child development class is to give a speech about teaching children the value of money, so you decide to create a PowerPoint presentation to add a little interest to your speech. Prepare the slides shown in Figures 2–79a through 2–79e. The pictures for this presentation are available on the Data Files for Students.

*Note:* To complete this assignment, you will be required to use the Data Files for Students. See the inside back cover of this book for instructions on downloading the Data Files for Students, or contact your instructor for information about accessing the required files.

*Instructions:* Perform the following tasks:

1. Create a new presentation using the Median document theme, and then change the presentation theme colors to Flow. This presentation should have five slides; apply the Title Slide layout to Slide 1, the Picture with Caption layout to Slides 2 and 5, the Comparison layout to Slide 3, and the Blank layout to Slide 4.

2. Type the title and content text for the title slide and the four text slides shown in Figure 2–79a–d.

3. On Slide 1, change the title text font size to 54 point. To make the letter 's' appear smaller than the other letters in the first word of the title slide title text placeholder, change the font size of this letter to 44 point. Insert the Oval shape, resize it so that it is approximately 0.5" × 0.5", and change the shape fill to white, which is the second color in the first row of the Theme Colors gallery. Type **$**, increase the font size to 48 point, change the color to green, and bold this dollar sign. Cover the letter 'o' in the word, Do, with this shape.

4. Insert the picture called Piggy Bank. Apply the Rounded Diagonal Corner, White picture style. Resize the picture so that it is approximately 4.4" × 5.03", change the border color to Light Blue, change the border weight to 3 pt, and then move the picture, as shown in Figure 2–79a. Change the subtitle font size to 32 point and then bold this text.

5. On Slide 2, insert the picture called Child Doing Dishes and then decrease the picture's contrast to −20%. Change the title text size to 36 point and bold this text. Change the caption text size to 32 point.

6. On Slide 3, change the background style to Style 6. Bold the title text. Change the heading title text size in both placeholders to 32 point. In the right placeholder, insert the picture called Father and Daughter and then apply the Reflected Bevel, White picture style. Resize the picture so that it is approximately 3" × 4", change the border color to Light Blue, and then change the border weight to 3 pt, as shown in Figure 2–79c.

7. On Slide 4, create a background by inserting the picture called Piggy Bank and Coins. Insert the Cloud shape located in the Basic Shapes area and then increase the cloud shape size so that it is approximately 3" × 5.6". Change the shape outline color to Yellow and then change the shape outline weight to 3 pt. Type **Teach your children to save for a big purchase.** as the shape text, and then change the font to Comic Sans MS. Bold and italicize this text and then change the font size to 32 point.

8. On Slide 5, create a background by inserting the picture called Coins. Insert the picture called Father and Child Shopping and then decrease the picture's brightness to −20%. Change the title text font size to 36 point and bold this text.

9. Apply the Box transition to all slides. Change the duration to 02.00. Check the spelling and correct any errors.

10. Change the document properties, as specified by your instructor. Save the presentation using the file name, Lab 2-3 ABCs of Money.

11. Submit the revised document in the format specified by your instructor.

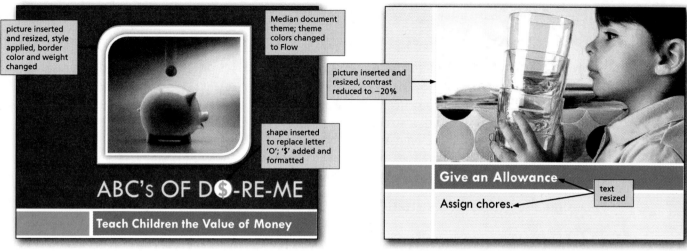

**(a) Slide 1**               **(b) Slide 2**

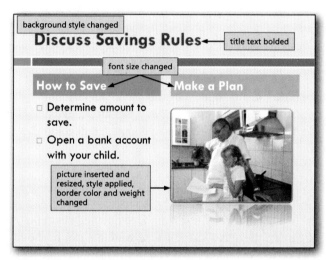 

**(c) Slide 3**               **(d) Slide 4**

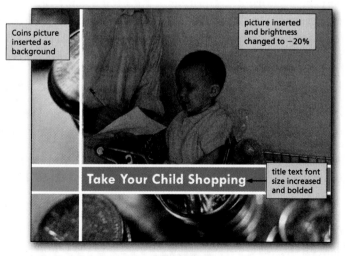

**(e) Slide 5**

**Figure 2–79**

# Cases and Places

Apply your creative thinking and problem-solving skills to design and implement a solution.

*Note:* To complete these assignments, you may be required to use the Data Files for Students. See the inside back cover of this book for instructions on downloading the Data Files for Students, or contact your instructor for information about accessing the required files.

As you design the presentations, remember to use the 7 × 7 rule: a maximum of seven words on a line and a maximum of seven lines on one slide.

## 1: Design and Create a Presentation about Acid Rain

**Academic**

Nature depends on the correct pH balance. Although some rain is naturally acidic with a pH level of around 5.0, human activities have increased the amount of acid in this water. Burning fossil fuels, including coal, oil, and natural gas, produces sulfur dioxide. Exhaust from vehicles releases nitrogen oxides. Both of these gases, when released into the atmosphere, mix with water droplets, forming acid rain. In your science class, you are studying about the causes and effects of acid rain. Create a presentation to show what causes acid rain and what effects it can have on humans, animals, plant life, lakes, and rivers. The presentation should contain at least three pictures appropriately resized. The Data Files for Students contains five pictures called Factory, Rain, Soil, Tree and Clouds, and Vehicles; you can use your own digital pictures or pictures from Office.com if they are appropriate for this topic. These pictures also should have appropriate styles and border colors. Use shapes such as arrows to show what gases are released into the atmosphere. Apply at least three objectives found at the beginning of this chapter to develop the presentation. Add a title slide with a shape and a closing slide. Be sure to check spelling.

## 2: Design and Create a Presentation about Tutoring

**Personal**

You have been helping some of your classmates with their schoolwork, and you have decided that you should start a small tutoring business. In the student center, there is a kiosk where students can find out about programs and activities on campus. The student center manager gave you permission to submit a short PowerPoint presentation promoting your tutoring business; this presentation will be added to the kiosk. The presentation should contain pictures appropriately resized. The Data Files for Students contains four pictures called Tutoring 1, Tutoring 2, Tutoring 3, and Tutoring 4, or you can use your own digital pictures or pictures from Office.com if they are appropriate for this topic. Change the contrast and brightness for at least one picture. Insert shapes and WordArt to enhance your presentation. Apply a transition in the Subtle area to all slides and increase the duration. Be sure to check spelling.

## 3: Design and Create a Presentation on Setting Up Children's Fish Tanks

**Professional**

Fish make great pets for young children, but there is a lot to learn before they can set up a fish tank properly. The owner of the pet store where you work has asked you to create a presentation for the store to give parents an idea of what they need to purchase and consider when setting up a fish tank. He would like you to cover the main points such as the appropriate size bowl or tank, setup procedures, filtration, water quality, types of fish, care, and feeding. The presentation should contain pictures appropriately resized. The Data Files for Students contains five pictures called Fish 1, Fish 2, Fish 3, Fish 4, and Fish 5, or you can use your own digital pictures or pictures from Office.com if they are appropriate for this topic. Add a title slide and closing slide to complete your presentation. Format the title slide with a shape and change the theme color scheme. Change the title text font on the title slide. Format the background with at least one picture and apply a background texture to at least one slide. This presentation is geared to parents of young children, so keep it colorful, simple, and fun.

# 3 Reusing a Presentation and Adding Media

## Objectives

You will have mastered the material in this chapter when you can:

- Color a picture
- Add an artistic effect to a picture
- Delete and move placeholders
- Align paragraph text
- Copy a slide element from one slide to another

- Ungroup, change the color, and regroup a clip
- Insert and edit a video clip
- Insert audio
- Control audio and video clips
- Check for spelling errors
- Print a presentation as a handout

# 3 | Reusing a Presentation and Adding Media

## Introduction

At times, you will need to revise a PowerPoint presentation. Changes may include inserting and adding effects to pictures, altering the colors of clips and pictures, and updating visual elements displayed on a slide. Applying a different theme, changing fonts, and substituting graphical elements can give a slide show an entirely new look. Adding media, including sounds, video, and music, can enhance a presentation and help audience members retain the information being presented.

## Project — Presentation with Video, Audio, and Pictures with Effects

**BTW**

**PowerPoint 2010 Video Enhancements**
New video tools in PowerPoint 2010 enable you to develop a presentation filled with professional-quality features. You now can embed and edit videos from within PowerPoint instead of needing to use a separate program to customize your media files. You can add fades and effects to captivate your audience, and you can trim specific pieces of the video file to show the exact scenes needed to make a point. Video and audio files now are embedded in your PowerPoint file, so they become part of the entire presentation. These enhanced features help make your media fit the message you are sending to your audience.

The project in this chapter follows graphical guidelines and uses PowerPoint to create the presentation shown in Figure 3–1. The slides in this revised presentation, which discusses Bird Migration, have a variety of audio and visual elements. For example, the pictures have artistic effects applied that soften the pictures and help the audience focus on other elements on the slides. The bird clip has colors that blend well with the background. The video has been edited to play only the portion with Bird Migration and has effects to add audience interest. Bird calls integrate with the visual elements. Overall, the slides have myriad media elements and effects that are exciting for your audience to watch and hear.

## Overview

As you read through this chapter, you will learn how to create the presentation shown in Figure 3–1 by performing these general tasks:

- Format pictures by recoloring and adding artistic effects.
- Insert and format video and audio clips.
- Modify clip art.
- Vary paragraph alignment.
- Check a presentation for spelling errors.
- Print a handout of your slides.

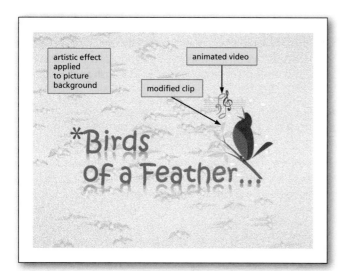

**(a) Slide 1 (Title Slide with Picture Background, Modified Clip, and Animated Clip)**

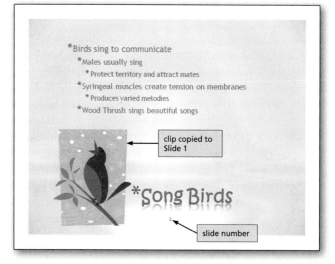

**(b) Slide 2 (Bulleted List)**

**(c) Slide 3 (Picture Background and Video Clip)**

**(d) Slide 4 (Video Playing Full Screen)**

**Figure 3–1**

Plan
Ahead

**General Project Guidelines**

When creating a PowerPoint presentation, the actions you perform and the decisions you make will affect the appearance and characteristics of the finished document. As you create a presentation with illustrations, such as the project shown in Figure 3–1, you should follow these general guidelines:

1. **Use the color wheel to determine color choices.** Warm colors and cool colors evoke opposite effects on audience members. As you make decisions to color pictures, consider the emotions you want to generate and choose colors that match these sentiments.

2. **Vary paragraph alignment.** Different effects are achieved when text alignment shifts in a presentation. Themes dictate whether paragraph text is aligned left, center, or right in a placeholder, but you can modify these design decisions when necessary.

3. **Use multimedia selectively.** Video, music, and sound files can add interest to your presentation. Use these files only when necessary, however, because they draw the audience's attention away from the presenter and toward the slides. Using too many multimedia files can be overwhelming.

4. **Use handouts to organize your speech.** Effective speakers take much time to prepare their verbal message that will accompany each slide. They practice their speeches and decide how to integrate the material displayed. Viewing the thumbnails, or miniature versions of the slides, will help you associate the slide image with the script. These thumbnails also can be cut out and arranged when organizing the presentation.

5. **Evaluate your presentation.** As soon as you finish your presentation, critique your performance. You will improve your communication skills by eliminating the flaws and accentuating the positives.

When necessary, more specific details concerning the above guidelines are presented at appropriate points in the chapter. The chapter also will identify the actions performed and decisions made regarding these guidelines during the creation of the presentation shown in Figure 3–1.

For an introduction to Windows 7 and instruction about how to perform basic Windows 7 tasks, read the Office 2010 and Windows 7 chapter at the beginning of this book, where you can learn how to resize windows, change screen resolution, create folders, move and rename files, use Windows Help, and much more.

# Starting PowerPoint

Chapter 1 introduced you to starting PowerPoint, selecting a document theme, creating slides with clip art and a bulleted list, and printing a presentation. Chapter 2 enhanced slides by adding pictures, shapes, and WordArt. The following steps, which assume Windows 7 is running, start PowerPoint and open the Birds presentation. For a detailed example of the procedure summarized below, refer to the Office 2010 and Windows 7 chapter at the beginning of this book.

## To Start PowerPoint and Open and Save a Presentation

**BTW**

**The Ribbon and Screen Resolution**
PowerPoint may change how the groups and buttons within the groups appear on the Ribbon, depending on the computer's screen resolution. Thus, your Ribbon may look different from the ones in this book if you are using a screen resolution other than 1024 × 768.

**1** Click the Start button on the Windows 7 taskbar to display the Start menu, type **Microsoft PowerPoint** as the search text in the 'Search programs and files' text box, and then click Microsoft PowerPoint 2010 in the search results on the Start menu to start PowerPoint and display a new blank document.

**2** If the PowerPoint window is not maximized, click the Maximize button.

**3** Open the presentation, Birds, from the Data Files for Students. See the inside back cover of this book for instructions on downloading the Data Files for Students, or contact your instructor for more information on accessing the required files.

**4** Save the presentation using the file name, Bird Migration.

# Inserting Pictures and Adding Effects

The Bird Migration presentation consists of four slides that have some text, a clip art image, a formatted background, and a transition applied to all slides. You will insert pictures into two slides and then modify them by adding artistic effects and recoloring. You also will copy the clip art from Slide 2 to Slide 1 and modify the objects in this clip. In Chapter 2, you inserted pictures, made corrections, and added styles and effects; the new effects you apply in this chapter will add to your repertoire of picture enhancements that increase interest in your presentation.

In the following pages, you will perform these tasks:

1. Insert the first digital picture into Slide 1.
2. Insert the second digital picture into Slide 3.
3. Recolor the Slide 3 picture.
4. Recolor and add an artistic effect to the Slide 1 picture.
5. Add an artistic effect to the Slide 3 picture.
6. Send the Slide 3 picture back behind all other slide objects.
7. Send the Slide 1 picture back behind all other slide objects.

For an introduction to Office 2010 and instruction about how to perform basic tasks in Office 2010 programs, read the Office 2010 and Windows 7 chapter at the beginning of this book, where you can learn how to start a program, use the Ribbon, save a file, open a file, quit a program, use Help, and much more.

## To Insert and Resize Pictures into Slides without Content Placeholders

The next step is to insert digital pictures into Slides 1 and 3. These pictures are available on the Data Files for Students. See the inside back cover of this book for instructions on downloading the Data Files for Students, or contact your instructor for information about accessing the required files.

The following steps insert pictures into Slides 1 and 3.

**1** With Slide 1 displaying and your USB flash drive connected to one of the computer's USB ports, click Insert on the Ribbon to display the Insert tab and then click the Picture button (Insert tab | Images group) to display the Insert Picture dialog box.

**2** If necessary, navigate to the picture location (in this case, the PowerPoint folder in the CIS 101 folder [or your class folder] on the USB flash drive). For a detailed example of this procedure, refer to Steps 3a–3c on pages OFF 28 and OFF 29 in the Office 2010 and Windows 7 chapter at the beginning of this book.

**3** Click Birds in Sky to select the file.

**4** Click the Insert button (Insert Picture dialog box) to insert the picture into Slide 1.

**5** Resize the picture so that it covers the entire slide (approximately 7.5" × 10").

**6** Display Slide 3, display the Insert tab, click the Picture button to display the Insert Picture dialog box, and then insert the Bird Reflect picture into Slide 3.

**7** Resize the picture so that it covers the entire slide (approximately 7.5" × 10") (Figure 3–2).

**Q&A**

How do I resize the picture so that it maintains its proportions?

Press and hold the SHIFT key while dragging a sizing handle away from or toward the center of the picture. To maintain the picture's proportions and keep its center in the same location, press and hold down both the CTRL and SHIFT keys while you drag a sizing handle.

**BTW**

**Inserting Text Boxes**

If you want to add text in an area of the slide where a content placeholder is not located, you can insert a text box. This object allows you to emphasize or set off text that you consider important for your audience to read. To create a text box, click the Text Box button (Insert tab | Text group), click the slide, and then drag this object to the desired location on the slide. Click inside the text box to add or paste text. You also can change the look and style of the text box characters by using formatting features (Home tab | Font group).

**Figure 3–2**

Plan
Ahead

**Use the color wheel to determine color choices.**
The color wheel is one of designers' basic tools. Twelve colors on the wheel are arranged in a specific order, with the three primary colors — red, yellow, and blue — forming a triangle. Between the primary colors are the secondary colors that are formed when the primary colors are mixed. For example, red and yellow mixed together form orange; red and blue form purple; and yellow and blue form green. The six other colors on the wheel are formed when the primary colors are mixed with the secondary colors.

Red, orange, and yellow are considered warm colors, and they display adjacent to each other on one side of the wheel. They are bold and lively, so you should use them when your message is intended to invigorate an audience and create a pleasing effect. Opposite the warm colors are the cool colors: green, blue, and purple. They generate a relaxing, calming atmosphere.

If you put a primary and secondary color together, such as red and purple, your slide will make a very bold and vivid statement. Be certain that effect is one you intend when planning your message.

## Adjusting Picture Colors

BTW

**Q&As**
For a complete list of the Q&As found in many of the step-by-step sequences in this book, visit the PowerPoint 2010 Q&A Web page (scsite.com/ppt2010/qa).

PowerPoint allows you to adjust colors to match or add contrast to slide elements by coloring pictures. The Color Picture gallery has a wide variety of preset formatting combinations. The thumbnails in the gallery display the more common color saturation, color tone, and recolor adjustments. **Color saturation** changes the intensity of colors. High saturation produces vivid colors; low saturation produces gray tones. **Color tone** affects the coolness, called blue, or the warmness, called orange, of pictures. When a digital camera does not measure the tone correctly, a **color cast** occurs, and, as a result, one color dominates the picture. **Recolor** effects convert the picture into a wide variety of hues. The more common are **grayscale**, which changes the color picture into black, white, and shades of gray, and **sepia**, which changes the picture colors into brown, gold, and yellow, reminiscent of a faded photo. You also can fine-tune the color adjustments by clicking Picture Color Options and More Variations commands in the Color gallery.

## To Color a Picture

The Slipstream theme and text on Slides 1 and 3 have many shades of blue. The inserted pictures, in addition, have blue backgrounds. The following steps recolor the Slide 3 picture to coordinate with the blue colors on the slide.

**1**

- With Slide 3 displaying and the Bird Reflect picture selected, click the Color button (Picture Tools Format tab | Adjust group) to display the Color gallery (Figure 3–3).

**Q&A** Why does the Adjust group look different on my screen?

Your monitor is set to a different resolution. See Chapter 1 for an explanation of screen resolution and the appearance of the Ribbon.

**Q&A** Why are yellow borders surrounding the thumbnails in the Color Saturation and Color Tone areas in the gallery?

The image on Slide 3 currently has normal color saturation and a normal color tone.

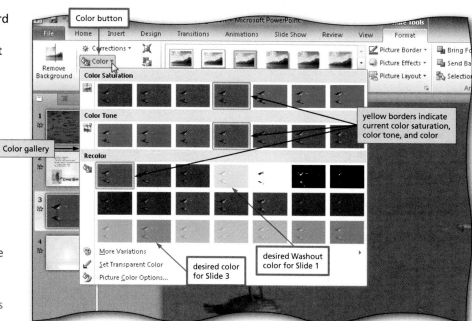

**Figure 3–3**

**2**

- Point to Blue, Accent color 1 Light (second picture in last row of Recolor area) to display a live preview of this adjustment on the picture.

**Experiment**

- Point to various thumbnails in the Recolor area and watch the hues change on the picture in Slide 3.

- Click Blue, Accent color 1 Light to apply this correction to the Bird Reflect picture (Figure 3–4).

**Q&A** Could I have applied this correction to the picture if it had been a background instead of a file inserted into the slide?

No. Artistic effects cannot be applied to backgrounds.

**Figure 3–4**

## To Color a Second Picture

The Slide 1 picture has rich hues and is very prominent on the slide. To soften its appearance and to provide continuity with the Slide 3 picture, you can color this picture. The following steps color the picture on the title slide.

**1** Display Slide 1 and then click the picture to select it. Click the Color button (Picture Tools Format tab | Adjust group) to display the Color gallery.

**2** Click Washout (fourth picture in first row of Recolor area) to apply this correction to the Bird Reflect picture (Figure 3–5).

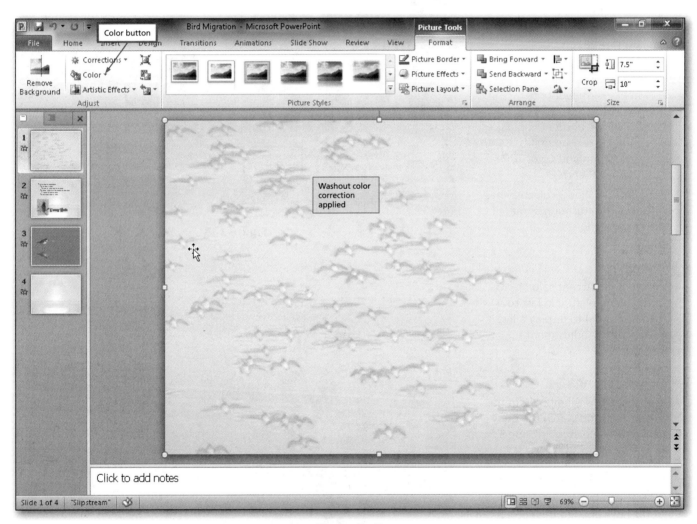

**Figure 3–5**

## To Add an Artistic Effect to a Picture

Artists use a variety of techniques to create effects in their paintings. For example, they can vary the amount of paint on their brushstroke, use fine bristles to add details, mix colors to increase or decrease intensity, and smooth their paints together to blend the colors. You, likewise, can add similar effects to your pictures using PowerPoint's built-in artistic effects. The following steps add an artistic effect to the Slide 3 picture.

**1**

- With the Birds in Sky picture selected in Slide 1, click the Artistic Effects button (Picture Tools Format tab | Adjust group) to display the Artistic Effects gallery (Figure 3–6).

**Q&A** Why does the Adjust group look different on my screen?

Your monitor is set to a different resolution. See Chapter 1 for an explanation of screen resolution and the appearance of the Ribbon.

**Q&A** Why is a yellow border surrounding the first thumbnail in the gallery?

The first thumbnail shows a preview of the image on Slide 1 with no artistic effect applied.

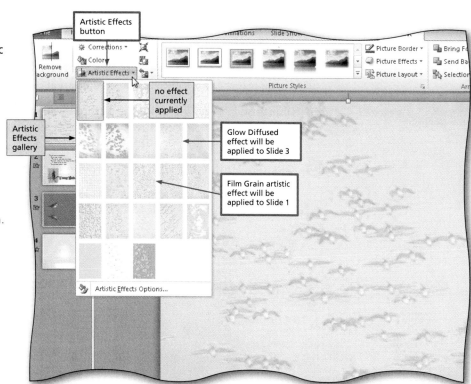

**Figure 3–6**

**2**

- Point to Film Grain (third picture in third row) to display a live preview of this adjustment on the picture.

🔍 **Experiment**

- Point to various thumbnails and watch the hues change on the picture in Slide 1.

- Click Film Grain to apply this correction to the Birds in Sky picture (Figure 3–7).

**Q&A** Must I adjust a picture by recoloring and applying an artistic effect?

No. You can apply either a color or an effect. You may prefer at times to mix these adjustments to create a unique image.

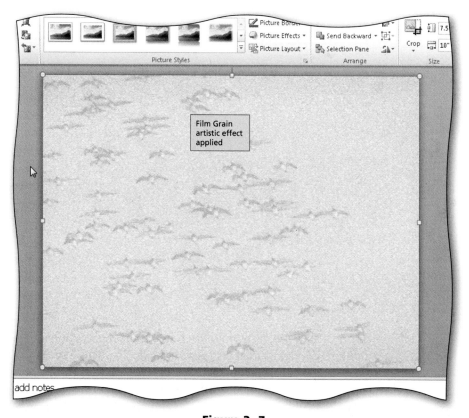

**Figure 3–7**

## To Add an Artistic Effect to a Second Picture

The Slide 3 picture was softened when you applied a blue accent color. You can further change the images and provide continuity with the Slide 1 picture by applying an artistic effect. The following steps add an artistic effect to the Slide 3 picture.

**1** Display Slide 3 and then click the picture to select it. If necessary, click the Picture Tools Format tab and then click the Artistic Effects button (Picture Tools Format tab | Adjust group) to display the Artistic Effects gallery.

**2** Click Glow Diffused (fourth picture in second row) to apply this effect to the Bird Reflect picture (Figure 3–8).

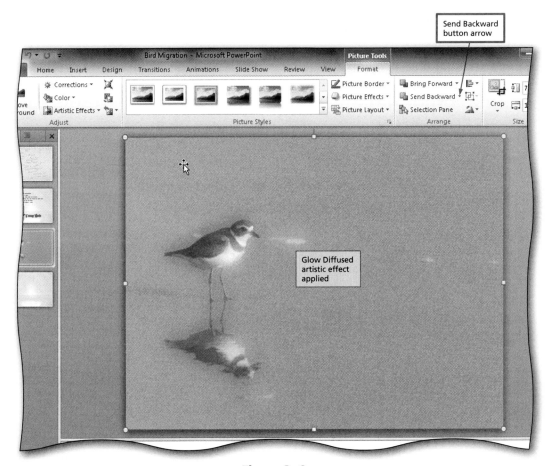

**Figure 3–8**

## To Change the Stacking Order

The objects on a slide stack on top of each other, much like individual cards in a deck. On Slides 1 and 3, the pictures you inserted are on top of text placeholders. To change the order of these objects, you use the Bring Forward and Send Backward commands. **Bring Forward** moves an object toward the top of the stack, and **Send Backward** moves an object underneath another object. When you click the Bring Forward button arrow, PowerPoint displays a menu with an additional command, **Bring to Front**, which moves a selected object to the top of the stack. Likewise, when you click the Send Backward button arrow, the **Send to Back** button moves the selected object underneath all objects on the slide. The following steps arrange the Slide 3 and Slide 1 pictures by sending them to the bottom of the stack on each slide.

**1**

- With the Bird Reflect picture selected in Slide 3, click the Send Backward button arrow (Picture Tools Format tab | Arrange group) to display the Send Backward menu (Figure 3–9).

**Q&A**

How can I see objects that are not on the top of the stack?

Press TAB or SHIFT+TAB to display each slide object.

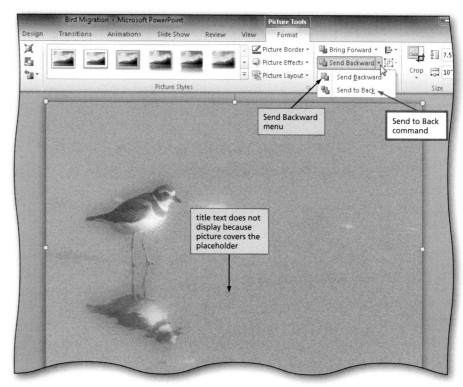

Figure 3–9

**2**

- Click Send to Back to move the picture underneath all slide objects (Figure 3–10).

Figure 3–10

**3**

- Display Slide 1, select the Birds in Sky picture, and then click the Send Backward button arrow (Picture Tools Format tab | Arrange group).

- Click Send to Back to move the picture underneath all slide objects (Figure 3–11).

Figure 3–11

| Other Ways |
|---|
| 1. Click Send to Back (Picture Tools Format tab \| Arrange group), press K    2. Point to Send to Back on shortcut menu, click Send to Back |

# Modifying Placeholders and Deleting a Slide

**BTW**

**BTWs**
For a complete list of the BTWs found in the margins of this book, visit the PowerPoint 2010 BTW Web page (scsite.com/ppt2010/btw).

You have become familiar with inserting text and graphical content in the three types of placeholders: title, subtitle, and content. These placeholders can be moved, resized, and deleted to meet desired design requirements. In addition, placeholders can be added to a slide when needed. After you have modified the placeholder locations, you can view thumbnails of all your slides simultaneously by changing views.

In the following pages, you will perform these tasks:

1. Resize and move the Slide 1 title text placeholder.
2. Delete the Slide 1 subtitle text placeholder.
3. Align the Slide 1 and Slide 3 paragraph text.
4. Delete Slide 4.
5. Change views.

## To Resize a Placeholder

The AutoFit button displays on the left side of the Slide 1 title text placeholder because the two lines of text exceed the placeholder's borders. PowerPoint attempts to reduce the font size when the text does not fit, and you can click this button to resize the existing text in the placeholder so the spillover text will fit within the borders. You also can resize the placeholder so that the letters fit within the rectangle. The following step increases the Slide 1 title text placeholder.

- With Slide 1 displaying, click somewhere in the title text paragraph to position the insertion point in the paragraph. Click the border of the title text placeholder to select it. Point to the bottom-middle sizing handle so that the mouse pointer changes to a two-headed arrow.

- Drag the bottom border downward to enlarge the text placeholder (Figure 3–12).

**Q&A** Can I drag other sizing handles to enlarge or shrink the placeholder?

Yes, you also can drag the left, right, top, and corner sizing handles to resize a placeholder.

**Q&A** How do the square sizing handles differ from circle sizing handles?

Dragging a square handle alters the shape of the text box so that it is wider or taller. Dragging a circle handle keeps the box in the same proportion and simply enlarges the overall shape.

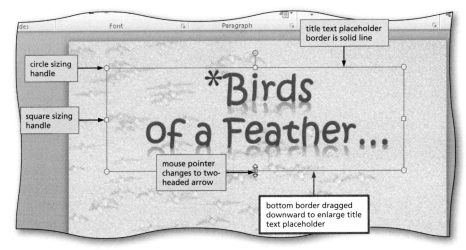

**Figure 3–12**

## To Move a Placeholder

The theme layouts determine where the text and content placeholders display on the slide. If you desire to have a placeholder appear in a different area of the slide, you can move it to a new location. The Slide 1 title text placeholder currently displays in the upper third of the slide, but the text in this placeholder would be more aesthetically pleasing if it were moved toward the center of the slide. The following step moves the Slide 1 title text placeholder.

**1**

- With the Slide 1 title text placeholder border displaying as a solid line, point to an area of the bottom border between two sizing handles so that the mouse pointer changes to a four-headed arrow.

**Q&A** What if the placeholder border displays as a dotted line?

Click the border to change the line from dotted to solid.

**Q&A** Can I click any part of the border, or do I need to click the bottom edge?

You can click any of the four border lines.

- Drag the placeholder downward so that it overlaps part of the subtitle text placeholder (Figure 3–13).

- Click to set the placeholder in its new location.

**Figure 3–13**

## To Delete a Placeholder

When you run a slide show, empty placeholders do not display. You may desire to delete unused placeholders from a slide so that they are not a distraction when you are designing slide content. The subtitle text placeholder on Slide 1 is not required for this presentation, so you can remove it. The following steps remove the Slide 1 subtitle text placeholder.

**1** Click a border of the subtitle text placeholder so that it displays as a solid line or fine dots (Figure 3–14).

**Q&A** What if the placeholder border is displaying as a dotted line?

Click the border to change the line from dotted to solid or fine dots.

**2** Press the DELETE key to remove the placeholder.

**Q&A** Can I click the Cut button (Home tab | Clipboard group) to delete the placeholder?

Yes. Clicking the Cut button deletes the placeholder if it does not contain any text.

**BTW**

**Reusing Placeholders**
If you need to show the same formatted placeholder on multiple slides, you may want to customize a slide master and insert a placeholder into a slide layout. Using a slide master saves you time because you do not need to type the same information in more than one slide. The slide master is useful when you have extremely long presentations. Every document theme has several slide masters that indicate the size and position of text and object placeholders. Any change you make to a slide master results in changing that component in every slide of the presentation.

**Figure 3–14**

| Plan Ahead | **Vary paragraph alignment.** |
|---|---|
|  | Designers use alignment within paragraphs to aid readability and to indicate relationships among slide elements. English language readers are accustomed to seeing paragraphs that are aligned left. When paragraphs are aligned right, the viewer's eyes are drawn to this unexpected text design. If your paragraph is short, consider centering or right-aligning the text for emphasis. |

## To Align Paragraph Text

The presentation theme determines the formatting characteristics of fonts and colors. It also establishes paragraph formatting, including the alignment of text. Some themes center the text paragraphs between the left and right placeholder borders, while others **left-align** the paragraph so that the first character of a text line is near the left border or **right-align** the paragraph so that the last character of a text line is near the right border. The paragraph also can be **justified** so that the text is aligned to both the left and right borders. When PowerPoint justifies text, it adds extras spaces between the words to fill the entire line.

The words, Birds of a Feather, are centered in the Slide 1 title text placeholder. Later, you will add clip art above the word, Feather, so you desire to left-align the paragraph to make room for this art. In addition, the words in the Slide 3 title text placeholder, Bird Migration, are covering the bird in the picture. You can right-align these words to uncover the bird in the lower-left corner. The following steps change the alignment of the Slide 1 and Slide 3 title placeholders.

- With the Home tab displayed, click somewhere in the title text paragraph of Slide 1 to position the insertion point in the paragraph to be formatted (Figure 3–15).

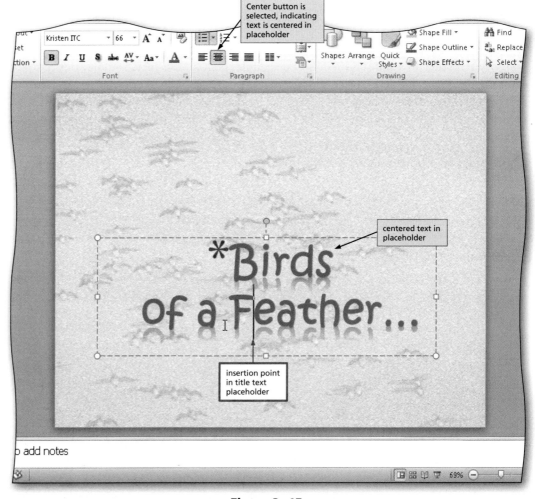

**Figure 3–15**

**2**

- Click the Align Text Left button (Home tab | Paragraph group) to left-align the paragraph (Figure 3–16).

**Q&A** What if I want to return the paragraph to center alignment?

Click the Center button (Home tab | Paragraph group).

**3**

- Display Slide 3. Click somewhere in the title text paragraph to position the insertion point in the paragraph to be formatted.

**4**

- Click the Align Text Right button (Home tab | Paragraph group) to right-align the paragraph.

**Figure 3–16**

**5**

- Move the Slide 3 title text placeholder downward so that it displays approximately as shown in Figure 3–17.

**Figure 3–17**

---

**Other Ways**

1. Right-click paragraph, click Align Text Right button on Mini toolbar

2. Right-click paragraph, click Paragraph on shortcut menu, click Indents and Spacing tab (Paragraph dialog box), click Alignment box arrow, click Right, click OK button

3. Click Paragraph Dialog Box Launcher (Home tab | Paragraph group), click Indents and Spacing tab (Paragraph dialog box), click Alignment box arrow, click Right, click OK button

4. Press CTRL+R

## To Delete a Slide

The Bird Migration presentation has a blank slide at the end. You decide that you will not use this slide, so you need to remove it from the file. The following steps delete Slide 4 from the presentation.

**1**

• Right-click the Slide 4 thumbnail in the Slides tab to display the shortcut menu (Figure 3–18).

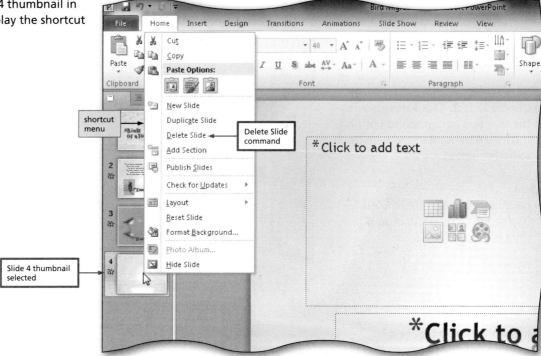

**Figure 3–18**

**2**

• Click Delete Slide to delete Slide 4 from the presentation (Figure 3–19).

**Figure 3–19**

**Q&A**

Can I delete multiple slides simultaneously?

Yes. If the slides are sequential, click the first slide you want to delete, press and hold the SHIFT key, click the last slide that you want to delete, right-click any selected slide, and then click Delete Slide on the shortcut menu. If the slides are not sequential, press and hold the CTRL key while you click each slide that you want to delete, right-click any selected slide, and then click Delete Slide on the shortcut menu.

# Changing Views

You have been using Normal view to create and edit your slides. Once you completed your slides, you reviewed the final products by displaying each slide in Slide Show view, which occupies the full computer screen. You were able to view how the transitions, graphics, and effects will display in an actual presentation before an audience.

PowerPoint has other views to help review a presentation for content, organization, and overall appearance. Slide Sorter view allows you to look at several slides at one time. Reading view is similar to Slide Show view because each slide displays individually, but the slides do not fill the entire screen. Using this view, you easily can control the progression through the slides forward or backward with simple controls at the bottom of the window. Switching between Slide Sorter view, Reading view, and Normal view helps you review your presentation, assess whether the slides have an attractive design and adequate content, and make sure they are organized for the most impact. After reviewing the slides, you can change the view to Normal so that you may continue working on the presentation.

## To Change Views

You have made several modifications to the slides, so you should check for balance and consistency. The following steps change the view from Normal view to Slide Sorter view, then Reading view, and back to Normal view.

**1**
- Click the Slide Sorter view button in the lower right of the PowerPoint window to display the presentation in Slide Sorter view (Figure 3–20).

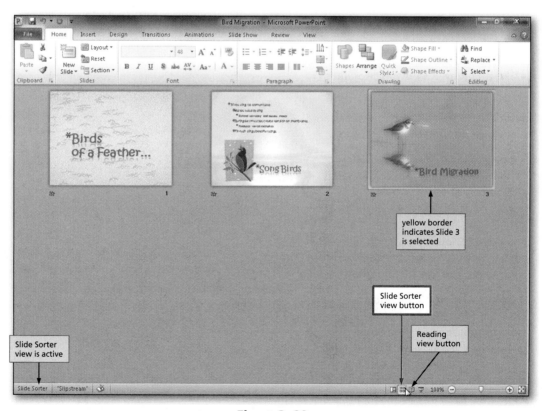

**Figure 3–20**

 Why is Slide 3 selected?

It is the current slide in the Slide pane.

- Click the Reading view button in the lower right of the PowerPoint window to display Slide 3 of the presentation in Reading view (Figure 3–21).

**Figure 3–21**

- Click the Previous button two times to display Slide 2 and then Slide 1.

- Click the Next button two times to advance through the presentation.

- Click the Menu button to display a menu of commonly used commands (Figure 3–22).

- Click End Show to return to Slide Sorter view, which is the view you were using before Reading view.

- Click the Normal view button to display the presentation in Normal view.

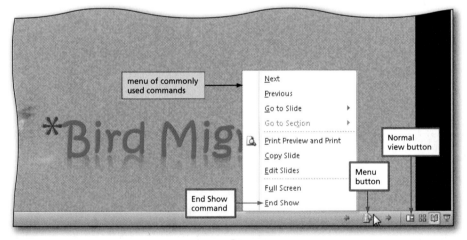

**Figure 3–22**

## Copying and Modifying a Clip

Slide 1 (shown in Figure 3–1a on PPT 139) contains a modified version of a songbird. You may want to modify a clip art picture for various reasons. Many times, you cannot find a clip art picture that precisely illustrates your topic. For example, you want a picture of a red sports car, but the only available clip art picture is painted black.

Occasionally, you may want to remove or change a portion of a clip art picture or you might want to combine two or more clip art pictures. For example, you can use one clip art picture for the background and another picture as the foreground. Other times, you may want to combine a clip art picture with another type of object. In this presentation, the bird picture has a yellow background that is not required to display on the slide, so you will ungroup the clip art picture and remove the background.

Modifying the clip on Slide 1 requires several steps. You first must copy it using the Office Clipboard and then paste it in the desired location. The **Office Clipboard** is a temporary storage location that can hold a maximum of 24 text or graphics items copied from any Office program. The same procedure of copying and pasting objects works for copying and pasting text from one placeholder to another. In the following pages, you will perform these tasks:

1. Copy the clip from Slide 2 to Slide 1.
2. Zoom Slide 1 to examine the clip.
3. Ungroup the clip.
4. Edit and change the clip colors.
5. Delete a clip object.
6. Regroup the clip.

## To Copy a Clip from One Slide to Another

The bird clip on Slide 2 also can display in a modified form on the title slide. The following steps copy this slide element from Slide 2 to Slide 1.

**1**

- Display Slide 2. With the Home tab displayed, click the bird clip to select it and then click the Copy button (Home tab | Clipboard group) (Figure 3–23).

**Q&A** Why are some words on Slide 2 underlined with red wavy lines?

Those words are not in PowerPoint's main or custom dictionaries, so PowerPoint indicates that they may be misspelled. For example, the word, Syringeal, is spelled correctly, but is not in PowerPoint's dictionaries.

**2**

- Display Slide 1 and then click the Paste button (Home tab | Clipboard group) to insert the bird clip into the title slide.

**Q&A** Is the clip deleted from the Office Clipboard when I paste it into the slide?

No.

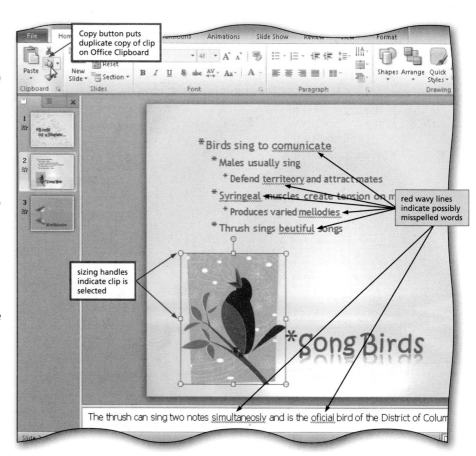

**Figure 3–23**

- Decrease the clip size by dragging one of the corner sizing handles inward until the clip is the size shown in Figure 3–24. Drag the clip to the location shown in this figure.

**Figure 3–24**

## To Zoom a Slide

You will be modifying small areas of the clip, so it will help you select the relevant pieces if the graphic is enlarged. The following step changes the zoom to 150 percent.

- Drag the Zoom slider to the right to change the zoom level to 150% (Figure 3–25).

**Other Ways**

1. Click Zoom button (View tab | Zoom group), change percentage in Percent text box (Zoom dialog box), click OK button

2. Click Zoom In button at end of slider

3. Click Zoom level on left side of slider, change percentage in Percent text box (Zoom dialog box), click OK button

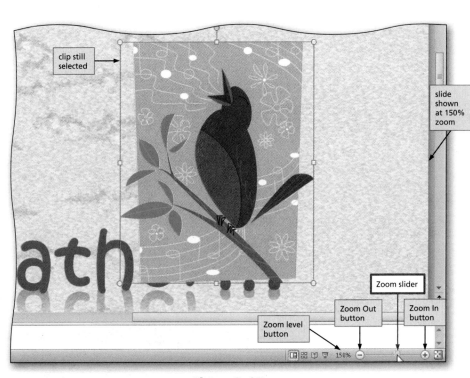

**Figure 3–25**

## To Ungroup a Clip

The next step is to ungroup the bird clip on Slide 1. When you **ungroup** a clip art picture, PowerPoint breaks it into its component objects. A clip may be composed of a few individual objects or several complex groups of objects. These groups can be ungrouped repeatedly until they decompose into individual objects. Because a clip art picture is a collection of complex groups of objects, you may need to ungroup a complex object into less complex objects before being able to modify a specific object. When you ungroup a clip and click the Yes button in the Microsoft PowerPoint dialog box, PowerPoint converts the clip to a PowerPoint object. The following steps ungroup a clip.

**1**

- With the bird clip selected, click Format on the Ribbon to display the Picture Tools Format tab.

- Click the Group button (Picture Tools Format tab | Arrange group) to display the Group menu (Figure 3–26).

Why does the Group button look different on my screen?

Your monitor is set to a different resolution. See Chapter 1 for an explanation of screen resolution and the appearance of the Ribbon.

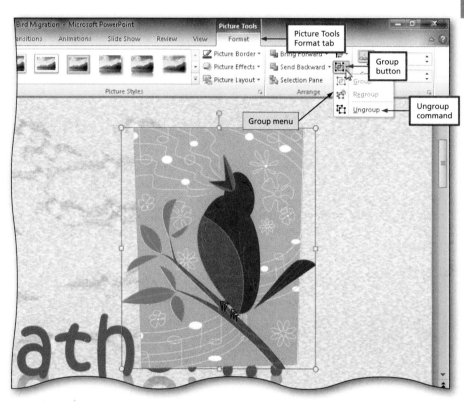

**Figure 3–26**

**2**

- Click Ungroup on the Group menu to display the Microsoft PowerPoint dialog box (Figure 3–27).

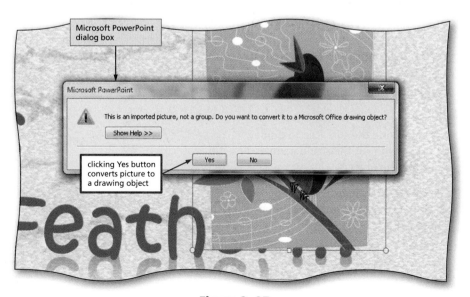

**Figure 3–27**

- Click the Yes button (Microsoft PowerPoint dialog box) to convert the clip to a Microsoft Office drawing.

**Q&A** What happens if I click the No button?

The clip will remain displayed on the slide as a clip art picture and will not ungroup.

- Click Format on the Ribbon to display the Drawing Tools Format tab. Click the Group button (Drawing Tools Format tab | Arrange group) and then click Ungroup again.

**Q&A** Why does the Drawing Tools Format tab show different options this time?

The clip has become a drawing object, so tools related to drawing now display.

- With the Drawing Tools Format tab displayed, click the Group button (Drawing Tools Format tab | Arrange group), and then click Ungroup a third time to display the objects that constitute the bird clip (Figure 3–28).

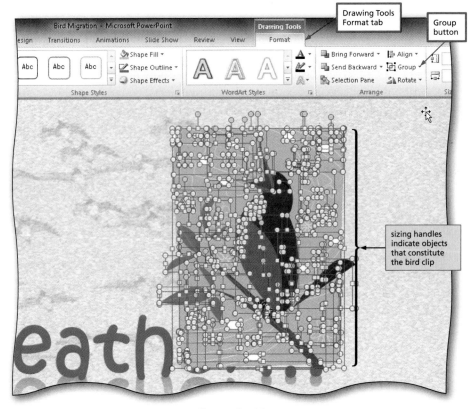

**Figure 3–28**

**Q&A** Why do all those circles and squares display in the clip?

The circles and squares are sizing handles for each of the clip's objects, which resemble pieces of a jigsaw puzzle.

**Other Ways**

1. Right-click clip, point to Group on shortcut menu, click Ungroup
2. Press SHIFT+CTRL+G

## To Change the Color of a Clip Object

Now that the bird picture is ungrouped, you can change the color of the objects. The clip is composed of hundreds of objects, so you must exercise care when selecting the correct object to modify. The following steps change the color of the bird's mouth and the leaves.

- Click outside the clip area to display the clip without the sizing handles around the objects.

- Click the bird's mouth to display sizing handles around the colored area (Figure 3–29).

**Q&A** What if I selected a different area by mistake?

Click outside the clip and retry.

**Figure 3–29**

**2**

- Click the Shape Fill button arrow (Drawing Tools Format tab | Shape Styles group) to display the Shape Fill gallery.

- Point to Yellow in the Standard Colors area (fourth color) to display a live preview of the mouth color (Figure 3–30).

 **Experiment**

- Point to various colors and watch the bird's mouth color change.

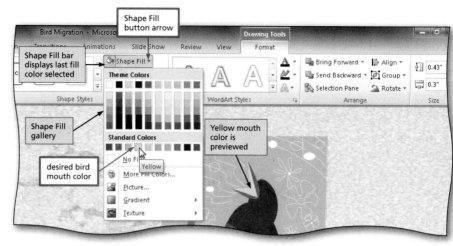

**Figure 3–30**

**3**

- Click the color Yellow to change the bird's mouth color.

**Q&A** Why is the bar under the Shape Fill button now yellow?

The button displays the last fill color selected.

- Click a leaf on the branch to display the sizing handles around the colored area (Figure 3–31).

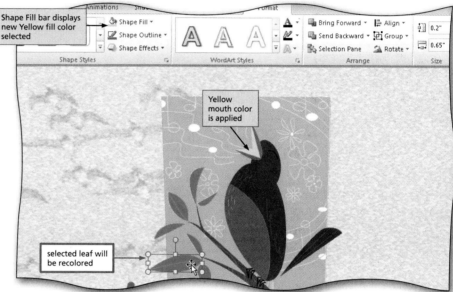

**Figure 3–31**

**4**

- Click the Shape Fill button arrow (Drawing Tools Format tab | Shape Styles group) and then point to Green, Accent 3 in the Theme Colors area (seventh color in first row) to display a live preview of the color of the selected leaf in the graphic (Figure 3–32).

 **Experiment**

- Point to various colors and watch the leaf color change.

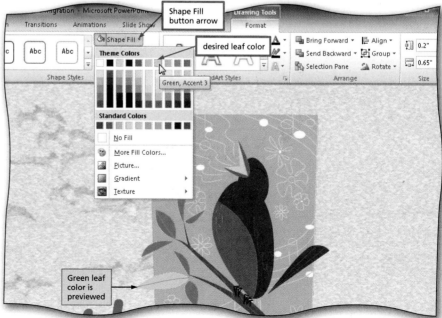

**Figure 3–32**

● Click the Green, Accent 3 color to change the leaf color.

● Click another leaf on the branch to select it.

● Click the Shape Fill button to change the leaf color to Green, Accent 3 (Figure 3–33).

**Q&A**

Why did I not need to click the Shape Fill button arrow to select this color?

PowerPoint uses the last fill color selected. This color displays in the bar under the bucket icon on the button.

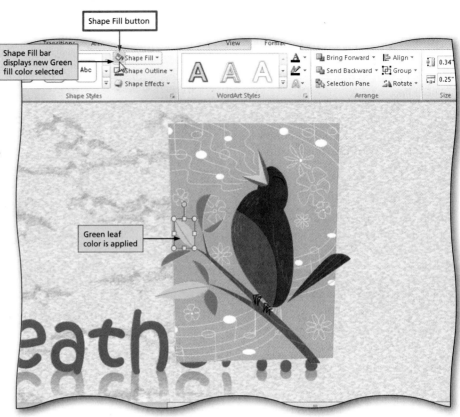

**Figure 3–33**

● Repeat Step 6 until all the leaves have been recolored (Figure 3–34).

**Q&A**

Can I open the Microsoft Clip Organizer when I am not using PowerPoint?

Yes. On the Start menu, point to All Programs, point to Microsoft Office, point to Microsoft Office 2010 Tools, and then click Microsoft Clip Organizer.

**Other Ways**

1. Right-click object, click Format Shape on shortcut menu, click Color button

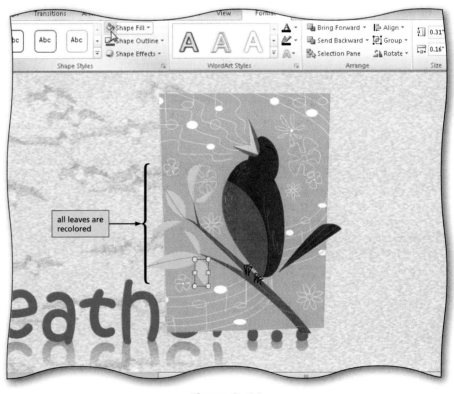

**Figure 3–34**

## To Delete a Clip Object

With the bird mouth and leaf colors changed, you want to delete the gold background object. The following steps delete this object.

**1**

• Click the background in any area where the gold color displays to select this object (Figure 3–35).

 Can I select multiple objects so I can delete them simultaneously?

Yes. While pressing the SHIFT key, click the unwanted elements to select them.

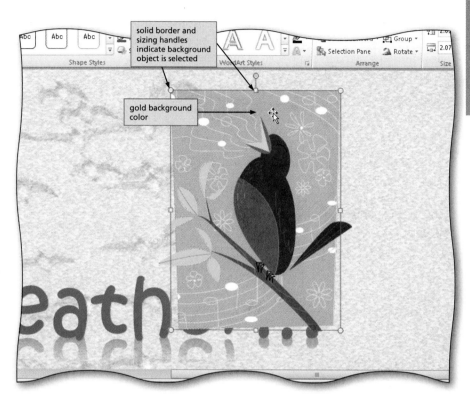

**Figure 3–35**

**2**

• Press the DELETE key to delete this object (Figure 3–36).

 Should the white musical staff display on the slide?

Yes. It is part of the bird clip.

**Figure 3–36**

## To Regroup Objects

When you ungrouped the bird clip, you eliminated the embedding data or linking information that tied all the individual pieces together. If you attempt to move or size this clip now, you might encounter difficulties because it consists of hundreds of objects and is no longer one unified piece. Dragging or sizing affects only a selected object, not the entire collection of objects, so you must use caution when objects are not completely regrouped. All of the ungrouped objects in the bird clip must be regrouped so they are not accidentally moved or manipulated. The following steps regroup these objects into one object.

- With the clip selected, click the Drawing Tools Format tab and then click the Group button (Drawing Tools Format tab | Arrange group) to display the Group menu (Figure 3–37).

- Click Regroup to combine all the objects.

- Use the Zoom slider to change the zoom level to 69%.

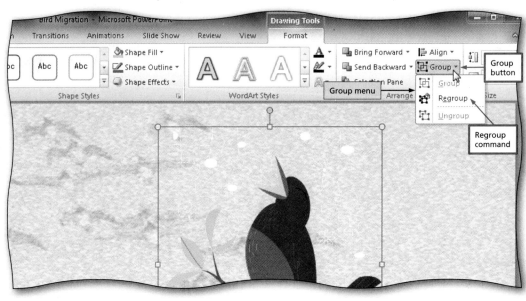

**Figure 3–37**

| Other Ways |
| --- |
| 1. Right-click clip, point to Group on shortcut menu, click Regroup |
| 2. Press CTRL+G |

Plan Ahead

**Use multimedia selectively.**
PowerPoint makes it easy to insert multimedia into a presentation. Well-produced video clips add value when they help explain a procedure or show movement that cannot be captured in a photograph. Music can help calm or energize an audience, when appropriate. A sound, such as applause when a correct answer is given, can emphasize an action. Before you insert these files on a slide, however, consider whether they really add any value to your overall slide show. If you are inserting them just because you can, you might want to reconsider your decision. Audiences quickly tire of extraneous sounds and movement on slides, and they will find these media clips annoying. Keep in mind that the audience's attention should focus primarily on the presenter; extraneous or inappropriate media files may divert their attention and, in turn, decrease the quality of the presentation.

**Break Point:** If you wish to take a break, this is a good place to do so. Be sure to save the Bird Migration file again and then you can quit PowerPoint. To resume at a later time, start PowerPoint, open the file called Bird Migration, and continue following the steps from this location forward.

# Adding Media to Slides

Media files can enrich a presentation if they are used correctly. Movies files can have two formats: digital video produced with a camera and editing software or animated GIF (Graphics Interchange Format) files composed of multiple images combined into a single file. Sound files can be from the Microsoft Clip Organizer, files stored on your computer, or an audio track on a CD. To hear the sounds, you need a sound card and speakers on your system.

In the following pages, you will perform these tasks:

1. Insert a video file into Slide 3.
2. Trim the video file so only the final few seconds play.
3. Add video options that determine the clip's appearance and playback.
4. Insert audio files.
5. Add audio options that determine the clips' appearance and playback.
6. Add a video style to the Slide 3 clip.
7. Resize the video.
8. Insert a movie clip into Slide 1.

## To Insert a Video File

Slide 3 has the title, Bird Migration, and you have a video clip that is composed of many scenes featuring various animals and birds. A short segment of this clip shows a flock of birds on a beach, and you want to use only this part of the clip in your presentation. PowerPoint allows you to insert this clip into your slide and then trim the file so that just a portion will play when you preview the clip or run the slide show. This clip is available on the Data Files for Students. See the inside back cover of this book for instructions on downloading the Data Files for Students, or contact your instructor for more information about accessing the required file. The following steps insert this video clip into Slide 3.

• Display Slide 3 and then display the Insert tab. With your USB flash drive connected to one of the computer's USB ports, click the Insert Video button (Insert tab | Media group) to display the Insert Video dialog box.

• If the list of files and folders on the selected USB flash drive are not displayed in the Insert Video dialog box, double-click your USB flash drive to display them.

• Click Wildlife to select the file (Figure 3–38).

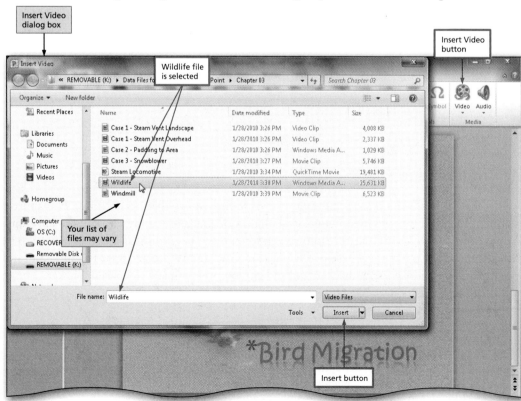

**Figure 3–38**

**2**
- Click the Insert button (Insert Video dialog box) to insert the movie clip into Slide 3 (Figure 3–39).

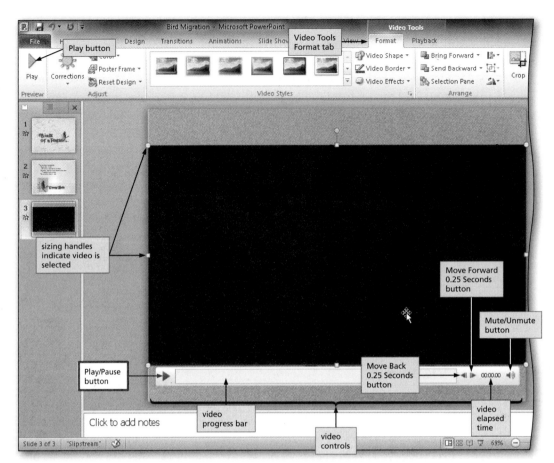

**Figure 3–39**

**Q&A**

Can I adjust the color of a video clip?

Yes. You correct the brightness and contrast, and you also recolor a video clip using the same methods you learned in this chapter to color a picture.

## To Trim a Video File

The Wildlife video has a running time of slightly more than 30 seconds. The approximately six-second segment that you want to use in your presentation begins 24 seconds into the file and finishes at the end of the clip. PowerPoint's **Trim Video** feature allows you to trim the beginning and end of your clip by designating your desired Start Time and End Time. These precise time measurements are accurate to one-thousandth of a second. The start point is indicated by a green marker, and the end point is indicated by a red marker. The following steps trim the Wildlife video clip.

**BTW**

**Using Codecs**

Digital media file sizes often are quite large, so video and audio content developers use a codec (**co**mpressor/**dec**ompressor) to reduce the required storage space and to transfer the files across the Internet quickly and smoothly. Your computer can play any compressed file if the specific codec used to compress the file is available on your computer. If the codec is not installed or is not recognized, your computer attempts to download this file from the Internet. Microsoft Windows Media Encoder is a free program that makes some media files compatible with PowerPoint.

**1**

• With the video clip selected on Slide 3, click the Play/Pause button to play the entire video.

**Q&A** Can I play the video by clicking the Play button in the Preview group?

Yes. This Play button plays the entire clip. You may prefer to click the Play/Pause button displayed in the Video Controls to stop the video and examine one of the frames.

• Click Playback on the Ribbon to display the Video Tools Playback tab. Click the Trim Video button (Editing group) to display the Trim Video dialog box (Figure 3–40).

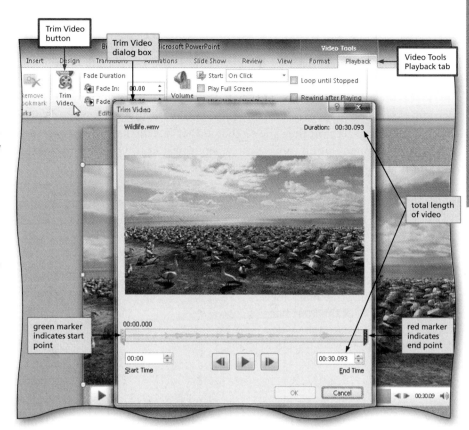

**Figure 3–40**

**2**

• Point to the start point, which is indicated by the green marker on the left side, so that the mouse pointer changes to a two-headed arrow.

• Drag the green marker to the right until the Start Time is 00:24:634 (Figure 3–41).

**Q&A** Can I specify the start or end times without dragging the markers?

Yes. You can enter the time in the Start Time or End Time boxes, or you can click the Start Time or End Time box arrows. You also can click the Next Frame and Previous Frame buttons (Trim Video dialog box).

**Q&A** How would I indicate an end point if I want the clip to end at a time other than at the end of the clip?

You would drag the red marker to the left until the desired end time displays.

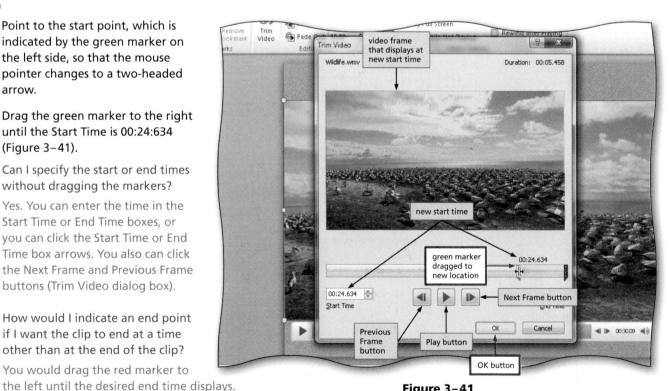

**Figure 3–41**

**3**

• Click the Play button (Trim Video dialog box) to review the shortened video clip.

• Click the OK button to set the Start Time and End Time and to close the Trim Video dialog box.

**Other Ways**

1. Right-click clip, click Trim Video on shortcut menu

## To Add Video Options

Once the video clip is inserted into Slide 3, you can specify options that affect how the file is displayed and played. For example, you can have the video play automatically when the slide is displayed, or you can click the slide when you are ready to start the playback. You also can have the video fill the entire slide, which is referred to as **full screen**. If you decide to play the slide show automatically and have it display full screen, you can drag the video frame to the gray area off the slide so that it does not display briefly before going to full screen. You can select the Loop until Stopped option to have the video repeat until you click the next slide, or you can choose to not have the video frame display on the slide until you click the slide.

If your video clip has recorded sounds, the volume controls give you the option to set how loudly this audio will play. They also allow you to mute the sound so that your audience will hear no background noise or music.

The following steps add the options of playing the video full screen automatically when Slide 3 is displayed and also mutes the background music recorded on the video clip.

● If necessary, click Playback on the Ribbon to display the Video Tools Playback tab. Click the Start box (Video Tools Playback tab | Video Options group) to view the Start menu (Figure 3–42).

**Q&A**

What does the On Click option do?

The video clip would begin playing when a presenter clicks the slide during the slide show.

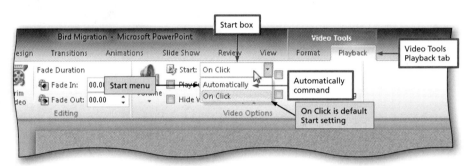

**Figure 3–42**

● Click Automatically in the Start menu (Figure 3–43).

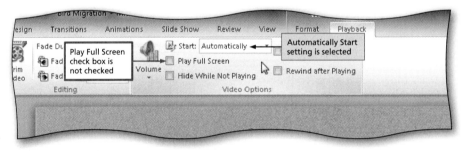

**Figure 3–43**

● Click the Play Full Screen check box (Video Tools Playback tab | Video Options group) to place a check mark in it.

● Click the Volume button (Video Tools Playback tab | Video Options group) to display the Volume menu (Figure 3–44).

● Click Mute in the Volume menu.

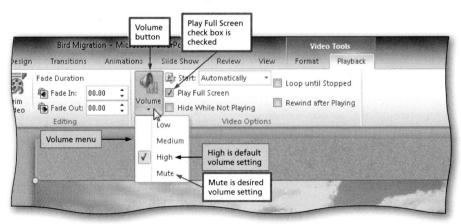

**Figure 3–44**

## To Insert an Audio File

Avid bird watchers listen to the songs and calls birds make to each other. The Microsoft Clip Organizer and Office.com have several of these sounds in audio files that you can download and insert into your presentation. Once these audio files are inserted into a slide, you can add options that specify how long and how loudly the clip will play; these options are similar to the video options you just selected for the Wildlife video clip. The following steps insert an audio clip into Slide 3.

**1**

- With Slide 3 displaying, click Insert on the Ribbon to display the Insert tab and then click the Insert Audio button arrow (Insert tab | Media group) to display the Insert Audio menu (Figure 3–45).

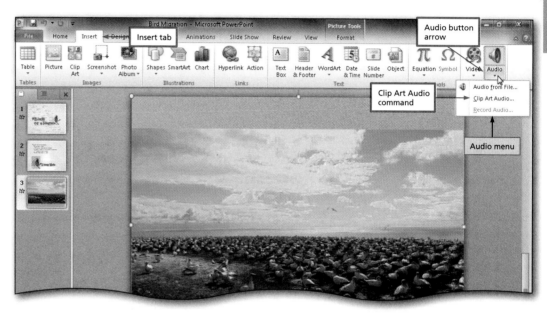

**Figure 3–45**

**2**

- Click Clip Art Audio in the Insert Audio menu to open the Clip Art task pane.

- Click the 'Results should be' box arrow and then click the 'All media types' check box to remove the check mark from each of the four types of media files.

- Click the Audio check box to place a check mark in it (Figure 3–46).

**Q&A**
Can I use this technique to search solely for videos, photographs, or illustrations?

Yes. You also can search for a combination of these file types, such as both video and audio files.

**Figure 3–46**

- If necessary, delete any letters that are present in the Search for text box and then type **Glade Birds** in the Search for text box. If necessary, click the 'Include Office.com content' check box to select it.

- Click the Go button so that the Microsoft Clip Organizer will search for and display all clips having the keyword or title, Glade Birds.

**4**

- Point to the Glade Birds clip to display the properties of this file (Figure 3–47).

**Q&A** What if the Glade Birds audio clip is not shown in my Clip Art task pane?

Select a similar clip. Your clips may be different depending on the clips installed on your computer and if you have an active Internet connection.

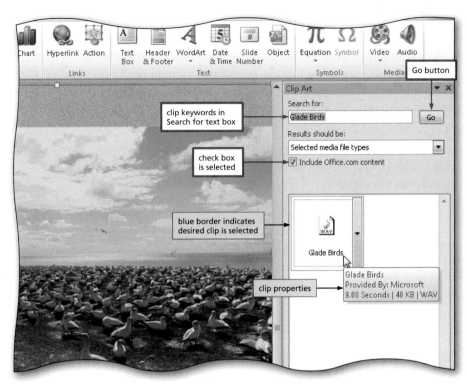

**Figure 3–47**

**Q&A** What are the properties associated with this clip?

The properties include the number of seconds of playing time, the file size, and the type of audio file. This file is a **Windows waveform (.wav)** file, which uses a standard format to encode and communicate music and sound between computers, music synthesizers, and instruments.

**5**

- Right-click the Glade Birds clip to select the clip and to display the Edit menu (Figure 3–48).

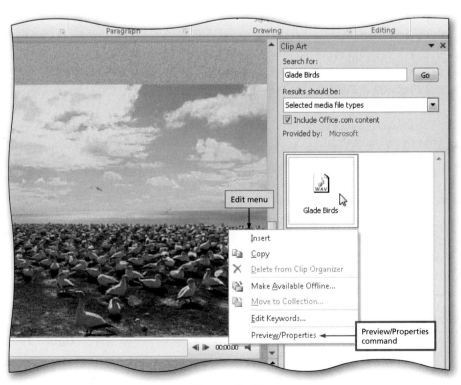

**Figure 3–48**

**6**

• Click Preview/
Properties to display
the Preview/Properties
dialog box and to hear
the clip (Figure 3–49).

**Q&A** What are the
words listed in the
Keywords box?

Those words are the
search terms associated
with the file. If you
enter any of those
words in the Search for
text box, this audio file
would display in the
results list.

**Q&A** Can I preview the clip
again?

Yes. Click the Play
button in the Preview/
Properties dialog box.

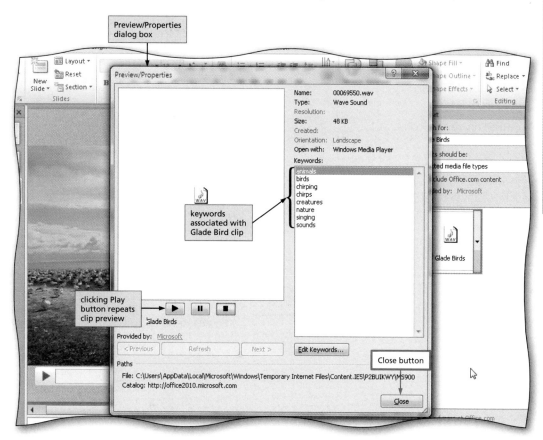

Figure 3–49

**7**

• Click the Close button
(Preview/Properties
dialog box) to close
the dialog box.

• Click Glade Birds in
the results list (Clip Art
task pane) to insert
that file into Slide 3
(Figure 3–50).

**Q&A** Why does a sound icon
display in the video?

The icon indicates an
audio file is inserted.

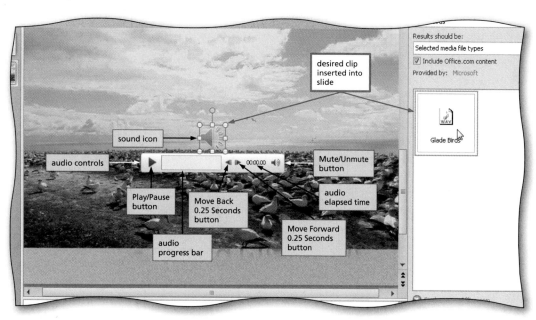

Figure 3–50

**Q&A** Do the Audio Controls buttons have the same functions as the Video Controls buttons that
displayed when I inserted the Wildlife clip?

Yes. The controls include playing and pausing the sound, moving back or forward 0.25
seconds, audio progress, elapsed time, and muting or unmuting the sound.

• Drag the sound icon to the upper-left corner of the slide (Figure 3–51).

**Q&A** Must I move the icon on the slide?

No. Although your audience will not see the icon when you run the slide show, it is easier for you to see the media elements when they are separated on the slide rather than stacked on top of each other.

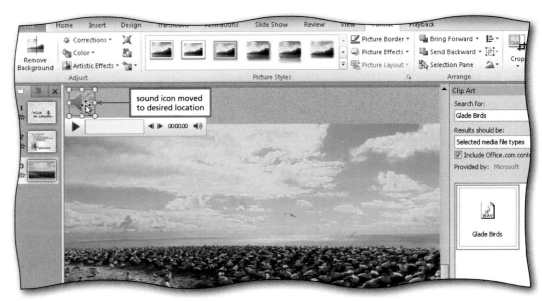

**Figure 3–51**

## To Add Audio Options

Once an audio clip is inserted into a slide, you can specify options that control playback and appearance. As with the video options you applied to the Wildlife clip, the audio clip can play either automatically or when clicked, it can repeat the clip while a particular slide is displayed, and you can drag the sound icon off the slide and set the volume.

The following steps add the options of starting automatically and playing until the slide no longer is displayed, hiding the sound icon on the slide, and increasing the volume.

• Click Playback on the Ribbon to display the Audio Tools Playback tab. Click the Start box (Audio Tools Playback tab | Audio Options group) to display the Start box menu (Figure 3–52).

**2**

• Click Automatically in the Start menu.

**Q&A** Does the On Click option function the same way for an audio clip as On Click does for a video clip?

Yes. If you were to select On Click, the sound would begin playing only after the presenter clicks Slide 1 during a presentation.

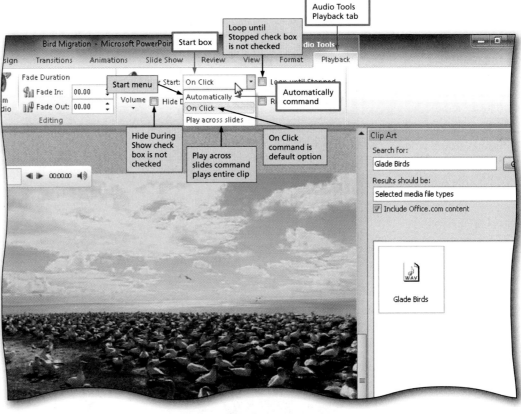

**Figure 3–52**

**3**

- Click the Loop until Stopped check box (Audio Tools Playback tab | Audio Options group) to place a check mark in it.

 **What is the difference between the Loop until Stopped option and the Play across slides option?**

The audio clip in the Loop until Stopped option repeats for as long as one slide is displayed. In contrast, the Play across slides option clip would play only once, but it would continue to play while other slides in the presentation are displayed. Once the end of the clip is reached, the sound would end and not repeat.

**4**

- Click the Hide During Show check box (Video Tools Playback tab | Audio Options group) to place a check mark in it (Figure 3–53).

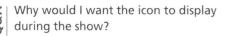 **Why would I want the icon to display during the show?**

If you had selected the On Click start option, you would need to find this icon on the slide and click it to start playing the clip.

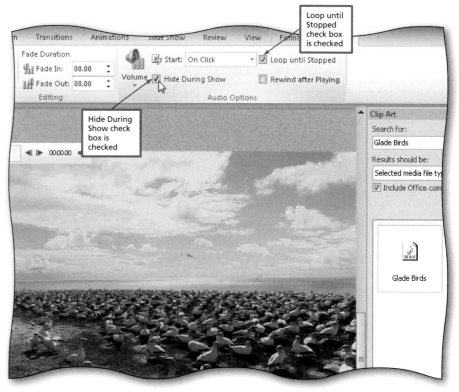

**Figure 3–53**

## To Insert an Additional Audio File and Set Options

Having an audio clip play when Slide 1 is displayed would add interest and help set the tone of the presentation. Only one bird appears on that slide, and it appears to be singing heartily. A single bird singing would coordinate nicely with this clip art image. The following steps insert a songbird audio clip into Slide 1 and set playback options.

**1** Display Slide 1, delete any letters that are present in the Search for text box, and then type **Birds at dawn** in the Search for text box (Clip Art task pane), and search for this audio clip.

**2** Insert the Birds at dawn clip into Slide 1 and then drag the sound icon to the lower-left corner of the slide.

**3** Close the Clip Art task pane.

**4** Display the Audio Tools Playback tab. Click the Start box (Audio Tools Playback tab | Audio Options group) and then click Automatically in the Start menu.

**5** Click the Loop until Stopped check box (Audio Tools Playback tab | Audio Options group) to place a check mark in it.

**BTW**

**Playing Audio Continuously**
You can play one audio file throughout an entire presentation instead of only when one individual slide is displayed. When you select the 'Play across slides' option in the Start box (Audio Tools Playback tab | Audio Options group), the audio clip will play continuously as you advance through the slides in your presentation. If you select this option, be certain the length of the clip exceeds the total time you will display all slides in your slide show.

**6** Click the Hide During Show check box (Audio Tools Playback tab | Audio Options group).

**7** Click the Volume button (Audio Tools Playback tab | Audio Options group) and then change the volume to Medium (Figure 3–54).

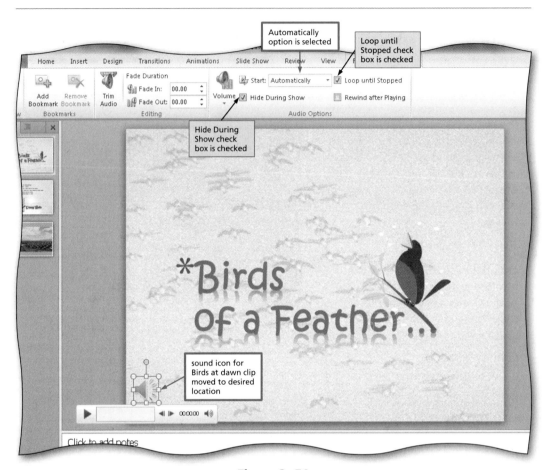

**Figure 3–54**

## To Add a Video Style

The Wildlife video clip on Slide 3 displays full screen when it is playing, but you can increase the visual appeal of the clip when it is not playing by applying a video style. The video styles are similar to the picture styles you applied in Chapter 2 and include various shapes, angles, borders, and reflections. The following steps apply a video style to the Wildlife clip on Slide 3.

**1**

• Display Slide 3 and select the video. Click Format on the Ribbon to display the Video Tools Format tab (Figure 3–55).

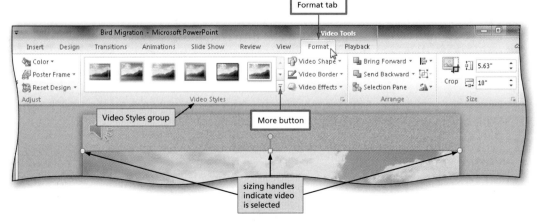

**Figure 3–55**

**2**

- With the video selected, click the More button in the Video Styles gallery (Video Tools Format tab | Video Styles group) (shown in Figure 3–55) to expand the gallery.

- Point to Bevel Perspective in the Intense area of the Video Styles gallery to display a live preview of that style applied to the video on the slide (Figure 3–56).

 **Experiment**

- Point to various picture styles in the Video Styles gallery and watch the style of the video frame change in the document window.

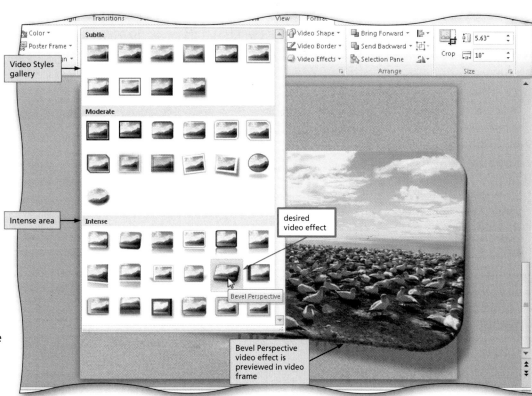

**Figure 3–56**

**3**

- Click Bevel Perspective in the Video Styles gallery to apply the style to the selected video (Figure 3–57).

**Q&A** Can I preview the movie clip?

Yes. Point to the clip and then click the Play/Pause button on the Video Controls below the video.

**Q&A** Can I add a border to a video style?

Yes. You add a border using the same method you learned in Chapter 2 to add a border to a picture. Click the Video Border button (Video Tools Format tab | Video Styles gallery) and then select a border line weight and color.

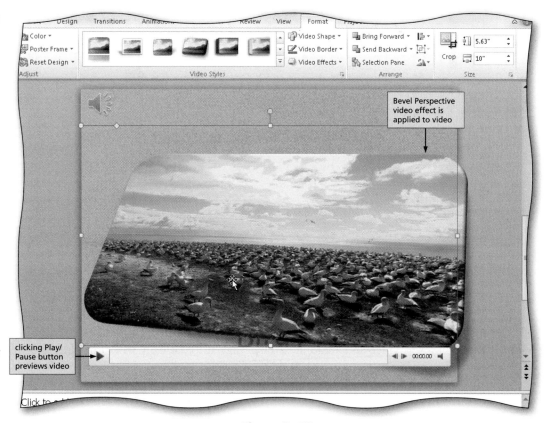

**Figure 3–57**

## To Resize a Video

The Wildlife video size can be decreased to fill the space on the right side of the slide. You resize a video clip in the same manner that you resize clip art and pictures. The following steps resize this video using a sizing handle.

- With the video clip selected, drag the lower-left corner sizing handle on the photograph diagonally inward until the photograph is resized to approximately 3.9″ × 6.93″.

- Drag the clip to the location shown in Figure 3–58.

**Figure 3–58**

## To Insert a Movie Clip

PowerPoint classifies animated GIF files as a type of video or movie because the clips have movement or action. These files are commonplace on Web sites. They also are found in PowerPoint presentations when you want to call attention to material on a particular slide. You can insert them into a PowerPoint presentation in the same manner that you insert video and audio files. They play automatically when the slide is displayed. The following steps insert a music notes video clip into Slide 1.

**1**

- Display Slide 1 and then display the Insert tab.

- Click the Picture button (Insert tab | Images group) to display the Insert Picture dialog box.

- If necessary, navigate to the Chapter 3 files on your USB drive.

- Click Music Notes to select the file (Figure 3–59).

**Q&A** Why does my list of files look different?

The list of picture files can vary depending upon the contents of your USB drive and the organization of those files into folders for each chapter.

**Q&A** Can I search for animated GIF files in the Microsoft Clip Organizer?

Yes. Click the Video button arrow (Insert tab | Media group), click Clip Art Video, click the Videos check box (Clip Art task pane), type the search text, and then click the Go button.

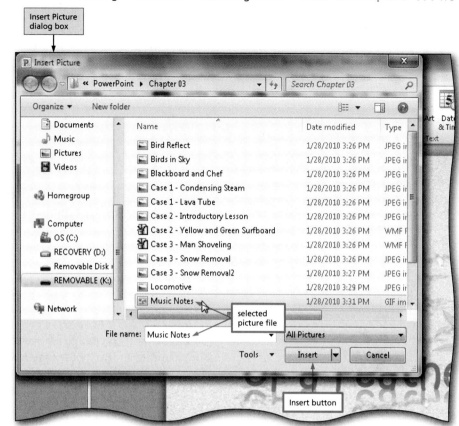

**Figure 3–59**

**2**

- Click the Insert button (Insert Picture dialog box) to insert the Music Notes animated GIF clip into Slide 1.

- Resize the clip so that it is approximately 1" × 1.47".

- Drag the clip to the location shown in Figure 3–60.

**Q&A** Why is the animation not showing?

Animated GIF files move only in Slide Show view and Reading view.

**Figure 3–60**

**Break Point:** If you wish to take a break, this is a good place to do so. Be sure to save the Bird Migration file again and then you can quit PowerPoint. To resume at a later time, start PowerPoint, open the file called Bird Migration, and continue following the steps from this location forward.

**BTW**

**Revising Your Text**
Generating ideas, revising slides, editing graphics and text, and then proofreading all slide text are required as part of the development process. A good PowerPoint developer has the ability to write and then revise slide content. Multiple drafts generally are needed to complete a successful presentation. PowerPoint's Find and Replace feature is useful if you need to change all instances of a word throughout a large presentation when you are revising slides.

# Reviewing and Revising Individual Slides

The text and graphics for all slides in the Bird Migration presentation have been entered. Once you complete a slide show, you might decide to change elements. PowerPoint provides several tools to assist you with making changes. They include finding and replacing text, inserting a synonym, and checking spelling. The following pages discuss these tools.

## Replace Dialog Box

At times, you might want to change all occurrences of a word or phrase to another word or phrase. For example, an instructor may have one slide show to accompany a lecture for several introductory classes, and he wants to update slides with the particular class name and section that appear on several slides. He manually could change the characters, but PowerPoint includes an efficient method of replacing one word with another. The Find and Replace feature automatically locates specific text and then replaces it with desired text.

In some cases, you may want to replace only certain occurrences of a word or phrase, not all of them. To instruct PowerPoint to confirm each change, click the Find Next button in the Replace dialog box instead of the Replace All button. When PowerPoint locates an occurrence of the text, it pauses and waits for you to click either the Replace button or the Find Next button. Clicking the Replace button changes the text; clicking the Find Next button instructs PowerPoint to disregard that particular instance and look for the next occurrence of the Find what text.

## To Find and Replace Text

While reviewing your slides, you realize that you could give more specific information regarding the type of thrush discussed in Slide 2. The Wood Thrush's songs especially are melodic and beautiful, so you decide to add the word, Wood, to the bird's name. In addition, you want to capitalize the word, Thrush, because it is a specific type of thrush. To perform this action, you can use PowerPoint's Find and Replace feature, which automatically locates each occurrence of a word or phrase and then replaces it with specified text. The word, thrush, displays twice on Slide 2. The following steps use Find and Replace to replace all occurrences of the word, thrush, with the words, Wood Thrush.

**BTW**

**Matching Case and Finding Whole Words**
Two options in the Replace dialog box are useful when revising slides. Match case maintains the upper- or lowercase letters within a word, such as a capitalized word at the beginning of a sentence. In addition, the 'Find whole words only' option specifies that PowerPoint makes replacements only when the word typed in the Find what box is a complete word and is not embedded within another word. For example, if you want to change the word 'diction' to 'pronunciation,' clicking the 'Find whole words only' option prevents PowerPoint from changing the word, dictionary, to 'pronunciationary.'

**1**

- Display the Home tab and then display Slide 2. Click the Replace button (Home tab | Editing group) to display the Replace dialog box.

- Type **thrush** in the Find what text box (Replace dialog box).

- Press the TAB key. Type **Wood Thrush** in the Replace with text box (Figure 3–61).

 Do I need to display the slide that contains the words for which I want to search?

No. But to allow you to see the results of this search and replace action, you can display the slide where the changes will occur.

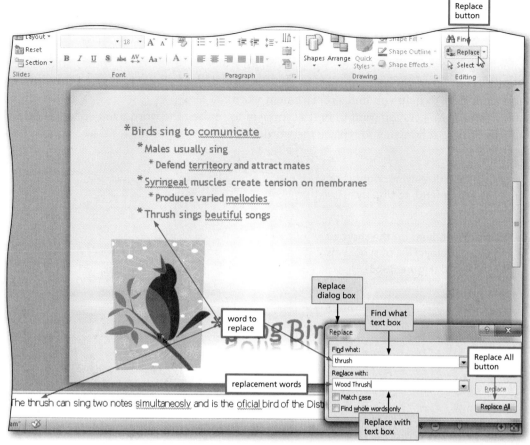

Figure 3–61

**2**

- Click the Replace All button (Replace dialog box) to instruct PowerPoint to replace all occurrences of the Find what word, thrush, with the Replace with words, Wood Thrush (Figure 3–62).

 If I accidentally replaced the wrong text, can I undo this replacement?

Yes. Click the Undo button on the Quick Access Toolbar to undo all replacements. If you had clicked the Replace button instead of the Replace All button, PowerPoint would undo only the most recent replacement.

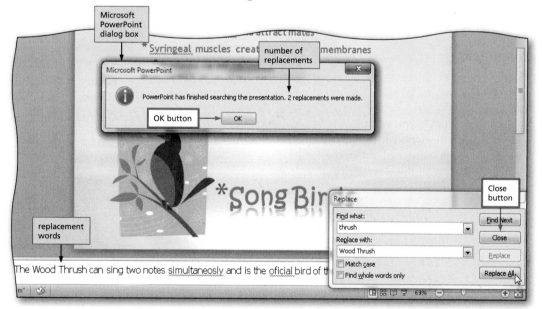

Figure 3–62

**3**

- Click the OK button (Microsoft PowerPoint dialog box).

- Click the Close button (Replace dialog box).

| Other Ways |
|---|
| 1. Press CTRL+H |

## To Find and Insert a Synonym

When reviewing your slide show, you may decide that a particular word does not express the exact usage you intended or that you used the same word on multiple slides. In these cases, you could find a **synonym**, or word similar in meaning, to replace the inappropriate or duplicate word. PowerPoint provides a **thesaurus**, which is a list of synonyms and antonyms, to help you find a replacement word.

In this project, you want to find a synonym to replace the word, Defend, on Slide 2. The following steps locate an appropriate synonym and replace the word.

**1**

- With Slide 2 displaying, right-click the word, Defend, to display a shortcut menu.

- Point to Synonyms on the shortcut menu to display a list of synonyms for this word (Figure 3–63).

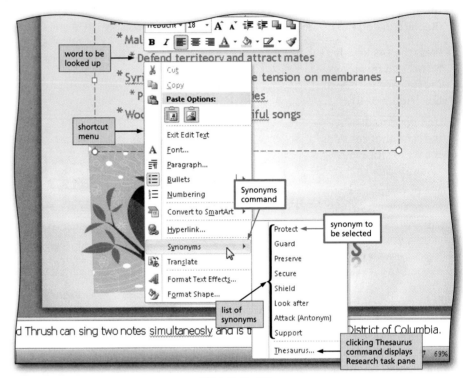

**Figure 3–63**

**2**

- Click the synonym you want (Protect) on the Synonyms submenu to replace the word, Defend, in the presentation with the word, Protect (Figure 3–64).

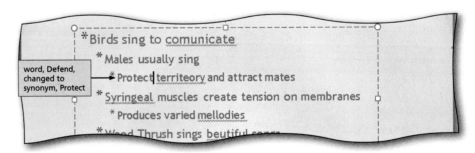

**Figure 3–64**

**Q&A** What if a suitable word does not display in the Synonyms submenu?

You can display the thesaurus in the Research task pane by clicking Thesaurus on the Synonyms submenu. A complete thesaurus with synonyms displays in the Research task pane along with an **antonym**, which is a word with an opposite meaning.

**BTW**

**Foreign Language Synonyms**
The thesaurus contains synonyms for languages other than English. To look up words in the thesaurus of another language, click the Thesaurus button (Review tab | Proofing group), click Research options (Research task pane), select the desired languages in the Reference Books area, and then click the OK button.

**Other Ways**

1. Click Thesaurus (Review tab | Proofing group)
2. Press SHIFT+F7

## To Add Notes

As you create slides, you may find material you want to state verbally and do not want to include on the slide. You can type and format notes in the **Notes pane** as you work in Normal view and then print this information as **notes pages**. After adding comments, you can print a set of speaker notes. These notes will print below a small image of the slide. Charts, tables, and pictures added to the Notes pane also print on these pages. In this project, comments were included on Slide 2 when you opened that file. The following steps add text to the Notes pane on Slides 1 and 3.

**1**

- Display Slide 1, click the Notes pane, and then type **More than 10,000 species of birds exist in the world. The largest bird is the ostrich, and the smallest is the hummingbird. They generally live in small groups, but some form huge flocks with thousands of members and a variety of species. Flocks help keep the birds safe while they search for food.** (Figure 3–65).

**Figure 3–65**

**Q&A**

What if I cannot see all the lines I typed?

You can drag the splitter bar up to enlarge the Notes pane. Clicking the Notes pane scroll arrows allows you to view the entire text.

**2**

- Display Slide 3, click the Notes pane, and then type **Birds migrate to benefit from warm weather. Some can fly more than 6,000 miles without stopping. We can help bird migration by providing food, shelters, nest sites, and water.** (Figure 3–66).

**Figure 3–66**

**BTW**

**Using AutoCorrect Features**
Microsoft Office programs use the AutoCorrect feature to correct typing mistakes and commonly misspelled words. When you install Microsoft Office, a default list of typical misspellings is created. You can modify the AutoCorrect list with words you are apt to misspell. The first column of this list contains the word that you often mistype, and the second column contains the replacement text. The AutoCorrect feature also inserts symbols, such as replacing (c) with the copyright symbol, ©.

# Checking Spelling

After you create a presentation, you should check it visually for spelling errors and style consistency. In addition, you use PowerPoint's Spelling tool to identify possible misspellings on the slides and in the notes. Do not rely on the spelling checker to catch all your mistakes. Although PowerPoint's spelling checker is a valuable tool, it is not infallible. You should proofread your presentation carefully by pointing to each word and saying it aloud as you point to it. Be mindful of commonly misused words such as its and it's, through and though, and to and too.

PowerPoint checks the entire presentation for spelling mistakes using a standard dictionary contained in the Microsoft Office group. This dictionary is shared with the other Microsoft Office applications such as Word and Excel. A **custom dictionary** is available if you want to add special words such as proper names, cities, and acronyms. When checking a presentation for spelling errors, PowerPoint opens the standard dictionary and the custom dictionary file, if one exists. When a word appears in the Spelling dialog box, you can perform one of several actions, as described in Table 3–1.

**Table 3–1 Spelling Dialog Box Buttons and Actions**

| Button Name | When To Use | Action |
|---|---|---|
| Ignore | Word is spelled correctly but not found in dictionaries | PowerPoint continues checking rest of the presentation but will flag that word again if it appears later in document. |
| Ignore All | Word is spelled correctly but not found in dictionaries | PowerPoint ignores all occurrences of the word and continues checking rest of presentation. |
| Change | Word is misspelled | Click proper spelling of the word in Suggestions list. PowerPoint corrects word, continues checking rest of presentation, but will flag that word again if it appears later in document. |
| Change All | Word is misspelled | Click proper spelling of word in Suggestions list. PowerPoint changes all occurrences of misspelled word and continues checking rest of presentation. |
| Add | Add word to custom dictionary | PowerPoint opens custom dictionary, adds word, and continues checking rest of presentation. |
| Suggest | Correct spelling is uncertain | Lists alternative spellings. Click the correct word from the Suggestions box or type the proper spelling. Corrects the word and continues checking the rest of the presentation. |
| AutoCorrect | Add spelling error to AutoCorrect list | PowerPoint adds spelling error and its correction to AutoCorrect list. Any future misspelling of word is corrected automatically as you type. |
| Close | Stop spelling checker | PowerPoint closes spelling checker and returns to PowerPoint window. |

The standard dictionary contains commonly used English words. It does not, however, contain many proper names, abbreviations, technical terms, poetic contractions, or antiquated terms. PowerPoint treats words not found in the dictionaries as misspellings.

## To Check Spelling

The following steps check the spelling on all slides in the Bird Migration presentation.

**1**

- Click Review on the Ribbon to display the Review tab.

- Click the Spelling button (Review Tab | Proofing group) to start the spelling checker and display the Spelling dialog box (Figure 3–67).

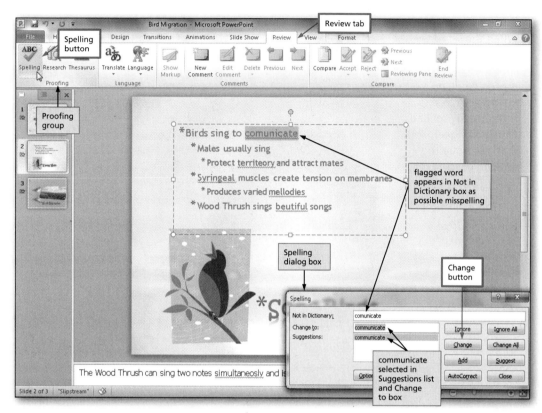

**Figure 3–67**

**2**

- With the word, communicate, selected in the Suggestions list, click the Change button (Spelling dialog box) to replace the misspelled flagged word, comunicate, with the selected correctly spelled word, communicate, and then continue the spelling check (Figure 3–68).

**Q&A**

Could I have clicked the Change All button instead of the Change button?

Yes. When you click the Change All button, you change the current and future occurrences of the misspelled word. The misspelled word, comunicate, appears only once in the presentation, so clicking the Change or the Change All button in this instance produces identical results.

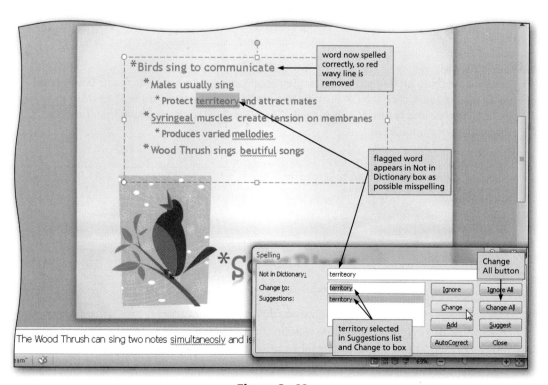

**Figure 3–68**

**3**

- Replace the misspelled word, territeory, with the word, territory (Figure 3–69).

- When the word, Syringeal, is flagged, click the Ignore button (Spelling dialog box) to skip the correctly spelled word, Syringeal, and then continue the spelling check.

**Q&A** Syringeal is flagged as a possible misspelled word. Why?

Your custom dictionary does not contain the word, so it is recognized as spelled incorrectly. You can add this word to a custom dictionary to prevent the spelling checker from flagging it as a mistake.

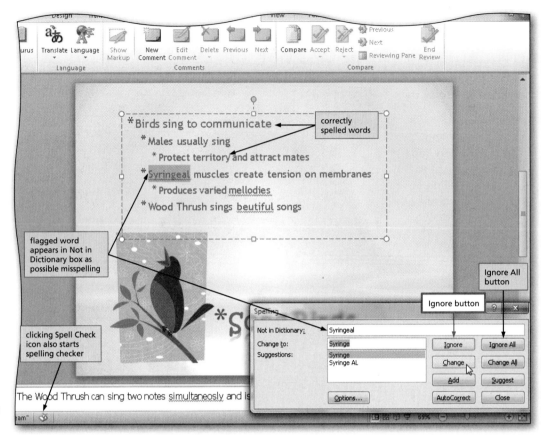

Figure 3–69

**Q&A** Could I have clicked the Ignore All button instead of the Ignore button?

Yes. When you click the Ignore All button, you ignore the current and future occurrences of the word.

**4**

- Continue checking all flagged words in the presentation. When the Microsoft PowerPoint dialog box appears, click the OK button (Microsoft PowerPoint dialog box) to close the spelling checker and return to the current slide, Slide 2, or to the slide where a possible misspelled word appeared.

| Other Ways |  |
| --- | --- |
| 1. Click Spell Check icon on status bar, click Spelling on shortcut menu | click Spelling on shortcut menu |
| 2. Right-click flagged word, click correct word or | 3. Press F7 |

## To Insert a Slide Number

PowerPoint can insert the slide number on your slides automatically to indicate where the slide is positioned within the presentation. The number location on the slide is determined by the presentation theme. You have the option to not display this slide number on the title slide. The following steps insert the slide number on all slides except the title slide.

**1**

- If a word in the Notes pane is selected, click the Slide 2 Slide pane. Display the Insert tab and then click the Insert Slide Number button (Insert tab | Text group) to display the Header and Footer dialog box (Figure 3–70).

**Q&A**

Why did I need to click the Slide pane?

The page number would have been inserted in the Notes pane instead of on the slide.

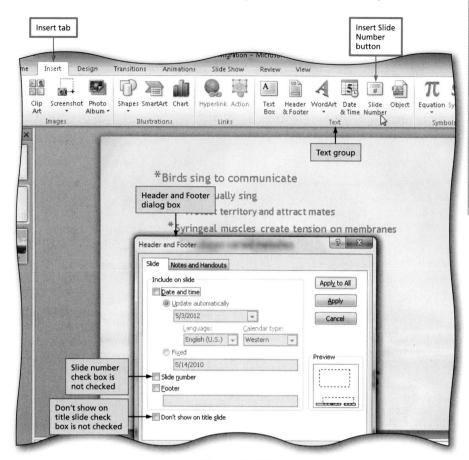

Figure 3–70

**2**

- Click the Slide number check box (Header and Footer dialog box) to place a check mark in it.

- Click the 'Don't show on title slide' check box (Header and Footer dialog box) to place a check mark in it (Figure 3–71).

**Q&A**

Where does the slide number display on the slide?

Each theme determines where the slide number is displayed in the footer. In the Slipstream theme, the slide number location is the center of the footer, as indicated by the black box at the bottom of the Preview area.

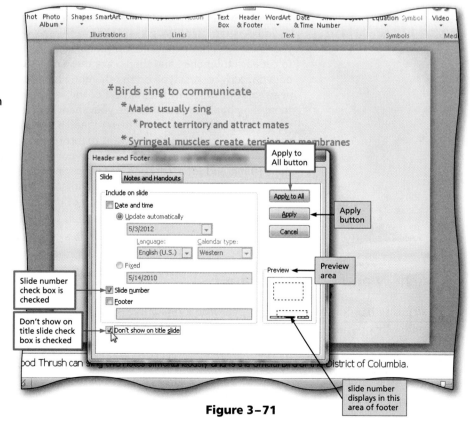

Figure 3–71

● Click the Apply to All button (Header and Footer dialog box) to close the dialog box and insert the slide number on all slides except Slide 1 (Figure 3–72).

**Figure 3–72**

**Q&A**

How does clicking the Apply to All button differ from clicking the Apply button?

The Apply button inserts the slide number only on the currently displayed slide whereas the Apply to All button inserts the slide number on every slide.

**Other Ways**

1. Click Header & Footer button (Insert tab | Text group), click Slide Number box (Header and Footer dialog box), click 'Slide number' and 'Don't show on title slide' boxes, click Apply to All button

**Plan Ahead**

**Use handouts to organize your speech.**

As you develop a lengthy presentation with many visuals, handouts may help you organize your material. Print handouts with the maximum number of slides per page. Use scissors to cut each thumbnail and then place these miniature slide images adjacent to each other on a flat surface. Any type on the thumbnails will be too small to read, so the images will need to work with only the support of the verbal message you provide. You can rearrange these thumbnails as you organize your speech. When you return to your computer, you can rearrange the slides on your screen to match the order of your thumbnail printouts. Begin speaking the actual words you want to incorporate in the body of the talk. This process of glancing at the thumbnails and hearing yourself say the key ideas of the speech is one of the best methods of organizing and preparing for the actual presentation. Ultimately, when you deliver your speech in front of an audience, the images on the slides or on your note cards should be sufficient to remind you of the accompanying verbal message.

## To Preview and Print a Handout

Printing handouts is useful for reviewing a presentation because you can analyze several slides displayed simultaneously on one page. Additionally, many businesses distribute handouts of the slide show before or after a presentation so attendees can refer to a copy. Each page of the handout can contain reduced images of one, two, three, four, six, or nine slides. The three-slides-per-page handout includes lines beside each slide so that your audience can write notes conveniently. The following steps preview and print a presentation handout.

- Click File on the Ribbon to open the Backstage view and then click the Print tab to display Slide 2 in the Print gallery.

- Click Full Page Slides in the Settings area to display the Full Page Slides gallery (Figure 3–73).

**Q&A**

Why does the preview of my slide appear in color?

Your printer determines how the preview appears. If your printer is not capable of printing color images, the preview will not appear in color.

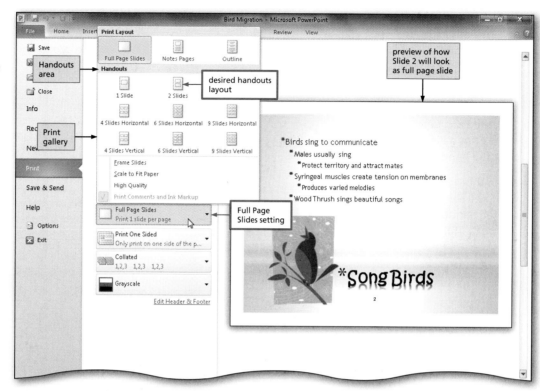

**Figure 3–73**

②

- Click 2 Slides in the Handouts area to select this option and display a preview of the handout (Figure 3–74).

**Q&A**

The current date displays in the upper-right corner of the handout, and the page number displays in the lower-right corner of the footer. Can I change their location or add other information to the header and footer?

Yes. Click the Edit Header & Footer link at the bottom of the Print gallery, click the Notes and Handouts tab (Header and Footer dialog box), and then decide what content to include on the handout page.

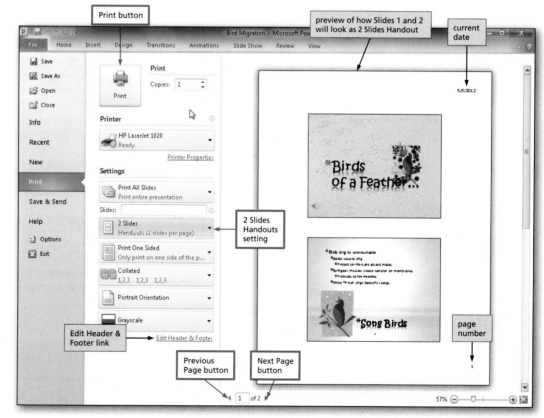

**Figure 3–74**

- Click the Next Page and Previous Page buttons to display previews of the two pages in the presentation.

- Click the Print button in the Print gallery to print the handout.

- When the printer stops, retrieve the printed handout (Figure 3–75).

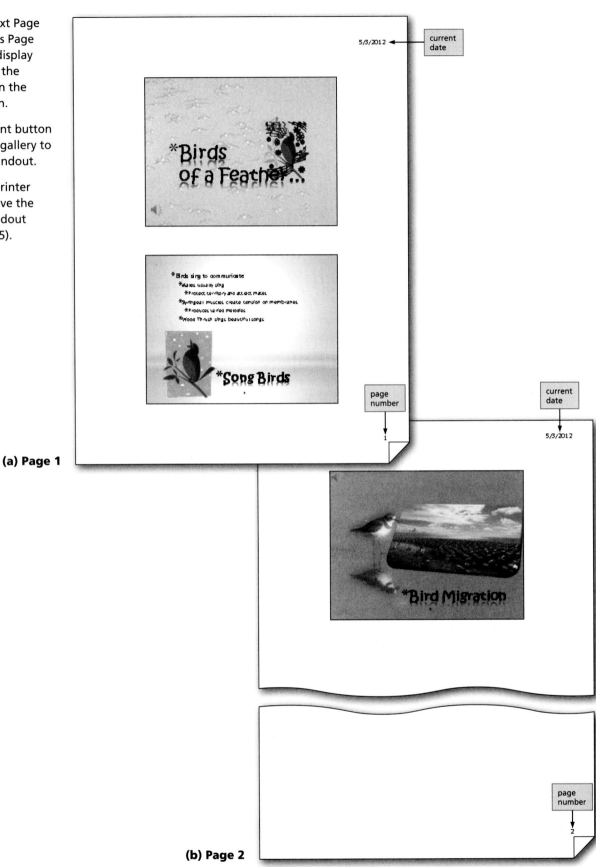

**(a) Page 1**

**(b) Page 2**

**Figure 3–75**

## To Print Speaker Notes

Comments added to slides in the Notes pane give the speaker information that supplements the text on the slide. They will print with a small image at the top and the comments below the slide. The following steps print the speaker notes.

**1**

- Click the Print tab in the Backstage view and then click 2 Slides in the Settings area to display the gallery (Figure 3–76).

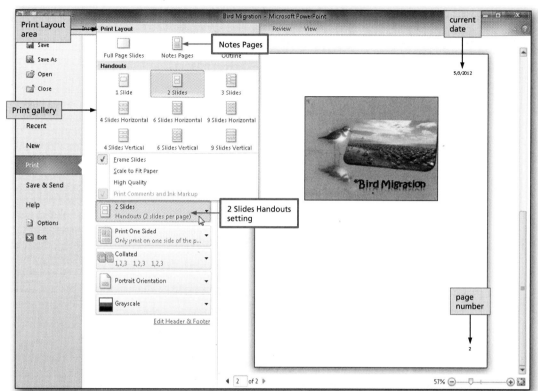

**Figure 3–76**

**2**

- Click Notes Pages in the Print Layout area to select this option and display a preview of the current page (Figure 3–77).

- Click the Previous Page and Next Page buttons to display previews of other pages in the presentation.

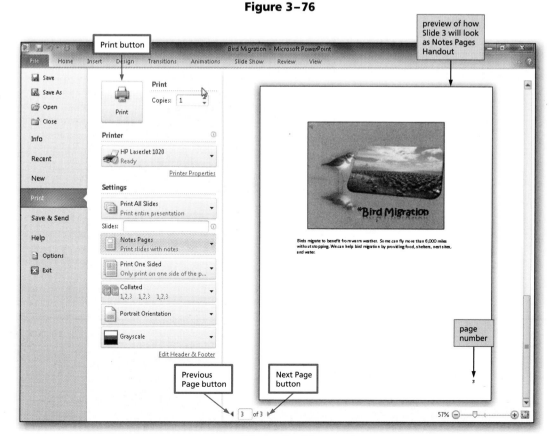

**Figure 3–77**

- Click the Print button in the Print gallery to print the notes.

- When the printer stops, retrieve the printed pages (Figure 3–78).

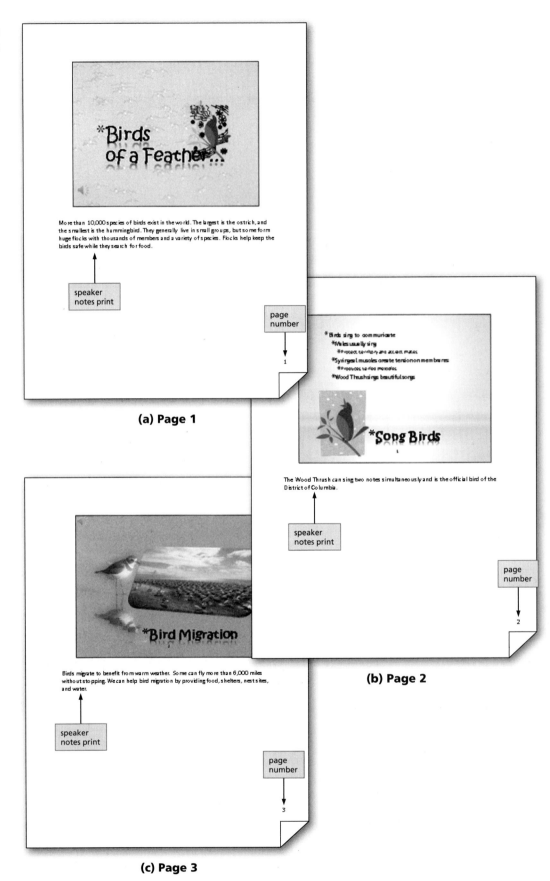

Figure 3–78

**Evaluate your presentation.**
One of the best methods of improving your communication skills is to focus on what you learned from the experience. Respond to these questions:

Plan
Ahead

- How successfully do you feel you fulfilled your assignment?
- What strategies did you use to develop your slides and the accompanying oral presentation?
- What revisions did you make?
- If you could go back to the speaking engagement and change one thing, what would it be?
- What feedback did you receive from your instructor or audience?

## To Change Document Properties

Before saving the presentation again, you want to add your name, class name, and some keywords as document properties. The following steps use the Document Information Panel to change document properties.

**BTW**

**Quick Reference**
For a table that lists how to complete the tasks covered in this book using the mouse, Ribbon, shortcut menu, and keyboard, see the Quick Reference Summary at the back of this book, or visit the PowerPoint 2010 Quick Reference Web page (scsite.com/ppt2010/qr).

1. In the Backstage view, click the Properties button in the right pane of the Info gallery, and then click Show Document Panel on the Properties menu to close the Backstage view and display the Document Information Panel.

2. Enter your name in the Author text box. Enter your course and section in the Subject text box. Enter the text, `bird, migration, singing` in the Keywords text box.

3. Close the Document Information Panel.

4. Click the Save button on the Quick Access Toolbar to overwrite the previous Bird Migration file on the USB flash drive.

## To Run a Slide Show with Media

All changes are complete, and the presentation is saved. You now can view the Bird Migration presentation. The following steps start Slide Show view.

**BTW**

**Certification**
The Microsoft Office Specialist (MOS) program provides an opportunity for you to obtain a valuable industry credential — proof that you have the PowerPoint 2010 skills required by employers. For more information, visit the PowerPoint 2010 Certification Web page (scsite.com/ppt2010/cert).

1. Click the Slide 1 thumbnail in the Slide pane to select and display Slide 1.

2. Click the Slide Show button to display the title slide, watch the animations, and listen to the bird calls. Allow the audio clip to repeat several times.

3. Press the SPACEBAR to display Slide 2.

4. Press the SPACEBAR to display Slide 3. Listen to the audio clip, watch the video clip, and then allow the audio clip to repeat several times.

5. Press the SPACEBAR to end the slide show and click to exit the slide show.

## To Quit PowerPoint

This project is complete. The following steps quit PowerPoint.

1. Click the Close button on the right side of the title bar to close the document and then quit PowerPoint.

2. If a Microsoft PowerPoint dialog box appears, click the Save button to save any changes made to the presentation since the last save.

# Chapter Summary

In this chapter you have learned how to enhance an existing presentation by adding video, audio, and pictures with effects. You also learned to modify placeholders, align text, and review a presentation by checking spelling and creating handouts. The items listed below include all the new PowerPoint skills you have learned in this chapter.

1. Color a Picture (PPT 143)
2. Add an Artistic Effect to a Picture (144)
3. Change the Stacking Order (PPT 146)
4. Resize a Placeholder (PPT 148)
5. Move a Placeholder (PPT 148)
6. Delete a Placeholder (PPT 149)
7. Align Paragraph Text (PPT 150)
8. Delete a Slide (PPT 152)
9. Change Views (PPT 153)
10. Copy a Clip from One Slide to Another (PPT 155)
11. Zoom a Slide (PPT 156)
12. Ungroup a Clip (PPT 157)
13. Change the Color of a Clip Object (PPT 158)
14. Delete a Clip Object (PPT 161)
15. Regroup Objects (PPT 162)
16. Insert a Video File (PPT 163)
17. Trim a Video File (PPT 164)
18. Add Video Options (PPT 166)
19. Insert an Audio File (PPT 167)
20. Add Audio Options (PPT 170)
21. Add a Video Style (PPT 172)
22. Resize a Video (PPT 174)
23. Insert a Movie Clip (PPT 174)
24. Find and Replace Text (PPT 176)
25. Find and Insert a Synonym (PPT 178)
26. Add Notes (PPT 179)
27. Check Spelling (PPT 181)
28. Insert a Slide Number (PPT 182)
29. Preview and Print a Handout (PPT 184)
30. Print Speaker Notes (PPT 187)

 If you have a SAM 2010 user profile, your instructor may have assigned an autogradable version of this assignment. If so, log into the SAM 2010 Web site at www.cengage.com/sam2010 to download the instruction and start files.

## Learn It Online

Test your knowledge of chapter content and key terms.

*Instructions:* To complete the Learn It Online exercises, start your browser, click the Address bar, and then enter the Web address **scsite.com/ppt2010/learn**. When the PowerPoint 2010 Learn It Online page is displayed, click the link for the exercise you want to complete and then read the instructions.

### Chapter Reinforcement TF, MC, and SA
A series of true/false, multiple choice, and short answer questions that test your knowledge of the chapter content.

### Flash Cards
An interactive learning environment where you identify chapter key terms associated with displayed definitions.

### Practice Test
A series of multiple choice questions that test your knowledge of chapter content and key terms.

### Who Wants To Be a Computer Genius?
An interactive game that challenges your knowledge of chapter content in the style of a television quiz show.

### Wheel of Terms
An interactive game that challenges your knowledge of chapter key terms in the style of the television show *Wheel of Fortune*.

### Crossword Puzzle Challenge
A crossword puzzle that challenges your knowledge of key terms presented in the chapter.

# Apply Your Knowledge

Reinforce the skills and apply the concepts you learned in this chapter.

### Adding Artistic Effects to Pictures, Moving a Placeholder, and Inserting and Controlling Audio Clips

*Note:*  To complete this assignment, you will be required to use the Data Files for Students. See the inside back cover of this book for instructions on downloading the Data Files for Students, or contact your instructor for information about accessing the required files.

*Instructions:*  Start PowerPoint. Open the presentation, Apply 3-1 SAD, from the Data Files for Students.
The five slides in the presentation, shown in Figure 3–79, present information about Seasonal Affective Disorder, also known as SAD, which is a mood disorder that occurs generally during the winter months. The document you open is composed of slides containing pictures and clip art, and you will apply artistic effects or modify some of these graphic elements. You also will insert audio clips from Office.com. In addition, you will move the placeholder on the final slide.

*Perform the following tasks:*
1. Insert the audio clip, Sad Piano Music, into Slide 1 (Figure 3–79a). Change the volume to Medium, start the clip automatically, and hide the sound icon during the slide show. Then copy this audio clip to Slides 2, 3, and 4 with the same options. Insert the audio clip, Variety Hour, into Slide 5, change the volume to Medium, start the clip automatically, and hide the sound icon during the slide show.
2. On Slide 2, color the picture by selecting Yellow, Accent color 2 Dark from the Recolor area, as shown in Figure 3–79b.
3. On Slide 3, apply the Watercolor Sponge artistic effect to the picture, as shown in Figure 3–79c.
4. On Slide 4, select the lamp clip and then change the Zoom level to 120%. Ungroup the lamp clip and then recolor the arms to Dark Teal, Text 2, Lighter 10% (last color in fourth Theme Colors column), as shown in Figure 3–79d. Regroup the clip. Change the Zoom level to 69%.
5. On Slide 5, move the WordArt placeholder above the bird in the picture, as shown in Figure 3–79e.
6. On Slide 1, type **Up to 9 percent of U.S. adults may suffer from SAD.** in the Notes pane.
7. Check the slides for spelling errors and then run the revised presentation.
8. Change the document properties, as specified by your instructor. Save the presentation using the file name, Apply 3-1 Seasonal Affective Disorder.
9. Submit the revised document in the format specified by your instructor.

**(a) Slide 1**

**(b) Slide 2**

**Figure 3–79**

*Continued >*

**Apply Your Knowledge** *continued*

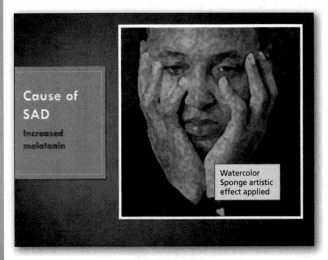

**(c) Slide 3**

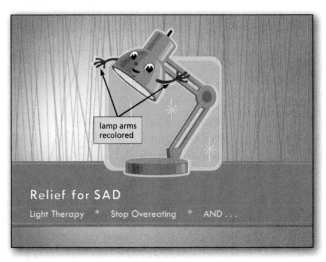

**(d) Slide 4**

**(e) Slide 5**

**Figure 3–79 (Continued)**

# Extend Your Knowledge

Extend the skills you learned in this chapter and experiment with new skills. You may need to use Help to complete the assignment.

### Formatting a Video Border, Deleting Audio, Adding a Font Effect, and Pausing and Resuming Video Playback

*Note:* To complete this assignment, you will be required to use the Data Files for Students. See the inside back cover of this book for instructions on downloading the Data Files for Students, or contact your instructor for information about accessing the required files.

*Instructions:* Start PowerPoint. Open the presentation, Extend 3-1 Nature, from the Data Files for Students. You will add the Small Caps font effect to the title text on the title slide, delete an audio clip, and format a video border, as shown in Figure 3–80a. While the slide show is running, you will adjust the video playback to pause and then resume playing the clip.

*Perform the following tasks:*

1. On Slide 1, move the title text placeholder up so that it is positioned in the upper-right corner of the slide, as shown in Figure 3–80a. Right-align the title text and then add the Small Caps font effect to these letters. *Hint:* Font effects are located in the Font dialog box (Home tab | Font group).

2. On the title slide, delete the audio clip positioned in the upper-left corner of the slide. The three audio clips on the right side of the slide will remain.

3. Change the video style from Soft Edge Oval to Beveled Oval, Black (in the Moderate area). Then change the video border color to Gold, Accent 2 and change the border weight to 10 pt. *Hint:* Click More Lines in the Video Border Weight gallery and then change the Border Style Width.

4. On Slide 2, add a border to each of the six pictures that surround the center deer video frame, and then change the border colors and the border weights. Use Figure 3–80b as a guide. Add the Compound Frame, Black video style (in the Moderate area) to the bird feeder clip.

5. Change the document properties, as specified by your instructor. Save the presentation using the file name, Extend 3-1 Observing Nature.

6. Start the slide show. When a few seconds of the video have elapsed, pause the video and then move your mouse pointer to an area other than the video and listen to the bird audio clips. Then move the mouse pointer over the video clip to display the Video Controls. Resume the video playback.

7. Submit the revised document in the format specified by your instructor.

**(a) Slide 1**

**(b) Slide 2**

**Figure 3–80**

## Make It Right

Analyze a presentation and correct all errors and/or improve the design.

### Editing Clips, Finding and Replacing Text, and Correcting Spelling

*Note:* To complete this assignment, you will be required to use the Data Files for Students. See the inside back cover of this book for instructions on downloading the Data Files for Students, or contact your instructor for information about accessing the required files.

*Instructions:* Start PowerPoint. Open the presentation, Make It Right 3-1 Flamingos, from the Data Files for Students.

Correct the formatting problems and errors in the presentation while keeping in mind the guidelines presented in this chapter.

*Perform the following tasks:*

1. On Slide 1 (Figure 3–81), change the audio clip volume to High and hide the sound icon during the show. Loop this clip for the duration of the slide show.

2. On Slide 2, add the Reflection video effect located in the Reflection Variations area, Tight Reflection 4 pt offset (first reflection in second row) to the video.

3. Trim the Slide 2 video so that the Start Time is 00:21.087 and the End Time is 01:44.273. The duration should be 01:23.186 minutes.

4. Copy the flamingo clip from Slide 4 to Slide 3 and then delete Slide 4. Place this clip on the left side of the picture frame and then adjust the picture frame size so it is the appropriate dimension for the slide content. Ungroup the flamingo clip and then recolor the flamingo to match the color of its legs, the palm tree leaves to a shade of green, and the bird to a shade of blue. Regroup the clip.

5. Find the word, Antarctica, in the Slide 1 Notes pane, and then replace it with the words, South America. Then find the number, 14, and replace it with the number, 4.

6. Check the slides for spelling errors and then run the revised presentation.

7. Change the document properties, as specified by your instructor. Save the presentation using the file name, Make It Right 3-1 Chilean Flamingos.

8. Submit the revised document in the format specified by your instructor.

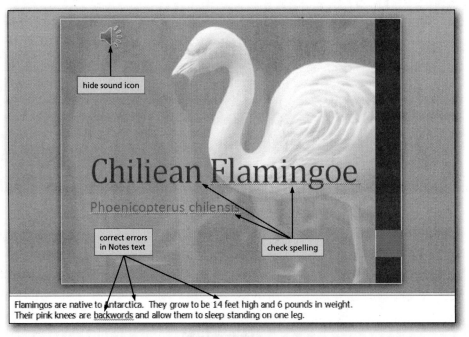

**Figure 3–81**

## In the Lab

Design and/or create a presentation using the guidelines, concepts, and skills presented in this chapter. Labs 1, 2, and 3 are listed in order of increasing difficulty.

### Lab 1: Inserting Audio Clips, Coloring a Picture, and Applying Artistic Effects to Pictures

*Note:* To complete this assignment, you will be required to use the Data Files for Students. See the inside back cover of this book for instructions on downloading the Data Files for Students, or contact your instructor for information about accessing the required files.

*Problem:* Start PowerPoint. Open the presentation, Lab 3-1 Cooking, from the Data Files for Students.

Your college has an outstanding culinary program, and you are preparing a PowerPoint presentation to promote an upcoming seafood cooking class. The slides will feature audio clips and graphics with applied effects. Create the slides shown in Figure 3–82.

*Instructions:* Perform the following tasks.

1. On Slide 1, insert the Mr. Light music audio clip from Office.com. Change the volume to Low, play across slides, and hide the sound icon during the show. Move the subtitle text placeholder downward to the location shown in Figure 3–82a and center both paragraphs.

2. On Slide 2, insert the picture called Blackboard and Chef, which is available on the Data Files for Students. Change the color of the picture to Gold, Accent color 3 Dark (Recolor area). Add a border to this picture using Dark Red, Accent 5, and then change the border weight to 6 pt., as shown in Figure 3–82b.

**(a) Slide 1**

**(b) Slide 2**

**Figure 3–82**

*Continued >*

**STUDENT ASSIGNMENTS**

**In the Lab** *continued*

3. On Slide 3, right-align all the text. Insert the Chef video clip from Office.com and resize this clip so that it is approximately 4.08" × 3.99", as shown in Figure 3–82c. Insert the Pepper Grinder video clip from Office.com and resize this clip so that it is approximately 3.81" × 2.25". Move the Pepper Grinder video clip to the lower-left corner of the slide. Insert the audio clips, Pepper Grinder and Cartoon Crash, from Office.com. Start these clips automatically, hide the sound icons during the show, and loop until stopped.

4. On Slide 4, apply the Watercolor Sponge artistic effect to the lobster picture in the left content placeholder and the Plastic Wrap artistic effect to the paella picture in the right content placeholder, as shown in Figure 3–82d.

5. On Slide 5, insert the Bottle Open audio clip from Office.com. Move the sound icon to the lower-right corner of the slide. Start this clip on click. Center the text in the caption placeholder and then move this placeholder downward to the location shown in Figure 3–82e.

6. Review the slides in Slide Sorter view to check for consistency, and then change the view to Normal.

7. Drag the scroll box to display Slide 1. Start Slide Show view and display each slide.

8. Change the document properties, as specified by your instructor. Save the presentation using the file name, Lab 3-1 Cooking Classes.

9. Submit the revised document in the format specified by your instructor.

**(c) Slide 3**

**(d) Slide 4**

**(e) Slide 5**

**Figure 3–82 (Continued)**

# In the Lab

## Lab 2: Adding Slide Numbers, Applying Artistic Effects to Pictures, and Recoloring a Video

*Note:* To complete this assignment, you will be required to use the Data Files for Students. See the inside back cover of this book for instructions on downloading the Data Files for Students, or contact your instructor for information about accessing the required files.

*Problem:* The Dutch tradition is continuing with Klompen dancers, who take their name from their traditional wooden clog shoes. You attended an annual festival this past spring and captured some video clips of teenagers dancing a traditional dance. In addition, you have some video of a hand-built windmill. In your speech class, you desire to inform your classmates of a few aspects of Dutch life, so you prepare the presentation shown in Figure 3–83.

*Instructions:* Perform the following tasks.

1. Start PowerPoint. Open the presentation, Lab 3-2 Dancers, from the Data Files for Students. On Slide 1, apply the Mosaic Bubbles artistic effect to the tulips picture, as shown in Figure 3–83a. Insert the audio clip, Spring Music, from Office.com. Start this clip automatically, hide the sound icon during the show, and change the volume to Medium.

2. On Slide 2, apply the Marker artistic effect to the wooden shoe picture, as shown in Figure 3–83b. Change the Start option for the video clip from On Click to Automatically. Apply the Rotated, Gradient video style (Moderate area) to the video clip, change the video border color to Tan, Accent 6, and then change the border width to 18 pt.

3. On Slide 2, type `Many dancers wear traditional, hand-sewn Dutch costumes. Dancers wear thick socks to make the wooden shoes comfortable during this annual event.` in the Notes pane.

**(a) Slide 1**

**(b) Slide 2**

**Figure 3–83**

*Continued >*

**In the Lab** *continued*

4. On Slide 3, insert the video clip called Windmill from the Data Files for Students. Apply the Reflected Bevel, White video style (Intense area). Change the color of the video to Dark Blue, Accent color 3 Dark (Recolor area). Start this clip automatically and loop until stopped. Center the text in the title placeholder, as shown in Figure 3–83c.

5. Use the thesaurus to change the word, Custom, to Tradition. Check the slides for spelling errors.

6. Add the slide number to all slides except the title slide.

7. Review the slides in Slide Sorter view to check for consistency. Then click the Reading view button to display the current slide and click the Next and Previous buttons to display each slide. Change the view to Normal.

8. Change the document properties, as specified by your instructor. Save the presentation using the file name, Lab 3-2 Klompen Dancers.

9. Submit the revised document in the format specified by your instructor.

video style applied

video clip recolored to Dark Blue

title text centered

thesaurus used to find synonym

A Long-Time Dutch Tradition

3

**(c) Slide 3**

**Figure 3–83 (Continued)**

# In the Lab

## Lab 3: Applying Artistic Effects to and Recoloring Pictures, Inserting Audio, and Trimming Video

*Note:* To complete this assignment, you will be required to use the Data Files for Students. See the inside back cover of this book for instructions on downloading the Data Files for Students, or contact your instructor for information about accessing the required files.

*Problem:* Your Uncle Barney is an avid railroad buff, and he especially is interested in viewing steam locomotives. He has a collection of video clips and photographs of historic steam engines, and he asks you to create a presentation for the next Hessville Train Club meeting he is planning to attend. Start PowerPoint and then open the presentation, Lab 3-3 Locomotives, from the Data Files for Students. Prepare the slides shown in Figures 3–84a through 3–84c.

*Instructions:* Perform the following tasks.

1. Delete the subtitle text placeholder on Slide 1. Then insert the picture, Steamer 624, from the Data Files for Students and apply the Glow Diffused artistic effect. Position the picture as shown in Figure 3–84a. Center the title text. Insert the audio clip, Train Whistle By, from Office.com. Start this clip automatically, hide the sound icon during the show, and loop until stopped.

2. On Slide 2, insert the picture, Locomotive, from the Data Files for Students and resize it so that it fills the entire slide height and width (approximately 7.5" × 10"). Change the color of the picture to Tan, Accent color 1 Light (Recolor area), as shown in Figure 3–84b.

3. Insert the video clip, Steam Locomotive, from the Data Files for Students. Resize this clip to approximately 4.54" × 8.07" and move the clip to the location shown in Figure 3–84b. Apply the Metal Rounded Rectangle video style (Intense area). Change the color of the border to Olive Green, Accent 2. Trim the Slide 2 video so that the Start Time is 00:06.186 and the End Time is 00:23.432. The duration should be 00:17.246 seconds. Start this clip automatically and loop until stopped.

4. On Slide 3, insert the picture, Railroad Track Border, and the video clip, Red Locomotive, from the Data Files for Students. Resize the Red Locomotive clip to approximately 2.78" × 5.36" and move it to the location shown in Figure 3–84c. Also, insert the audio clip, Steam Train Pass, from Office. com, and move this sound icon to the lower-left corner of the slide. Copy the audio clip, Train Whistle By, from Slide 1 and then move the sound icon to the upper-right corner of the slide. Start both audio clips automatically, hide the sound icons during the show, and loop until stopped.

5. Review the slides in Slide Sorter view. Then click the Reading view button to display the current slide and click the Next and Previous buttons to display each slide. Change the view to Normal.

6. Change the document properties, as specified by your instructor. Save the presentation using the file name, Lab 3-3 Steam Locomotives.

7. Submit the revised document in the format specified by your instructor.

**(a) Slide 1**

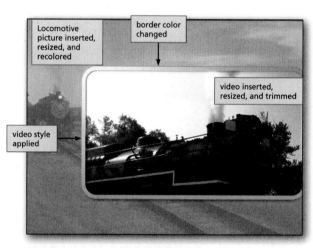

**(b) Slide 2**

**(c) Slide 3**

**Figure 3–84**

# Cases and Places

Apply your creative thinking and problem-solving skills to design and implement a solution.

*Note:* To complete these assignments, you will be required to use the Data Files for Students. See the inside back cover of this book for instructions on downloading the Data Files for Students, or contact your instructor for information about accessing the required files.

As you design the presentations, remember to use the 7 × 7 rule: a maximum of seven words on a line and a maximum of seven lines on one slide.

## 1: Design and Create a Presentation about Kilauea Volcano

**Academic**

Most of the volcanic eruptions in Hawaii have occurred within Hawaii Volcanoes National Park. One of these volcanoes, Kilauea, has been erupting since 1983, and visitors to the National Park can drive on two roads to see lava tubes, steam vents, and plants returning to the barren landscape. Rainwater drains through cracks in the ground, is heated, and then is released through fissures and condenses in the cool air. Lava flows in underground tubes, and vents release volcanic gases that consist mainly of carbon dioxide, steam, and sulfur dioxide. During your recent trip to Hawaii Volcanoes National Park, you drove on these roads and captured these geological wonders with your video and digital cameras. You want to share your experience with your Geology 101 classmates. Create a presentation to show the pictures and video clips, which are located in the Data Files for Students and begin with the file name, Case 1. You also can use pictures from Office.com if they are appropriate for this topic. Apply appropriate styles and effects, and use at least three objectives found at the beginning of this chapter to develop the presentation. Be sure to check spelling.

## 2: Design and Create a Presentation about Surfing

**Personal**

During your summer vacation, you took surfing lessons and enjoyed the experience immensely. You now want to share your adventure with friends, so you decide to create a short PowerPoint presentation with video clips of the surf and of your paddling on your surfboard to the instruction area in the ocean. You also have pictures of your introductory lesson on shore and of your first successful run catching a wave. The Data Files for Students contains these media files that begin with the file name, Case 2. You also can use your own digital pictures or pictures from Office.com if they are appropriate for this topic. Use the clip, Case 2 - Yellow and Green Surfboard, on one slide, but ungroup this clip and then change the surfboard's colors to your school's team colors. Trim the video clips and apply appropriate styles and effects. Use at least three objectives found at the beginning of this chapter to develop the presentation. Be sure to check spelling.

## 3: Design and Create a Presentation to Promote Your Snow Removal Business

**Professional**

Record snowfalls have wreaked havoc in your neighborhood, so you have decided to earn tuition money by starting a snow removal business. You are willing to clear sidewalks and driveways when snowfall exceeds three inches. To promote your business, you desire to create a PowerPoint presentation to run behind the counter at the local hardware store. The Data Files for Students contains pictures and a video clip that begin with the file name, Case 3. You also can use your own digital pictures or pictures from Office.com if they are appropriate for this topic. Use the clip, Case 3 - Man Shoveling, on one slide, but ungroup this clip and then zoom in and delete the white area of the clip depicting the man's breath. Also, recolor at least one picture and apply an artistic effect. Be sure to check spelling.

# 4 Working with Information Graphics

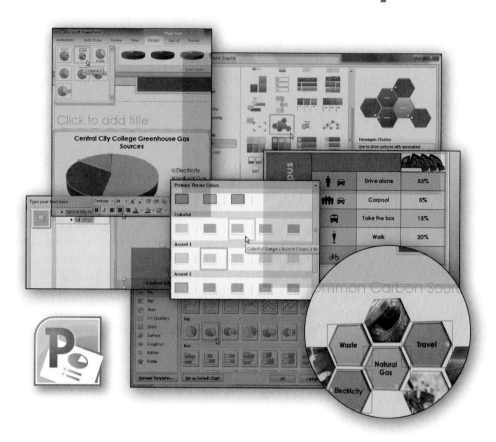

## Objectives

You will have mastered the material in this chapter when you can:

- Insert a SmartArt graphic
- Insert images from a file into a SmartArt graphic
- Convert text to a SmartArt graphic
- Format a SmartArt graphic
- Create and format a chart
- Change the chart slice outline weight and color

- Rotate a chart
- Change the chart title and legend
- Create and format a table
- Change table text alignment and orientation
- Add an image to a table
- Insert a symbol

# 4 | Working with Information Graphics

## Introduction

Audiences generally focus first on the visual elements displayed on a slide. Graphical elements increase **visual literacy**, which is the ability to examine and assess these images. They can be divided into two categories: images and information graphics. Images are the clips and photographs you have used in Chapters 1, 2, and 3, and information graphics are tables, charts, graphs, and diagrams. Both sets of visuals help audience members interpret and retain material, so they should be designed and presented with care.

## Project — Presentation with SmartArt, a Chart, and a Table

The project in this chapter follows visual content guidelines and uses PowerPoint to create the presentation shown in Figure 4–1. The slide show uses several visual elements to help audience members understand the carbon footprint, or carbon dioxide emissions, created by college students and staff. The first two slides are enhanced with SmartArt graphics and pictures. The three-dimensional pie chart on Slide 3 shows four contributors to the carbon footprint and emphasizes that the largest contributor is electricity. The four-column table on Slide 4 lists the five most common transportation methods students use to arrive on campus.

## Overview

As you read through this chapter, you will learn how to create the presentation shown in Figure 4–1 by performing these general tasks:

- Insert and modify a SmartArt graphic.
- Add styles and effects to SmartArt.
- Create a table and a chart.
- Add borders to tables and charts.
- Change table text alignment and orientation.
- Change chart and table styles and colors.

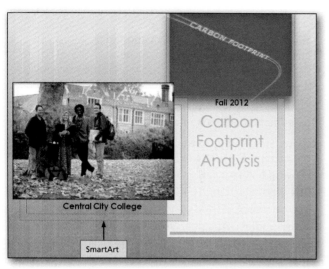

**(a) Slide 1 (Title Slide with SmartArt Enhanced with a Picture)**

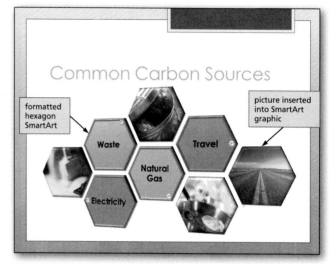

**(b) Slide 2 (SmartArt Enhanced with Pictures)**

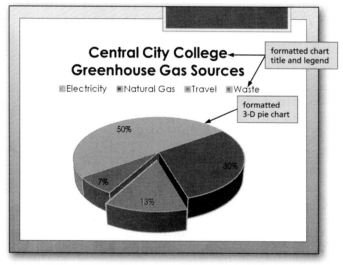

**(c) Slide 3 (3-D Chart)**

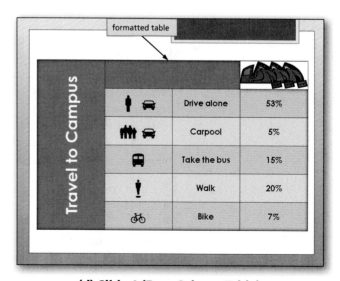

**(d) Slide 4 (Four-Column Table)**

**Figure 4–1**

<table>
<tr><td>Plan<br>Ahead</td><td>

**General Project Guidelines**

When creating a PowerPoint presentation, the actions you perform and the decisions you make will affect the appearance and characteristics of the finished document. As you create a presentation with illustrations, such as the project shown in Figure 4–1 on the previous page, you should follow these general guidelines:

1. **Consider the graphic's function.** Decide precisely what message you want the chart, table, or illustration to convey to the audience. Determine the graphic's purpose.

2. **Choose an appropriate SmartArt layout.** SmartArt illustrations represent ideas and concepts graphically. Audiences can grasp these visual concepts and recall them more quickly and accurately than when viewing text alone. Many SmartArt layouts are available (see Table 4–1), so select the one that best represents the concept you are attempting to present.

3. **Choose an appropriate chart style.** Most audience members like charts to help them understand the relationships between groups of data. Charts express numbers visually, but you must decide which chart type best conveys the points you are attempting to make in your presentation. PowerPoint presents a variety of chart layouts, and you must decide which one is effective in presenting the relationships between numbers and indicating important trends.

4. **Obtain information for the graphic from credible sources.** The text or numbers in the graphics should be current and correct. Verify the sources of the information and be certain you have typed the data correctly. On the slide or during your presentation, acknowledge the source of the information. If necessary, give credit to the person or organization that supplied the information for your graphics.

5. **Test your visual elements.** Show your slides to several friends or colleagues and ask them to interpret what they see. Time the duration they studied each slide. Have them verbally summarize the information they perceived.

When necessary, more specific details concerning the above guidelines are presented at appropriate points in the chapter. The chapter also will identify the actions performed and decisions made regarding these guidelines during the creation of the presentation shown in Figure 4–1.

</td></tr>
</table>

**BTW**

**BTWs**
For a complete list of the BTWs found in the margins of this book, visit the PowerPoint 2010 BTW Web page (scsite.com/ppt2010/btw).

## To Start PowerPoint and Open and Save a Presentation

To begin this presentation, you will open a file located on the Data Files for Students. See the inside back cover of this book for instructions on downloading the Data Files for Students, or contact your instructor for more information about accessing the required files. If you are using a computer to step through the project in this chapter and you want your screens to match the figures in this book, you should change your screen's resolution to $1024 \times 768$.

The following steps start PowerPoint, open the Carbon presentation, and save the file with a new name.

**1** Start PowerPoint. If necessary, maximize the PowerPoint window.

**2** Open the presentation, Carbon, located on the Data Files for Students.

**3** Save the presentation using the file name, Carbon Footprint.

Plan
Ahead

**Consider the graphic's function.**
Determine why you are considering using an information graphic. The SmartArt, chart, or table should introduce meaningful information, support information in your speech, and help you convey details. If you are inserting the graphic simply for the sake of enlivening the presentation, do not use it. Graphics should help your audience understand and retain information and should not merely repeat details they have seen or heard up to this point in the slide show.

Take care in placing a manageable amount of information in your chart or table. Avoid overwhelming your audience with numerous lines in your table or slices or bars in your chart. If your audience is confused or struggling with comprehending the graphic, chances are they simply will abandon the task and wait for you to display the next slide.

# Creating and Formatting a SmartArt Graphic

An illustration often can help convey relationships between key points in your presentation. Numerous studies have shown that audience members recall information more readily and accurately when it is presented graphically rather than textually. Microsoft Office 2010 includes **SmartArt graphics**, which are visual representations of your ideas. The SmartArt layouts have a variety of shapes, arrows, and lines to correspond to the major points you want your audience to remember.

You can create a SmartArt graphic in two ways: Select a type and then add text and pictures or convert text or pictures already present on a slide to a graphic. Once the SmartArt graphic is present, you can customize its look by changing colors, adding and deleting shapes, adding fill and effects, adding pictures, and including animation. Table 4–1 lists the SmartArt types and their uses.

**BTW**

**Improving Audience Retention**
Audience members need to use both senses of sight and hearing when they view graphics and listen to a speaker. When they become engaged in the presentation, they tune out distractions, which ultimately increases their retention of the material being presented. Although the exact amount of measured retention varies, one study found that an audience recalled five times more material when it was presented both verbally and visually.

| Table 4–1 SmartArt Graphic Layout Types and Purposes | |
|---|---|
| **Type** | **Purpose** |
| List | Show non sequential information |
| Process | Show steps in a process or timeline |
| Cycle | Show a continual process |
| Hierarchy | Create an organizational chart |
| Relationship | Illustrate connections |
| Matrix | Show how parts relate to a whole |
| Pyramid | Show proportional relationships with the largest component at the top or bottom |
| Picture | Include a placeholder for pictures within the graphic |
| Office.com | Use SmartArt available on the Office.com Web site |

In the following pages, you will follow these general steps to create two SmartArt graphics:

1. Insert a SmartArt graphic.
2. Add text and then format these characters.
3. Insert a picture from a file into the SmartArt graphic.
4. Add a SmartArt Style to the graphics.
5. Change the SmartArt color.
6. Convert text to a SmartArt graphic.
7. Adjust the SmartArt size and location on the slide.

Plan
Ahead

**Choose an appropriate SmartArt layout.**
If a slide contains key points that show a process or relationship, consider using a SmartArt graphic to add visual appeal and enhance audience comprehension. As you select a layout, determine the number of ideas you need to present and then select a graphic that contains the same number of shapes. For example, the Counterbalance Arrows layout in the Relationship area resembles a teeter-totter; it represents the notion that one concept conversely affects another concept, such as the economic principle that supply has an inverse relationship to demand.

## To Insert a SmartArt Graphic

A picture of Central City students and staff would complement the theme of showing the results of the campus's carbon footprint survey. Several SmartArt graphics have placeholders for one or more pictures, and they are grouped in the Picture category. The Snapshot Picture List graphic has one area for a picture and another for text. The following steps insert the Snapshot Picture List SmartArt graphic on Slide 1.

- Display the Insert tab and then click the SmartArt button (Insert tab | Illustrations group) to display the Choose a SmartArt Graphic dialog box.

- Click Picture in the left pane to display the Picture gallery.

- Click the Snapshot Picture List graphic (last graphic in first row) to display a preview of this graphic in the right pane (Figure 4–2).

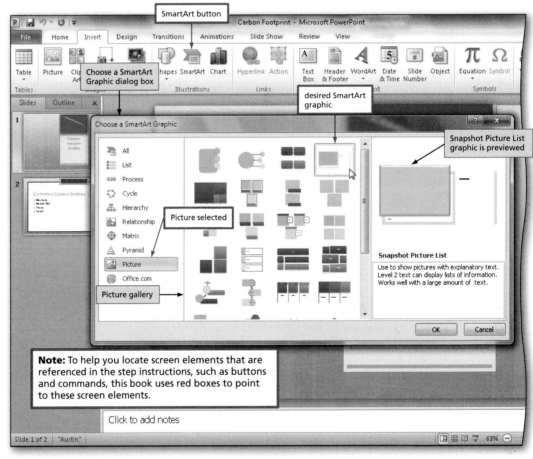

Figure 4–2

**②**

- Click the OK button to insert this SmartArt graphic on Slide 1 (Figure 4–3).

- If necessary, click the Text Pane button (SmartArt Tools Design tab | Create Graphic group) to open the Text pane if it does not display automatically.

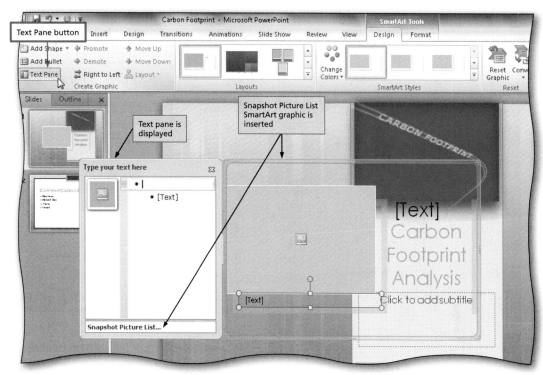

**Figure 4–3**

## Text Pane

The **Text pane** assists you in creating a graphic because you can direct your attention to developing and editing the message without being concerned with the actual graphic. This Text pane consists of two areas: The top portion has the text that will appear in the SmartArt graphic and the bottom portion gives the name of the graphic and suggestions of what type of information is best suited for this type of visual. Each SmartArt graphic has an associated Text pane with bullets that function as an outline and map directly to the image. You can create new lines of bulleted text and then indent and demote these lines. You also can check spelling. Table 4–2 shows the character shortcuts you can use to enter Text pane characters.

**BTW**

**The Ribbon and Screen Resolution**
PowerPoint may change how the groups and buttons within the groups appear on the Ribbon, depending on the computer's screen resolution. Thus, your Ribbon may look different from the ones in this book if you are using a screen resolution other than 1024 × 768.

| Table 4–2 Text Pane Keyboard Shortcuts | |
|---|---|
| **Activity** | **Shortcut** |
| Indent text | TAB or ALT+SHIFT+RIGHT ARROW |
| Demote text | SHIFT+TAB or ALT+SHIFT+LEFT ARROW |
| Add a tab character | CTRL+TAB |
| Create a new line of text | ENTER |
| Check spelling | F7 |
| Merge two lines of text | DELETE at the end of the first text line |
| Display the shortcut menu | SHIFT+F10 |
| Switch between the SmartArt drawing canvas and the Text pane | CTRL+SHIFT+F2 |
| Close the Text pane | ALT+F4 |
| Switch the focus from the Text pane to the SmartArt graphic border | ESC |

## To Enter Text in a SmartArt Graphic

The following steps insert two lines of text in the Text pane and in the corresponding SmartArt shapes on Slide 1.

- Type **Central City College** in the first bullet line and then press the DOWN ARROW key to move the insertion point to the second bullet line (Figure 4–4).

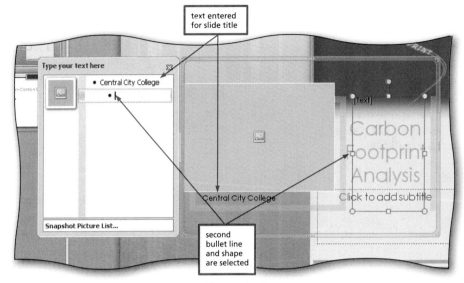

**Figure 4–4**

- Type **Fall 2012** in the second bullet line. Do not press the ENTER or DOWN ARROW keys (Figure 4–5).

**Q&A** I mistakenly pressed the ENTER key. How can I delete the bullet line I just added?

Press the BACKSPACE key twice to delete the line.

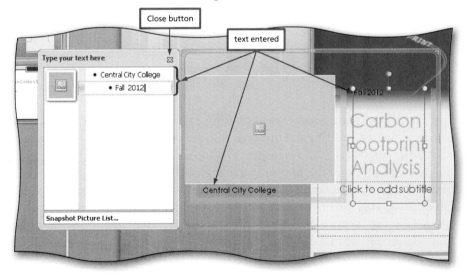

**Figure 4–5**

## To Format Text Pane Characters

Once the desired characters are entered in the Text pane, you can change the font size and apply formatting features, such as bold, italic, and underlined text. The following steps format the text by changing the shape text font color and bolding the letters.

- With the Text pane open, drag through both bulleted lines to select the text and display the Mini toolbar.

**Q&A** If my Text pane no longer is displayed, how can I get it to appear?

Click the control, which is the tab with two arrows pointing to the right and left, on the left side of the SmartArt graphic.

**2**

- Display the Font Color gallery and change the font color to Dark Blue.

- Bold the text.

- Center the text (Figure 4–6).

**Q&A** These formatting changes did not appear in the Text pane. Why?

Not all the formatting changes are evident in the Text pane, but they appear in the corresponding shape.

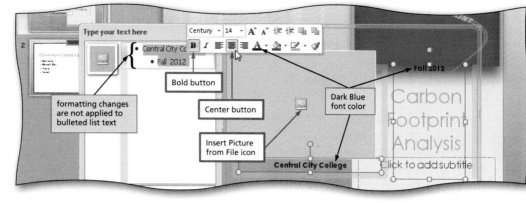

Figure 4–6

**3**

- Click the Close button in the SmartArt Text pane so that it no longer is displayed.

## To Insert a Picture from a File into a SmartArt Graphic

The picture icon in the middle of the Snapshot Picture List SmartArt graphic indicates that the rectangular shape is designed to hold an image. You can select files from the Clip Organizer or from images you have obtained from other sources, such as a photograph taken with your digital camera. The following steps insert an image located on the Data Files for Students into the SmartArt graphic.

**1**

- With your USB flash drive connected to one of the computer's USB ports, click the Insert Picture from File icon in the rectangle picture placeholder to display the Insert Picture dialog box.

- If the list of files and folders on the selected USB flash drive are not displayed in the Insert Picture dialog box, double-click your USB flash drive to display them.

- Click Students and Staff to select the file name (Figure 4–7).

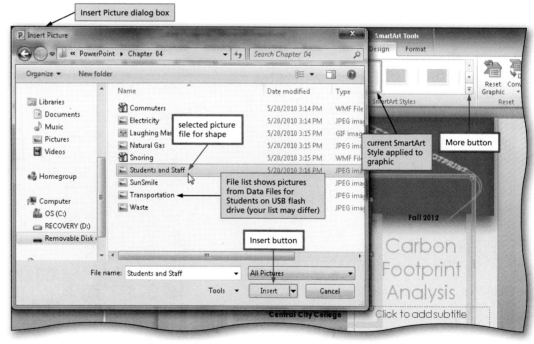

Figure 4–7

**Q&A** What if the picture is not on a USB flash drive?

Use the same process, but be certain to select the location containing the picture in the File list.

**2**

- Click the Insert button (Insert Picture dialog box) to insert the picture into the SmartArt picture placeholder.

## To Apply a SmartArt Style

You can change the look of your SmartArt graphic easily by applying a **SmartArt Style**. These professionally designed effects have a variety of shape fills, edges, shadows, line styles, gradients, and three-dimensional styles that allow you to customize the appearance of your presentation. The following steps add the Cartoon Style to the Snapshot Picture List SmartArt graphic.

- With the SmartArt graphic still selected, click the More button in the SmartArt Styles group (SmartArt Tools Design tab) to expand the SmartArt Styles gallery (Figure 4–8).

**Q&A** How do I select the graphic if it no longer is selected?

Click the graphic anywhere except the picture you just added.

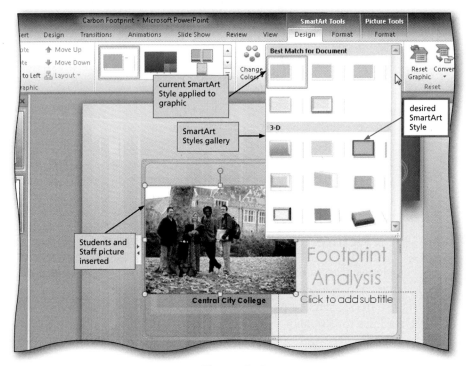

**Figure 4–8**

- Point to the Cartoon Style in the 3-D area (third style in first row) in the SmartArt Styles gallery to display a live preview of this style (Figure 4–9).

 **Experiment**

- Point to various styles in the SmartArt Styles gallery and watch the Snapshot Picture List graphic change styles.

❸

- Click Cartoon to apply this style to the graphic.

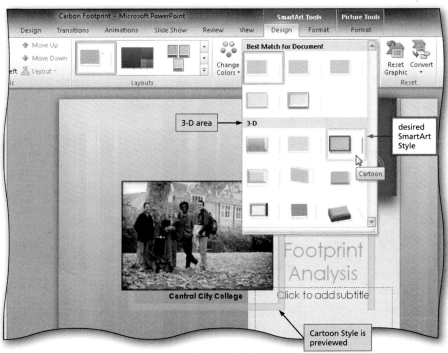

**Figure 4–9**

## To Change SmartArt Color

Another modification you can make to your SmartArt graphic is to change its color. As with the WordArt Style gallery, PowerPoint provides a gallery of color options you can preview and evaluate. The following steps change the SmartArt graphic color to a Colorful range.

- With the SmartArt graphic still selected, click the Change Colors button (SmartArt Tools Design tab | SmartArt Styles group) to display the Change Colors gallery (Figure 4–10).

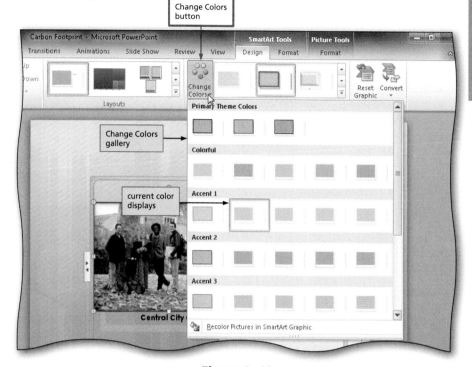

**Figure 4–10**

- Point to Colorful Range – Accent Colors 3 to 4 in the Colorful area (third color) to display a live preview of these colors (Figure 4–11).

**Experiment**

- Point to various colors in the Change Colors gallery and watch the shapes change colors.

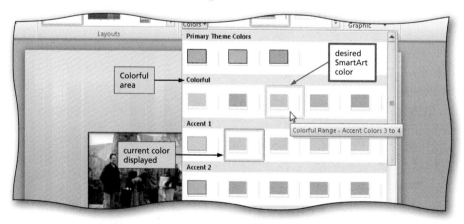

**Figure 4–11**

- Click Colorful Range – Accent Colors 3 to 4 to apply this color variation to the graphic (Figure 4–12).

**Figure 4–12**

# To Resize a SmartArt Graphic

When you view the completed graphic, you may decide that individual shapes or the entire piece of art needs to be enlarged or reduced. If you change the size of one shape, the other shapes also may change size to maintain proportions. Likewise, the font size may change in all the shapes if you increase or decrease the font size of one shape. On Slide 1, the SmartArt graphic size can be increased to fill the space and add readability. All the shapes will enlarge proportionally when you adjust the graphic's height and width. The following steps resize the SmartArt graphic.

- With the SmartArt graphic still selected, point to the lower-left sizing handle and drag downward and to the left, as shown in Figure 4–13.

**Figure 4–13**

- Release the mouse button to resize the graphic.

- Press the UP and RIGHT ARROW keys to position the graphic, as shown in Figure 4–14.

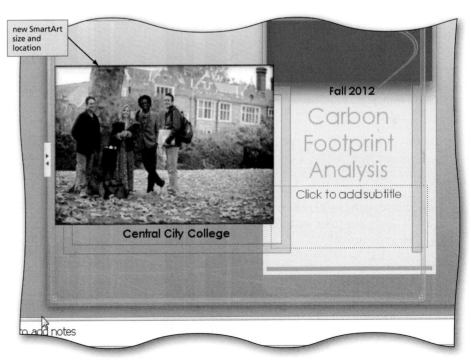

**Figure 4–14**

## To Convert Text to a SmartArt Graphic

You quickly can convert small amounts of slide text and pictures into a SmartArt graphic. Once you determine the type of graphic, such as process or cycle, you then have a wide variety of styles from which to choose in the SmartArt Graphic gallery. As with other galleries, you can point to the samples and view a live preview if you desire. The following steps convert the four bulleted text paragraphs on Slide 2 to the Hexagon Cluster graphic, which is part of the Picture category.

- Click the Next Slide button to display Slide 2.

- With the Home tab displayed, select the four bulleted list items and then click the Convert to SmartArt Graphic button (Home tab | Paragraph group) to display the SmartArt Graphics gallery (Figure 4–15).

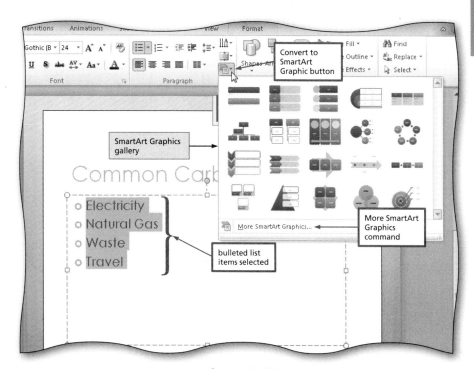

**Figure 4–15**

**2**

- Click More SmartArt Graphics in the SmartArt Graphics gallery to display the Choose a SmartArt Graphic dialog box.

- Click Picture in the left pane to display the Picture gallery.

- Scroll down and then click the Hexagon Cluster graphic (second graphic in sixth row) to display a preview of this graphic in the right pane (Figure 4–16).

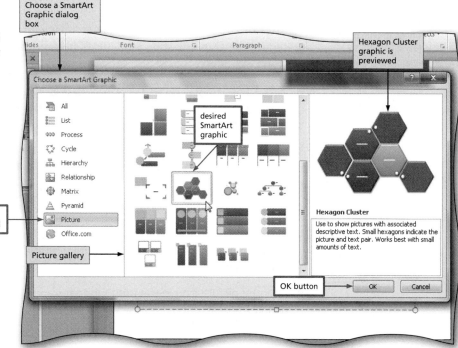

**Figure 4–16**

**3**

- Click the OK button (Choose a SmartArt Graphic dialog box) to apply this shape and convert the text (Figure 4–17).

**Q&A**

How can I edit the text that displays in the four shapes?

You can click the text and then make the desired changes. Also, if you display the Text pane on the left side of the graphic, you can click the text you want to change and make your edits.

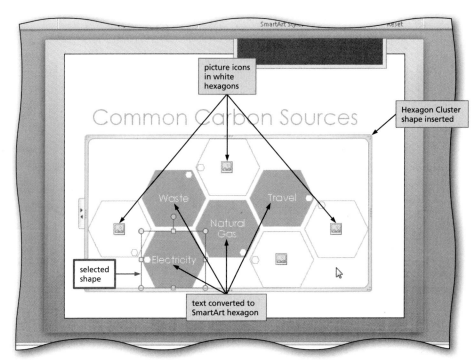

**Figure 4–17**

**Other Ways**

1. Click Convert to SmartArt on shortcut menu

**BTW**

**Q&As**
For a complete list of the Q&As found in many of the step-by-step sequences in this book, visit the PowerPoint 2010 Q&A Web page (scsite.com/ppt2010/qa).

## To Insert Pictures from a File into a SmartArt Graphic

The picture icon in each of the four white hexagons in the SmartArt graphic indicates the shape is designed to hold an image. In this presentation, you will add images located on the Data Files for Students. The following steps insert pictures into the SmartArt graphic.

**1** With Slide 2 displaying and your USB flash drive connected to one of the computer's USB ports, click the Insert picture from file icon in the top white hexagon under the word, Carbon, to display the Insert Picture dialog box.

**2** Click Waste in the list of picture files and then click the Insert button (Insert Picture dialog box) to insert the picture into the top SmartArt picture placeholder.

**3** Click the Insert picture from file icon in the left white hexagon to display the Insert Picture dialog box and then insert the picture with the file name, Electricity, into the placeholder.

**4** Click the picture icon in the white hexagon to the right of the word, Natural Gas (below the word, Travel), and insert the picture with the file name, Natural Gas, into the placeholder.

**5** Click the picture icon in the right white hexagon and then insert the picture with the file name, Transportation, into the placeholder (Figure 4–18).

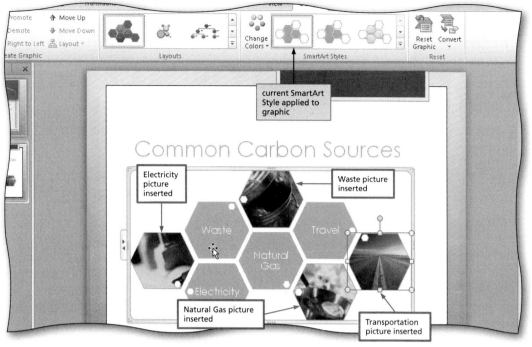

**Figure 4–18**

## To Add a SmartArt Style to the Graphic

To enhance the appearance of the group of hexagons, you can add a three-dimensional style. The following steps add the Metallic Scene Style to the Hexagon Cluster graphic.

**1** With the SmartArt graphic still selected, Click the More button in the SmartArt Styles group (SmartArt Tools Design tab) to expand the SmartArt Styles gallery.

**2** Click Metallic Scene in the 3-D area (first graphic in third row) to apply this style to the graphic (Figure 4–19).

**BTW**

**Addressing Your Audiences**
As you show your information graphics, resist the urge to turn to the screen and talk to the graphics instead of talking to your audience. If you turn toward the screen, your audience will get the impression that you are not prepared and must read information displayed on the graphics. Point with your hand nearest the screen and keep eye contact with your audience.

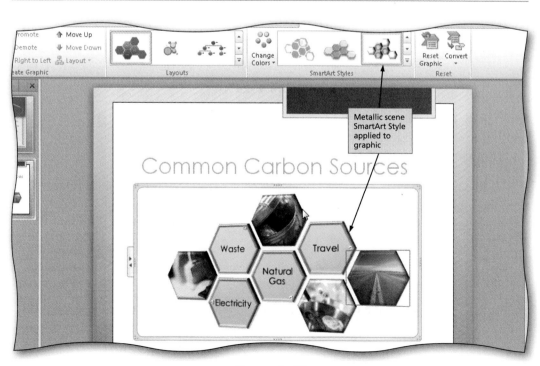

**Figure 4–19**

**BTW**

**Choosing Contrasting Colors**
Black or dark blue type on a white screen is an extremely effective color combination because the contrast increases readability. If you add a background color, be certain it has sufficient contrast with the font color. This contrast is especially important if your presentation will be delivered in a room with bright lighting that washes out the screen.

## To Change the SmartArt Color

Adding more colors to the SmartArt graphic would enhance its visual appeal. The following steps change the SmartArt graphic color to a Colorful range.

**1** With the SmartArt graphic still selected, click the Change Colors button (SmartArt Tools Design tab | SmartArt Styles group) to display the Change Colors gallery.

**2** Click Colorful Range – Accent Colors 3 to 4 to apply this color variation to the graphic (Figure 4–20).

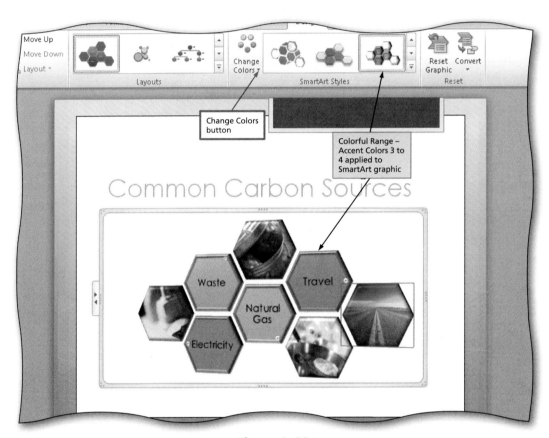

**Figure 4–20**

**BTW**

**Avoid Distorting Graphics**
Take care in preparing your visual elements so that you do not distort their physical appearance and mislead the audience. Edward R. Tufte's classic book, *The Visual Display of Quantitative Information,* presents guidelines for presenting information graphics and gives examples of accurate and inaccurate representations of data.

## To Resize a SmartArt Graphic

Although white space on a slide generally is good to have, Slide 2 has sufficient space to allow the SmartArt graphic size to increase slightly. When you adjust the graphic's height and width, all the hexagons will enlarge proportionally. The following steps resize the SmartArt graphic.

**1** With the SmartArt graphic still selected, drag one of the corner sizing handles diagonally outward, as shown in Figure 4–21.

**2** Position the graphic so it is centered in the lower area of the slide (shown in Figure 4–22).

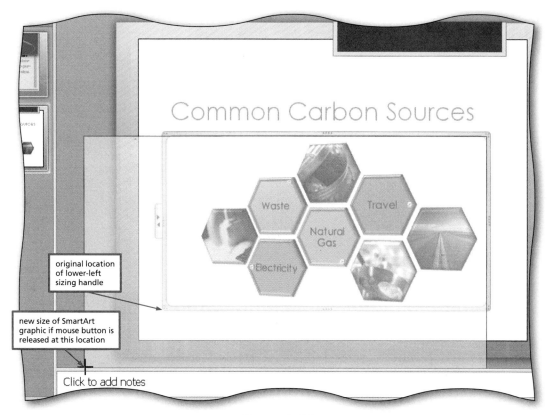

original location of lower-left sizing handle

new size of SmartArt graphic if mouse button is released at this location

**Figure 4–21**

## To Bold SmartArt Graphic Text

The text in the four hexagons can be bolded for readability. For consistency and efficiency, you can select all four hexagons and then change the text simultaneously. These hexagons are separate items in the SmartArt graphic, so you select these objects by selecting one hexagon, pressing and holding down the CTRL key, and then selecting the second, third, and fourth hexagons. The following steps simultaneously bold the hexagon text.

**1**
- Click the hexagon labeled Waste to select it. Press and hold down the CTRL key and then click the Electricity, Natural Gas, and Travel hexagons (Figure 4–22).

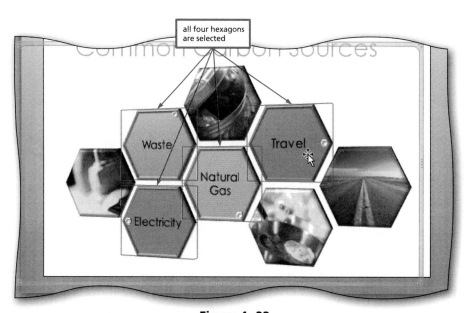

all four hexagons are selected

**Figure 4–22**

**2**
- Display the Home tab and then click the Bold button (Home tab | Font group) (Figure 4–23).

**Q&A**

Can I make other formatting changes to the graphics' text?

Yes. You can format the text by making such modifications as increasing the font size, changing the text color, and adding an underline and shadow.

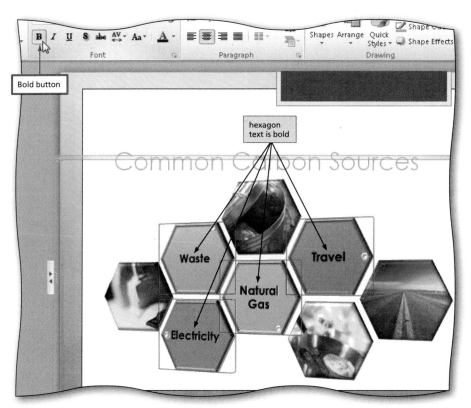

**Figure 4–23**

## To Save an Existing Presentation with the Same File Name

You have made several modifications to the presentation since you last saved it. Thus, you should save it again. The following step saves the presentation again.

**1** Click the Save button on the Quick Access Toolbar to overwrite the previously saved file.

**Break Point:** If you wish to take a break, this is a good place to do so. You can quit PowerPoint now. To resume at a later time, start PowerPoint, open the file called Carbon Footprint, and continue following the steps from this location forward.

# Adding a Chart to a Slide and Formatting

Carbon dioxide is a natural by-product of combustion, and administrators at Central City College have determined that four major elements contribute to the campus's carbon ("greenhouse gas") footprint. One-half of the greenhouse gas comes from using electricity, most of which is produced from hydropower dams, coal-burning generators, and nuclear reactors. Another large contributor is natural gas, which is used on campus to heat buildings. Transportation to and from campus adds to carbon dioxide production because most of Central City College's students and staff commute to campus using cars or buses. A fourth carbon footprint contributor is waste; microscopic bacteria eat trash in landfills and convert this garbage into carbon dioxide and methane. The chart on Slide 3, shown in Figure 4–1c on page PPT 203, shows the proportion of these four greenhouse gas sources on campus.

# Microsoft Excel and Microsoft Graph

PowerPoint uses one of two programs to develop a chart. It opens Microsoft Excel if that software is installed on your system. If Excel is not installed, PowerPoint opens Microsoft Graph and displays a chart with its associated data in a table called a datasheet. Microsoft Graph does not have the advanced features found in Excel. In this chapter, the assumption is made that Excel has been installed. When you start to create a chart, Excel opens and displays a chart in the PowerPoint slide. The default chart type is a **Clustered Column chart**. The Clustered Column chart is appropriate when comparing two or more items in specified intervals, such as comparing how inflation has risen during the past 10 years. Other popular chart types are line, bar, and pie, the latter of which you will use in Slide 3.

The figures for the chart are entered in a corresponding **Microsoft Excel worksheet**, which is a rectangular grid containing vertical columns and horizontal rows. Column letters display above the grid to identify particular **columns**, and row numbers display on the left side of the grid to identify particular **rows**. **Cells** are the intersections of rows and columns, and they are the locations for the chart data and text labels. For example, cell A1 is the intersection of column A and row 1. Numeric and text data are entered in the **active cell**, which is the one cell surrounded by a heavy border. You will replace the sample data in the worksheet by typing entries in the cells, but you also can import data from a text file, import an Excel worksheet or chart, or paste data obtained from another program. Once you have entered the data, you can modify the appearance of the chart using menus and commands.

In the following pages, you will perform these tasks:

1. Insert a chart and then replace the sample data.
2. Apply a chart style.
3. Change the line and shape outline weights.
4. Change the chart layout.
5. Resize the chart and then change the title and legend font size.
6. Separate a pie slice.
7. Rotate the chart.

**BTW**

**Giving Credit to Your Sources**
If you insert a chart that was created by someone else, you must give credit to this person and might need to ask permission to reproduce this graphic. This attribution informs your audience that you did not conduct your own research to construct this chart and that you are relying upon the expertise of another person.

---

**Plan Ahead**

**Choose an appropriate chart style.**
General adult audiences are familiar with bar and pie charts, so those chart types are good choices. Specialized audiences, such as engineers and architects, are comfortable reading scatter and bubble charts.

Common chart types and their purposes are as follows:

- Column — Vertical bars compare values over a period of time.

- Bar — Horizontal bars compare two or more values to show how the proportions relate to each other.

- Line — A line or lines show trends, increases and decreases, levels, and costs during a continuous period of time.

- Pie — A pie chart divides a single total into parts to illustrate how the segments differ from each other and the whole.

- Scatter — A scatterplot displays the effect on one variable when another variable changes.

In general, three-dimensional charts are more difficult to comprehend than two-dimensional charts. The added design elements in a three-dimensional chart add clutter and take up space. Also, legends help keep the chart clean, so use them prominently on the slide.

## To Insert a Chart

The next step in developing the presentation is to insert a chart. The following steps insert a chart with sample data into Slide 3.

- Click the New Slide button to add Slide 3 to the presentation (Figure 4–24).

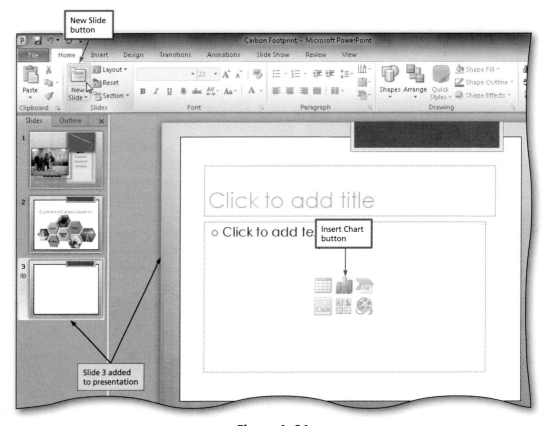

**Figure 4–24**

- Click the Insert Chart button in the content placeholder to display the Insert Chart dialog box.

- Scroll down and then click the Pie in 3-D chart button in the Pie area to select that chart style (Figure 4–25).

**Q&A**

Can I change the chart style after I have inserted a chart?

Yes. Click the Change Chart Type button in the Type group on the SmartArt Tools Design tab to display the Change Chart Type dialog box and then make another selection.

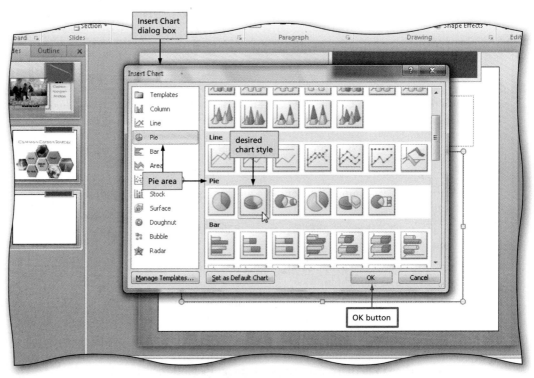

**Figure 4–25**

**3**

- Click the OK button (Insert Chart dialog box) to start the Microsoft Excel program and open a worksheet tiled on the right side of your Carbon Footprint presentation (Figure 4–26).

**Q&A** What do the numbers in the worksheet and the chart represent?

Excel places sample data in the worksheet and charts the sample data in the default chart type.

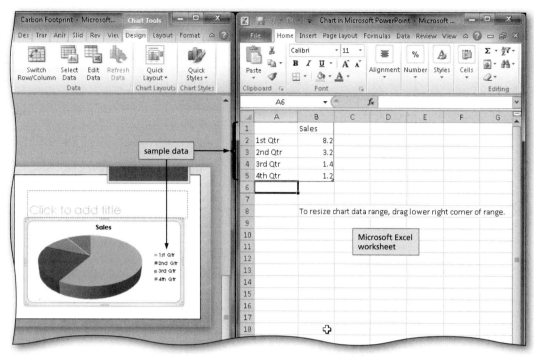

**Figure 4–26**

---

**Obtain information for the graphic from credible sources.**

At times, you are familiar with the data for your chart or table because you have conducted in-the-field, or primary, research by interviewing experts or taking measurements. Other times, however, you have gathered the data from secondary sources, such as magazine articles, newspaper articles, or Web sites. General circulation magazines and newspapers, such as *Newsweek* and the *Wall Street Journal*, use experienced journalists and editors to verify their information. Also, online databases, such as EBSCOhost, OCLC FirstSearch, LexisNexis Academic, and NewsBank Info Web contain articles from credible sources.

On the other hand, some sources have particular biases and present information that supports their causes. Political, religious, and social publications and Web sites often are designed for specific audiences who share a common point of view. You should, therefore, recognize that data from these sources can be skewed.

If you did not conduct the research yourself, you should give credit to the source of your information. You are acknowledging that someone else provided the data and giving your audience the opportunity to obtain the same materials you used. Type the source at the bottom of your chart or table, especially if you are distributing handouts of your slides. At the very least, state the source during the body of your speech.

**Plan Ahead**

## To Replace Sample Data

The next step in creating the chart is to replace the sample data, which will redraw the chart. The sample data is displayed in two columns and five rows. The first row and left column contain text labels and will be used to create the chart title and legend. A **legend** is a box that identifies each slice of the pie chart and coordinates with the colors assigned to the slice categories. The other cells contain numbers that are used to determine the size of the pie slices. The following steps replace the sample data in the worksheet.

**1**

- Click cell B1, which is the intersection of column B and row 1, to select it.

**Q&A**

Why did my mouse pointer change shape?

The mouse pointer changes to a block plus sign to indicate a cell is selected.

- Type **Central City College Greenhouse Gas Sources** in cell B1 to replace the sample chart title (Figure 4–27).

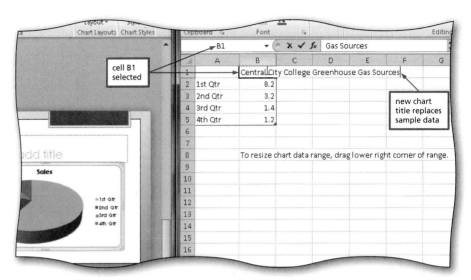

**Figure 4–27**

**2**

- Click cell A2 to select that cell.

- Type **Electricity** in cell A2 (Figure 4–28).

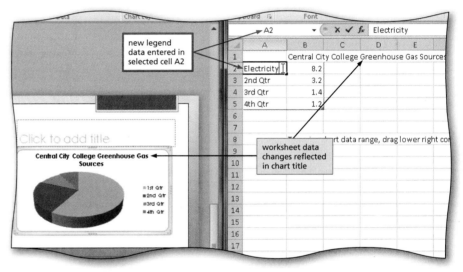

**Figure 4–28**

**3**

- Press the DOWN ARROW key to move the mouse pointer to cell A3.

- Type **Natural Gas** in cell A3 and then press the DOWN ARROW key to move the mouse pointer to cell A4.

**4**

- Type **Travel** in cell A4 and then press the DOWN ARROW key.

- Type **Waste** in cell A5 (Figure 4–29).

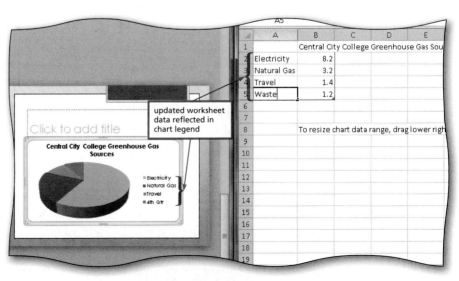

**Figure 4–29**

- Click cell B2, type 50 in that cell, and then press the DOWN ARROW key to move the mouse pointer to cell B3.

- Type 30 in cell B3 and then press the DOWN ARROW key.

- Type 13 in cell B4 and then press the DOWN ARROW key.

- Type 7 in cell B5. Do not press the DOWN ARROW key (Figure 4–30).

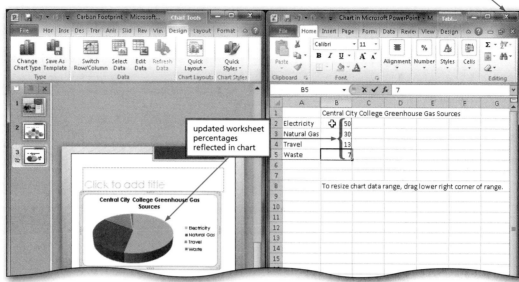

**Figure 4–30**

**Q&A** Why do the slices in the PowerPoint pie chart change locations?

As you enter data in the Excel worksheet, the chart slices rotate to reflect these new figures.

- Close Excel by clicking its Close button.

**Q&A** Can I open the Excel spreadsheet once it has been closed?

Yes. Click the chart to select it and then click the Edit Data button (Chart Tools Design tab | Data group).

## To Apply a Chart Style

Each chart type has a variety of styles that can change the look of the chart. If desired, you can change the chart from two dimensions to three dimensions, add borders, and vary the colors of the slices, lines, and bars. When you inserted the Pie in 3-D chart, a style was applied automatically. Thumbnails of this style and others are displayed in the Chart Styles gallery. The following steps apply a chart style to the Slide 3 pie chart.

- If the entire pie chart area is not selected, click a white space near the pie chart and then click the Chart Tools Design tab to display the Chart Tools Design Ribbon (Figure 4–31).

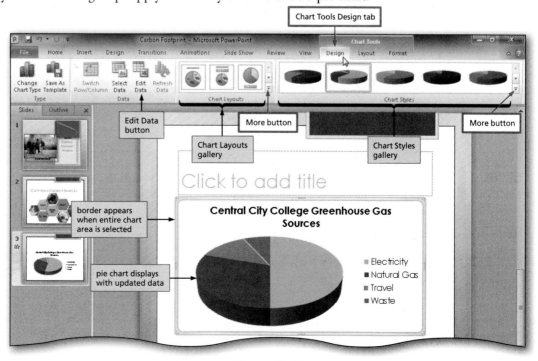

**Figure 4–31**

**2**

- Click the More button in the Chart Styles gallery to expand the gallery.

- Point to Style 10 (second chart in second row) (Figure 4–32).

**Q&A**  Does the Chart Styles gallery have a live preview feature?

This feature is not available.

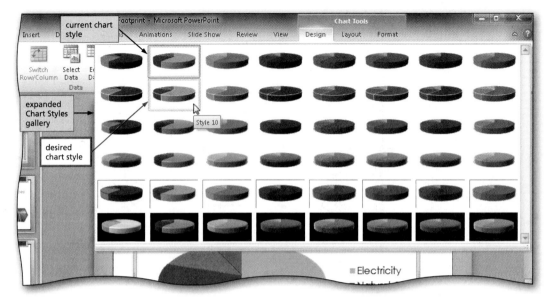

Figure 4–32

**3**

- Click Style 10 in the Chart Styles gallery to apply the selected style to the chart (Figure 4–33).

**Q&A**  Can I change the chart type?

Yes. Click the Change Chart Type button (Chart Tools Design tab | Type group) and then select a different type.

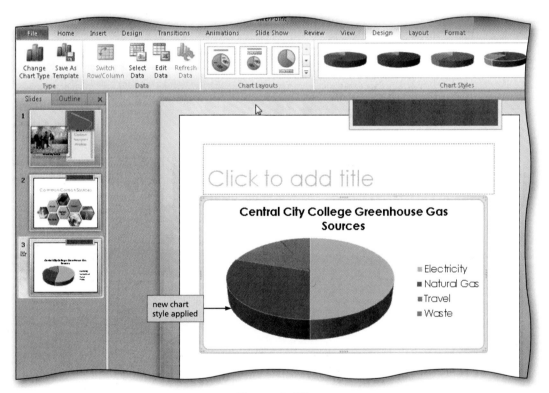

Figure 4–33

## To Change the Shape Outline Weight

Chart Style 10 has thin white outlines around each pie slice and around each color square in the legend. You can change the weight of these lines to accentuate each slice. The following steps change the outline weight.

**1**

- Click the Chart Tools Format tab to display the Chart Tools Format Ribbon.

- Click the center of the pie chart to select it and display the sizing handles around each slice.

- Click the Shape Outline button arrow (Chart Tools Format tab | Shape Styles group) to display the Shape Outline gallery.

- Point to Weight in the Shape Outline gallery to display the Weight list (Figure 4–34).

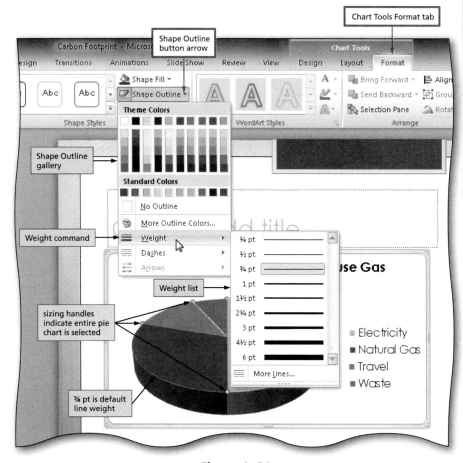

**Figure 4–34**

**2**

- Point to 4½ pt to display a live preview of this outline line weight (Figure 4–35).

 **Experiment**

- Point to various weights on the submenu and watch the border weights on the pie slices change.

**3**

- Click 4½ pt to increase the border around each slice to that width.

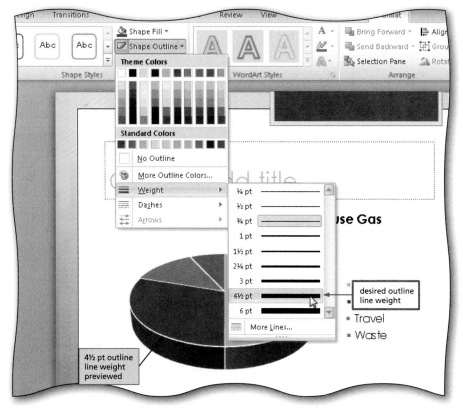

**Figure 4–35**

## To Change the Shape Outline Color

Style 10 has white outlines around each pie slice and around each color square in the legend. At this point, you can't see the border around the legend squares because it is white. You can change this color to add contrast to each slice and legend color square. The following steps change the border color.

- Click the Shape Outline button arrow (Chart Tools Format tab | Shape Styles group) and then point to Orange in the Standard Colors area to display a live preview of that border color on the pie slice shapes and legend squares.

**Experiment**

- Point to various colors in the Shape Outline gallery and watch the border colors on the pie slices change.

- Click Orange to add orange borders around each slice and also around the color squares in the legend (Figure 4–36).

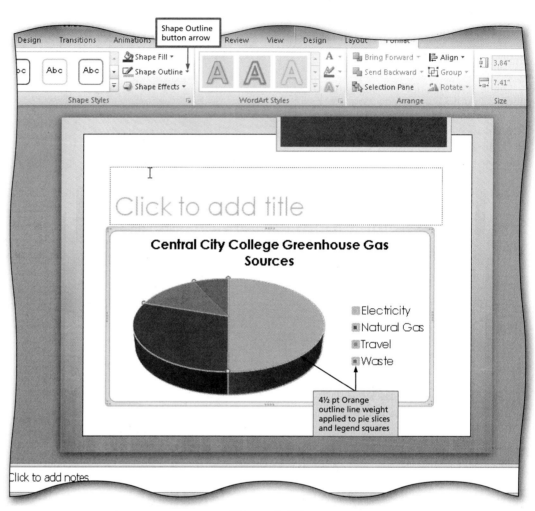

**Figure 4–36**

## To Change a Chart Layout

Once you have selected a chart style, you can modify the look of the chart elements by changing its layout. The various layouts move the legend above or below the chart, or they move some or all of the legend data directly onto the individual chart pieces. For example, in the pie chart type, seven different layouts display only percentages on the pie slices, only the identifying information, such as the word, Electricity, or combinations of this data. If the chart layout displays a title that provides sufficient information to describe the chart's purpose, you may want to delete the slide title text placeholder. The following steps apply a chart layout with a title, legend, and percentages to the Slide 3 pie chart and then delete the title text placeholder.

**①**

- With the chart still selected, click the Chart Tools Design tab to display the Chart Tools Design Ribbon and then click the More button in the Chart Layouts gallery to expand the gallery.

- Point to Layout 2 (second chart in first row) (Figure 4–37).

**Q&A** Does the Chart Layouts gallery have a live preview feature?

This feature is not available.

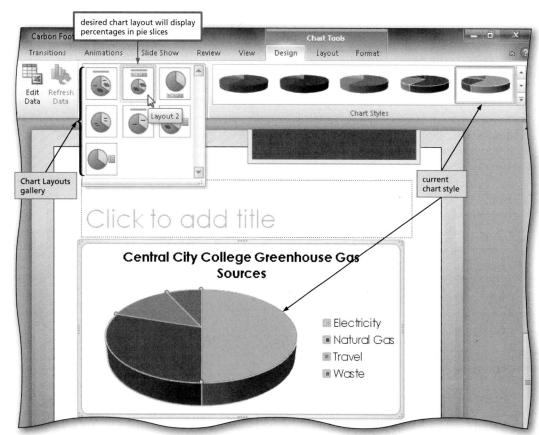

**Figure 4–37**

**②**

- Click Layout 2 in the Chart Layouts gallery to apply the selected layout to the chart (Figure 4–38).

**Q&A** Can I change the chart layout?

Because a live preview is not available, you may want to sample the various layouts to evaluate their effectiveness. To change these layouts, repeat Steps 1 and 2 with different layouts.

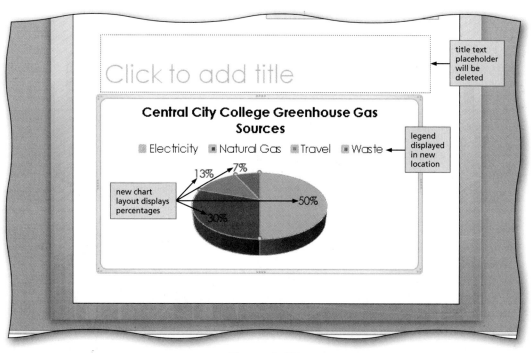

**Figure 4–38**

## To Resize a Chart

Removing the title text placeholder increases the white space on the slide, so you are able to enlarge the chart and aid readability. You resize a chart the same way you resize a SmartArt graphic or any other graphical object. The following steps delete the title text placeholder and resize the chart to fill Slide 3.

- Click a border of the title text placeholder so that it displays as a solid line and then press the DELETE key to remove the placeholder.

- Select the chart, point to a corner sizing handle, and then drag diagonally outward, as shown in Figure 4–39.

- Release the mouse button to resize the chart. Position the chart so it is centered in the slide.

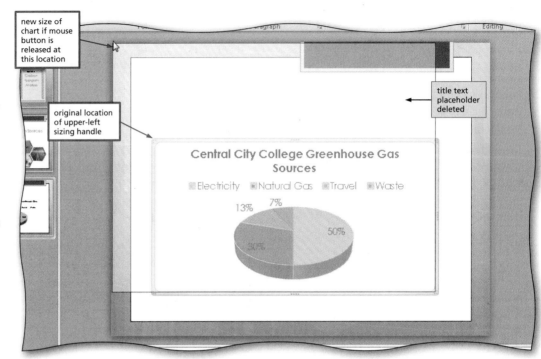

**Figure 4–39**

## To Change the Title and Legend Font Size

Depending upon the complexity of the chart and the overall slide, you may want to increase the font size of the chart title and legend to increase readability. The following steps change the font size of both of these chart elements.

- Click the chart title, Central City College Greenhouse Gas Sources, and then triple-click to select the paragraph of text and display the Mini toolbar.

- Click the Increase Font Size button to increase the font size of the selected text to 32 point (Figure 4–40).

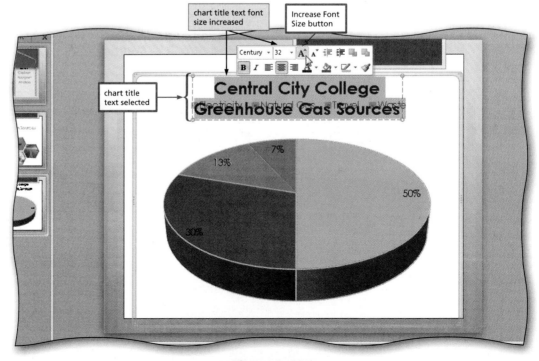

**Figure 4–40**

- Click an area of the chart other than the title to position the new title text.

- Right-click the legend in the chart to display the Mini toolbar and a legends shortcut menu.

- Click the Increase Font Size button on the Mini toolbar to increase the font size of the legend text to 20 point (Figure 4–41).

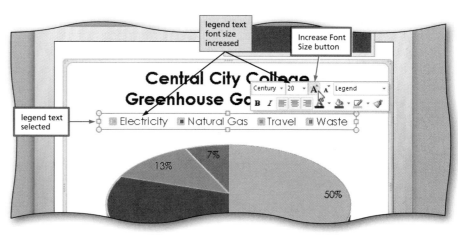

**Figure 4–41**

## To Separate a Pie Slice

At times, you may desire to draw the viewers' attention to a particular area of the pie chart. To add this emphasis, you can separate, or explode, one or more slices. For example, you can separate the orange Travel slice of the chart to stress that Central City College students and staff contribute significantly to greenhouse gas production when traveling to and from campus. The following steps separate a chart slice.

- Click the orange Travel slice of the pie chart to select it.

- Click and hold down the mouse button and then drag the Travel slice diagonally toward the word, Electricity (Figure 4–42).

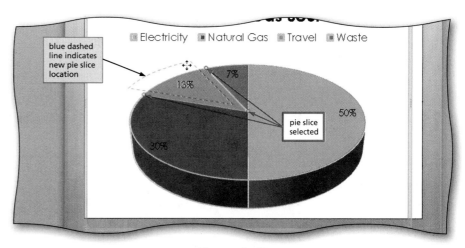

**Figure 4–42**

- Release the mouse button to position the slice in a new location on the slide (Figure 4–43).

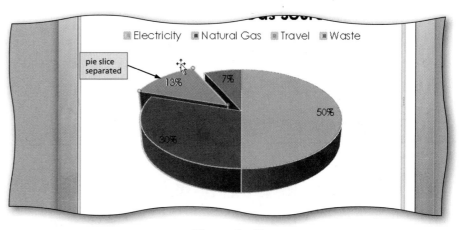

**Figure 4–43**

## To Rotate a Chart

Excel determines where each slice of pie is positioned in the chart. You may desire to have a specific slice display in a different location, such as at the top or bottom of the circle. You can rotate the entire chart clockwise until a particular part of the chart displays where you desire. A circle's circumference is 360 degrees, so if you want to move a slice from the top of the chart to the bottom, you would rotate it halfway around the circle, or 180 degrees. Similarly, if you a want a slice to move one-quarter of the way around the slide, you would rotate it either 90 degrees or 270 degrees. The following steps rotate the chart so that the orange Travel slice displays at the bottom of the chart.

- With the orange Travel slice of the pie chart still selected, click the Chart Tools Format tab to display the Chart Tools Format Ribbon.

- Click the Format Selection button (Chart Tools Format tab | Current Selection group) to display the Format Data Point dialog box (Figure 4–44).

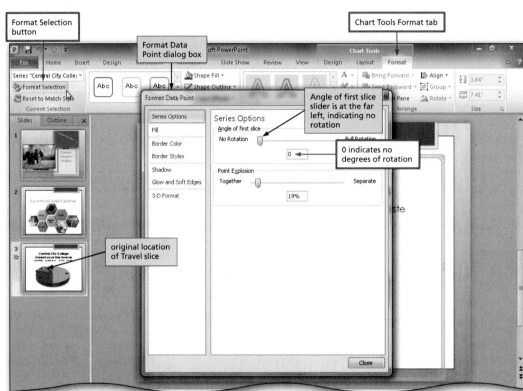

**Figure 4–44**

- Click the 'Angle of first slice' text box, delete the text, and then type **235** in the box to specify that the Travel slice rotates 235 degrees to the right (Figure 4–45).

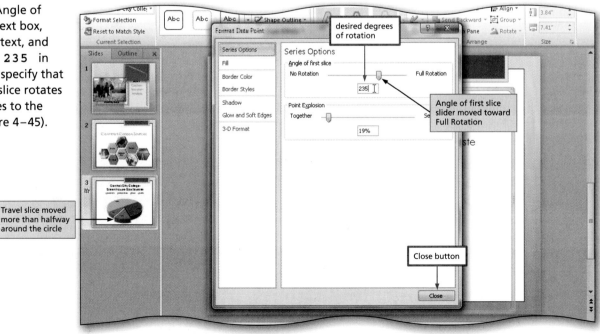

**Figure 4–45**

● Click the Close button to close the dialog box and rotate the chart (Figure 4–46).

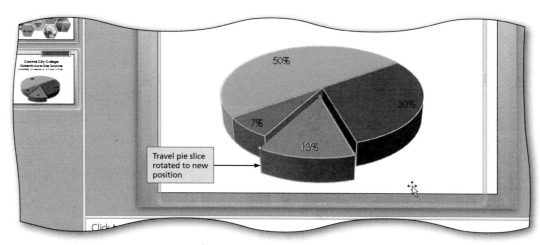

**Figure 4–46**

**Break Point:** If you wish to take a break, this is a good place to do so. Be sure to save the Carbon Footprint file again and then you can quit PowerPoint. To resume at a later time, start PowerPoint, open the file called Carbon Footprint, and continue following the steps from this location forward.

# Adding a Table to a Slide and Formatting

One effective method of organizing information on a slide is to use a **table**, which is a grid consisting of rows and columns. You can enhance a table with formatting, including adding colors, lines, and backgrounds, and changing fonts.

In the following pages, you will perform these tasks:

1. Insert a table and then enter data and symbols.
2. Apply a table style.
3. Add borders and an effect.
4. Resize the table.
5. Add an image.
6. Merge cells and then display text in the cell vertically.
7. Align text in cells.
8. Format table data.

## Tables

The table on Slide 4 (shown in Figure 4–1d on page PPT 203) contains information about the five major methods students and staff use to travel to campus. This data is listed in four columns and six rows. The intersections of these rows and columns are **cells**.

To begin developing this table, you first must create an empty table and insert it into the slide. You must specify the table's **dimension**, which is the total number of rows and columns. This table will have a 4 × 6 dimension; the first number indicates the number of columns, and the second specifies the number of rows. You will fill the cells with data pertaining to transportation to campus. Then you will format the table using a table style.

**BTW**

**Entering Table Data**
The table you create on Slide 4 has four columns and six rows. Many times, however, you may need to create much larger tables and then enter data into many cells. In these cases, experienced PowerPoint designers recommend clearing all formatting from the table so that you can concentrate on the numbers and letters and not be distracted by the colors and borders. To clear formatting, click the Clear Table command at the bottom of the Table Styles gallery (Table Tools Design tab | Table Styles group). Then, add a table style once you have verified that all table data is correct.

## To Insert an Empty Table

The next step in developing the presentation is to insert an empty table. The following steps insert a table with four columns and six rows into Slide 4.

**1**
- Add a new slide to the presentation (Figure 4–47).

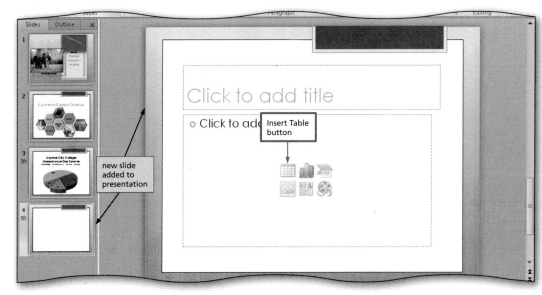

**Figure 4–47**

**2**
- Click the Insert Table button in the content placeholder to display the Insert Table dialog box.

- Click the down arrow to the right of the 'Number of columns' text box one time so that the number 4 appears in the box.

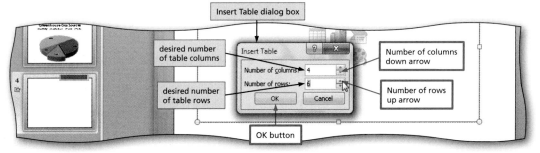

**Figure 4–48**

- Click the up arrow to the right of the 'Number of rows' text box four times so that the number 6 appears in the box (Figure 4–48).

**3**
- Click the OK button (Insert Table dialog box) to insert the table into Slide 4 (Figure 4–49).

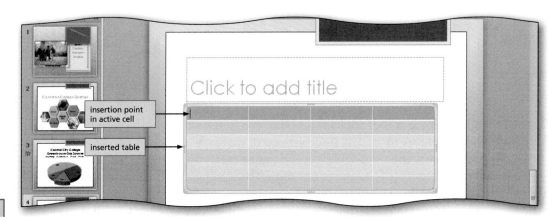

**Other Ways**

1. Click Table on Insert tab, drag to select columns and rows, press ENTER

**Figure 4–49**

## To Enter Data in a Table

The Slide 4 table title will display vertically in the first column. The three columns to the right of this title will contain data with symbols representing the type of travel, words describing this travel, and the percent of students and staff using these modes of travel. The next step is to enter data in the cells of the empty table. To place data in a cell, you click the cell and then type text. The following steps enter the data in the table.

- Click the second cell in the third column to place the insertion point in this cell. Type **Drive alone** and then press the TAB key to advance the insertion point to the adjacent right column cell.

- Type **53%** and then press the TAB key three times to advance to the cell below the words, Drive Alone.

- Type **Carpool** and then press the TAB key.

- Type **5%** and then press the TAB key three times (Figure 4–50).

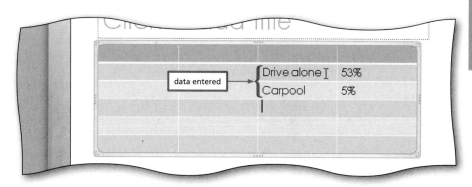

**Figure 4–50**

Q&A | How do I correct cell contents if I make a mistake?
Click the cell and then correct the text.

Q&A | Can I use the arrow keys to move the insertion point in the table cells?
Yes.

- Enter the data for the remaining table cells in the third and fourth columns, using Figure 4–51 as a guide.

Q&A | What if I pressed the TAB key after filling in the last cell and added another row?

Right-click the unnecessary row and then click Delete Rows on the shortcut menu.

Q&A | How would I add more rows to the table?

When the insertion point is positioned in the bottom-right cell, press the TAB key.

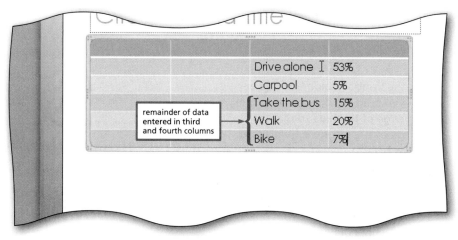

**Figure 4–51**

## To Insert a Symbol

The Slide 4 table title will display vertically in the first column. The three columns to the right of this title will contain symbols and words describing the type of travel and the percent of students and staff using these modes of travel. The second column of the table contains symbols depicting the various modes of transportation. Although you could add clip art or pictures to these table cells, you also can insert special symbols. You insert symbols, such as mathematical characters and dots, using the Symbol dialog box.

The following steps insert symbols in the second table column.

● Click the second cell in the second column to place the insertion point in this cell.

● Display the Insert tab.

● Click the Symbol button (Insert tab | Symbols group) to display the Symbol dialog box (Figure 4–52).

**Q&A** What if the symbol I want to insert already appears in the Symbol dialog box?

You can click any symbol shown in the dialog box to insert it in the slide.

**Q&A** Why does my 'Recently used symbols' list display different symbols from those shown in Figure 4–52?

As you insert symbols, PowerPoint places them in the 'Recently used symbols' list.

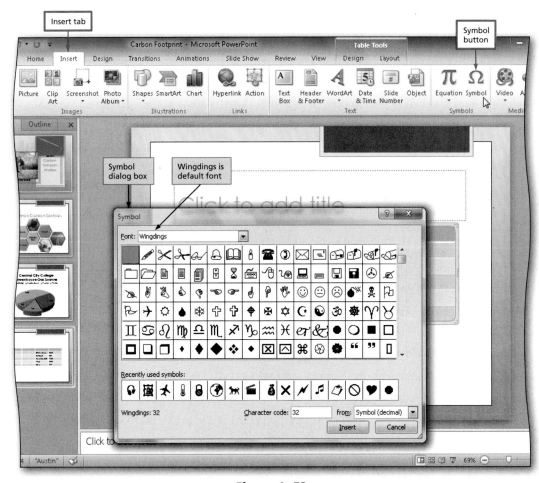

Figure 4–52

● Click the Symbol dialog box title bar and then drag the dialog box to the right edge of the slide so that the left side of the second column in the table is visible.

● If Webdings is not the font displayed in the Font box, click the Font box arrow (Symbol dialog box) and then scroll to Webdings and click it.

● In the list of symbols, if necessary, scroll to and then click the man symbol shown in Figure 4–53.

● Click the Insert button (Symbol dialog box) to place the man symbol in the selected table cell (Figure 4–53).

**Q&A** Why is the Symbol dialog box still open?

The Symbol dialog box remains open, allowing you to insert additional symbols.

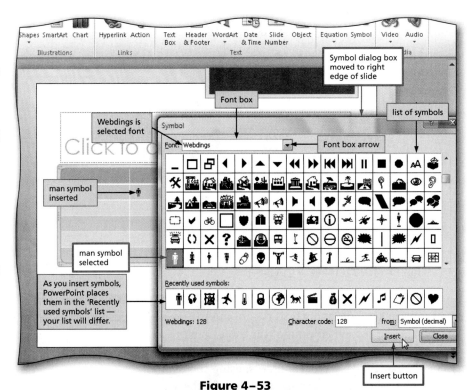

Figure 4–53

**4**

- In the list of symbols, click the car symbol shown in Figure 4–54.

- Click the Insert button (Symbol dialog box) to place the car symbol beside the man symbol in the selected table cell (Figure 4–54).

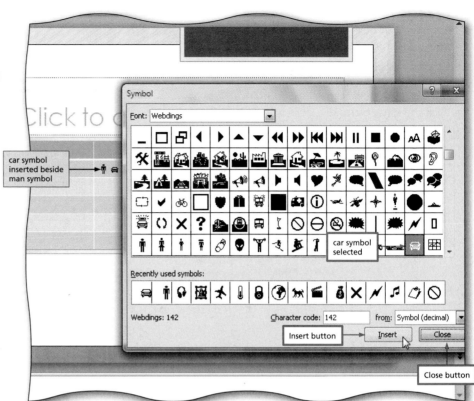

**Figure 4–54**

**5**

- Click the Close button (Symbol dialog box).

**6**

- Press the DOWN ARROW key to move the insertion point to the third cell in the second table column.

- Display the Symbol dialog box and then insert the people and car symbols shown in Figure 4–55.

**Q&A**

Can I insert the car symbol from the 'Recently used symbols' list?

Yes. PowerPoint designers generally reuse a set of symbols, which conveniently are displayed in this list for this purpose.

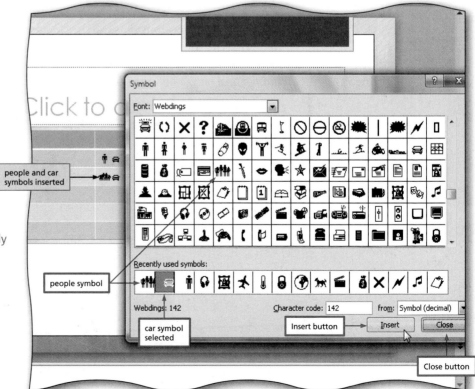

**Figure 4–55**

● Using Figure 4–56 as a guide, continue inserting symbols in the second column.

● Click the Close button (Symbol dialog box).

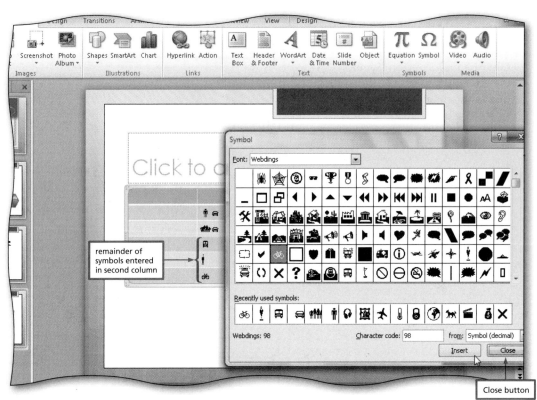

**Figure 4–56**

## To Apply a Table Style

A table style is a combination of formatting options that use the theme colors applied to the presentation. When you inserted the table, PowerPoint automatically applied a style. Thumbnails of this style and others are displayed in the Table Styles gallery. These styles use a variety of colors and shading and are grouped in the categories of Best Match for Document, Light, Medium, and Dark. The following steps apply a table style to the Slide 4 table.

● With the insertion point in the table, display the Table Tools Design tab (Figure 4–57).

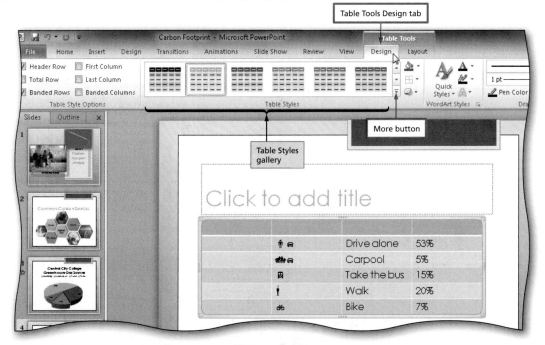

**Figure 4–57**

**2**

- Click the More button in the Table Styles gallery to expand the Table Styles gallery.

- Scroll down and then point to Dark Style 2 - Accent 3/Accent 4 in the Dark area (third table in last row) (Figure 4–58).

 Does the Table Styles gallery have a live preview feature?

Yes, but the gallery is covering most of the table, greatly limiting your ability to preview table styles.

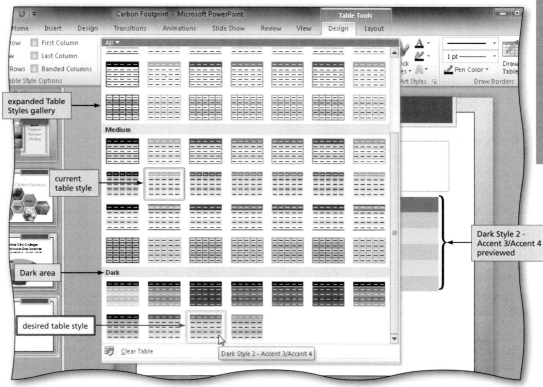

**Figure 4–58**

**3**

- Click Dark Style 2 - Accent 3/Accent 4 in the Table Styles gallery to apply the selected style to the table (Figure 4–59).

**Q&A** Can I resize the columns and rows or the entire table?

Yes. To resize columns or rows, drag a **column boundary** (the border to the right of a column) or the **row boundary** (the border at the bottom of a row) until the column or row is the desired width or height. To resize the entire table, drag a **table resize handle**.

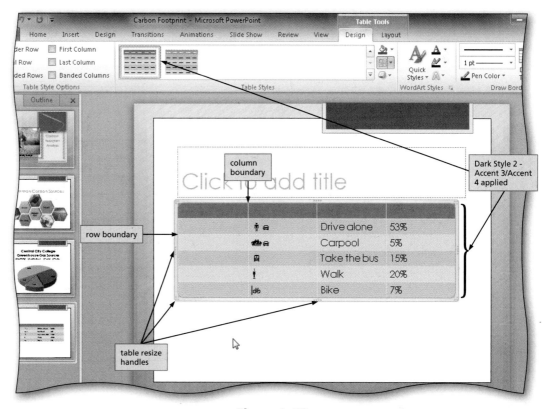

**Figure 4–59**

## To Add Borders to a Table

The Slide 4 table does not have borders around the entire table or between the cells. The following steps add borders to the entire table.

- Click the edge of the table so that the insertion point does not appear in any cell.

- Click the Border button arrow (Table Tools Design tab | Table Styles group) to display the Border gallery (Figure 4–60).

 Why is the button called No Border in the ScreenTip?

The ScreenTip name for the button will change based on the type of border, if any, present in the table. Currently no borders are applied.

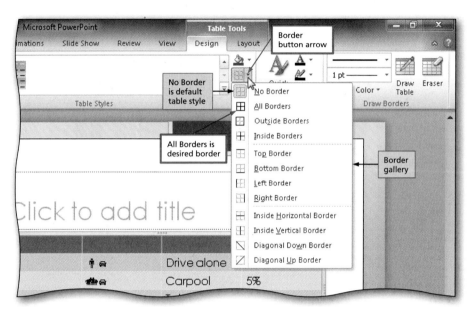

**Figure 4–60**

- Click All Borders in the Border gallery to add borders around the entire table and to each table cell (Figure 4–61).

 Why is the border color black?

PowerPoint's default border color is black. This color is displayed on the Pen Color button (Table Tools Design tab | Draw Borders group).

 Can I apply any of the border options in the Border gallery?

Yes. You can vary the look of your table by applying borders only to the cells, around the table, to the top, bottom, left or right edges, or a combination of these areas.

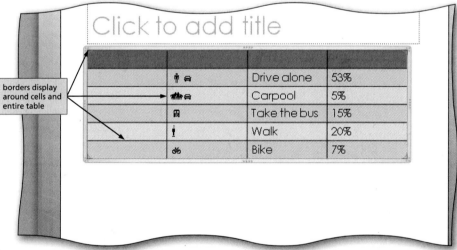

**Figure 4–61**

## To Add an Effect to a Table

To enhance the visual appeal of the table, you can add an effect. PowerPoint gives you the option of applying a bevel to specified cells so they have a three-dimensional appearance. You also can add a shadow or reflection to the entire table. The following steps add a shadow and give a three-dimensional appearance to the entire table.

**1**

- With the table selected, click the Effects button (Table Tools Design tab | Table Styles group) to display the Effects menu.

**Q&A** What is the difference between a shadow and a reflection?

A shadow gives the appearance that a light is displayed on the table, which causes a shadow behind the graphic. A reflection gives the appearance that the table is shiny, so a mirror image appears below the actual graphic.

**2**

- Point to Shadow to display the Shadow gallery (Figure 4–62).

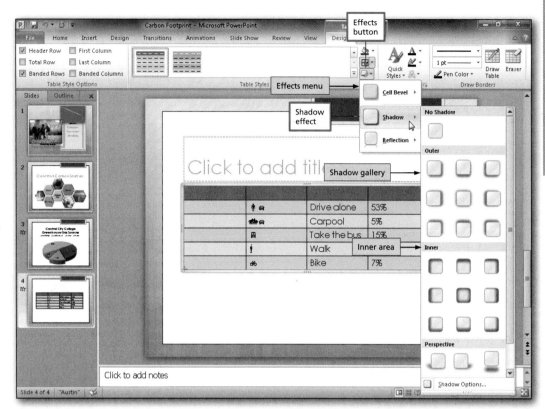

**Figure 4–62**

**Q&A** How do the shadows differ in the Outer, Inner, and Perspective categories?

The Outer shadows are displayed on the outside of the table, whereas the Inner shadows are displayed in the interior cells. The Perspective shadows give the illusion that a light is shining from the right or left side of the table or from above, and the table is casting a shadow.

**3**

- Point to Inside Center in the Inner category (second shadow in second row) to display a live preview of this shadow (Figure 4–63).

**Experiment**

- Point to the various shadows in the Shadow gallery and watch the shadows change in the table.

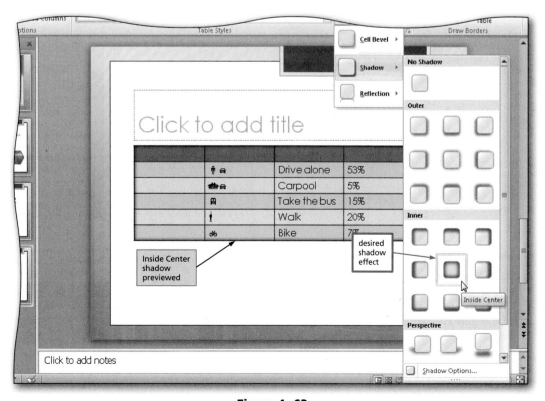

**Figure 4–63**

● Click Inside Center to apply this shadow to the table (Figure 4–64).

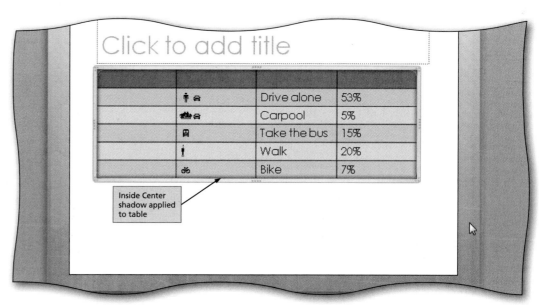

**Figure 4–64**

## To Resize a Table

You resize a table the same way you resize a chart, a SmartArt graphic, or any other graphical object. On Slide 4, you can remove the title text placeholder because the table will have the title, Travel to Campus, in the first column. The following steps resize the table to fill Slide 4.

● Click a border of the title text placeholder so that it displays as a solid line and then press the DELETE key to remove the placeholder.

● Select the table, point to a corner sizing handle, and then drag diagonally outward, as shown in Figure 4–65.

● Release the mouse button to resize the chart. Position the table so it is centered in the slide (shown in Figure 4–66).

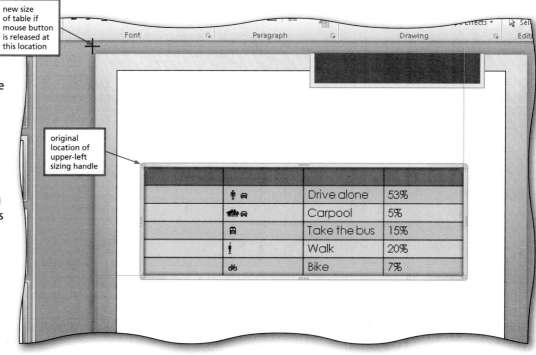

**Figure 4–65**

## To Add an Image to a Table

Another table enhancement you can make is to add a picture or clip to a table cell. The following steps add a commuter picture to the upper-right table cell.

- Right-click the upper-right table cell to display the shortcut menu and Mini toolbar (Figure 4–66).

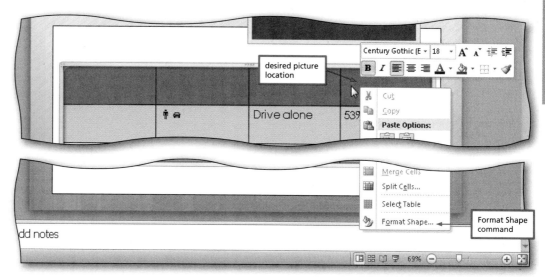

**Figure 4–66**

- Click Format Shape to display the Format Shape dialog box and then click 'Picture or texture fill' (Figure 4–67).

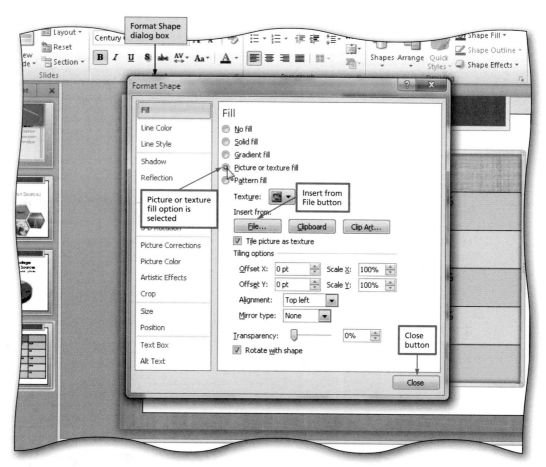

**Figure 4–67**

- Click the Insert from File button to display the Insert Picture dialog box.

- Select the Commuters picture located on the Data Files for Students and then click the Insert button in the Insert Picture dialog box to insert the picture into the table cell.

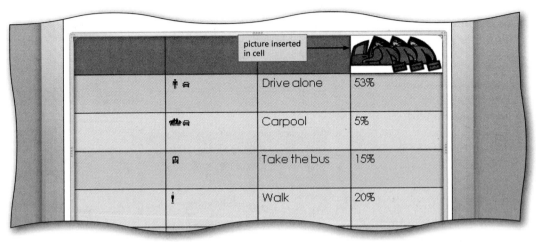

**Figure 4–68**

- Click the Close button (Format Shape dialog box) (Figure 4–68).

## To Merge Cells

To provide space for the table title to stretch across the entire table height, you can merge all the cells in the first column. In addition, the top row of the table will contain only the picture you added to the upper-right cell, so you can merge cells in the top row so it looks like a single cell. The following steps merge the six cells in the first column into a single cell and merge two cells in the first table row.

- Drag through all six cells in the first table column to select these cells (Figure 4–69).

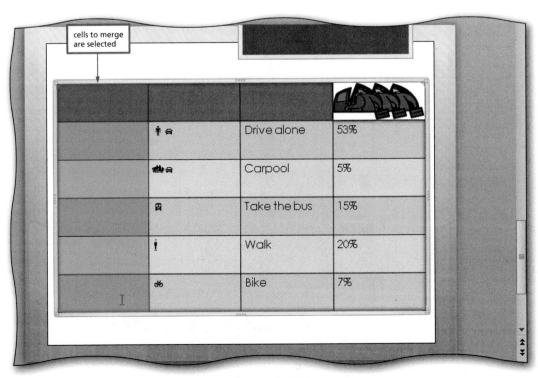

**Figure 4–69**

**2**

• Click the Table Tools Layout tab to display the Table Tools Layout Ribbon.

• Click the Merge Cells button (Table Tools Layout tab | Merge group) to merge the six column cells into one cell (Figure 4–70).

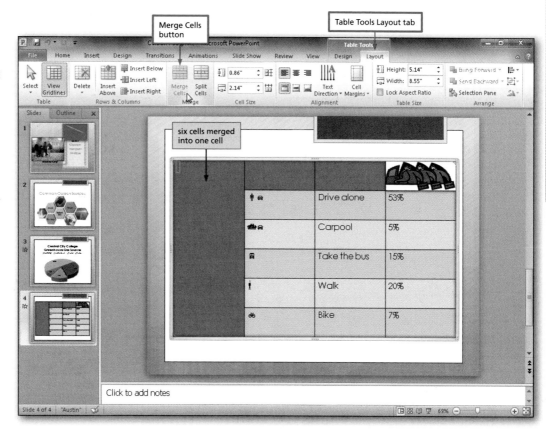

**Figure 4–70**

**3**

• Drag through the second and third column cells in the first table row to select these two cells (Figure 4–71).

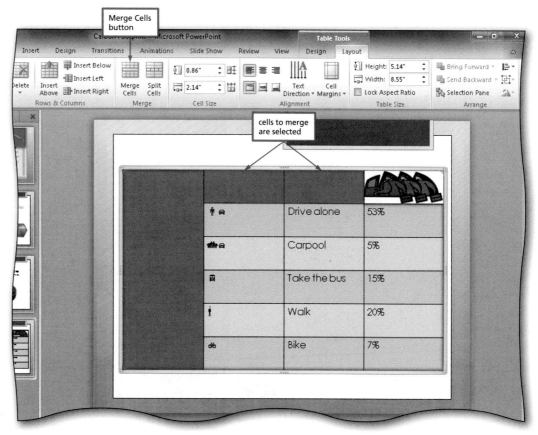

**Figure 4–71**

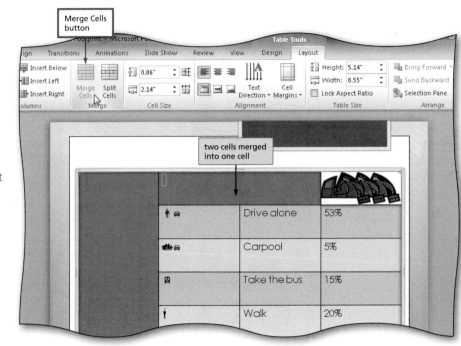

**Figure 4–72**

**4**

- Click the Merge Cells button to merge these cells (Figure 4–72).

 Could I have merged the cells in the first row before merging the first column cells?

Yes, but you would have achieved different results. If you merge the row one cells, then you would need to merge all first column cells except the first cell.

**Other Ways**

1. Right-click selected cells, click Merge Cells on shortcut menu

## To Display Text in a Cell Vertically

The default orientation of table cell text is horizontal. You can change this direction to stack the letters so they display above and below each other, or you can rotate the direction in 90-degree increments. The following steps rotate the text in the first column cell.

**1**

- With the Table Tools Layout tab displayed, click the column 1 cell.

- Type **Travel to Campus** in the table cell.

- Click the Text Direction button (Table Tools Layout tab | Alignment group) to display the Text Direction gallery (Figure 4–73).

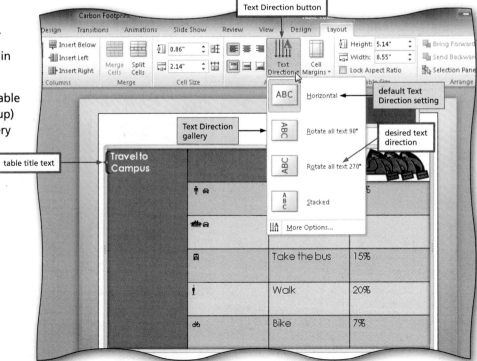

**Figure 4–73**

**2**
- Click 'Rotate all text 270°' to rotate the text in the cell (Figure 4–74).

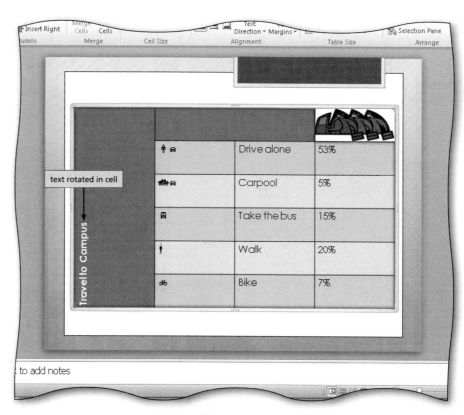

text rotated in cell

Figure 4–74

**Other Ways**
1. Right-click selected cells, click Format Shape on shortcut menu, click Text Box, click Text direction arrow

## To Align Text in Cells

The data in each cell can be aligned horizontally and vertically. You change the horizontal alignment of each cell in a similar manner as you center, left-align, or right-align text in a placeholder. You also can change the vertical alignment so that the data displays at the top, middle, or bottom of each cell. The following steps center the text both horizontally and vertically in each table cell.

- With the Table Tools Layout tab displayed, click the Select button (Table group) to display the Select menu (Figure 4–75).

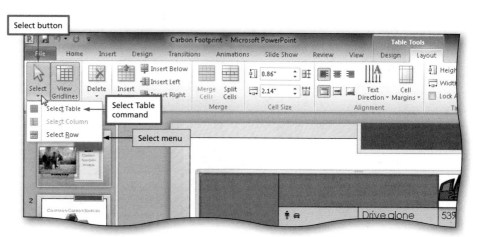

Select button

Select Table command

Select menu

Figure 4–75

**2**

- Click Select Table in the Select menu to select the entire table.

- Click the Center button (Table Tools Layout tab | Alignment group) to center the text between the left and right borders of each cell in the table (Figure 4–76).

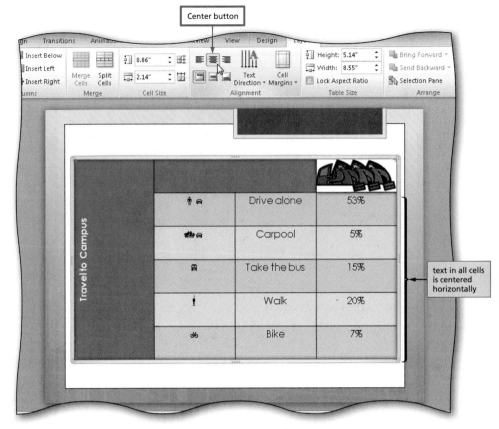

Figure 4–76

**3**

- Click the Center Vertically button (Table Tools Layout tab | Alignment group) to center the text between the top and bottom borders of each cell in the table (Figure 4–77).

**Q&A**

Must I center all the table cells, or can I center only specific cells?

You can center as many cells as you desire at one time by selecting one or more cells.

**Other Ways**

1. Right-click selected cells, click Format Shape on shortcut menu, click Text Box, click Vertical alignment arrow

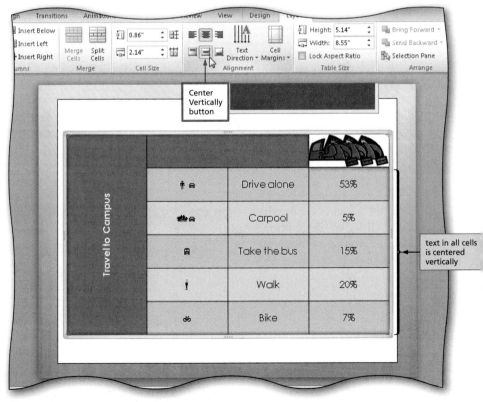

Figure 4–77

## To Format Table Data

The final table enhancement is to bold the text in all cells and increase the font size of the title and the symbols. The entire table is selected, so you can bold all text simultaneously. The title and symbols will have different font sizes. The following steps format the data.

**1** Display the Home tab and then click the Bold button (Font group) to bold all text in the table.

**2** Select the table title text in the first column and then increase the font size to 36 point.

**3** Select the symbols in the second column and then increase the font size to 44 point (Figure 4–78).

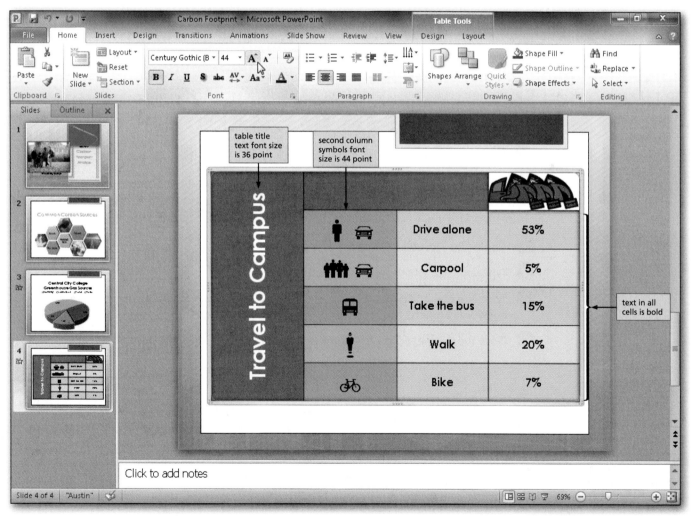

**Figure 4–78**

Plan
Ahead

**Test your visual elements.**

Proofread your charts and tables carefully using these guidelines:

* Verify that your charts and tables contain the correct data. It is easy to make mistakes when inputting large quantities of numbers or entering many lines of text. Check that numbers are not transposed and that pie chart percentages total 100.

* Be certain that graphics are clearly labeled. The slide title text or the chart title should state the graphic's purpose. Table column headings must indicate the data below them. Chart legends must accompany the graphic if the data is not displayed on the chart itself. Units of measurement, such as degrees, dollars, or inches, should appear for clarity.

* Show your graphic to people unfamiliar with your topic. Ask them to explain verbally what they gather from viewing the material. Determine how long it takes them to state their interpretations. If they pause or look confused, your graphic either has too much or too little information and needs revision.

**BTW**

**Quick Reference**
For a table that lists how to complete the tasks covered in this book using the mouse, Ribbon, shortcut menu, and keyboard, see the Quick Reference Summary at the back of this book, or visit the PowerPoint 2010 Quick Reference Web page (scsite.com/ppt2010/qr).

## To Add a Transition between Slides

A final enhancement you will make in this presentation is to apply the Orbit transition in the Dynamic Content category to all slides and change the transition speed to 3.00. The following steps apply this transition to the presentation.

**1** Apply the Orbit transition in the Dynamic Content category to all four slides in the presentation.

**2** Change the transition speed from 01.60 to 03.00.

## To Change Document Properties

Before saving the presentation again, you want to add your name, class name, and some keywords as document properties. The following steps use the Document Information Panel to change document properties.

**1** Display the Document Information Panel and then type your name as the Author property.

**2** Type your course and section in the Subject property.

**3** Type `carbon footprint, greenhouse gas, transportation` as the Keywords property.

**4** Close the Document Information Panel.

**BTW**

**Certification**
The Microsoft Office Specialist (MOS) program provides an opportunity for you to obtain a valuable industry credential — proof that you have the PowerPoint 2010 skills required by employers. For more information, visit the PowerPoint 2010 Certification Web page (scsite.com/ppt2010/cert).

## To Save, Print, and Quit PowerPoint

The presentation now is complete. You should save the slides, print a handout, and then quit PowerPoint.

**1** Save the presentation again with the same file name.

**2** Print the slide as a handout with two slides per page (Figure 4–79).

**3** Quit PowerPoint, closing all open documents.

**(a) Page 1**

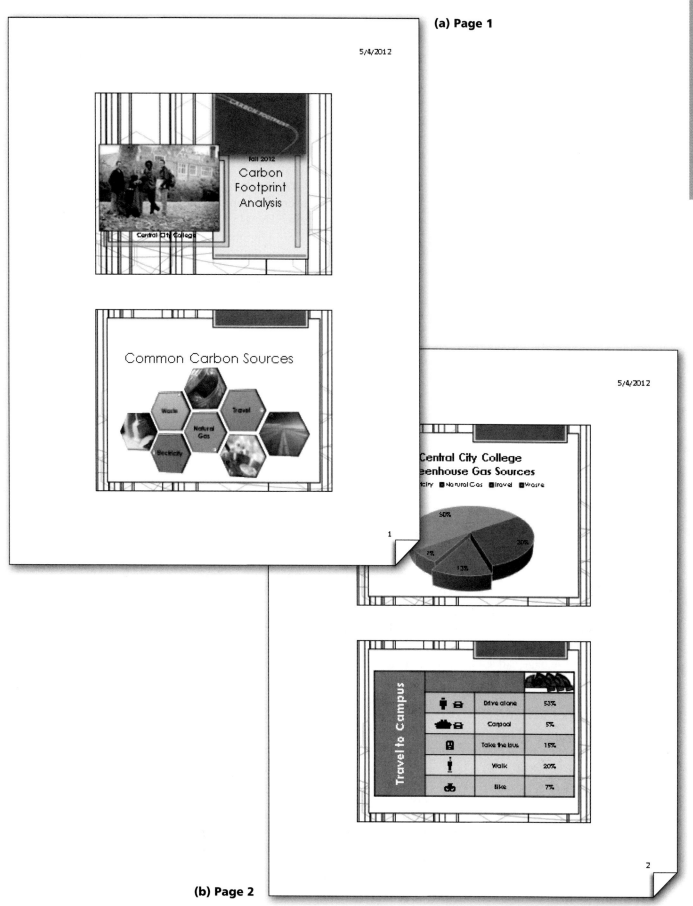

**(b) Page 2**

**Figure 4–79**

# Chapter Summary

In this chapter you have learned how to insert a SmartArt graphic and then add a picture and text, convert pictures to a SmartArt graphic, create and format a chart and a table, change table text alignment and orientation, and insert symbols. The items listed below include all the new PowerPoint skills you have learned in this chapter.

1. Insert a SmartArt Graphic (PPT 206)
2. Enter Text in a SmartArt Graphic (PPT 208)
3. Format Text Pane Characters (PPT 208)
4. Insert a Picture from a File into a SmartArt Graphic (PPT 209)
5. Apply a SmartArt Style (PPT 210)
6. Change SmartArt Color (PPT 211)
7. Resize a SmartArt Graphic (PPT 212)
8. Convert Text to a SmartArt Graphic (PPT 213)
9. Bold SmartArt Graphic Text (PPT 217)
10. Insert a Chart (PPT 220)
11. Replace Sample Data (PPT 221)
12. Apply a Chart Style (PPT 223)
13. Change the Shape Outline Weight (PPT 224)
14. Change the Shape Outline Color (PPT 226)
15. Change a Chart Layout (PPT 226)
16. Resize a Chart (PPT 228)
17. Change the Title and Legend Font Size (PPT 228)
18. Separate a Pie Slice (PPT 229)
19. Rotate a Chart (PPT 230)
20. Insert an Empty Table (PPT 232)
21. Enter Data in a Table (PPT 233)
22. Insert a Symbol (PPT 233)
23. Apply a Table Style (PPT 236)
24. Add Borders to a Table (PPT 238)
25. Add an Effect to a Table (PPT 238)
26. Resize a Table (PPT 240)
27. Add an Image to a Table (PPT 241)
28. Merge Cells (PPT 242)
29. Display Text in a Cell Vertically (PPT 244)
30. Align Text in Cells (PPT 245)

If you have a SAM 2010 user profile, your instructor may have assigned an autogradable version of this assignment. If so, log into the SAM 2010 Web site at www.cengage.com/sam2010 to download the instruction and start files.

## Learn It Online

Test your knowledge of chapter content and key terms.

*Instructions:*    To complete the Learn It Online exercises, start your browser, click the Address bar, and then enter the Web address **scsite.com/ppt2010/learn**. When the PowerPoint 2010 Learn It Online page is displayed, click the link for the exercise you want to complete and then read the instructions.

### Chapter Reinforcement TF, MC, and SA
A series of true/false, multiple choice, and short answer questions that test your knowledge of the chapter content.

### Flash Cards
An interactive learning environment where you identify chapter key terms associated with displayed definitions.

### Practice Test
A series of multiple choice questions that test your knowledge of chapter content and key terms.

### Who Wants To Be a Computer Genius?
An interactive game that challenges your knowledge of chapter content in the style of a television quiz show.

### Wheel of Terms
An interactive game that challenges your knowledge of chapter key terms in the style of the television show *Wheel of Fortune*.

### Crossword Puzzle Challenge
A crossword puzzle that challenges your knowledge of key terms presented in the chapter.

## Apply Your Knowledge

Reinforce the skills and apply the concepts you learned in this chapter.

### Converting Text to a SmartArt Graphic

*Note:* To complete this assignment, you will be required to use the Data Files for Students. See the inside back cover of this book for instructions on downloading the Data Files for Students, or contact your instructor for information about accessing the required files.

*Instructions:* Start PowerPoint. Open the presentation, Apply 4-1 Medical, located on the Data Files for Students.

The slide in the presentation presents information about when injured people should seek medical care at a hospital emergency room or an urgent care facility. The document you open is an unformatted presentation. You are to convert the two separate lists to SmartArt and format these graphics so the slide looks like Figure 4–80.

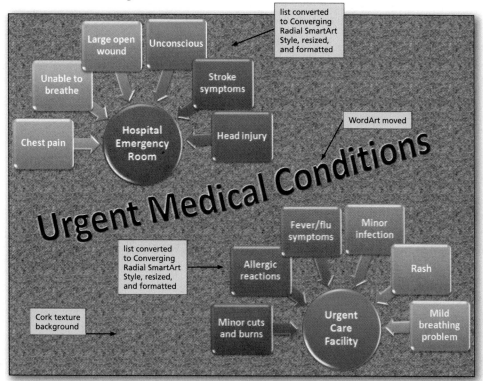

**Figure 4–80**

*Perform the following tasks:*

1. Convert the upper-left Hospital Emergency Room list to SmartArt by applying the Converging Radial Style (Relationship area). Change the colors to Colorful Range – Accent Colors 3 to 4.

2. Resize this SmartArt graphic to approximately 4.5" × 5.25". With the Text pane open, select the six Level 2 bulleted lines and then increase the font size to 16 point and bold this text. Select all six SmartArt graphic squares and then click the Larger button (SmartArt Tools Format tab | Shapes group) three times to increase the size of the selected shapes.

3. Select the center Hospital Emergency Room circle, increase the font size to 18 point, and bold this text. Click the Larger button two times to increase the size of the selected shape.

4. Apply the Polished (3-D area) Style and then move this SmartArt graphic to the area shown in Figure 4–80.

5. Convert the lower-right Urgent Care Facility list to SmartArt by applying the Converging Radial Style (Relationship area). Change the colors to Colorful Range – Accent Colors 2 to 3.

*Continued >*

*Apply Your Knowledge* continued

6. Resize this SmartArt graphic to approximately 4.5" × 5.25". With the Text pane open, select the six Level 2 bulleted lines and then increase the font size to 16 point and bold this text. Select all six SmartArt graphic squares and then click the Larger button (SmartArt Tools Format tab | Shapes group) three times to increase the size of the selected shapes.

7. Select the center Urgent Care Facility circle, decrease the font size to 18 point, and bold this text. Click the Larger button two times to increase the size of the selected shape.

8. Apply the Polished (3-D area) Style to this SmartArt graphic.

9. Move the center WordArt title, Urgent Medical Conditions, to the location shown in Figure 4–80 on the previous page.

10. Insert the Cork texture to format the background.

11. Apply the Clock transition (Exciting area) and then change the duration to 2.00 seconds.

12. Check the spelling and then change the document properties as specified by your instructor. Save the presentation using the file name, Apply 4-1 Urgent Medical. Submit the revised document in the format specified by your instructor.

# Extend Your Knowledge

Extend the skills you learned in this chapter and experiment with new skills. You may need to use Help to complete the assignment.

### Changing Chart Type and Style and Creating a SmartArt Graphic from Text

*Note:* To complete this assignment, you will be required to use the Data Files for Students. See the inside back cover of this book for instructions on downloading the Data Files for Students, or contact your instructor for information about accessing the required files.

*Instructions:* Start PowerPoint. Open the presentation, Extend 4-1 College, located on the Data Files for Students.

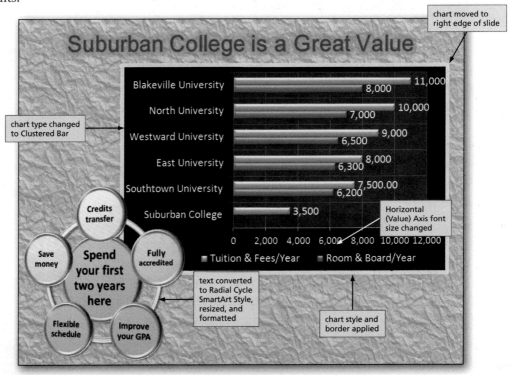

**Figure 4–81**

You will format a chart by applying a type and style, and then you will create a graphic by converting text to SmartArt.

*Perform the following tasks:*

1. Change the chart type from Clustered Column to Clustered Bar. *Hint:* Click the chart to select it and then click the Change Chart Type button (Chart Tools Design tab | Type group).

2. Apply chart Style 43 (last style in blue column) and then add a 6 pt. Yellow border to the chart. Move the chart to the right edge of the slide, as shown in Figure 4–81 on the previous page. Right-click the Horizontal (Value) Axis to display the Mini toolbar and then decrease the font size to 16 point.

3. Convert the text in the lower-left corner of the slide to the Radial Cycle layout (first layout in third row in Cycle area) SmartArt graphic. Change the color to Colored Fill – Accent 3 (second color in Accent 3 area). Apply the Metallic Scene design in the 3-D area.

4. Resize this SmartArt graphic to approximately 3.8" × 6.5" and then move the graphic to the location shown in Figure 4–81.

5. Select all six SmartArt graphic circles and then click the Larger button (SmartArt Tools Format tab | Shapes group) three times to increase the size of the selected shapes. Select the center shape and then click the Larger button once to increase the size of this circle. Increase the font size of the center circle text to 24 point and the outer circle text to 16 point. Change the font size of the word, Accredited, to 14 point so it displays on one line. Bold the text in the six circles.

6. Change the document properties, as specified by your instructor. Save the presentation using the file name, Extend 4-1 Suburban College.

7. Submit the revised document in the format specified by your instructor.

## Make It Right

Analyze a presentation and correct all errors and/or improve the design.

### Modifying a Table

*Note:* To complete this assignment, you will be required to use the Data Files for Students. See the inside back cover of this book for instructions on downloading the Data Files for Students, or contact your instructor for information about accessing the required files.

*Instructions:* Start PowerPoint. Open the presentation, Make It Right 4-1 Media World, located on the Data Files for Students.

In your sociology class, you have learned that women tend to have more friends than men do in their personal and online relationships. Table 4–3 lists the more popular social networking Web sites and the percentages of women and men who participate in these groups. This table is displayed partially on the slide in the Media World presentation (Figure 4–82 on the next page). Correct the formatting problems and errors in the presentation while keeping in mind the guidelines presented in this chapter.

| Table 4–3 Social Media World | | |
|---|---|---|
| **Males** | | **Females** |
| 43% | Facebook | 57% |
| 45% | Flickr | 55% |
| 36% | MySpace | 64% |
| 43% | Twitter | 57% |

*Continued >*

**Make It Right** *continued*

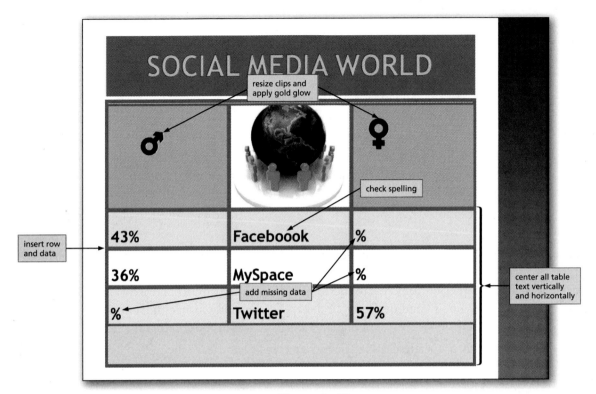

**Figure 4–82**

*Perform the following tasks:*

1. Resize the male symbol clip in the cell at the upper-left corner of the table to approximately 1.25" × 1.25". Apply the Gold, 18 pt glow, Accent color 4 (Glow Variations area) picture effect to this clip. Resize the female symbol clip in the cell at the upper-right corner of the table to approximately 1.35" × 0.88". Apply the Pink, 18 pt glow, Accent color 5 (Glow Variations area) picture effect to this clip. Center the male and female clips in the cells.

2. Use Table 4–3 on the previous page to add the missing data in three table cells. Insert a row for the Flickr data by right-clicking any cell in the Facebook row, pointing to Insert on the shortcut menu, and then clicking Insert Rows Below. Using Table 4–3, type the percentages and the word, Flickr, in this new row.

3. Select the table and then apply the Circle effect (Cell Bevel, Bevel area) to the table.

4. Select the four social media rows, center the text horizontally in the cells, and then middle-align this text vertically.

5. Change the slide transition from Shred to Orbit (Dynamic Content area) and then change the duration to 3.00 seconds.

6. Check the slide for spelling errors and then change the document properties, as specified by your instructor. Save the presentation using the file name, Make It Right 4-1 Social Media World.

7. Submit the revised document in the format specified by your instructor.

## In the Lab

Design and/or create a presentation using the guidelines, concepts, and skills presented in this chapter. Labs 1, 2, and 3 are listed in order of increasing difficulty.

### Lab 1: Inserting and Formatting SmartArt

*Note:* To complete this assignment, you will be required to use the Data Files for Students. See the inside back cover of this book for instructions on downloading the Data Files for Students, or contact your instructor for information about accessing the required files.

*Problem:* A pineapple is a type of fruit enjoyed throughout the world. People living in the Caribbean first called this fruit *anana*, meaning excellent fruit. European explorers to the Caribbean then changed the name to pineapple because they thought the outside looked like a pinecone and the inside texture resembled an apple. You visited Hawaii recently and toured a pineapple plantation. Several of the pictures you took are on the slides shown in Figure 4–83 and are on the Data Files for Students. You will convert the four pictures on Slide 1 to SmartArt and add descriptive text. Then you will convert the bulleted list on Slide 2 to a SmartArt graphic, change colors, apply a style, and add a shape fill.

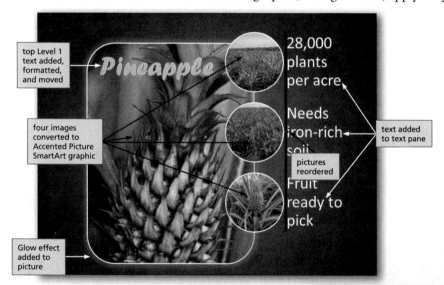

**(a) Slide 1**

**(b) Slide 2**

**Figure 4–83**

*Continued >*

**In the Lab** *continued*

*Perform the following tasks:*

1. Open the presentation, Lab 4-1 Pineapples, located on the Data Files for Students.

2. On Slide 1, change the order of the pictures to match the order shown in Figure 4-83a on the previous page by selecting the picture you want to move and then clicking the Move Up or Move Down buttons (SmartArt Tools Design tab | Create Graphic group).

3. In the SmartArt Text pane, type `Pineapple` as the top Level 1 text that will appear over the central pineapple picture. Type `28,000 plants per acre` as the second Level 1 text that will appear to the right of the first circle, `Needs iron-rich soil` as the text for the middle circle, and `Fruit ready to pick` for the third circle.

4. Change the font for the word, Pineapple, to Forte. Bold this word and then change the font color to Orange. Decrease the size of the placeholder for the word, Pineapple, by dragging the bottom square sizing handle upward being careful not to decrease the size of the word, Pineapple. Move the placeholder toward the top of the slide, as shown in Figure 4–83a on the previous page.

5. Apply the Orange, 18 pt glow, Accent color 6 (Glow Variations area) picture effect to the large pineapple picture.

6. On Slide 2, convert the bulleted list to the Circle Accent Timeline (Process area) SmartArt Graphic. Change the color to Colored Fill – Accent 3 (Accent 3 area). Apply the Subtle Effect (Best Match for Document area) SmartArt Style to the entire graphic.

7. Select all text in the Text pane and then add a shape fill by clicking the Shape Fill button arrow (SmartArt Tools Format tab | Shape Styles group) and then clicking the color, Orange, Accent 6, Lighter 40% (Theme Colors area), as shown in Figure 4–83b on the previous page.

8. For all slides, apply the Reveal transition (Subtle area) and change the duration to 5.00 seconds.

9. Change the document properties, as specified by your instructor. Save the presentation using the file name, Lab 4-1 Growing Pineapples.

10. Submit the revised document in the format specified by your instructor.

## In the Lab

### Lab 2: Creating a Presentation by Inserting SmartArt and a Chart

*Note:* To complete this assignment, you will be required to use the Data Files for Students. See the inside back cover of this book for instructions on downloading the Data Files for Students, or contact your instructor for information about accessing the required files.

*Problem:* Adults generally have four or five sleep cycles every night. Each cycle lasts approximately 90 minutes and is composed of four steps, which are light sleep, intermediate sleep, deep sleep, and rapid eye movement (REM) sleep. Nearly one-fifth of people sleep fewer than six hours each night, and the average hours slept are indicated in Table 4–4. Your speech teacher has assigned an informative speech, and you desire to explain the sleep cycle and the hours slept as part of your talk. You create two slides of a PowerPoint presentation shown in Figure 4–84a and Figure 4–84b. These slides contain clips that are on the Data Files for Students.

| Table 4–4 Hours Slept | | | |
|---|---|---|---|
| Fewer than 6 | 6 – 6.9 | 7 – 7.9 | More than 8 |
| 19% | 27% | 30% | 24% |

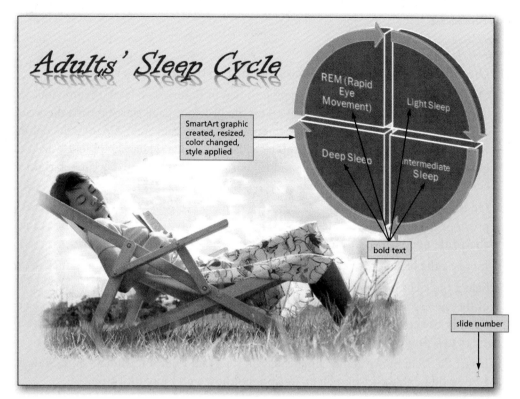

(a) Slide 1

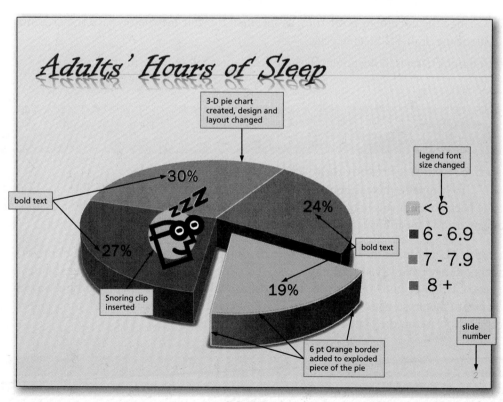

(b) Slide 2

**Figure 4–84**

*Continued >*

**In the Lab** *continued*

*Perform the following tasks:*

1. Open the presentation, Lab 4-2 Sleep, located on the Data Files for Students.

2. On Slide 1, create the SmartArt graphic shown in Figure 4–84a on the previous page. Replace the sample data with the data in Table 4–4 on the previous page starting with the words, Light Sleep, and moving clockwise. Apply the Segmented Cycle (Cycle area). Change the colors to Colored Fill – Accent 5 (Accent 5 group). Apply the Brick Scene (3-D area) Style. Resize the SmartArt graphic to approximately 5" × 7" and then move this graphic to the upper-right corner of the slide. Bold all words in the graphic.

3. On Slide 2, create the Pie in 3-D chart (second chart in Pie area) shown in Figure 4–84b on the previous page. Apply chart design Style 10 and then change the chart layout to Layout 6. Select the chart title text, Sales, and then press the DELETE key to delete this text.

4. Increase the legend font size to 28 point and the percentages on each pie slice to 24 point bold.

5. Select the chart and rotate it approximately 120 degrees so that the green slice is at the bottom of the pie. Explode the green slice, which represents the percentage of people sleeping fewer than 6 hours, as shown in Figure 4–84. Add a 6 pt border to this slice and then change the border color to Orange.

6. Insert the Man Snore audio clip located on the Data Files for Students into Slide 1, play the clip across slides, hide the sound icon during the show, and loop until stopped.

7. Insert the Snoring clip located on the Data Files for Students into Slide 2 and move it to the location shown in Figure 4–84.

8. Insert the slide number on both slides. Apply the Ripple transition (Exciting area) to all slides. Change the duration to 3.00 seconds. Check the spelling and correct any errors.

9. Change the document properties, as specified by your instructor. Save the presentation using the file name, Lab 4-2 Sleep Cycle.

10. Submit the revised document in the format specified by your instructor.

## In the Lab

### Lab 3: Creating a Presentation with SmartArt and a Table

*Note:* To complete this assignment, you will be required to use the Data Files for Students. See the inside back cover of this book for instructions on downloading the Data Files for Students, or contact your instructor for information about accessing the required files.

*Problem:* Laughter is the best medicine, according to the adage. Sharing a humorous situation with others can have many health benefits, as outlined in Table 4–5. You have read about the positive effects of laughter, and you want to share your knowledge with students enrolled in your health class. You create the presentation in Figure 4–85 that consists of three slides. Pictures and a clip for the presentation are on the Data Files for Students.

**Table 4–5 Benefits of Laughter**

| Benefits of Laughter | | | |
|---|---|---|---|
| **Physical** | Lowers blood pressure | Boosts immunity | Decreases pain |
| **Mental** | Relieves stress | Eases anxiety | Improves mood |
| **Social** | Strengthens relationships | Promotes teamwork | Minimizes conflict |

*Perform the following tasks:*

1. Open the presentation, Lab 4-3 Laughter, located on the Data Files for Students. Change the presentation theme colors to Austin.

2. On Slide 1, insert the Funnel graphic (Process area) SmartArt graphic shown in Figure 4–85a. Type the keywords, Smile, Laugh, Love, in the first three Level 1 bulleted lines in the Text pane, and type the word, HEALTH, in the fourth line. Bold the word, HEALTH.

3. Resize the SmartArt graphic to approximately 5.4" × 7.58". Change the graphic's colors to Colorful Range – Accent Colors 3 to 4. Add the Sunset Scene (3-D area) Style. Move this graphic to the left side of the slide.

**(a) Slide 1**

**Figure 4–85**

*Continued >*

**In the Lab** *continued*

4. On Slide 2, create a background by inserting the SunSmile picture located on the Data Files for Students and then change the transparency to 80%. Create the SmartArt graphic shown in Figure 4–85b using the Vertical Box List graphic (List area) and the text shown in Figure 4–85b. Change the graphic's colors to Colorful Range – Accent Colors 5 to 6. Apply the Cartoon (3-D area) Style and the Tight Reflection 4 pt offset (Reflection Variations area) shape effect reflection to the graphic.

5. Apply the Shape Outline Green, Accent 1 color to the four blank rectangle shapes in the SmartArt graphic and then change the weight to 4½ pt.

6. Insert the clip of the person laughing, shown in Figure 4–85b, from Office.com. Resize the clip to approximately 2.33" × 1.96" and then move this clip to the lower-left corner of the slide.

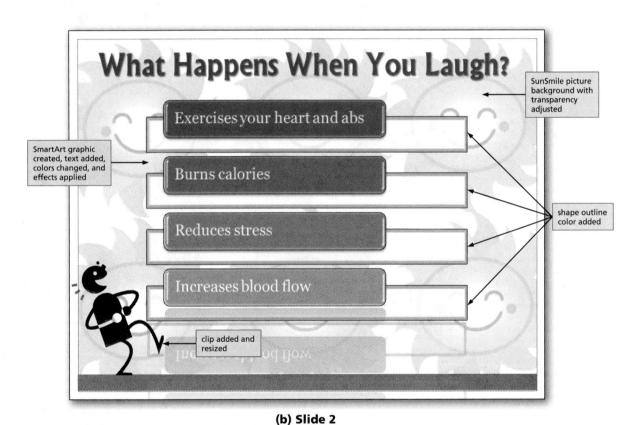

**(b) Slide 2**

**Figure 4–85 (Continued)**

7. On Slide 3, insert a table with four columns and four rows, as shown in Figure 4–85c. Merge the second, third, and fourth cells in the Header Row and then change the font size to 48 point.

8. Type the table header and text using the data in Table 4–5 on page PPT 258. Change the font for all cells to Narkisim and then middle-align this text vertically and center this text horizontally.

9. For all cells other than the Header Row, change the font size to 24 point. Bold the text in the first column and rotate the text direction to 270 degrees.

10. Move the table to the location shown in Figure 4–85c and increase the table size. Change the shading of the second, third, and fourth cells in the first column to Green, Accent 1. If the upper-left table cell has a green fill, apply a No Fill format to this cell so that only the cells below it have a green fill.

11. In the first table cell, insert the picture called Laughing Man located on the Data Files for Students. If necessary, increase the size of this clip in the cell, as shown in Figure 4-85c. Then insert the audio clip, Long Laugh, located on the Data Files for Students. Start the audio clip automatically, hide the sound icon during the show, and loop until stopped.

12. Apply the Riblet (Bevel area) Cell Bevel effect to the table.

13. Apply the Doors transition and change the duration to 03.00. Check the spelling and correct any errors.

14. Change the document properties, as specified by your instructor. Save the presentation using the file name, Lab 4-3 Laughter Benefits.

15. Submit the revised document in the format specified by your instructor.

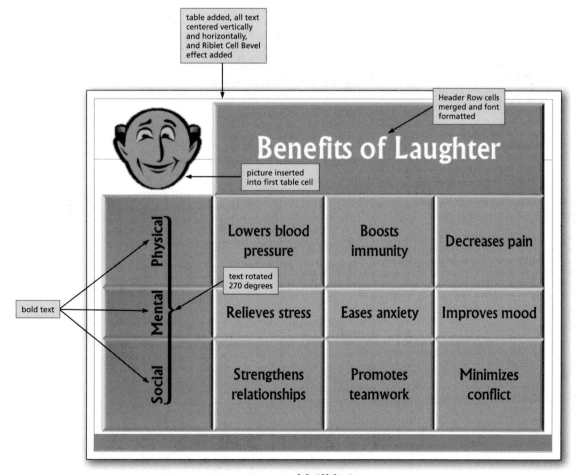

**(c) Slide 3**

**Figure 4–85 (Continued)**

# Cases and Places

Apply your creative thinking and problem-solving skills to design and implement a solution.

*Note:* To complete these assignments, you may be required to use the Data Files for Students. See the inside back cover of this book for instructions on downloading the Data Files for Students, or contact your instructor for information about accessing the required files.

As you design the presentations, remember to use the 7 × 7 rule: a maximum of seven words on a line and a maximum of seven lines on one slide.

## 1: Designing and Creating a Presentation about Temperature Conversions

### Academic

Students in your chemistry class are struggling to convert temperatures from Fahrenheit to Celsius to Kelvin, so you have decided to help them understand the formulas. In addition, you provide some facts to help them see the relationship among the numbers, such as ice melting at 32 degrees Fahrenheit, 0 degrees Celsius, and 273 degrees Kelvin, and water boiling at 212 degrees Fahrenheit, 100 degrees Celsius, and 373 degrees Kelvin. Create a presentation to show the formulas and temperature conversions in two tables. Use the data in Tables 4-6 and 4-7 to create your tables. Apply table styles and add borders and effects, and use at least three objectives found at the beginning of this chapter to develop the presentation. Use pictures from Office.com if they are appropriate for this topic. Be sure to check spelling.

| Table 4–6 Temperature Conversion Formulas | | |
| --- | --- | --- |
| Temperature | | |
| From | To | Formula |
| Fahrenheit (degrees F) | Celsius (degrees C) | 5 ÷ 9 (F − 32) |
| Celsius (degrees C) | Fahrenheit (degrees F) | 9 ÷ 5 C + 32 |
| Fahrenheit (degrees F) | Kelvin (degrees K) | (F + 459.67) × (5/9) |

| Table 4–7 Temperature Conversions | | |
| --- | --- | --- |
| Quick Temperature Conversions | | |
| Fahrenheit | Celsius | Kelvin |
| 212 | 100 | 373 |
| 86 | 30 | 303 |
| 68 | 20 | 293 |
| 50 | 10 | 283 |
| 32 | 0 | 273 |
| 14 | −10 | 263 |
| −4 | −20 | 253 |

## 2: Designing and Creating a Presentation about Dogs and Cats

**Personal**

On weekends, you volunteer at an animal shelter, and you notice that fewer dogs and cats are adopted by people living alone than by households having multiple people. You decide to survey the adopting families to see how likely a household is to adopt a dog or a cat if the household has one, two, three, or four members. The data you collect is summarized in Tables 4–8 and 4–9. Share your findings by creating a PowerPoint presentation that contains two pie charts representing survey results. Use at least three objectives found at the beginning of this chapter to develop the presentation. Be sure to check spelling.

**Table 4–8 Dogs by Family Size**

| Dogs by Family Size | |
|---|---|
| Household Size | Percent |
| 4 or more people | 33 |
| 3 people | 21 |
| 2 people | 32 |
| 1 person | 14 |

**Table 4–9 Cats by Family Size**

| Cats by Family Size | |
|---|---|
| Household Size | Percent |
| 4 or more people | 29 |
| 3 people | 20 |
| 2 people | 33 |
| 1 person | 18 |

*Continued >*

**Cases and Places** *continued*

### 3: Designing and Creating a Presentation about Light Bulbs

**Professional**

You are employed at a local hardware store, and many customers desire to change their light bulbs from incandescent to compact fluorescent (CFL). Your manager has asked you to develop a presentation that provides information about equivalent light output, which is measured in lumens. In addition, she wants you to include an explanation that describes the color temperatures recommended for indoor general and task lighting. For example, warm colors (2700–3600 K) are preferred for living spaces because they complement clothing and skin tones; cool colors (3600–5500 K) are best for reading and household tasks because they provide contrast. These temperatures are not related to the heat generated from bulb usage. You decide to create a table using the data in Table 4–10 and a SmartArt graphic using the data in Table 4–11. Insert images in the table and SmartArt graphics from Office.com or your own digital pictures if they are appropriate for this topic. Apply at least one style, border, and effect. Be certain to check spelling.

**Table 4–10 Light Bulbs**

| Incandescent Bulbs vs. CFL Bulbs | | |
|---|---|---|
| Incandescent | Minimum Light Output | CFL |
| 40 watts | 450 lumens | 9–13 watts |
| 60 watts | 800 lumens | 13–15 watts |
| 75 watts | 1,100 lumens | 18–25 watts |
| 100 watts | 1,600 lumens | 23–30 watts |
| 150 watts | 2,600 lumens | 30–52 watts |

**Table 4–11 Color Temperatures**

| Light Sources Warmth and Coolness | |
|---|---|
| Kelvin (K) Temperature | Bulb Type |
| 2600 | Incandescent |
| 3000 | Warm white |
| 3100 | Halogen |
| 4200 | Cool white |
| 5000 | Daylight |

# 5 | Collaborating on and Delivering a Presentation

## Objectives

You will have mastered the material in this chapter when you can:

- Combine slide shows
- Accept and reject a reviewer's proposed changes
- Insert, modify, and delete comments
- Reuse slides from an existing presentation
- Capture part of a slide using screen clipping
- Insert slide footer content

- Set slide and presentation resolution
- Save a file as a PowerPoint show
- Package a presentation for storage on a compact disc
- Save a presentation in a previous PowerPoint format
- Inspect and protect files
- Annotate slide shows with a pen and highlighter

# 5 | Collaborating on and Delivering a Presentation

BTW

**Integrating Differing Perspectives**
Audience members often have diverse educational levels, technical skills, and cultural backgrounds. It is important for you to understand how they may interpret material on your slides. Terms and graphics that seem clear to you may raise questions among people viewing your slides. The issues raised and the comments made during the review cycle play an important role in the development of a successful PowerPoint presentation.

## Introduction

Often presentations are enhanced when individuals collaborate to fine-tune text, visuals, and design elements on the slides. A **review cycle** occurs when a slide show designer shares a file with reviewers so they can make comments and changes to their copies of the slides and then return the file to the designer. A **comment** is a description that normally does not display as part of the slide show. It can be used to clarify information that may be difficult to understand, to pose questions, or to communicate suggestions. The designer then can display the comments, modify their content, and ask the reviewers to again review the presentation, and continue this process until the slides are satisfactory. Once the presentation is complete, the designer can protect the file so no one can open it without a password or alter comments and other information. The designer also can save the presentation to an optical disc or as a PowerPoint show that will run without opening the PowerPoint application. In addition, a presenter can use PowerPoint's variety of tools to run the show effectively and to emphasize various elements on the screen.

## Project — Presentation with Comments, Inserted Slides, and Protection

The six slides in the Windstorms presentation (Figure 5 – 1) give information on and provide images of two particular types of windstorms: tornadoes and hurricanes. The initial presentation began with three slides, which were sent to a reviewer, Mary Halen. She suggested changes and created a new slide.

When you are developing a presentation, it often is advantageous to ask a variety of people to review your work in progress. These individuals can evaluate the wording, art, and design, and experts in the subject can check the slides for accuracy. They can add comments to the slides in specific areas, such as a paragraph, a graphic, or a table. You then can review their comments and use them to modify and enhance your work. You also can insert slides from other presentations into your file. The Windstorms presentation includes two slides from the file, Hurricanes.pptx.

Once you develop the final set of slides, you can complete the file by removing any comments and personal information, by adding a password so that unauthorized people cannot see or change the file contents without your permission, by saving the file as a PowerPoint show that runs automatically when you open a file, and by saving the file to an optical disc.

When running your presentation, you may decide to show the slides nonsequentially. For example, you may need to review a slide you discussed already, or you may want to skip slides and jump forward. You also may want to emphasize, or **annotate**, material on the slides by highlighting text or writing on the slides. You can save your annotations to review during or after the presentation.

BTW

**Documenting Your Thoughts**
Your PowerPoint slides are formal documentation of the thoughts you are attempting to present to an audience, so you should seek comments to help ensure that your words and graphic elements are as clear as possible. The words you use on your slides and the handouts you provide are important documents that audience members may reference in the future. Your efforts, consequently, may be visible long after the verbal presentation has concluded.

**(a) Slide 1 (Title Slide Enhanced from Reviewer)**

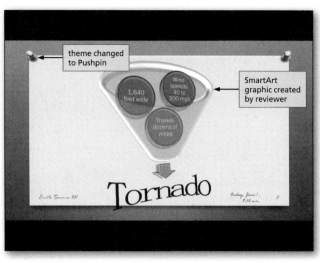

**(b) Slide 2 (SmartArt from Reviewer)**

**(c) Slide 3 (Inserted from Reviewer's Presentation)**

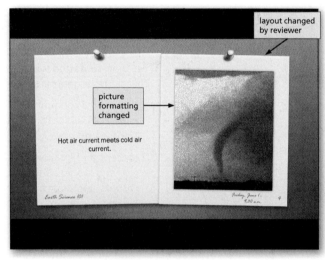

**(d) Slide 4 (Enhanced from Reviewer)**

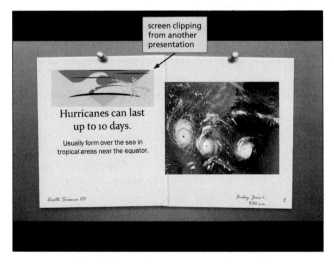

**(e) Slide 5 (Inserted from Reviewer's Presentation)**

**(f) Slide 6 (Inserted from Reviewer's Presentation)**

**Figure 5–1**

**BTW**

**Considering Reviewers' Technology**
People who receive copies of your presentation to review may not be able to open a PowerPoint 2010 file saved in the default .pptx format because they may have a previous version of this software or may not have Internet access available readily. For these reasons, you need to know their software and hardware limitations and distribute your file or handouts accordingly.

# Overview

As you read through this chapter, you will learn how to create the presentation shown in Figure 5–1 on the previous page by performing these general tasks:

- Review a merged presentation.
- Insert slides and content clipped from slides.
- Secure and share a presentation.
- Use presentation tools.
- Package a presentation for a CD or DVD.
- Save a presentation in a variety of formats.
- Annotate a presentation.

**Plan Ahead**

### General Project Guidelines

When creating a PowerPoint presentation, the actions you perform and the decisions you make will affect the appearance and characteristics of the finished document. As you create a presentation with illustrations, such as the project shown in Figure 5–1, you should follow these general guidelines:

1. **Develop a collaboration plan.** Planning tasks for group members to follow helps ensure success. Collaborators must understand the overall group goal, set short-term and long-term goals, identify subtasks that must be completed, and set a schedule.

2. **Accept and evaluate criticism.** Feedback, both positive and negative, that enables you to improve yourself and your work, is called **criticism**. Written and oral comments from others can help reinforce the positive aspects and also identify flaws. Seek comments from a variety of people who genuinely want to help you develop an effective slide show.

3. **Give constructive criticism.** If you are asked to critique a presentation, begin and end with positive comments. Give specific details about a few key areas that can be improved. Be honest, but be tactful.

4. **Use slide numbers to guide your speech.** A speaker can view the slide numbers to organize the speech, jump to particular slides, and control timing.

5. **Determine the screen show ratio.** Consider where the presentation will be shown and the type of hardware that will be available. Wide-screen displays are prevalent in the home office and corporate world, but their dimensions present design challenges for the PowerPoint developer.

6. **Select an appropriate password.** A **password** is a private combination of characters that allows users to open a file. To prevent unauthorized people from viewing your slides, choose a good password and keep it confidential.

When necessary, more specific details concerning the above guidelines are presented at appropriate points in the chapter. The chapter also will identify the actions performed and decisions made regarding these guidelines during the creation of the presentation shown in Figure 5–1.

## To Start PowerPoint and Open and Save a Presentation

To begin this presentation, you will open a file located on the Data Files for Students. See the inside back cover of this book for instructions on downloading the Data Files for Students, or contact your instructor for more information about accessing the required files. If you are using a computer to step through the project in this chapter and you want your screens to match the figures in this book, you should change your screen's resolution to $1024 \times 768$.

The following steps start PowerPoint, open a file, and then save it with a new file name.

**1** Start PowerPoint. If necessary, maximize the PowerPoint window.

**2** Open the presentation, Windstorms, located on the Data Files for Students.

**3** Save the presentation using the file name, Windstorms Final.

---

**Plan Ahead**

**Develop a collaboration plan.**
Working with your classmates can yield numerous benefits. Your peers can assist in brainstorming, developing key ideas, revising your project, and keeping you on track so that your presentation meets the assignment goals.

The first step when collaborating with peers is to define success. What, ultimately, is the goal? For example, are you developing a persuasive presentation to school administrators in an effort to fund a new club? Next, you can set short-term and long-term goals that help lead you to completing the project successfully. These goals can be weekly tasks to accomplish, such as interviewing content experts, conducting online research, or compiling an annotated bibliography. After that, you can develop a plan to finish the project by stating subtasks that each member must accomplish. Each collaborator should inform the group members when the task is complete or if problems are delaying progress. When collaborators meet, whether in person or online, they should establish an agenda and have one member keep notes of topics discussed.

**BTW**

**Slide Library**
In a business environment, PowerPoint presentations may be stored on a centrally located Slide Library that resides on a server. These slide shows may be shared, reused, and accessed by many individuals who then can copy materials into their individual presentations. The Slide Library time stamps when an individual has borrowed a particular slide or presentation and then time stamps the slide or presentation when it is returned. If a particular slide in the Slide Library has been updated, anyone who has borrowed that slide is notified that the content has changed. People creating PowerPoint presentations can track the changes to presentations, locate the latest versions of slides, and check for slide updates.

# Collaborating on a Presentation

PowerPoint provides several methods to collaborate with friends or coworkers who can view your slide show and then provide feedback. When you **collaborate**, you work together on a document with other PowerPoint users who are cooperating jointly and assisting willingly with the endeavor. You can distribute your slide show physically to others by exchanging a compact disc or a flash drive. You also can share your presentation through the Internet by sending the file as an e-mail attachment or saving the file to a storage location, such as Windows Live SkyDrive.

In the following pages, you will follow these general steps to collaborate with Mary Halen, who has reviewed your Windstorms presentation:

1. Combine a presentation.
2. Print slides and comments.
3. Review and accept or reject changes.
4. Delete a comment.
5. Modify a comment.
6. Insert a comment.

## To Merge a Presentation

Mary Halen reviewed the Windstorms presentation and made several comments about the design. She converted the Slide 1 title text to WordArt and the Slide 2 bulleted list to a SmartArt graphic. She also added a transition to all slides, changed the theme, edited some paragraphs, and added two slides. The following steps merge this reviewer's file with the original Windstorms presentation.

**1**

• With the Windstorms Final presentation active, display the Review tab (Figure 5–2).

Q&A

Can I track my changes in PowerPoint as I can in other Office 2010 products, such as Word 2010?

No. To detect differences between your presentation and another presentation, you must merge the files.

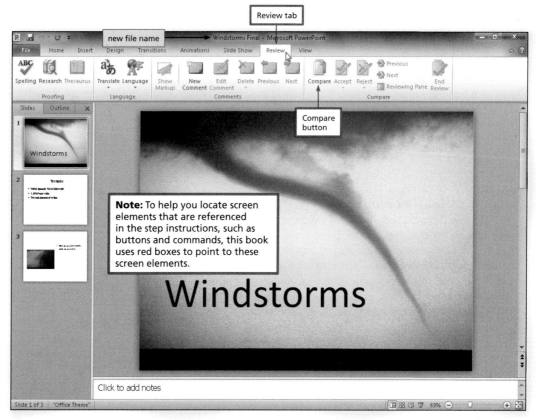

**Figure 5–2**

**2**

• Click the Compare button (Review tab | Compare group) to display the Choose File to Merge with Current Presentation dialog box.

• With the list of files and folders on your USB flash drive displaying, click Windstorms – Mary Halen to select the file name (Figure 5–3).

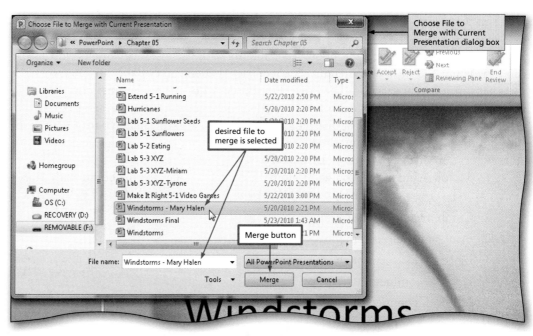

**Figure 5–3**

**3**

- Click the Merge button (Choose File to Merge with Current Presentation dialog box) to merge Mary Halen's presentation with the Windstorms presentation and to display the Revisons task pane (Figure 5–4).

**Q&A**

If several reviewers have made comments and suggestions, can I merge their files, too?

Yes. Repeat Steps 1 and 2. Each reviewer's initials display in a color-coded comment box.

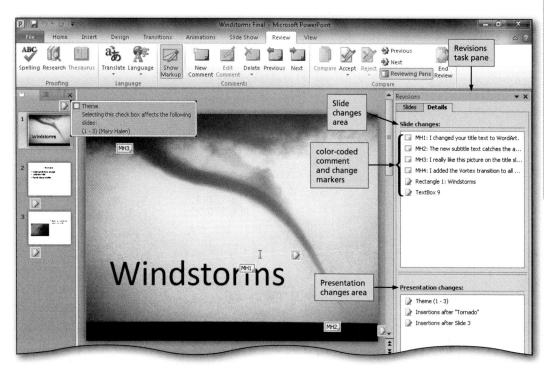

**Figure 5–4**

## To Print Comments

As owner of the original presentation, you want to review the comments and modifications and then make decisions about whether to accept these suggestions. You can print each slide and the comments a reviewer has made before you begin to accept and reject each suggestion. PowerPoint can print these slides and comments on individual pages. The following steps use this slide show to illustrate printing these suggestions.

**1**

- Open the Backstage view and then click the Print tab to display the Print gallery.

- Click Full Page Slides to display the Print Layout gallery.

- If necessary, click Print Comments and Ink Markup to select this option (Figure 5–5).

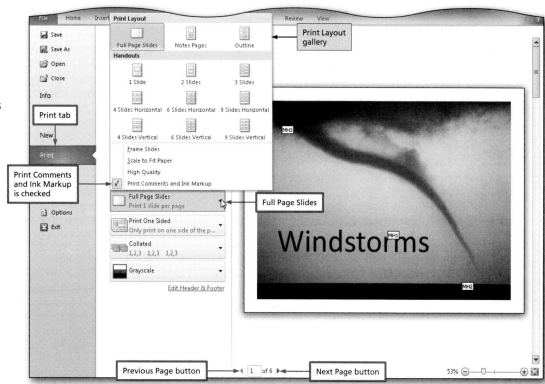

**Figure 5–5**

● Click the Next Page and Previous Page buttons to scroll through the previews of the three slides and the three comment pages.

● Click the Print button to print the six pages (Figure 5–6).

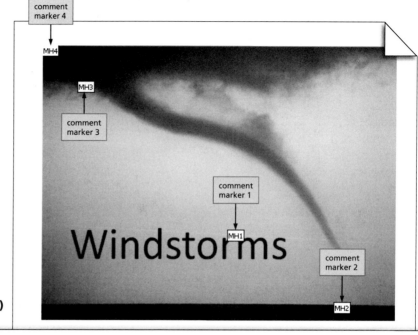

**(a) Page 1 (Title Slide)**

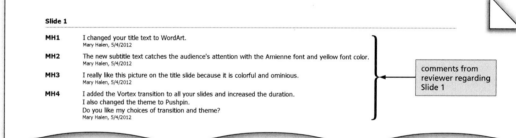

**(b) Page 2 (Comments from Reviewer)**

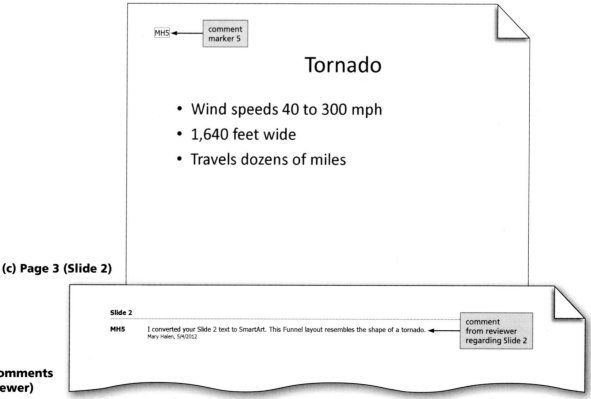

**(c) Page 3 (Slide 2)**

**(d) Page 4 (Comments from Reviewer)**

**Figure 5–6**

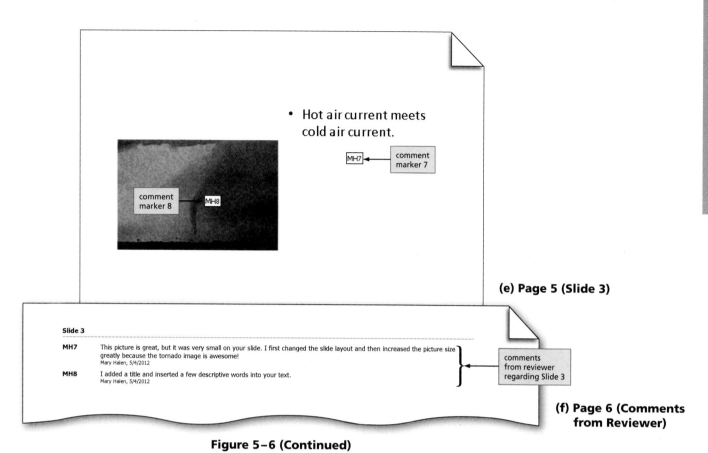

- Hot air current meets cold air current.

MH7 ← comment marker 7

comment marker 8 — MH8

**(e) Page 5 (Slide 3)**

**Slide 3**

**MH7**   This picture is great, but it was very small on your slide. I first changed the slide layout and then increased the picture size greatly because the tornado image is awesome!
Mary Halen, 5/4/2012

**MH8**   I added a title and inserted a few descriptive words into your text.
Mary Halen, 5/4/2012

} comments from reviewer regarding Slide 3

**(f) Page 6 (Comments from Reviewer)**

**Figure 5–6 (Continued)**

## To Preview Presentation Changes

The reviewer made several changes to the overall presentation and then edited your three slides. You can preview her modifications to obtain an overview of her suggestions. Seeing her edits now can help you decide later whether to accept or reject each change as you step through each revision. The following steps preview the merged presentation.

- If necessary, display the Review tab and then click the Reviewing Pane button (Review tab | Compare group) to display the Revisions task pane. With Slide 1 displaying, click the Slides tab in the Revisions task pane to display a thumbnail of merged Slide 1 (Figure 5–7).

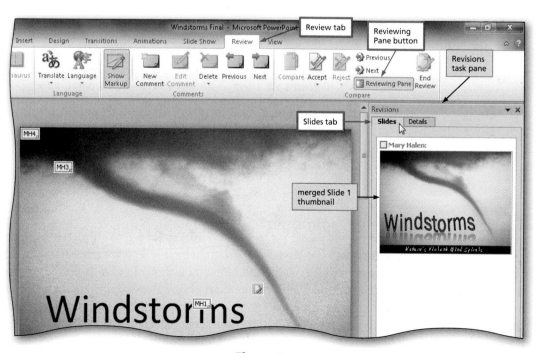

**Figure 5–7**

● Click the Mary Halen check box above the Slide 1 thumbnail to view the proposed changes in the Slide pane (Figure 5–8).

● Click the Mary Halen check box again to reject the changes.

**Q&A**

Can I make some, but not all, of the reviewer's changes on Slide 1?

Yes. PowerPoint allows you to view each proposed change individually and then either accept or reject the modification.

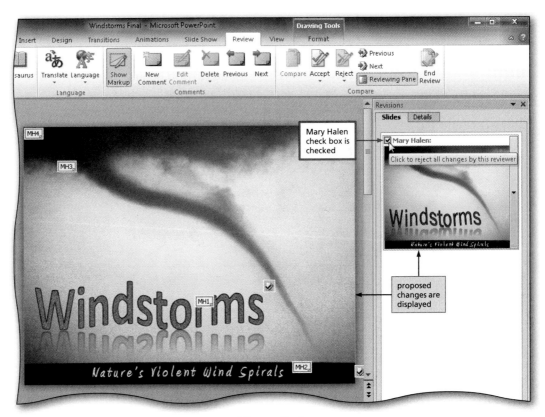

**Figure 5–8**

**Plan Ahead**

**Accept and evaluate criticism.**
Receiving feedback from others ultimately should enhance your presentation. If several of your reviewers make similar comments, such as too much text appears on one slide or that a chart would help present your concept, then you should heed their criticism and modify your slides. Criticism from a variety of people, particularly if they are from different cultures or vary in age, gives a wide range of viewpoints. Some reviewers might focus on the font size, others on color and design choices, while others might single out the overall message. These individuals should make judgments on your work, such as saying that the overall presentation is good or that a particular paragraph is confusing, and then offer reasons why elements are effective or how you can edit a paragraph.

When you receive these comments, do not get defensive. Ask yourself why your reviewers would have made these comments. Perhaps they lack a background in the subject matter, or, on the other hand, they may have a particular interest in this topic and can add their expertise.

## To Review and Delete Comments

The Revisions task pane and the Reviewing group help you review each comment. These notes from the reviewer may guide you through the revisions and help you ultimately to decide whether to accept changes or delete the suggestions. Color-coded comment and change markers are displayed in the Revisions task pane. The reviewer's initials display in the rectangular comment marker on the slide and next to the comment marker in the task pane; the initials are followed by a numeral that indicates the sequence by which the reviewer added comments to the presentation. The following steps view and then delete the reviewer's comments for Slide 1.

**1**

- Click the Details tab in the Revisions task pane to display the comment markers and the change markers in the Slide changes and Presentation changes areas.

**Q&A**  How do I distinguish between the comment markers and the change markers?

The comment markers are horizontal rectangles followed by the reviewer's initials and a number; the change markers are vertical rectangles with a pencil overlay.

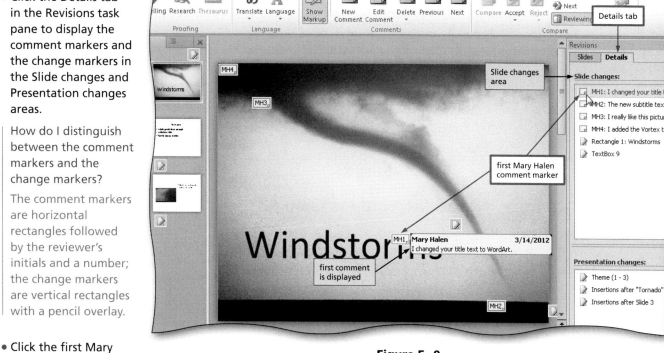

**Figure 5–9**

- Click the first Mary Halen comment marker, MH1, in the Slides changes area to display the comment (Figure 5–9).

**Q&A**  Why does the number 1 display after the commenter's initials?

The number indicates it is the first comment the reviewer inserted.

**Q&A**  Can I read the comment without clicking the comment marker on the Details tab?

Yes. You can mouse over or click the comment marker on the slide.

**2**

- Read the comment and then click the Delete Comment button (Review tab | Comments group) to delete Mary Halen's first comment.

- Click the Next Comment button (Review tab | Comments group) to view the second comment (Figure 5–10).

**Q&A**  Can I click the comment marker on the Details tab to display the comment instead of clicking the Next button?

Yes. Either method displays the comment.

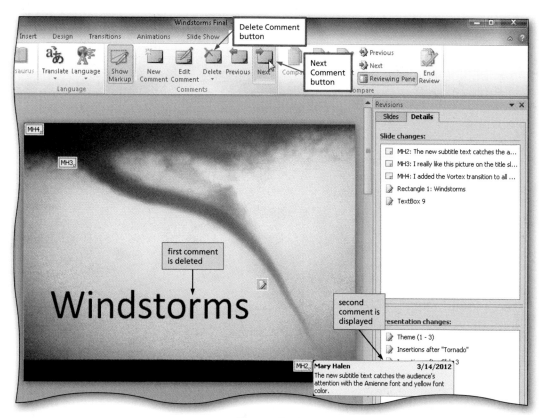

**Figure 5–10**

- Delete the second comment.

- Review the third comment for Slide 1 and then delete this comment marker.

- Review the fourth comment for Slide 1 but do not delete this comment marker.

**Q&A** Why should I not delete Mary Halen's fourth comment?

Mary indicates that she added a transition and changed the presentation theme. You have not accepted her changes yet, so you do not know if you agree with her modifications. You will respond to her question after you have made the changes.

## To Review, Accept, and Reject Presentation Changes

Changes that affect the entire presentation are indicated in the Presentation changes area of the Revisions task pane. These changes can include transitions, color schemes, fonts, backgrounds, and slide insertions. The following steps display and accept the reviewer's three revisions in the presentation.

- Click the first presentation change marker, Theme (1 – 3), in the Presentation changes area to display the Theme box with an explanation of the proposed change for all slides in the presentation (Figure 5–11).

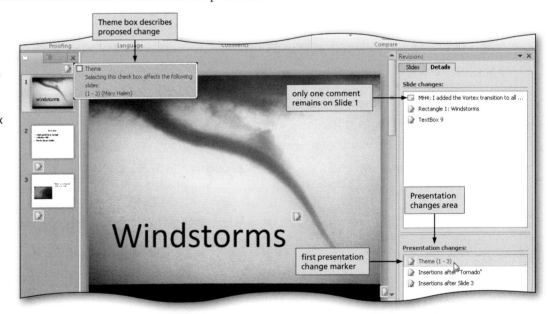

**Figure 5–11**

- Click the Accept Change button (Review tab | Compare group) to view the new Pushpin theme on all slides (Figure 5–12).

**Q&A** Can I also apply the change by clicking the Theme check box?

Yes. Either method applies the Pushpin theme.

**Q&A** If I decide to not apply the new theme, can I reverse this change?

Yes. Click the Reject Change button (Review tab | Compare group) or click the check box to remove the check mark and reject the reviewer's theme modification.

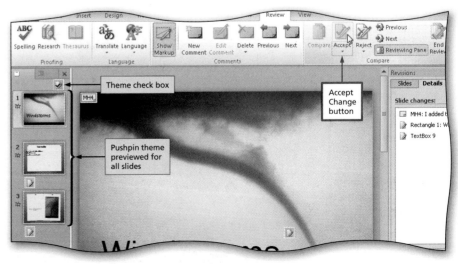

**Figure 5–12**

**3**

- Click the second presentation change marker, Insertions after "Tornado", in the Presentation changes area to display the review content thumbnail with an explanation of the proposed new slide (Figure 5–13).

**Q&A**

Why does a check mark appear in the Theme (1 – 3) change marker?

The check mark indicates you have applied the proposed change.

**4**

- Click the Accept Change button to insert the new slide.

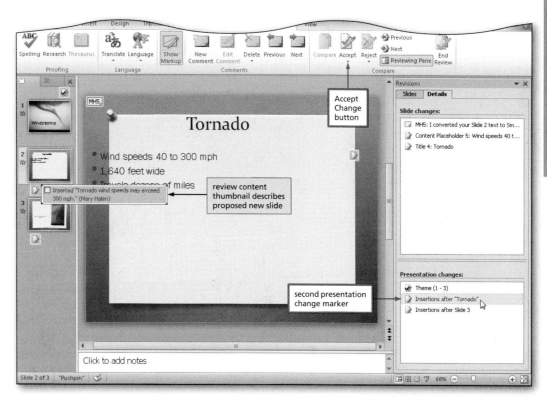

**Figure 5–13**

**5**

- Click the third presentation change marker, Insertions after Slide 4, to display the review content thumbnail with a proposed slide to insert in the presentation (Figure 5–14).

**6**

- Click the Insertions check box to insert the new Slide 5.

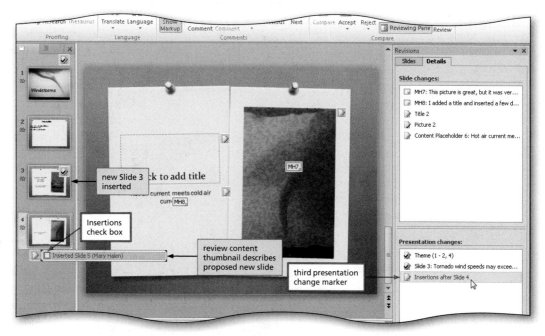

**Figure 5–14**

## To Review, Accept, and Reject Slide Changes

Changes that affect only the displayed slide are indicated in the Slide changes area of the Revisions task pane. A reviewer can modify many aspects of the slide, such as adding and deleting pictures and clips, editing text, and moving placeholders. The following steps display and accept the reviewer's revisions to Slide 1.

- Click the first slide change, Rectangle 1: Windstorms, in the Slide changes area to display the Rectangle 1 box with Mary Halen's three proposed changes for the Windstorms text in the rectangle (Figure 5–15).

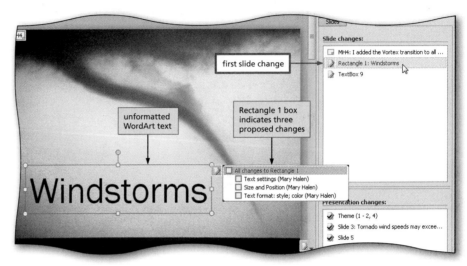

Figure 5–15

- Click the All changes to Rectangle 1 check box to preview the three proposed changes to the Windstorms text (Figure 5–16).

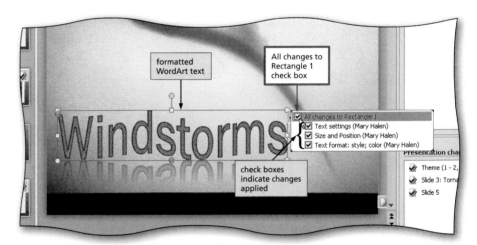

Figure 5–16

- Click the Size and Position check box to preview only the proposed Text settings and the Text format: style, color changes to the Windstorms text (Figure 5–17).

**Q&A**

Can I select any combination of the check boxes to modify the text in the rectangle?

Yes. Click the individual check boxes to preview the reviewer's modifications.

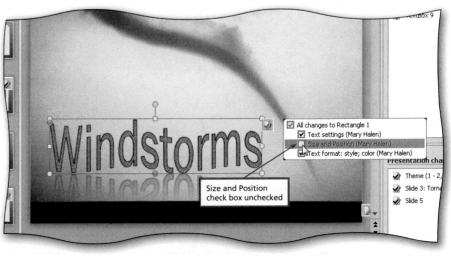

Figure 5–17

**4**

- Click the second slide change, TextBox, in the Slide changes area to display the Inserted TextBox box.

- Click the Inserted TextBox check box to view the proposed text box (Figure 5–18).

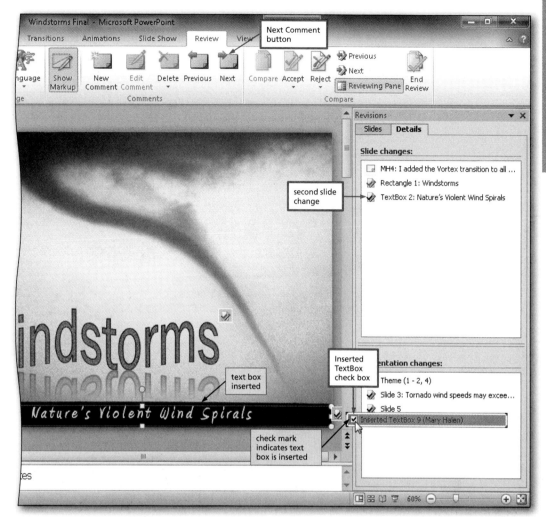

**Figure 5–18**

## To Review and Accept Slide Changes on the Remaining Slides

You have accepted all of Mary Halen's presentation changes and most of her Slide 1 changes. She also inserted comments in and made changes to other slides. The following steps review her comments and accept her modifications.

**1** Click the Next Comment button (Review tab | Comments group) to display Slide 2.

**2** Read comment 5 and then delete the comment.

**3** Click the Content Placeholder 5 slide change and then apply the Canvas contents change.

**4** Click the Title 4: Tornado slide change and then accept the change to delete the title text placeholder.

**5** Click the Next Comment button to display Slide 3. Read comment 6, but do not delete it.

**6** Click the Next Comment button to display Slide 4. Read comments 7 and 8 and then delete them.

**7** Click the Next Comment button to display Slide 5. Read comment 9, but do not delete it (Figure 5–19).

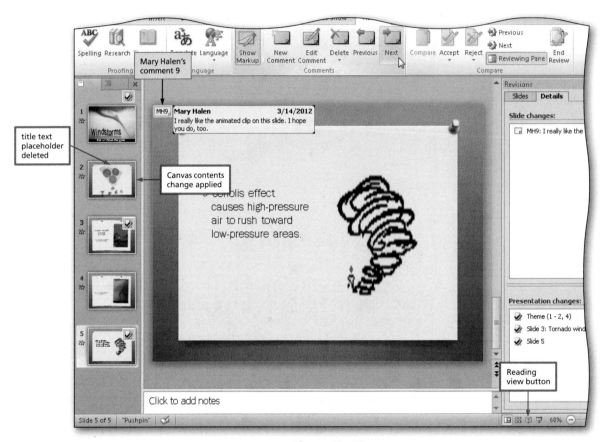

**Figure 5–19**

**BTW**

**Q&As**
For a complete list of the Q&As found in many of the step-by-step sequences in this book, visit the PowerPoint 2010 Q&A Web page (scsite.com/ppt2010/qa).

## To Run the Revised Presentation in Reading View

Mary's changes modified the original presentation substantially, so it is a good idea to review the new presentation. The following steps review the revised slides.

**1** Display Slide 1 and then click the Reading view button.

**2** Click the Next and Previous buttons to review the changes on each slide.

**3** After viewing the animated tornado on Slide 5, click the Normal view button.

## To Reject a Slide Revision

After running the presentation, you decide that the animation on Slide 5 is distracting and that the text is not part of the material you desire to display in the slide show. Although you initially accepted Mary's change to insert the slide, you decide to reject this modification. The following steps display and reject the reviewer's revision to insert Slide 5.

- Click the change marker on the Slide 5 thumbnail in the Slides tab to display the Inserted Slide 5 box (Figure 5–20).

**2**

- Click the Reject Change button (Review tab | Compare group) to delete Slide 5 from the presentation.

**Q&A** Could I have deleted the slide by clicking the Inserted Slide 5 check box to remove the check mark?

Yes.

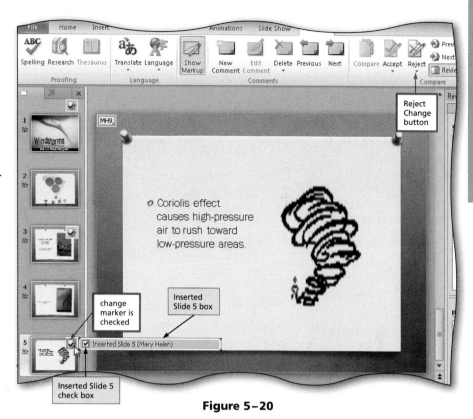

Figure 5–20

---

**Give constructive criticism.**
If you are asked to critique a presentation, begin and end with positive comments. Give specific details about a few key areas that can be improved. Be honest, but be tactful. Avoid using the word, you. For example, instead of writing, "You need to give some statistics to support your viewpoint," write "I had difficulty understanding which departments' sales have declined in the past five months. Perhaps a chart with specific losses would help depict how dramatically revenues have fallen."

**Plan Ahead**

## To Insert a Comment

Mary Halen's comments and changes greatly enhanced your slide show, and you would like to send her a copy of the presentation so that she can see what modifications you accepted. You want to insert a comment to her on Slide 1 to thank her for taking the time to review your original slides. The following steps insert a comment on Slide 1.

- With Slide 1 displaying, click the Slide pane. Click the Insert Comment button, which displays as New Comment, (Review tab | Comments group) to open a comment box at the top of the slide (Figure 5–21).

**Q&A** Why do my initials and name differ from those shown in the figure?

The initials and name reflect the information that was entered when Microsoft Office 2010 was installed on your computer.

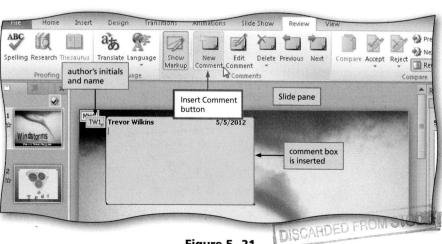

Figure 5–21

• Type **Your suggestions and modifications are excellent, Mary. I really appreciate the work you did to enhance my slides.** in the comment box (Figure 5–22).

• Click anywhere outside the comment box to hide the text and lock in the comment.

**Q&A** Can I move the comment on the slide?

Yes. Select the comment and then drag it to another location on the slide.

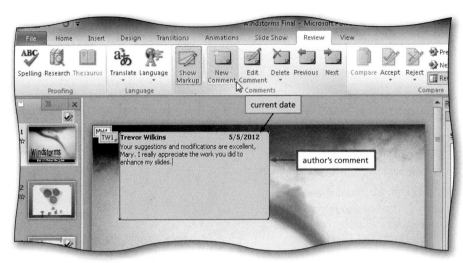

**Figure 5–22**

## To Edit a Comment

Mary asked some questions in the comments she made in her presentation. You want to provide feedback to her by responding to her queries. One method of responding is by editing the comments she made. The following steps edit the comments on Slides 1 and 3.

• With Slide 1 displaying, click the MH4 comment marker on the slide to display Mary's fourth comment.

**Q&A** Can I click the MH4 comment marker in the Revisions task pane to display Mary's comment?

Yes.

• Click the Edit Comment button (Review tab | Comments group) to change the marker comment color and display your initials and name (Figure 5–23).

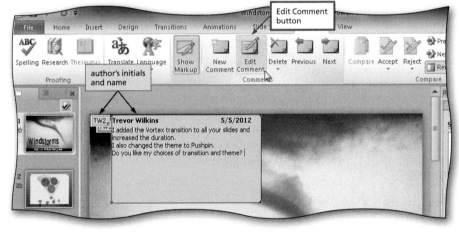

**Figure 5–23**

• Press the ENTER key to move the insertion point below Mary's comment. Press the ENTER key again to insert a blank line and then type **The Vortex transition complements the windstorm topic well. The Pushpin theme is excellent for displaying the photos.** in the comment box (Figure 5–24).

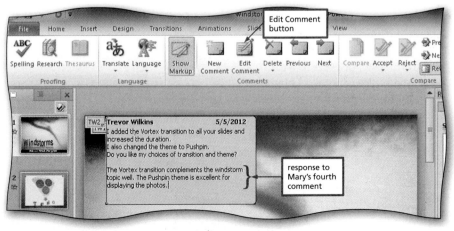

**Figure 5–24**

**3**

- Display Slide 3 and then click the MH6 comment marker on the slide to display Mary's comment.

- Click the Edit Comment button (Review tab | Comments group), press the ENTER key twice, and then type **The devastation from that tornado is amazing! Your slide is outstanding.** in the comment box immediately after Mary's comment (Figure 5–25).

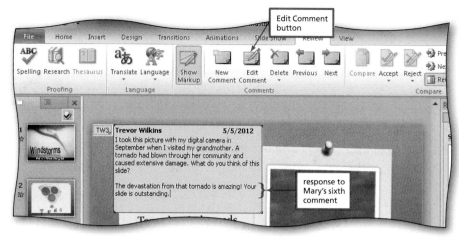

**Figure 5–25**

## To End the Review

You have analyzed all of the reviewer's proposed changes and replied to some of her questions. Your review of the merged presentation is complete, so you can apply all the changes and close the Revisions task pane. Be mindful that you cannot undo these changes after the review has ended. The following steps end the review of the merged slides.

**1**

- Click the End Review button (Review tab | Compare group) to display the Microsoft PowerPoint dialog box (Figure 5–26).

**2**

- Click the Yes button (Microsoft PowerPoint dialog box) to apply the changes you accepted and discard the changes you rejected.

**Q&A**

Which changes are discarded?

You did not apply the size and position change to the Windstorms rectangle on Slide 1, and you did not insert Mary's proposed Slide 5.

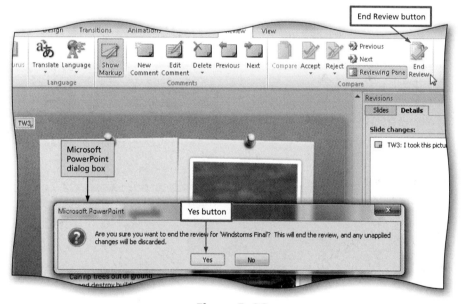

**Figure 5–26**

# Reusing Slides from an Existing Presentation

Occasionally you may want to insert a slide from another presentation into your presentation. PowerPoint offers two methods of obtaining these slides. One way is to open the second presentation and then copy and paste the desired slides. The second method is to use the Reuse Slides task pane to view and then select the desired slides. The presentation can be stored on a storage medium or in a Slide Library, which is a folder where individual slides are saved.

**BTW**

**BTWs**
For a complete list of the BTWs found in the margins of this book, visit the PowerPoint 2010 BTW Web page (scsite.com/ppt2010/btw).

The PowerPoint presentation with the file name, Hurricanes, has colorful pictures and useful text. It contains three slides, and you would like to insert two of these slides, shown in Figure 5–27, into your Windstorms Final presentation. You will capture part of the diamond graphic on Slide 3 and copy this snip to one Windstorms Final slide. The Hurricanes presentation is located on your Data Files for Students. See the inside back cover of this book for instructions on downloading the Data Files for Students, or contact your instructor for more information about accessing the required files.

**(a) Slide 1 (Insert and Use Pushpin Formatting)**

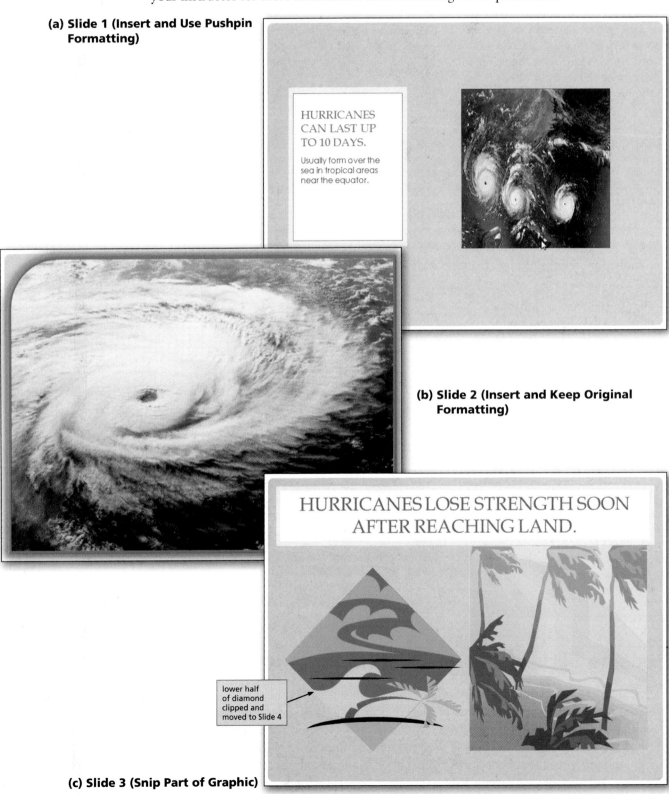

**(b) Slide 2 (Insert and Keep Original Formatting)**

**(c) Slide 3 (Snip Part of Graphic)**

**Figure 5–27**

The inserted slides will be placed in the presentation directly after Slide 4. PowerPoint converts inserted slides to the theme and styles of the current presentation, so the first slide will inherit the styles of the current Pushpin theme and Windstorms Final presentation. You will, in contrast, specify that the second slide keep the source formatting of the Hurricanes presentation, which uses the Apothecary theme. You will need to add the Vortex transition to the second slide because you are not applying the Windstorms Final formatting.

## To Reuse Slides from an Existing Presentation

The following steps add two slides from the Hurricanes presentation to your presentation.

**1**

- With your USB flash drive connected to one of the computer's USB ports, display Slide 4 and then display the Home tab.

- Click the New Slide button arrow to display the Pushpin layout gallery (Figure 5–28).

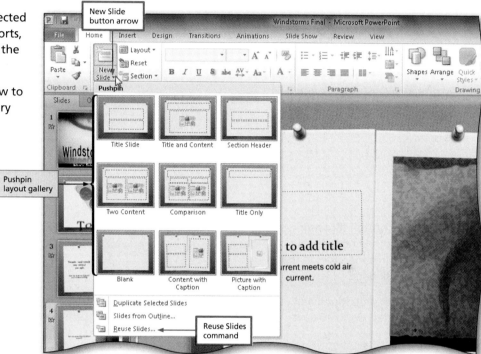

**Figure 5–28**

**2**

- Click Reuse Slides in the Pushpin layout gallery to display the Reuse Slides task pane.

- Click the Browse button (Figure 5–29).

**Q&A**

What are the two Browse options shown?

If the desired slides are in a Slide Library, you would click Browse Slide Library to select individual slides that you want to use. The slides you need, however, are on your Data Files for Students, so you need to click Browse File.

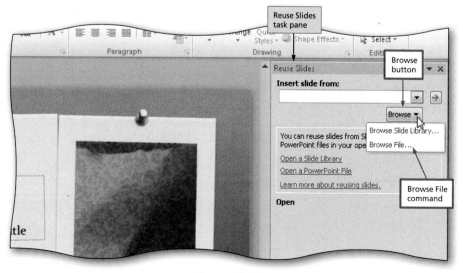

**Figure 5–29**

- Click Browse File to display the Browse dialog box.

- If necessary, double-click your USB flash drive in the list of available storage devices to display a list of files and folders on the selected USB flash drive.

- Click Hurricanes to select the file (Figure 5–30).

**Q&A** What if the file is not on a USB flash drive?

Use the same process, but select the drive containing the file.

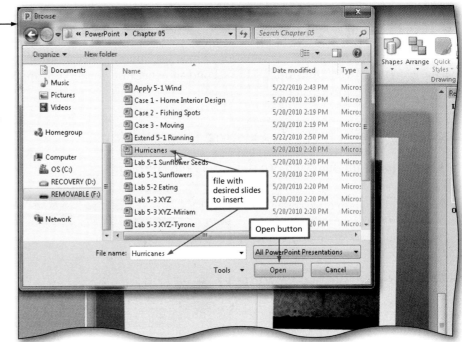

**Figure 5–30**

- Click the Open button (Browse dialog box) to display thumbnails of the three Hurricane slides in the Reuse Slides task pane.

- Point to the first slide thumbnail, Hurricanes can last up to 10 days (Figure 5–31).

 **Experiment**

- Point to each of the thumbnails in the Reuse Slides task pane to see a larger preview of that slide.

- Click the Hurricanes can last up to 10 days thumbnail to insert this slide into the Windstorms Final presentation after Slide 4.

**Q&A** Can I insert all the slides in the presentation in one step instead of selecting each one individually?

Yes. Right-click any thumbnail and then click Insert All Slides.

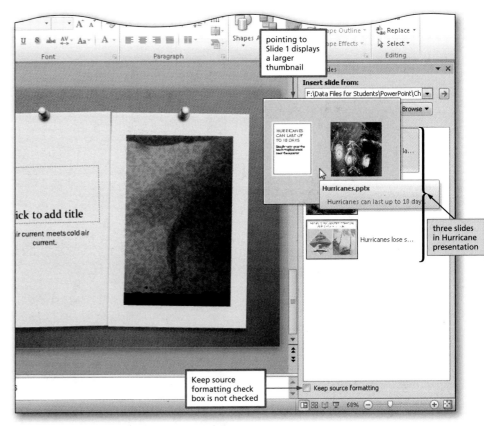

**Figure 5–31**

**6**

- Click the 'Keep source formatting' check box at the bottom of the Reuse Slides task pane to preserve the Hurricanes presentation formatting.

**Q&A** What would happen if I did not check this box?

PowerPoint would change the formatting to the characteristics found in the Pushpin theme.

- Point to the second slide, which has an aerial picture of a hurricane (Figure 5–32).

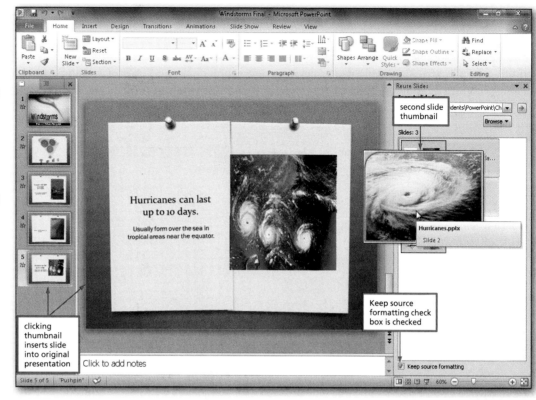

**Figure 5–32**

**7**

- Click the second slide thumbnail to insert this slide into the presentation as the last slide in the Windstorms Final presentation (Figure 5–33).

**8**

- Click the Close button in the Reuse Slides task pane so that it no longer is displayed.

- Apply the Vortex transition to Slide 6.

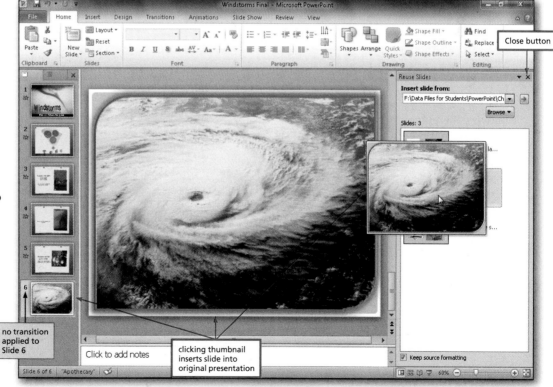

**Figure 5–33**

## To Capture Part of a Screen Using Screen Clipping

At times you may be developing a presentation and need a portion of a clip or picture in another presentation. You can capture, or **snip**, part of an object on a slide in another presentation that is open. PowerPoint refers to this presentation as being available. When you click the Screenshot button, PowerPoint displays a dialog box and asks you to select a particular available presentation. You then click the Screen Clipping command, and PowerPoint displays a white overlay on the available slide until you capture the snip. The following steps snip part of an image on Slide 3 of the Hurricanes presentation and paste it on Slide 5 in the Windstorms Final presentation.

- Open the Hurricanes presentation from your USB flash drive. Display Slide 3 of the Hurricanes presentation.

- Display Slide 5 of the Windstorms Final presentation.

- Display the Insert tab and then click the Screenshot button (Insert tab | Images group) to display the Available Windows gallery (Figure 5–34).

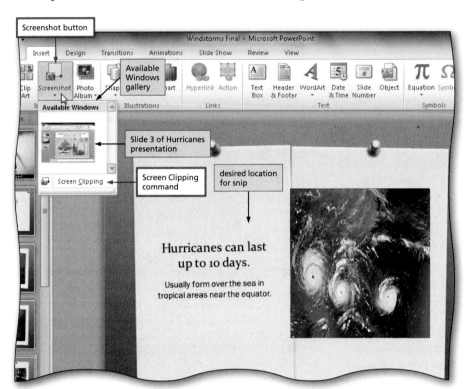

**Figure 5–34**

- Click Screen Clipping (Available Windows gallery) to display Slide 3 of the Hurricanes presentation.

- When the white overlay displays on Slide 3, move the mouse pointer near the left point of the diamond until the pointer changes to a crosshair.

- Drag downward and to the right to select the lower half of the diamond (Figure 5–35).

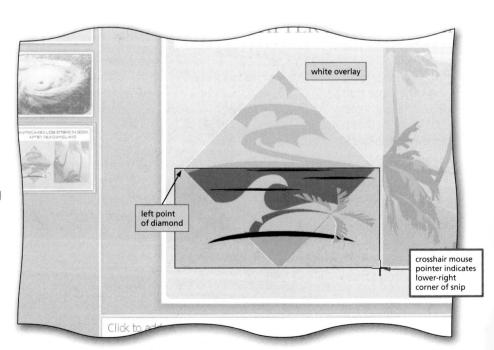

**Figure 5–35**

**3**

- Release the mouse button. When the snip displays on Slide 5 of the Windstorms Final presentation, drag the snip above the title text (Figure 5–36).

**Figure 5–36**

Plan
Ahead

**Use slide numbers to guide your speech.**
Slide numbers help a presenter organize a talk. While few audience members are cognizant of this aspect of a slide, the presenter can glance at the number and know which slide contains particular information. If an audience member asks a question pertaining to information contained on a slide that had been displayed previously or is on a slide that has not been viewed yet, the presenter can jump to that slide in an effort to answer the question. In addition, the slide number helps pace the slide show. For example, a speaker could have the presentation timed so that Slide 4 is displaying three minutes into the talk.

## To Add a Footer with Fixed Information

Slides can contain information at the top or bottom. The area at the top of a slide is called a **header**, and the area at the bottom is called a **footer**. As a default, no information is displayed in the header or footer. You can choose to apply only a header, only a footer, or both a header and footer. In addition, you can elect to have the header or footer display on single slides, all slides, or all slides except the title slide.

PowerPoint gives the option of displaying the current date and time obtained from the system or a fixed date and time that you specify. In addition, you can add relevant information, such as your name, your school or business name, or the purpose of your presentation in the footer. The following steps add a slide number, a fixed date, and footer text to all slides in the presentation except the title slide.

**1**

- Display the Insert tab.

- Click the Header & Footer button (Insert tab | Text group) to display the Header and Footer dialog box.

- If necessary, click the Slide tab to display the Slide sheet (Figure 5–37).

**Q&A** Can I change the starting slide number?

Yes. The first slide number is 1 by default. To change this number, click the Page Setup button (Design tab | Page Setup group) and then click the 'Number slides from' up button (Page Setup dialog box).

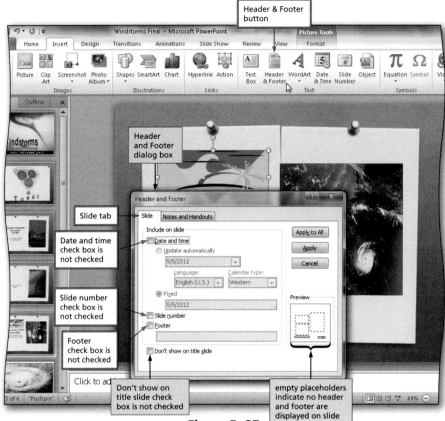

**Figure 5–37**

**2**

- Click 'Date and time' to select this check box.

- If necessary, click Fixed to select this option. Type **Friday, June 1 - 9:30 a.m.** in the Fixed box.

- Click Slide number to select this check box.

- Click Footer to select this check box.

- Type **Earth Science 101** in the Footer box (Figure 5–38).

**Q&A** What are the black boxes in the Preview area?

The black box in the left footer placeholder indicates where the footer information will appear on the slide; the black box in the right footer placeholder indicates where the date and time information and the page number will appear.

**Q&A** What if I want the current date and time to appear?

Click the Update automatically option in the 'Date and time' area.

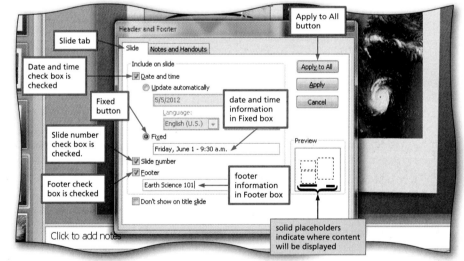

**Figure 5–38**

**3**

- Click the Apply to All button to display the date, time, footer text, and slide number on all slides.

**Q&A** When would I click the Apply button instead of the Apply to All button?

Click the Apply button when you want the slide number to appear only on the slide currently selected.

## To Clear Formatting and Apply an Artistic Effect

PowerPoint provides myriad options to enhance pictures. You can, for example, format the images by recoloring, changing the color saturation and tone, adding artistic effects, and altering the picture style. After adding various effects, you may desire to reset the picture to its original state. The tornado picture on Slide 4 has several formatting adjustments, and now you want to see the original unformatted picture. The following steps remove all formatting applied to the tornado picture on Slide 4 and then apply the Film Grain artistic effect.

**1**
- Display Slide 4, select the tornado picture, and then display the Picture Tools Format tab (Figure 5–39).

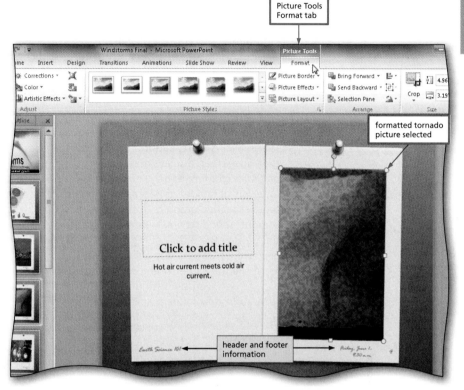

**Figure 5–39**

**2**
- Click the Reset Picture button (Picture Tools Format tab | Adjust group) to remove all formatting from the picture.

- Click the Artistic Effects button (Picture Tools Format tab | Adjust group) to display the Artistic Effects gallery (Figure 5–40).

**3**
- Apply the Film Grain effect (third effect in the third row) to the tornado picture.

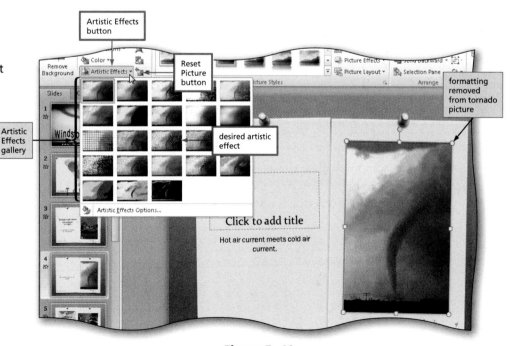

**Figure 5–40**

**Break Point:** If you wish to take a break, this is a good place to do so. Be sure to save the Windstorms Final file again and then you can quit PowerPoint. To resume at a later time, start PowerPoint, open the file called Windstorms Final, and continue following the steps from this location forward.

Plan
Ahead

**Determine the screen show ratio.**

Your presentation can be viewed on one of three different screen sizes. A standard monitor has a ratio of 4:3. Many new wide-screen notebook computers have a 16:10 ratio, and high-definition televisions have displays with a 16:9 ratio. These numbers describe the dimensions of the screen. For example, a display with a 4:3 ratio would be four feet wide if it were three feet high. Similarly, a notebook computer screen would be 16 inches wide if it were 10 inches high. While these exact measurements do not fit all displays and screens, the hardware height and width dimensions remain in the same proportion using these ratios.

Changing the default ratio offers many advantages. Audience members perceive a presentation in the wide-screen format as being trendy and new. In addition, the wider screen allows more layout area to display photographs and clips. In rooms with low ceilings, the wide-screen displays mirror the room dimensions and blend with the environment.

Slides created in the 4:3 format and then converted to 16:9 or 16:10 may look distorted, especially if images of people or animals are inserted. You consequently may need to adjust these stretched graphics if they look unnatural. If you present your slide show frequently on computers and screens with varying formats, you may want to save the slide show several times using the different ratios and then open the presentation that best fits the environment where it is being shown.

While the wide screen presents the opportunity to place more text on a slide, resist the urge to add words. Continue to use the 7 × 7 guideline (a maximum of seven lines on a slide and a maximum of seven words on a line).

**BTW**

**Pixels**
Screen resolution specifies the amount of pixels displayed on your screen. The word, pixel, combines the words pix ("pictures") and el ("element").

# Setting Slide Size and Slide Show Resolution

Today's technology presents several options you should consider when developing your presentation. The on-screen show ratio determines the height and width proportions. The screen resolution affects the slides' clarity.

## To Set Slide Size

By default, PowerPoint sets a slide in a 4:3 ratio, which is the proportion found on a standard monitor. If you know your presentation will be viewed on a wide-screen high-definition television (HDTV) or you are using a wide-screen notebook computer, you can change the slide size to optimize the proportions. The following steps change the default size ratio to 16:9, which is the proportion of most notebook computers.

**1**

- Display the Design tab and then click the Page Setup button (Design tab | Page Setup group) to display the Page Setup dialog box.

- Click the 'Slides sized for' box arrow to display the size list (Figure 5–41).

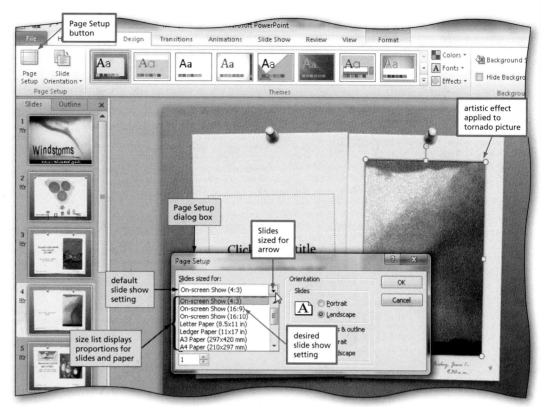

**Figure 5–41**

**2**

- Click On-screen Show (16:9) to change the slide size setting (Figure 5–42).

**Q&A**

Can I also change the default slide orientation from Landscape to Portrait?

Yes, but all slides in the presentation will change to this orientation. You cannot mix Portrait and Landscape orientations in one presentation. If you need to use both orientations during a speech, you can use a hyperlink to seamlessly jump from one slide show in Landscape orientation to another in Portrait orientation. Hyperlinks are discussed in Chapter 6.

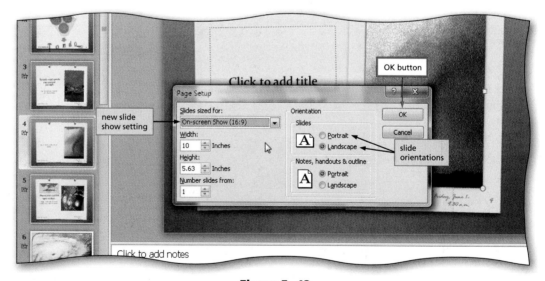

**Figure 5–42**

**3**

- Click the OK button to change the slide size in the presentation.

**4**

- Save the Windstorms Final presentation.

## To Select Slide Show Resolution

Screen, or presentation, resolution affects the number of pixels that are displayed on your screen. When screen resolution is increased, more information is displayed, but it is decreased in size. Conversely, when screen resolution is decreased, less information is displayed, but that information is increased in size. Throughout this book, the screen resolution has been set to $1024 \times 768$. The following steps change the presentation resolution to $800 \times 600$.

- Display the Slide Show tab and then click the Resolution box arrow (Slide Show tab | Monitors group) to display the Resolution list (Figure 5–43).

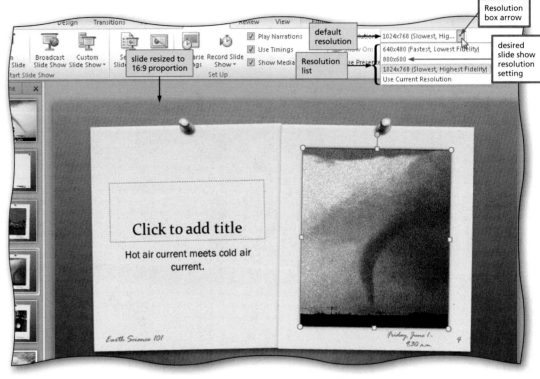

**Figure 5–43**

- Click $800 \times 600$ to change the slide show resolution setting (Figure 5–44).

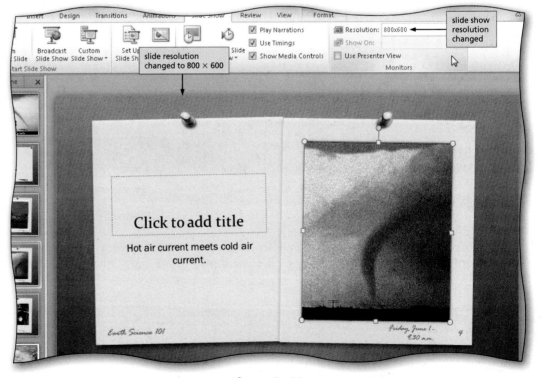

**Figure 5–44**

# Saving and Packaging a Presentation

Both PowerPoint 2010 and PowerPoint 2007 save files, by default, as a PowerPoint Presentation with a .pptx file extension. You can, however, select other file types that allow other computer users to view your slides if they do not have one of the newer PowerPoint versions installed. You also can save the file as a PowerPoint show so that it runs automatically when opened. Another option is to save one slide as an image that can be inserted into another program, such as Microsoft Word, or can be e-mailed.

In the following pages, you will follow these general steps to save the slides in four file types:

1. Save the presentation as a PowerPoint show.
2. Save one slide as an image.
3. Package the presentation for a CD.
4. Save the presentation in the PowerPoint 97–2003 format.

## To Save a File as a PowerPoint Show

To simplify giving a presentation in front of an audience, you may want your slide show to start running without having to start PowerPoint, open a file, and then click the Slide Show button. When you save a presentation as a **PowerPoint show (.ppsx)**, it automatically begins running when opened. The following steps save the Windstorms Final file as a PowerPoint show.

**1**

- Open the Backstage view, display the Save & Send tab, and then click Change File Type in the File Types area.

- Click PowerPoint Show in the Presentation File Types area (Figure 5–45).

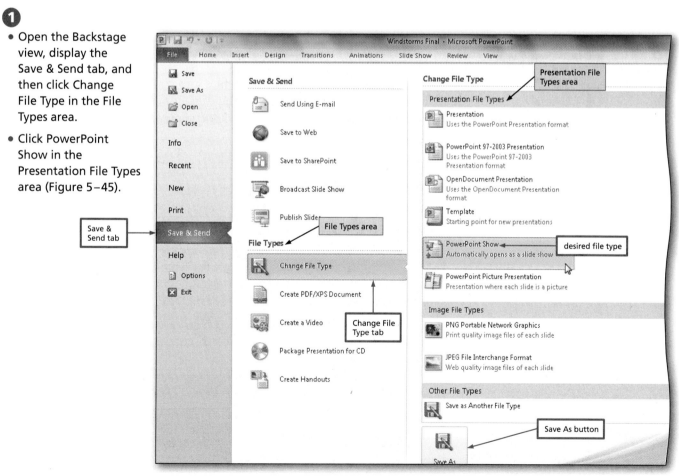

**Figure 5–45**

**2**

- Click the Save As button below the Other File Types area to display the Save As dialog box.

- Type **Windstorms Final Show** in the File name text box (Figure 5–46).

**3**

- Click the Save button (Save As dialog box) to save the Windstorms Final presentation as a PowerPoint show.

**4**

- Close both the current PowerPoint file and the Hurricanes presentation.

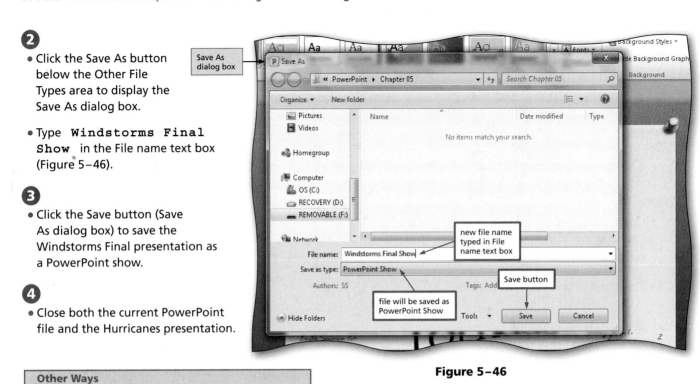

**Figure 5–46**

**Other Ways**

1. Click File on Ribbon, click Save As in Backstage view, click 'Save as type' arrow, select PowerPoint Show, click Save button

2. Double-click PowerPoint Show in Presentation File Types area

## To Save a Slide as an Image

To create visually interesting slides, you insert pictures, clips, and video files into your presentation. Conversely, the need may arise for you to insert a PowerPoint slide into another file. For example, you can save the information on a slide as an image and insert the image into a Microsoft Word document. The following steps save Slide 2 as a JPEG File Interchange Format image.

**1**

- Open the Windstorms Final presentation from your USB flash drive.

**Q&A** Why do I want to open this presentation?

It is best to use the final .pptx version of the presentation to complete the remaining tasks in this chapter.

- Display Slide 2.

- Open the Backstage view, display the Save & Send tab, and then click Change File Type in the File Types area.

- Click JPEG File Interchange Format in the Image File Types area (Figure 5–47).

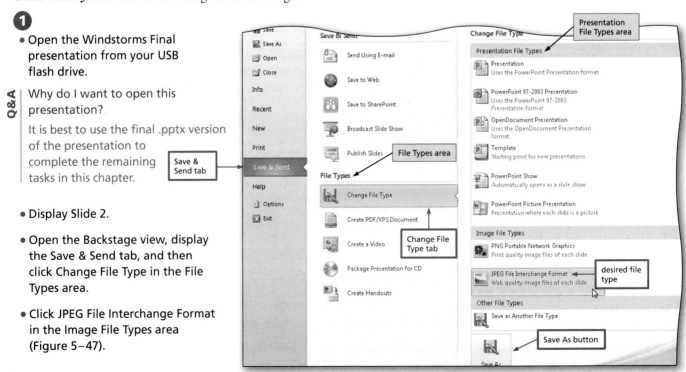

**Figure 5–47**

**2**

- Click the Save As button to display the Save As dialog box.
- Type `Tornadoes SmartArt` in the File name text box (Figure 5–48).

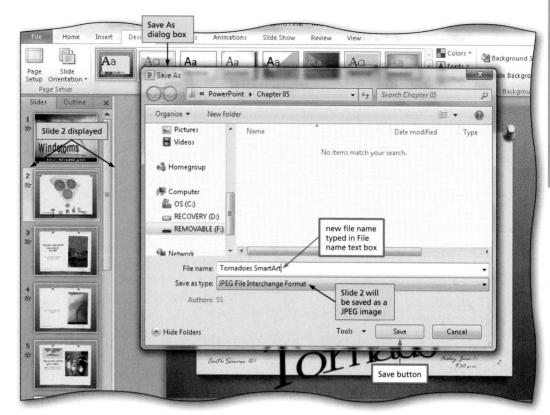

**Figure 5–48**

**3**

- Click the Save button (Save As dialog box) to display the Microsoft PowerPoint dialog box (Figure 5–49).

**4**

- Click the Current Slide Only button (Microsoft PowerPoint dialog box) to save only Slide 2 as a file in JPEG (.jpg) format.

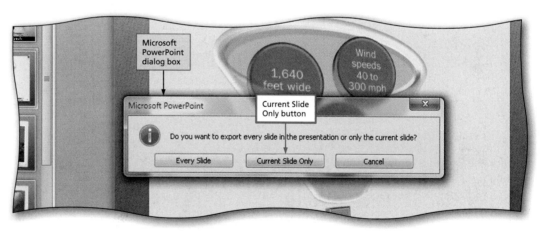

**Figure 5–49**

| Other Ways | |
|---|---|
| 1. Click File on Ribbon, click Save As in Backstage view, click 'Save as type' arrow, select JPEG File Interchange Format, click Save button | 2. Double-click JPEG File Interchange Format in Image File Types area |

## To Package a Presentation for Storage on a CD or DVD

If your computer has compact disc (CD) or digital video disc (DVD) burning hardware, the Package for CD option will copy a PowerPoint presentation and linked files onto a CD or DVD. Two types of CDs or DVDs can be used: recordable (CD-R or DVD-R) and rewritable (CD-RW or DVD-RW). You must copy all the desired files in a single operation if you use PowerPoint for this task because you cannot add any more files after the first set is copied. If, however, you want to add more files to the CD or DVD, you can use Windows Explorer to copy additional files. If you are using a CD-RW or DVD-RW with existing content, these files will be overwritten.

The PowerPoint Viewer is included so you can show the presentation on another computer that has Microsoft Windows but does not have PowerPoint installed. The **PowerPoint Viewer** also allows users to view presentations created with PowerPoint 2003, 2000, and 97.

The Package for CD dialog box allows you to select the presentation files to copy, linking and embedding options, whether to add the Viewer, and passwords to open and modify the files. The following steps show how to save a presentation and related files to a CD or DVD using the Package for CD feature.

- Insert a blank CD-R or DVD-R or a CD-RW or DVD-RW into your CD or DVD drive.

- Open the Backstage view, display the Save & Send tab, and then click Package Presentation for CD in the File Types area (Figure 5–50).

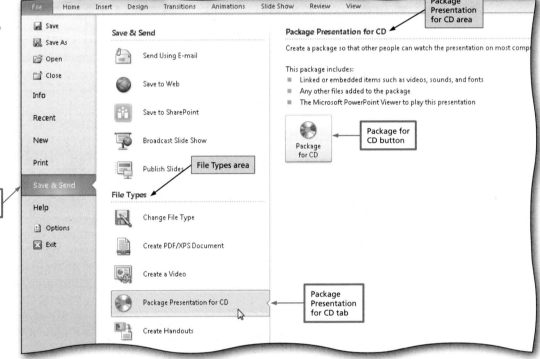

**Figure 5–50**

**2**

- Click the Package for CD button in the Package Presentation for CD area to display the Package for CD dialog box.

- Type **Windstorms** in the Name the CD text box (Package for CD dialog box) (Figure 5–51).

**Q&A**

What if I want to add more files to the CD?

Click the Add button and then locate the files you want to write on the CD.

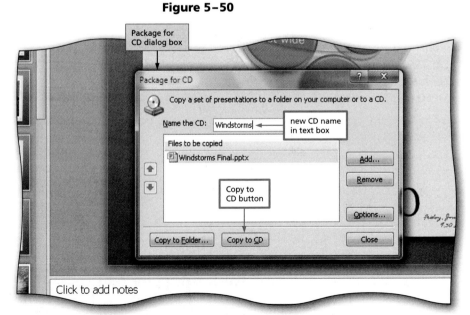

**Figure 5–51**

**3**

- Click the Copy to CD button to begin packaging the presentation files and to display the Microsoft PowerPoint dialog box (Figure 5–52).

**Q&A**

What is the purpose of the Copy to Folder button?

If you are copying your presentation to a folder on a network or on your storage device instead of on a CD, you would click this button.

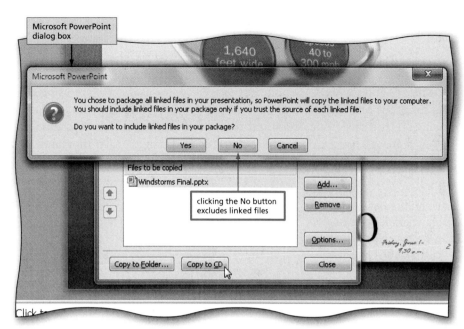

Figure 5–52

**4**

- Click the No button (Microsoft PowerPoint dialog box) to not include linked files and to display another Microsoft PowerPoint dialog box (Figure 5–53).

**5**

- Click the Continue button (Microsoft PowerPoint dialog box) to continue copying the presentation to a CD without the comments added to the slides.

**6**

- When the files have been written, click the No button (Microsoft PowerPoint dialog box) to not copy the files to another CD.

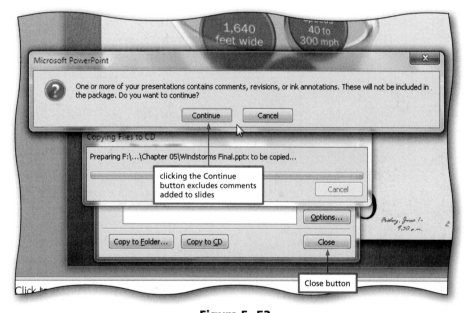

Figure 5–53

**7**

- Click the Close button (Package for CD dialog box) to finish saving the presentation to a CD.

---

### To View a PowerPoint Show Using the PowerPoint Viewer

When you arrive at a remote location, you will run the packaged presentation. The following steps explain how you would run the presentation using the PowerPoint Viewer.

1. Insert your CD or DVD into the CD or DVD drive.

2. Accept the licensing agreement for the PowerPoint Viewer to open and run the slide show.

## To Save a File in a Previous PowerPoint Format

Prior to Microsoft Office 2007, PowerPoint saved files, by default, as a .ppt type. The earlier versions of PowerPoint cannot open the .pptx type that PowerPoint 2010 and 2007 create by default. The Microsoft Office Downloads and Updates Web site has converters for users who are using these earlier versions of the program and also for other Microsoft Office software. The Microsoft Compatibility Pack for Word, Excel, and PowerPoint will open, edit, and save Office 2010 and 2007 documents. You cannot assume that people who obtain a .pptx file from you have installed the Compatibility Pack, so to diminish frustration and confusion, you can save a presentation as a .ppt type. The following steps save the Windstorms Final file as a PowerPoint 97–2003 Presentation.

**1**
- Open the Backstage view, display the Save & Send tab, and then click Change File Type in the File Types area.
- Click PowerPoint 97–2003 Presentation in the Presentation File Types area (Figure 5–54).

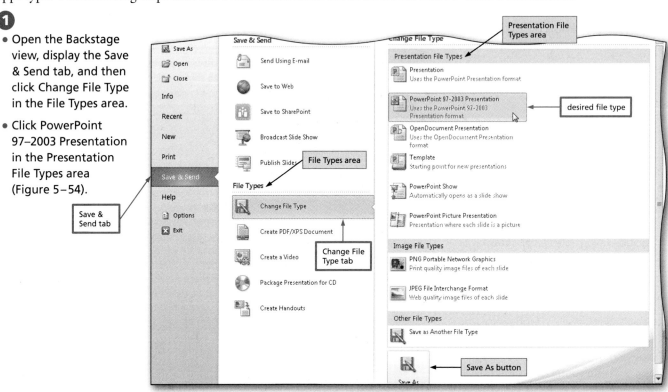

**Figure 5–54**

**2**
- Click the Save As button to display the Save As dialog box.
- Type **Windstorms Final Previous Version** in the File name text box (Figure 5–55).

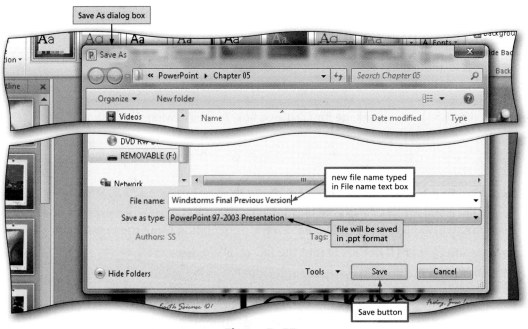

**Figure 5–55**

- Click the Save button (Save As dialog box) to save the Windstorms Final Previous Version presentation as a .ppt type and display the Microsoft PowerPoint Compatibility Checker.

**Q&A** Why does this Compatibility Checker dialog box display?

PowerPoint is alerting you that the older file version will not keep some of the features used in the presentation. You will learn more about the Compatibility Checker in the next section of this chapter.

**4**

- Click the Continue button (Microsoft PowerPoint Compatibility Checker) to continue to save the presentation.

**5**

- Close the current PowerPoint file and then open the Windstorms Final presentation from your USB flash drive.

**Q&A** Why do I want to open this presentation instead of using the current file?

The current file is saved in a previous version of PowerPoint, so some features are not available when you run the final version of the slide show. It is best to use the more current version of the presentation to complete the remaining tasks in this chapter.

> **Other Ways**
>
> 1. Click File on Ribbon, click Save As in Backstage view, click 'Save as type' arrow, select PowerPoint 97–2003 Presentation, click Save button
>
> 2. Double-click PowerPoint 97–2003 Presentation in Presentation File Types area

# Protecting and Securing a Presentation

When your slides are complete, you can perform additional functions to finalize the file and prepare it for distributing to other users or for running on a computer other than the one used to develop the file. For example, the Compatibility Checker reviews the file for any feature that will not work properly or display on computers running a previous PowerPoint version. In addition, the Document Inspector locates inappropriate information, such as comments, in a file and allows you to delete these slide elements. With passwords and digital signatures, you add security levels to prevent people from distributing, viewing, or modifying your slides. When the review process is complete, you can indicate this file is the final version.

In the following pages, you will follow these general steps to ensure your presentation contains appropriate information and that the contents will not be changed without authorization:

1. Identify features not supported by versions prior to PowerPoint 2007.
2. Remove personal information.
3. Select a password to open the file.
4. Identify the presentation as the final version.
5. Create a digital certificate to state the file contents have not been altered.

**BTW**

**Digital Signatures**
A digital signature verifies that the contents of a file have not been altered and that an imposter is not trying to commit forgery by taking ownership of the document. This signature encrypts, or converts, readable data into unreadable characters. To read the file, a user must decrypt, or decipher, the data into a readable form.

## To Identify Presentation Features Not Supported by Previous Versions

PowerPoint 2010 has many new features not found in some previous versions of PowerPoint, especially versions older than PowerPoint 2007. For example, WordArt formatted with Quick Styles is an enhancement found only in PowerPoint 2010 and PowerPoint 2007. If you give your file to people who have an earlier PowerPoint version installed on their computers, they will be able to open the file but may not be able to see or edit some special features and effects. You can use the **Compatibility Checker** to see which presentation elements will not function in earlier versions of PowerPoint. The following steps run the Compatibility Checker and display a summary of the elements in your Windstorms Final presentation that will be lost if your file is opened in some earlier PowerPoint versions.

**1**
- Open the Backstage view and then click the Check for Issues button (Info tab | Prepare for Sharing area) to display the Prepare for Sharing menu (Figure 5–56).

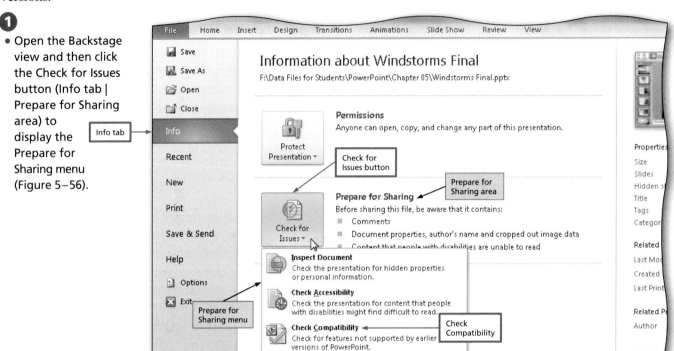

**Figure 5–56**

**2**
- Click Check Compatibility to have PowerPoint examine the file and then, after a short period, display the Microsoft PowerPoint Compatibility Checker dialog box.

- In the Summary area, view the comments regarding the three features that are not supported by earlier versions of PowerPoint (Figure 5–57).

**Q&A**

Why do the numbers 1, 1, and 6 display in the Occurrences column in the right side of the Summary area?

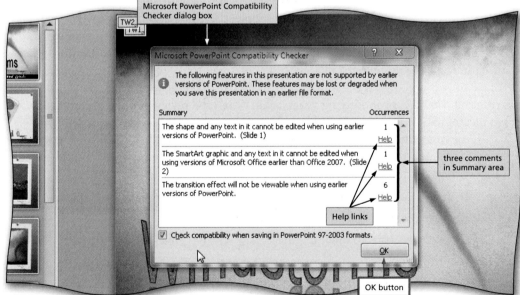

**Figure 5–57**

The Compatibility Checker found one shape and one SmartArt graphic in your presentation that cannot be edited in previous versions. These graphics will be converted to bitmap images in older versions, so they cannot be ungrouped and modified. In addition, the Vortex transition applied to all six slides will not display if the presentation is opened with any previous version of PowerPoint.

**Q&A** What happens if I click the Help links in the Summary area?

PowerPoint will provide additional information about the particular incompatible slide element.

**3**
- Click the OK button (Microsoft PowerPoint Compatibility Checker dialog box) to close the dialog box and return to the presentation.

## To Remove Inappropriate Information

As you work on your presentation, you might add information meant only for you to see. For example, you might write comments to yourself or put confidential information in the Document Information Panel. You would not want other people to access this information if you give a copy of the presentation file to them. You also added a comment and replied to Mary Halen's questions, and you may not want anyone other than Mary to view this information. The Document Inspector provides a quick and efficient method of searching for and deleting inappropriate or confidential information.

If you tell the Document Inspector to delete content, such as personal information, comments, invisible slide content, or notes, and then decide you need to see those slide elements, quite possibly you will be unable to retrieve the information by using the Undo command. For that reason, it is a good idea to make a duplicate copy of your file and then inspect this new second copy. The following steps save a duplicate copy of your Windstorms Final presentation, run the Document Inspector on this new file, and then delete comments.

**1**
- Open the Backstage view, click Save As to open the Save As dialog box, and then type **Windstorms Final Duplicate** in the File name text box.

- Click the Save button to change the file name and save another copy of this presentation.

**2**
- Open the Backstage view and then click the Check for Issues button (Info tab | Prepare for Sharing area) to display the Prepare for Sharing menu (Figure 5–58).

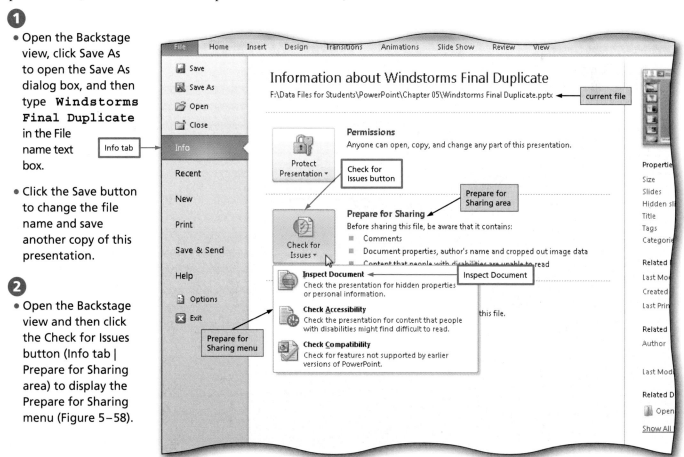

**Figure 5–58**

**3**

- Click Inspect Document to display the Document Inspector dialog box (Figure 5–59).

What information does the Document Inspector check?

This information includes text in the Document Information Panel, such as your name and company. Other information includes details of when the file was last saved, objects formatted as invisible, graphics and text you dragged off a slide, presentation notes, and e-mail headers.

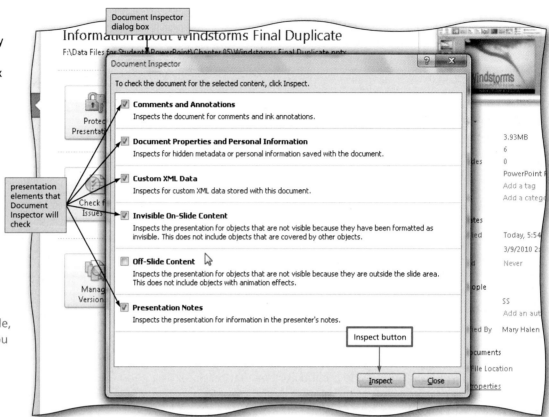

**Figure 5–59**

**4**

- Click the Inspect button to check the document and display the inspection results (Figure 5–60).

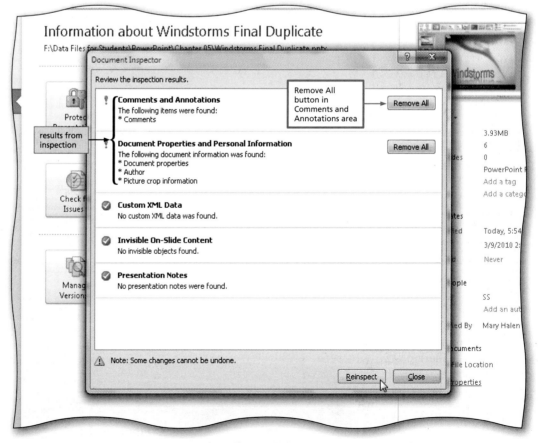

**Figure 5–60**

**5**
- Click the Remove All button in the Comments and Annotations area of the inspection results to remove the comments from the presentation (Figure 5–61).

**Q&A**

Should I also remove the document properties and personal information?

You might want to delete this information so that no identifying information is saved. This information includes text that displays in the Document Information Panel, such as your name, course number, and keywords.

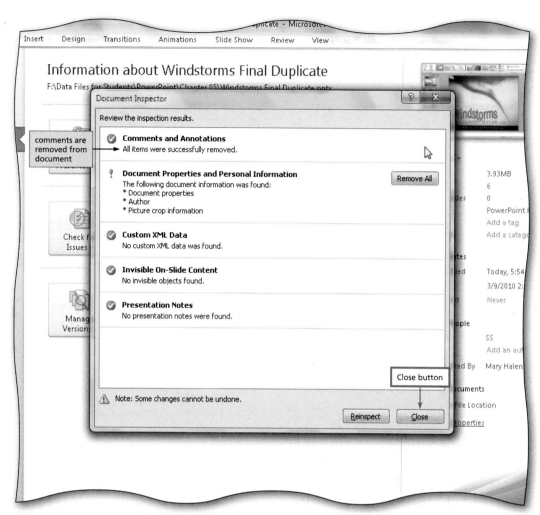

**Figure 5–61**

**6**
- Click the Close button (Document Inspector dialog box) to close the dialog box.

---

**Select an appropriate password.**
A password should be at least eight characters and contain a combination of letters and numbers. Using both uppercase and lowercase letters is advised. Do not use a password that someone could guess, such as your first or last name, spouse's or child's name, telephone number, birth date, street address, license plate number, or Social Security number.

Once you develop this password, write it down in a secure place. Underneath your keyboard is not a secure place, nor is your middle desk drawer.

**Plan Ahead**

## To Set a Password

You can protect your slide content by using passwords. The passwords specify whether a user can look at or modify a file. The following steps set a password for the Windstorms Final Duplicate file.

- With the Backstage view open and the Info tab displaying, click the Protect Presentation button (Info tab | Permissions area) menu to display the Permissions menu (Figure 5–62).

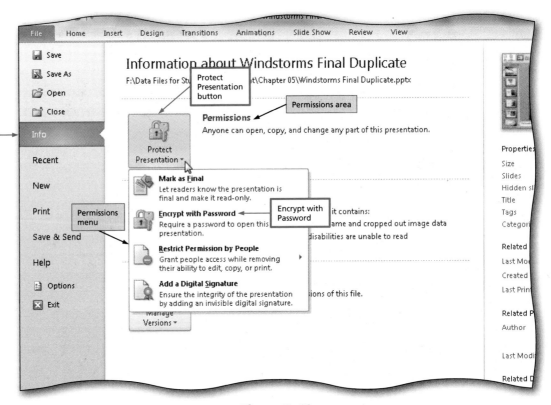

**Figure 5–62**

- Click Encrypt with Password to display the Encrypt Document dialog box.

- Type **Tornado2Windy** in the Password text box (Figure 5–63).

**Q&A**

Why do dots appear instead of the characters I typed?

PowerPoint does not display the actual letters and numbers for security reasons. In the next step, you are prompted to reenter the characters to ensure you pressed the desired keys.

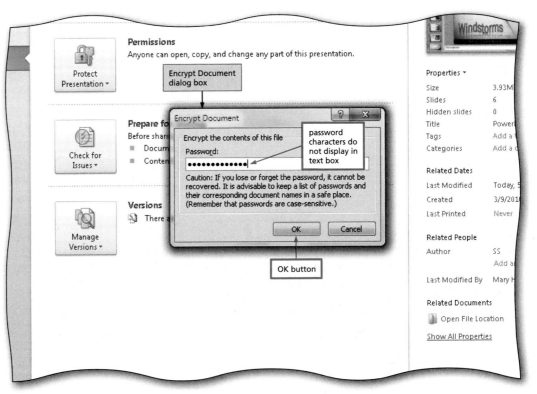

**Figure 5–63**

**3**
- Click the OK button to display the Confirm Password dialog box.

- Type **Tornado2Windy** in the Reenter password text box (Figure 5–64).

**Q&A** What if I forget my password?

You will not be able to open your file. For security reasons, Microsoft or other companies cannot retrieve a lost password.

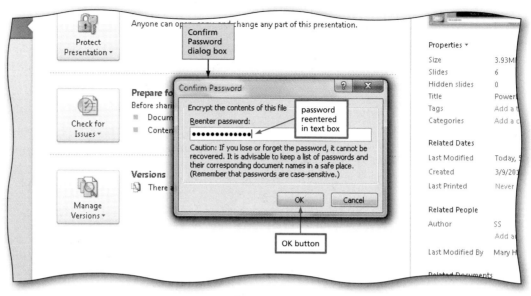

**Figure 5–64**

**4**
- Click the OK button in the Confirm Password dialog box.

**Q&A** When does the password take effect?

You will need to enter your password the next time you open your presentation.

### TO OPEN A PRESENTATION WITH A PASSWORD

To open a file that has been protected with a password, you would perform the following steps.

1. Display the Open dialog box, locate the desired file, and then click the Open button to display the Password dialog box.
2. When the Password dialog box appears, type the password in the Password text box and then click the OK button to display the presentation.

### TO CHANGE THE PASSWORD OR REMOVE PASSWORD PROTECTION

To change a password that you added to a file or to remove all password protection from the file, you would perform the following steps.

1. Display the Open dialog box, locate the desired file, and then click the Open button to display the Password dialog box.
2. When the Password dialog box appears, type the password in the Password text box and then click the OK button to display the presentation.
3. Open the Backstage view and then click Save As to display the Save As dialog box. Click the Tools button and then click General Options in the Tools list.
4. Select the contents of the 'Password to open' text box or the 'Password to modify' text box. To remove the password, delete the password text. To change the password, type the new password and then click the OK button. When prompted, retype your password to reconfirm it, and then click the OK button.
5. Click the OK button, click the Save button, and then click the Yes button to resave the presentation.

**BTW**

**Selecting Passwords**
Common passwords are 123456, 12345, 123456789, password, and iloveyou. Security experts recommend using passwords or passphrases that have at least eight characters and are a combination of numbers, letters, and capital letters.

## To Mark a Presentation as Final

When your slides are completed, you may want to prevent others or yourself from accidentally changing the slide content or features. If you use the **Mark as Final** command, the presentation becomes a read-only document and cannot be edited. The following steps mark the presentation as a final (read-only) document.

- With the Backstage view open and the Info tab displaying, click Protect Presentation to display the Permissions menu (Figure 5–65).

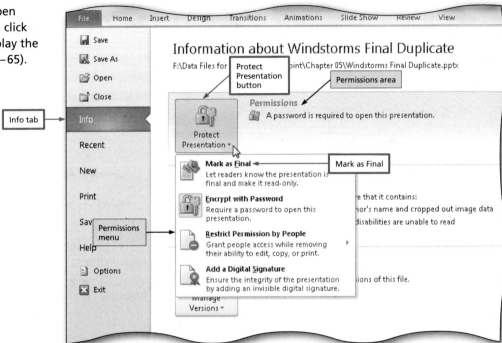

**Figure 5–65**

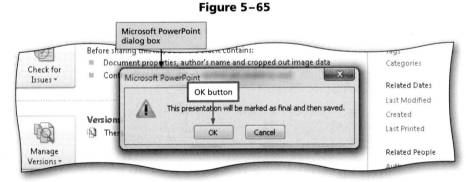

**2**

- Click Mark as Final to display the Microsoft PowerPoint dialog box indicating that the presentation will be saved as a final document (Figure 5–66).

**Figure 5–66**

- Click the OK button (Microsoft PowerPoint dialog box) to save the file and to display another Microsoft PowerPoint dialog box with information about a final version of a document and indicating that the presentation is final (Figure 5–67).

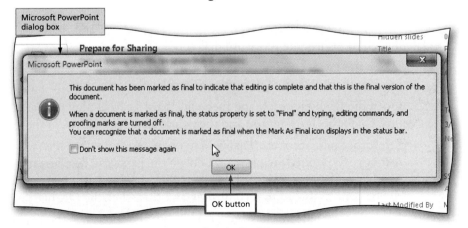

**Figure 5–67**

**Q&A**  Can I turn off this read-only status so that I can edit the file?

Yes. Click Mark as Final in the Permissions menu to toggle off the read-only status.

**4**

• Click the OK button (Microsoft PowerPoint dialog box) to return to the Backstage view.

## To Create a Digital Signature and Add It to a Document

A digital signature or ID is more commonly known as a **digital certificate**. It verifies that file contents are authentic and valid. Files protected with this certificate cannot be viewed in the PowerPoint Viewer or sent as an e-mail attachment. You can add a digital signature to files that require security, such as a presentation about a company's prototype or a patent application that will be submitted shortly. Only users with Office PowerPoint 2003 or later can view presentations protected by the digital signature. You can obtain an authentic digital certificate from a Microsoft partner, or you can create one yourself. The following steps create a digital signature and add it to the Windstorms Final Duplicate file.

**1**

• With the Backstage view open and the Info tab displaying, click the Protect Presentation button (Info tab | Permissions area) to display the Permissions menu (Figure 5–68).

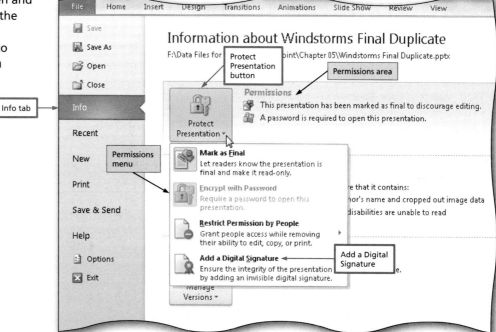

**Figure 5–68**

**2**

• Click Add a Digital Signature to display the Microsoft PowerPoint dialog box (Figure 5–69).

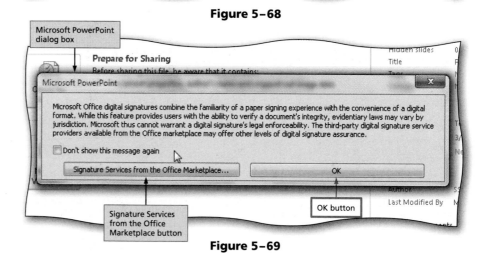

**Figure 5–69**

- Click the OK button to display the Get a Digital ID dialog box.

- Click 'Create your own digital ID' (Get a Digital ID dialog box) (Figure 5–70).

**Q&A** What would have happened if I had clicked the Signature Services from the Office Marketplace button instead of the OK button?

You would have been connected to the Microsoft Office Marketplace, which is the same process that will occur if you click the 'Get a digital ID from a Microsoft partner' option button.

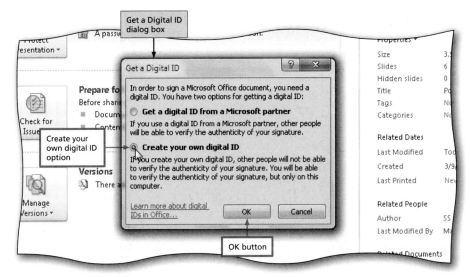

**Figure 5–70**

- Click the OK button to display the Create a Digital ID dialog box.

- If necessary, select the text in the Name text box, and then type **Mary Halen** in this text box.

- Type **mary_halen@hotmail.com** in the E-mail address text box.

- Type **Mary's Weather** in the Organization text box.

- Type **Chicago, IL** in the Location text box (Figure 5–71).

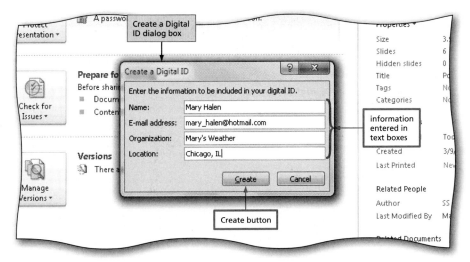

**Figure 5–71**

**5**

- Click the Create button to display the Sign dialog box (Figure 5–72).

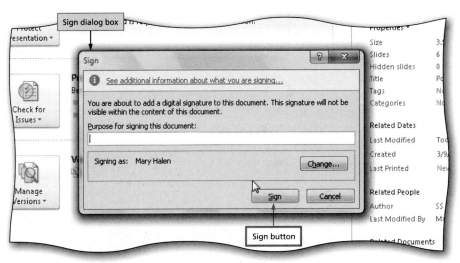

**Figure 5–72**

**6**

- Click the Sign button to display the Signature Confirmation dialog box (Figure 5–73).

**Q&A** Why would a company want to add a digital signature to a document?

The publisher, who is the signing person or organization, is trusted to ensure the source and integrity of the digital information. A signature confirms that the file contents have not been altered since it was signed.

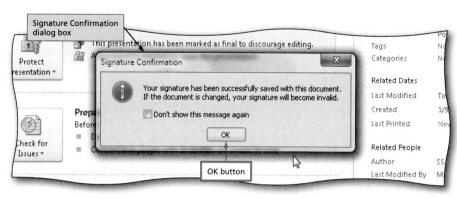

**Figure 5–73**

**Q&A** Can I remove a digital signature that has been applied?

Yes. Point to a signature in the Signatures task pane, click the list arrow, click Remove Signature, click the Yes button, and then, if necessary, click the OK button.

**7**

- Click the OK button to close the Signature Confirmation dialog box and return to the Backstage view.

# Using Presentation Tools to Navigate

When you display a particular slide and view the information, you may want to return to one of the other slides in the presentation. Jumping to particular slides in a presentation is called **navigating**. A set of keyboard shortcuts can help you navigate to various slides during the slide show. When running a slide show, you can press the F1 key to see a list of these keyboard controls. These navigational features are listed in Table 5–1.

**BTW**

**Displaying a Black or White Screen**
If an audience member interrupts your planned presentation and asks a question not pertaining to the current slide, you should consider displaying a black or white screen temporarily while you are answering the query.

| Table 5–1 Slide Show Navigation Shortcut Keys | |
|---|---|
| **Keyboard Shortcut** | **Purpose** |
| N<br>Click<br>SPACEBAR<br>RIGHT ARROW<br>DOWN ARROW<br>ENTER<br>PAGE DOWN | Advance to the next slide |
| P<br>BACKSPACE<br>LEFT ARROW<br>UP ARROW<br>PAGE UP | Return to the previous slide |
| Number followed by ENTER | Go to a specific slide |
| B<br>PERIOD | Display a black screen<br>Return to slide show from a black screen |
| W<br>COMMA | Display a white screen<br>Return to slide show from a white screen |
| ESC<br>CTRL+BREAK<br>HYPHEN | End a slide show |

# Delivering and Navigating a Presentation Using the Slide Show Toolbar

When you begin running a slide show and move the mouse pointer, the Slide Show toolbar is displayed. The **Slide Show toolbar** contains buttons that allow you to navigate to the next slide or previous slide, mark up the current slide, or change the current display. When you move the mouse, the toolbar displays faintly in the lower-left corner of the slide; it disappears after the mouse has not been moved for three seconds. Table 5–2 describes the buttons on the Slide Show toolbar.

**Table 5–2 Slide Show Toolbar Buttons**

| Description | Image | Function |
|---|---|---|
| Previous | | Previous slide or previous animated element on the slide |
| Pointer | | Shortcut menu for arrows, pens, and highlighters |
| Navigation | | Shortcut menu for slide navigation and screen displays |
| Next | | Next slide or next animated element on the slide |

## To Highlight Items on a Slide

You click the arrow buttons on either end of the toolbar to navigate backward or forward through the slide show. The Pointer button has a variety of functions, most often to emphasize, or **highlight**, words or to add **ink** notes or drawings to your presentation in order to emphasize aspects of slides or make handwritten notes. When the presentation ends, PowerPoint will prompt you to keep or discard the ink annotations. The following steps highlight items on a slide in Slide Show view.

- Display the Home tab and then click the Edit Anyway button in the yellow Marked as Final Message Bar near the top of the screen to enable editing the presentation.

- Click the Slide 1 thumbnail in the Slides tab and then run the slide show.

- If the Slide Show toolbar is not visible, move the mouse pointer on the slide.

- Click the Pointer button on the Slide Show toolbar to display the shortcut menu (Figure 5–74).

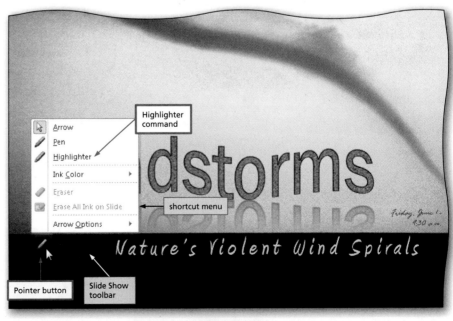

**Figure 5–74**

**2**

- Click Highlighter and then drag the mouse over the word, Windstorms. Repeat this action until all the letters are highlighted (Figure 5–75).

word is highlighted

**Figure 5–75**

## To Change Ink Color

Instead of the Highlighter, you also can click Pen to draw or write notes on the slides. The following steps change the pointer to a pen and change the color of ink during the presentation.

**1**

- Display Slide 2. Click the Pointer button on the Slide Show toolbar and then click Pen on the shortcut menu.

- Click the Pointer button on the Slide Show toolbar and then point to Ink Color (Figure 5–76).

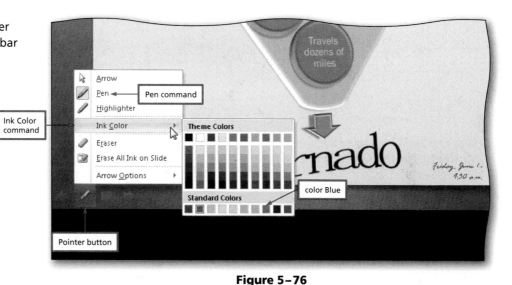

Pen command

Ink Color command

Pointer button

color Blue

**Figure 5–76**

**2**

- Click the color Blue in the Standard Colors row.

- Drag the mouse around the SmartArt graphic to draw a circle around this object (Figure 5–77).

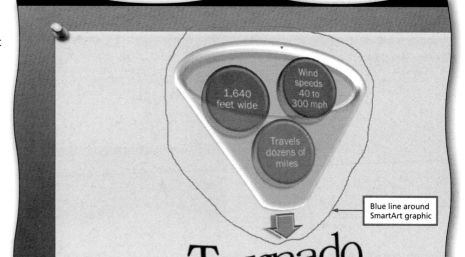

Blue line around SmartArt graphic

**Figure 5–77**

- Right-click the slide to display the shortcut menu (Figure 5–78).

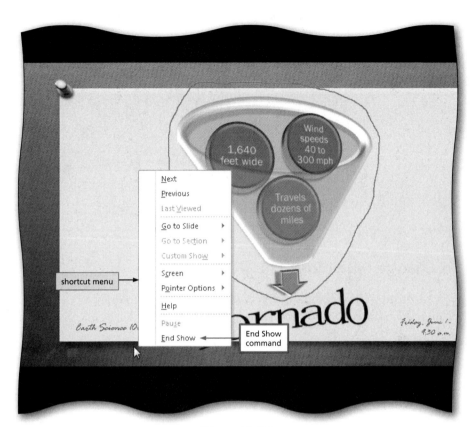

**Figure 5–78**

**4**

- Click End Show to display the Microsoft PowerPoint dialog box (Figure 5–79).

**5**

- Click the Discard button (Microsoft PowerPoint dialog box) to end the presentation without saving the annotations.

**Q&A** If I clicked the Keep button in error, can I later discard the annotations?

Yes. Display the slide, click the annotation line to select it, and then press the DELETE key.

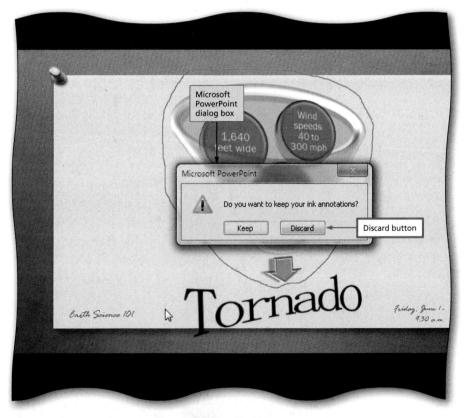

**Figure 5–79**

### TO HIDE THE MOUSE POINTER AND SLIDE SHOW TOOLBAR

To hide the mouse pointer and Slide Show toolbar during the slide show, you would perform the following step.

1. Click the Pointer button on the Slide Show toolbar, point to Arrow Options, and then click Hidden.

### TO CONSTANTLY DISPLAY THE MOUSE POINTER AND SLIDE SHOW TOOLBAR

By default, the mouse pointer and toolbar are set at Automatic, which means they are hidden after three seconds of no movement. After you hide the mouse pointer and toolbar, they remain hidden until you choose one of the other commands on the Pointer Options submenu. They are displayed again when you move the mouse.

To keep the mouse pointer and toolbar displayed at all times during a slide show, you would perform the following step.

1. Click the Pointer button on the Slide Show toolbar, point to Arrow Options, and then click Visible.

## To Change Document Properties

Before saving the presentation again, you want to add your name, class name, and some keywords as document properties. The following steps use the Document Information Panel to change document properties.

**1** Display the Document Information Panel and then type your name as the Author property.

**2** Type your course and section in the Subject property.

**3** Type `windstorm, hurricane, tornado` as the Keywords property.

**4** Close the Document Information Panel.

## To Save, Print, and Quit PowerPoint

The presentation now is complete. You should save the slides, print a handout, and then quit PowerPoint.

**1** Save the Windstorms Final presentation again with the same file name.

**2** Print the presentation as a handout with two slides per page. Do not print the comment pages (Figure 5–80 on the following page).

**3** Click the Page Setup button (Design tab | Page Setup group) and then change the slide size to On-screen Show (4:3).

**4** Click the Resolution box arrow (Slide Show tab | Monitors group) and then change the slide show resolution to 1024 × 768.

**5** Quit PowerPoint, closing all open documents.

**BTW**

**Quick Reference**
For a table that lists how to complete the tasks covered in this book using the mouse, Ribbon, shortcut menu, and keyboard, see the Quick Reference Summary at the back of this book, or visit the PowerPoint 2010 Quick Reference Web page (scsite.com/ppt2010/qr).

**BTW**

**Certification**
The Microsoft Office Specialist (MOS) program provides an opportunity for you to obtain a valuable industry credential — proof that you have the PowerPoint 2010 skills required by employers. For more information, visit the PowerPoint 2010 Certification Web page (scsite.com/ppt2010/cert).

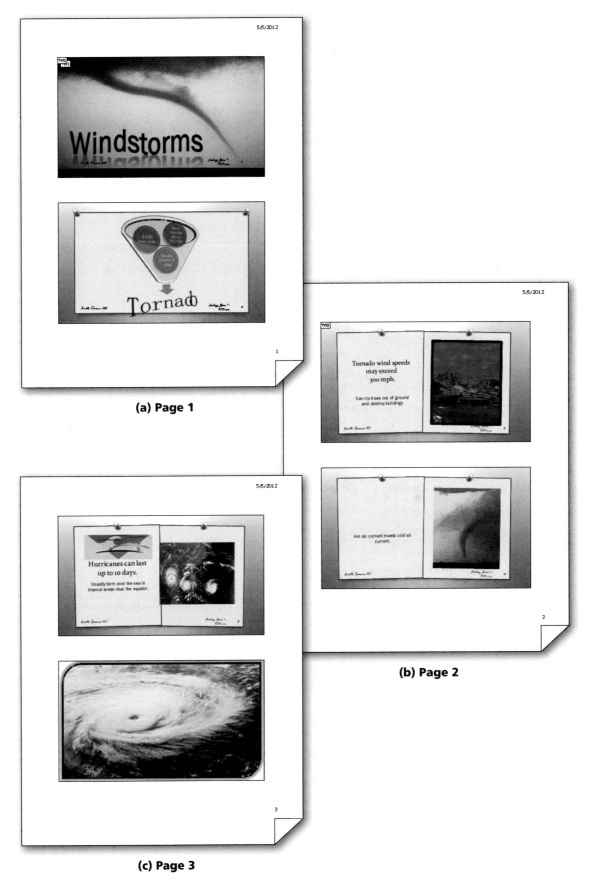

(a) Page 1

(b) Page 2

(c) Page 3

**Figure 5–80**

# Chapter Summary

In this chapter you have learned how to merge presentations, review a reviewer's comments, and then accept or reject proposed changes. You changed the slide size and presentation resolution, protected and secured the file with a password and digital signature, checked compatibility, removed inappropriate information, and then saved the presentation in a variety of formats. Finally, you ran the presentation and annotated the slides with a highlighter and pen. The items listed below include all the new PowerPoint skills you have learned in this chapter.

1. Merge a Presentation (PPT 270)
2. Print Comments (PPT 271)
3. Preview Presentation Changes (PPT 273)
4. Review and Delete Comments (PPT 274)
5. Review, Accept, and Reject Presentation Changes (PPT 276)
6. Review, Accept, and Reject Slide Changes (PPT 278)
7. Reject a Slide Revision (PPT 280)
8. Insert a Comment (PPT 281)
9. Edit a Comment (PPT 282)
10. End the Review (PPT 283)
11. Reuse Slides from an Existing Presentation (PPT 285)
12. Capture Part of a Screen Using Screen Clipping (PPT 288)
13. Add a Footer with Fixed Information (PPT 289)
14. Clear Formatting and Apply an Artistic Effect (PPT 291)
15. Set Slide Size (PPT 292)
16. Select Slide Show Resolution (PPT 294)
17. Save a File as a PowerPoint Show (PPT 295)
18. Save a Slide as an Image (PPT 296)
19. Package a Presentation for Storage on a CD or DVD (PPT 297)
20. Save a File in a Previous PowerPoint Format (PPT 300)
21. Identify Presentation Features Not Supported by Previous Versions (PPT 301)
22. Remove Inappropriate Information (PPT 303)
23. Set a Password (PPT 305)
24. Mark a Presentation as Final (PPT 308)
25. Create a Digital Signature and Add It to a Document (PPT 309)
26. Highlight Items on a Slide (PPT 312)
27. Change Ink Color (PPT 313)

 If you have a SAM 2010 user profile, your instructor may have assigned an autogradable version of this assignment. If so, log into the SAM 2010 Web site at www.cengage.com/sam2010 to download the instruction and start files.

# Learn It Online

**Test your knowledge of chapter content and key terms.**

*Instructions:*   To complete the Learn It Online exercises, start your browser, click the Address bar, and then enter the Web address **scsite.com/ppt2010/learn**. When the PowerPoint 2010 Learn It Online page is displayed, click the link for the exercise you want to complete and then read the instructions.

### Chapter Reinforcement TF, MC, and SA
A series of true/false, multiple choice, and short answer questions that test your knowledge of the chapter content.

### Flash Cards
An interactive learning environment where you identify chapter key terms associated with displayed definitions.

### Practice Test
A series of multiple choice questions that test your knowledge of chapter content and key terms.

### Who Wants To Be a Computer Genius?
An interactive game that challenges your knowledge of chapter content in the style of a television quiz show.

### Wheel of Terms
An interactive game that challenges your knowledge of chapter key terms in the style of the television show *Wheel of Fortune*.

### Crossword Puzzle Challenge
A crossword puzzle that challenges your knowledge of key terms presented in the chapter.

# Apply Your Knowledge

Reinforce the skills and apply the concepts you learned in this chapter.

### Inserting Comments, Adding a Header and a Footer, Marking as Final, and Saving As a Previous Version

*Note:* To complete this assignment, you will be required to use the Data Files for Students. See the inside back cover of this book for instructions on downloading the Data Files for Students, or contact your instructor for information about accessing the required files.

*Instructions:* Start PowerPoint. Open the presentation, Apply 5-1 Wind, located on the Data Files for Students.

The slides in the presentation present information about wind energy. You will insert a comment, add a footer, and then save the file as PowerPoint 2010 (.pptx) document. The slides should look like Figure 5–81a and 5–81b. You then will remove inappropriate information, mark the presentation as final, and save the files as a PowerPoint 97–2003 (.ppt) document. Figure 5–81c shows the new Slide 1.

*Perform the following tasks:*

1. On Slide 1, add a comment on the picture with the following text: **To be consistent with kilowatts, I suggest you show wind speeds in kilometers per hour instead of miles per hour. I converted them for you: 12 mph = 19.31 Km/H and 14 mph = 22.53 Km/H.**

2. Display the Header and Footer dialog box and add the slide number and the automatic date and time. Type your name as the footer text. Do not show on title slide.

3. Check the spelling and then change the document properties, as specified by your instructor. Save the presentation using the file name, Apply 5-1 Wind Energy.

4. Remove all inappropriate information.

5. Mark the presentation as final.

6. Save the presentation as a PowerPoint 97-2003 (.ppt) document using the file name, Apply 5-1 Wind Energy PPT. Submit the revised documents in the format specified by your instructor.

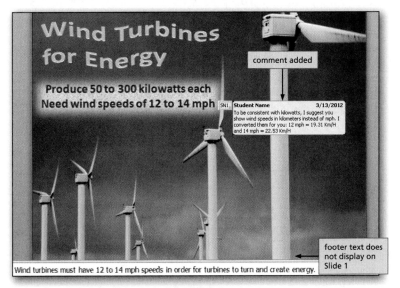

**(a) Slide 1**

**(b) Slide 2**

**Figure 5–81**

**(c) Revised Slide 1**

**Figure 5–81 (Continued)**

# Extend Your Knowledge

Extend the skills you learned in this chapter and experiment with new skills. You may need to use Help to complete the assignment.

## Changing Headers and Footers on Slides and Handouts and Inserting a Screenshot

*Note:* To complete this assignment, you will be required to use the Data Files for Students. See the inside back cover of this book for instructions on downloading the Data Files for Students, or contact your instructor for information about accessing the required files.

*Instructions:* Start PowerPoint. Open the presentation, Extend 5-1 Running, located on the Data Files for Students.

You will add a footer and a fixed date to all slides in the presentation (Figure 5–82) and format this text on the title slide. You also will insert a screenshot of marathon information on one slide.

*Perform the following tasks:*

1. Display the Header and Footer dialog box and then add your next birthday as the fixed date footer text on all slides. Type your school's name as the footer text, followed by the words, Running Club.

2. Display the Notes and Handouts tab (Header and Footer dialog box) and then add the same date and footer text to the notes and handouts.

3. Increase the font size of the Slide 1 footer date to 16 point and change the font color to Red. Italicize this text (Figure 5–82a).

**(a) Slide 1**

**Figure 5–82**

*Continued >*

**Extend Your Knowledge** *continued*

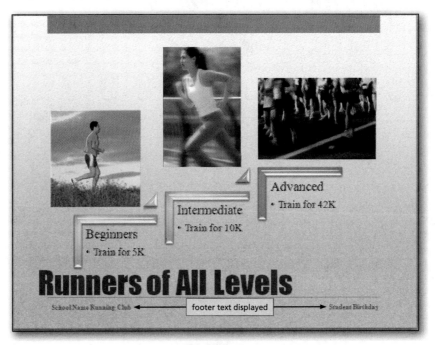

**(b) Slide 2**

**(c) Slide 3**

**Figure 5–82 (Continued)**

4. Insert a comment on Slide 1 as a reminder to yourself to verify the training dates and times with your school's running club president.

5. Locate information about marathons on the Internet. This information could list previous winners, record times, or routes. Insert a screenshot of one Web page on Slide 3 (Figure 5–82c). You may need to make the screenshot smaller or reduce the size of the two photos at the top of Slide 3.

6. Change the document properties, as specified by your instructor. Save the presentation using the file name, Extend 5–1 Running Club.

7. Submit the revised document in the format specified by your instructor.

## Make It Right

Analyze a presentation and correct all errors and/or improve the design.

### Clearing Formatting and Correcting Headers and Footers

*Note:* To complete this assignment, you will be required to use the Data Files for Students. See the inside back cover of this book for instructions on downloading the Data Files for Students, or contact your instructor for information about accessing the required files.

*Instructions:* Start PowerPoint. Open the presentation, Make It Right 5-1 Video Games, located on the Data Files for Students.

In your psychology class, you are studying the habits of teenagers and if playing video games can have negative effects on their behavior. You contact a local high school and get permission to conduct a survey among the students to find out how they spend their leisure time. Correct the formatting problems and errors in the presentation, shown in Figure 5–83, while keeping in mind the guidelines presented in this chapter.

*Perform the following tasks:*
1. Change the design from Trek to Slipstream.
2. Set the slide size to On-screen Show (16:9). Change the slide show resolution to 800 × 600.
3. On Slide 1, adjust the chart size so that all text on the chart is visible. Decrease the slide title text font size to 44 point.
4. Adjust the size of the picture and move it to the upper-right corner of the slide so that it is not covering the title text.
5. On Slide 2, decrease the font size of the bulleted text to 20 point and decrease the title text font size to 54 point.
6. Clear the formatting from the picture and adjust the size so that it fits below the bulleted text in the right text placeholder.
7. Display the Header and Footer dialog box, remove the student name from the footer on Slide 2, and do not show the slide number on the title slide.
8. Change the Transition from Fly Through to Cube on all slides.
9. Change the document properties, as specified by your instructor. Save the presentation using the file name, Make It Right 5-1 Teens and Video Games.
10. Submit the revised document in the format specified by your instructor.

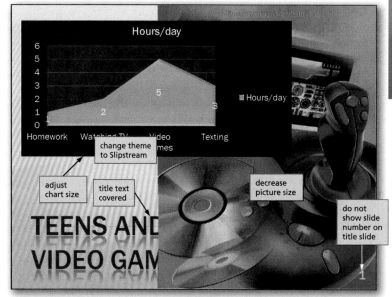

**(a) Slide 1**

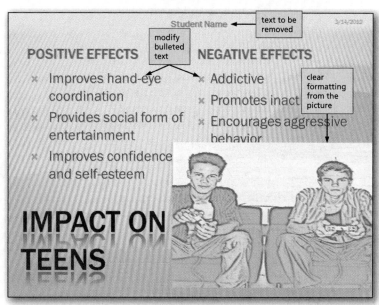

**(b) Slide 2**

**Figure 5–83**

# In the Lab

Design and/or create a presentation using the guidelines, concepts, and skills presented in this chapter. Labs 1, 2, and 3 are listed in order of increasing difficulty.

### Lab 1: Adding Comments to and Protecting a Presentation and Inserting a Slide

*Note:* To complete this assignment, you will be required to use the Data Files for Students. See the inside back cover of this book for instructions on downloading the Data Files for Students, or contact your instructor for information about accessing the required files.

*Problem:* The garden center where you work is putting together small gift baskets to hand out to local senior citizens at an upcoming fair. One of the items in the gift basket is a packet of sunflower seeds. Last spring your manager, John Wind, created a PowerPoint presentation about sunflower seeds. He sent you two sets of slides and requested comments. One PowerPoint presentation that he sent to you includes instructions for roasting sunflower seeds, and he would like those instructions to be added to the presentation. In addition, he will print out the instructions to include with the sunflower seeds. You add several comments, insert a slide, check the slides for compatibility with previous PowerPoint versions, and then protect the presentation with a password. When you run the presentation, you add annotations. The annotated slides are shown in Figure 5–84.

*Perform the following tasks:*

1. Open the presentation, Lab 5-1 Sunflowers, located on the Data Files for Students.

2. On Slide 1, replace Calista Lindy's name with your name. Add a comment on the picture with the following text: **I suggest you enlarge this picture and add a 6 pt Gold border.**

3. On Slide 2, add a comment in the SmartArt graphic with the following text: **I would change the text color and size and then bold the words in this SmartArt graphic so that it is more readable.**

4. On Slide 3, add a comment on the title text placeholder with the following text: **I would change the title text font so it matches the title text font on Slide 2.**

5. After Slide 2, insert Slide 2 (which becomes the new Slide 3, and former Slide 3 becomes Slide 4) from the Lab 5-1 Sunflower Seeds file located on the Data Files for Students. Keep the source formatting.

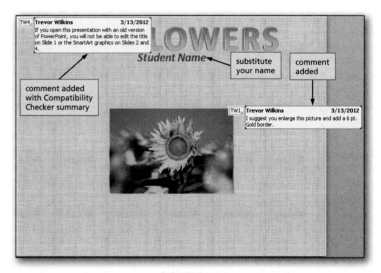

**(a) Slide 1**

**(b) Slide 2**

**Figure 5–84**

6. On the new Slide 3, clear the formatting from the picture.

7. Run the Compatibility Checker to identify the presentation features not supported in previous PowerPoint versions. Summarize these features in a comment placed on Slide 1.

8. Protect the presentation with the password, Sunflowers2Grow.

9. Change the document properties, as specified by your instructor. Save the presentation using the file name, Lab 5-1 Growing Sunflowers.

10. Print the slides. In addition, print Slide 3 again.

11. Run the presentation. On Slide 2, click the Pointer button, point to Ink Color on the shortcut menu, and then click Blue in the Standard Colors row. Click the Pen, draw a circle around the text, Miniature – 2 to 4 feet, in the SmartArt graphic. Click the Next button on the toolbar, click Highlighter, point to Ink Color, and then click Light Green in the Standard Colors row. Highlight the text, Soak seeds overnight in salted water. Save the annotations.

12. Print the slides with annotations.

13. Submit the revised document in the format specified by your instructor.

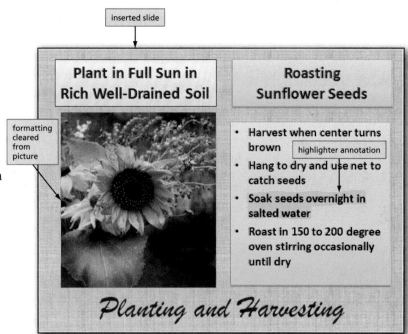

**(c) Slide 3 (Inserted Slide)**

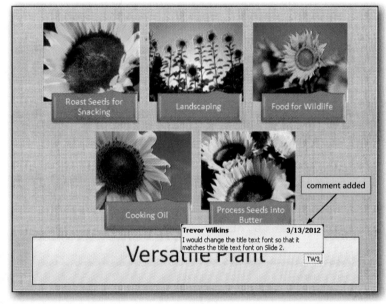

**(d) Slide 4**

**Figure 5–84 (Continued)**

# In the Lab

## Lab 2: Modifying and Deleting Comments in a Protected Presentation

*Note:* To complete this assignment, you will be required to use the Data Files for Students. See the inside back cover of this book for instructions on downloading the Data Files for Students, or contact your instructor for information about accessing the required files.

*Problem:* In an effort to eat healthy and shop economically, stocking up on vegetables and fruits is a good idea. The manager of your local grocery store contacts you about doing a display for the produce department. He is listening to his customers and trying to provide more healthy choices of fresh produce at reasonable prices. Several customers have expressed a concern about handling the fresh produce to get the best value from them. He knows you are studying biology in school and thought you might be able to help. He gives you a password-protected file that he created and asks you to review the slides, which are shown in Figure 5–85. He has inserted comments with questions. You offer some suggestions by modifying his comments and removing inappropriate information.

*Perform the following tasks:*

1. Open the presentation, Lab 5-2 Eating, located on the Data Files for Students. The password is Produce4Us.

2. Insert the date, time, and your name in the footer on all slides except the title slide. On Slide 1, modify the comment on the title by adding the following text: `Yes, I think the title is a great attention-getter. You really want your customers to eat healthy and make better food choices.`

3. On Slide 2, modify the comment by adding the following text: `You could change the word microbial to bacterial. The statement is good because a lot of people might not know they should not wash produce before storing.`

4. On Slide 3, modify comment 3 by adding the following text: `The presentation will be printed in color and displayed throughout the produce department. These slides will be enlarged, so shoppers should see the pictures easily.` Delete comment 4 on the title text placeholder.

**(a) Slide 1**

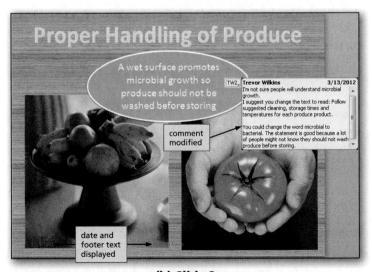

**(b) Slide 2**

**Figure 5–85**

5. Mark the presentation as final.

6. Add a digital signature by creating your own digital ID. Enter your name in the Name text box, `mary_halen@hotmail.com` in the E-mail address text box, `John's Supermarket` in the Organization text box, and `Chicago, IL` in the Location text box.

7. Inspect the document and then remove all document properties and personal information.

8. Save the presentation using the file name, Lab 5-2 Healthy Eating. Then save the slides as a PowerPoint 97-2003 Presentation (.ppt) type using the same file name.

9. Print the slides and comments.

10. Submit the revised document in the format specified by your instructor.

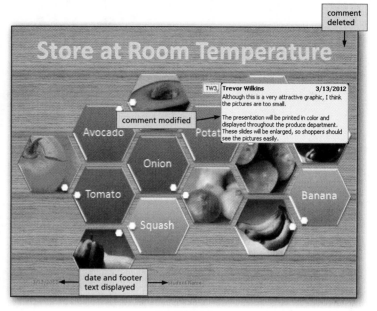

**(c) Slide 3**

**Figure 5–85 (Continued)**

# In the Lab

## Lab 3: Reviewing and Accepting Comments, Using Screen Clipping, and Packaging the Presentation for Storage on a Compact Disc

*Note:* To complete this assignment, you will be required to use the Data Files for Students. See the inside back cover of this book for instructions on downloading the Data Files for Students, or contact your instructor for information about accessing the required files.

*Problem:* The XYZ Corporation is promoting its software products. You work in the Marketing department and have developed a PowerPoint presentation, which is shown in Figures 5–86a and 5–86b on the next page, as part of the marketing strategy. You ask your coworker, Miriam Lind, to review the presentation by inserting comments and making revisions on the slides. You use her input to create the final presentation shown in Figures 5–86c through 5–86e on page PPT 327. You also obtain a picture of your department's new director, Sanjai Rukah, from another PowerPoint presentation. In addition, you use the Package for CD feature to distribute the presentation to local businesses.

*Perform the following tasks:*

1. Open the presentation, Lab 5-3 XYZ, located on the Data Files for Students.

2. Merge Miriam's revised file, Lab 5-3 XYZ-Miriam, located on the Data Files for Students. Accept both presentation changes so that the transition is added and Slide 3 is inserted. Review all of Miriam's comments on Slide 1 and Slide 2. Preview the slides, and then print the slides and the comments.

*Continued >*

**In the Lab** *continued*

3. On Slide 1, accept all changes except Miriam's computer clip (Picture 6) at the bottom of the slide.

4. On Slide 2, accept the SmartArt change.

5. On Slide 3, review all of Miriam's comments. Change the layout to Picture with Caption. Type **Meet Our New IT Director** as the title text. Type **Sanjai Rukah** as the caption text below the title text placeholder, as shown in Figure 5–86e. Increase the title text and the caption text font size. Bold and italicize the caption text.

6. Open the presentation, Lab 5-3 XYZ-Tyrone, located on the Data Files for Students. Then display Lab 5-3 XYZ. With Slide 3 still displayed, use screen clipping to capture Sanjai's head shot in Lab 5-3 XYZ-Tyrone. Resize the screen clipping and move it to the location shown in Figure 5–86e.

7. Delete all markup in the presentation.

8. On Slide 1, enhance the building picture by applying the Reflected Bevel, White picture style. Change the color to Tan, Accent color 1 Dark. Resize the picture.

9. Change the document properties, as specified by your instructor. Save the presentation using the file name, Lab 5-3 XYZ Corporation.

10. Save Slide 3 as a .jpg image with the file name, Lab 5-3 XYZ-Sanjai Rukah.

11. Save the presentation using the Package for CD feature. Name the CD XYZ Corporation.

12. Submit the revised PowerPoint file, the Slide 3 .jpg file, and the CD in the format specified by your instructor.

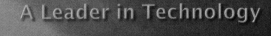

**(a) Slide 1**

**(b) Slide 2**

**Figure 5–86**

**(c) Slide 3 (Revised Slide 1)**

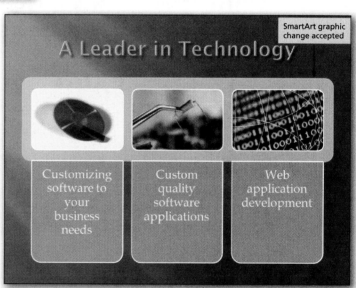

**(d) Slide 4 (Revised Slide 2)**

**(e) Slide 5 (Inserted Slide 3)**

**Figure 5–86 (Continued)**

## Cases and Places

Apply your creative thinking and problem-solving skills to design and implement a solution.

*Note:* To complete these assignments, you will be required to use the Data Files for Students. See the inside back cover of this book for instructions on downloading the Data Files for Students, or contact your instructor for information about accessing the required files.

As you design the presentations, remember to use the 7 × 7 rule: a maximum of seven words on a line and a maximum of seven lines on one slide.

### 1: Designing and Creating a Presentation about Interior Design

**Academic**

For an assignment in your Interior Design class, you must put together a slide presentation showing a variety of home interior designs. Create a presentation to show at least two examples of living rooms, bedrooms, kitchens, and dining rooms. Apply at least three objectives found at the beginning of this chapter to develop the presentation. Use the file, Home Interior Design, located on the Data Files for Students and insert at least two pictures from each slide. Use pictures from Office.com if they are appropriate for this topic. Insert and modify comments, set slide size, and select a presentation resolution. Add a header and footer with your name included. Be sure to check spelling. Save the presentation in a previous PowerPoint format.

### 2: Designing and Creating a Presentation about Fishing

**Personal**

You and your friends have decided to take a summer fishing trip. You volunteered to find the best fishing spots. You have found several destinations, and you want to relay the information to your friends. Use at least three objectives found at the beginning of this chapter to develop the presentation. Using the file, Fishing Spots, located on the Data Files for Students, insert slides into your presentation and capture part of a screen using screen clipping. Add comments to the presentation. Encrypt the presentation with a password and create a digital signature. Be sure to check spelling. Save an individual slide and save the presentation in the PowerPoint 97-2003 format.

### 3: Designing and Creating a Presentation about Moving

**Professional**

You are employed at a moving company. Your manager has asked you to develop a presentation to promote the business and show the many services your company provides. He wants you to give customers some hints for making their moving experience a little easier. You create a presentation using at least three of the pictures in the file, Moving, located on the Data Files for Students. Insert comments so you can share your thoughts with your boss. Create two similar presentations and compare and combine the presentations. Be certain to check spelling. Save the file as a slide show so that when your manager opens the file, it displays automatically as a slide show. Package the presentation for storage on a compact disc.

# 6 | Navigating Presentations Using Hyperlinks and Action Buttons

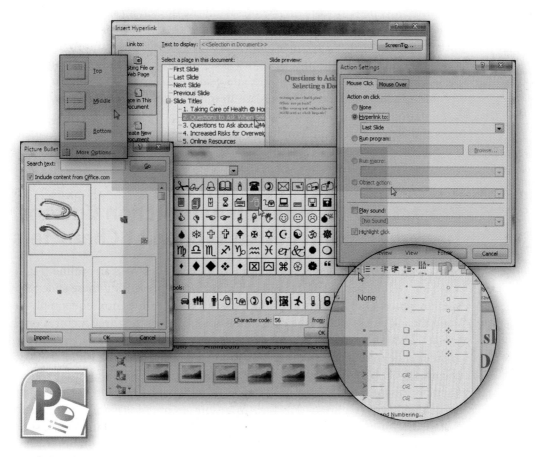

## Objectives

You will have mastered the material in this chapter when you can:

- Create a presentation from a Microsoft Word outline
- Add hyperlinks to slides and objects
- Hyperlink to other Microsoft Office documents
- Add action buttons and action settings
- Display guides to position slide elements

- Set placeholder margins
- Create columns in a placeholder
- Change paragraph line spacing
- Format bullet size and color
- Change bullet characters to pictures and numbers
- Hide slides

# 6 | Navigating Presentations Using Hyperlinks and Action Buttons

**BTW**

**Using Outlines to Organize Thoughts**
Two types of outlines can help you get and stay organized. As you plan a speech, a scratch outline is a type of rough sketch of possible major points you would like to make and the order in which they might appear. Once you determine your material and the sequence of topics, you can develop a formal outline to arrange your thoughts in multiple levels of major and supporting details.

**BTW**

**Organizing with Sections**
One of PowerPoint 2010's new features can help you organize presentations composed of dozens of slides. You can create logical sections, which are groups of related slides, and then customize and give them unique names to help identify their content or purpose. While giving a presentation, you can jump to a particular section. You also can print the slides in a specific section.

## Introduction

Many writers begin composing reports and documents by creating an outline. Others review their papers for consistency by saving the document with a new file name, removing all text except the topic headings, and then saving the file again. An outline created in Microsoft Word or another word-processing program works well as a shell for a PowerPoint presentation. Instead of typing text in PowerPoint, as you did in previous projects, you can import this outline, add visual elements such as clip art, photos, and graphical bullets, and ultimately create an impressive slide show. When delivering the presentation, you can navigate forward and backward through the slides using hyperlinks and action buttons to emphasize particular points, to review material, or to address audience concerns.

## Project — Presentation with Action Buttons, Hyperlinks, and Formatted Bullet Characters

Speakers may elect to begin creating their presentations with an outline (Figure 6–1a) and then add formatted bullets and columns. When presenting these slides during a speaking engagement, they can run their PowerPoint slides nonsequentially depending upon the audience's needs and comprehension. Each of the three pictures on the Home Health title slide (Figure 6–1b on page PPT 332) branches, or hyperlinks, to another slide in the presentation. Action buttons and hyperlinks on Slides 2, 3, and 4 (Figures 6–1c – 6–1e) allow the presenter to jump to Slide 5 (Figure 6–1f), slides in another presentation (Figures 6–1g and 6–1h on page PPT 333), or to a Microsoft Word document (Figure 6–1i). The five resources on Slide 5 are hyperlinks that display specific health-related Web sites when clicked during a presentation. The slides in the presentation have a variety of embellishments, including a two-column list on Slide 4 that provides details of the factors associated with obesity, formatted graphical bullets on Slides 2 and 5 in the shape of stethoscopes and computer mice, and a numbered list on Slide 3.

# Overview

As you read through this chapter, you will learn how to create the presentation shown in Figure 6–1 by performing these general tasks:

- Open a Microsoft Word outline as a presentation.
- Insert, use, and remove hyperlinks.
- Insert and format action buttons.
- Indent and align text in placeholders.
- Create columns and adjust column spacing.
- Change and format bullet characters.
- Run a slide show with hyperlinks and action buttons.

**BTW**

**Defining Outline Levels**
Imported outlines can contain up to nine outline levels, whereas PowerPoint outlines are limited to six levels (one for the title text and five for body paragraph text). When you import an outline, all text in outline levels six through nine is treated as a fifth-level paragraph.

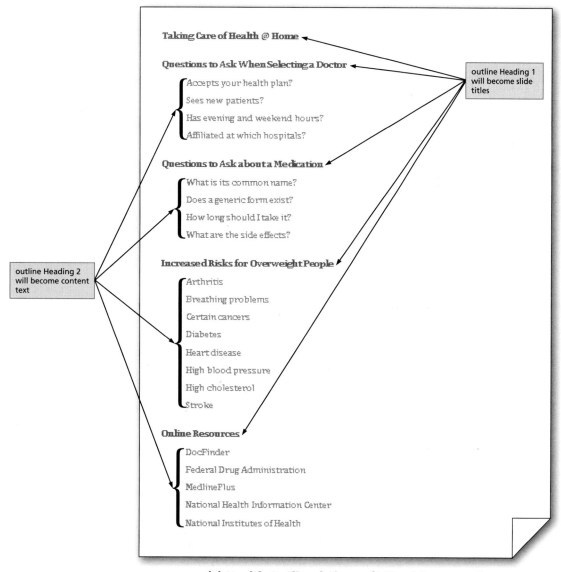

**(a) Health Outline (Microsoft Word Document)**

**Figure 6–1**

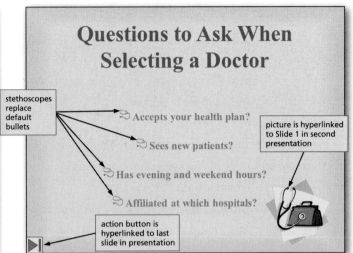

**(b) Slide 1 (Title Slide with Picture Hyperlinks)**

**(c) Slide 2 (Centered List with Graphical Bullets)**

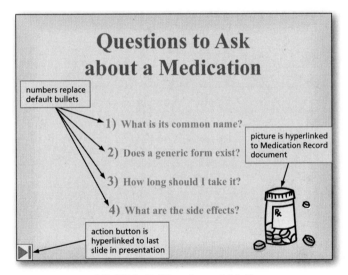

**(d) Slide 3 (Numbered List)**

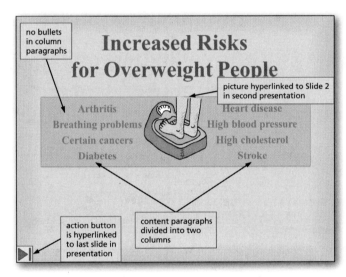

**(e) Slide 4 (Two-Column List)**

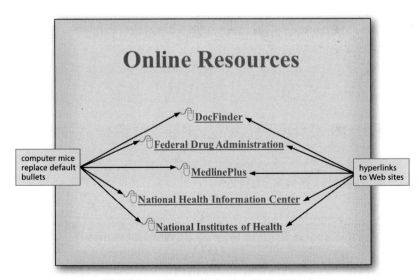

**(f) Slide 5 (Hyperlinks to Web Sites)**

**Figure 6 – 1 (Continued)**

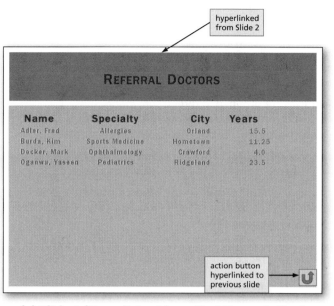

**(g) Slide 1 (Hyperlinked from First Presentation)**

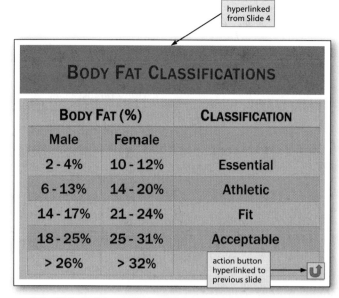

**(h) Slide 2 (Hyperlinked from First Presentation)**

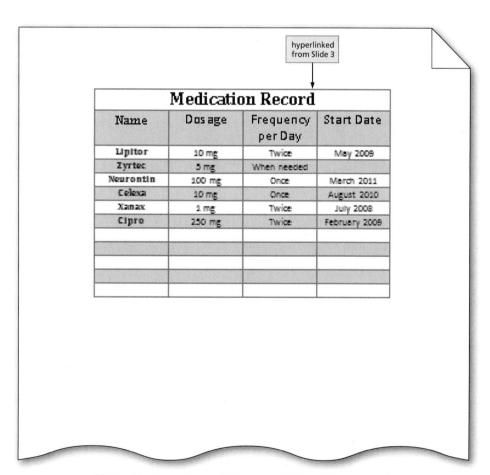

**(i) Medication Record (Microsoft Word Document)**

**Figure 6–1 (Continued)**

**General Project Guidelines**

When creating a PowerPoint presentation, the actions you perform and the decisions you make will affect the appearance and characteristics of the finished document. As you create a presentation with illustrations, such as the project shown in Figure 6–1 on pages PPT 331 through PPT 333, you should follow these general guidelines:

1. **Think threes.** Many aspects of our lives are grouped in threes: sun, moon, stars; reduce, reuse, recycle; breakfast, lunch, dinner. Your presentation and accompanying presentation likewise can be grouped in threes: introduction, body, and conclusion.

2. **Choose outstanding hyperlink images or text.** Make the hypertext graphics or letters large so a speaker is prompted to click them easily during a speaking engagement.

3. **Customize action buttons for a unique look.** The icons on the action buttons indicate their functions, but you also can add clip art, pictures, and other graphic elements to add interest or make the button less obvious to your viewers.

4. **Be mindful of prepositional phrases.** A preposition at the end of a title or a bulleted line is disconcerting to audience members. For example, if you say, "This is something I am thinking about," or "Retiring soon is something I dream of," your audience could be waiting for you to continue your thought.

5. **Consider the audience's interests.** Audience members desire to hear speeches and view presentations that benefit them in some way based on their personal needs. A presenter, in turn, must determine the audience's physical and psychological needs and then tailor the presentation to fit each speaking engagement.

When necessary, more specific details concerning the above guidelines are presented at appropriate points in the chapter. The chapter also will identify the actions performed and decisions made regarding these guidelines during the creation of the presentation shown in Figure 6–1.

# Creating a Presentation from a Microsoft Word 2010 Outline

An outline created in Microsoft Word or another word-processing program works well as a shell for a PowerPoint presentation. Instead of typing text in PowerPoint, you can import this outline, add visual elements such as clip art, pictures, and graphical bullets, and ultimately create an impressive slide show.

## To Start PowerPoint

To begin this presentation, you will open a file located on the Data Files for Students. See the inside back cover of this book for instructions on downloading the Data Files for Students, or contact your instructor for more information about accessing the required files. If you are using a computer to step through the project in this chapter and you want your screens to match the figures in this book, you should change your screen's resolution to $1024 \times 768$.

The following step starts PowerPoint.

 Start PowerPoint. If necessary, maximize the PowerPoint window.

# Converting Documents for Use in PowerPoint

PowerPoint can produce slides based on an outline created in Microsoft Word, another word-processing program, or a Web page if the text was saved in a format that PowerPoint can recognize. Microsoft Word 2010 and 2007 files use the **.docx** file extension in their file names. Text originating in other word-processing programs for later use with PowerPoint should be saved in Rich Text Format (.rtf) or plain text (.txt). Web page documents that use an HTML extension (.htm or .html) also can be imported.

PowerPoint automatically opens Microsoft Office files, and many other types of files, in the PowerPoint format. The **Rich Text Format (.rtf)** file type is used to transfer formatted documents between applications, even if the programs are running on different platforms, such as Windows and Macintosh. When you insert a Word or Rich Text Format document into a presentation, PowerPoint creates an outline structure based on heading styles in the document. A Heading 1 in a source document becomes a slide title in PowerPoint, a Heading 2 becomes the first level of content text on the slide, a Heading 3 becomes the second level of text on the slide, and so on.

If the original document contains no heading styles, PowerPoint creates an outline based on paragraphs. For example, in a .docx or .rtf file, for several lines of text styled as Normal and broken into paragraphs, PowerPoint turns each paragraph into a slide title.

## To Open a Microsoft Word Outline as a Presentation

The text for the Home Health presentation is contained in a Microsoft Word 2010 file. The following steps open this Microsoft Word outline as a presentation located on the Data Files for Students.

**1**

- With your USB flash drive connected to one of the computer's USB ports, open the Backstage view and then click the Open command in the Backstage view to display the Open dialog box.

- If necessary, navigate to the PowerPoint folder on your USB flash drive (Open dialog box) so that you can open the Health Outline file in that location.

- Click the File Type arrow to display the File Type list (Figure 6–2).

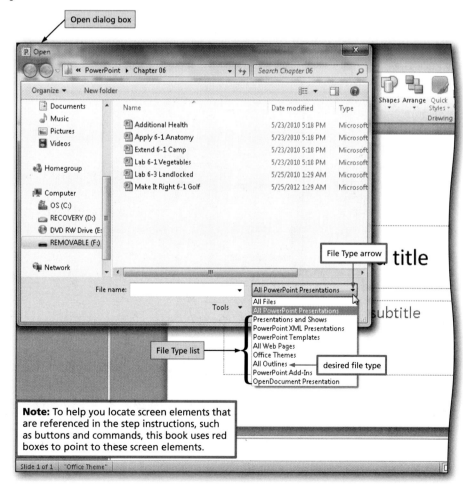

**Figure 6–2**

**2**

- Click All Outlines to select this file type.

- Click Health Outline to select the file (Figure 6–3).

**Q&A**

What if the file is not on a USB flash drive?

Use the same process, but select the drive containing the file.

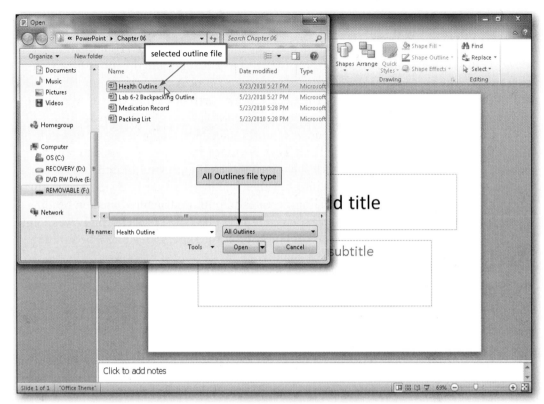

Figure 6–3

**3**

- Click Open to create the five slides in your presentation (Figure 6–4).

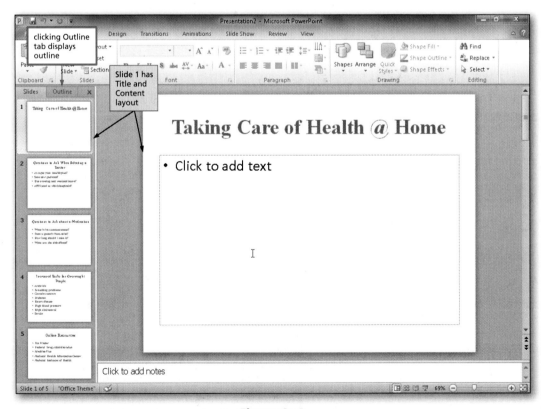

Figure 6–4

**4**

- Click the Outline tab in the Tabs pane to view the outline (Figure 6–5).

**Q&A** Do I need to see the text as an outline in the Outline tab now?

No, but sometimes it is helpful to view the content of your presentation in this view before looking at individual slides.

**Q&A** Do I need to change to the Slides tab to navigate between slides?

No, you can click the slide number in Outline view to navigate to slides.

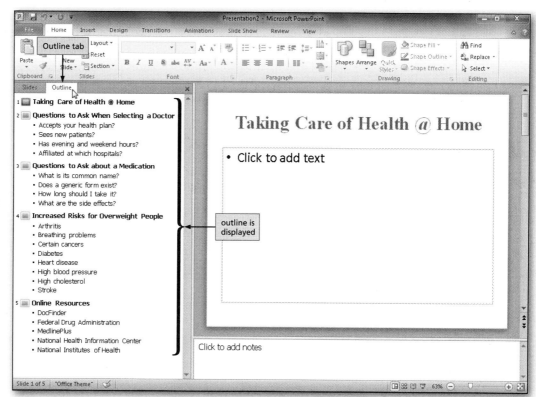

**Figure 6–5**

## To Change the Slide 1 Layout, Apply a Document Theme, and Change the Theme Colors

When you created the new slides from the Word outline, PowerPoint applied the Title and Text slide layout to all slides. You want to apply the Title Slide layout to Slide 1 to introduce the presentation. The following steps change the Slide 1 slide layout.

**1** With Slide 1 displaying, click the Layout button (Home tab | Slides group) and then click Title Slide to apply that layout to Slide 1.

**2** Apply the Hardcover document theme.

**3** Change the presentation theme colors to Clarity.

**Think threes.**
Speechwriters often think of threes as they plan their talks and PowerPoint presentations. The number three is considered a symbol of balance, as in an equilateral triangle that has three 60-degree angles, the three meals we eat daily, or the three parts of our day — morning, noon, and night. A speech generally has an introduction, a body, and a conclusion. Audience members find balance and harmony seeing three objects on a slide, so whenever possible, plan visual components on your slides in groups of three.

**Plan Ahead**

**BTW**

**The Ribbon and Screen Resolution**
PowerPoint may change how the groups and buttons within the groups appear on the Ribbon, depending on the computer's screen resolution. Thus, your Ribbon may look different from the ones in this book if you are using a screen resolution other than 1024 × 768.

## To Insert and Size Pictures

Health-related pictures will serve two purposes in this presentation. First, they will add visual interest and cue the viewers to the three topics of doctor visits, medications, and weight-control measures. The three pictures are located on the Data Files for Students. Later in this chapter, you will position the pictures in precise locations. The following steps insert and then size the three pictures on Slides 1, 2, 3, and 4.

**1** On the title slide, insert the pictures called Stethoscope, Prescription, and Scale, which are located on the Data Files for Students, in the area below the title text.

**2** Display the Picture Tools Format tab and then resize the three pictures so that they are approximately 2″ × 2″ (Figure 6–6).

**3** Copy the stethoscope picture to the lower-right corner of Slide 2, the prescription picture to the lower-right corner of Slide 3, and the scale picture to the lower-right corner of Slide 4.

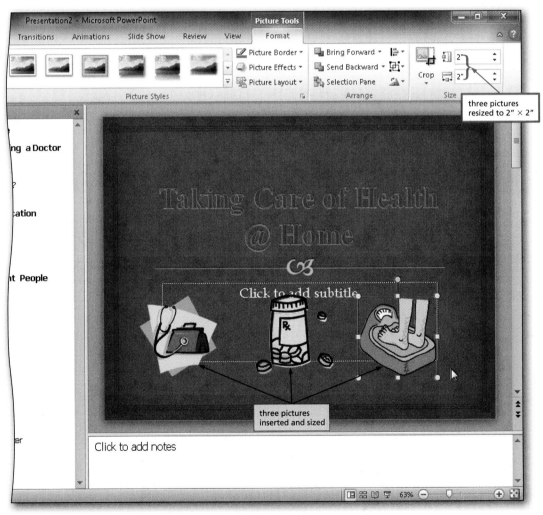

**Figure 6–6**

## To Save the Presentation

With all five slides created, you should save the presentation. The following steps save the slides.

**1** Click the Save button on the Quick Access Toolbar to display the Save As dialog box.

**2** Save the file on your USB flash drive using **Home Health** as the file name.

---

**Choose outstanding hyperlink images or text.**
Good speakers are aware of their audiences and know their speech material well. They have rehearsed their presentations and know where the hypertext is displayed on the slides. During a presentation, however, they sometimes need to divert from their planned material. Audience members may interrupt with questions, the room may not have optimal acoustics or lighting, or the timing may be short or long. It is helpful, therefore, to make the slide hyperlinks as large and noticeable to speakers as possible. The presenters can glance at the slide and receive a visual cue that it contains a hyperlink. They then can decide whether to click the hyperlink to display a Web page.

**Plan Ahead**

# Adding Hyperlinks and Action Buttons

Speakers sometimes skip from one slide to another in a presentation in response to audience needs or timing issues. In addition, if Internet access is available, they may desire to display a Web page during a slide show to add depth to the presented material and to enhance the overall message. When presenting the Home Health slide show and discussing medical information on Slides 1, 2, 3, or 4, a speaker might want to skip to the last slide in the presentation and then access a Web site for further specific health information. Or the presenter may be discussing information on Slide 5 and want to display Slide 1 to begin discussing a new topic.

One method of jumping nonsequentially to slides is by clicking a hyperlink or an action button on a slide. A **hyperlink**, also called a **link**, connects one slide to a Web page, another slide, a custom show consisting of specific slides in a presentation, an e-mail address, or a file. A hyperlink can be any element of a slide. This includes a single letter, a word, a paragraph, or any graphical image such as a clip, picture, shape, or graph.

**BTW**

**BTWs**
For a complete list of the BTWs found in the margins of this book, visit the PowerPoint 2010 BTW Web page (scsite.com/ppt2010/btw).

## To Add a Hyperlink to a Picture

In the Home Health presentation, each piece of clip art on Slide 1 will hyperlink to another slide in the same presentation. When you point to a hyperlink, the mouse pointer becomes the shape of a hand to indicate the text or object contains a hyperlink. The following steps create the first hyperlink for the stethoscope picture on Slide 1.

- Display Slide 1, select the stethoscope picture, and then display the Insert tab.

- Click the Insert Hyperlink button (Insert tab | Links group) to display the Insert Hyperlink dialog box.

- If necessary, click the Place in This Document button in the Link to area.

- Click 2. Questions to Ask When Selecting a Doctor in the 'Select a place in this document' area (Insert Hyperlink dialog box) to select and display a preview of this slide (Figure 6–7).

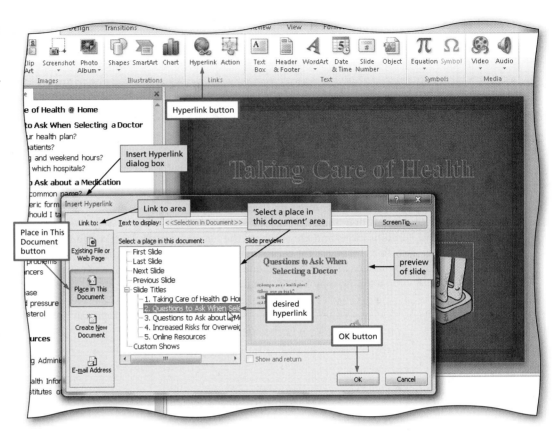

**Figure 6–7**

**Q&A** Could I also have selected the Next Slide link in the 'Select a place in this document' area?

Yes. Either action would create the hyperlink to Slide 2.

**2**
- Click the OK button to insert the hyperlink.

**Q&A** I clicked the stethoscope picture, but Slide 2 did not display. Why?

Hyperlinks are active only when you run the presentation, not when you are creating it in Normal, Reading, or Slide Sorter view.

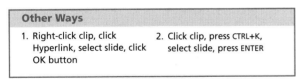

**Other Ways**

1. Right-click clip, click Hyperlink, select slide, click OK button
2. Click clip, press CTRL+K, select slide, press ENTER

## To Add a Hyperlink to the Remaining Slide 1 Pictures

The hyperlink for the stethoscope clip is complete. The next task is to create the hyperlinks for the other two pictures on Slide 1.

**1** On Slide 1, click the prescription picture.

**2** Click the Insert Hyperlink button and then click 3. Questions to Ask about a Medication to select this slide as the hyperlink. Click the OK button.

**3** Click the scale picture, click the Insert Hyperlink button, and then click 4. Increased Risks for Overweight People. Click the OK button.

## To Add a Hyperlink to a Paragraph

On Slide 5, each second-level paragraph will be a hyperlink to a health organization's Web page. If you are connected to the Internet when you run the presentation, you can click each of these paragraphs, and your Web browser will open a new window and display the corresponding Web page for each hyperlink. By default, hyperlinked text is displayed with an underline and in a color that is part of the color scheme. The following steps create a hyperlink for the first paragraph.

**1**

- Display Slide 5 and then double-click the second-level paragraph that appears first, DocFinder, to select the text.

- Display the Insert Hyperlink dialog box and then click the Existing File or Web Page button in the Link to area (Figure 6–8).

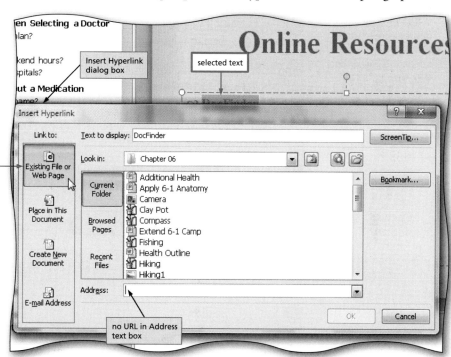

**Figure 6–8**

**2**

- Type **www.docboard.org** in the Address text box (Figure 6–9).

**3**

- Click the OK button to insert the hyperlink.

**Q&A**

Why is this paragraph now underlined and displaying a new font color?

The default style for hyperlinks is underlined text. The Clarity built-in theme hyperlink color is Blue, so PowerPoint formatted the paragraph to that color automatically.

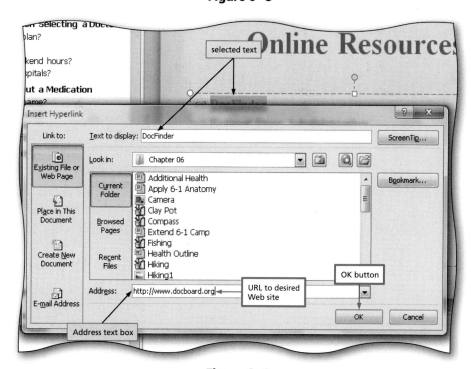

**Figure 6–9**

| Other Ways |
| --- |
| 1. Right-click selected text, click Hyperlink, type address, click OK button |
| 2. Select text, press CTRL+K, type address, press ENTER |

**BTW**

**Customizing ScreenTips**
You can create a custom ScreenTip that displays when you hover your mouse over a hyperlink. Click the ScreenTip button (Insert Hyperlink dialog box), type the desired ScreenTip text (Set Hyperlink ScreenTip dialog box), and then click the OK button.

## To Add a Hyperlink to the Remaining Slide 5 Paragraphs

The hyperlink for the second-level paragraph that appears first is complete. The next task is to create the hyperlinks for the other second-level paragraphs on Slide 5.

**1** Triple-click the second-level paragraph that appears second, Federal Drug Administration, to select this text.

**2** Display the Insert Hyperlink dialog box and then type `www.fda.gov` in the Address text box. Click the OK button.

**3** Select the third paragraph, MedlinePlus, display the Insert Hyperlink dialog box, type `www.medlineplus.gov` in the Address text box, and then click the OK button.

**4** Select the fourth paragraph, National Health Information Center, display the Insert Hyperlink dialog box, type `www.health.gov/nhic` in the Address text box, and then click the OK button.

**5** Select the fifth paragraph, National Institutes of Health, display the Insert Hyperlink dialog box, type `www.nih.gov` in the Address text box, and then click the OK button (Figure 6–10).

**Q&A** I clicked the hyperlink, but the Web page did not display. Why?

Hyperlinks are active only when you run the presentation, not when you are creating it in Normal, Reading, or Slide Sorter view.

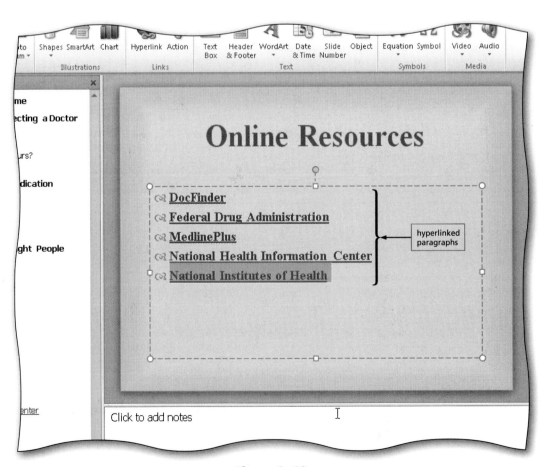

**Figure 6–10**

**Plan
Ahead**

**Customize action buttons for a unique look.**
PowerPoint's built-in action buttons have icons that give the presenter an indication of their function. Designers frequently customize these buttons with images related to the presentation. For example, in a grocery store presentation, the action buttons may have images of a coupon, dollar sign, and question mark to indicate links to in-store coupons, sale items, and the customer service counter. Be creative when you develop your own presentations and attempt to develop buttons that have specific meanings for your intended audience.

## Action Buttons

PowerPoint provides 12 built-in action buttons. An **action button** is a particular type of hyperlink that has a built-in function. Each action button performs a specific task, such as displaying the next slide, providing help, giving information, or playing a sound. In addition, the action button can activate a hyperlink that allows users to jump to a specific slide in the presentation. The picture on the action button indicates the type of function it performs. For example, the button with the house icon represents the home slide, or Slide 1. To achieve a personalized look, you can customize an action button with a photograph, piece of clip art, logo, text, or any graphic you desire. Table 6–1 describes each of the built-in action buttons.

**BTW**

**Q&As**
For a complete list of the Q&As found in many of the step-by-step sequences in this book, visit the PowerPoint 2010 Q&A Web page (scsite.com/ppt2010/qa).

### Table 6–1 Built-In Action Buttons

| Button Name | Image | Description |
| --- | --- | --- |
| Back or Previous | | Returns to the previous slide displayed in the same presentation. |
| Forward or Next | | Jumps to the next slide in the presentation. |
| Beginning | | Jumps to Slide 1. This button performs the same function as the Home button. |
| End | | Jumps to the last slide in the presentation. |
| Home | | Jumps to Slide 1. This button performs the same function as the Beginning button. |
| Information | | Does not have any predefined function. Use it to direct a user to a slide with details or facts. |
| Return | | Returns to the previous slide displayed in any presentation. For example, you can place it on a hidden slide or on a slide in a custom slide show and then return to the previous slide. |
| Movie | | Does not have any predefined function. You generally would use this button to jump to a slide with an inserted video clip. |
| Document | | Opens a program other than PowerPoint. For example, you can open Microsoft Word or Microsoft Excel and display a page or worksheet. |
| Sound | | Does not have any predefined function. You generally would use this button to jump to a slide with an inserted audio clip. |
| Help | | Does not have any predefined function. Use it to direct a user to a slide with instructions or contact information. |
| Custom | | Does not have any predefined function. You can add a clip, picture, graphic, or text and then specify a unique purpose. |

## To Insert an Action Button

In the Home Health slide show, the action buttons on Slides 2, 3, and 4 hyperlink to the last slide, Slide 5. You will insert and format the action button shape on Slide 2 and copy it to Slides 3 and 4, and then create a link to Slide 5 so that you will be able to display Slide 5 at any point in the presentation by clicking the action button. When you click the action button, a sound will play. This sound will vary depending upon which slide is displayed. The following steps insert an action button on Slide 2 and link it to Slide 5.

**1**

- Display Slide 2 and then click the Shapes button (Insert tab | Illustrations group) to display the Shapes gallery.

- Point to the Action Button: End shape in the Action Buttons area (fourth image) (Figure 6–11).

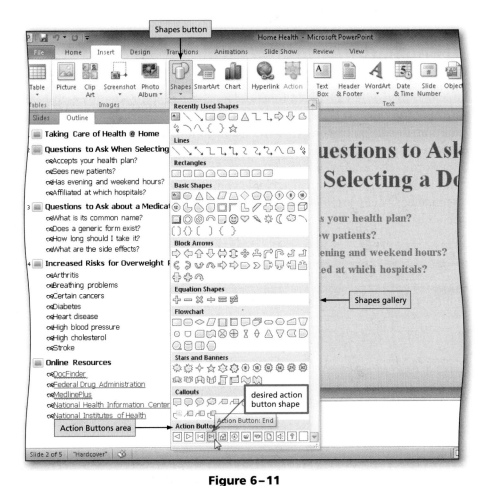

**Figure 6–11**

**2**

- Click the Action Button: End shape.

- Click the lower-left corner of the slide to insert the action button and to display the Action Settings dialog box.

- If necessary, click the Mouse Click tab (Action Settings dialog box) (Figure 6–12).

**Q&A** Why is the default setting the action to hyperlink to the last slide?

The End shape establishes a hyperlink to the last slide in a presentation.

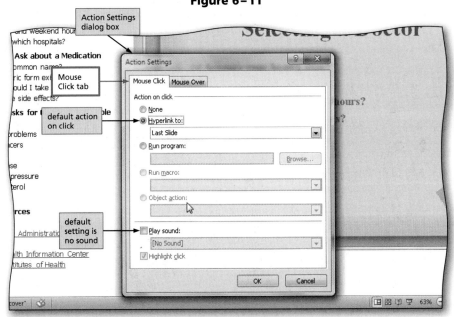

**Figure 6–12**

• Click the Play sound check box and then click the Play sound arrow to display the Play Sound list (Figure 6–13).

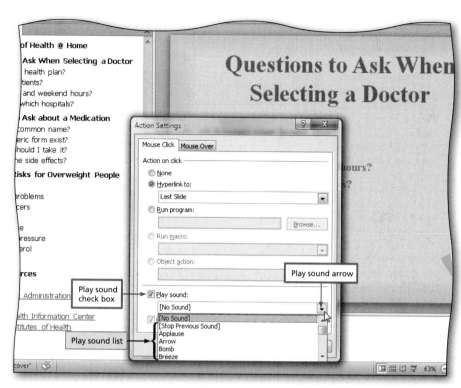

**Figure 6–13**

• Scroll down and then click Push to select that sound (Figure 6–14).

**Q&A**

I did not hear the sound when I selected it. Why not?

The Push sound will play when you run the slide show and click the action button.

• Click the OK button to apply the hyperlink setting and sound to the action button and to close the Action Settings dialog box.

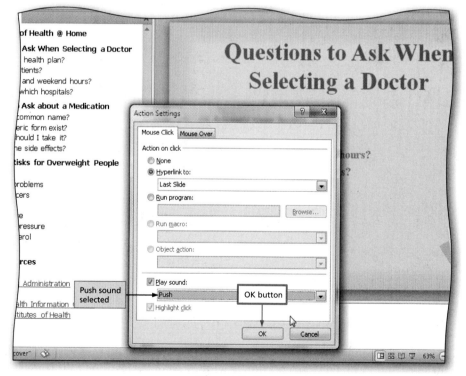

**Figure 6–14**

**BTW**

**Customizing Action Buttons**

This project uses one of PowerPoint's built-in action buttons. Designers frequently customize these buttons with images related to the presentation. For example, in a school the action buttons may have images of a book, silverware, and question mark to indicate links to the library, the cafeteria, and the information desk. Be creative when you develop your own presentations and attempt to develop buttons that have a specific meaning for your intended audience.

## To Size an Action Button

The action button size can be decreased to make it less obvious on the slide. The following step resizes the selected action button.

**1** With the action button still selected, display the Drawing Tools Format tab and then size the action button so that it is approximately 0.5" × 0.5". If necessary, move the action button to the location shown in Figure 6–15.

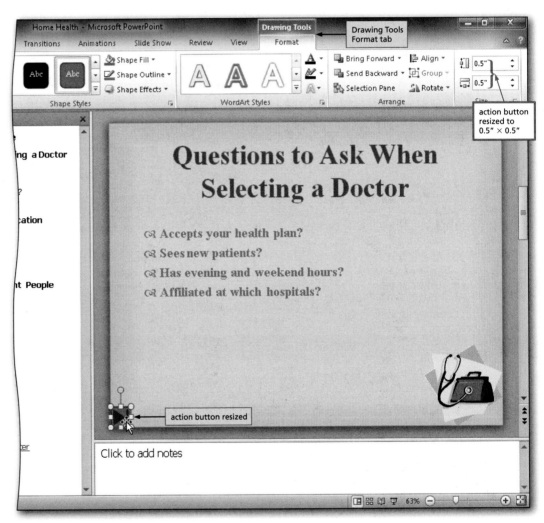

**Figure 6–15**

## To Change an Action Button Fill Color

The action button's Gray interior color does not blend well with the light yellow border on the slide. You can select a new fill color to coordinate with the slide edges. The following steps change the fill color from Gray to Light Yellow.

- With the action button still selected, click the Shape Fill button arrow (Drawing Tools Format tab | Shape Styles gallery) to display the Shape Fill gallery (Figure 6–16).

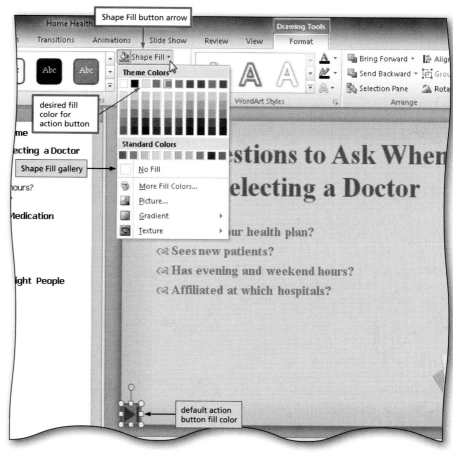

**Figure 6–16**

- Point to Light Yellow, Background 2 (third color from left in first row) to display a live preview of that fill color on the action button (Figure 6–17).

**Experiment**

- Point to various colors in the Shape Fill gallery and watch the fill color change in the action button.

- Click Light Yellow, Background 2 to apply this color to the action button.

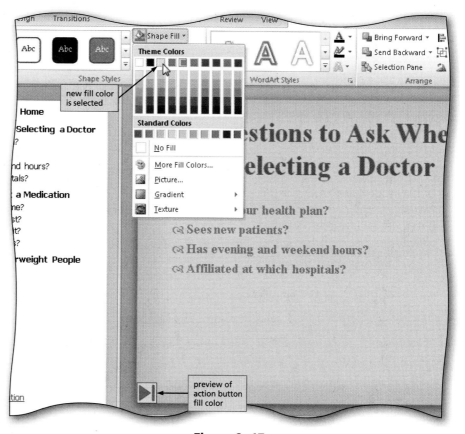

**Figure 6–17**

## To Copy an Action Button

The Slide 2 action button is formatted and positioned correctly. You can copy this shape to Slides 3 and 4. The following steps copy the Slide 2 action button to the next two slides in the presentation.

**1**

- Right-click the action button on Slide 2 to display the shortcut menu (Figure 6–18).

**Q&A**

Why does my shortcut menu have different commands?

Depending upon where you right-clicked, you might see a different shortcut menu. As long as this menu displays the Copy command, you can use it. If the Copy command is not visible, click the slide again to display another shortcut menu.

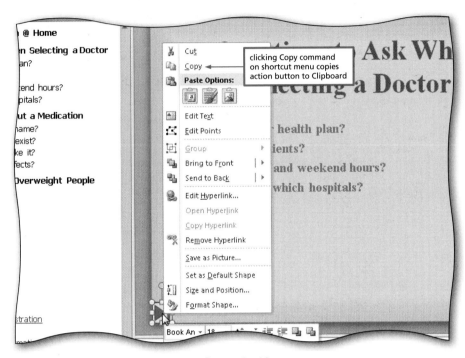

**Figure 6–18**

**2**

- Click Copy on the shortcut menu to copy the action button to the Clipboard.

- Display Slide 3 and then click the Paste button (Home tab | Clipboard group) to paste the action button in the lower-left corner of Slide 3 (Figure 6–19).

**3**

- Display Slide 4 and then click the Paste button to paste the action button in the lower-left corner of Slide 4.

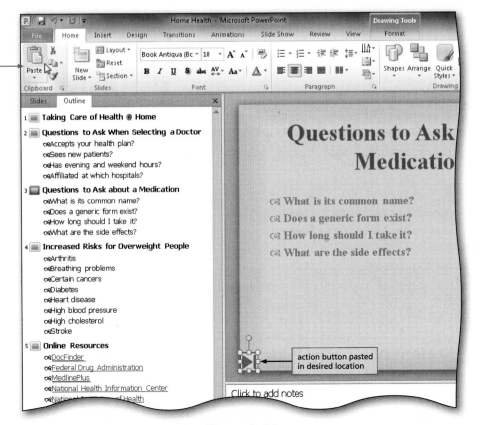

**Figure 6–19**

## To Edit an Action Button Action Setting

When you copied the action button, PowerPoint retained the settings to hyperlink to the last slide and to play the Push sound. For variety, you want to change the sounds that play for the Slide 3 and Slide 4 action buttons. The following steps edit the Slide 3 and Slide 4 hyperlink sound settings.

**1**

- With the action button still selected on Slide 4, display the Insert tab and then click the Action button (Insert tab | Links group) to display the Action Settings dialog box.

- Click the Play sound arrow to display the Play sound menu (Figure 6–20).

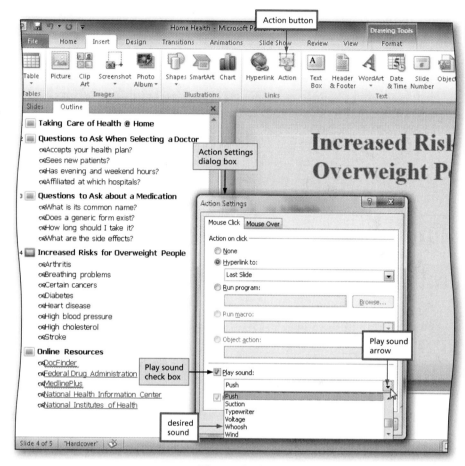

**Figure 6–20**

**2**

- Click Whoosh in the Play sound list to select the Whoosh sound to play when the action button is clicked (Figure 6–21).

**3**

- Click the OK button (Action Settings dialog box) to apply the new sound setting to the Slide 4 action button.

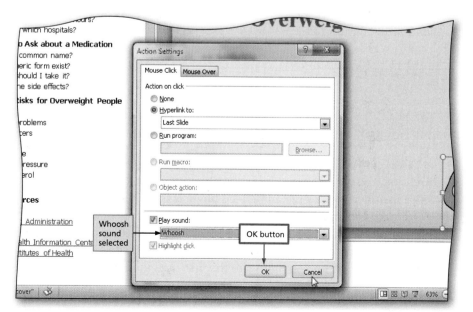

**Figure 6–21**

• Display Slide 3, select the action button, and then click the Action button (Insert tab | Links group) to display the Action Settings dialog box.

• Click the Play sound arrow to display the Play sound menu.

• Scroll up and then click Breeze in the Play sound list (Figure 6–22).

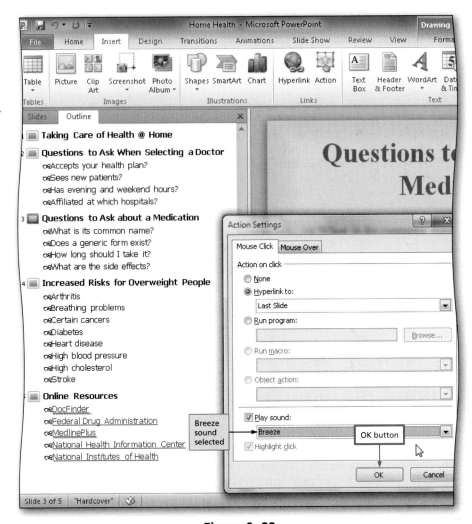

**Figure 6–22**

• Click the OK button (Action Settings dialog box) to apply the new sound setting to the Slide 3 action button.

## To Hyperlink to Another PowerPoint File

Slide 2 in your presentation provides information for patients to ask a potential doctor. When running a presentation, the speaker may decide some useful information might be a list of referral doctors, especially if an audience member asks for recommended physicians. While hyperlinks are convenient tools to navigate through the current PowerPoint presentation or to Web pages, they also allow you to open a second PowerPoint presentation and display a particular slide in that file. The first slide in another presentation, Additional Home Health, lists details about several doctors, including their names, specialties, and number of years of practice. The following steps hyperlink the stethoscope on Slide 2 to the first slide in the second presentation.

**1**

- Display Slide 2 and then select the stethoscope picture.

- If necessary, display the Insert tab and then click the Action button (Insert tab | Links group) to display the Action Settings dialog box.

- Click Hyperlink to in the 'Action on click' area and then click the Hyperlink to arrow to display the Hyperlink to menu (Figure 6–23).

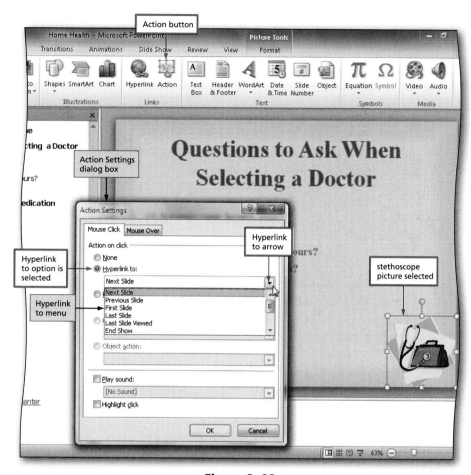

**Figure 6–23**

**2**

- Scroll down and then click Other PowerPoint Presentation to display the Hyperlink to Other PowerPoint Presentation dialog box.

- Click Additional Health to select this file as the hyperlinked presentation (Figure 6–24).

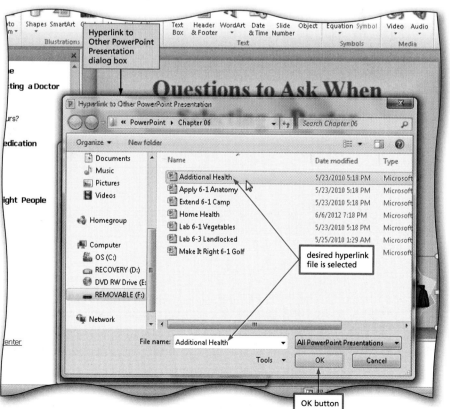

**Figure 6–24**

**3**

- Click the OK button to display the Hyperlink to Slide dialog box (Figure 6–25).

**Q&A**

What are the two items listed in the Slide title area?

They are the title text of the two slides in the Additional Health file.

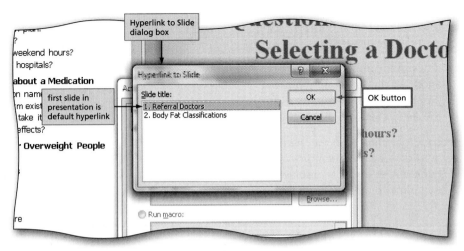

**Figure 6–25**

**4**

- Click the OK button (Hyperlink to Slide dialog box) to hyperlink the first slide in the Additional Health presentation to the stethoscope picture (Figure 6–26).

**5**

- Click the OK button (Action Settings dialog box) to apply the new action setting to the Slide 2 picture.

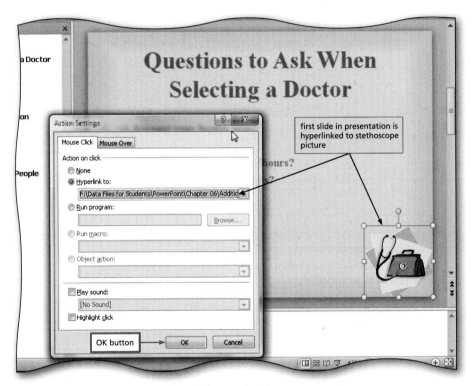

**Figure 6–26**

## To Hyperlink to a Second Slide in Another PowerPoint File

A table on the second slide in the Additional Health presentation has information regarding the five classifications of male and female body fat. This slide might be useful to display during a presentation when a speaker is discussing the information on Slide 4, which describes the health risks associated with being overweight. If the speaker has time to discuss the material and the audience needs to know these specific body fat percentages, he could click the scale picture on Slide 4 and then hyperlink to Slide 2 in the second presentation. The following steps hyperlink Slide 4 to the second slide in the Additional Health presentation.

**1** Display Slide 4, select the scale picture, and then click the Action button (Insert tab | Links group) to display the Action Settings dialog box.

**2** Click Hyperlink to in the 'Action on click' area, click the Hyperlink to arrow, and then scroll down and click Other PowerPoint Presentation in the Hyperlink to menu.

**3** Click Additional Health in the Hyperlink to Other PowerPoint Presentation dialog box to select this file as the hyperlinked presentation and then click the OK button.

**4** Click 2. Body Fat Classifications (Hyperlink to Slide dialog box) (Figure 6–27).

**5** Click the OK button (Hyperlink to Slide dialog box) to hyperlink the second slide in the Additional Health presentation to the scale picture.

**6** Click the OK button (Action Settings dialog box) to apply the new action setting to the Slide 4 picture.

**BTW**

**Verifying Hyperlinks**
Always test your hyperlinks prior to giving a presentation. Web addresses change frequently, so if your hyperlinks are to Web sites, be certain your Internet connection is working, the Web sites are active, and that the content on these pages is appropriate for your viewers. If your hyperlinks direct PowerPoint to display specific slides and to open files, click the hyperlinks to verify your desired actions are followed and that the files exist.

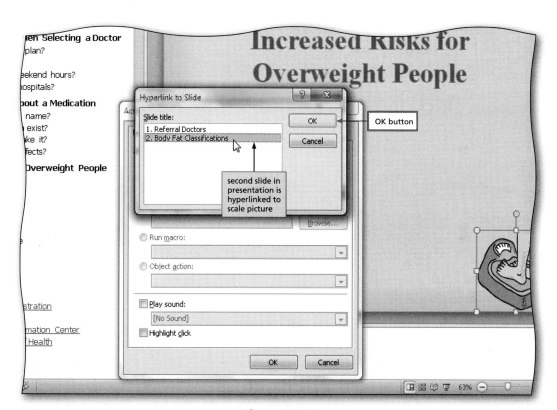

**Figure 6–27**

## To Hyperlink to a Microsoft Word File

Doctors recommend their patients keep a current record of all prescribed and over-the-counter medications. This list should include the name of the drug, the amount taken per day, and the date when the patient started taking this medication. A convenient form for recording these details is located on the Data Files for Students. The file, Medication Record, was created using Microsoft Word, and it would be useful to display this document when discussing the information on Slide 3 of your presentation. PowerPoint allows a speaker to hyperlink to other Microsoft Office documents in a similar manner as linking to another PowerPoint file. The following steps hyperlink the prescription picture on Slide 3 to the Microsoft Word document with the file name, Medication Record.

**1**

- Display Slide 3, select the prescription picture, and then click the Action button (Insert tab | Links group) to display the Action Settings dialog box.

- Click Hyperlink to, click the Hyperlink to arrow to display the Hyperlink to menu, and then scroll down to the end of the Hyperlink to list (Figure 6–28).

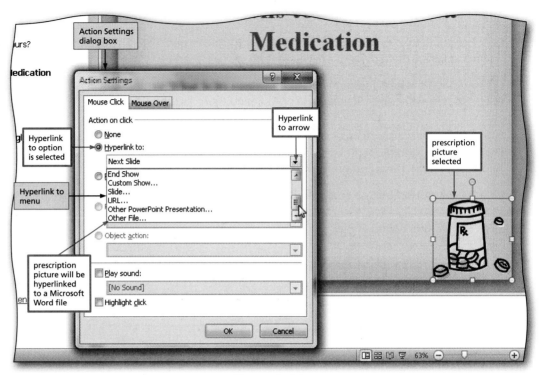

Figure 6–28

**2**

- Click Other File to display the Hyperlink to Other File dialog box, scroll down, and then click Medication Record to select this file as the hyperlinked document (Figure 6–29).

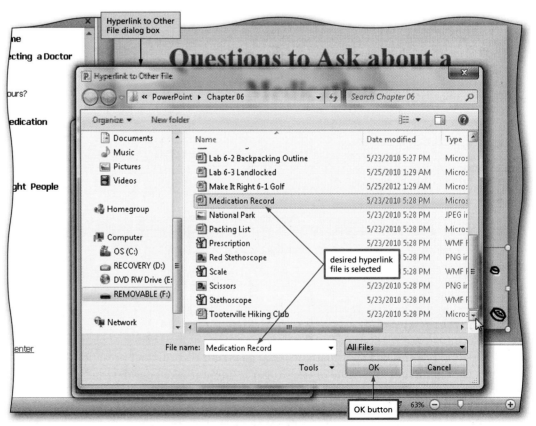

Figure 6–29

**3**
- Click the OK button (Hyperlink to Other File dialog box) to hyperlink this file to the prescription picture action button (Figure 6–30).

**4**
- Click the OK button (Action Settings dialog box) to apply the new action setting to the Slide 3 picture.

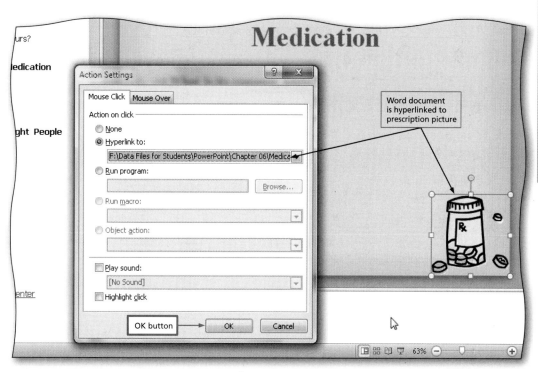

Figure 6–30

## To Insert and Format Action Buttons on the Hyperlinked File

The action buttons on Slide 2 and Slide 3 hyperlink to slides in the Additional Health file. While running the presentation, if you click an action button that opens and then displays either Slide 1 or Slide 2, you may need to review this slide and then return to the previous slide displayed in the first presentation. The Return action button performs this function. The following steps open the Additional Health file and then insert and format the Return action button on both slides.

**1** In the Backstage view, click the Open command to display the Open dialog box, click the File Type arrow to display the File Type list, and then click All PowerPoint Presentations to select this file type.

**2** Open the Additional Health file located on the Data Files for Students.

**3** With Slide 1 displaying, click the Shapes button (Insert tab | Illustrations group), and then click the Action Button: Return shape (seventh image).

**4** Insert the action button in the lower-right corner of the slide.

**5** Display the Action Settings dialog box and then hyperlink the action button to Slide 2 (Questions to Ask When Selecting a Doctor) in the Home Health presentation.

**6** Size the action button so that it is approximately 0.5" × 0.5".

**7** Change the action button fill color to Tan, Background 2, Lighter 40% (fourth color in third column).

**8** Copy the action button to the same location on Slide 2 (Figure 6–31 on the next page). Display the Action Settings dialog box and then hyperlink this action button to Slide 4 (Increased Risks for Overweight People) in the Home Health presentation.

**BTW**

**Showing a Range of Slides**
If your presentation consists of many slides, you may want to show only a portion of them in your slide show. For example, if your 30-slide presentation is designed to accompany a 30-minute speech and you are given only 10 minutes to present, you may elect to display only the first 10 slides. Rather than have the show end abruptly after Slide 10, you can elect to show a range of slides. To specify this range, display the Slide Show tab, click the Set Up Slide Show button, and then specify the starting and ending slide numbers in the From and To boxes in the Show slides area (Set Up Show dialog box).

⑨ Save the file using the same file name.

⑩ Close the Additional Health file.

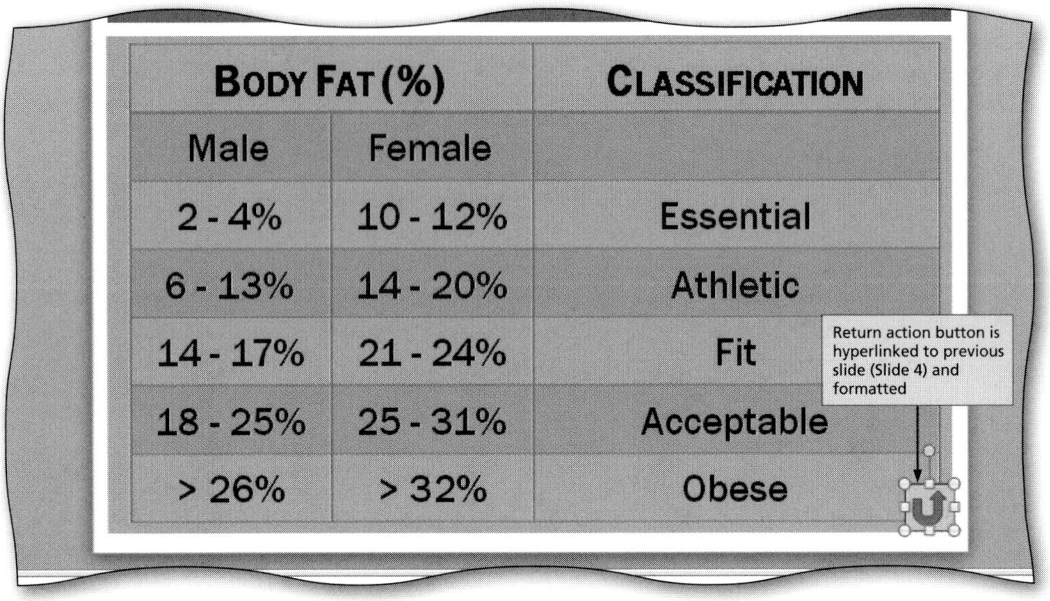

| Body Fat (%) | | Classification |
|---|---|---|
| Male | Female | |
| 2 - 4% | 10 - 12% | Essential |
| 6 - 13% | 14 - 20% | Athletic |
| 14 - 17% | 21 - 24% | Fit |
| 18 - 25% | 25 - 31% | Acceptable |
| > 26% | > 32% | Obese |

Return action button is hyperlinked to previous slide (Slide 4) and formatted

**Figure 6–31**

**Break Point:** If you wish to take a break, this is a good place to do so. Be sure to save the Home Health file again and then you can quit PowerPoint. To resume at a later time, start PowerPoint, open the file called Home Health, and continue following the steps from this location forward.

**BTW**

**Measurement System**
The vertical and horizontal rulers display the units of measurement in inches by default. This measurement system is determined by the settings in Microsoft Windows. You can change the measurement system to centimeters by customizing the numbers format in the Clock, Language, and Region area of Control Panel.

# Positioning Slide Elements

At times you may desire to arrange slide elements in precise locations. PowerPoint provides useful tools to help you position shapes and objects on slides. **Drawing guides** are two straight dotted lines, one horizontal and one vertical. When an object is close to a guide, its corner or its center (whichever is closer) **snaps**, or aligns precisely on top of the guide. You can drag a guide to a new location to meet your alignment requirements. Another tool is the vertical or horizontal **ruler**, which can help you drag an object to a precise location on the slide. The center of a slide is 0.00 on both the vertical and the horizontal rulers.

## Aligning and Distributing Objects

If you display multiple objects, PowerPoint can **align** them above and below each other (vertically) or side by side (horizontally). The objects, such as SmartArt graphics, clip art, shapes, text boxes, and WordArt, can be aligned relative to the slide so that they display along the top, left, right, or bottom borders or in the center or middle of the slide. They also can be aligned relative to each other, meaning that you position either the first or last object in the desired location and then command PowerPoint to move the remaining objects in the series above, below, or beside it. Depending on the alignment option that you click, objects will move straight up, down, left, or right, and might cover an object already located on the slide. Table 6–2 describes alignment options.

| Table 6–2 Alignment Options | |
| --- | --- |
| **Alignment** | **Action** |
| Left | Aligns the edges of the objects to the left |
| Center | Aligns the objects vertically through the centers of the objects |
| Right | Aligns the edges of the objects to the right |
| Top | Aligns the top edges of the objects |
| Middle | Aligns the objects horizontally through the middles of the objects |
| Bottom | Aligns the bottom edges of the objects |
| to Slide | Aligns one object to the slide |

One object remains stationary when you align objects relative to each other by their edges. For example, Align Left aligns the left edges of all selected objects with the left edge of the leftmost object. The leftmost object remains stationary, and the other objects are aligned relative to it. Objects aligned to a SmartArt graphic are aligned to the leftmost edge of the SmartArt graphic, not to the leftmost shape in the SmartArt graphic. Objects aligned relative to each other by their middles or centers are aligned along a horizontal or vertical line that represents the average of their original positions. All of the objects might move.

**Smart Guides** appear automatically when two or more shapes are in spatial alignment with each other, even if the shapes vary in size. To evenly space multiple objects horizontally or vertically, you **distribute** them. PowerPoint determines the total length between either the outermost edges of the first and last selected object or the edges of the entire slide. It then inserts equal spacing among the items in the series. You also can distribute spacing by using the Size and Position dialog box, but the Distribute command automates this task.

## To Display the Drawing Guides

Guides help you align objects on slides. When you point to a guide and then press and hold the mouse button, PowerPoint displays a box containing the exact position of the guide on the slide in inches. An arrow is displayed below the guide position to indicate the vertical guide either left or right of center. An arrow also is displayed to the right of the guide position to indicate the horizontal guide either above or below center. The following step displays the guides.

- With the Home Health presentation displayed, click the View tab, and then click the Guides check box (View tab | Show group) to display the horizontal and vertical guides (Figure 6–32).

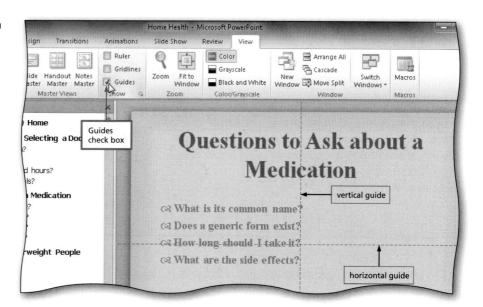

**Other Ways**

1. Right-click area of slide other than a placeholder or object, click Grid and Guides on shortcut menu, click 'Display drawing guides on screen' check box
2. Press ALT+F9

**Figure 6–32**

## To Position a Picture Using Guides

The three pictures on Slides 2, 3, and 4 should be displayed in precisely the same location so they appear static as you transition from one slide to the next during the slide show. In addition, the top border of the three pictures on Slide 1 should align evenly. The following steps position the picture on Slide 3.

- Point to the horizontal guide anywhere except the text.

Why does 0.00 display when I hold down the mouse button?

The ScreenTip displays the horizontal guide's position. A 0.00 setting means that the guide is precisely in the middle of the slide and is not above or below the center.

- Click and then drag the horizontal guide to 1.50 inches below the center. Do not release the mouse button (Figure 6–33).

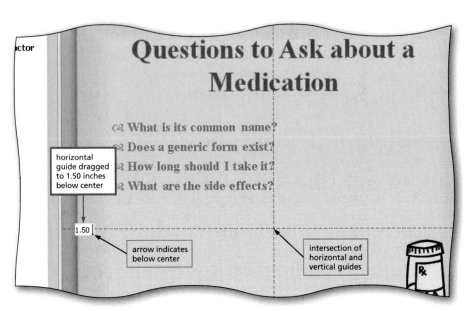

**Figure 6–33**

- Release the mouse button to position the horizontal guide at 1.50, which is the intended location of the picture's top border.

- Point to the vertical guide anywhere except the text in the content placeholder.

- Click and then drag the vertical guide to 2.50 inches right of the center and then release the mouse button to position the vertical guide.

- Drag the upper-left corner of the picture to the intersection of the vertical and horizontal guides to position the picture in the desired location (Figure 6–34).

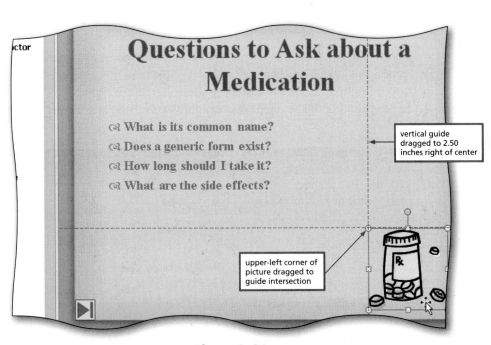

**Figure 6–34**

Can I add guides to help me align multiple objects?

Yes. Position the mouse pointer over one guide and then press the CTRL key. When you drag your mouse pointer, a second guide appears.

## To Position the Slide 4 and Slide 2 Pictures

The pictures on Slide 4 and Slide 2 should be positioned in the same location as the Slide 3 picture. The guides will display in the same location as you display each slide, so you easily can align similar objects on multiple slides. The following steps position the pictures on Slide 4 and Slide 2.

**1** Display Slide 4 and then drag the upper-left corner of the scale picture to the intersection of the guides.

**2** Repeat Step 1 to position the stethoscope picture on Slide 2 (Figure 6–35).

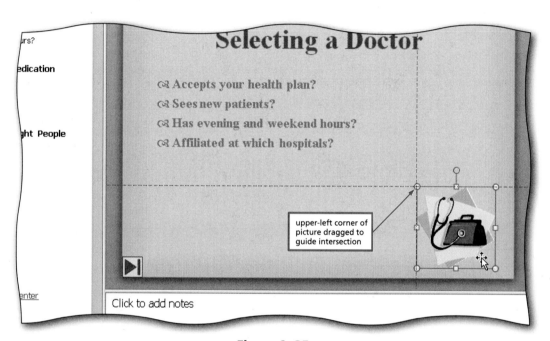

**Figure 6–35**

## To Hide Guides

The three pictures on Slides 2, 3, and 4 are positioned in the desired locations, so the guides no longer are needed. The following step hides the guides.

**1** If necessary, display the View tab and then click the Guides check box to remove the check mark.

| Other Ways |
| --- |
| 1. Right-click area of slide other than a placeholder or object, click Grid and Guides on shortcut menu,     click 'Display drawing guides on screen' check box<br>2. Press ALT+F9 |

## To Display the Rulers

To begin aligning the three Slide 1 objects, you need to position either the left or the right object. The vertical or horizontal **ruler** can help you drag an object to a precise location on the slide. The center of a slide is 0.00 on both the vertical and the horizontal rulers. The following step displays the rulers.

**1**

- If necessary, display the View tab and then click the Ruler check box (View tab | Show group) to display the vertical and horizontal rulers (Figure 6–36).

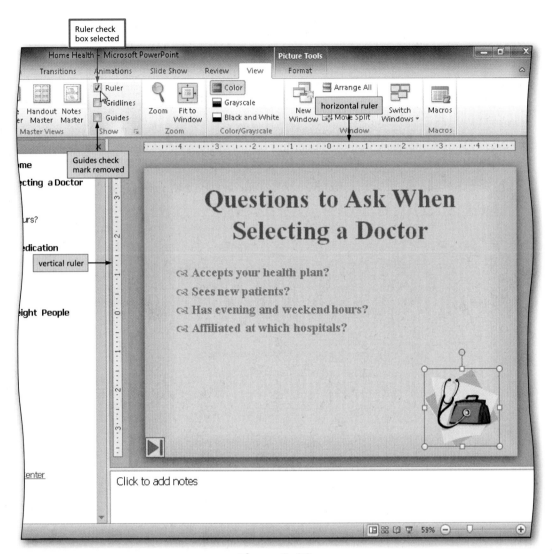

**Figure 6–36**

**Other Ways**

1. Right-click area of slide other than a placeholder or object, click Ruler

## To Align Pictures

The three pictures on Slide 1 will look balanced if the bottom edges are aligned. One method of creating this orderly appearance is by dragging the borders to a guide. Another method that is useful when you have multiple objects is to use one of PowerPoint's align commands. On Slide 1, you will position the far left picture of the stethoscope and then align its bottom edge with those of the prescription and scale pictures. The following steps align the Slide 1 pictures.

**1**

- Display Slide 1 and then position the mouse pointer over the handle of the doctor's bag in the stethoscope picture.

- Drag the picture so that the bag handle is positioned 3 inches left of the center and 2½ inches below the center (Figure 6–37).

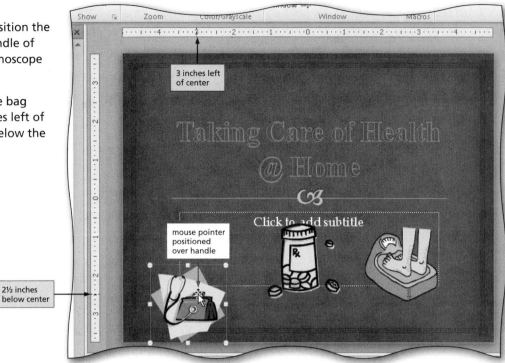

Figure 6–37

**2**

- Drag the prescription picture toward the bottom of the slide until the Smart Guide appears in the center of the stethoscope and prescription pictures (Figure 6–38).

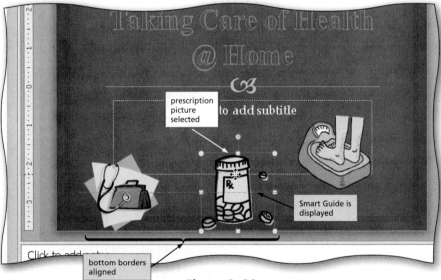

Figure 6–38

**3**

- Drag the scale picture toward the bottom of the slide until the Smart Guide appears in the center of all three pictures on the slide (Figure 6–39).

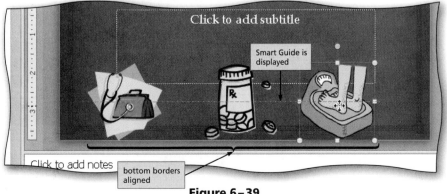

Figure 6–39

## To Distribute Pictures

Now that the three Slide 1 pictures are aligned along their bottom edges, you can have PowerPoint place the same amount of space between the first and second pictures and the second and third pictures. You have two distribution options: Align to Slide spaces all the selected objects evenly across the entire width of the slide; Align Selected Objects spaces only the middle objects between the fixed right and left objects. The following steps use the Align to Slide option to horizontally distribute the Slide 1 pictures.

**1**
• Select the three Slide 1 pictures, display the Picture Tools Format tab, and then click the Align button (Picture Tools Format tab | Arrange group) to display the Align menu.

**2**
• If necessary, click Align to Slide so that PowerPoint will adjust the spacing of the pictures evenly between the slide edges and then click the Align button to display the Align menu again (Figure 6–40).

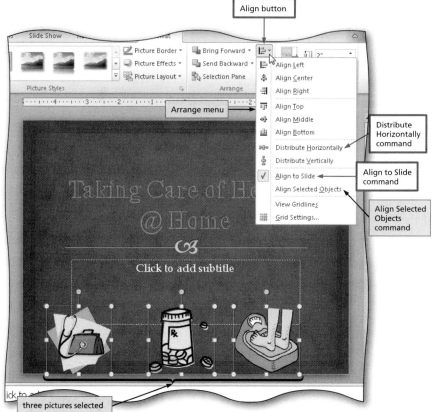

**Figure 6–40**

**3**
• Click Distribute Horizontally to adjust the spacing (Figure 6–41).

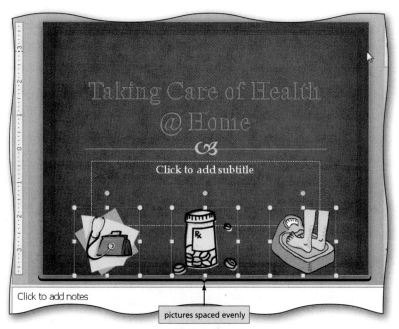

**Figure 6–41**

## To Hide Rulers

The three pictures on Slide 1 are positioned in the desired locations, so the rulers no longer need to display. The following step hides the rulers.

 Display the View tab and then click the Ruler check box to remove the check mark.

# Hiding a Slide

Slides 2, 3, and 4 present a variety of health information with hyperlinks. Depending on the audience's needs and the time constraints, you may decide not to display one or more of these slides. If need be, you can use the **Hide Slide** command to hide a slide from the audience during the normal running of a slide show. When you want to display the hidden slide, press the H key. No visible indicator displays to show that a hidden slide exists. You must be aware of the content of the presentation to know where the supporting slide is located.

When you run your presentation, the hidden slide does not display unless you press the H key when the slide preceding the hidden slide is displaying. For example, Slide 4 does not display unless you press the H key when Slide 3 displays in Slide Show view. You continue your presentation by clicking the mouse or pressing any of the keys associated with running a slide show. You skip the hidden slide by clicking the mouse and advancing to the next slide.

## To Hide a Slide

Slide 4 discusses health problems that overweight people face. If time permits, or if the audience requires information on this subject, you can display Slide 4. As the presenter, you decide whether to show Slide 4. You hide a slide in Slide Sorter view so you can see the slashed square surrounding the slide number, which indicates a slide is hidden. The following steps hide Slide 4.

- Click the Slide Sorter view button to display the slide thumbnails.

- Click Slide Show on the Ribbon to display the Slide Show tab and then click the Slide 4 thumbnail to select it (Figure 6–42).

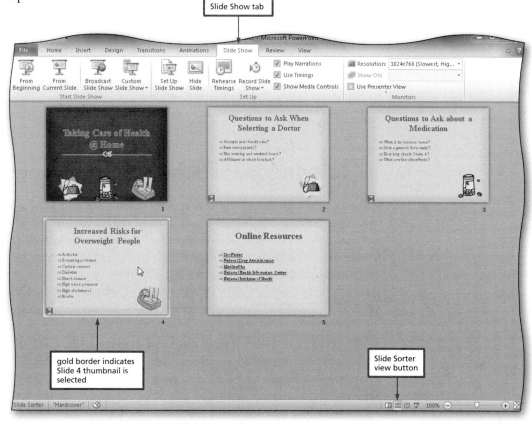

**Figure 6–42**

**2**

- Click the Hide Slide button (Slide Show tab | Set Up group) to hide Slide 4 (Figure 6–43).

**Q&A** How do I know that Slide 4 is hidden?

The rectangle with a slash surrounds the slide number to indicate Slide 4 is a hidden slide.

**Q&A** What if I decide I no longer want to hide a slide?

Repeat Steps 1 and 2. The Hide Slide button is a toggle; it either hides or displays a slide.

**3**

- Click the Normal view button to display Slide 4.

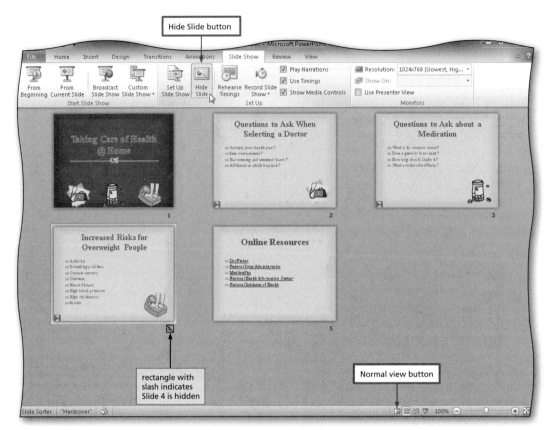

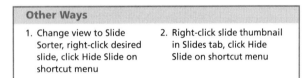

**Figure 6–43**

| Other Ways |
|---|
| 1. Change view to Slide Sorter, right-click desired slide, click Hide Slide on shortcut menu | 2. Right-click slide thumbnail in Slides tab, click Hide Slide on shortcut menu |

**Break Point:** If you wish to take a break, this is a good place to do so. Be sure to save the Home Health file again and then you can quit PowerPoint. To resume at a later time, start PowerPoint, open the file called Home Health, and continue following the steps from this location forward.

# Modifying Placeholder Text Settings

The PowerPoint design themes specify default alignment of and spacing for text within a placeholder. For example, the text in most paragraphs is **left-aligned**, so the first character of each line is even with the first character above or below it. Text alignment also can be horizontally **centered** to position each line evenly between the left and right placeholder edges; **right-aligned**, so that the last character of each line is even with the last character of each line above or below it; and **justified**, where the first and last characters of each line are aligned and extra space is inserted between words to spread the characters evenly across the line.

When you begin typing text in most placeholders, the first paragraph is aligned at the top of the placeholder with any extra space at the bottom. You can change this default **paragraph alignment** location to position the paragraph lines centered vertically between the top and bottom placeholder edges, or you can place the last line at the bottom of the placeholder so that any extra space is at the top.

The design theme also determines the amount of spacing around the sides of the placeholder and between the lines of text. An internal **margin** provides a cushion of space between text and the top, bottom, left, and right sides of the placeholder. **Line spacing** is the amount of vertical space between the lines of text in a paragraph, and **paragraph spacing** is the amount of space above and below a paragraph. PowerPoint adjusts the line spacing and paragraph spacing automatically to accommodate various font sizes within the placeholder.

Long lists of items can be divided into several **columns** to fill the placeholder width and maximize the slide space. Once you have created columns, you can adjust the amount of space between the columns to enhance readability.

## To Center Placeholder Text

By default, all placeholder text in the Hardcover document theme is left-aligned. For variety, you want the text to be centered, or placed with equal space horizontally between the left and right placeholder edges. The following steps center the text in the content placeholders on Slides 2, 3, 4, and 5.

**1**
- Display Slide 2 and then select the four paragraphs in the content placeholder (Figure 6–44).

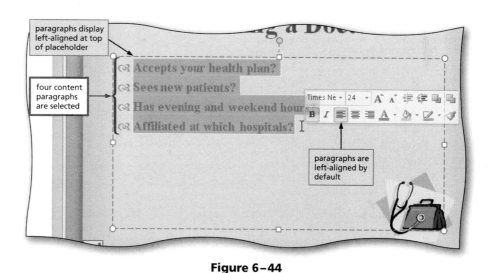

**Figure 6–44**

**2**
- Click the Center button on the Mini toolbar to center these paragraphs (Figure 6–45).

**3**
- Repeat Steps 1 and 2 to center the paragraph text in the content placeholders on Slides 3, 4, and 5.

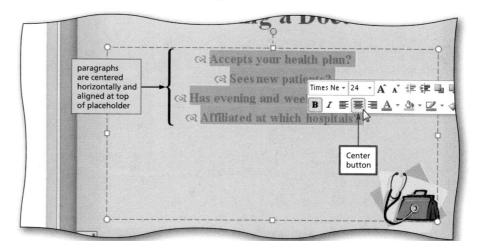

**Figure 6–45**

| Other Ways |
|---|
| 1. Click Center button (Home tab \| Font group)  2. Right-click selected text, click Paragraph on shortcut menu, click Alignment box | arrow (Paragraph dialog box), click Centered, click OK button  3. Click Paragraph Dialog Box Launcher (Home tab \| | Paragraph group), click Alignment box arrow (Paragraph dialog box), click Centered, click OK button  4. Press CTRL+E |

## To Align Placeholder Text

The Hardcover document theme aligns the text paragraphs at the top of the content placeholders. This default setting can be changed easily so that the paragraphs either are centered or aligned at the bottom of the placeholder. The following steps align the paragraphs vertically in the center of the content placeholders on Slides 2, 3, 4, and 5.

- With the Slide 5 paragraphs still selected, display the Home tab and then click the Align Text button (Home tab | Paragraph group) to display the Align Text gallery.

- Point to Middle in the Align Text gallery to display a live preview of the four paragraphs aligned in the center of the content placeholder (Figure 6–46).

🔎 **Experiment**

- Point to the Bottom option in the gallery to see a preview of that alignment.

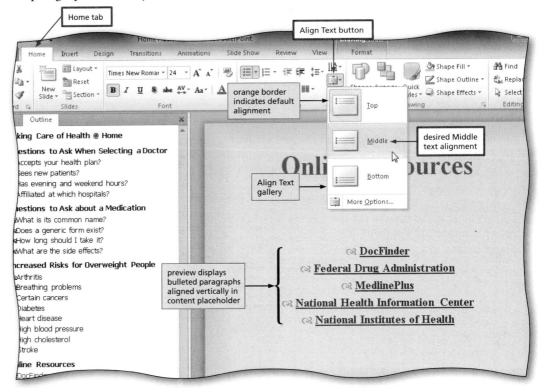

**Figure 6–46**

**2**

- Click Middle in the Align Text gallery to align the paragraphs vertically in the center of the content placeholder (Figure 6–47).

**Q&A**

What is the difference between centering the paragraphs in the placeholder and centering the text?

Clicking the Align Text button and then clicking Middle moves the paragraphs up or down so that the first and last paragraphs are equal distances from the top and bottom placeholder borders. The Center button, on the other hand, moves the paragraphs left or right so that the first and last words in each line are equal distances from the left and right text box borders.

**Figure 6–47**

- Repeat Steps 1 and 2 to center the paragraph text in the middle of the content placeholders on Slides 2, 3, and 4.

## To Change Paragraph Line Spacing

The vertical space between paragraphs is called **line spacing**. PowerPoint adjusts the amount of space based on font size. Default line spacing is 1.0, which is considered single spacing. Other preset options are 1.5, 2.0 (double spacing), 2.5, and 3.0 (triple spacing). You can specify precise line spacing intervals between, before, and after paragraphs in the Indents and Spacing tab of the Paragraph dialog box. The following steps increase the line spacing of the content paragraphs from single (1.0) to double (2.0) on Slides 2, 3, and 5.

- With the Home tab displayed, display Slide 2 and select the four content paragraphs.

- Click the Line Spacing button (Home tab | Paragraph group) to display the Line Spacing gallery.

- Point to 2.0 in the Line Spacing gallery to display a live preview of this line spacing (Figure 6–48).

  **Experiment**

- Point to each of the line spacing options in the gallery to see a preview of that paragraph spacing.

- Click 2.0 in the Line Spacing gallery to change the paragraph line spacing to double.

- Repeat Steps 1 and 2 to change the line spacing for the paragraph text in the content placeholders on Slides 3 and 5. Do not change the line spacing on Slide 4.

**Q&A** Why is the line spacing not changing on Slide 4?

The content placeholder paragraphs will be changed into columns, so spacing is not a design concern at this time.

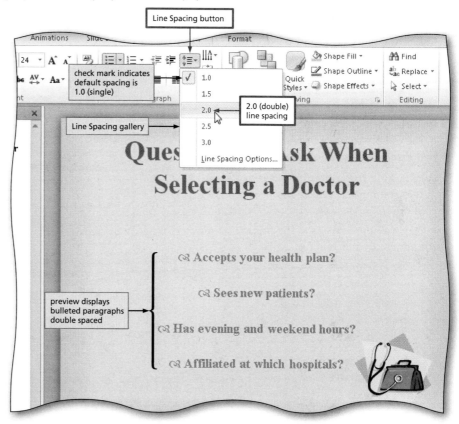

**Figure 6–48**

| Other Ways |
|---|
| 1. Right-click selected text, click Paragraph on shortcut menu, click Line Spacing box arrow (Paragraph dialog box), click Double, click OK button     2. Click Paragraph Dialog Box Launcher (Home tab \| Paragraph group), click Line Spacing box arrow (Paragraph dialog box), click Double, click OK button |

## To Create Columns in a Placeholder

The list of health risks in the Slide 4 placeholder is lengthy and lacks visual appeal. You can change these items into two, three, or more columns and then adjust the column widths. The following steps change the placeholder elements into columns.

- Display Slide 4 and then click the content placeholder to select it.

- With the Home tab displayed, click the Columns button (Home tab | Paragraph group) to display the Columns gallery.

- Point to Two Columns in the Columns gallery to display a live preview of the text in the first column (Figure 6–49).

 **Experiment**

- Point to each of the column options in the gallery to see a preview of the text displaying in various columns.

**Q&A** Why doesn't the content display in two columns if I selected two columns?

Because all the text fits in the first column in the placeholder.

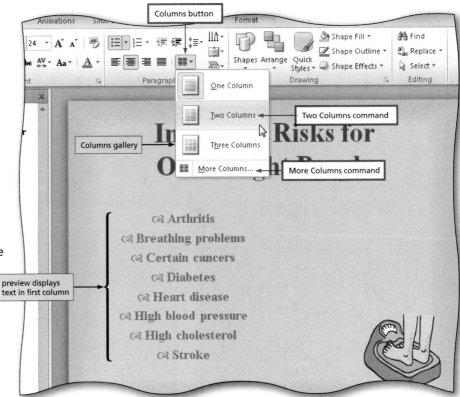

Figure 6–49

- Click Two Columns to create two columns of text.

- Drag the bottom sizing handle up to the location shown in Figure 6–50.

**Q&A** Why is the bottom sizing handle between the Diabetes and Heart Disease paragraphs?

Eight risks are listed in the content placeholder, so dividing the paragraphs in two groups of four will balance the layout.

**3**

- Release the mouse button to resize the content placeholder and create the two columns of text.

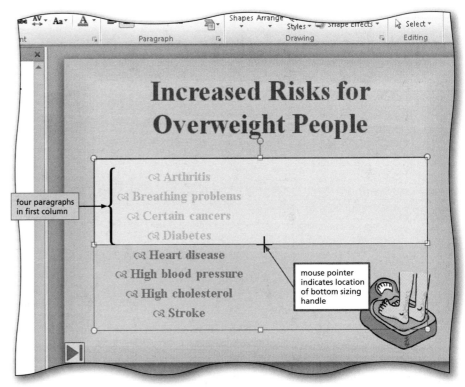

Figure 6–50

## To Adjust Column Spacing

The space between the columns in the placeholder can be increased to make room for the scale picture in the lower-right corner. The following steps increase the spacing between the columns.

**1**

• With the placeholder selected, click the Columns button and then click More Columns.

• Click the Spacing box up arrow (Columns dialog box) until 1.5" is displayed (Figure 6–51).

**Q&A** Can I type a number in the text box instead of clicking the up arrow?

Yes. Double-click the text box and then type the desired measurement expressed in inches.

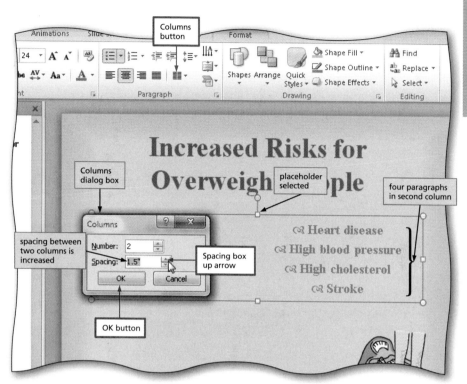

**Figure 6–51**

**2**

• Click the OK button to increase the spacing between the columns (Figure 6–52).

**Q&A** Can I change the paragraphs back to one column easily?

Yes. Click the Columns button and then click One Column.

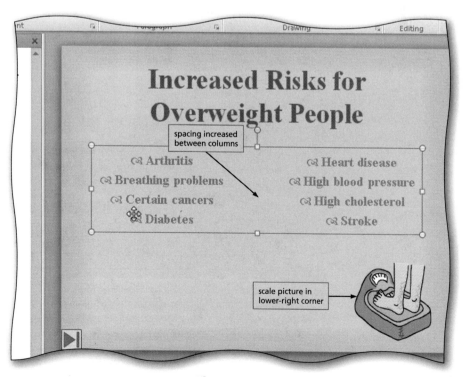

**Figure 6–52**

## To Format the Content Placeholder

To add interest to the Slide 4 content placeholder, apply a Quick Style and then move the scale picture from the lower-right corner to the space between the columns. The following steps apply a green Subtle Effect style to the placeholder and then change the picture location.

**1** With the placeholder selected, click the Quick Styles button (Home tab | Drawing group) to display the Quick Styles gallery.

**2** Click Subtle Effect – Gray-50%, Accent 1 (second style in fourth row).

**3** Move the scale clip from the lower-right corner to the area between the two columns (Figure 6–53).

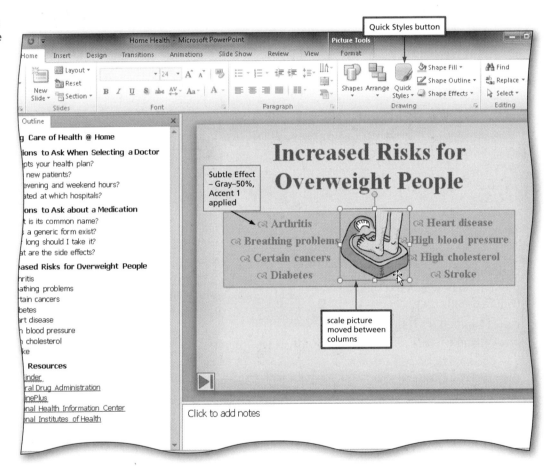

**Figure 6–53**

**Plan Ahead**

**Be mindful of prepositional phrases.**
A prepositional phrase links nouns and pronouns to the rest of a sentence. The phrase begins with a preposition and ends with a noun or pronoun. For example, in the sentence, I left my textbook on my desk, the word "on" is a preposition and the word "desk" is a noun. The more commonly used prepositions are at, by, for, from, in, of, on, to, and with. Because the words in the prepositional phrase work together as a unit, PowerPoint audience members often find it awkward when the entire prepositional phrase does not appear together in one line on the slide. It therefore is best to reword slide text or split multiple paragraph lines so that the prepositional phrase stays intact.

## To Enter a Line Break

Slides 3 and 4 in your presentation have prepositional phrases in the title text placeholders. On Slide 3, the words, about a Medication, and on Slide 4 the words, for Overweight People, start on the first line and then continue to the second line. This break in the middle of the phrase can be disconcerting to your viewers who interpret each line as a separate thought. It is advisable to display all words in a prepositional phrase together on one line. If you press the ENTER key at the end of a line, PowerPoint automatically applies paragraph formatting, which could include indents and bullets. To prevent this formatting from occurring, you can press SHIFT+ENTER to place a **line break** at the end of the line, which moves the insertion point to the beginning of the next line. The following steps place a line break at the beginning of the prepositional phrases on Slide 3 and Slide 4.

- Display Slide 3 and then place the insertion point before the word, about (Figure 6–54).

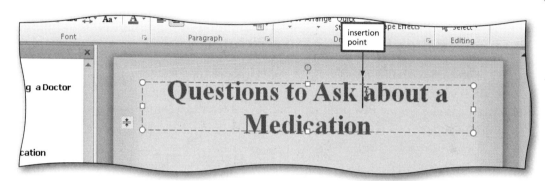

**Figure 6–54**

- Press SHIFT+ENTER to insert a line break character and move the word, about, to the second line in the placeholder.

- Display Slide 4, place the insertion point before the word, for, and then press SHIFT+ENTER to insert a line break character and move the word, for, to the second line (Figure 6–55).

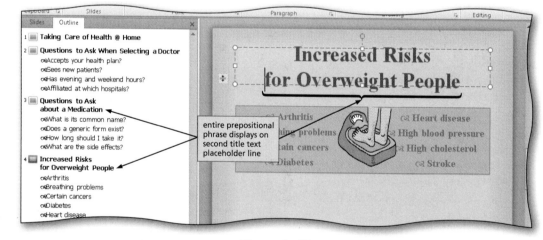

**Figure 6–55**

## Modifying Bullets

PowerPoint allows you to change the default appearance of bullets in a slide show. The document themes determine the bullet character. A **bullet character** is a symbol, traditionally a closed circle, that sets off items in a list. It can be a predefined style, a variety of fonts and characters displayed in the Symbol gallery, or a picture from a file or the Clip Organizer. You may want to change a character to add visual interest and variety. Once you change the bullet character, you also can change its size and color.

If desired, you can change every bullet in a presentation to a unique character. If your presentation has many bulleted slides, however, you would want to have a consistent look on all slides by making the bullets a similar color and size.

To customize your presentation, you can change the default slide layout bullets to numbers by changing the bulleted list to a numbered list. PowerPoint provides a variety of numbering options, including Arabic and Roman numerals. These numbers can be sized and recolored, and the starting number can be something other than 1 or I. In addition, PowerPoint's numbering options include upper- and lowercase letters.

## To Change a Bullet Character to a Picture

The decorative bullet characters for the Hardcover document theme do not fit the serious nature of a presentation with the topic of medicine. One method of modifying these bullets is to use a relevant picture. The following steps change the first paragraph bullet character to a stethoscope picture, which is located on the Data Files for Students.

**1**

- With the Home tab still displaying and your USB flash drive connected to one of the computer's USB ports, display Slide 2 and then select all four content placeholder paragraphs.

**Q&A** Can I insert a different bullet character in each paragraph?

Yes. Select only a paragraph and then perform the steps below for each paragraph.

- Click the Bullets arrow (Home tab | Paragraph group) to display the Bullets gallery (Figure 6–56).

**Q&A** Why is an orange box displayed around the three characters?

They are the default first-level bullet characters for the Hardcover document theme.

**Experiment**

- Point to each of the bullets displayed in the gallery to see a preview of the characters.

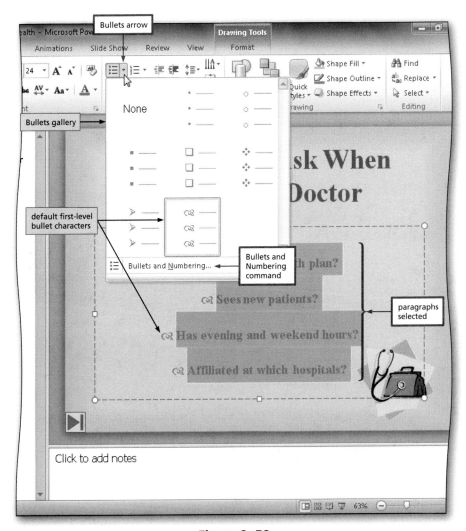

**Figure 6–56**

**2**

- Click Bullets and Numbering to display the Bullets and Numbering dialog box (Figure 6–57).

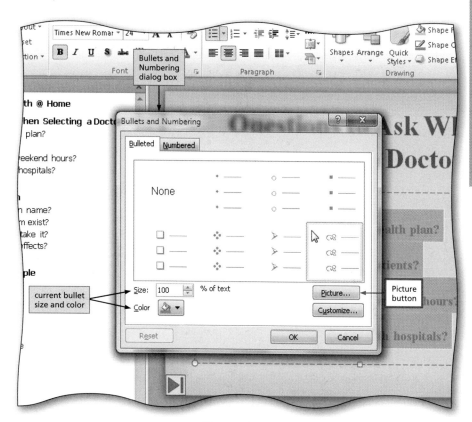

**Figure 6–57**

**3**

- Click the Picture button (Bullets and Numbering dialog box) to display the Picture Bullet dialog box (Figure 6–58).

**Q&A** | Why are my bullets different from those displayed in Figure 6–58?

The bullets most recently inserted are displayed as the first items in the dialog box.

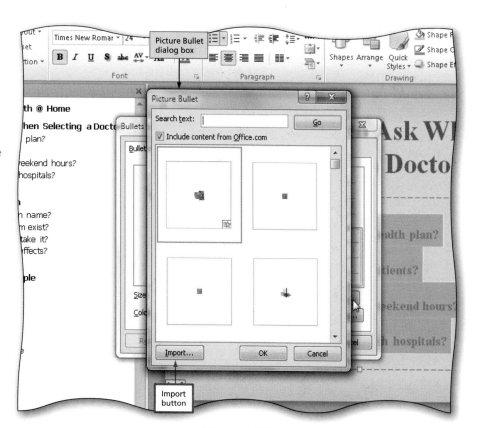

**Figure 6–58**

**4**
- Click the Import button (Picture Bullet dialog box) to display the Add Clips to Organizer dialog box.

- If necessary, double-click your USB flash drive in the list of available storage devices to display a list of files and folders on the selected USB flash drive.

- Click Red Stethoscope to select the file (Figure 6–59).

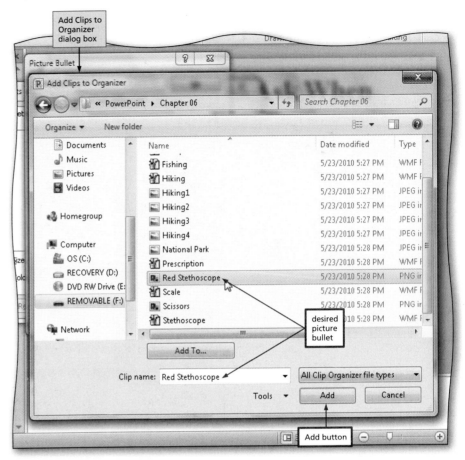

**Figure 6–59**

**5**
- Click the Add button (Add Clips to Organizer dialog box) to import the clip to the Microsoft Clip Organizer (Figure 6–60).

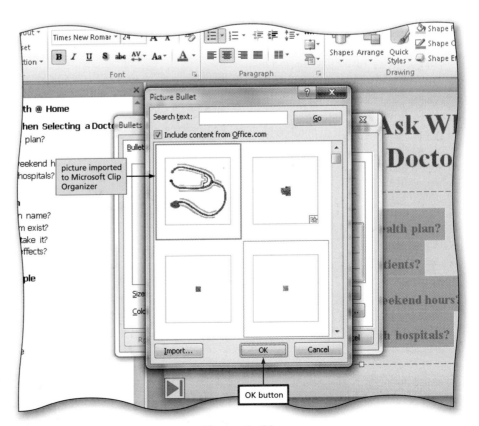

**Figure 6–60**

**6**

- Click the OK button (Picture Bullet dialog box) to insert the Red Stethoscope picture as the paragraph bullet character (Figure 6–61).

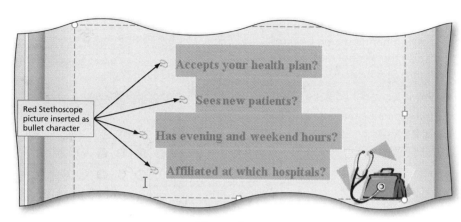

Red Stethoscope picture inserted as bullet character

**Figure 6–61**

> **Other Ways**
>
> 1. Right-click paragraph, point to Bullets on shortcut menu, click Bullets and Numbering

## To Change a Bullet Character to a Symbol

Picture bullets add a unique quality to your presentations. Another bullet change you can make is to insert a symbol as the character. Symbols are found in several fonts, including Webdings, Wingdings, Wingdings 2, and Wingdings 3. The following steps change the bullet character on Slide 5 to a computer mouse symbol in the Wingdings font.

**1**

- Display Slide 5, select all five hyperlinked paragraphs, click the Bullets arrow, and then click Bullets and Numbering to display the Bullets and Numbering dialog box (Figure 6–62).

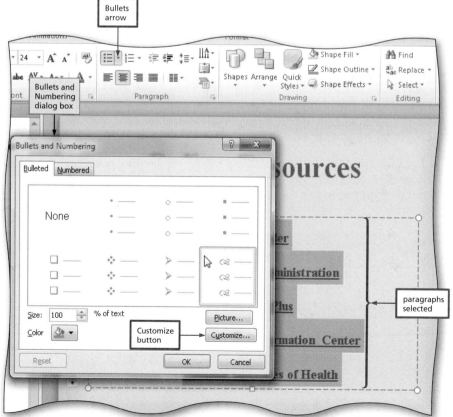

Bullets arrow

Bullets and Numbering dialog box

paragraphs selected

Customize button

**Figure 6–62**

- Click the Customize button (Bullets and Numbering dialog box) to display the Symbol dialog box (Figure 6–63).

**Q&A** Why is a symbol selected?

That symbol is the default bullet for the first-level paragraphs in the Hardcover document theme.

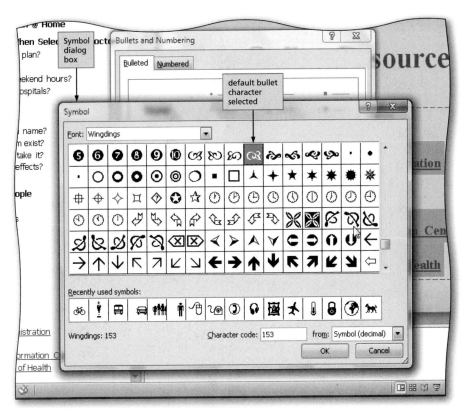

**Figure 6–63**

- Scroll up to locate the computer mouse symbol.

- Click the computer mouse symbol to select it (Figure 6–64).

**Q&A** Why does my dialog box have more rows of symbols and different fonts from which to choose?

The rows and fonts displayed depend upon how PowerPoint was installed on your system.

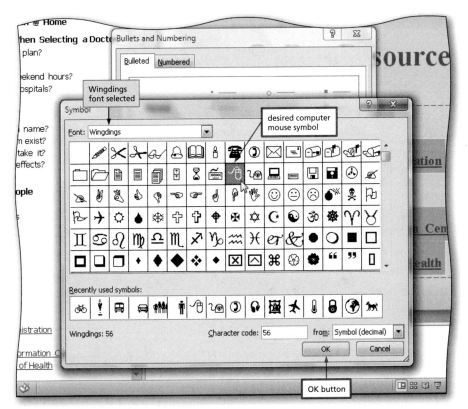

**Figure 6–64**

**4**

- Click the OK button (Symbol dialog box) to display the computer mouse bullet in the Bullets and Numbering dialog box (Figure 6–65).

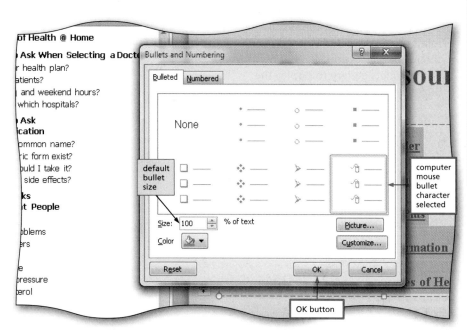

**Figure 6–65**

**5**

- Click the OK button (Bullets and Numbering dialog box) to insert the computer mouse symbol as the paragraph bullet (Figure 6–66).

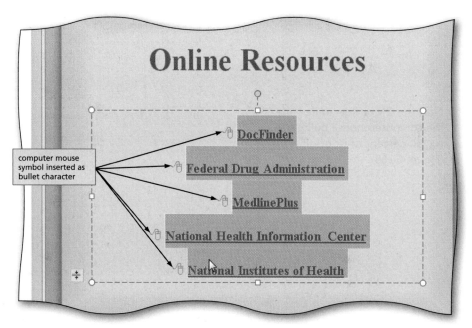

**Figure 6–66**

## To Format a Bullet Size

Bullets have a default size determined by the document theme. **Bullet size** is measured as a percentage of the text size and can range from 25 to 400 percent. The following steps change the computer mouse character size.

- With the Slide 5 paragraphs still selected, click the Bullets arrow and then click Bullets and Numbering in the Bullets gallery to display the Bullets and Numbering dialog box.

- Click and hold down the mouse button on the Size box up arrow until 150 is displayed (Figure 6–67).

 Can I type a number in the text box instead of clicking the up arrow?

Yes. Double-click the text box and then type the desired percentage.

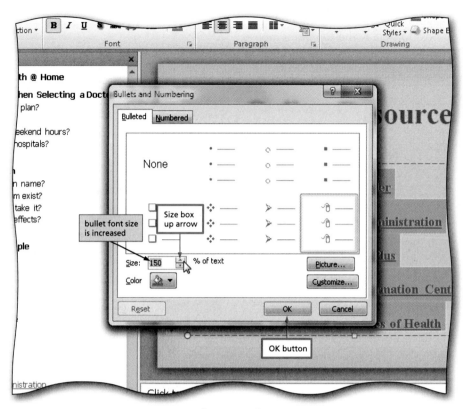

**Figure 6–67**

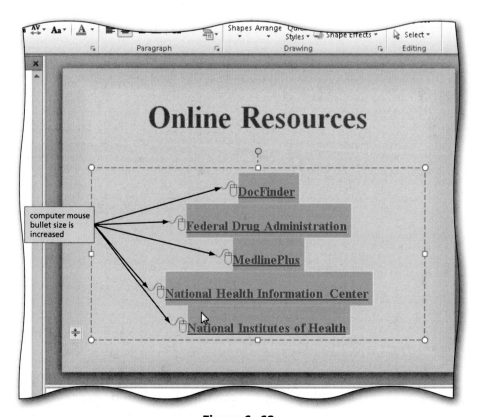

- Click the OK button to increase the computer mouse bullet size to 150 percent of its original size (Figure 6–68).

**Figure 6–68**

## To Change the Size of Other Bullet Characters

For consistency, the bullet character on Slide 2 should have a similar size as that on Slide 5. The following steps change the size of the Red Stethoscope bullets.

**1** Display Slide 2 and then select the four paragraphs in the content placeholder.

**2** Display the Bullets and Numbering dialog box, increase the bullet size to 160% of text, and then click the OK button (Figure 6–69).

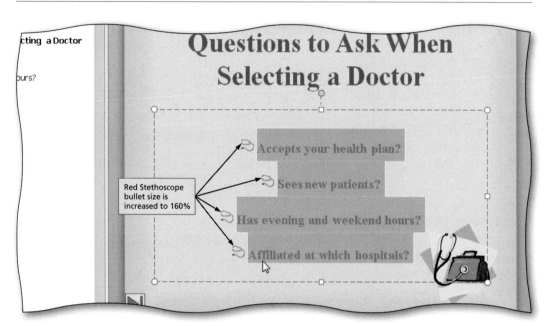

**Figure 6–69**

## To Format a Bullet Color

A default **bullet color** is based on the eight colors in the design theme. Additional standard and custom colors also are available. The following steps change the computer mouse bullet color to Red.

**1**

- Display Slide 5, select the five hyperlinked paragraphs, display the Bullets and Numbering dialog box, and then click the Color button to display the Color gallery (Figure 6–70).

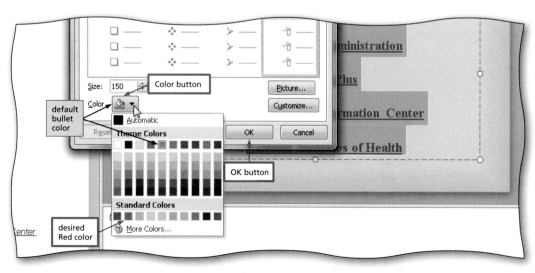

**Figure 6–70**

● Click the color Red in the Standard Colors area to change the bullet color to Red (second color in the Standard Colors area) (Figure 6–71).

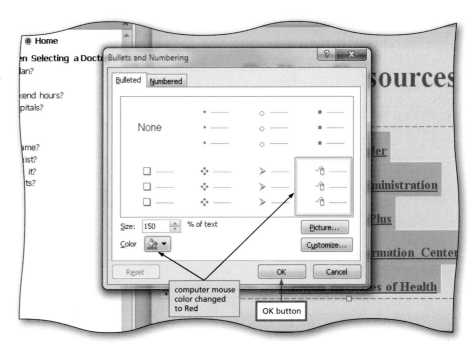

**Figure 6–71**

● Click the OK button to apply the color Red to the computer mouse bullet (Figure 6–72).

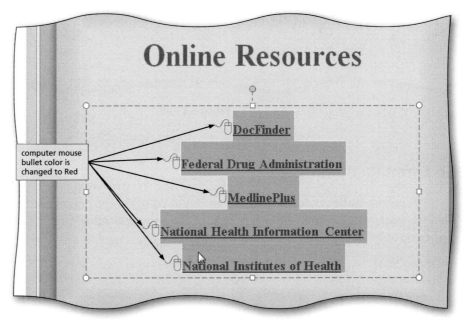

**Figure 6–72**

## To Change a Bullet Character to a Number

PowerPoint allows you to change the default bullets to numbers. The process of changing the bullet characters is similar to the process of changing bullets to symbols. The following steps change the first-level paragraph bullet characters on Slide 3 to numbers.

**1**

- Display Slide 3 and then select all four content paragraphs.

- With the Home tab still displaying, click the Numbering button arrow (Home tab | Paragraph group) to display the Numbering gallery.

- Point to the 1) 2) 3) numbering option in the Numbering gallery to display a live preview of these numbers (Figure 6–73).

 **Experiment**

- Point to each of the numbers in the Numbering gallery to watch the numbers change on Slide 3.

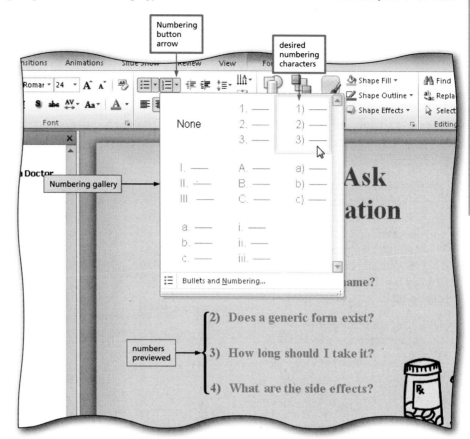

**Figure 6–73**

**2**

- Click the 1) 2) 3) numbering option to insert these numbers as the first-level paragraph characters (Figure 6–74).

**Q&A**

How do I change the first number in the list?

Click Bullets and Numbering at the bottom of the Numbering gallery and then click the up or down arrow in the Start at text box to change the number.

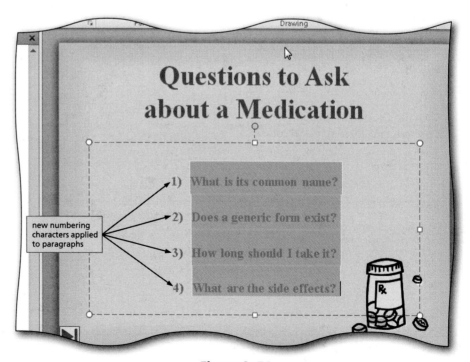

**Figure 6–74**

**Other Ways**

1. Right-click paragraph, point to Numbering on shortcut menu, select numbering characters

## To Format a Numbered List

To add emphasis, you can increase the size of the new numbers inserted in Slide 3. As with bullets, these characters are measured as a percentage of the text size and can range from 25 to 400 percent. The color of these numbers also can change. The original color is based on the eight colors in the design theme. Additional standard and custom colors are available. The following steps change the size and colors of the numbers to 125 percent and Red, respectively.

- With the Slide 3 content paragraphs still selected, click the Numbering button arrow (Home tab | Paragraph group) to display the Numbering gallery and then click Bullets and Numbering to display the Bullets and Numbering dialog box.

- Click the Size box up arrow several times to change the size to 125%.

**Q&A** Can I type a number in the text box instead of clicking the up arrow?

Yes. Double-click the text box and then type the desired percentage.

- Click the Color button to display the Color gallery and then click Red (second color in the Standard Colors area) to change the numbers' font color (Figure 6–75).

- Click the OK button to apply the new numbers' font size and color.

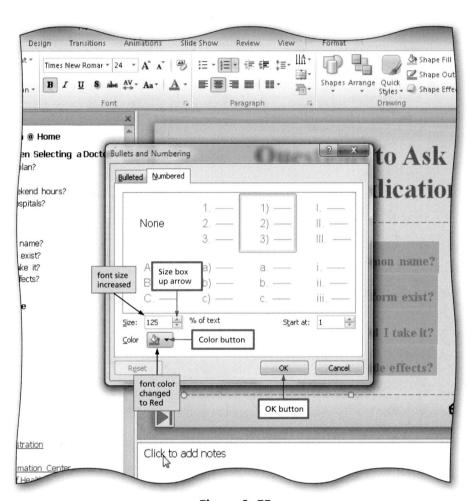

**Figure 6–75**

**Other Ways**

1. Right-click paragraph, point to Numbering on shortcut menu, click Bullets and Numbering, click up or down Size arrow until desired size is displayed, click Color button, select color, click OK button

## To Remove Bullet Characters

The health risks listed in the two Slide 4 columns are preceded by an ornate bullet character. The slide may appear less cluttered if you remove the bullets. The following steps remove the bullet characters from the items in the two columns on Slide 4.

**1**

- Display Slide 4, select all the text in the two columns, and then click the Bullets button arrow.

- Point to the None option in the Bullets gallery to display a live preview of how the slide will appear without bullets (Figure 6–76).

**2**

- Click the None option to remove the bullet characters on Slide 4.

- If necessary, move the scale picture to center it between the two columns.

**Q&A**

Would I use the same technique to remove numbers from a list?

Yes. The None option also is available in the Numbering gallery.

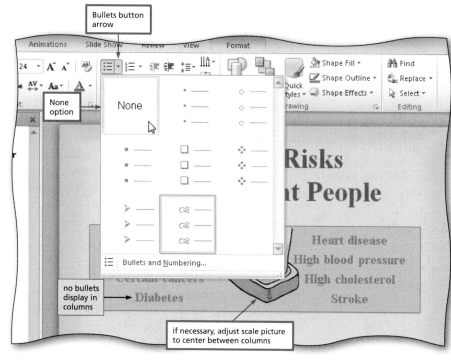

**Figure 6–76**

## To Change Document Properties

Before saving the presentation again, you want to add your name, class name, and some keywords as document properties. The following steps use the Document Information Panel to change document properties.

**1** Display the Document Information Panel and then type your name as the Author property.

**2** Type your course and section in the Subject property.

**3** Type `home health, medication record, doctor selection, overweight risks` as the Keywords property.

**4** Close the Document Information Panel.

**Consider the audience's interests.**
As audience members start to view your presentation, they often think about their personal needs and wonder, "How will this presentation benefit me?" As you may have learned in your psychology classes, Maslow's hierarchy of needs drives much of your behavior, starting with basic sustenance and moving on to safety, belonging, ego-status, and self-actualization. Audience members cannot move to the next higher level of needs until their current level is satisfied. For example, an individual must first satisfy his needs of hunger and thirst before he can consider partaking in leisure time activities. Your presentations must meet the requirements of your audience members; otherwise, these people will not consider your talk as benefiting their needs. Having hyperlinks and action buttons can help you tailor a presentation to fulfill the audience's satisfaction level.

**Plan Ahead**

# Running a Slide Show with Hyperlinks and Action Buttons

The Home Health presentation contains a variety of useful features that provide value to an audience. The graphics should help viewers understand and recall the information being presented. The hyperlinks on Slide 5 show useful Web sites that give current medical information. In addition, the action button allows a presenter to jump to Slide 5 while Slides 2 or 3 are being displayed. If an audience member asks a question or if the presenter needs to answer specific questions regarding weight when Slide 3 is displaying, the information on the hidden Slide 4 can be accessed immediately by pressing the H key.

## To Run a Slide Show with Hyperlinks, Action Buttons, and a Hidden Slide

Running a slide show that contains hyperlinks and action buttons is an interactive experience. A presenter has the option to display slides in a predetermined sequence or to improvise based on the audience's reaction and questions. When a presentation contains hyperlinks and the computer is connected to the Internet, the speaker can click the links to command the default browser to display the Web sites. The following steps run the Home Health presentation.

**1** Click Slide 1 on the Outline tab. Click the Slide Show button to run the slide show and display Slide 1.

**2** Click the stethoscope picture to display Slide 2.

**3** On Slide 2, click the stethoscope picture to link to the first slide in the Additional Health presentation.

**4** Click the Return action button on the first slide to return to Slide 2 in the Home Health presentation.

**5** Press the ENTER key to display Slide 3. Click the prescription picture to start Microsoft Word and open the Medication Record file. View the information and then click the Close button on the title bar to quit Word and return to Slide 3.

**6** Press the H key to display Slide 4. Click the scale picture to link to the second slide in the Additional Health presentation. Click the Return action button on the second slide to return to Slide 4 in the Home Health presentation.

**7** Press the ENTER key to display Slide 5. Click the first hyperlink to start your browser and access the DocFinder online physician directory Web page. If necessary, maximize the Web page window when the page is displayed. Click the Close button on the Web page title bar to close the browser.

**8** Continue using the hyperlinks and action buttons and then end the presentation.

## To Save, Print, and Quit PowerPoint

The presentation now is complete. You should save the slides, print a handout, and then quit PowerPoint.

**1** Save the Home Health presentation again with the same file name.

**2** Print the presentation as a handout with two slides per page (Figure 6–77).

**3** Quit PowerPoint, closing all open documents.

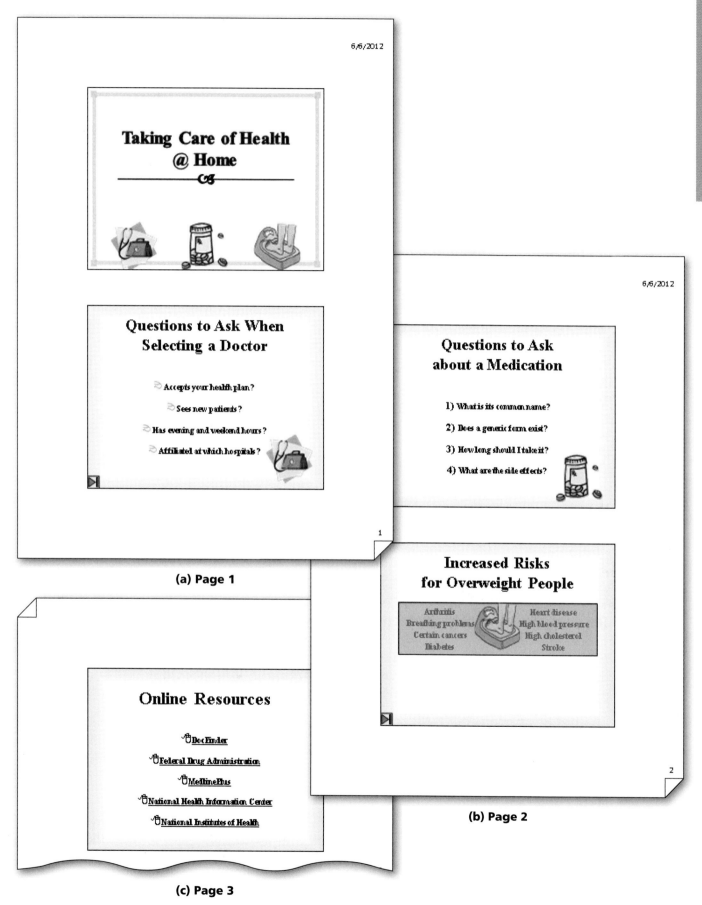

(a) Page 1

(b) Page 2

(c) Page 3

**Figure 6–77**

# Chapter Summary

In this chapter you have learned how to open a Microsoft Word outline as a PowerPoint presentation, develop slides with hyperlinks and action buttons, position slide elements using the drawing guides and rulers, align and distribute pictures, center and align placeholder text, and create columns and then adjust the width. You then learned to change a bullet character to a picture or a symbol and then change its size and color. Finally, you ran the presentation using the action buttons and hyperlinks. The items listed below include all the new PowerPoint skills you have learned in this chapter.

1. Open a Microsoft Word Outline as a Presentation (PPT 335)
2. Add a Hyperlink to a Picture (PPT 339)
3. Add a Hyperlink to a Paragraph (PPT 341)
4. Insert an Action Button (PPT 344)
5. Change an Action Button Fill Color (PPT 346)
6. Copy an Action Button (PPT 348)
7. Edit an Action Button Action Setting (PPT 349)
8. Hyperlink to Another PowerPoint File (PPT 350)
9. Hyperlink to a Microsoft Word File (PPT 353)
10. Display the Drawing Guides (PPT 357)
11. Position a Picture Using Guides (PPT 358)
12. Display the Rulers (PPT 359)
13. Align Pictures (PPT 360)
14. Distribute Pictures (PPT 362)
15. Hide a Slide (PPT 363)
16. Center Placeholder Text (PPT 365)
17. Align Placeholder Text (PPT 366)
18. Change Paragraph Line Spacing (PPT 367)
19. Create Columns in a Placeholder (PPT 367)
20. Adjust Column Spacing (PPT 369)
21. Enter a Line Break (PPT 371)
22. Change a Bullet Character to a Picture (PPT 372)
23. Change a Bullet Character to a Symbol (PPT 375)
24. Format a Bullet Size (PPT 377)
25. Format a Bullet Color (PPT 379)
26. Change a Bullet Character to a Number (PPT 380)
27. Format a Numbered List (PPT 382)
28. Remove Bullet Characters (PPT 382)

 If you have a SAM 2010 user profile, your instructor may have assigned an autogradable version of this assignment. If so, log into the SAM 2010 Web site at www.cengage.com/sam2010 to download the instruction and start files.

## Learn It Online

Test your knowledge of chapter content and key terms.

*Instructions:* To complete the Learn It Online exercises, start your browser, click the Address bar, and then enter the Web address **scsite.com/ppt2010/learn**. When the Office 2010 Learn It Online page is displayed, click the link for the exercise you want to complete and then read the instructions.

**Chapter Reinforcement TF, MC, and SA**
A series of true/false, multiple choice, and short answer questions that test your knowledge of the chapter content.

**Flash Cards**
An interactive learning environment where you identify chapter key terms associated with displayed definitions.

**Practice Test**
A series of multiple choice questions that test your knowledge of chapter content and key terms.

**Who Wants To Be a Computer Genius?**
An interactive game that challenges your knowledge of chapter content in the style of a television quiz show.

**Wheel of Terms**
An interactive game that challenges your knowledge of chapter key terms in the style of the television show *Wheel of Fortune*.

**Crossword Puzzle Challenge**
A crossword puzzle that challenges your knowledge of key terms presented in the chapter.

# Apply Your Knowledge

Reinforce the skills and apply the concepts you learned in this chapter.

## Revising a Presentation with Action Buttons, Bullet Styles, and Hidden Slides

*Note:* To complete this assignment, you will be required to use the Data Files for Students. See the inside back cover of this book for instructions on downloading the Data Files for Students, or contact your instructor for information about accessing the required files.

*Instructions:* Start PowerPoint. Open the presentation, Apply 6-1 Anatomy, located on the Data Files for Students.

The six slides in the presentation identify names seldom used for parts of the body. You plan to use the presentation as a study guide for your anatomy class. The document you open is an unformatted presentation. You are to add a style to the pictures; insert action buttons on Slide 1; hide Slides 2, 3, 4, and 5; and format the bullets on Slides 2 through 6 so the slides look like Figure 6–78 on the next page.

*Perform the following tasks:*

1. Change the document theme to Grid. Apply the WordArt style, Fill – Tan, Accent 2, Warm Matte Bevel, to the title text and add the Chevron Up text effect.

2. On Slide 1, apply the Rotated, White picture style to the upper-left picture, apply the Metal Frame picture style to the upper-right picture, apply the Metal Rounded Rectangle picture style to the lower-left picture, and apply the Bevel Perspective Left, White picture style to the lower-right picture, as shown in Figure 6–78a.

3. Hyperlink each picture to the corresponding slide. For example, the upper-left picture should hyperlink to Slide 2. The other three pictures should hyperlink to Slides 3, 4, and 5, respectively.

4. Center the subtitle text and then bold this text.

5. On Slide 2, insert a Home action button and hyperlink it to the first slide. Change the action button fill color to Yellow, and then change the transparency to 60%. Do not play a sound. Size the button so that it is approximately 0.75" × 0.75" and then move it to the location shown in Figure 6–78b. Copy this action button to Slides 3, 4, and 5.

6. On Slides 2 through 6, add Arrow Bullets to the content text paragraphs and then increase the size of the bullets to 135% of text. Change the color of the body part terms at the beginning of each paragraph to Tan, Accent 1 on all slides.

7. Hide Slides 2, 3, 4, and 5.

8. Change the Transition from Zoom to Split. Change the duration to 02.50.

9. Display the revised presentation in Slide Sorter view to check for consistency.

10. Change the document properties, as specified by your instructor. Save the presentation using the file name, Apply 6-1 Parts of the Body. Submit the revised document in the format specified by your instructor.

*Continued >*

**Apply Your Knowledge** *continued*

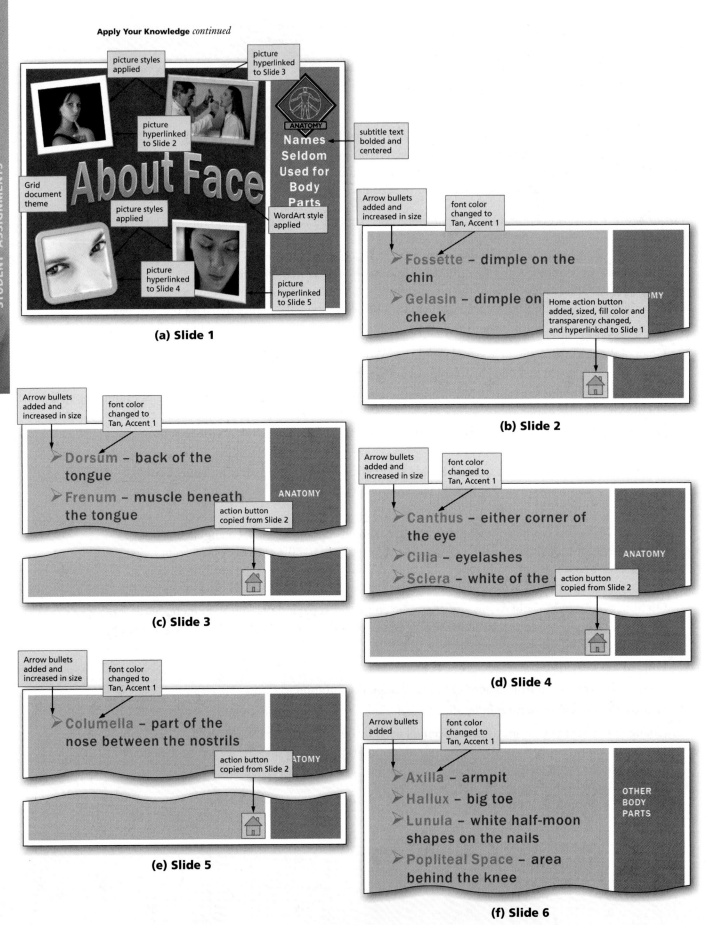

**Figure 6–78**

# Extend Your Knowledge

Extend the skills you learned in this chapter and experiment with new skills. You may need to use Help to complete the assignment.

---

### Inserting a Picture into an Action Button and Changing a Bullet Character to a Picture

*Note:*   To complete this assignment, you will be required to use the Data Files for Students. See the inside back cover of this book for instructions on downloading the Data Files for Students, or contact your instructor for information about accessing the required files.

*Instructions:*   Start PowerPoint. Open the presentation, Extend 6-1 Camp, located on the Data Files for Students.

You will insert hyperlinks on the title slide; enter the data from Table 6–3 on Slide 2; insert action buttons on Slides 2, 3, and 4; and change the bullet characters to pictures on Slides 5 and 6, as shown in Figure 6–79 on the next page.

| Table 6–3 Adams Family Camp Trails | | |
| --- | --- | --- |
| **Trail** | **Length** | **Trail Head** |
| Mountainview | 10.2 miles | Behind clubhouse |
| Lakeside | 11.5 miles | Main dock |
| Upper Bend | 12.8 miles | Behind clubhouse |

*Perform the following tasks:*

1. On Slide 1, hyperlink each picture to the corresponding slide. For example, the top picture should hyperlink to Slide 2. The other two pictures should hyperlink to Slides 3 and 4, respectively. Use the Smart Guides to align the three pictures to the slide and then distribute these images vertically. Once the pictures are distributed vertically, use the Arrange list to align their centers as well.

2. On Slide 2, insert a Custom action button in the lower-left area of the slide and hyperlink it to the first slide. Format this shape by inserting the picture, Hiking, located on the Data Files for Students, as shown in Figure 6–79b.

3. Enter the data from Table 6–3 in the text box on Slide 2. Change the paragraph line spacing to 1.5 and center all text.

4. On Slide 3, insert a Custom action button in the lower-left corner of the slide and hyperlink it to the first slide. Format this shape by inserting the picture, Fishing, located on your Data Files for Students, as shown in Figure 6–79c.

5. On Slide 4, insert a Forward or Next action button in the lower-right corner of the slide.

6. On Slide 5, change the bullet character to the Scissors picture located on the Data Files for Students. Increase the size of the bullets to 150% of text.

7. On Slide 6, insert a picture bullet by importing the Camera picture located on the Data Files for Students, and then increase the size of the bullets to 150% of text.

8. Change the title text paragraph alignment on Slides 5 and 6 to Distributed by selecting the title text, displaying the Home tab, clicking the Paragraph Dialog Box Launcher button (Home tab | Paragraph group), clicking the Alignment box arrow, and then clicking Distributed.

9. Apply a transition to all slides.

10. Change the document properties, as specified by your instructor. Save the presentation using the file name, Extend 6-1 Family Summer Camp.

11. Submit the revised document in the format specified by your instructor.

*Continued >*

**Extend Your Knowledge** *continued*

**(a) Slide 1**

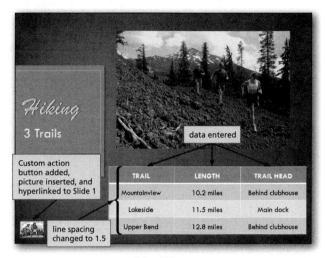

**(b) Slide 2**

**(c) Slide 3**

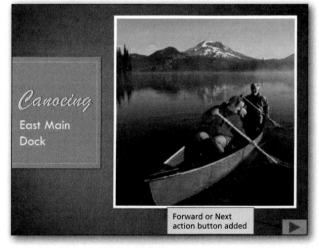

**(d) Slide 4**

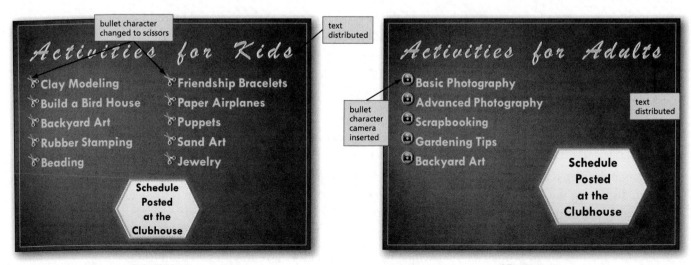

**(e) Slide 5**

**(f) Slide 6**

**Figure 6–79**

## Make It Right

Analyze a presentation and correct all errors and/or improve the design.

### Modifying Text and Line Spacing in a Placeholder

*Note:* To complete this assignment, you will be required to use the Data Files for Students. See the inside back cover of this book for instructions on downloading the Data Files for Students, or contact your instructor for information about accessing the required files.

*Instructions:* Start PowerPoint. Open the presentation, Make It Right 6-1 Golf, located on the Data Files for Students. Correct the formatting problems and errors in the presentation while keeping in mind the guidelines presented in this chapter.

*Perform the following tasks:*

1. On Slide 1, shown in Figure 6–80, select the four words, What's in Your Bag?, at the top of the slide and then decrease the font size to 28 point. Make sure that these four words show in the box. Change the title text font size to 40 point and then right-align this text. Center the text in both subtitle placeholders.
2. Remove the artistic effect from the picture and change the style to Rotated, White.
3. Increase the font size of the text in the right placeholder to 22 point.
4. Align the text in both placeholders vertically in the center.
5. Increase the size of the bullets to 200% of the text size.
6. Check the spelling and correct the misspellings.
7. Change the document properties, as specified by your instructor. Save the presentation using the file name, Make It Right 6-1 Golf Clubs.
8. Submit the revised document in the format specified by your instructor.

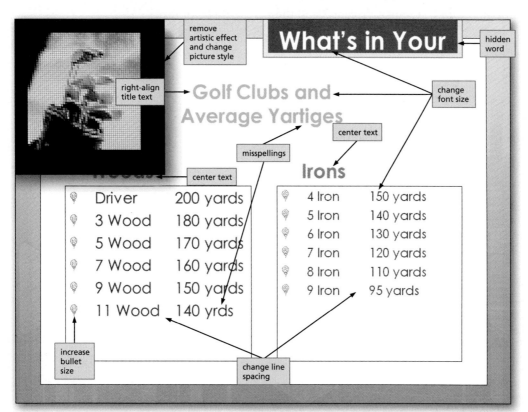

**Figure 6–80**

**In the Lab**

Design and/or create a presentation using the guidelines, concepts, and skills presented in this chapter. Labs 1, 2, and 3 are listed in order of increasing difficulty.

### Lab 1: Aligning Text and Creating Columns in a Text Box, Moving a Placeholder, and Changing a Bullet Character to a Picture

*Note:* To complete this assignment, you will be required to use the Data Files for Students. See the inside back cover of this book for instructions on downloading the Data Files for Students, or contact your instructor for information about accessing the required files.

*Problem:* You belong to a garden club in the city and find that many members have limited yard space for planting a garden. The president of the club asked if you would modify an existing presentation that describes the basics of container gardening. You create the slides shown in Figure 6–81 using files located on the Data Files for Students.

*Perform the following tasks:*

1. Open the presentation, Lab 6-1 Vegetables, located on the Data Files for Students.

2. Change the presentation theme colors to Hardcover.

3. On Slide 1, change the title text placeholder vertical alignment to Top. Insert a line break after the dash in the first line and then delete the space before the word, No, in the second line. Change the font size to 54 points, and the font color to Light Green, and then bold this text. Change the subtitle text font to Vani and the font size to 36 point. Increase the size of the three clips, as shown in Figure 6–81a, and then use the Smart Guides to align the two flowerpots.

4. On Slide 2, add bullets and then change the bullet character to the Clay Pot picture located on the Data Files for Students. Increase the size of these bullets to 250% of text.

5. On Slide 3, change the four bullet characters to the 1) 2) 3) numbering format. Change the numbering color to Orange, Accent 2 and the size to 100% of text.

6. On Slide 4, create three columns in the text box, adjust the column spacing to 1", and then change the line spacing to 1.5. Move the two clips to the locations shown in Figure 6–81d.

7. Apply the Window transition and change the duration to 2.25 for all slides.

8. Change the document properties, as specified by your instructor. Save the presentation using the file name, Lab 6-1 Container Vegetable Garden.

9. Submit the revised document in the format specified by your instructor.

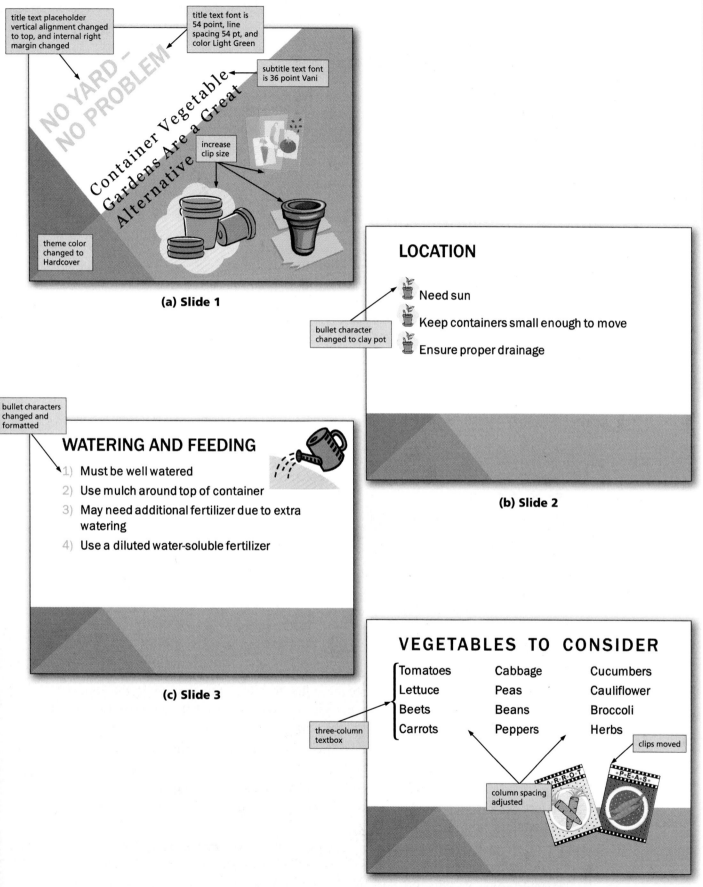

**(a) Slide 1**

**(b) Slide 2**

**(c) Slide 3**

**(d) Slide 4**

**Figure 6–81**

# In the Lab

## Lab 2: Creating a Presentation from a Microsoft Word Outline, Inserting Hyperlinks to Other Office Documents, Hiding Slides, and Copying and Editing Action Buttons

*Note:* To complete this assignment, you will be required to use the Data Files for Students. See the inside back cover of this book for instructions on downloading the Data Files for Students, or contact your instructor for information about accessing the required files.

*Problem:* The members of your school's hiking club are planning an eight-day backpacking trip in a national park. As program chairman, you are working on the details of the trip. The president asks you to give a presentation at your next meeting to discuss some of the trip's details and gives you a Microsoft Word outline with points to cover during your speech. To supplement your talk, the treasurer gives you an Excel file that has the club's membership information, and you have created a Microsoft Word document that lists items everyone should pack and bring on the trip. You will use the outline as the basis for your presentation and create hyperlinks to the other documents to display during your presentation. You borrowed photos from your cousin, who took a trip to this park, and you will use those pictures in your presentation. The trip will include visits to Baer Woods, Ruff Summit, Pine Cone Valley, and Stoop Falls. You create the slides shown in Figure 6–82 using files located on the Data Files for Students.

*Perform the following tasks:*

1. Create a new presentation using the Office Theme. Import the outline, Lab 6-2 Backpacking Outline, shown in Figure 6–82a, located on the Data Files for Students. Change the new Slide 1 layout to Title Slide.

2. On Slide 1, create a background by inserting the picture called National Park located on the Data Files for Students. Change the transparency to 62%.

3. Increase the title text font size to 54 point. Create a hyperlink for all the title text to the Excel document, Tooterville Hiking Club (Figure 6–82i), located on the Data Files for Students. Bold the subtitle text.

4. On Slide 2, convert the bulleted list to SmartArt by applying the Continuous Picture List (List area). Change the colors to Colorful Range – Accent Colors 2 to 3 and then apply the Polished 3D style to the graphic. Insert the pictures, Hiking1, Hiking2, Hiking3, and Hiking4, from the Data Files for Students, as shown in Figure 6–82b.

5. On all slides except the title slide, change the background to Style 10.

6. On Slide 3 (Figure 6–82c), change the bullet character to the Compass picture located on the Data Files for Students. Increase the size of the bullets to 110% of the text. Insert the Return action button in the lower-right corner of this slide and then hyperlink the button to the Last Slide Viewed, which will be Slide 2 when you run the presentation.

7. Duplicate Slide 3 three times to add the new three slides to create new Slides 4, 5, and 6. The current Slide 4 becomes Slide 7.

8. On Slide 2, insert a hyperlink on each picture. Link the Baer Woods picture to Slide 3, the Ruff Summit picture to Slide 4, the Pine Cone Valley picture to Slide 5, and the Stoop Falls picture to Slide 6. Play the sound, Camera, for each hyperlink.

9. On Slides 3, 4, 5, and 6, change the font color of the bulleted paragraphs to match the corresponding SmartArt graphic color, as shown in Figures 6–82d through 6–82g. The Baer Woods color is Red, Accent 2; the Ruff Summit color is Orange, Accent 6; the Pine Cone Valley color is Orange; and the Stoop Falls color is Olive Green, Accent 3, Darker 50%. Bold each of the colored paragraphs.

10. Hide Slides 3, 4, 5, and 6.

11. On Slide 7 (Figure 6–82h), insert a hyperlink in the title text to the Word document, Packing List (Figure 6–82j), located on the Data Files for Students. Change the six bullet characters to the 1.2.3. numbering format, the color to Blue, and the size to 125% of the text. Bold all the numbered paragraphs on the slide.

12. Apply the Honeycomb transition and then change the duration to 3.25 for all slides.

13. Check the spelling and correct any errors.

14. Change the document properties, as specified by your instructor. Save the presentation using the file name, Lab 6-2 Backpacking Trip.

15. Submit the revised document in the format specified by your instructor.

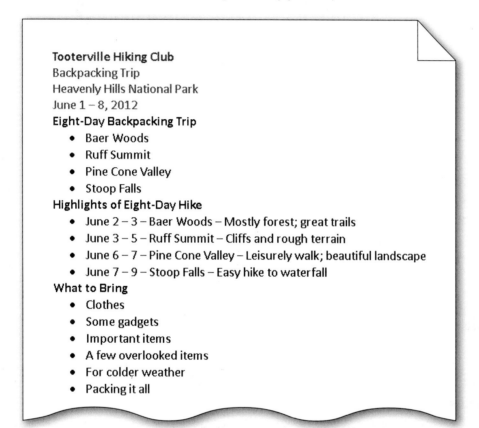

**Tooterville Hiking Club**
Backpacking Trip
Heavenly Hills National Park
June 1 – 8, 2012
**Eight-Day Backpacking Trip**
- Baer Woods
- Ruff Summit
- Pine Cone Valley
- Stoop Falls

**Highlights of Eight-Day Hike**
- June 2 – 3 – Baer Woods – Mostly forest; great trails
- June 3 – 5 – Ruff Summit – Cliffs and rough terrain
- June 6 – 7 – Pine Cone Valley – Leisurely walk; beautiful landscape
- June 7 – 9 – Stoop Falls – Easy hike to waterfall

**What to Bring**
- Clothes
- Some gadgets
- Important items
- A few overlooked items
- For colder weather
- Packing it all

**(a) Backpacking Outline — Microsoft Word Document**

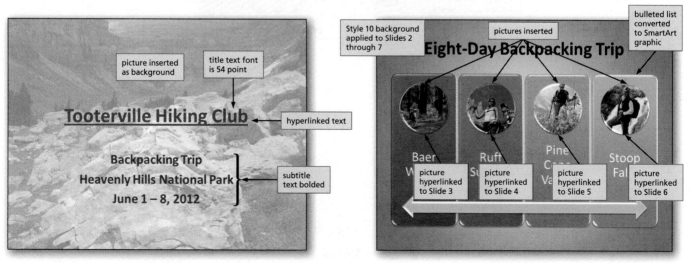

**(b) Slide 1**

**(c) Slide 2**

**Figure 6–82**

*Continued >*

**In the Lab** *continued*

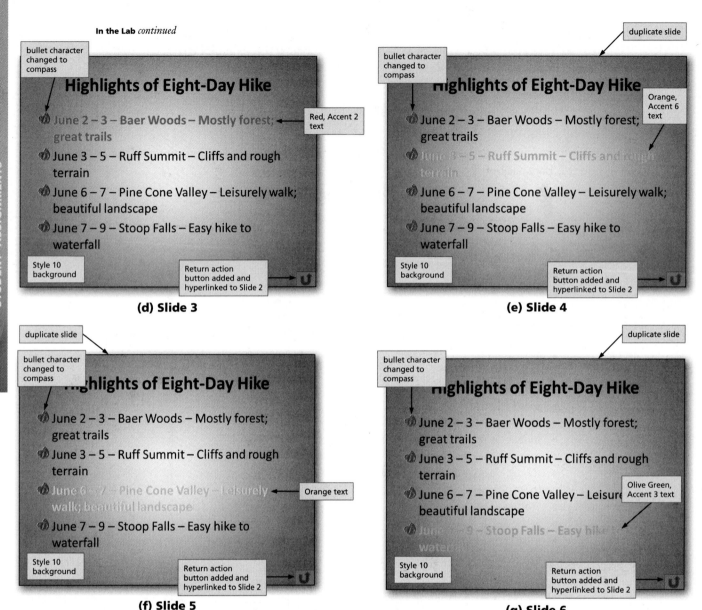

**(d) Slide 3**

**(e) Slide 4**

**(f) Slide 5**

**(g) Slide 6**

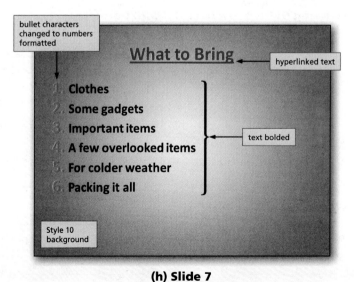

**(h) Slide 7**

**Figure 6–82 (Continued)**

**(i) Membership Roster — Microsoft Excel File**

**Clothes**
- Shirts (long- and short-sleeved)
- Thin fleece jacket
- Socks and underwear
- Two pair of jeans
- Baseball hat, sun hat
- Swimming gear
- Hiking boots/shoes and sandals

**Some gadgets**
- Camera and spare battery
- Chargers and plug adaptor if needed
- Mini LED flashlight or head light
- Cell phone
- Calculator

**Important Items**
- ATM, credit card, and cash
- Sun glasses
- Glasses and contacts lenses and solutions
- First aid/medicine kit
- Shower kit
- Mosquito net and tape
- Documents: emergency numbers, insurance cards, flight details, etc.
- Guidebook

**A few overlooked items**
- Pen and notepad
- Packets of tissues
- Towel
- Sleeping sac
- Entertainment: book(s), magazine(s), cards, MP3 player, handheld games
- Umbrella or waterproof shell
- Earplugs, eye mask
- Snacks

**For colder weather**
- Heavy fleece jacket
- Thermal vest
- Gloves, knit hat, thick socks, an outer windproof shell, thermal leggings

**Packing it all**
- Money belt
- Mini padlock and cable lock
- Shoulder bag or fanny pack for day use
- Small plastic bags and containers for storage
- A bag/backpack to store everything

**(j) Packing List — Microsoft Word File**

**Figure 6–82 (Continued)**

# In the Lab

### Lab 3: Inserting Hyperlinks and Action Buttons, Hiding Slides, Using Guides, and Formatting Bullets

*Note:* To complete this assignment, you will be required to use the Data Files for Students. See the inside back cover of this book for instructions on downloading the Data Files for Students, or contact your instructor for information about accessing the required files.

*Problem:* Your public speaking instructor has assigned an informative speech, and you have decided to discuss landlocked countries. You create the presentation in Figure 6–83 that consists of six slides with hyperlinks, and you decide to hide four slides. Required files are located on the Data Files for Students.

*Perform the following tasks:*

1. Open the presentation, Lab 6-3 Landlocked, from the Data Files for Students. Change the document theme to Civic and then change the presentation theme colors to Adjacency.

2. On Slide 1, change the title text font to Algerian. Increase the font size of the first line of the title text to 48 point, and then decrease the second line's font size to 36 point. Convert the bulleted list to SmartArt by applying the Vertical Circle List (List area). Decrease the font size of the first line to 30 point and the countries' names to 24 point. Apply the Bevel Perspective picture style to the picture.

3. On Slides 2, 3, and 4, resize the globe and map pictures so that they are approximately 3.39" × 5.4" and then move them to the locations shown in Figure 6–83. Display the rulers, click to the left and below the center of the globe, and then move the graphic so that the mouse pointer is positioned at the center of both the vertical and horizontal rulers. Hide the rulers.

4. On Slides 2, 3, and 4, resize the country symbols in the lower-right corners so that they are approximately 0.75" × 1.67". Display the drawing guides. Set the horizontal guide to 2.33 below center and the vertical guide to 3.17 right of center. Move the country symbols so that their upper-left sizing handles align with the intersection of the guides. Hide the guides.

5. On Slide 5, change the color of the map to Tan, Accent color 5 Dark.

6. On Slide 6, center all six content text paragraphs and then align these paragraphs in the middle of the placeholder.

7. On Slide 1, insert a hyperlink for each country. Kazakhstan should be hyperlinked to Slide 2, Mongolia should be hyperlinked to Slide 3, and Hungary should be hyperlinked to Slide 4.

8. On Slides 2, 3, and 4, insert a hyperlink for each country symbol to Slide 1. Then insert a hyperlink for each country's name to the country's Web site shown in Slide 6.

9. On Slide 5, change the bullets to the Star Bullets, change the color to Orange, and then increase the size of the two first-level paragraph bullets to 130% of text and the four countries to 120% of text. Right-align all six bulleted paragraphs.

10. Hide Slides 2, 3, 4, and 6.

11. Apply the Flip transition to all slides and then change the duration to 2.50.

12. Click the Slide Sorter view button, view the slides for consistency, and then click the Normal view button.

13. Change the document properties, as specified by your instructor. Save the presentation using the file name, Lab 6-3 Landlocked Countries.

14. Submit the revised document in the format specified by your instructor.

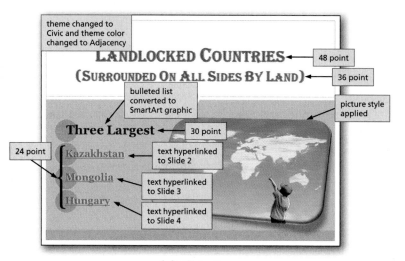

**(a) Slide 1**

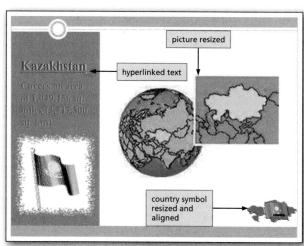

**(b) Slide 2**

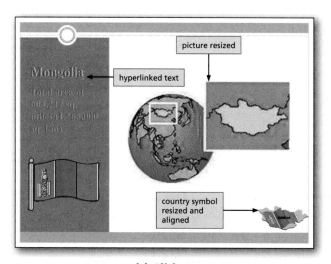

**(c) Slide 3**

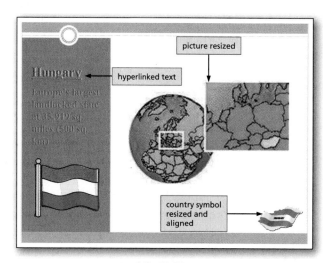

**(d) Slide 4**

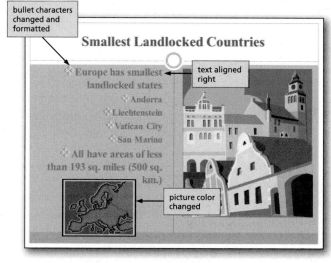

**(e) Slide 5**

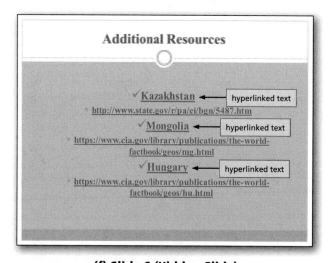

**(f) Slide 6 (Hidden Slide)**

**Figure 6–83**

# Cases and Places

Apply your creative thinking and problem-solving skills to design and implement a solution.

*Note:* To complete these assignments, you may be required to use the Data Files for Students. See the inside back cover of this book for instructions on downloading the Data Files for Students, or contact your instructor for information about accessing the required files.

As you design the presentations, remember to use the 7 × 7 rule: a maximum of seven words on a line and a maximum of seven lines on one slide.

### 1: Designing and Creating a Presentation about Hurricane Names

**Academic**

You are studying tropical cyclones in your Earth Science class and learning about the names given to hurricanes worldwide. The World Meteorological Organization (WMO) manages the 10 lists of agreed-upon names for the storms throughout the world. The National Hurricane Center developed the original lists of names in 1953. Create a presentation for your class with columns of hurricane names for the Atlantic and North Pacific oceans. Also include the history of naming hurricanes, including when men's names were added to the rotation, when names are retired, and how often the lists are rotated. Apply at least three objectives found at the beginning of this chapter to develop the presentation. Hide at least one slide. Be sure to check spelling.

### 2: Designing and Creating a Presentation about First Aid Kits

**Personal**

To be prepared for emergencies, it is a good idea to have a first aid kit in your home and vehicle. You can purchase a kit at a local store or you can assemble one yourself. The Red Cross (www.redcross.org) and the Ready America (www.ready.gov) Web sites provide lists of recommended items to include in a first aid kit. Visit these Web sites and use the information regarding basic first aid kit supplies to create a presentation to share with your family, urging them to buy their own kits or check their current kits. Create a title slide introducing the topic, and create text slides containing columns of supplies that should be included in a first aid kit. Create another slide reminding your family to check the kit contents' expiration dates and flashlight batteries. Also include a hyperlink to your local Red Cross chapter for details on taking a class, donating blood, and volunteering. Use at least three objectives found at the beginning of this chapter to develop the presentation. Use bullets related to medical or emergency themes. Be sure to check spelling.

### 3: Designing and Creating a Presentation about Sound Levels

**Professional**

You work in a noisy factory and are concerned about the sound levels and how they are affecting your hearing. More than nine million workers are subjected to loud noises on the job that can lead to hearing loss. Sound levels are measured in decibels (dB). According to the American Speech-Language-Hearing Association (ASHA), noises louder than 80 dB can damage the inner ear and the auditory nerve. Visit the ASHA (www.asha.org) and National Institute on Deafness and Other Communication Disorders (NIDCD) (www.nidcd/nih.org) Web sites and read the information regarding noise levels in the workplace and the relationship to noise-induced hearing loss (NIHL).

Develop a Microsoft Word outline regarding specific sounds and the decibel levels, prolonged exposure to loud noises, and hearing protection. Insert this outline into a PowerPoint presentation that you can share with your boss and your coworkers about working around hazardous noise. Include a table showing the decibel levels of various sounds. Also include information about how employees can benefit physiologically and psychologically from reduced noise levels in the workplace and how they can protect their hearing. Include hyperlinks to the ASHA, NIDCD, and the National Institute for Occupational Safety and Health (www.cdc.gov/niosh) Web sites. Include action buttons and bullet characters that have been changed to pictures or symbols. Be certain to check spelling.

# 7 | Creating a Self-Running Presentation Containing Animation

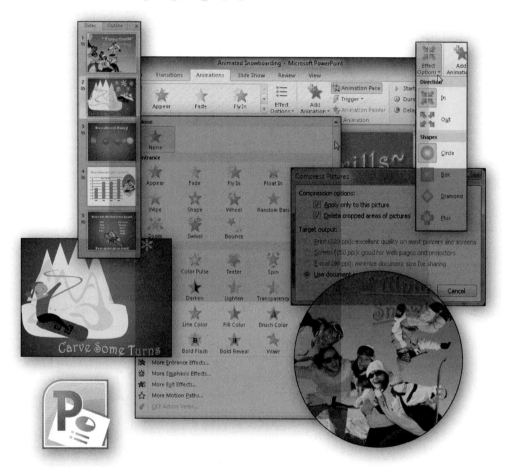

## Objectives

You will have mastered the material in this chapter when you can:

- Remove a picture background
- Crop and compress a picture
- Insert entrance, emphasis, and exit effects
- Add and adjust motion paths
- Reorder animation sequences
- Associate sounds with animations

- Control animation timing
- Animate SmartArt graphics and charts
- Insert and animate a text box
- Animate bulleted lists
- Rehearse timings
- Set slide show timings manually

# 7 | Creating a Self-Running Presentation Containing Animation

**BTW**

**Animation Enhancements**
Microsoft made many changes and enhancements to animation features in PowerPoint 2010. The Animation tab is reorganized and contains the Animation group to add effects to slide objects. The Timing group allows designers to change the order of elements and set the precise time when they appear on each slide. In addition, the transitions that appeared on the PowerPoint 2007 Animation tab are moved to their own tab.

## Introduction

One method used for disseminating information is a **kiosk**. This freestanding, self-service structure is equipped with computer hardware and software and is used to provide information or reference materials to the public. Some have a touch screen or keyboard that serves as an input device and allows users to select various options so they can browse or find specific information. Advanced kiosks allow customers to place orders, make payments, and access the Internet. Many kiosks have multimedia devices for playing sound and video clips.

Various elements on PowerPoint slides can have movement to direct the audience's attention to the point being made. For example, each paragraph in a bulleted list can fade or disappear after being displayed for a set period of time. Each SmartArt graphic component can appear in sequence. A picture can grow, shrink, bounce, or spin, depending upon its relationship to other slide content. PowerPoint's myriad animation effects allow you to use your creativity to design imaginative and distinctive presentations.

## Project — Presentation with Adjusted Pictures, Animated Content, and Slide Timings

**BTW**

**Animation Effect Icon Colors**
Animation effects allow you to control how objects enter, move on, and exit slides. Using a traffic signal analogy may help you remember the sequence of events. Green icons indicate when the animation effect starts on the slide. Yellow icons represent the object's motion; use them with caution so they do not distract from the message you are conveying to your audience. Red icons indicate when the object stops appearing on a slide.

Interest in the sport of snowboarding, which also is called boarding, has grown since its commercial start in the 1970s and its entry into the Olympics in 1998. Today, almost every North American ski resort allows snowboarders to perform their jumps and aerial feats. Downhill enthusiasts of all ages have experienced the sport, with the average age ranging between 18 and 24 years. Approximately 25 percent of the boarding population is women. The snowboarding project in this chapter (Figure 7–1) explores the sport and uses animation to give a feeling of the twists and turns the boarders experience while on the slopes. The title slide (Figure 7–1a) has animated title text and a snowboarder who performs a flip as she cruises down the mountain. The second slide (Figure 7–1b) shows a snowboarder clip that carves graceful turns during a gentle snowfall. The third slide (Figure 7–1c) uses animated SmartArt to explain how to find the correct snowboard length based on the boarder's height. The growth of the snowboarding industry is depicted in the animated chart on Slide 4 (Figure 7–1d). The last slide (Figure 7–1e) has two lists that describe the essential gear a snowboarder needs to have an enjoyable day on the slopes and an upward-rolling credit line to end the presentation.

**(a) Slide 1 (Title Slide with Animated WordArt and Picture)**

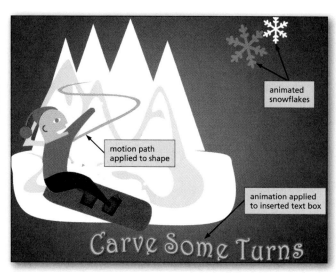

**(b) Slide 2 (Animated Clip with Motion Path and Sound)**

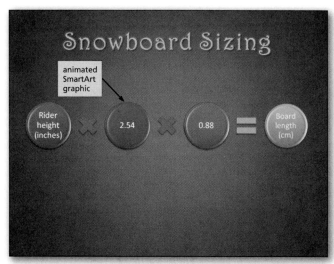

**(c) Slide 3 (Animated SmartArt)**

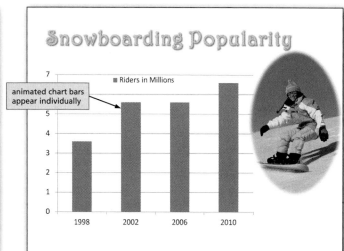

**(d) Slide 4 (Animated Chart)**

**(e) Slide 5 (Animated Bulleted List and Credits)**

**Figure 7–1**

**BTW**

**The Ribbon and Screen Resolution**
PowerPoint may change how the groups and buttons within the groups appear on the Ribbon, depending on the computer's screen resolution. Thus, your Ribbon may look different from the ones in this book if you are using a screen resolution other than 1024 × 768.

# Overview

As you read through this chapter, you will learn how to create the presentation shown in Figure 7 – 1 by performing these general tasks:

- Remove picture backgrounds.
- Crop and compress pictures.
- Add entrance, emphasis, and exit animations.
- Create custom animations.
- Animate text boxes, SmartArt, and charts.
- Change transition effect options.
- Set slide show timings.

**Plan Ahead**

---

**General Project Guidelines**

When creating a PowerPoint presentation, the actions you perform and the decisions you make will affect the appearance and characteristics of the finished document. As you create a presentation with illustrations, such as the project shown in Figure 7 – 1 on the previous page, you should follow these general guidelines:

1. **Use animation sparingly.** Prior to using an animation effect, think about why you need it and how it will affect your presentation. Do not use animation merely for the sake of using animation.

2. **Select colors for dimming text.** Paragraphs of text can change color after they display on the slide. This effect, called dimming, can be used effectively to emphasize important points and draw the audience's attention to another area of the slide. Select dimming colors that suit the purpose of the presentation.

3. **Use quotations judiciously.** At times, the words of noted world leaders, writers, and prominent entertainers can create interest in your presentation and inspire audiences. If you choose to integrate their quotations into your slide show, give credit to the source and keep the original wording.

4. **Give your audience sufficient time to view your slides.** On average, an audience member will spend only eight seconds viewing a basic slide with a simple graphic or a few words. They need much more time to view charts, graphs, and SmartArt graphics. When you are setting slide timings, keep this length of time in mind, particularly when the presentation is viewed at a kiosk without a speaker's physical presence.

When necessary, more specific details concerning the above guidelines are presented at appropriate points in the chapter. The chapter also will identify the actions performed and decisions made regarding these guidelines during the creation of the presentation shown in Figure 7 – 1.

---

## To Start PowerPoint, Open a Presentation, and Rename the Presentation

To begin this presentation, you will open a file located on the Data Files for Students. See the inside back cover of this book for instructions on downloading the Data Files for Students, or contact your instructor for more information about accessing the required files. If you are using a computer to step through the project in this chapter and you want your screens to match the figures in this book, you should change your screen's resolution to 1024 × 768.

The following steps start PowerPoint, open a file, and then save it with a new file name.

**1** Start PowerPoint. If necessary, maximize the PowerPoint window.

**2** Open the presentation, Snowboarding, located on the Data Files for Students.

**3** Save the presentation using the file name, Animated Snowboarding.

# Adjusting and Cropping a Picture

At times you may desire to emphasize one section of a picture and eliminate distracting background content. PowerPoint includes picture formatting tools that allow you to edit pictures. The **Remove Background** command isolates the foreground from the background, and the **Crop** command removes content along the top, bottom, left, or right edges. Once you format the picture to include only the desired content, you can **compress** the image to reduce the file size.

## To Remove a Background

The title slide in the Animated Snowboarding presentation has a picture of a snowboarder wearing tan and white clothes in the foreground. Snow is present in the background of this picture, and you want to eliminate it to direct the viewers' attention to the snowboarder. PowerPoint 2010's Background Removal feature makes it easy to eliminate extraneous aspects. When you click the Remove Background button, PowerPoint attempts to select the foreground of the picture and overlay a magenta marquee selection on this area. You then can adjust the marquee shape and size to contain all foreground picture components you want to keep. The following steps remove the background from the snowboarder picture.

- With the title slide displaying, double-click the snowboarder picture in the foreground to display the Picture Tools Format tab.

- Click the Remove Background button (Picture Tools Format tab | Adjust group) to display the Background Removal tab and a marquee selection area (Figure 7–2).

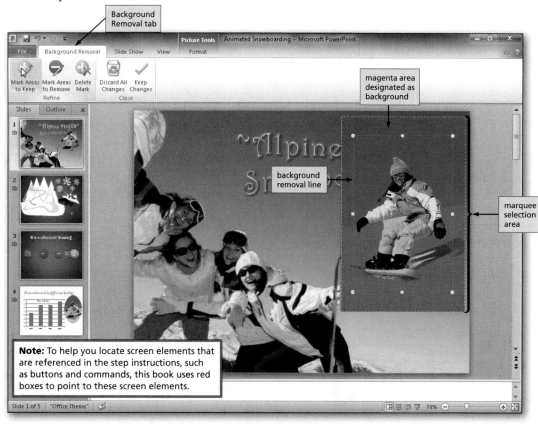

**Note:** To help you locate screen elements that are referenced in the step instructions, such as buttons and commands, this book uses red boxes to point to these screen elements.

**Figure 7–2**

**Q&A** How does PowerPoint determine the area to display within the marquee?

Microsoft Research software engineers developed the algorithms that determine the portions of the picture in the foreground.

**2**

• Click and drag the handles on the background removal lines so that the snowboarder and her snowboard are contained within the marquee (Figure 7–3).

**Q&A**

Why do some parts of the background, such as the area under her right arm and below her knees, still display?

The removal tool was not able to determine that those areas are part of the background. You will remove them in the next set of steps.

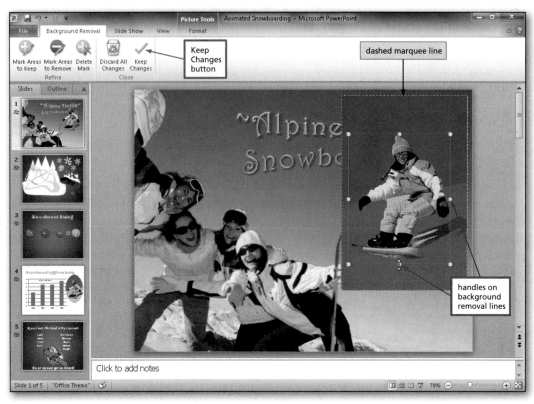

Figure 7–3

**3**

• Click the Keep Changes button (Background Removal tab | Close group) to discard the unwanted picture background (Figure 7–4).

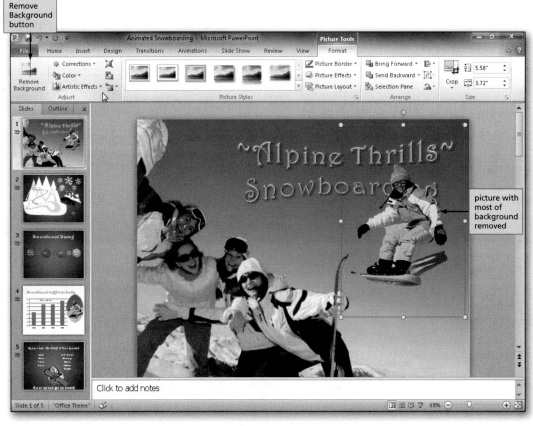

Figure 7–4

## To Refine Background Removal

In many cases, the Remove Background command discards all the undesired picture components. Occasionally, however, some pieces remain when the background is integrated closely with the foreground picture. In the title slide snowboarding picture, for example, the algorithms could not distinguish the snow and sky between the boarder's right arm and torso, below her knees, and directly behind her. Tools on the Background Removal tab allow you to mark specific areas to remove. The following steps remove the unwanted background areas from around the snowboarder.

- Click the Remove Background button again to display the Background Removal tab and the marquee selection area.

- Click the Mark Areas to Remove button (Background Removal tab | Refine group) and then position the mouse pointer in the white area above the snowboarder's right knee (Figure 7–5).

**Q&A** Why did my mouse pointer change shape?

The mouse pointer changed to a pencil to indicate you are about to draw on a precise area of the picture.

**Figure 7–5**

- Click and then drag the mouse pointer to the snowboarder's jacket to indicate the portion of the background to delete (Figure 7–6).

**Q&A** Why does a circle with a minus sign display on the dotted line?

That symbol indicates that you manually specified the deletion of a portion of the background.

**Q&A** Why does some of the background remain on my picture?

The location where you drew your line determines the area that PowerPoint deletes. You may need to make several passes to remove all of the unwanted background.

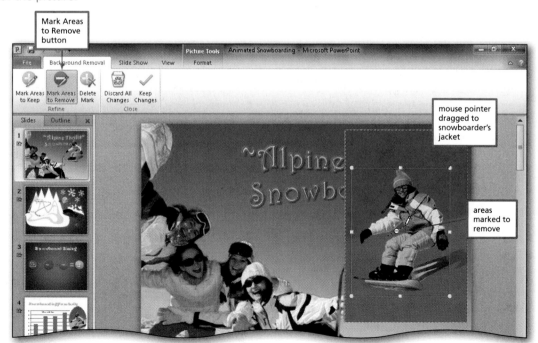

**Figure 7–6**

**3**

- Repeat Step 2 to delete the white area below her knees and the area to the right of her left boot (Figure 7–7).

**Q&A**
I mistakenly removed the snowboard when I tried to remove some of the background. How can I keep the snowboard in the picture?

You can mark the snowboard as an area to keep and then delete the background.

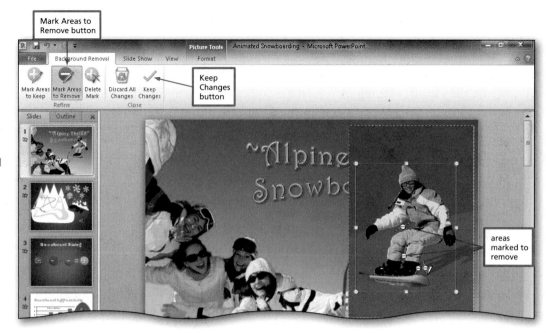

**Figure 7–7**

**Q&A**
If I marked an area with a line and now want to keep it, can I reverse my action?

Yes. Click the Delete Mark button (Background Removal tab | Refine area) and then click the line to remove it. You also can press CTRL+Z immediately after you draw the line.

**4**

- Click the Keep Changes button to review the results of your background refinements.

**Q&A**
The tail no longer is connected to the rest of the board, or my entire board is removed. Can I add this missing piece?

Yes. In the next step, you will instruct PowerPoint to keep any necessary area that was discarded.

**5**

- Click the Remove Background button again, click the Mark Areas to Keep button (Background Removal tab | Refine group), and then position the mouse pointer on the snow on the tail of the snowboard.

- Click and then drag the mouse pointer to the front of the snowboard (Figure 7–8).

**6**

- Click the Keep Changes button to review the results of your background refinement.

**Figure 7–8**

**Q&A**
If I want to see the original picture at a later time, can I display the components I deleted?

Yes. If you click the Discard All Changes button (Background Removal tab | Close area), all the deleted pieces will reappear.

## To Crop a Picture

The Remove Background command deleted the snow and sky components of the picture from your view, but they still remain in the picture. Because you will not need to display the background in this presentation, you can remove the unnecessary edges of the picture. When you crop a picture, you trim the vertical or horizontal sides so that the most important area of the picture is displayed. Any picture file type except animated GIF can be cropped. The following steps crop the title slide snowboarder picture.

- With the snowboarder picture still selected, click the Crop button (Picture Tools Format tab | Size group) to display the cropping handles on the picture.

- Position the mouse pointer over the center cropping handle on the right side of the picture (Figure 7–9).

**Q&A** Why did my mouse pointer change shape?

The mouse pointer changed to indicate you are about to crop a picture.

**Figure 7–9**

- Drag the center cropping handle inward so that the right edge of the marquee is beside the snowboarder's glove on her left hand.

- Drag the center cropping handles on the left, upper, and lower edges of the background removal lines inward to frame the picture (Figure 7–10).

**Q&A** Does cropping actually cut the picture's edges?

No. Although you cannot see the cropped edges, they exist until you save the file.

- Click an area of the slide other than the picture to crop the edges.

**Q&A** Can I change the crop lines?

If you have not saved the file, you can undo your crops by clicking the Undo button on the Quick Access Toolbar, clicking the Reset Picture button (Picture Tools Format tab | Adjust group), or pressing CTRL+Z.

**Figure 7–10**

| Other Ways |
|---|
| 1. Enter dimensions in Left, Right, Top, and Bottom boxes in Crop position    area (Format Picture dialog box \| Crop tab) |

## To Compress a Picture

Pictures inserted into slides greatly increase the total PowerPoint file size. PowerPoint automatically compresses picture files inserted into slides by eliminating details, generally with no visible loss of quality. You can increase the compression and, in turn, decrease the file size if you instruct PowerPoint to compress a picture you have cropped so you can save space on a storage medium such as a hard disk, USB flash drive, or optical disk. Although these storage devices generally have a large storage capacity, you might want to reduce the file size for e-mailing the file or reducing the download time from an FTP or Web site.

The snowboard picture on the title slide picture is cropped and displays only the female snowboarder. You will not need any of the invisible portions of the picture, so you can delete them permanently and reduce the picture file size. The following steps compress the title slide snowboarder picture.

**1**

- Double-click the snowboarder picture to display the Picture Tools Format tab. Click the Compress Pictures button (Picture Tools Format tab | Adjust group) to display the Compress Pictures dialog box (Figure 7–11).

**Q&A** Should I apply an artistic effect prior to or after compressing a picture?

Compress a picture and then apply the artistic effect.

**2**

- Click the OK button (Compress Pictures dialog box) to delete the cropped portions of this picture and compress the image.

**Q&A** Can I undo the compression?

Yes, as long as you have not closed the file.

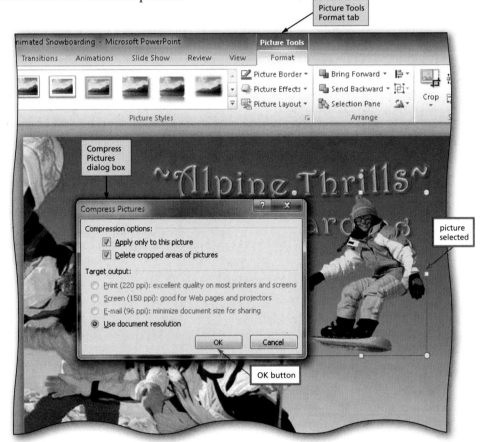

Figure 7–11

## Animating Slide Content

**Animation** includes special visual and sound effects applied to text or other content. You already are familiar with one form of animation: transitions between slides. To add visual interest and clarity to a presentation, you can animate various parts of an individual slide, including clips, shapes, text, and other slide elements. For example, each paragraph on the slide can spin as it is displayed. Individual letters and shapes also can spin or move in a wide variety of motions. PowerPoint has a variety of built-in animations that will fade, wipe, or fly-in text and graphics.

# Custom Animations

You can create your own **custom animations** to meet your unique needs. Custom animation effects are grouped in categories: entrance, exit, emphasis, and motion paths. **Entrance** effects, as the name implies, determine how slide elements first appear on a slide. **Exit** animations work in the opposite manner as entrance effects: They remove slide elements. **Emphasis** effects modify text and objects displayed on the screen. For example, letters may darken or increase in font size. The entrance, exit, and emphasis animations are grouped into categories: Basic, Subtle, Moderate, and Exciting. You can set the animation speed to Very Fast, Fast, Medium, Slow, or Very Slow.

The Slide 1 background picture shows skiing enthusiasts posing on a ski slope. When the presentation begins, the audience will view these skiers and then see a snowboarder enter from the upper-left corner, slide down the slope, perform an aerial trick as she reaches the center of the slide, and then continue down the slope toward the lower-right corner. To create this animation on the slide, you will use entrance, emphasis, and exit effects.

If you need to move objects on a slide once they are displayed, you can define a **motion path**. This predefined movement determines where an object will be displayed and then travel. Motion paths are grouped into the Basic, Lines & Curves, and Special categories. You can draw a **custom path** if none of the predefined paths meets your needs.

**Plan Ahead**

**Use animation sparingly.**
PowerPoint audience members usually take notice the first time an animation is displayed on the screen. When the same animation effect is applied throughout a presentation, the viewers generally become desensitized to the effect unless it is highly unusual or annoying. Resist the urge to use animation effects simply because PowerPoint provides the tools to do so. You have options to decide how text or a slide element enters and exits a slide and how it is displayed once it is present on the slide; your goal, however, is to use these options wisely. Audiences soon tire of a presentation riddled with animations, causing them to quickly lose their impact.

## To Animate a Picture Using an Entrance Effect

The snowboarder you modified will not appear on Slide 1 when you begin the presentation. Instead, she will enter the slide from the uphill part of the slope, which is in the upper-left corner of the slide, to give the appearance she is snowboarding down the mountain. She will then continue downhill until she reaches the center of the slide. Entrance effects are colored green in the Animation gallery. The following steps apply an entrance effect to the snowboarder picture.

- With Slide 1 displaying, move the snowboarder picture to the center of the slide, as shown in Figure 7–12.

 **Why am I moving the picture to this location?**

This area of the slide is where you want the picture to stop moving after she enters the slide in the upper-left corner.

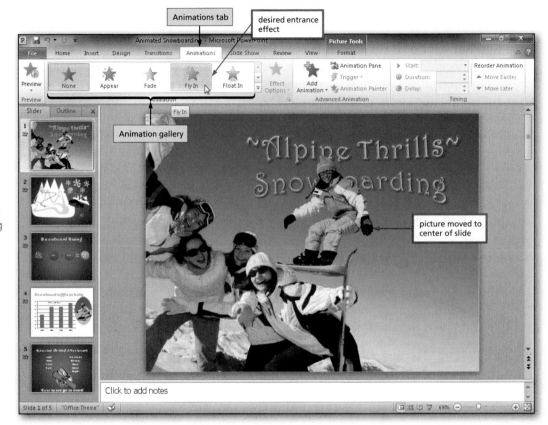

**Figure 7–12**

- Click the Animations tab on the Ribbon and then point to the Fly In animation in the Animation gallery (Animation group) to display a live preview of this animation (Figure 7–12).

### Experiment

- Point to three other animations shown in the Animation gallery and watch the snowboarder enter the slide.

 Are more entrance animations available?

Yes. Click the More button in the Animation gallery to see additional animations. You can select one of the 13 entrance animations that are displayed, or you can click the More Entrance Effects command to expand the selection.

- Click Fly In to apply this entrance animation to the snowboarder picture.

Why does the number 1 appear in a box on the left side of the picture?

The 1 is a sequence number and indicates Fly In is the first animation that will appear on the slide when you click the mouse.

## To Change Animation Direction

By default, the picture appears on the slide by entering from the bottom edge. You can modify this direction and specify that it enters from another side or from a corner. The following steps change the snowboard picture entrance animation direction to the upper-left corner.

**1**

● Click the Effect Options button (Animations tab | Animation group) to display the Direction gallery (Figure 7–13).

**Q&A** Why does a gold box appear around the From Bottom arrow?

From Bottom is the default entrance direction applied to the animation.

● Point to From Top-Left in the Direction gallery to display a live preview of this animation effect.

**Experiment**

● Point to various arrows in the Direction gallery and watch the snowboarder enter the slide from different sides and corners.

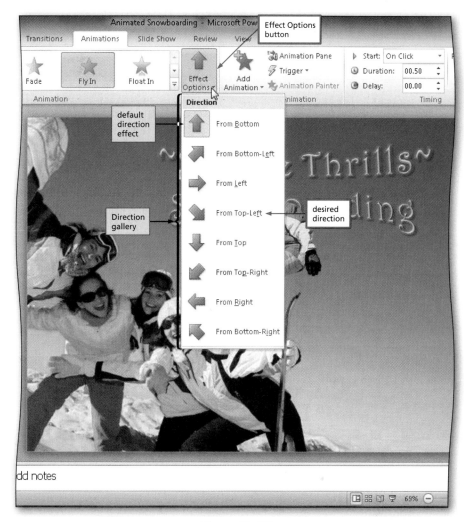

**Figure 7–13**

**2**

● Click the From Top-Left arrow to apply this direction to the entrance animation.

**Q&A** Can I change this entrance effect?

Yes. Repeat Step 1 to select another direction.

## To Animate a Picture Using an Emphasis Effect

The snowboarder will enter the slide from the upper-left corner and stop in the center of the slide. You then want her to perform an acrobatic trick. PowerPoint provides several effects that you can apply to a picture once it appears on a slide. These movements are categorized as emphasis effects, and they are colored yellow in the Animation gallery. You already have applied an entrance effect to the snowboarder picture, so you want to add another animation to this picture. The following steps apply an emphasis effect to the snowboarder picture after the entrance effect.

- With the snowboarder picture still selected, click the Add Animation button (Animations tab | Advanced Animation group) to expand the Animation gallery.

- Point to Spin in the Emphasis area to display a live preview of this effect (Figure 7–14).

**Experiment**

- Point to various effects in the Emphasis area and watch the snowboarder.

**Q&A** Are more emphasis effects available in addition to those shown in the Animation gallery?

Yes. To see additional emphasis effects, click More Emphasis Effects in the lower portion of the Animation gallery. The effects are arranged in the Basic, Subtle, Moderate, and Exciting categories.

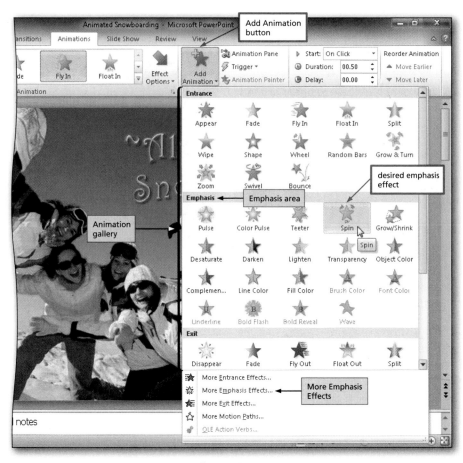

**Figure 7–14**

- Click Spin to apply this emphasis effect to the snowboarder picture.

**Q&A** Do I need to use both an entrance and an emphasis effect, or can I use only an emphasis effect?

You can use one or the other effect, or both effects.

**Q&A** Why does the number 2 appear in a box below the number 1 on the left side of the picture?

The 2 in the numbered tag indicates a second animation is applied in the animation sequence.

## To Animate a Picture Using an Exit Effect

The animated snowboarder picture will enter the slide from the upper-left corner, stop in the center of the slide, and then perform a spin trick. She then will continue down the slope and snowboard off the slide in the lower-right corner. To continue this animation sequence, you first need to apply an exit effect. As with the entrance and emphasis effects, PowerPoint provides a wide variety of effects that you can apply to remove a picture from a slide. These exit effects are colored red in the Animation gallery. You already have applied the Fly In entrance effect, so the Fly Out exit effect would give continuity to the animation sequence. The following steps add this exit effect to the snowboarder picture after the emphasis effect.

**1**

- With the snowboarder picture still selected, click the Add Animation button again to expand the Animation gallery.

- Point to Fly Out in the Exit area to display a live preview of this effect (Figure 7–15).

 **Experiment**

- Point to various effects in the Exit area and watch the snowboarder. You will not be able to view all the effects because they are hidden by the Animation gallery, but you can move the snowboarder clip to the left side of the slide to view the effects and then move her back to the middle of the slide.

**Q&A** Are more exit effects available in addition to those shown in the Animation gallery?

Yes. To see additional exit effects, click More Exit Effects in the lower portion of the Animation gallery. The effects are arranged in the Basic, Subtle, Moderate, and Exciting categories.

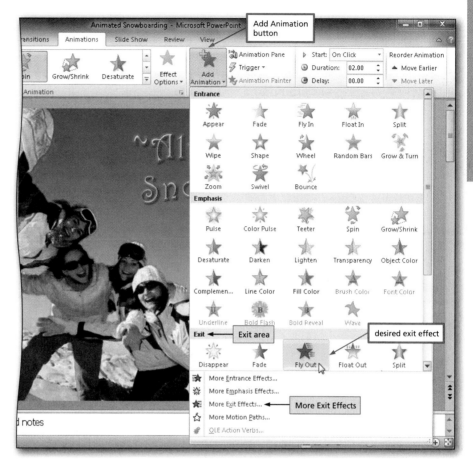

**Figure 7–15**

**2**

- Click Fly Out to add this exit effect to the sequence of snowboarder picture animations (Figure 7–16).

**Q&A** How can I tell that this exit effect has been applied?

The Fly Out effect is displayed in the Animation gallery (Animations tab | Animation group), and the number 3 is displayed to the left of the snowboarder picture.

**Figure 7–16**

## To Change Exit Animation Direction

The default direction for a picture to exit a slide is To Bottom. In this presentation, you want the snowboarder to exit in the lower-right corner to give the impression she is continuing down the slope. The following steps change the exit animation direction from To Bottom to To Bottom-Right.

**1** Click the Effect Options button (Animations tab | Animation group) to display the Direction gallery.

**2** Click the To Bottom-Right arrow to apply this direction to the exit animation effect.

## To Preview an Animation Sequence

Although you have not completed developing the presentation, you should view the animation you have added. By default, the entrance, emphasis, and exit animations will be displayed when you run the presentation and click the mouse. The following step runs the presentation and displays the three animations.

- Click the Preview button (Animations tab | Preview group) to view all the Slide 1 animations (Figure 7–17).

**Q&A**

Why does a red square appear in the middle of the circle on the Preview button when I click that button?

The red square indicates the animation sequence is in progress. Ordinarily, a green arrow is displayed in the circle.

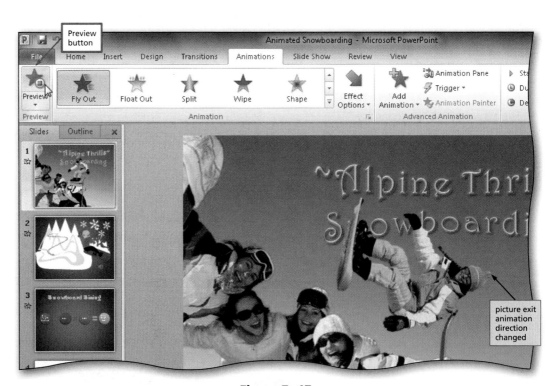

**Figure 7–17**

## To Modify Entrance Animation Timing

The three animation effects are displayed quickly. To create a dramatic effect, you can change the timing so that the background picture displays and then, a few seconds later, the snowboarder starts to glide down the mountain slowly. The default setting is to start each animation with a mouse click, but you can change this setting so that the entrance effect is delayed until a specified number of seconds has passed. The following steps modify the start, delay, and duration settings for the entrance animation.

**1**

- Click the 1 numbered tag on the left side of the snowboarder picture and then click the Start Animation Timing button arrow (Animations tab | Timing group) to display the Start menu (Figure 7–18).

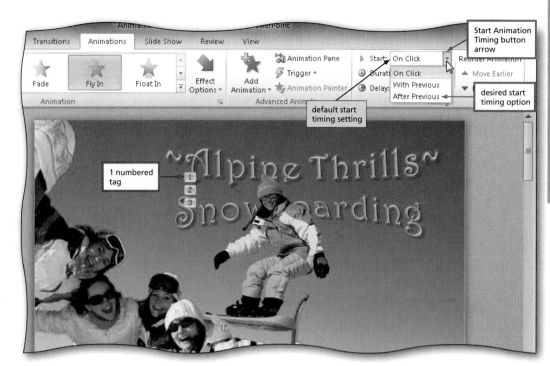

Figure 7–18

**2**

- Click After Previous to change the start timing setting.

**Q&A** Why did the numbered tags change from 1, 2, 3 to 0, 1, 2?

The first animation now occurs automatically without a mouse click. The first and second mouse clicks now will apply the emphasis and exit animations.

**Q&A** What is the difference between the With Previous and After Previous settings?

The With Previous setting starts the effect simultaneously with any prior animation; the After Previous setting starts the animation after a prior animation has ended. If the prior animation is fast or a short duration, it may be difficult for a viewer to discern the difference between these two settings.

**3**

- Click the Animation Duration up arrow (Animations tab | Timing group) several times to increase the time from 00.50 second to 05.00 seconds (Figure 7–19).

- Click the Preview button to view the animations.

**Q&A** What is the difference between the duration time and the delay time?

The duration time is the length of time in which the animation occurs; the delay time is the length of time that passes before the animation begins.

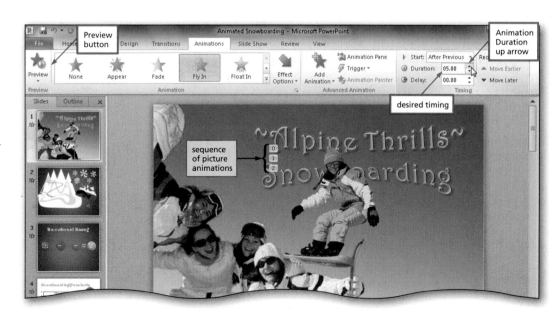

Figure 7–19

**Q&A** Can I type the speed in the Duration text box instead of clicking the arrow to adjust the speed?

Yes. Typing the numbers allows you to set a precise timing.

**4**

- Click the Animation Delay up arrow (Animations tab | Timing group) several times to increase the time from 00.00 seconds to 04.00 seconds (Figure 7–20).

- Click the Preview button to view the animations.

**Q&A** Can I adjust the delay time I just set?

Yes. Click the Animation Delay up or down arrows and run the slide show to display Slide 1 until you find the time that best fits your presentation.

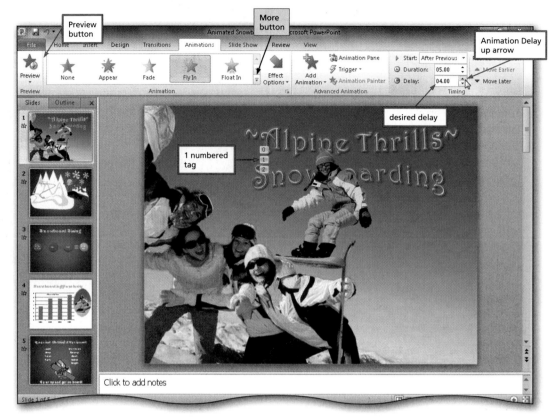

**Figure 7–20**

**BTW**

**Q&As**
For a complete list of the Q&As found in many of the step-by-step sequences in this book, visit the PowerPoint 2010 Q&A Web page (scsite.com/ppt2010/qa).

## To Modify Emphasis and Exit Timings

Now that the entrance animation settings have been modified, you then can change the emphasis and exit effects for the snowboarder picture. The emphasis effect can occur once the entrance effect has concluded, and then the exit effect can commence. With gravity's effect, the snowboarder should be able to glide more quickly down the lower part of the mountain, so you will shorten the duration of her exit effect compared with the duration of the entrance effect. The animation sequence should flow without stopping, so you will not change the default delay timing of 00.00 seconds. The following steps modify the start and duration settings for the emphasis and exit animations.

**1** Click the 1 sequence number, which represents the emphasis effect, on the left side of the snowboarder picture, click the Start Animation Timing button arrow (Animations tab | Timing group) to display the Start menu and then click After Previous to change the start timing option setting.

**2** Click the Animation Duration up arrow (Animations tab | Timing group) several times to increase the time to 03.00 seconds.

**3** Click the 1 sequence number, which now represents the exit effect, click the Start Animation Timing button arrow, and then click After Previous.

**4** Click the Animation Duration up arrow several times to increase the time to 04.00 seconds.

**5** Preview the Slide 1 animation.

## To Animate Title Text Placeholder Paragraphs

The snowboarder picture on Slide 1 has one entrance, one emphasis, and one exit animation, and you can add similar animations to the two paragraphs in the Slide 1 title text placeholder. For a special effect, you can add several emphasis animations to one slide element. The following steps add one entrance and two emphasis animations to the title text paragraphs.

- Double-click the Slide 1 title text placeholder border so that it displays as a solid line.

- Click the More button (shown in Figure 7–20) in the Animation gallery (Animations tab | Animation group) to expand the Animation gallery (Figure 7–21).

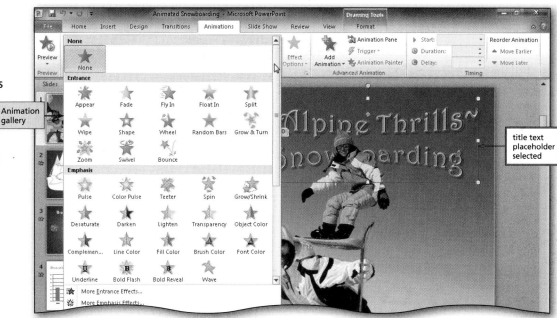

**Figure 7–21**

- Point to the Zoom entrance effect in the Animation gallery to display a live preview of this effect.

**Experiment**

- Point to various effects in the Entrance area and watch the title text. You will not be able to view all the effects because they are hidden by the Animation gallery, but you can move the title text placeholder to the left side of the slide to view the effects and then move the placeholder back to its original position.

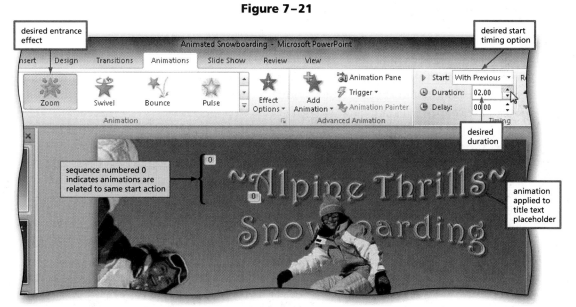

**Figure 7–22**

- Click the Zoom entrance effect in the Animation gallery to add this animation.

- Change the start timing option to With Previous.

- Change the duration time to 02.00 seconds (Figure 7–22).

**Q&A**

Do I need to change the delay time?

No. The title text placeholder can start appearing on the slide when the snowboarder exit effect is beginning.

**3**

- Click the Add Animation button and then click the Font Color emphasis animation effect.

- Change the start timing option to After Previous.

- Click the Add Animation button and then click the Underline emphasis animation effect.

- Change the start timing option to With Previous (Figure 7–23).

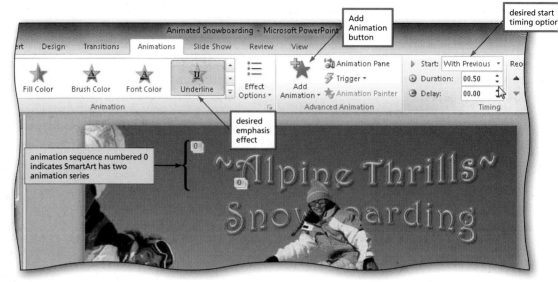

Figure 7–23

**Q&A**

Why is a second set of animation numbered tags starting with 0 displaying on the left side of the title text placeholder?

They represent the three animations associated with the paragraphs in that placeholder.

## To Change Animation Order

Two title slide elements have animations: the snowboarder picture and the title text placeholder. PowerPoint applies the animations in the order you created them, so on this slide the snowboarder picture animations will appear first and then the title text placeholder animation will follow. You can reorder animation elements if you decide one set of animation should appear before another set, and you also can reorder individual animation elements within an animation group. In this presentation, you decide to display the title text placeholder animation first, and then you decide that the Underline emphasis effect should appear before the Font Color emphasis effect. The following steps reorder the two animation groups on the slide and then reorder the Font Color and Underline emphasis effects.

- Double-click the Slide 1 title text placeholder border so that it displays as a solid line. Click the far-left orange sequence order tag to display the Animation Pane task pane (Figure 7–24).

Figure 7–24

**Q&A** Why do blue lines appear around the three Rectangle effects?

The lines correspond to the three animation effects that you applied to the title text placeholder. The green star indicates the entrance effect, the A with the multicolor underline indicates the Font Color emphasis effect, and the black B indicates the Underline emphasis effect.

**Q&A** Why do I see a different number after the Rectangle label?

PowerPoint numbers slide elements consecutively, so you may see a different number if you have added and deleted pictures, text, and other graphics. You will rename these labels in a later set of steps.

**2**

- Click the Move Earlier button (Animations tab | Timing group) three times to move the three Rectangle animations above the Picture animations (Figure 7–25).

- Click the Play button (Animation Pane task pane) to see the reordered animation.

**Q&A** Can I click the Re-Order up button at the bottom of the Animation Pane task pane instead of the Move Earlier button on the Ribbon?

Yes. Either button will change the animation order.

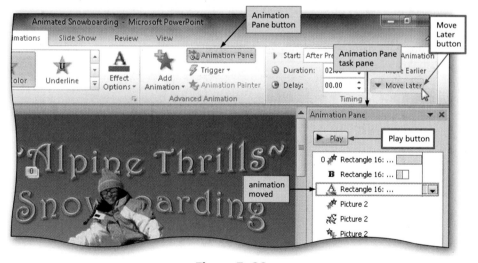

Figure 7–25

**3**

- In the Animation Pane task pane, click the second Rectangle label representing the Font Color animation to select it and then click the Move Later button (Animations tab | Timing group) to move this animation below the Rectangle label representing the Underline animation (Figure 7–26).

- Click the Play button (Animation Pane task pane) to see the reordered text placeholder animation.

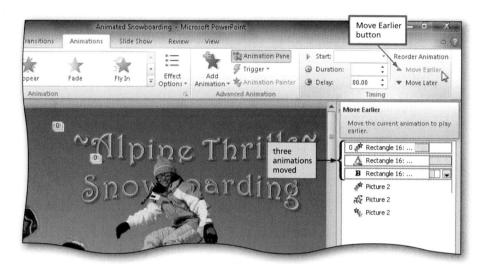

Figure 7–26

**Q&A** Can I view the Animation Pane task pane at any time when I am adding and adjusting animation effects?

Yes. Click the Animation Pane button (Animations tab | Advanced Animation group) to display the Animation Pane task pane.

## To Rename Slide Objects

The two animated title slide elements are listed in the Animation Pane task pane as Rectangle and Picture. You can give these objects meaningful names so that you can identify them in the animation sequence. The following steps rename the animated Slide 1 objects.

- Display the Home tab and then click Select (Home tab | Editing group) to display the Select menu (Figure 7–27).

**Figure 7–27**

- Click Selection Pane in the Select menu to display the Selection and Visibility task pane.

- Click the Picture label in the Shapes on this Slide area and then click the label again to place the insertion point in the text box (Figure 7–28).

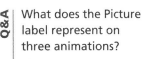 What does the Picture label represent on three animations?

The green entry, yellow emphasis, and red exit animations are applied to the snowboarder picture.

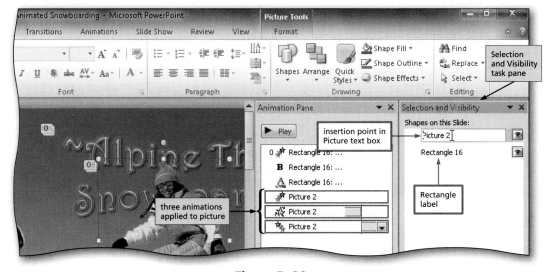

**Figure 7–28**

- Delete the text and then type **Snowboarder** in the Picture text box.

- Click the Rectangle label in the Shapes on this Slide area, click the label again, delete the text, and then type **Title Text** in the Rectangle text box (Figure 7–29).

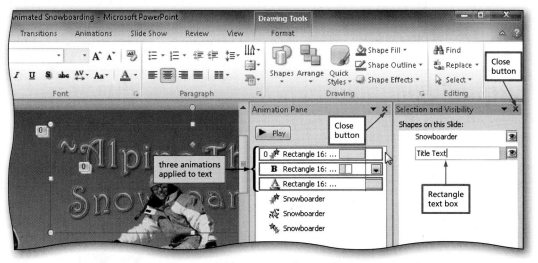

**Figure 7–29**

**Q&A** What does the Rectangle label represent on three animations?

The green entry and two emphasis animations are applied to the title text placeholder.

**4**

- Click the Close button on the Selection and Visibility task pane.

- Click the Close button on the Animation Pane task pane.

**Break Point:** If you wish to take a break, this is a good place to do so. Be sure to save the Animated Snowboarding file again and then you can quit PowerPoint. To resume at a later time, start PowerPoint, open the file called Animated Snowboarding, and continue following the steps from this location forward.

## To Insert a Text Box and Format Text

Slide 2 contains three elements that you will animate. First, you will add a text box, format and animate the text, and add a motion path and sound. Next, you will add an entrance effect and custom motion path to the snowboarder clip. Finally, you will animate one snowflake and copy the animation to the other snowflakes using the Animation Painter.

You can add the parts of the animation in any order and then change the sequence. You can save time, however, if you develop the animation using the sequence in which the elements will display on the slide. The first sequence will be a text box in the lower-left corner of the slide. The following steps add a text box to Slide 2.

 **1**

- Display Slide 2 and then display the Insert tab.

- Click the Text Box button (Insert tab | Text group) and then position the mouse pointer in the blue area in the lower-left corner of the slide (Figure 7–30).

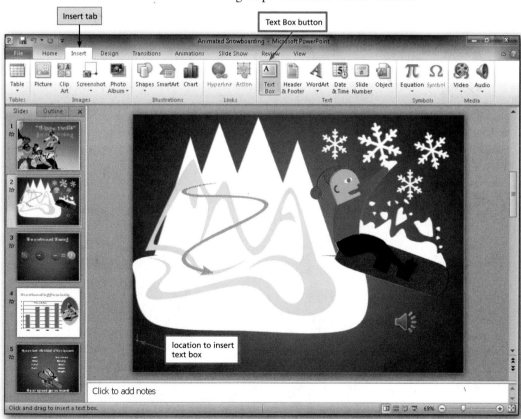

**Figure 7–30**

**2**

• Click the slide and then type **Carve Some Turns** in the text box (Figure 7–31).

Figure 7–31

**3**

• Display Slide 1, position the mouse pointer in the second line of the title text placeholder, and then double-click the Format Painter button (Home tab | Clipboard group) (Figure 7–32).

Figure 7–32

**4**

- Display Slide 2 and then triple-click the inserted text box to apply the Slide 1 title text format to the text in the text box.

- Press the ESC key to turn off the Format Painter feature.

- Display the Drawing Tools Format tab, click the Text Effects button (Drawing Tools Format tab | WordArt Styles group), and then apply the Wave 1 WordArt text effect (first effect in fifth row of the Warp area

**Figure 7–33**

of the Transform gallery) to the words in the text box (Figure 7–33). If necessary, move the text box so that all the letters display on the slide.

## To Animate a Text Box Using an Entrance Effect

Text boxes can have the same animation effects applied to pictures and placeholders. Entrance, emphasis, and exit animations can add interest to slides, and the default timings can be changed to synchronize with the slide content. The 13 effects shown in the Entrance area of the Animation gallery are some of the more popular choices; PowerPoint provides many more effects that are divided into the Basic, Subtle, Moderate, and Exciting categories. The following steps add an entrance effect to the text box.

**1**

- If necessary, click the text box to select it and then display the Animations tab.

- Click the More button in the Animation gallery (Animations tab | Animation group) to expand the Animation gallery (Figure 7–34).

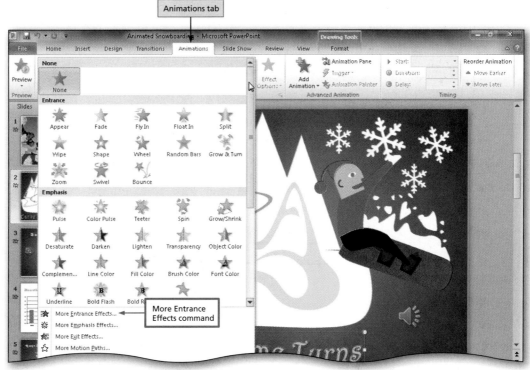

**Figure 7–34**

- Click More Entrance Effects in the Animation gallery to display the Change Entrance Effect dialog box (Figure 7–35).

🔍 **Experiment**

- Click some of the entrance effects in the various areas and watch the effect preview in the text box on Slide 2.

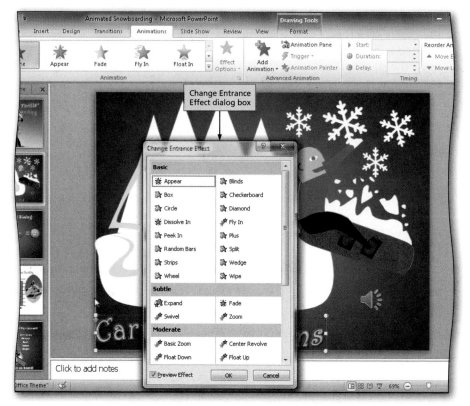

**Figure 7–35**

**Q&A** Can I move the dialog box so that I can see the effect preview?
Yes. Drag the dialog box title bar so that the dialog box does not cover the text box.

❸

- Scroll down and then click Flip in the Exciting area (Figure 7–36).

**Q&A** Why do I see a preview of the effects when I click their names?
The Preview Effect box is selected. If you do not want to see previews, click the box to deselect it.

**Figure 7–36**

**4**

- Click the OK button to apply the Flip entrance effect to the text.

- Change the start timing option to With Previous.

- Change the duration to 02.00 seconds (Figure 7–37).

**Q&A** Can I remove an animation?

Yes. Click None (Animations tab | Animation group). You may need to click the More button to see None.

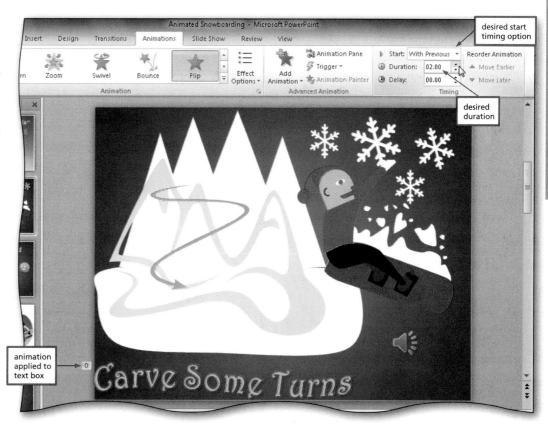

**Figure 7–37**

## To Animate a Text Box by Applying a Motion Path

One of the more effective methods of animating slide objects is to use a motion path to predetermine the route the object will follow. In your presentation, the text box will move from the left side of the slide to the right side in a curving motion that simulates a snowboarder's sideslip ride across the slope. The following steps apply a motion path to the Slide 2 text box.

**1**

- Click the Add Animation button (Animations tab | Advanced Animation group) to expand the Animation gallery.

- Scroll down until the Motion Paths area is visible (Figure 7–38).

**Experiment**

- Point to some of the motion paths and watch the animation preview in the text box.

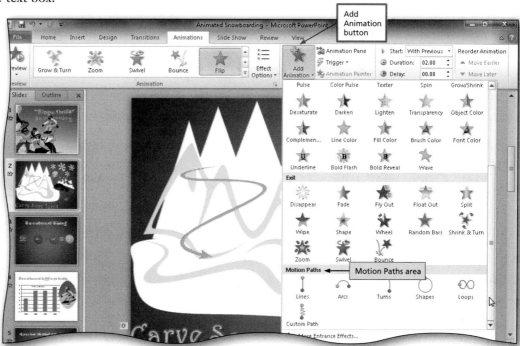

**Figure 7–38**

**2**

- Click the Arcs motion path to apply the animation to the text box.

- Change the start timing option to After Previous.

- Change the duration to 04.00 seconds (Figure 7–39).

**Figure 7–39**

**Q&A**

Are more motion paths available in addition to those shown in the Animation gallery?

Yes. To see additional motion paths, click More Motion Paths in the lower portion of the Animation gallery. The motion paths are arranged in the Basic, Lines & Curves, and Special categories.

## To Adjust a Motion Path

The Arcs motion path moves the text box in the correct directions, but the path can be extended to move across the entire width of the slide. The green triangle in the middle of the word, Some, indicates the starting point, and the red triangle in the middle of the word, Turns, indicates the stopping point. For the maximum animation effect on the slide, you would like to move the starting point toward the left edge and the stopping point toward the right edge. The following steps move the starting and stopping points on the Slide 2 text box and then reverse the direction of the arc.

**1**

• With the motion path selected in the text box, click the red stopping point and position the cursor over the upper-right sizing handle so that your cursor is displayed as a two-headed arrow.

• Drag the red stopping point to the location shown in Figure 7–40.

My entire motion path moved. How can I move only the red stopping point arrow?

Be certain your cursor is a two-headed arrow and not a four-headed arrow.

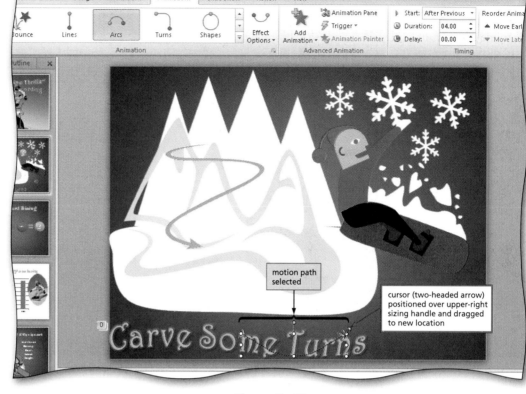

Figure 7–40

**2**

• Drag the green starting point to the location shown in Figure 7–41.

• Drag the upper-center sizing handle to the location shown in Figure 7–41.

• Preview the custom animation (Figure 7–41).

My animation is not exactly like the path shown in Figure 7–41. Can I change the path?

Yes. Continue adjusting the starting and stopping points and playing the animation until you are satisfied with the effect.

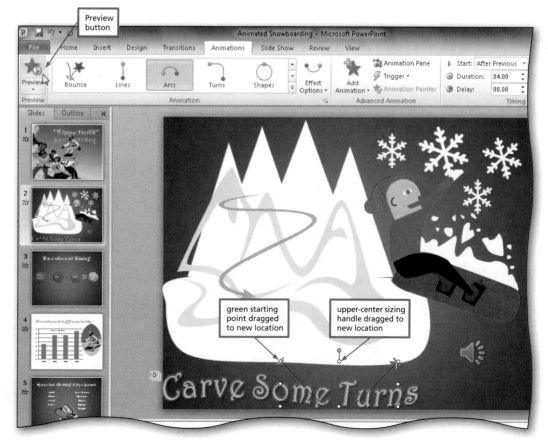

Figure 7–41

- Click the Effect Options button (Animations tab | Animation group) to display the Effect Options gallery (Figure 7–42).

- Click Up in the Direction area to reverse the direction from Down to Up.

- Preview the custom animation.

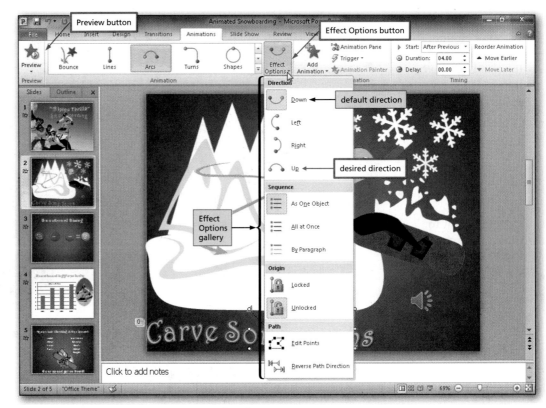

**Figure 7–42**

## To Associate a Sound with an Animation

Sounds can enhance a presentation if used properly, and they can be linked to other animations on the slide. Slide 2 already has the inserted sound of a snowboarder carving turns. The following step associates a sound with the text box on Slide 2.

- Click the sound icon on Slide 2 and then click Play animation (Animations tab | Animation group).

- Change the start timing option to With Previous (Figure 7–43).

**Q&A** What does the duration Auto setting control?

The sound will play automatically and will repeat as long as the text box is animated.

**Figure 7–43**

## To Draw a Custom Motion Path

Although PowerPoint supplies a wide variety of motion paths, at times they may not fit the precise animations your presentation requires. In that situation, you can draw a custom path that specifies the unique movement your slide element should make. Slide 2 has a clip of a mountain and another clip of a snowboarder. The mountain has an orange curvy line running down the face of the slope, and you can animate the snowboarder to follow this line. No preset motion path presents the exact motion you want to display, so you will draw your own custom path.

Drawing a custom path requires some practice and patience. You click the mouse to begin drawing the line. If you want the line to change direction, such as to curve, you click again. When you have completed drawing the path, you double-click to end the line. The following steps draw a custom motion path.

**1**

- Select the snowboarder clip, apply the Fade entrance effect, and then change the start timing option to After Previous.

- Click the Add Animation button and then scroll down until the entire Motion Paths area is visible (Figure 7–44).

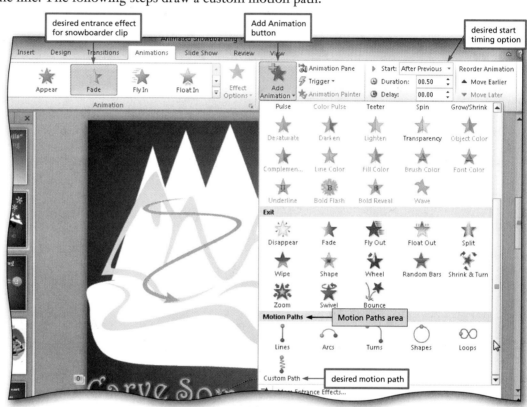

**Figure 7–44**

**2**

- Click Custom Path in the Motion Paths gallery to add this animation.

- Click the Effect Options button (Animations tab | Animation group) to display the Type gallery (Figure 7–45).

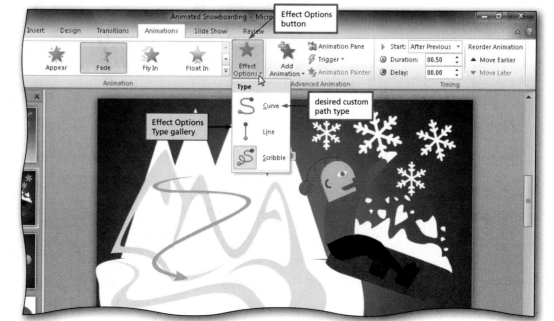

**Figure 7–45**

**3**

- Click Curve in the Type gallery and then position the mouse pointer at the beginning of the orange line at the top of the mountain.

**Q&A** Why did I need to change the option from Scribble to Curve?

Your custom motion path will follow the orange curves on the mountain clip, and the Curve type will create rounded edges to connect the lines you draw. The Scribble option would draw only straight lines, so the snowboarder would not carve smooth turns as he comes downhill.

- Click the mouse to indicate where the curve will start and then move the mouse pointer to the location shown in Figure 7–46, which is where the curve will change direction.

**Figure 7–46**

**4**

- Click the mouse, position the mouse pointer at the top of the far-right orange curve, and then click to indicate the end of this direction of travel.

- Position the mouse pointer at the top of the lower-left curve and then click to indicate the end of this curve (Figure 7–47).

**Figure 7–47**

**5**

- Position the mouse pointer at the tip of the orange arrowhead and then double-click to indicate the end of the motion path and preview the animation (Figure 7–48).

- Change the start timing option to With Previous and the duration setting to 05.00 seconds.

**Q&A** If my curve is not correct, can I delete it?

Yes. Select the motion path, press the DELETE key, and then repeat the previous steps.

**Figure 7–48**

## To Use the Animation Painter to Animate a Clip

At times, you may desire to apply the same animation effects to several objects on a slide. On Slide 2, for example, you want to animate the four snowflakes with identical entrance, emphasis, and exit effects. As with the Format Painter that is used to duplicate font and paragraph attributes, the Animation Painter copies animation effects. Using the Animation Painter can save time by duplicating numerous animations quickly and consistently. The following steps animate one snowflake and then use the Animation Painter to copy these effects to three other snowflakes.

**1**

- Select the snowflake in the upper-right corner of the slide and then apply the Fly In entrance effect.

- Click the Effect Options button and then change the direction to From Top.

- Change the start timing option to With Previous and the duration to 06.00 seconds (Figure 7–49).

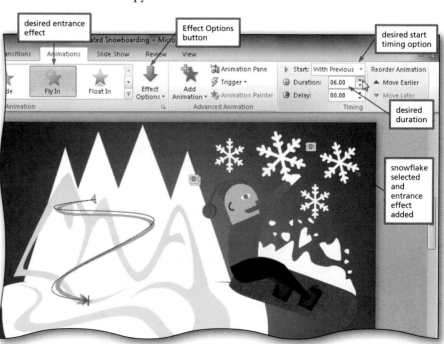

**Figure 7–49**

**2**

• With the snowflake still selected, add the Teeter emphasis effect, change the start timing option to After Previous, and then change the duration to 01.50 seconds (Figure 7–50).

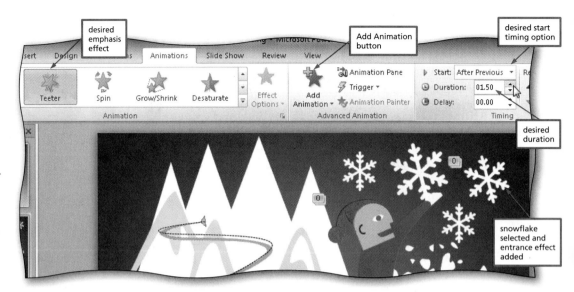

**Figure 7–50**

**3**

• Add the Fade exit effect, change the start timing option to After Previous, and then change the duration to 03.00 seconds (Figure 7–51).

Can I copy the animation to an object on another slide?

Yes. Once you establish the desired animation effects, you can copy them to any object that can be animated on any slide.

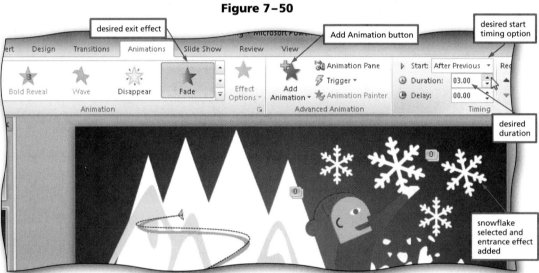

**Figure 7–51**

**4**

• Click the upper-right snowflake with the animation effects to select it and then click the Animation Painter button (Animations tab | Advanced Animation group).

• Position the mouse pointer over the upper-left snowflake (Figure 7–52).

Why did my mouse pointer change shape?

The mouse pointer changed shape by displaying a paintbrush to indicate that the Animation Painter function is active.

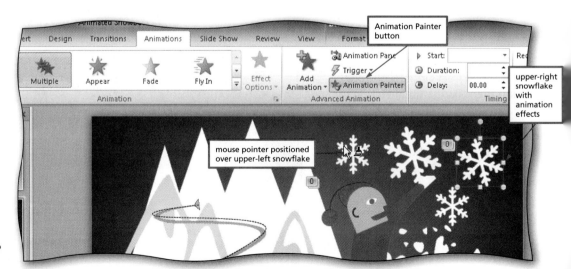

**Figure 7–52**

**5**

- Click the upper-left snowflake to apply the same entrance, emphasis, and exit animation effects as those added to the upper-right snowflake.

- Click the Animation Painter button and then click the center snowflake.

- Click the Animation Painter button again and then click the lower-right snowflake (Figure 7–53).

- Preview the animation effects.

**Q&A** Can I copy the animation to more than one object simultaneously?

No. Unlike using the Format Painter, you must click the Animation Painter button each time you want to copy the animation to an object on the slide.

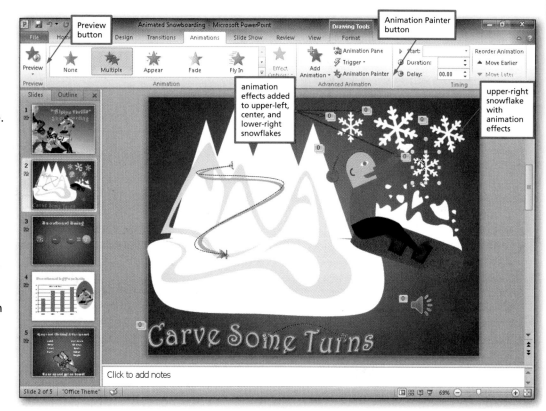

**Figure 7–53**

**Break Point:** If you wish to take a break, this is a good place to do so. Be sure to save the Animated Snowboarding file again and then you can quit PowerPoint. To resume at a later time, start PowerPoint, open the file called Animated Snowboarding, and continue following the steps from this location forward.

## To Animate a SmartArt Graphic

The bulleted lists on the text slides are animated, and you can build on this effect by adding animation to the Slide 3 SmartArt graphic. You can add a custom animation to each shape in the cycle, but you also can use one of PowerPoint's built-in animations to simplify the animation procedure. The following steps apply an entrance animation effect to the Equation diagram.

- Display Slide 3 and then select the SmartArt graphic.

- Display the Animation gallery and then point to the Zoom entrance effect to display a live preview of this effect (Figure 7–54).

**Experiment**

- Point to some of the entrance effects and watch the animation preview in the SmartArt objects.

- Select the Zoom entrance effect.

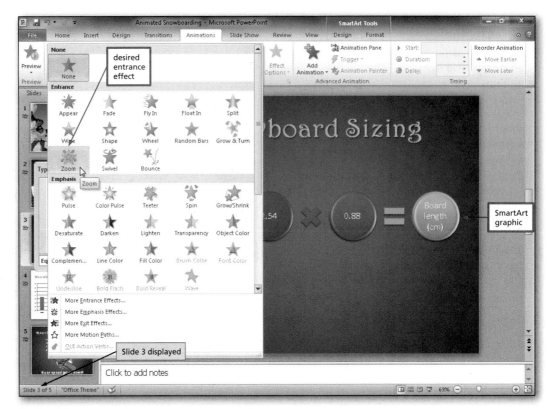

**Figure 7–54**

## To Change a SmartArt Graphic Animation Sequence

By default, all SmartArt graphic components enter the slide simultaneously. You can modify this setting and change the entrance sequence so that each element enters one at a time and builds the mathematical sequence from left to right. The following steps change the sequence for the SmartArt animation to One by One.

- Click the Effect Options button to display the Effect Options gallery (Figure 7–55).

**Q&A**

Can I reverse the order of individual shapes in the SmartArt sequence?

No. You can reverse the order of the entire SmartArt graphic but not individual shapes within the sequence.

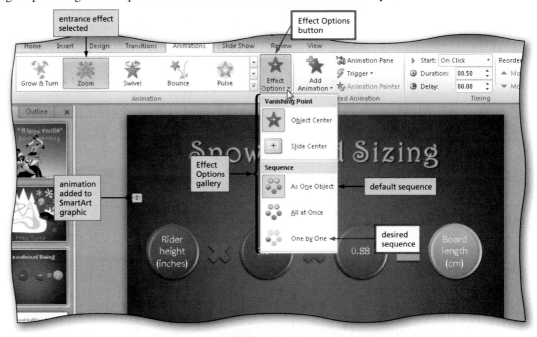

**Figure 7–55**

**2**
- Click One by One in the Sequence area to change the animation order.

- Change the start timing option to After Previous, the duration to 5.00 seconds, and the delay to 01.00 second (Figure 7–56).

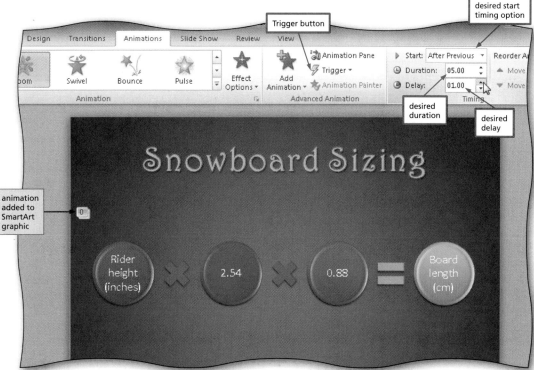

Figure 7–56

### TO TRIGGER AN ANIMATION EFFECT

If you select the On Click start timing option and run the slide show, PowerPoint starts the animation when you click any part of the slide or press the SPACEBAR. You may, however, want the option to play an animation in a particular circumstance. For example, you may have an animated sequence ready to show if time permits or if you believe your audience needs time to understand a process and would understand the concept more readily if you revealed one part of a SmartArt graphic at a time. A **trigger** specifies when an animation or other action should occur. It is linked to a particular component of a slide so that the action occurs only when you click this slide element. If you click any other part of the slide, PowerPoint will display the next slide in the presentation. If you need to set a slide object as the trigger to start an animation, you would follow these steps.

1. Click the Trigger button (Animations tab | Advanced Animation group) to display the Trigger menu and then point to On Click Of to display the list of slide elements.

2. Click the desired slide element to set the trigger on the click of that object.

**BTW**

**Displaying Equations**
One of PowerPoint 2010's enhancements is the Equation Tools Design tab. This feature allows you to type mathematical symbols and insert structures, including functions, integrals, operators, and radicals.

## To Animate a Chart

The chart on Slide 4 depicts the growth of the sport of snowboarding. In 10 years, the number of snowboarders practically has doubled. To emphasize this increase in popularity, you can animate the bars of the chart so that each one enters the slide individually. As with the SmartArt animation, PowerPoint gives you many options to animate the chart data. The following steps animate the Slide 4 chart bars.

- Display Slide 4 and then click an edge of the chart so that the frame is displayed. Display the Animation gallery (Figure 7–57).

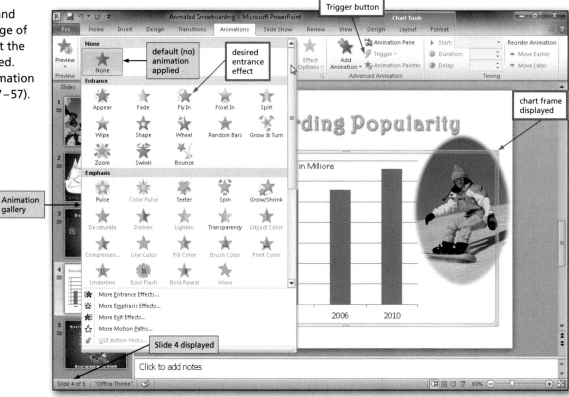

**Figure 7–57**

- Click the Fly In entrance effect, change the start timing option to After Previous, change the duration to 02.00 seconds, and change the delay to 02.50 seconds.

- Click the Effect Options button to display the Effect Options gallery (Figure 7–58).

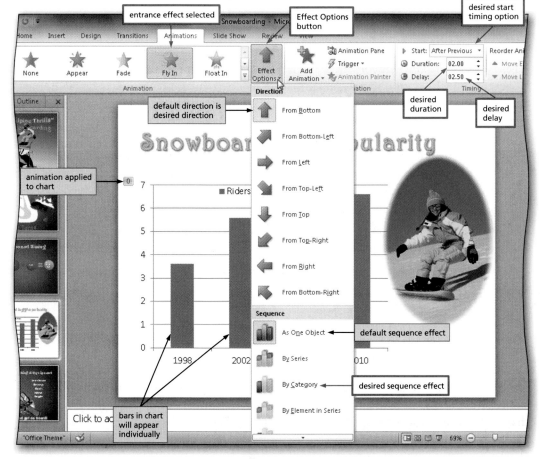

**Figure 7–58**

**4**

- Point to By Category to preview the chart animation so that each bar for the first category, Number of Snowboarders in Millions, appears individually for each year.

### Experiment

- Point to some of the animations in the various categories and watch the animations preview on Slide 4.

- Click By Category to change the chart animation for the first category.

- Change the start timing option to After Previous, change the duration to 03.00 seconds, and change the delay to 03.50 seconds.

## To Animate a List

The two lists on Slide 5 give the minimum clothing and equipment required to snowboard warmly and safely. Each item in the placeholder is a separate paragraph. To add interest during a presentation, you can have each paragraph in the left list enter the slide individually. When the entire list has displayed, the list can disappear and then each paragraph in the right list can appear. The following steps animate the Slide 5 paragraph lists.

**1**

- Display Slide 5 and then select the four items in the left text placeholder.

- Apply the Shape entrance animation effect, change the start timing option to After Previous, change the duration to 03.00 seconds, and change the delay to 01.50 seconds (Figure 7–59).

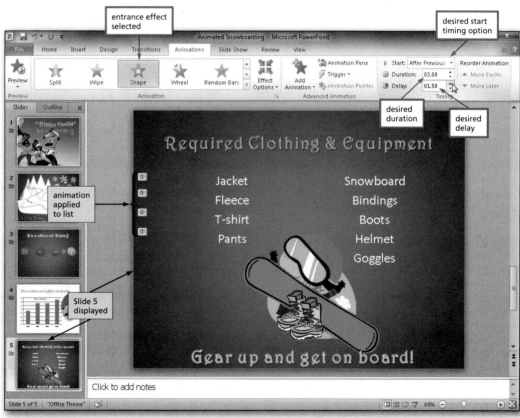

**Figure 7–59**

**2**

- Click the Effect Options button to display the Effect Options gallery (Figure 7–60).

**Experiment**

- Point to the Out direction and the Box, Diamond, and Plus Shapes and watch the animations preview on the Slide 5 left list paragraphs.

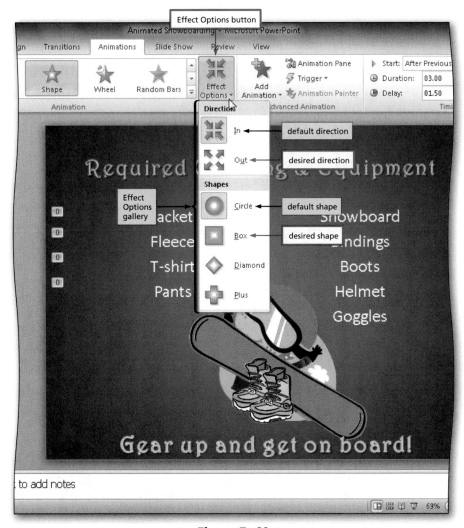

**Figure 7–60**

**3**

- Change the Shapes from Circle to Box.

- Click the Effect Options button again and then change the Direction to Out.

---

**Plan Ahead**

**Select colors for dimming text.**
After paragraphs of text are displayed, you can change the color, or dim the text, to direct the audience's attention to another area of the slide. Choose the dimming colors carefully. For example, use cool colors, such as blue, purple, and turquoise, as backgrounds so that the audience focuses on the next brighter, contrasting color on the slide. Avoid using light blue because it often is difficult to see, especially against a dark background. In addition, use a maximum of three colors unless you have a compelling need to present more variety.

## To Dim Text after Animation

As each item in the list is displayed, you may desire to have the previous item removed from the screen or to have the font color change, or **dim**. PowerPoint provides several options for you to alter this text by specifying an After Animation effect. The following steps dim each item in the left placeholder list by changing the font color to Purple.

- Select the four paragraphs in the left placeholder and then click the Animation Pane button (Animations tab | Advanced Animation) to display the Animation Pane task pane.

- Click the Pants Animation Order list arrow to display the Animation Order menu (Figure 7–61).

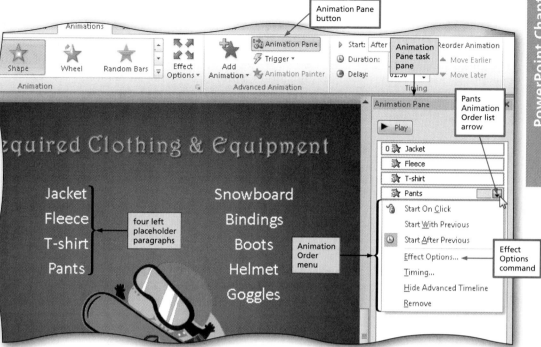

**Figure 7–61**

- Click Effect Options on the Animation Order list to display the Box dialog box.

- Click the After animation list arrow to display the After animation menu (Figure 7–62).

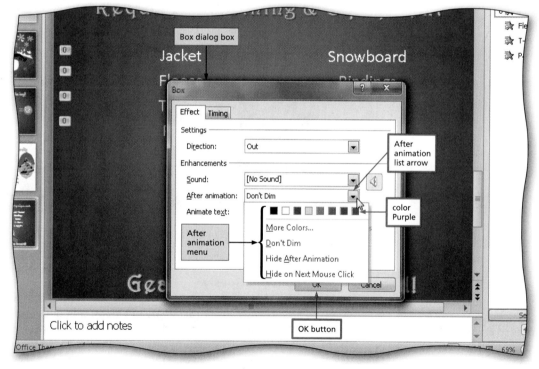

**Figure 7–62**

- Click the color Purple (last color in the row of colors) to select this color for the dim effect.

- Click the OK button (Box dialog box) to apply the dim effect to the four items in the left placeholder on Slide 5.

- Close the Animation Pane task pane.

## To Use the Animation Painter to Copy Animations

All animations have been applied to the left placeholder paragraphs. You now can copy these animations to the five items in the right text placeholder. The following steps use the Animation Painter to copy the animation.

**1** Click one item in the list in the left text placeholder and then click the Animation Painter button.

**2** Click the word, Snowboard, in the right list to copy the animations in the left list to the five words in the right list.

**3** Select the five words in the list in the right placeholder and then change the start timing option to After Previous, the duration to 03.00 seconds, and the delay to 01.50 seconds (Figure 7–63).

**Figure 7–63**

**Plan Ahead**

**Use quotations judiciously.**
Quotations and sayings are available from a variety of print sources, such as *Quotable Quotes, The Merriam-Webster Dictionary of Quotations,* and *Bartlett's Familiar Quotations.* Web sites, including bartleby.com and quotations.com, also provide direct quotes organized into specific categories. These words often add insight to the beginning or the end of a slide show. If you use a quotation, give credit to the person who said or wrote the words. Also, do not change the wording unless it is offensive or biased.

## To Create Credits

Many motion pictures use rolling credits at the end of the movie to acknowledge the people who were involved in the filmmaking process or to provide additional information about the actors or setting. You, too, can use a credit or closing statement at the end of your presentation to thank individuals or companies who helped you develop your slide show or to leave your audience with a final thought. The following steps display text as an ascending credit line on Slide 5.

**1**

- With Slide 5 displaying, click the text box with the words, Gear up and get on board!, at the bottom of the slide to select it.

- Display the Animation gallery and then click More Entrance Effects (Figure 7–64).

**Figure 7–64**

**2**

- Click the Credits entrance animation effect in the Exciting area and then click the OK button (Change Entrance Effect dialog box) to apply the effect.

**3**

- Change the start timing option to After Previous, the duration to 18.00 seconds, and the delay to 01.00 second (Figure 7–65).

- Preview the animation.

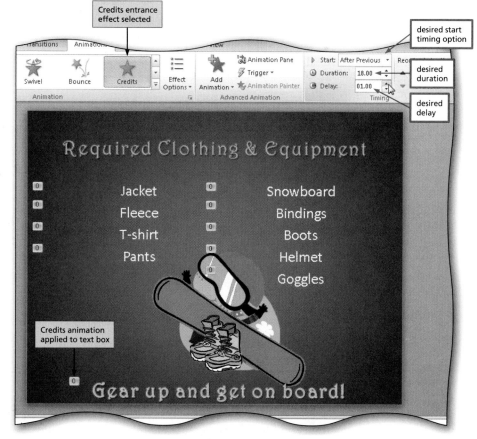

**Figure 7–65**

**Quick Reference**
For a table that lists how to complete the tasks covered in this book using the mouse, Ribbon, shortcut menu, and keyboard, see the Quick Reference Summary at the back of this book, or visit the PowerPoint 2010 Quick Reference Web page (scsite.com/ppt2010/qr).

# Preparing for a Self-Running Presentation

In previous slide shows, you clicked to advance from one slide to the next. Because all animations have been added to the slides in the presentation, you now can set the time each slide is displayed on the screen. You can set these times in one of two ways. The first method is to specify each slide's display time manually. The second method is to use PowerPoint's **rehearsal feature**, which allows you to advance through the slides at your own pace, and the amount of time you view each slide is recorded. You will use the second technique in this chapter and then adjust the last slide's timing manually.

When you begin rehearsing a presentation, the Rehearsal toolbar is displayed. The **Rehearsal toolbar** contains buttons that allow you to start, pause, and repeat viewing the slides in the slide show and to view the times for each slide as well as the elapsed time. Table 7–1 describes the buttons on the Rehearsal toolbar.

### Table 7–1 Rehearsal Toolbar Buttons

| Button Name | Image | Description |
| --- | --- | --- |
| Next | ➡ | Displays the next slide or next animated element on the slide. |
| Pause Recording | ‖ | Stops the timer. Click the Next or Pause Recording button to resume timing. |
| Slide Time | 0:00:00 | Indicates the length of time a slide has been displayed. You can enter a slide time directly in the Slide Time box. |
| Repeat | ↺ | Clears the Slide Time box and resets the timer to 0:00:00. |
| Elapsed Time | 0:00:00 | Indicates slide show total time. |

**Plan Ahead**

**Give your audience sufficient time to view a slide.**
The presentation in this chapter is designed to run continuously at a kiosk without a speaker's physical presence. Your audience, therefore, must read or view each slide and absorb the information without your help as a narrator. Be certain to give them time to read the slide and grasp the concept you are presenting. They will become frustrated if the slide changes before they have finished viewing and assimilating the material. As you set the slide timings, read each slide aloud and note the amount of time that elapses. Add a few seconds to this time and use this amount for the total time the slide is displayed.

## To Rehearse Timings

You need to determine the length of time each slide should be displayed. Audience members need sufficient time to read the text and watch the animations. Table 7–2 indicates the desired timings for the five slides in the snowboarding presentation. Slide 1 is displayed and then the title text and animated snowboarder picture appear for 25 seconds. The Slide 2 title text, sound, and clip are displayed for 50 seconds. Slide 3 has the animated SmartArt, and it takes one minute for the elements to display. The bars on the Slide 4 chart can display in 40 seconds, and the two lists and rolling credits on Slide 5 display for one minute, five seconds.

**Table 7–2 Slide Rehearsal Timings**

| Slide Number | Display Time | Elapsed Time |
|---|---|---|
| 1 | 0:00 | 0:25 |
| 2 | 0:50 | 1:15 |
| 3 | 1:00 | 2:15 |
| 4 | 0:40 | 2:55 |
| 5 | 1:05 | 4:00 |

The following steps add slide timings to the slide show.

**1**

- Display Slide 1 and then click Slide Show on the Ribbon to display the Slide Show tab (Figure 7–66).

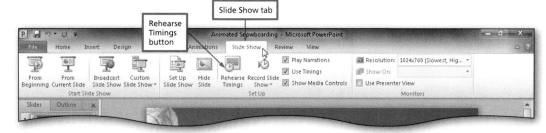

**Figure 7–66**

**2**

- Click the Rehearse Timings button (Slide Show tab | Set Up group) to start the slide show and the counter (Figure 7–67).

**Figure 7–67**

**3**

- When the Elapsed Time displays 0:25, click the Next button to display Slide 2.

- When the Elapsed Time displays 1:15, click the Next button to display Slide 3.

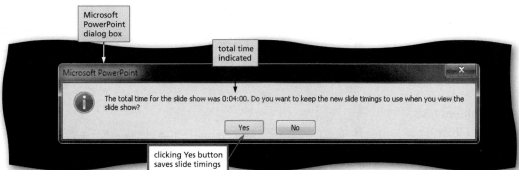

- When the Elapsed Time displays 2:15, click the Next button to display Slide 4.

**Figure 7–68**

- When the Elapsed Time displays 2:55, click the Next button to display Slide 5.

- When the Elapsed Time displays 4:00, click the Next button to display the black slide (Figure 7–68).

**4**

- Click the Yes button in the Microsoft Office PowerPoint dialog box to keep the new slide timings with an elapsed time of 4:00.

- Review each slide's timing displayed in the lower-left corner in Slide Sorter view (Figure 7–69).

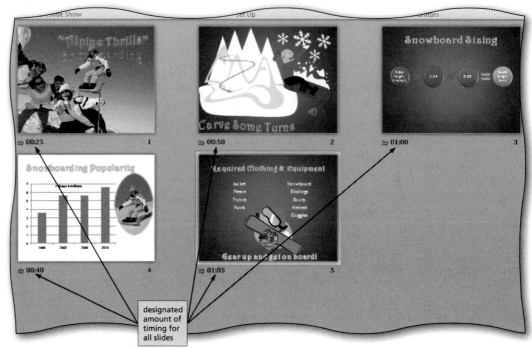

Figure 7–69

## To Adjust Timings Manually

If the slide timings need adjustment, you manually can change the length of time each slide is displayed. In this presentation, you decide to display Slide 4 for 30 seconds instead of 40 seconds. The following step decreases the Slide 4 timing.

- In Slide Sorter view, display the Transitions tab and then select Slide 4.

- Click and hold down the Advance Slide After down arrow (Transitions tab | Timing group) until 00:30.00 is displayed (Figure 7–70).

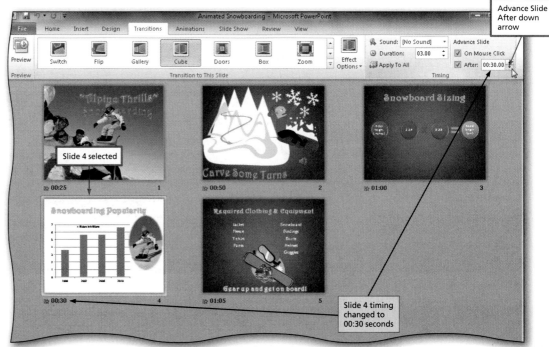

Figure 7–70

## To Modify a Transition Effect

The Cube transition is applied to the five slides in this presentation. The default rotation is From Right, so the current slide turns to the left while the new slide appears from the right side of the screen. To keep the downhill theme of the presentation in mind, you can change the Cube rotation so that the current slide moves to the bottom of the screen and the new slide appears from the top. The following steps modify the Transition Effect for all slides in the presentation.

**1**

- With the Transitions tab still selected, click the Effect Options button (Transitions tab | Transition to This Slide group) to display the Effect Options gallery (Figure 7–71).

**Q&A**  Are the same four effects available for all transitions?

No. The transition effects vary depending upon the particular transition selected.

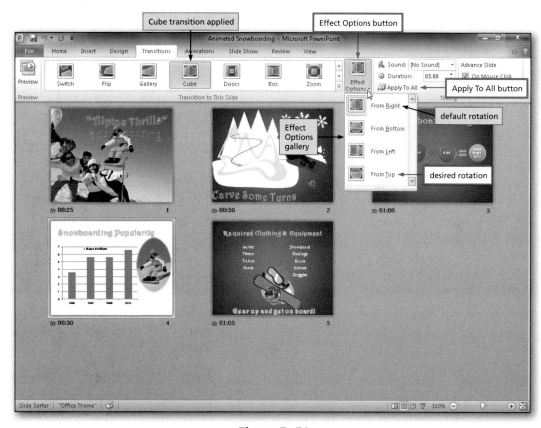

**Figure 7–71**

**2**

- Click the From Top effect to change the rotation.

- Click the Apply To All button (Transitions tab | Timing group) to set the From Top transition effect for all slides in the presentation.

## To Create a Self-Running Presentation

The snowboarding presentation can accompany a speech, but it also can run unattended at sporting goods stores and ski resorts. When the last slide in the presentation is displayed, the slide show **loops**, or restarts, at Slide 1. PowerPoint has the option of running continuously until the user presses the ESC key. The following steps set the slide show to run in this manner.

**1**

- Display the Slide Show tab and then click the Set Up Slide Show button (Slide Show tab | Set Up group) to display the Set Up Show dialog box (Figure 7–72).

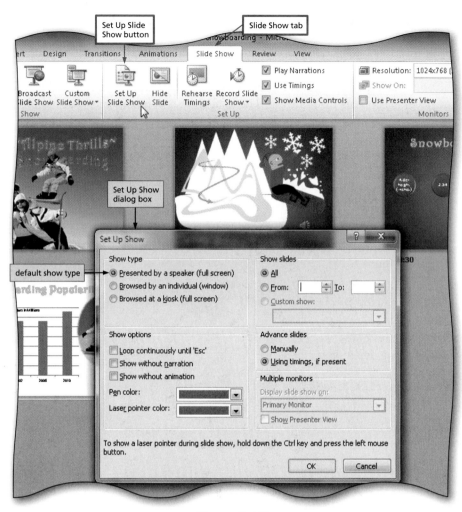

**Figure 7–72**

**2**

- Click 'Browsed at a kiosk (full screen)' in the Show type area (Figure 7–73).

**3**

- Click the OK button to apply this show type.

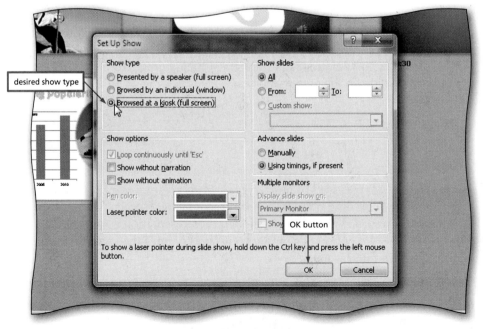

**Figure 7–73**

## To Run an Animated Slide Show

All changes are complete. You now can view the Animated Snowboarding presentation. The following steps run the slide show.

**1** Click the Normal View button, display the title slide, and then click the Slide Show button to start the presentation.

**2** As each slide automatically is displayed, review the information.

**3** When Slide 1 is displayed again, press the ESC key to stop the presentation.

## To Change Document Properties

Before saving the presentation again, you want to add your name, class name, and some keywords as document properties. The following steps use the Document Information Panel to change document properties.

**1** Display the Document Information Panel and then type your name as the Author property.

**2** Type your course and section in the Subject property.

**3** Type `snowboarding, snowboard size, popularity, clothing, equipment` as the Keywords property.

**4** Close the Document Information Panel.

## To Save, Print, and Quit PowerPoint

The presentation now is complete. You should save the slides, print a handout, and then quit PowerPoint.

**1** Save the Animated Snowboarding presentation again with the same file name.

**2** Print the presentation as a handout with two slides per page (Figure 7–74 on the next page).

**3** Quit PowerPoint, closing all open documents.

BTW

**Certification**
The Microsoft Office Specialist (MOS) program provides an opportunity for you to obtain a valuable industry credential — proof that you have the PowerPoint 2010 skills required by employers. For more information, visit the PowerPoint 2010 Certification Web page (scsite.com/ppt2010/cert).

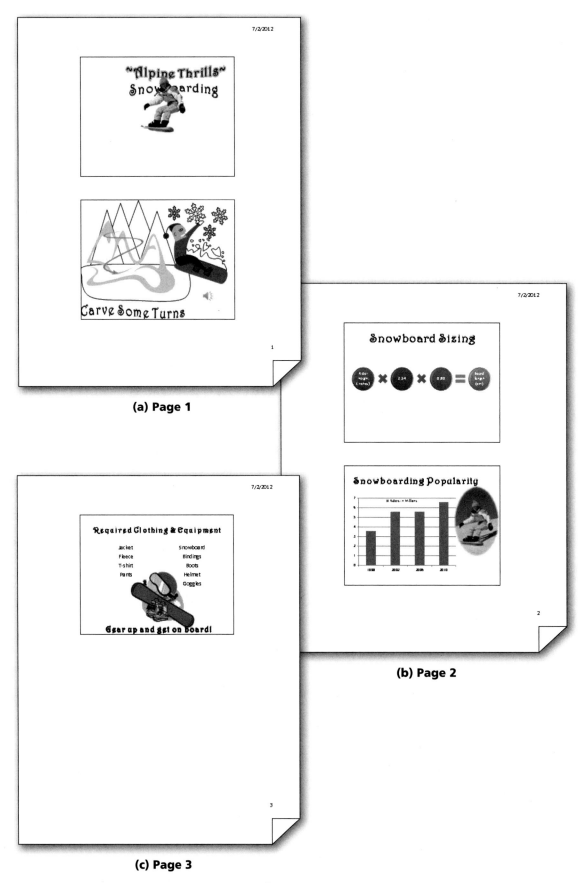

(a) Page 1

(b) Page 2

(c) Page 3

**Figure 7–74**

# Chapter Summary

In this chapter you have learned how to remove a background from a picture and then crop and compress the image. You then applied entrance, emphasis, and exit effects to slide content and created a custom animation using a motion path. Also, you inserted and animated a text box and associated a sound with this text. You animated a SmartArt graphic, a chart, and two lists. Then, you set timing so that the slide show runs automatically. The items listed below include all the new PowerPoint skills you have learned in this chapter.

1. Remove a Background (PPT 405)
2. Refine Background Removal (PPT 407)
3. Crop a Picture (PPT 409)
4. Compress a Picture (PPT 410)
5. Animate a Picture Using an Entrance Effect (PPT 411)
6. Change Animation Direction (PPT 412)
7. Animate a Picture Using an Emphasis Effect (PPT 413)
8. Animate a Picture Using an Exit Effect (PPT 414)
9. Preview an Animation Sequence (PPT 416)
10. Modify Entrance Animation Timing (PPT 416)
11. Animate Title Text Placeholder Paragraphs (PPT 419)
12. Change Animation Order (PPT 420)
13. Rename Slide Objects (PPT 422)
14. Insert a Text Box and Format Text (PPT 423)
15. Animate a Text Box Using an Entrance Effect (PPT 425)
16. Animate a Text Box by Applying a Motion Path (PPT 427)
17. Adjust a Motion Path (PPT 428)
18. Associate a Sound with an Animation (PPT 430)
19. Draw a Custom Motion Path (PPT 431)
20. Use the Animation Painter to Animate a Clip (PPT 433)
21. Animate a SmartArt Graphic (PPT 435)
22. Change a SmartArt Graphic Animation Sequence (PPT 436)
23. Animate a Chart (PPT 437)
24. Animate a List (PPT 439)
25. Dim Text after Animation (PPT 440)
26. Create Credits (PPT 442)
27. Rehearse Timings (PPT 444)
28. Adjust Timings Manually (PPT 446)
29. Modify a Transition Effect (PPT 447)
30. Create a Self-Running Presentation (PPT 447)

If you have a SAM 2010 user profile, your instructor may have assigned an autogradable version of this assignment. If so, log into the SAM 2010 Web site at www.cengage.com/sam2010 to download the instruction and start files.

## Learn It Online

Test your knowledge of chapter content and key terms.

*Instructions:* To complete the Learn It Online exercises, start your browser, click the Address bar, and then enter the Web address `scsite.com/ppt2010/learn`. When the Office 2010 Learn It Online page is displayed, click the link for the exercise you want to complete and then read the instructions.

**Chapter Reinforcement TF, MC, and SA**
A series of true/false, multiple choice, and short answer questions that test your knowledge of the chapter content.

**Flash Cards**
An interactive learning environment where you identify chapter key terms associated with displayed definitions.

**Practice Test**
A series of multiple choice questions that test your knowledge of chapter content and key terms.

**Who Wants To Be a Computer Genius?**
An interactive game that challenges your knowledge of chapter content in the style of a television quiz show.

**Wheel of Terms**
An interactive game that challenges your knowledge of chapter key terms in the style of the television show *Wheel of Fortune*.

**Crossword Puzzle Challenge**
A crossword puzzle that challenges your knowledge of key terms presented in the chapter.

## Apply Your Knowledge

Reinforce the skills and apply the concepts you learned in this chapter.

**Applying Entrance Effects**

*Note:* To complete this assignment, you will be required to use the Data Files for Students. See the inside back cover of this book for instructions on downloading the Data Files for Students or contact your instructor for information about accessing the required files.

*Instructions:* Start PowerPoint. Open the presentation, Apply 7-1 Losing Weight, located on the Data Files for Students.

The slide in this presentation gives a few suggestions on losing weight. The document you open is an unformatted presentation. You are to add an entrance effect to the title, convert the text to a SmartArt graphic, and then add an entrance effect to the SmartArt graphic so the slide looks like Figure 7–75.

*Perform the following tasks:*
1. Change the document theme to Angles and change the presentation theme colors to Clarity.
2. Apply the Brown, Accent 2 WordArt text fill and the Dark Red, Accent 6 WordArt text outline to the title text. Then change the text outline weight to 2¼ pt. Also apply the WordArt Transform text effect, Fade Right, in the Warp area, to this text. Increase the size of the WordArt to 1.27" × 8.23".
3. Click More Entrance Effects in the Animation gallery and then apply the Grow & Turn entrance effect in the Moderate category to the title text. Change the start timing setting to After Previous and the duration to 02.00 seconds.

4. Reduce the picture size to 3.62" × 2.42" and apply the Soft Edges, 10 Point effect. Move the picture to the lower-right corner of the slide, as shown in Figure 7–75. Then apply the Appear entrance effect and change the duration from Auto to 01.00 second. Change the start timing setting to After Previous.

5. Convert the bulleted text to the Basic Target layout (Relationship area) SmartArt graphic. Change the color to the Colorful Range - Accent Colors 5 to 6 in the Colorful area. Apply the Polished 3-D SmartArt Style and then resize this graphic to approximately 5.5" × 10".

6. Increase the font size of the SmartArt graphic to 22 point. Change the width of the first three text boxes in the SmartArt graphic to 3.5". Use the Ruler and Guides to align the first three text boxes with the fourth and fifth text boxes.

7. Apply the Zoom entrance effect to the SmartArt graphic. Add the One by One effect option. Change the duration to 02.50 seconds. Move the SmartArt graphic to the location shown in Figure 7–75.

8. Change the transition from Reveal to Shape and then change the duration to 03.50 seconds.

9. Change the document properties, as specified by your instructor. Save the presentation using the file name, Apply 7-1 Aim for Losing Weight. Submit the revised document in the format specified by your instructor.

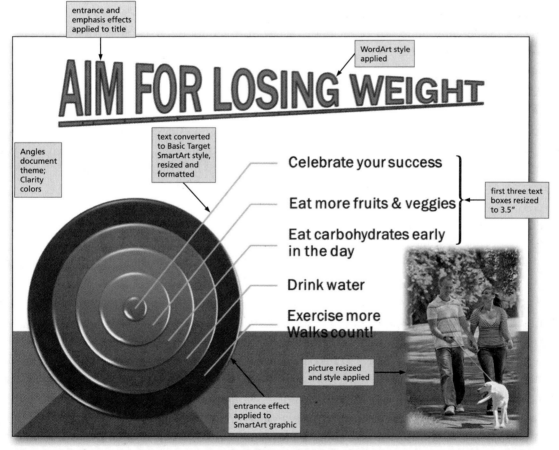

**Figure 7–75**

# Extend Your Knowledge

Extend the skills you learned in this chapter and experiment with new skills. You may need to use Help to complete the assignment.

### Changing and Reordering Animations, Adding Sound to Animations, Inserting a Text Box, and Cropping a Picture to a Shape

*Note:* To complete this assignment, you will be required to use the Data Files for Students. See the inside back cover of this book for instructions on downloading the Data Files for Students or contact your instructor for information about accessing the required files.

*Instructions:* Start PowerPoint. Open the presentation, Extend 7-1 Blue Moon, located on the Data Files for Students. You will change the title text animations, animate a bulleted list, dim text after animation, add sound to animations, and insert a text box, as shown in Figure 7–76. You will need to show more entrance, emphasis, and exit effects to locate the required animations.

*Perform the following tasks:*

1. On the Slide 1 title, change the Bounce entrance effect to the Float In entrance effect. Change the start timing option from On Click to After Previous, the duration to 02.00 seconds, and the direction to Float Down. Add the Wave emphasis effect in the Advanced Animation area, change the start timing option to After Previous, and change the duration to 05.50 seconds. Have the Brass Wind Chime sound, which is next to the title text on the slide, play with the Wave emphasis effect, and hide the sound icon during the show.

2. Apply the Fly In from Bottom Left Entrance animation to the three bulleted paragraphs so that they enter one at a time on click and then change the duration to 03.75 seconds.

3. Apply the Fly In from Left entrance animation to the moon clip. Change the duration to 03.00 seconds. Change the start timing option to After Previous. Have the Drum Roll Loud sound, which is next to the moon clip, play with this clip, change the volume to High, and hide the sound icon during the show.

4. Change the font of the vertically rotated text, Next Blue Moon 2015, to Eras Bold ITC, the color of the text to Dark Blue, and the font size to 40 point. Center this text. Add the Dissolve In entrance effect to this text. Change the start timing option to After Previous and the duration to 02.50 seconds. Add the Grow With Color emphasis to the text. Click the Effect Options button and select the teal color (ninth color in Theme Colors row). Change the start timing option to After Previous and change the duration to 03.00 seconds.

5. Apply the Flash transition to Slide 1 and change the duration to 04.50 seconds.

6. On Slide 2, select the moon picture, and, while holding down the CTRL key, move the picture to the right to duplicate it. Remove the background from the duplicate picture, click the handles on the marquee, and then drag the lines so that the moon is centered in the picture. Change the color of this picture to Blue, Accent Color 1 Dark and then move this picture on top of the original picture until the blue moon is lined up directly on top of the white moon.

7. Apply the Shrink & Turn exit effect to the blue moon picture, change the start timing option to After Previous, and change the duration to 05.00 seconds. Change the name of the blue moon picture in the Animation pane from Picture 4 to Blue Moon.

8. On Slide 2, select the Wave shape and add the Float In entrance effect. Change the direction to Float Down. Change the start timing option to After Previous and the duration to 2.00. Resize the oval shape so that it is approximately 2.19" × 2.25", and also reduce the font size to fit into the shape. Add the Fly In entrance effect, change the direction to From Right, and then change the start timing option to After Previous and the duration to 02.50 seconds.

9. Insert the Moon picture located on the Data Files for Students. Crop the picture so that the moon is centered within the black background. Increase the size of the picture to 3.28" × 3.66" and then

crop the picture to fill the Moon shape. You may need to use Help to learn how to crop to a shape. Move the Moon picture to the location shown in the figure.

10. Apply the Orbit transition to Slide 2 and change the duration to 04.50 seconds.

11. Change the document properties, as specified by your instructor. Save the presentation using the file name, Extend 7-1 Once in a Blue Moon.

12. Submit the revised document in the format specified by your instructor.

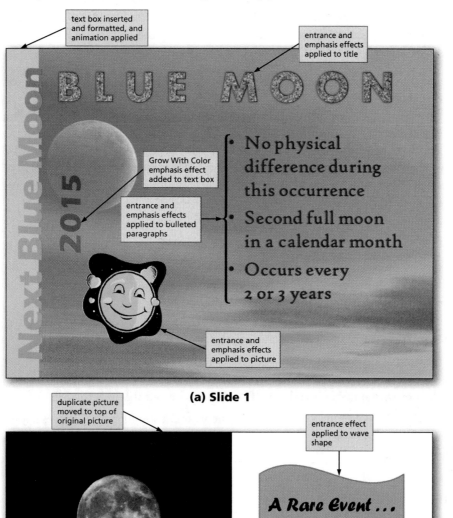

**(a) Slide 1**

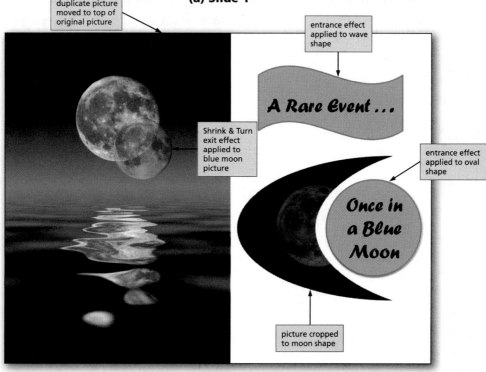

**(b) Slide 2**

**Figure 7–76**

## Make It Right

Analyze a presentation and correct all errors and/or improve the design.

### Removing and Changing Animation, and Copying Animation Using the Animation Painter

*Note:* To complete this assignment, you will be required to use the Data Files for Students. See the inside back cover of this book for instructions on downloading the Data Files for Students or contact your instructor for information about accessing the required files.

*Instructions:* Start PowerPoint. Open the presentation, Make It Right 7-1 Footprints, located on the Data Files for Students.

Correct the formatting problems and errors in the presentation while keeping in mind the guidelines presented in this chapter. This presentation was created as part of an interactive exhibit for children at the local nature center. The instructions for the matching game are as follows: First, select the green number 1; then, click on the animal's picture. The correct picture will display with a Grow & Turn animation and an orange border. Then click on green number 2. Continue selecting the green numbers to match all the animals with their tracks.

The footprints and pictures shown in Figure 7–77 are not in the correct order. You volunteer to modify the presentation so that the animals match their tracks.

*Perform the following tasks:*

1. Display the Animation tab, and remove the animation from all the footprints except number 1. Remove the animation from all the pictures except the skunk picture. Use the Animation Painter to copy the animation from the first footprint picture to the five remaining footprint pictures. Then copy the animation from the skunk picture to the five remaining animal pictures.

2. Reorder the animations so that the animal picture follows the footprint. Footprint number 1 is the skunk, footprint number 2 is the deer, footprint number 3 is the squirrel, footprint number 4 is the mink, footprint number 5 is the wolf, and footprint number 6 is the fox.

3. Change the Fade transition to Rotate, change the Camera sound to the Wolves sound, and then change the duration to 04.50 seconds.

4. Change the document properties, as specified by your instructor. Save the presentation using the file name, Make It Right 7-1 Animal Footprints.

5. Submit the revised document in the format specified by your instructor.

**Figure 7–77**

## In the Lab

Design and/or create a presentation using the guidelines, concepts, and skills presented in this chapter. Labs 1, 2, and 3 are listed in order of increasing difficulty.

### Lab 1: Creating a Presentation with an Animated Chart

*Note:*   To complete this assignment, you will be required to use the Data Files for Students. See the inside back cover of this book for instructions on downloading the Data Files for Students or contact your instructor for information about accessing the required files.

*Problem:*   In many countries around the world, people do not have clean drinking water. You belong to a science club, and your group has decided to develop a water project that can change salt water to fresh water. You decide to create a PowerPoint presentation to introduce the basic facts about water on Earth. You create the slides shown in Figure 7–78 on pages PPT 458 and PPT 459 using files located on the Data Files for Students. You will need to show more entrance and emphasis effects to locate the required animations.

*Perform the following tasks:*

1.  Open the presentation, Lab 7-1 Water, located on the Data Files for Students.

2.  On Slide 1, apply the Wedge entrance effect to the title text. Change the start timing option to With Previous and the duration to 03.50 seconds. Then add a Wave emphasis effect to the title text, change the start timing option to With Previous, and change the duration to 04.00 seconds.

*Continued >*

**In the Lab** *continued*

3. On Slide 2, apply the Wheel entrance effect to the title text. Change the start timing option to After Previous and change the duration to 03.50 seconds.

4. Apply the Random Bars entrance effect to the clip. Change the start timing option to After Previous and change the duration to 04.50 seconds.

5. Apply the Wipe entrance effect to the chart. Change the duration to 05.25 seconds.

6. Apply the Fly In From Left entrance effect to all paragraphs in the content placeholder. Change the duration to 02.50 seconds.

7. Dim the second bulleted paragraph (Ocean and seas), the third bulleted paragraph, and the three second-level paragraphs (Fresh water; Lakes, Rivers; Glaciers; Ground) after animation using a blue and a green color displayed in the pie chart. To select these colors, click the After animation arrow in the Enhancements area (Fly In dialog box), click More Colors in the After animation menu, and then click the colors that best match the chart colors.

8. Add the Style 5 background style to Slide 2. *Hint:* Right-click Style 5 and then click Apply to Selected Slides in the shortcut menu.

9. Apply the Ripple transition and change the duration to 03.00 seconds for all slides.

10. Change the document properties, as specified by your instructor. Save the presentation using the file name, Lab 7-1 Water on Earth.

11. Submit the revised document in the format specified by your instructor.

entrance and emphasis effects applied to title text

**(a) Slide 1**

**Figure 7–78**

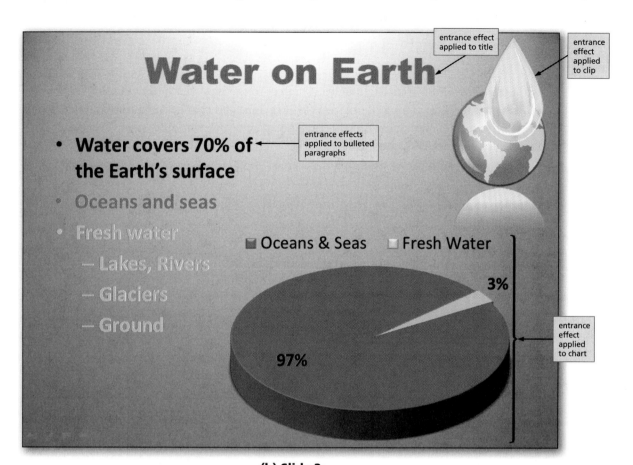

**(b) Slide 2**

**Figure 7–78**

# In the Lab

## Lab 2: Creating a Self-Running Presentation and Animating a Clip Using a Motion Path

*Note:* To complete this assignment, you will be required to use the Data Files for Students. See the inside back cover of this book for instructions on downloading the Data Files for Students or contact your instructor for information about accessing the required files.

*Problem:* You are studying botany and work part time at a local botanic garden. The garden's directors announced recently that a butterfly conservatory will be opening next year. In the interim, they are setting up a temporary exhibit. The master gardener, who is overseeing the planting of flowers and bushes that attract butterflies, has asked you to assist with the design of the conservatory. One of your assignments is to create a self-running PowerPoint presentation that will be viewed on a kiosk at the temporary exhibit. He asked you to gear your presentation to children because the botanic gardens are visited frequently by groups of children on field trips, and the butterfly conservatory will be designed with children in mind. You create the slides shown in Figure 7–79 on pages PPT 460 and PPT 461 using files located on the Data Files for Students.

*Perform the following tasks:*

1. Open the presentation, Lab 7-2 Butterfly, located on the Data Files for Students, and then add the Slipstream document theme.

2. On Slide 1, increase the size of the picture and add the Reflected Bevel, White picture style. Change the border to Turquoise, Accent 2.

3. Increase the title text font size to 54 point so that it is on two lines, as shown in Figure 7–79a.

*Continued >*

**In the Lab** *continued*

4. Change the subtitle font to Eurostyle or a similar font and then bold and italicize the author's name.

5. Apply the Fly In from Bottom-Right entrance effect to the butterfly in the upper-left corner of Slide 1. Change the start timing option to With Previous and change the duration to 02.50 seconds. Add the Loops motion path animation, change the start timing option to After Previous, and change the duration to 03.00 seconds.

6. Apply the Fly In from Bottom-Right entrance effect to the butterfly in the lower-right corner of Slide 1. Change the start timing option to After Previous and change the duration to 01.75 seconds. Add another animation to the butterfly by drawing a custom motion path. To draw the path, select the butterfly, click the More button in Animation group, click Custom Path, click the Effect Options button, and then click Scribble. Draw the motion path so it starts at the left side of the slide and moves upward toward the picture, and then loops down to the right corner of the slide. Change the start timing option to After Previous and change the duration to 02.75 seconds.

7. On Slide 2, insert the Butterfly picture located on the Data Files for Students. Crop the picture to show more of the butterfly and then resize the picture so that it is close to the size of the caterpillar picture (4.25" × 2.81"). Add the Beveled Oval Black picture style to both pictures and then move the pictures to the locations shown in Figure 7–79b.

8. Convert the bulleted text to the Block Cycle SmartArt graphic, change the color to Accent Colors 4 to 5, and apply the Sunset Scene style. Increase the size of the graphic to approximately 5.25" × 7.25" and move it to the location shown in Figure 7–79b. Apply the Fly In, One by One (in Sequence area), entrance effect to the SmartArt graphic. Change the start timing option to After Previous and change the duration to 02.75 seconds.

9. Apply the Honeycomb transition and then change the duration to 04.00 seconds for all slides.

10. Rehearse the presentation and then set the slide timings to 22 seconds for Slide 1 and 28 seconds for Slide 2.

11. Change the document properties, as specified by your instructor. Save the presentation using the file name, Lab 7-2 Butterfly Mystique.

12. Submit the revised document in the format specified by your instructor.

(a) Slide 1

**Figure 7–79**

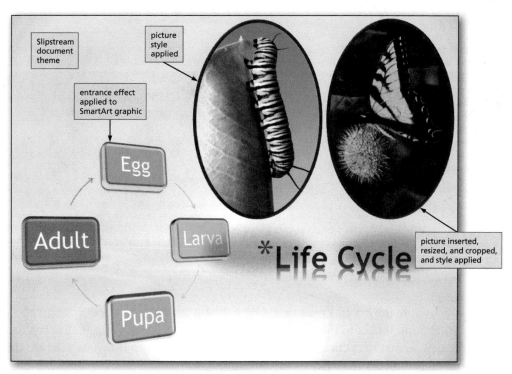

**(b) Slide 2**

**Figure 7–79**

## In the Lab

### Lab 3: Animating a Chart, Adding Credits, and Removing a Background from a Picture

*Note:* To complete this assignment, you will be required to use the Data Files for Students. See the inside back cover of this book for instructions on downloading the Data Files for Students or contact your instructor for information about accessing the required files.

*Problem:* You volunteer a few days each week at the local animal shelter, and the manager of the shelter asks if you would create a PowerPoint presentation to show to prospective dog owners. You create the presentation in Figure 7–80 on page PPT 463 consisting of three slides and a closing slide.

*Perform the following tasks:*

1. Open the presentation, Lab 7-3 Dog, located on the Data Files for Students, and change the document theme to Trek.

2. On Slide 1, add the Bounce entrance effect to the WordArt. Change the start timing option to After Previous and change the duration to 02.75 seconds.

3. Change the subtitle so that the text is on three lines, increase font size to 40 point, and then move the subtitle to the location shown in Figure 7–80a. Add the Fade entrance effect to the subtitle. Change the start timing option to After Previous and change the duration to 01.50 seconds. Add the Wipe From Top exit effect to this text, change the start timing option to After Previous, change the duration to 03.00 seconds, and change the delay to 02.25 seconds.

4. On Slide 2, remove the background from the German Shepherd picture and then increase the size of the picture to approximately 5.19" x 4.14", as shown in Figure 7–80b.

5. Apply the animation effects to the seven bulleted paragraphs and pictures using Table 7–3 as a guide.

*Continued >*

**In the Lab** *continued*

| Table 7–3 Slide 2 Animation Effects | | | | |
| --- | --- | --- | --- | --- |
| **Text or Picture** | **Entrance Effect** | **Start** | **Duration** | **Delay** |
| First bulleted paragraph | Appear | After Previous | 3.00 | 2.00 |
| Second bulleted paragraph | Fly In From Left | On Click | 2.50 | — |
| White dog picture | Float Down | With Previous | 2.50 | — |
| Third bulleted paragraph | Fly In From Left | On Click | 2.50 | — |
| Brown puppy picture | Float Down | With Previous | 2.50 | — |
| Fourth bulleted paragraph | Fly In From Left | On Click | 2.50 | — |
| German Shepherd picture | Fly In From Right | With Previous | 2.50 | — |
| Fifth, sixth, and seventh bulleted paragraphs | Fly In From Left | On Click | 2.50 | — |

6. On Slide 3, apply the Fly In From Left – By Element in Category (Sequence group in Effect Options) entrance effect to the chart, as shown in Figure 7–80c. Change the start timing option for only the first animation, which is the chart background, to After Previous. Change the duration for all animations to 03.25 seconds.

7. Apply Background Style 6 to Slides 2 and 3.

8. Create a fourth slide for a closing slide and use the Title and Content layout. In the title text placeholder, type **Thank You for Your Support**. Change the font color to Orange, Accent 1 and then center and italicize this text, as shown in Figure 7–80d. Apply the Dissolve In entrance animation effect (Basic group) and then change the duration to 07.00 seconds.

9. Insert the Bulldog picture located in the Data Files for Students on Slide 4. Remove the background from the picture and then refine the background removal by keeping and removing areas around the bulldog. Crop the picture, resize it so that it is approximately 5" × 6.76", and then move it to the location shown in the figure. Compress this picture.

10. Insert a text box at the bottom of the slide and type **Clifford Mason, Manager** as the first paragraph and **Southtown Animal Shelter** as the second paragraph. Change the font color to Light Yellow, Text 2 and the font size to 32 point. Center this text. Bring this text box forward so that the text will be in front of the bulldog. Apply the Credits entrance animation, change the start timing option to With Previous, and change the duration to 13.00 seconds. Add the Applause sound to this text and change the volume to the highest level.

11. Apply Background Style 3 to Slide 4.

12. Add a trigger to display the Thank You for Your Support text box when the bulldog picture is clicked. Rename the trigger animation Bulldog Picture.

13. Change the document properties, as specified by your instructor. Save the presentation using the file name, Lab 7-3 Adopting a Dog.

14. Submit the revised document in the format specified by your instructor.

**(a) Slide 1**

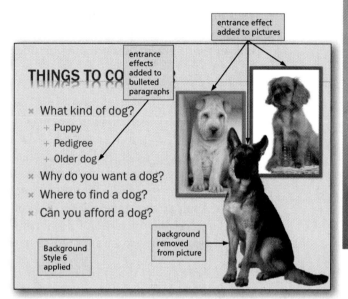

**(b) Slide 2**

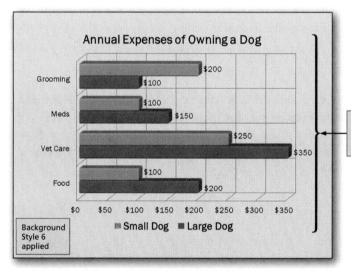

**(c) Slide 3**

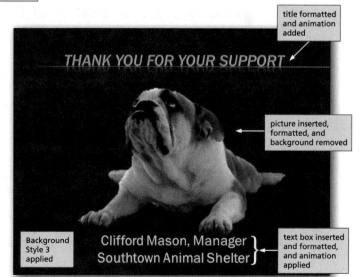

**(d) Slide 4**

**Figure 7–80**

# Cases and Places

Apply your creative thinking and problem-solving skills to design and implement a solution.

*Note:* To complete these assignments, you may be required to use the Data Files for Students. See the inside back cover of this book for instructions on downloading the Data Files for Students, or contact your instructor for information about accessing the required files.

As you design the presentations, remember to use the 7 × 7 rule: a maximum of seven words on a line and a maximum of seven lines on one slide.

### 1: Designing and Creating a Presentation about the Dwarf Planet Pluto

**Academic**

The International Astronomical Union (IAU) determined, after changing the definition of what constitutes a planet, that Pluto is now considered a dwarf planet. Even though Pluto was once considered the ninth planet in our solar system, other planets have been discovered since that are larger than Pluto. In your Astronomy class, you are studying the planets in our solar system. You decide to create a PowerPoint presentation to explain why Pluto is now considered a dwarf planet. Include information about other dwarf planets. Apply at least three objectives found at the beginning of this chapter to develop the presentation, including a cropped picture and an animated picture or a SmartArt graphic. Use pictures and diagrams from Office.com if they are appropriate for this topic. Be sure to check spelling.

### 2: Designing and Creating a Presentation about Sailing

**Personal**

You always have wanted to learn how to sail. You and a few friends have registered for sailing lessons and want to learn some things in advance to better prepare you for the sailing lessons. Use at least three objectives found at the beginning of this chapter to develop the presentation, including a motion path and dimmed text. Use pictures from Office.com if they are appropriate for this topic or use your personal digital pictures. Be sure to check spelling.

### 3: Designing and Creating a Presentation about Planning a Retirement Community

**Professional**

You work for an architectural firm that is developing a retirement village for people ages 55 and older. The 30-acre village will have condominiums, townhomes, and a few single-family homes. It will offer a community clubhouse with an indoor-outdoor swimming pool, a fitness center, party rooms, a large banquet room, a small movie theater, and a game room. Your firm has assigned you the job of putting together a presentation listing all the amenities this retirement village will offer. There will also be a community garden for residents to plant vegetables and flowers; tennis courts; shuffleboard courts; and a small landscaped park that will feature a fountain, a pond, benches, and picnic tables. You will be showing your slide show at a town hall meeting for community residents and also plan to run the self-running presentation at a kiosk. Use pictures from Office.com if they are appropriate for this topic or use your personal digital pictures. Add credits on the last slide. Be certain to check spelling.

# 8 | Customizing a Template and Handouts Using Masters

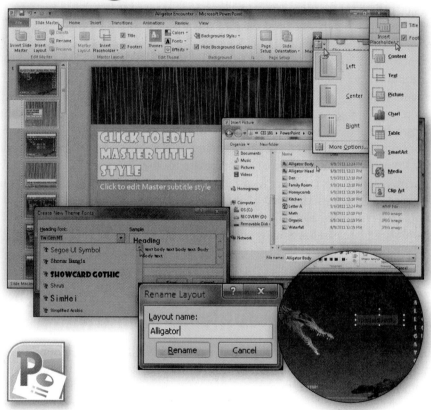

## Objectives

You will have mastered the material in this chapter when you can:

- Apply slide and font themes to a slide master
- Change a slide master background
- Add a background style and graphic to a slide master
- Insert a placeholder into a slide layout
- Apply a Quick Style to a placeholder
- Change text direction and character spacing

- Hide background graphics on individual slides
- Apply a fill to a text box and change transparency
- Rename a slide master
- Save a slide master as a template
- Create handouts using the handout master
- Create speaker notes using the notes master

# 8 | Customizing a Template and Handouts Using Masters

## Introduction

**BTW**

**The Power of Using Masters**
Use masters to give your presentation a unique and uniform look. They are convenient when you have presentations with many slides because they allow you to make universal style changes to every slide in your presentation, including ones added later. You can customize the presentation theme and slide layouts, including the background, color, fonts, effects, and placeholder sizes and location. Using slide masters saves time because you don't have to format every slide or type the same information repeatedly.

PowerPoint provides a variety of designs and layouts to meet most presenters' needs. At times, however, you may need a different set of colors, fonts, placeholders, or graphics to display throughout a presentation. PowerPoint allows you to customize the master layouts for slides, handouts, and speaker notes. These masters specify the precise locations and styles of placeholders, pictures, text boxes, and other slide and handout elements.

Once you determine your custom specifications in these masters, you can save the file as a template so that you can reuse these key elements as a starting point for multiple presentations. This unique **template** is a set of special slides you create and then use to create similar presentations. A template consists of a general master slide layout that has elements common to all the slide layouts. One efficient way to create similar presentations is to create a template, save the template, open the template, and then save the slides as a different PowerPoint presentation each time a new presentation is required.

Templates help speed and simplify the process of creating a presentation, so many PowerPoint designers create a template for common presentations they develop frequently. Templates can have a variable number of slide layouts depending upon the complexity of the presentation. A simple presentation can have a few slide layouts; for example, the Alligator Encounter presentation will have three slide layouts. A more complex template can have many slide masters and layouts.

## Project — Presentation with Customized Slide, Handout, and Notes Masters

**BTW**

**Multiple Slide Masters**
PowerPoint allows you to insert additional slide masters in one file so that one presentation can have two or more different styles. Each slide master has a related set of layout masters. In contrast, however, one presentation can have only one handout master and one notes master.

Alligators have existed on Earth for more than 200 million years. Found in the southeastern United States and in China, these reptiles can weigh more than 1,000 pounds and grow to a length of more than 19 feet. Having approximately 80 teeth, their bone-crushing jaws can catch unsuspecting prey, such as fish, mammals, and other reptiles. Many nature parks, including the Alligator Encounter you will feature in this project, offer excursions into freshwater swamps and allow visitors to view the alligators in a natural habitat. The project in this chapter (Figure 8–1) promotes these safaris. All three slides are created by starting with a template file that contains two basic slide elements: the nature center's name on a formatted placeholder and an alligator picture. The overall template, called the **slide master** (Figure 8–1a), is formatted with a theme, customized title and text fonts, and customized footer placeholders for the slide layouts. The Title Slide Layout (Figure 8–1b) is used to create Slide 1 (Figure 8–1c), which introduces audiences to the nature center. Similarly, the Blank Layout (Figure 8–1d) is used for Slide 2 (Figure 8–1e), which promotes the nighttime tours in June. The Title and Content Layout (Figure 8–1f) is used to create the text and graphic on Slide 3 (Figure 8–1g). In addition, the custom handout master (Figure 8–1h) is used to create a handout with an alligator picture and header and footer text (Figure 8–1i). Likewise, the custom notes master (Figure 8–1j) is used to create speaker notes pages (Figures 8–1k, 8–1l, and 8–1m).

# Overview

As you read through this chapter, you will learn how to create the presentation and handouts shown in Figure 8–1 on this page through page PPT 469 by performing these general tasks:

- Customize slide masters.
- Format and arrange slide master footers.
- Insert pictures and a placeholder into slide layouts.
- Insert and format text boxes.
- Rename and delete slide layouts.
- Customize handout and notes masters.
- Create a new presentation using a custom template.

**BTW**

**Inserting Objects into the Slide Master**
In this project you will add a placeholder, text box, and pictures to the layout. You can, however, insert other objects, including clip art and video and audio files. Corporations often insert their company logos into a slide master.

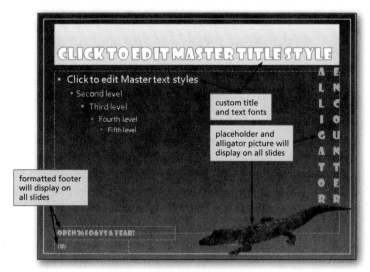

**(a) Slide Master**

**(b) Title Slide Layout**

**(c) Slide 1**

**Figure 8–1**

(d) Blank Layout

(e) Slide 2

(f) Title and Content Layout

(g) Slide 3

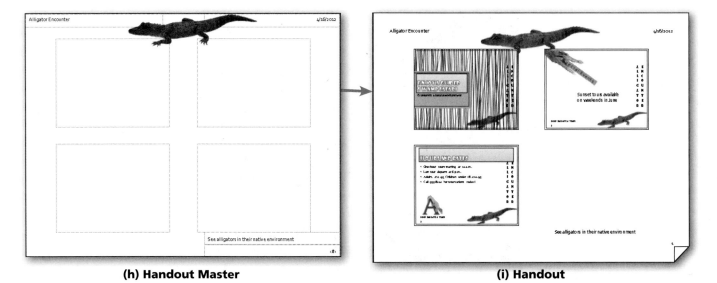

(h) Handout Master

(i) Handout

**Figure 8–1 (Continued)**

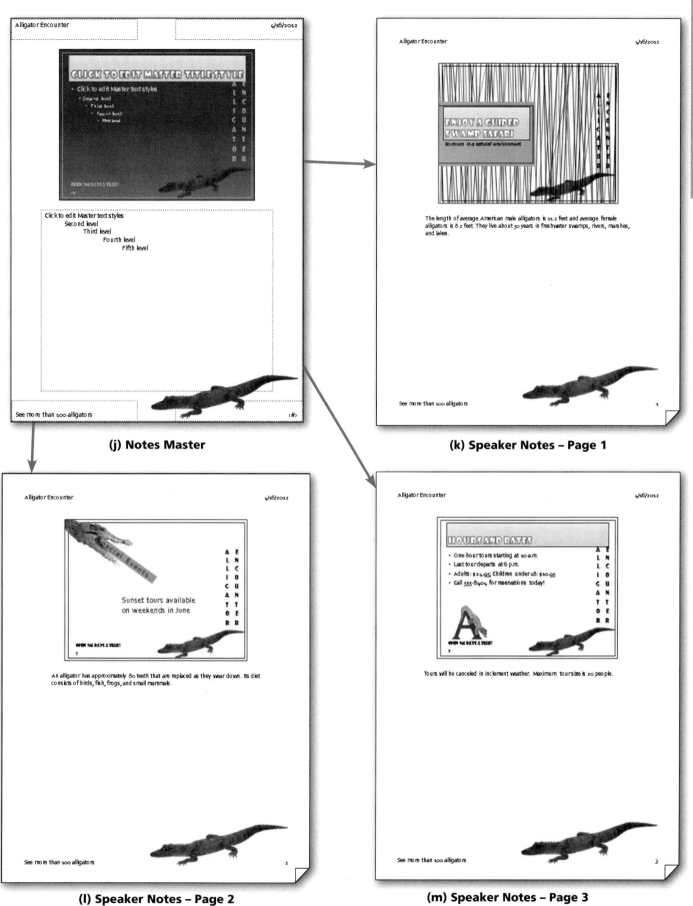

**(j) Notes Master**

**(k) Speaker Notes – Page 1**

**(l) Speaker Notes – Page 2**

**(m) Speaker Notes – Page 3**

**Figure 8–1 (Continued)**

Plan
Ahead

> **General Project Guidelines**
> When creating a PowerPoint presentation, the actions you perform and the decisions you make will affect the appearance and characteristics of the finished document. As you create a presentation with illustrations, such as the project shown in Figure 8–1 on pages PPT 467 to PPT 469, you should follow these general guidelines:
>
> 1. **Plan the slide master.** Using a new slide master gives you the freedom to plan every aspect of your slide. Take care to think about the overall message you are trying to convey before you start PowerPoint and select definite elements for this master.
>
> 2. **Develop the slide master prior to creating presentation slides.** You can save time and create consistency when you design and build your master at the start of your PowerPoint session rather than after you have created individual slides.
>
> 3. **Decide how to distribute copies of slides.** Some audience members will desire printed copies of your slides. To conserve paper and ink, you may decide to limit the number of copies you print or to post the presentation electronically in a shared location for users to print the presentation if they so choose.
>
> When necessary, more specific details concerning the above guidelines are presented at appropriate points in the chapter. The chapter also will identify the actions performed and decisions made regarding these guidelines during the creation of the presentation shown in Figure 8–1.

**BTW**

**The Ribbon and Screen Resolution**
PowerPoint may change how the groups and buttons within the groups appear on the Ribbon, depending on the computer's screen resolution. Thus, your Ribbon may look different from the ones in this book if you are using a screen resolution other than 1024 × 768.

## To Start PowerPoint and Save a File

If you are using a computer to step through the project in this chapter and you want your screens to match the figures in this book, you should change your computer's resolution to 1024 × 768. The following steps start PowerPoint and then save a file.

**1** Start PowerPoint. If necessary, maximize the PowerPoint window.

**2** Save the presentation using the file name, Alligator Encounter.

Plan
Ahead

> **Plan the slide master.**
> Using a new slide master gives you the freedom to specify every slide element. Like an artist with a new canvas or a musician with blank sheet music, only your imagination prevents you from creating an appealing master that conveys the overall look of your presentation.
> Before you start developing the master, give your overall plan some careful thought. The decisions you make at this point should be reflected on every slide. A presentation can have several master layouts, but you should change these layouts only if you have a compelling need to change them. Use the Plan Ahead concepts you have read throughout the chapters in this book to guide your decisions about fonts, colors, backgrounds, art, and other essential slide elements.

## Customizing Presentation Slide Master Backgrounds and Fonts

PowerPoint has many template files with the file extension .potx. Each template file has three masters: slide, handout, and notes. A slide master has at least one layout; you have used many of these layouts, such as Title and Content, Two Content, and Picture with

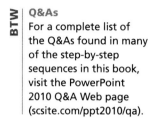

Caption, to create presentations. A **handout master** designates the placement of text, such as page numbers, on a sheet of paper intended to distribute to audience members. A **notes master** defines the formatting for speaker's notes.

## Slide Master

If you select a document theme and want to change one of its components on every slide, you can override that component by changing the slide master. In addition, if you want your presentation to have a unique design, you might want to create a slide master rather than attempt to modify a current document theme. A slide master indicates the size and position of text and object placeholders, font styles, slide backgrounds, transitions, and effects. Any change to the slide master results in changing that component on every slide in the presentation. For example, if you change the second-level bullet on the slide master, each slide with a second-level bullet will display this new bullet format.

One presentation can have more than one slide master. You may find two or more slide masters are necessary when your presentation reuses special slide layouts. In this Alligator Encounter presentation, for example, one slide will have the title slide to introduce the overall concept, another will have a blank slide to showcase a special event for the month, and a third slide will have a title and a bulleted list to give specific information about the nature park's hours, admission prices, and telephone number. All slides will have an alligator picture and the name of the safari company, Alligator Encounter, on the slide master.

**BTW**

**Q&As**
For a complete list of the Q&As found in many of the step-by-step sequences in this book, visit the PowerPoint 2010 Q&A Web page (scsite.com/ppt2010/qa).

## To Display a Slide Master

To begin developing a unique design for the Alligator Encounter slides, you need to display the slide master so that you can customize the slide components. The following steps display the slide master.

- Click View on the Ribbon to display the View tab (Figure 8–2).

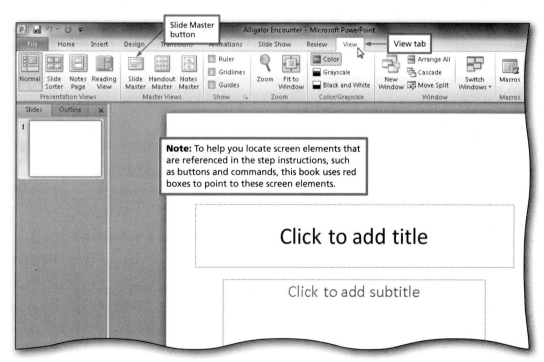

**Figure 8–2**

**2**

- Click the Slide Master button (View tab | Master Views group) to display the Slide Master tab and the slide thumbnails in the Overview pane.

- Click the Office Theme Slide Master layout (Figure 8–3).

What are all the other thumbnails in the left pane below the slide master?

They are all the slide layouts associated with this slide master. You have used many of these layouts in the presentations you have developed in the exercises in this book.

Why is the layout given this name?

The slide layout names begin with the theme applied to the slides. In this case, the default Office Theme is applied. The first slide layout in the list is called the master because it controls the colors, fonts, and objects that are displayed on all the other slides in the presentation.

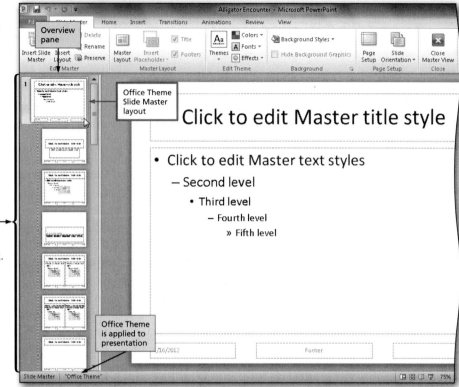

**Figure 8–3**

## To Apply Slide and Font Themes to a Slide Master

You can change the look of an entire presentation by applying formats to the slide master in the same manner that you apply these formats to individual slides. Alligators live in swampy areas, so you want your slides to reflect a marshy background and earthy tones. The following steps apply a theme and change the font theme colors.

**1**

- With the slide master displaying, click the Themes button (Slide Master tab | Edit Theme group) to display the Themes gallery.

- Scroll down to display the Thatch theme in the gallery (Figure 8–4).

🔍 **Experiment**

- Point to various themes in the Themes gallery and watch the colors and fonts change on the slide master.

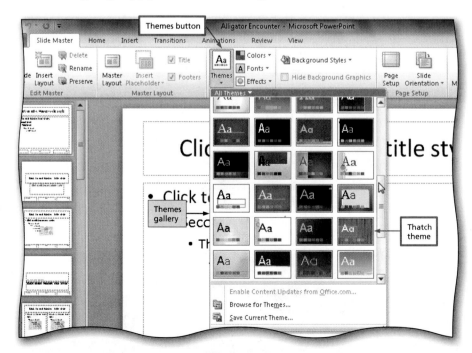

**Figure 8–4**

**2**

- Click the Thatch theme to apply this theme to the slide master.

- Click the Theme Colors button (Slide Master tab | Edit Theme group) to display the Theme Colors gallery.

- Scroll down to display the Paper theme color scheme in the gallery (Figure 8–5).

**Experiment**

- Point to various themes in the Theme Colors gallery and watch the colors and fonts change on the slide master.

**3**

- Click Paper in the Theme Colors gallery to change the slide master colors to Paper.

Can I insert another set of slide masters to give other slides in the presentation a unique look?

Yes. PowerPoint allows you to insert multiple masters into an existing presentation.

**Figure 8–5**

## To Customize Theme Fonts

Each theme has a heading font and a body font applied to it. At times both fonts are the same. For example, the Thatch theme you applied to the slide master uses the Twentieth Century MT font for both the heading and body. Other times, the heading font differs from the body font, but both fonts coordinate with each other. You can customize theme fonts by selecting your own combination of heading and body font and then giving the new theme font set a unique name. The following steps apply a new heading and body font to the Thatch theme.

**1**

- Click the Theme Fonts button (Slide Master tab | Edit Theme group) to display the Theme Fonts gallery (Figure 8–6).

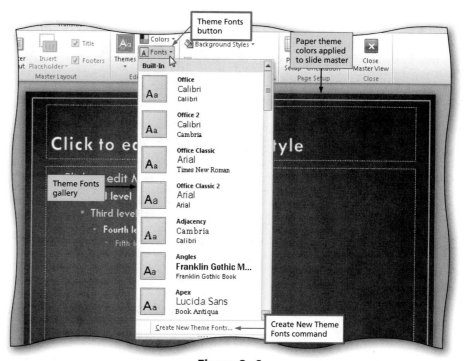

**Figure 8–6**

- Click Create New Theme Fonts in the Theme Fonts gallery to display the Create New Theme Fonts dialog box.

- Click the Heading font arrow and then scroll up to display Showcard Gothic in the list (Figure 8–7).

**Q&A** Can I preview the fonts to see how they are displayed on the slide master?

No preview is available when using the Create New Theme Fonts dialog box. Once you select the font, however, PowerPoint will display text in the Sample box.

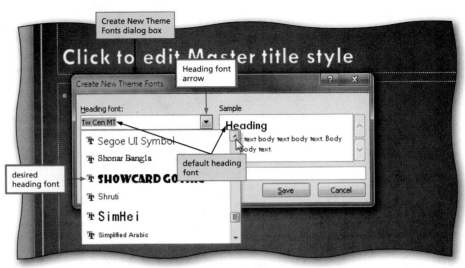

**Figure 8–7**

- Click Showcard Gothic to apply that font as the new heading text font.

- Click the Body font arrow and then scroll up to display Corbel in the list (Figure 8–8).

**Q&A** What if the Showcard Gothic or Corbel fonts are not in my list of fonts?

Select fonts that resemble the fonts shown in Figure 8–8.

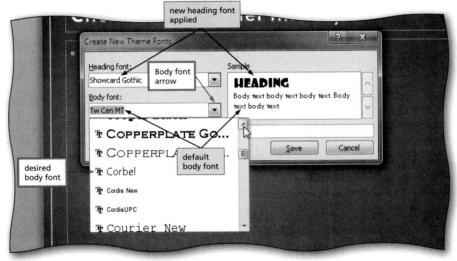

**Figure 8–8**

- Click Corbel to apply that font as the new body text font.

- Select the words, Custom 1, in the Name text box and then type **Alligator** to name the new font set (Figure 8–9).

**Q&A** Must I name this font set I just created?

No. If you name the set, however, you easily will recognize this combination in your font set if you want to use it in new presentations. It will display in the Custom area of the Fonts gallery fonts.

**Figure 8–9**

**⑤**

- Click the Save button (Create New Theme Fonts dialog box) to save this new font set with the name, Alligator.

# To Format a Slide Master Background and Apply a Quick Style

Once you have applied a theme to the slide master and determined the fonts for the presentation, you can further customize the presentation. The following steps format the slide master background and then apply a Quick Style.

- Click the Background Styles button (Slide Master tab | Background group) to display the Background Styles gallery (Figure 8–10).

**Experiment**

- Point to various styles themes in the Background Styles gallery and watch the backgrounds change on the slide master title text placeholder.

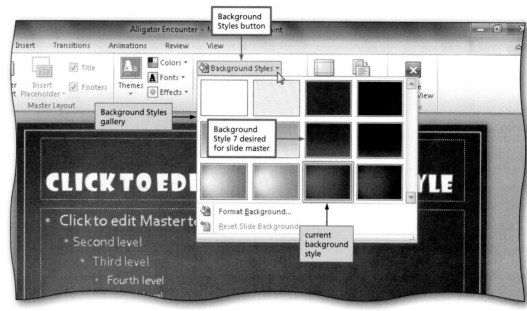

**Figure 8–10**

- Click Background Style 7 (third style in second row) to apply this background to the slide master (Figure 8–11).

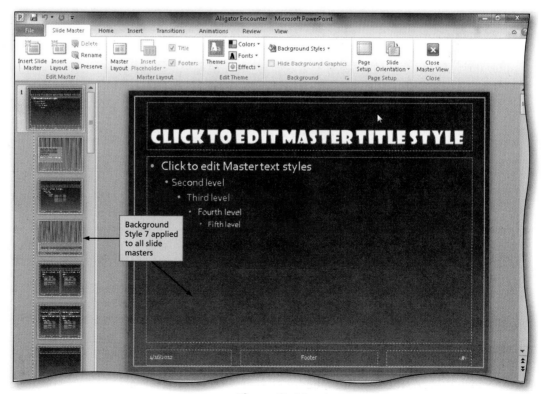

**Figure 8–11**

- Click the slide master title text placeholder to select it.
- Display the Home tab and then click the Quick Styles button (Home tab | Drawing group) to display the Quick Styles gallery (Figure 8–12).

 **Experiment**

- Point to various styles in the Quick Styles gallery and watch the background and borders change on the slide master title text placeholder.

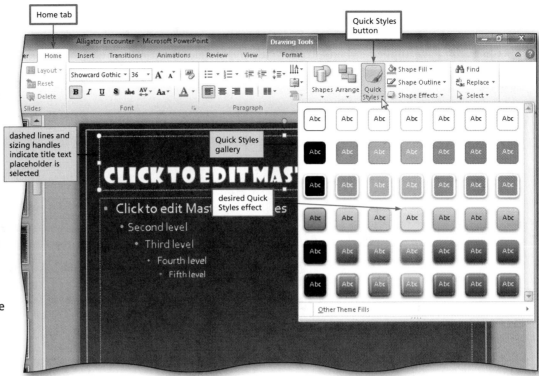

**Figure 8–12**

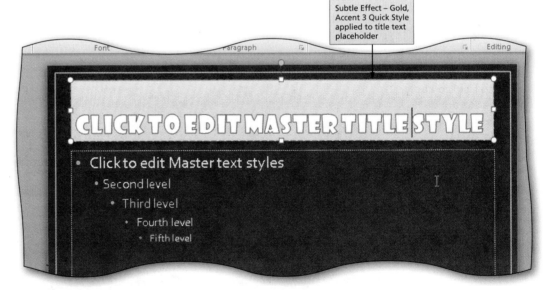

**Figure 8–13**

- Click the Subtle Effect – Gold, Accent 3 Quick Style (fourth style in fourth row) to apply this style to the title text placeholder (Figure 8–13).

## To Delete, Move, and Add Text to a Slide Master Footer

Slide numbers, the date and time, and footer text can be displayed anywhere on a slide, not just in the default footer placeholder locations. The following steps delete one footer placeholder, move the footer placeholders, and then add footer text.

**1**

- With the slide master displaying, click the border of the date footer placeholder to select it (Figure 8–14).

**Figure 8–14**

**2**

- Press the DELETE key to delete the date placeholder.

**Q&A** What should I do if the placeholder still is showing on the slide?

Be certain you clicked the placeholder border and not just the text. The border must display as a solid line before you can delete it.

- Click the page number footer placeholder to select it and then drag it to the location where the date placeholder originally appeared.

**3**

- Click the content footer placeholder and then drag it above the page number placeholder (Figure 8–15).

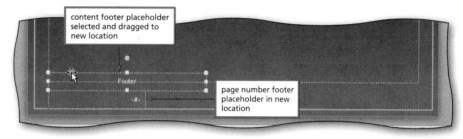

**Figure 8–15**

**4**

- Display the Insert tab, click the Header & Footer button (Insert tab | Text group), and then place a check mark in the Slide number check box.

- Place a check mark in the Footer check box and then type **Open 365 days a year!** in the Footer text box.

- Place a check mark in the 'Don't show on title slide' check box (Figure 8–16).

**Q&A** Can I verify where the footer placeholders will display on the slide layout?

Yes. The black boxes in the bottom of the Preview area indicate the footer placeholders' locations.

**5**

- Click the Apply to All button (Header and Footer dialog box) to add the slide number and footer text to the slide master.

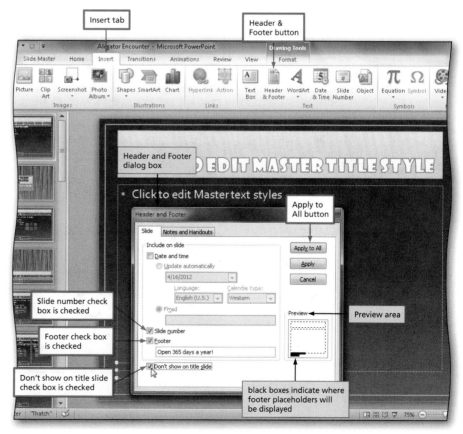

**Figure 8–16**

## To Format Slide Master Footer Text

You can format footer text using the same font styles and text attributes available to title and subtitle text. The following steps format the footer text.

- Select the content footer placeholder text and then click the Font box arrow on the Mini toolbar to display the Font gallery (Figure 8–17).

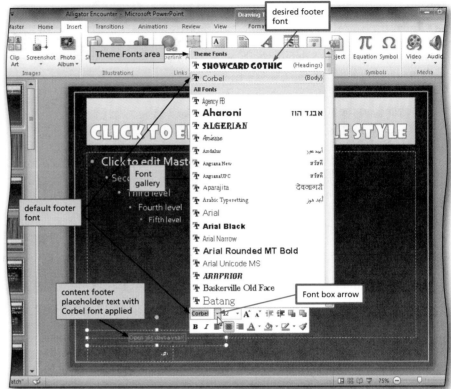

**Figure 8–17**

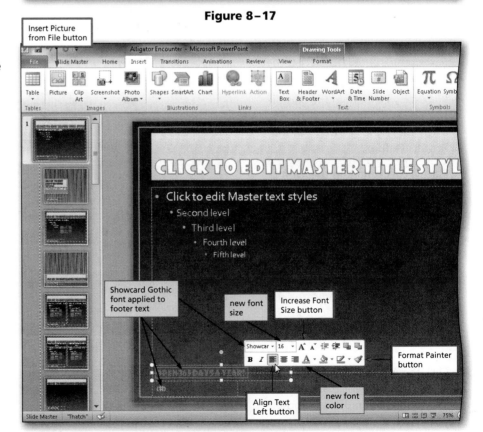

- Click Showcard Gothic in the Theme Fonts area of the Font gallery to change the footer font.
- Display the Mini toolbar again and then increase the font size from 12 to 16 point.
- Change the font color to Orange, Accent 2 (sixth color in first row).
- Use the Format Painter to apply the content footer placeholder formatting to the page number placeholder.
- Click the Align Text Left button to move both the content and page number footer text toward the left border of the placeholder (Figure 8–18).

**Figure 8–18**

## To Insert a Background Graphic into a Slide Master

The theme, fonts, footer, and background colors are set. The next step is to draw the viewers' attention to the presentation by placing Alligator Body picture, located on the Data Files for Students, in the same location on every slide. See the inside back cover of this book for instructions on downloading the Data Files for Students, or contact your instructor for more information on accessing the required files. The repetition of this picture creates consistency and helps reinforce the message. The following steps insert an alligator picture into the slide master.

**1**

• With the slide master and Insert tab displaying, click the Insert Picture from File button (Insert tab | Images group) to display the Insert Picture dialog box.

• With your USB flash drive connected to one of the computer's USB ports and the list of files and folders on your flash drive displaying, click Alligator Body to select the file name (Figure 8–19).

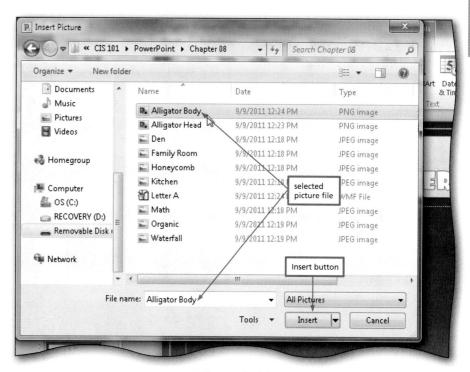

**Figure 8–19**

**What if the picture is not on a USB flash drive?**

Use the same process, but select the device containing the picture. Another option is to locate this picture or a similar one in the Microsoft Clip Organizer. You may need to remove the picture background to call attention to the alligator.

**2**

• Click the Insert button (Insert Picture dialog box) to insert the picture into the slide master.

• Drag the picture to the location shown in Figure 8–20.

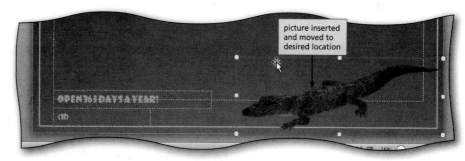

**Figure 8–20**

**Break Point:** If you wish to take a break, this is a good place to do so. Be sure to save the Alligator Encounter file again and then you can quit PowerPoint. To resume at a later time, start PowerPoint, open the file called Alligator Encounter, and continue following the steps from this location forward.

# Adding and Formatting Placeholders

Each design theme determines where placeholders appear on individual layouts. The slide master has placeholders for bulleted lists, title text, pictures, and other graphical elements. At times, you may find that you need a specific placeholder for a design element not found on any of the slide master layouts. You can add a placeholder in Slide Master view for text, SmartArt, charts, tables, and other graphical elements.

## To Insert a Placeholder into a Blank Layout

The words, Alligator Encounter, will appear on the title slide. To emphasize the name, you can add these words to every text slide. One efficient method of adding this text is to insert a placeholder, type the words, and, if necessary, format the characters. The following steps insert a placeholder into the Blank Layout.

- In the Overview pane, scroll down and then click the Blank Layout to display this layout.
- With the Slide Master tab displaying, click the Insert Placeholder button arrow (Slide Master tab | Master Layout group) to display the Insert Placeholder gallery (Figure 8–21).

**Q&A**

Why does the Insert Placeholder button on my screen differ from the button shown in Figure 8–21?

The image on the button changes based on the type of placeholder content that was last inserted. A placeholder can hold any content, including text, pictures, and tables. If the last type of placeholder inserted was for SmartArt, for example, the Insert Placeholder button would display the SmartArt icon.

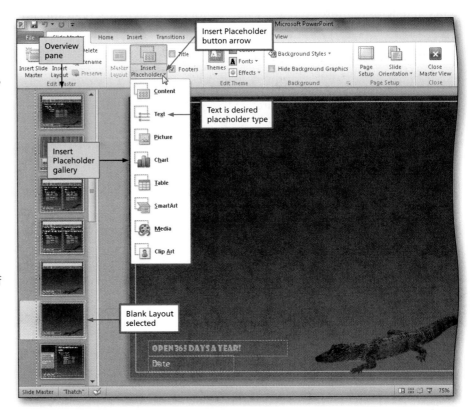

**Figure 8–21**

- Click Text in the gallery to change the mouse pointer to a crosshair.

Could I have inserted a Content placeholder rather than a Text placeholder?

Yes. The Content placeholder is used for any of the seven types of slide content: text, table, chart, SmartArt, picture, clip art, or media. In this project, you will insert text in the placeholder. If you know the specific kind of content you want to place in the placeholder, it is best to select that placeholder type.

- Position the mouse pointer at the upper-right area of the layout (Figure 8–22).

**Figure 8–22**

- Click to insert the new placeholder into the Blank Layout (Figure 8–23).

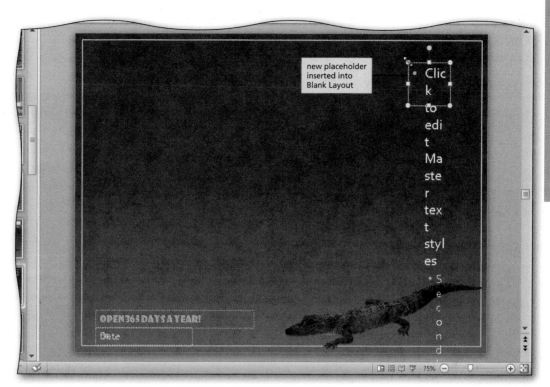

**Figure 8–23**

## To Add and Format Placeholder Text

Now that the text placeholder is positioned, you can add the desired text and then format the characters. You will need to delete the second-, third-, fourth-, and fifth-level bullets in this placeholder because they are not being used. The following steps add and format the words in the new Blank Layout placeholder.

- Click inside the new placeholder, press and hold down the CTRL key, and then press the A key to select all the text in the placeholder (Figure 8–24).

**Figure 8–24**

**2**

- Press the DELETE key to delete all the selected text in the placeholder.

- Display the Home tab and then click the Bullets button (Home tab | Paragraph group) to remove the bullet from the placeholder.

- Type **Alligator Encounter** in the placeholder.

- Drag the bottom sizing handle down until it is above the alligator picture, as shown in Figure 8–25.

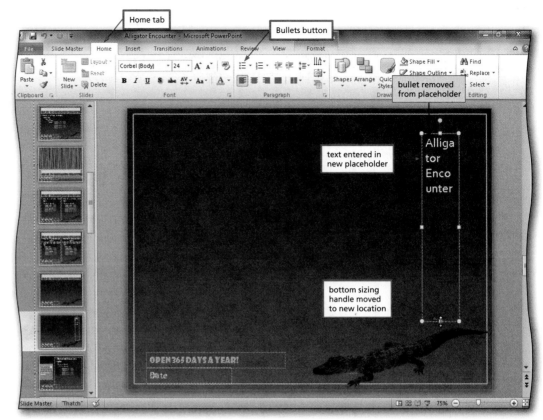

Figure 8–25

**3**

- Click the Text Direction button (Home tab | Paragraph group) to open the Text Direction gallery (Figure 8–26).

🔎 **Experiment**

- Point to various directions in the Text Direction gallery and watch the two words in the placeholder change direction on the layout.

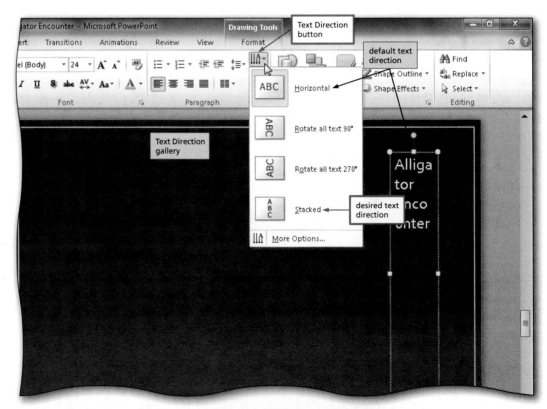

Figure 8–26

**4**

- Click Stacked to display the text vertically.

- Click the Align Text button (Home tab | Paragraph group) to display the Align Text gallery (Figure 8–27).

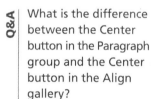 **Experiment**

- Point to the Center and Right icons in the Align Text gallery and watch the two words in the placeholder change alignment on the layout.

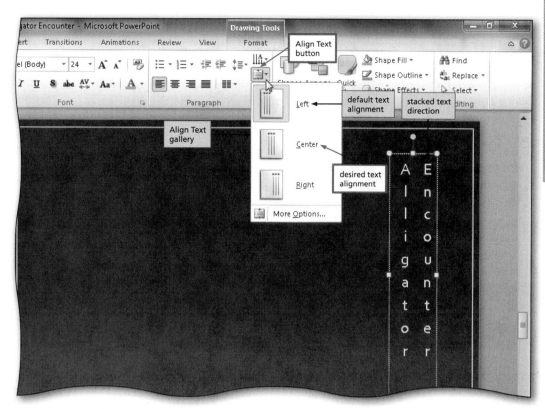

**Figure 8–27**

**5**

- Click Center to display the text in the middle of the placeholder (Figure 8–28).

 What is the difference between the Center button in the Paragraph group and the Center button in the Align gallery?

The Center button in the Paragraph group positions the text between the top and bottom borders of the placeholder. The Center button in the Align gallery centers the text between the left and right borders.

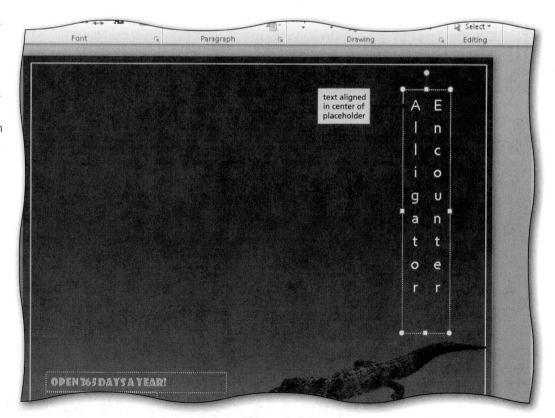

**Figure 8–28**

**6**

- Right-click the text in the placeholder to display the Mini toolbar and shortcut menu, click the Font box arrow on the Mini toolbar, and then select Showcard Gothic in the Theme Fonts area of the Font gallery.

- Click the Font Color button to change the font color to Orange, Accent 2 (Figure 8–29).

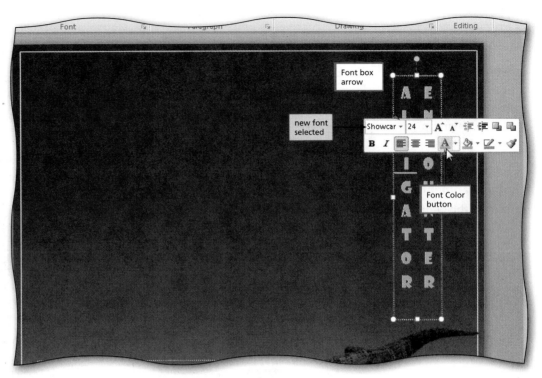

**Figure 8–29**

## To Cut a Placeholder and Paste It into a Slide Master

The new formatted placeholder appears only on the Blank Layout. If you selected any other layout in your presentation, such as Two Content or Title Only, this placeholder would not display. For consistency, this placeholder should appear on all text slides. You are not given the opportunity to insert a placeholder into the slide master, but you can paste a placeholder that you copied or cut from another slide. The following steps cut the new placeholder from the Blank Layout and paste it into the slide master.

**1**

- With the Home tab displaying, click the new placeholder border and then click the Cut button (Home tab | Clipboard group) to delete the placeholder from the layout and copy it to the Clipboard (Figure 8–30).

Q&A | Why did I click the Cut button instead of the Copy button?

Clicking the Cut button deletes the placeholder. Clicking the Copy button keeps the original placeholder on the slide, so if you paste the placeholder on the slide master, a second, identical placeholder would display on the Blank Layout.

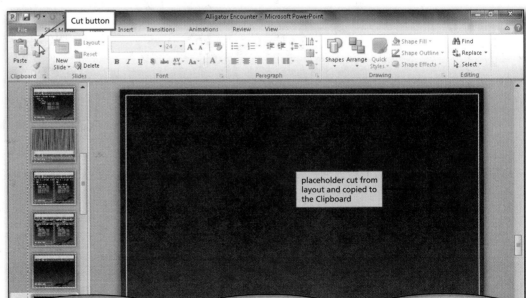

**Figure 8–30**

**2**

• Scroll up and then click the Thatch Slide Master thumbnail in the Overview pane to display the slide master.

• Click the Paste button (Home tab | Clipboard group) to copy the placeholder from the Clipboard to the slide master.

• Drag the placeholder to the location shown in Figure 8–31.

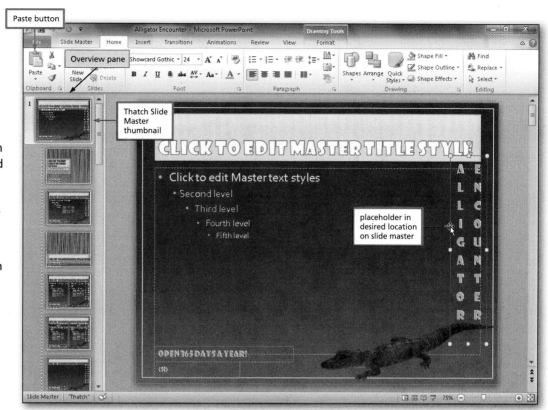

**Figure 8–31**

---

**Break Point:** If you wish to take a break, this is a good place to do so. Be sure to save the Alligator Encounter file again and then you can quit PowerPoint. To resume at a later time, start PowerPoint, open the file called Alligator Encounter, and continue following the steps from this location forward.

## To Insert a Picture and a Text Box into a Blank Layout

One slide in the completed presentation will feature the Alligator Encounter's new events. The content on this slide can vary depending upon the occasion; it might be photographs of newborn alligators, video from nighttime tours, or airboat rides. To ensure continuity when publicizing special events and promotions, you can insert another picture into the Blank Layout and then add and format a text box. This layout includes the Alligator Encounter placeholder you inserted into the slide master. The following steps insert a picture and a text box into the Blank Layout and then add text in the text box.

**1** Scroll down and then click the Blank Layout thumbnail in the Overview pane.

**2** Display the Insert tab, insert the Alligator Head picture from your USB flash drive into the Blank Layout, and then move the picture to the location shown in Figure 8–32.

**3** Display the Insert tab, click the Text Box button (Insert tab | Text group) and then insert a new text box in a blank area in the center of the layout.

**4** Type **Special Events** as the text box text, change the font color to Black, Background 1 (first color in first row), and then increase the font size to 28 point (Figure 8–32).

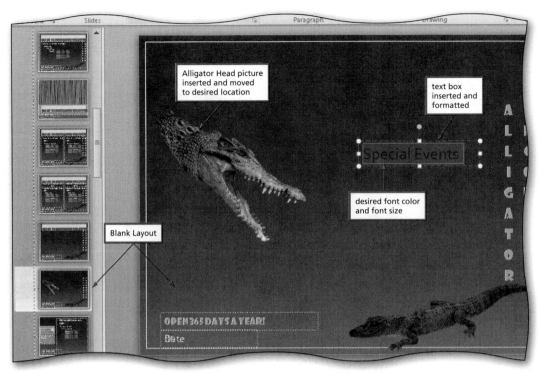

**Figure 8–32**

## To Change Character Spacing

Now that the text is added, you can change the spacing between the letters in the placeholder. The amount of space, called **character spacing**, can be increased or decreased from the Normal default in one of four preset amounts: Very Tight, Tight, Loose, or Very Loose. In addition, you can specify a precise amount of space in the Character Spacing tab of the Font dialog box. In this presentation, you will move the text box inside of the alligator's mouth, which is very long, so the letters in the text box can be stretched to fit the length of the mouth. The following steps increase the character spacing in the text box.

**1**

- With the text in the new text box selected, click the Character Spacing button (Home tab | Font group) to display the Character Spacing gallery (Figure 8–33).

**Experiment**

- Point to the spacing options in the gallery and watch the characters in the placeholder change.

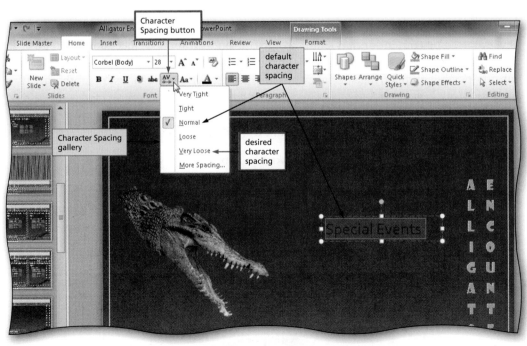

**Figure 8–33**

- Click Very Loose in the gallery to change the character spacing in the text box (Figure 8–34).

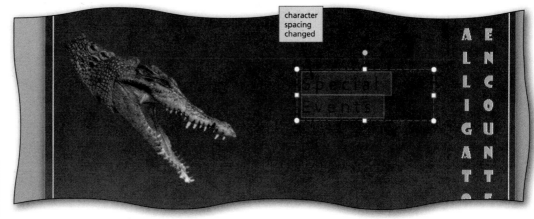

**Figure 8–34**

**Other Ways**

1. Click Character Spacing tab (Font dialog box), select Expanded or Condensed in Spacing box and point size in By text box

## To Apply a Fill to a Text Box and Increase Transparency

Now that the text is added, you can format the text box. A **fill** refers to the formatting of the interior of a shape. The fill can be a color, picture, texture, pattern, or the presentation background. If a color fill is desired, you can increase the transparency so that some of the background color or pattern mixes with the fill color. **Transparency** determines how much you can see through a picture or other slide element. A fully opaque object is solid, and it is represented by the default transparency percentage of 0. In contrast, the transparency percentage of 100 is fully transparent and allows all of the background to display. The following steps apply a fill to the text box on the Blank Layout and increase the transparency.

- Click the text inside the Special Events text box to remove the selection from the letters.

- Click the Shape Fill button arrow (Home tab | Drawing group) to display the Shape Fill gallery.

🄰 **Experiment**

- Point to various colors in the Shape Fill gallery and watch the placeholder background change.

- Click Red (second color in Standard Colors row) to fill the text box.

- Click the Drawing Dialog Box Launcher (Home tab | Drawing group) to display the Format Shape dialog box (Figure 8–35).

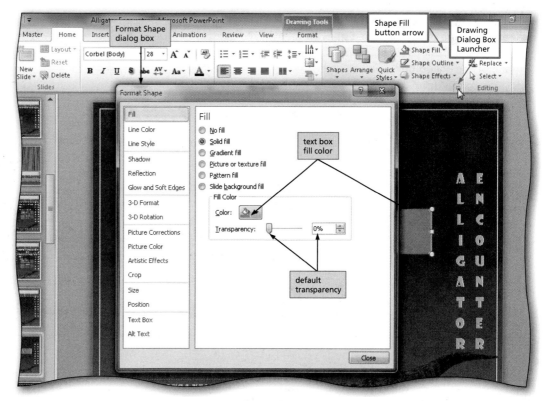

**Figure 8–35**

- If necessary, drag the Format Shape dialog box to the left side of the layout so that it does not cover the Special Events text box.

- Click the Transparency slider in the Fill pane and drag it to the right until 50% is displayed in the Transparency text box (Figure 8–36).

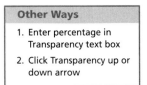
**Experiment**

- Drag the Transparency slider to the left and right, and watch the text box background change.

| **Other Ways** |
| --- |
| 1. Enter percentage in Transparency text box |
| 2. Click Transparency up or down arrow |

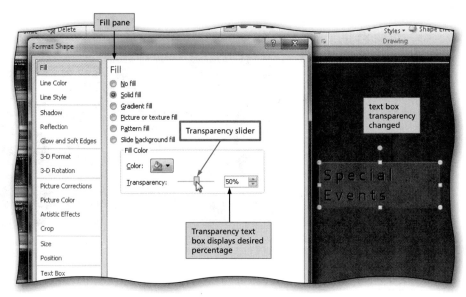

**Figure 8–36**

## To Change a Text Box Internal Margin

Each placeholder and text box has preset internal margins, which are the spaces between the border and the contents of the box. The default left and right margins are 0.1", and the default top and bottom margins are 0.05". In this project, you will drag the text box into the alligator's mouth, so you want the text to align as closely as possible against the left, top, and bottom borders of the box and the right margin to extend out of the alligator's mouth. The following steps change all four text box margins.

- Click Text Box in the left pane (Format Shape dialog box) to display the Text Box options in the right pane of the dialog box.

- Click the Left down arrow in the Internal margin area one time to decrease the margin to 0".

- Click the Right up arrow two times to increase the margin to 0.3".

- Click the Top down arrow one time to decrease the margin to 0".

- Click the Bottom down arrow one time to decrease the margin to 0".

- Click the 'Wrap text in shape' check box to remove the check mark in it (Figure 8–37).

**Q&A**    Must I change all the margins?

No. You can change one, two, three, or all four internal margins depending upon the placeholder shape and the amount of text entered.

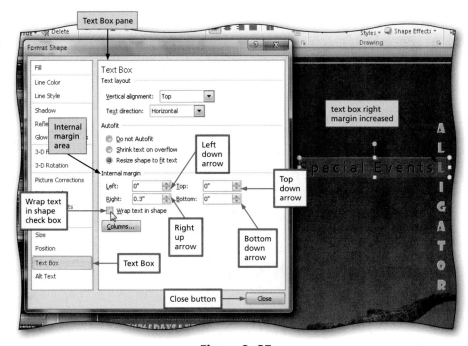

**Figure 8–37**

- Click the Close button (Format Shape dialog box).

## To Rotate a Picture and a Text Box

To balance the pictures on the slide, you can move the Alligator Head picture farther into the upper-left corner and then move the Special Events text box inside of the alligator's open mouth. For a dramatic effect, you can change the orientation of the picture and the placeholder on the slide by rotating them. Dragging the green **rotation handle** above a selected object allows you to rotate an object in any direction. The following steps move and rotate the Alligator Head picture and the Special Events text box.

**1**

- Click the Alligator Head picture to select it and then position the mouse pointer over the rotation handle so that it changes to a Free Rotate pointer (Figure 8–38).

**Q&A**
I selected the picture, but I cannot see the rotation handle. Why?

The rotation handle may not be visible at the top of the slide layout. Drag the picture downward, and the rotation hand will appear.

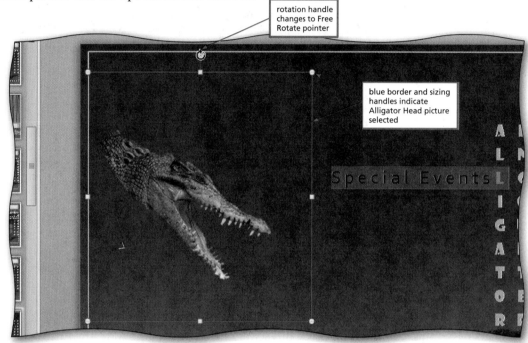

**Figure 8–38**

**2**

- Drag the mouse pointer counterclockwise so that it is displayed as shown in Figure 8–39.

**3**

- Drag the picture to position it in the upper-left corner of the slide layout.

**Q&A**
How do I move the picture in small increments?

To move or nudge the picture in very small increments, hold down the CTRL key with the picture selected while pressing the UP ARROW, DOWN ARROW, RIGHT ARROW, or LEFT ARROW keys.

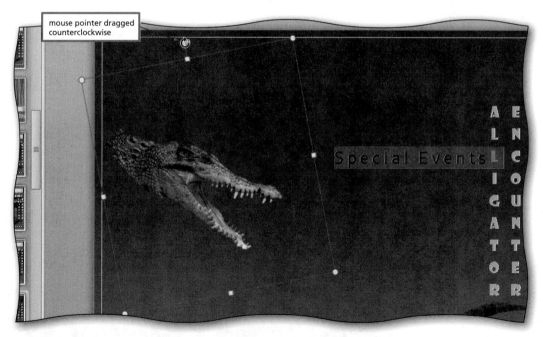

**Figure 8–39**

**4**

- Click the Special Events text box to select it, position the mouse pointer over the rotation handle so that it changes to a Free Rotate pointer, and then drag the text box clockwise so that it is at the same angle as the alligator's mouth.

- Drag the text box into the alligator's mouth as shown in Figure 8–40.

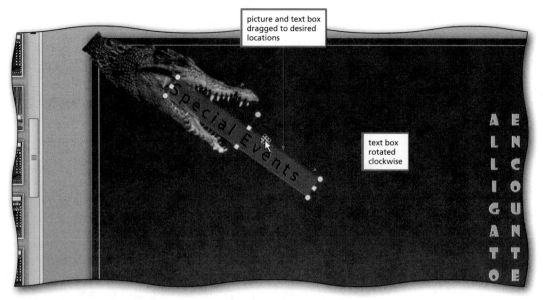

**Figure 8–40**

## To Hide and Unhide Background Graphics

The placeholder, text box, pictures, and other graphical elements are displayed on some slide master layouts and are hidden on others. You have the ability to change the default setting by choosing to hide or unhide the background graphics. The Title Slide Layout, by default, hides the background elements. Because alligators often hide in the marshy swamps, you want to convey this setting by displaying the Alligator Encounter placeholder and the alligator picture you inserted. The following steps unhide the background graphics on the Title Slide Layout, which is the first layout below the Thatch Slide Master in the Overview pane.

**1**

- Scroll up to display the Title Slide Layout and then display the Slide Master tab (Figure 8–41).

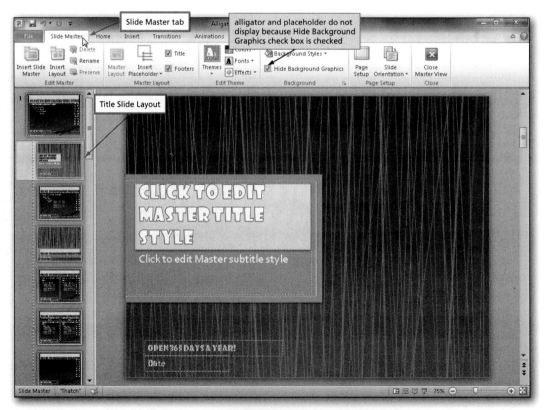

**Figure 8–41**

**2**

• Click the Hide Background Graphics check box (Slide Master tab | Background group) to remove the check mark in it (Figure 8–42).

**Q&A**

If I decide to hide the graphics, do I click the same check box to make them disappear?

Yes. The Hide Background Graphics check box is a toggle that displays and conceals the graphics.

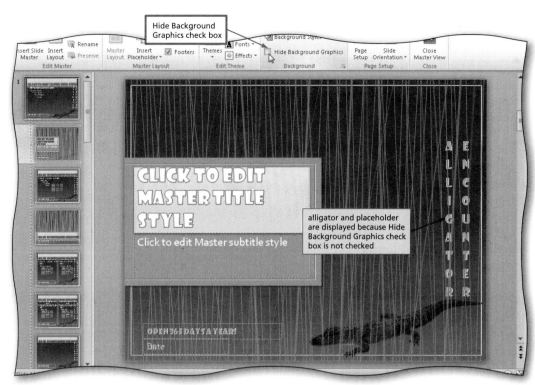

**Figure 8–42**

## To Rename a Slide Master and a Slide Layout

Once all the changes are made to a slide master and a slide layout, you may want to rename them with meaningful names that describe their functions or features. The new slide master name will be displayed on the status bar; the new layout name will be displayed in the Slide Layout gallery. The following steps rename the Thatch Slide Master, the Title Slide Layout, the Blank Layout, and the Title and Content Layout.

**1**

• Display the Thatch Slide Master and then click the Rename button (Slide Master tab | Edit Master group) to display the Rename Layout dialog box.

• Delete the text in the Layout name text box (Rename Layout dialog box) and then type **Alligator** in the text box (Figure 8–43).

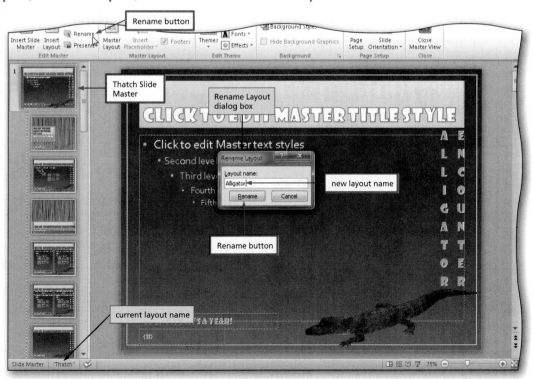

**Figure 8–43**

• Click the Rename button (Rename Layout dialog box) to give the layout the new name, Alligator Slide Master.

• Display the Title Slide Layout, click the Rename button (Slide Master tab | Edit Master group), and then type **Alligator Hiding** as the new layout name (Figure 8–44).

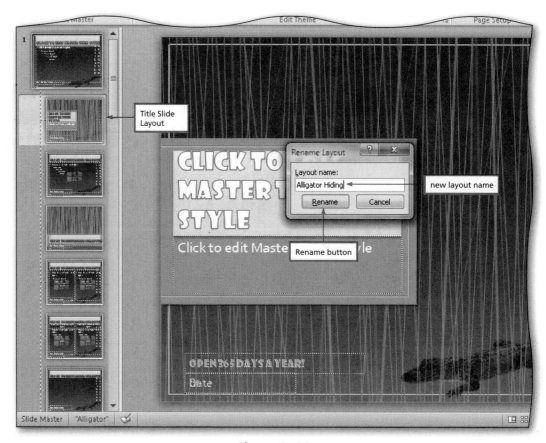

**Figure 8–44**

• Click the Rename button (Rename Layout dialog box) to rename the Title Slide layout.

• Scroll down to display the Blank Layout, click the Rename button (Slide Master tab | Edit Master group), and then type **Special Events** as the new layout name (Figure 8–45).

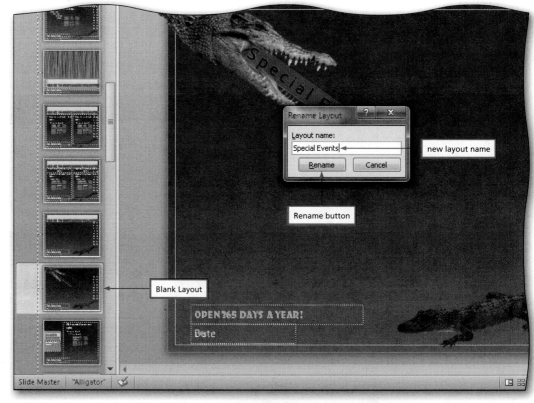

**Figure 8–45**

- Click the Rename button (Rename Layout dialog box).

- Scroll up to display the Title and Content Layout, click the Rename button (Slide Master tab | Edit Master group), and then type **Miscellaneous** as the new layout name (Figure 8–46).

- Click the Rename button (Rename Layout dialog box).

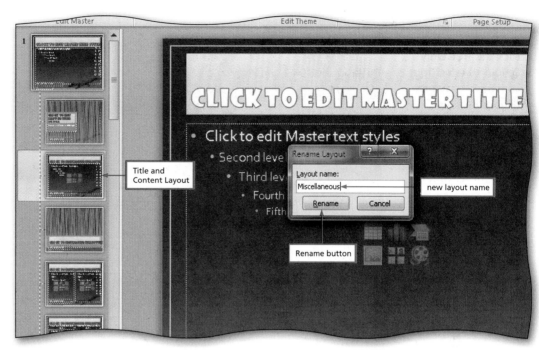

**Figure 8–46**

## To Delete a Slide Layout

You have made many changes to the slide master and two slide layouts. You will use these layouts and the Title and Content Layout, which is now called the Miscellaneous layout, when you close Master view and then add text, graphics, or other content to the presentation in Normal view. You can delete the other layouts in the Overview pane because you will not use them. The following steps delete slide layouts that will not be used to create the presentation.

- Click the Section Header Layout in the Overview pane to select it (Figure 8–47).

**Figure 8–47**

• Press and hold down the SHIFT key and then click the Title Only Layout to select four consecutive layouts (Figure 8–48).

**Q&A**

Why did I select only these four layouts?

The layout below the Title Only Layout is the Special Events Layout, and you will use that layout when you create Slide 2 in your presentation.

**Figure 8–48**

• Press the DELETE key to delete the four layouts.

• Click the Content with Caption Layout, press and hold down the SHIFT key, and then click the last layout, which is the Vertical Title and Text Layout, in the Overview pane (Figure 8–49).

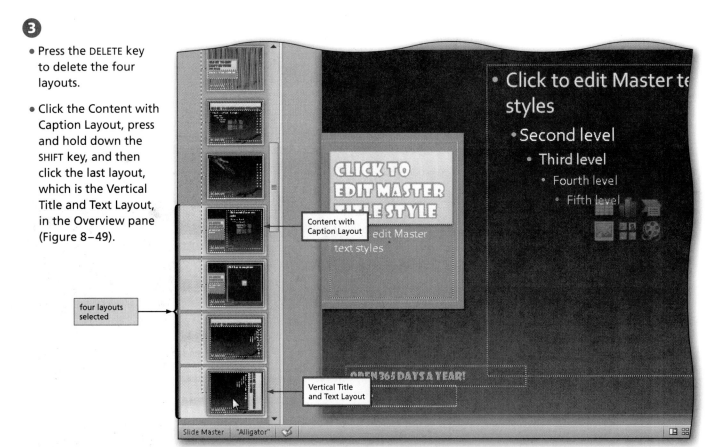

**Figure 8–49**

**4**

- Press the DELETE key to delete the four layouts (Figure 8–50).

**Q&A**

Now that I have created this slide master, can I ensure that it will not be changed when I create future presentations?

Yes. Normally a slide master is deleted when a new design template is selected. To keep the original master as part of your presentation, you can preserve it by selecting the thumbnail and then clicking the Preserve button in the Edit Master group. An icon in the shape of a pushpin is displayed below the slide number to indicate the master is preserved. If you decide to unpreserve a slide master, select this thumbnail and then click the Preserve button.

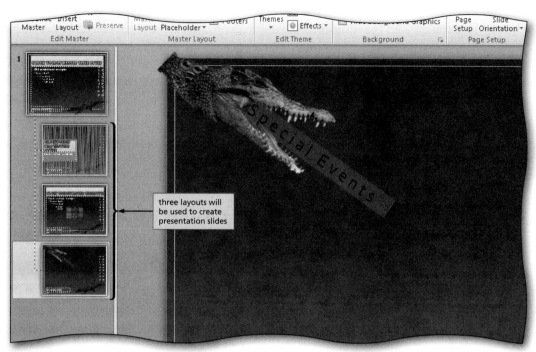

three layouts will be used to create presentation slides

**Figure 8–50**

| Other Ways |
| --- |
| 1. Click Delete button (Home tab \| Slides group)    2. Right-click selected slide, click Delete Layout on shortcut menu |

**Break Point:** If you wish to take a break, this is a good place to do so. You can quit PowerPoint now. To resume at a later time, start PowerPoint and continue following the steps from this location forward.

**Decide how to distribute copies of slides.**
Printed copies of your slides or handouts can give your audience the ability to follow the main points of your presentation and to write notes. Depending upon the venue and the audience, you might decide to limit the number of copies of the printed version of your presentation. As an alternative, you can put the file in a shared location, such as a Web site or a company's intranet. You can tell your audience members before the presentation where to locate the slides, and they can decide whether they want to download and print the copies. This option conserves ink and paper.

**Plan Ahead**

## Customizing Handout and Notes Masters

You have used PowerPoint's slide master template file to create unique slide layouts for the Alligator Encounter presentation. PowerPoint also has master template files to create handouts and notes. If you are going to distribute handouts to your audience, you can customize the handout master so that it coordinates visually with the presentation slides and reinforces your message. In addition, if you are going to use speaker notes to guide you through a presentation, you can tailor the notes master to fit your needs.

**BTW**

**Formatting the Date and Time Placeholder**
The 'Date and time' footer can have a variety of formats. When you click the Update automatically arrow, you can choose among formats that display the day, date, and time in a variety of combinations.

## To Customize a Handout Using a Handout Master

When you created the Alligator slide master, you specified the background, fonts, theme, and pictures for all slides. You likewise can create a specific handout master to determine the layout and graphics that will display on the printed page. Possible customization includes moving, restoring, and formatting the header and footer placeholders; setting the page number orientation; adding graphics; and specifying the number of slides to print on each page. The following steps use the handout master to create a custom handout.

- Display the View tab (Figure 8–51).

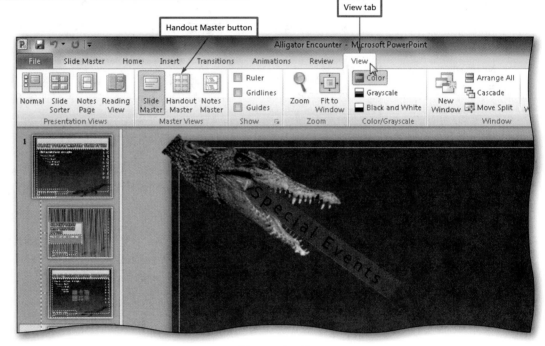

**Figure 8–51**

- Click the Handout Master button (View tab | Master Views group) to display the Handout Master tab and then click the Slides Per Page button (Handout Master tab | Page Setup group) to display the Slides Per Page gallery (Figure 8–52).

Is 6 Slides the default layout for all themes?

Yes. If you have fewer than six slides in your presentation or want to display slide details, then choose a handout layout with 1, 2, 3, or 4 slides per sheet of paper.

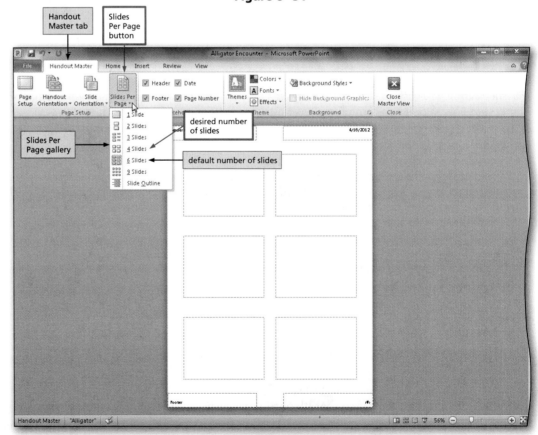

**Figure 8–52**

**3**

- Click 4 Slides in the gallery to change the layout from 6 slides to 4 slides.

- Click the Handout Orientation button (Handout Master tab | Page Setup group) to display the Handout Orientation gallery (Figure 8–53).

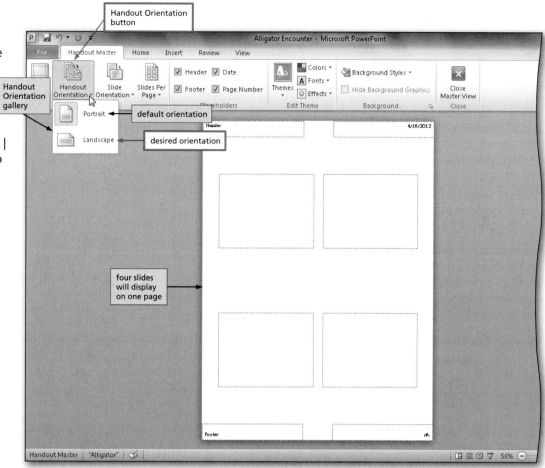

Figure 8–53

**4**

- Click Landscape in the gallery to display the page layout in landscape orientation (Figure 8–54).

When should I change the orientation from portrait to landscape?

If your slide content is dominantly vertical, such as an athlete running or a skyscraper in a major city, consider using the default portrait orientation. If, however, your slide content has long lines of text or pictures of four-legged animals, landscape orientation may be a more appropriate layout.

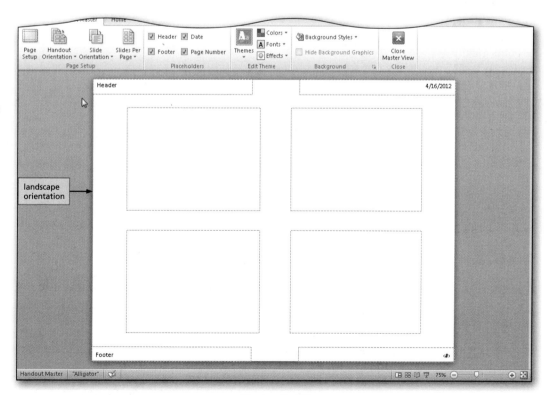

Figure 8–54

- Click the Header placeholder and then type **Alligator Encounter** as the header text.

- Click the Footer placeholder and then type **See alligators in their native environment** as the footer text.

- Drag the Footer placeholder above the page number placeholder (Figure 8–55).

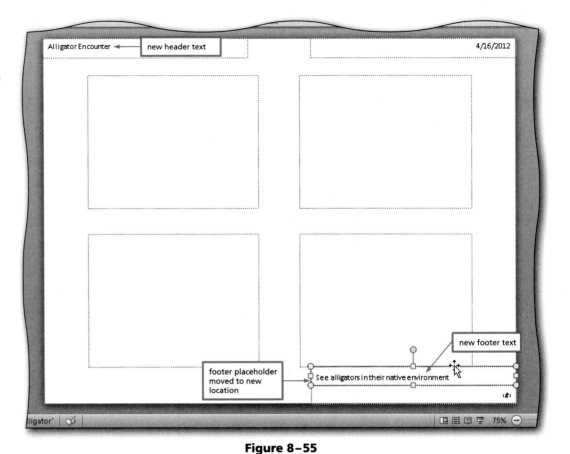

**Figure 8–55**

- Click the Theme Fonts button (Handout Master tab | Edit Theme group) to display the Theme Fonts gallery (Figure 8–56).

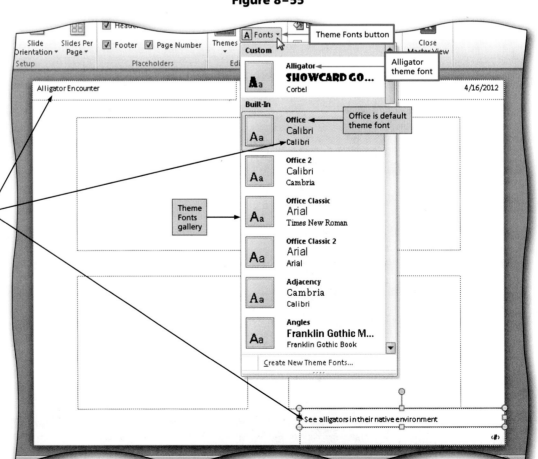

**Figure 8–56**

- Click Alligator in the Custom area of the gallery to apply the Corbel font to the text in the placeholders.

- Display the Insert tab, click the Insert Picture from File button (Insert tab | Images group), and then insert the Alligator Body picture located on the Data Files for Students.

- Rotate the Alligator Body picture clockwise, resize the picture so it is approximately 1.5" × 4.24", and then center it along the upper edge of the handout layout, as shown in Figure 8–57.

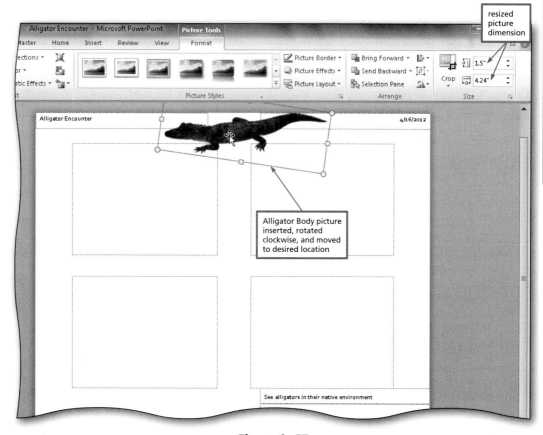

**Figure 8–57**

- Display the Insert tab, click the Header & Footer button (Insert tab | Text group), and then place a check mark in the 'Date and time' check box.

- Place a check mark in the Header check box.

- Place a check mark in the Footer check box (Figure 8–58).

- Click the Apply to All button (Header and Footer dialog box) to add the header and footer text and date to the handout master.

**Q&A**
Where will the header and footer display on the handout?

The black boxes in the Preview area show where these placeholders are located.

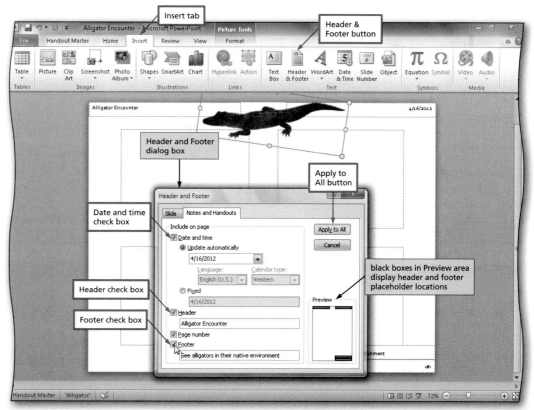

**Figure 8–58**

## To Customize a Notes Page Using a Notes Master

If you type notes in the Notes pane, you can print them for yourself or for your audience. The basic format found in the Backstage view generally suffices for handouts, but you may desire to alter the layout using the notes master. As with the slide master and handout master, you can add graphics and rearrange and format the header, footer, and page number placeholders. The following steps use the notes master to create a custom handout.

- Display the View tab (Figure 8–59).

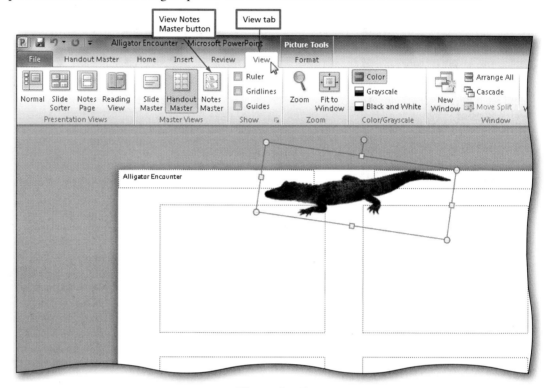

**Figure 8–59**

- Click the View Notes Master button (View tab | Master Views group) to display the Notes Master tab.

- Click the Footer placeholder, delete the text, and then type **See more than 100 alligators** as the new footer text.

- Click the Theme Fonts button (Notes Master tab | Edit Theme group) to display the Theme Fonts gallery (Figure 8–60).

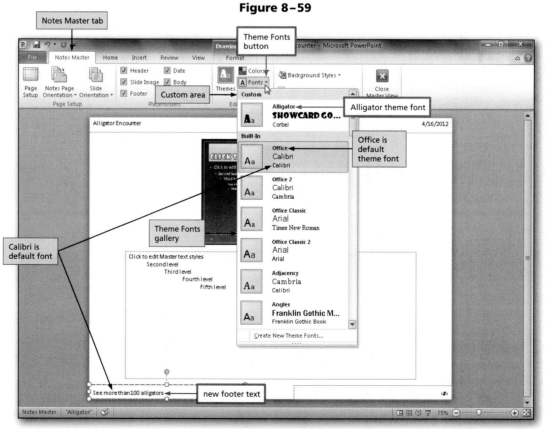

**Figure 8–60**

**4**

- Click Alligator in the Custom area of the Theme Fonts gallery to apply the Corbel font to the text in the header, footer, date, and page number placeholders.

- Click the Notes Page Orientation button (Notes Master tab | Page Setup group) to display the Notes Page Orientation gallery (Figure 8–61).

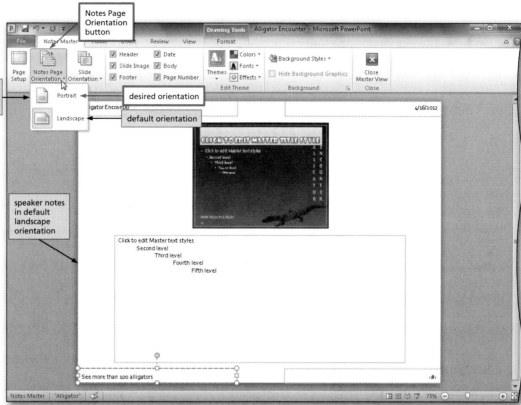

Figure 8–61

**5**

- Click Portrait in the gallery to display the page layout in portrait orientation.

- Display the Insert tab, click the Insert Picture from File button (Insert tab | Images group), and then insert the Alligator Body picture located on the Data Files for Students.

- Resize the picture so that it is approximately 1.25" × 4".

- Move the picture to the lower-right corner of the layout, as shown in Figure 8–62.

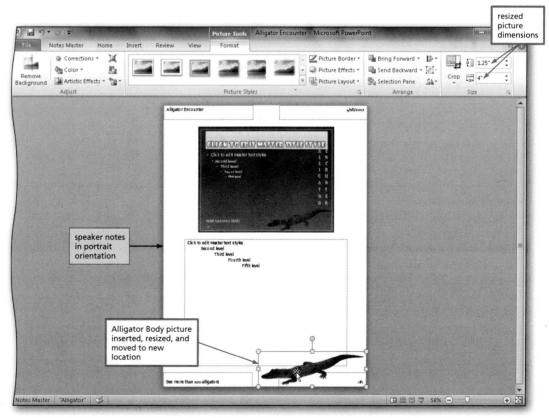

Figure 8–62

## To Close Master View

Now that all the changes to the slide master, handout master, and notes master are complete, you can exit Master view and return to Normal view. The following steps close Master view.

- Display the Notes Master tab (Figure 8–63).

- Click the Close Master View button (Notes Master tab | Close group) to exit Master view and return to Normal view.

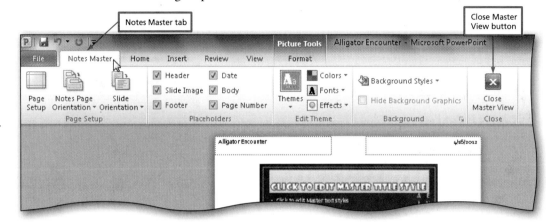

**Figure 8–63**

## To Save a Master as a Template

The changes and enhancements you have made to the Alligator Encounter slide master, handout master, and notes master are excellent starting points for future presentations. The background text and graphics allow users to add text boxes, pictures, SmartArt, tables, and other elements depending upon the specific message that needs to be communicated to an audience. You can save your slide layouts as a template to use for a new presentation and use the revised handout and notes masters to print unique pages. The following steps save the Alligator masters as a template on your USB drive.

**1**

- Open the Backstage view, display the Save & Send tab, and then click Change File Type in the File Types area.

- Click Template in the Presentation File Types area (Figure 8–64).

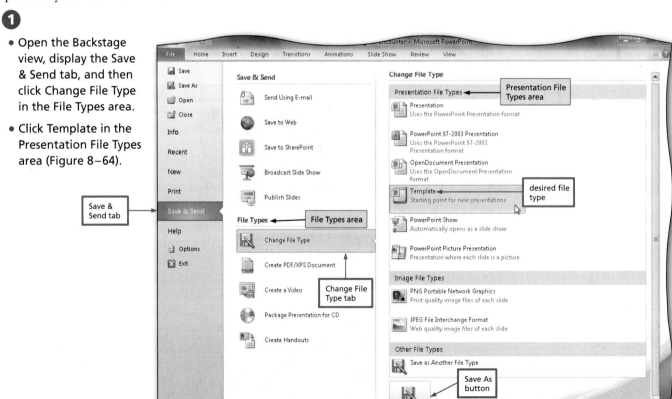

**Figure 8–64**

- Click the Save As button below the Other File Types area to display the Save As dialog box.

- Type **Alligator Template** in the File name text box (Figure 8–65).

- If necessary, navigate to the desired location to save the file and then click the Save button (Save As dialog box) to save the Alligator Encounter presentation as a template.

④

- Close the Alligator Template file.

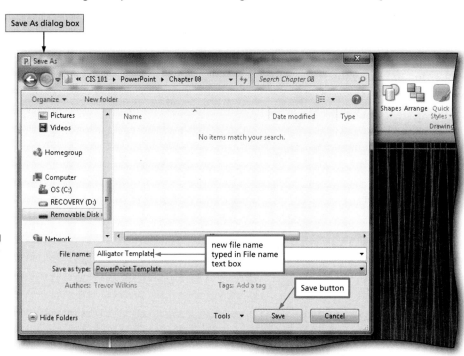

**Figure 8–65**

**Break Point:** If you wish to take a break, this is a good place to do so. You can quit PowerPoint now. To resume at a later time, start PowerPoint and continue following the steps from this location forward.

## To Open a Template and Save a Presentation

The Alligator Template file you created is a convenient start to a new presentation. The graphical elements and essential slide content are in place; you then can customize the layouts for a specific need, such as a new event or special program. The following steps open the Alligator Template file and save the presentation with the Alligator Encounter name.

- Open the file, Alligator Template, from your USB flash drive.

- Open the Backstage view, display the Save & Send tab, and then click Change File Type in the File Types area.

- Click Presentation in the Presentation File Types area (Figure 8–66).

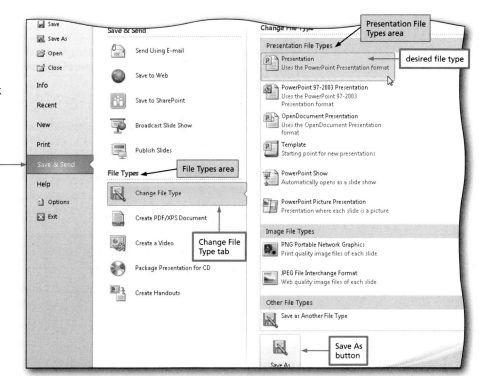

**Figure 8–66**

**2**

- Click the Save As button to display the Save As dialog box.

- Navigate to your USB drive and then click Alligator Encounter to select the file name (Figure 8–67).

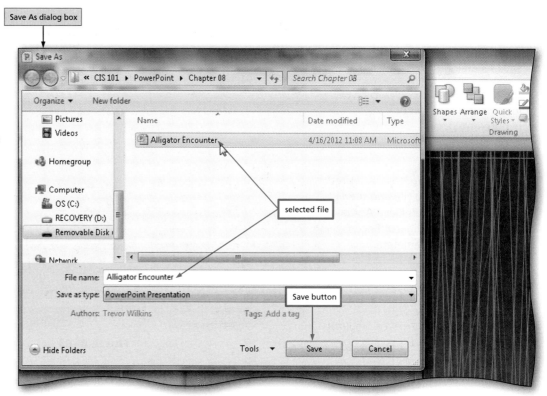

**Figure 8–67**

**3**

- Click the Save button (Save As dialog box) to display the Confirm Save As dialog box (Figure 8–68).

**4**

- Click the Yes button to replace the file.

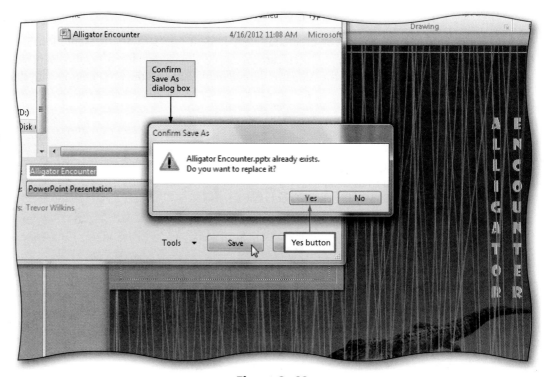

**Figure 8–68**

## To Add Text and Notes to the Title Slide

By default, the Title Slide Layout, which was renamed Alligator Hiding, is applied to the first slide. The following steps add text and speaker notes to Slide 1.

**1** With the title slide displaying, type **Enjoy a Guided Swamp Safari** as the title text and **Ecotours in a natural environment** as the subtitle text.

**2** Click the Notes pane and type **The length of average American male alligators is 11.2 feet and average female alligators is 8.2 feet. They live about 50 years in freshwater swamps, rivers, marshes, and lakes.** (Figure 8–69).

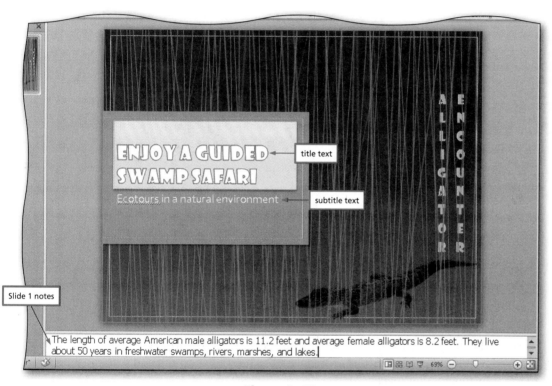

**Figure 8–69**

## To Add Text and Notes to the Blank Layout

The second slide in your presentation will feature the June special event, which is a night excursion into the swamp. The Special Events slide layout, which is the new name for the Blank Layout, is designed so that you can add variable slide content below the alligator picture in the upper-left corner. The following steps add a text box and speaker notes to Slide 2.

**1** Insert a slide with the Special Events layout and then insert a text box between the two alligator pictures. Type **Sunset tours available on weekends in June** as the text box text.

**2** Increase the text box font size to 32 point and then, if necessary, adjust the text box borders so the text is displayed on two lines.

**3** In the Notes pane, type **An alligator has approximately 80 teeth that are replaced as they wear down. Its diet consists of birds, fish, frogs, and small mammals.** (Figure 8–70).

**BTW**

**Showing Notes Pane Text Formatting**
The words you type in the Notes pane can be useful for outlining the important points you want to make during a presentation. You can format this text by increasing the font size and bolding and italicizing the letters. To view these formatting changes, display the Outline tab, right-click any text in the Outline pane, and then click Show Text Formatting on the shortcut menu.

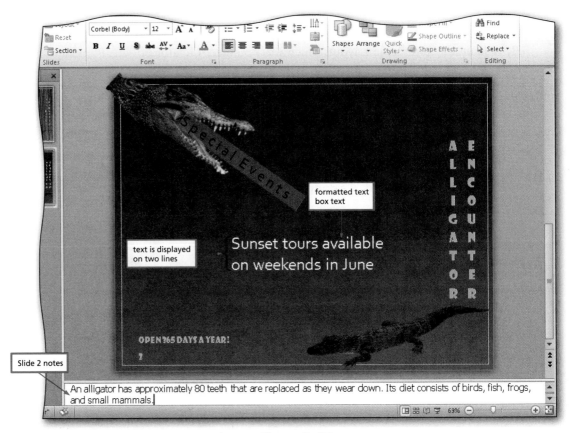

**Figure 8–70**

**Customer Experience Improvement Program**

You can contribute to the design and development of Microsoft products by participating in the company's Customer Experience Improvement Program (CEIP). If you choose to sign up for the program, your computer will send information to Microsoft automatically about how you use Microsoft products and other third-party applications. CEIP reports include your computer's configuration, the programs' performance and reliability, and how you use the programs' features. Microsoft uses the data to improve frequently used elements and to solve common problems.

## To Add Text, Notes, and a Picture to the Title and Content Layout

The third slide in your presentation will list details about the nature park's admission and tour prices, swamp tour hours, and telephone number. The Miscellaneous layout, which is the new name for the Title and Content slide layout, will allow you to insert text into the content placeholder. The following steps insert a slide and add text and a picture to the title and content placeholder.

1. Insert a slide with the Miscellaneous layout and then type `Hours and Rates` as the title text.

2. Type `One-hour tours starting at 10 a.m.` as the first content placeholder paragraph.

3. Type `Last tour departs at 6 p.m.` as the second paragraph.

4. Type `Adults: $24.95; Children under 18: $10.95` as the third paragraph.

5. Type `Call 555-8404 for reservations today!` as the fourth paragraph.

6. In the Notes pane, type `Tours will be canceled in inclement weather. Maximum tour size is 20 people.`

7. Insert the picture with the file name, Letter A, located on the Data Files for Students, and then move the picture above the content footer placeholder (Figure 8–71).

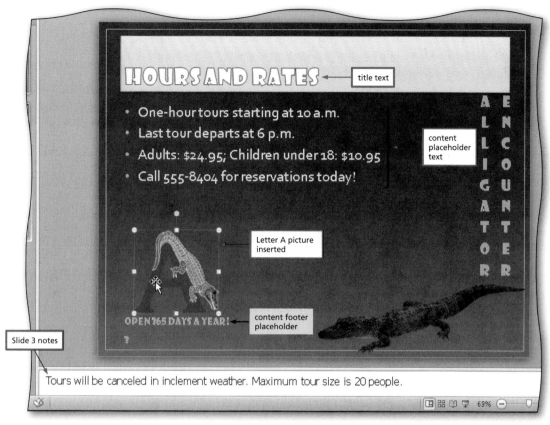

**Figure 8–71**

## To Apply a Fill Color to a Slide

Earlier in this project, you formatted the interior of the Special Event text box by applying a fill. In a similar manner, you can apply a fill to an entire slide by selecting a color from the Shape Fill gallery. If desired, you can increase the transparency to soften the color. Because the Special Events text box on Slide 2 is red, you can coordinate the Slide 3 fill color by changing the Slide 3 background to red. The following steps apply a fill to Slide 3 and increase the transparency.

**1**

- With Slide 3 displaying, right-click anywhere on the green background to display the shortcut menu.

- Click Format Background on the shortcut menu to display the Format Background dialog box (Figure 8–72).

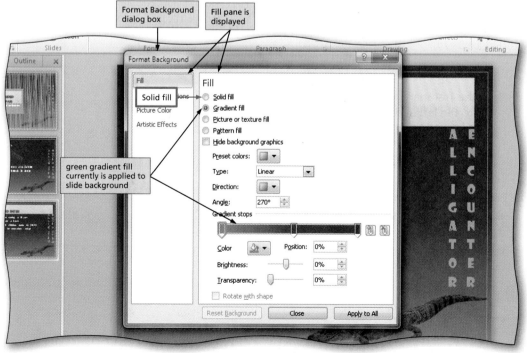

**Figure 8–72**

**2**

- With the Fill pane displaying, click Solid fill to reduce the fill options and to display the Fill Color area.

- Click the Color button in the Fill Color area to display the Fill Color gallery (Figure 8–73).

**Q&A**

Can I experiment with previewing the background colors?

No live preview feature is available.

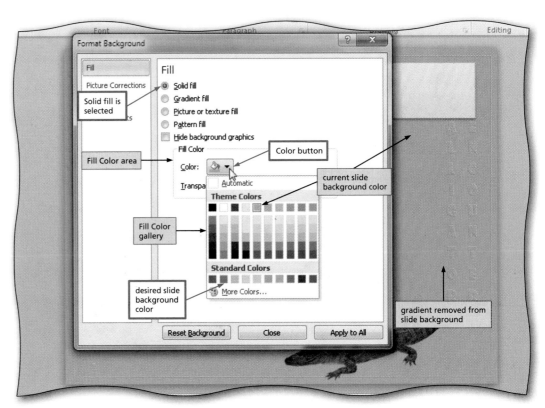

**Figure 8–73**

**3**

- Click Red (second color in Standard Colors row) to change the slide background color.

- Click the Transparency slider in the Fill Color area and drag it to the right until 20% is displayed in the Transparency text box (Figure 8–74).

**Experiment**

- Drag the Transparency slider to the left and right, and watch the text box background change.

**Q&A**

How can I delete a fill color if I decide not to apply one to my slide?

Any fill effect in the Format Background dialog box is applied immediately. If this dialog box is displayed, click the Reset Background button. If you already have applied the fill color, you must click the Undo button on the Quick Access Toolbar.

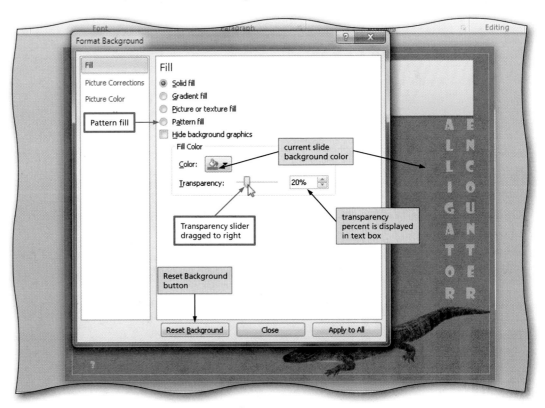

**Figure 8–74**

| Other Ways | |
| --- | --- |
| 1. Enter percentage in Transparency text box | 2. Click Transparency up or down arrow |

## To Apply a Pattern to a Slide

You add variety to a slide by adding a **pattern fill**. This design of repeating horizontal or vertical lines, dots, dashes, or stripes can enhance the visual appeal of one or more slides in the presentation. If you desire to change the colors in the pattern, PowerPoint allows you to select the fill foreground and background colors by clicking the Color button and then choosing the desired colors. The following steps apply a pattern to Slide 3.

**1**

- With the Format Background dialog box displaying, click Pattern fill to display the Pattern gallery and the 5% pattern on Slide 3 (Figure 8–75).

🔍 **Experiment**

- Click various patterns in the Pattern gallery and watch the patterns change on the slide.

**Q&A** How can I delete a pattern if I decide not to apply one to my slide?

If the Format Background dialog box is displayed, click the Reset Background button. If you already have applied the pattern, you must click the Undo button on the Quick Access Toolbar.

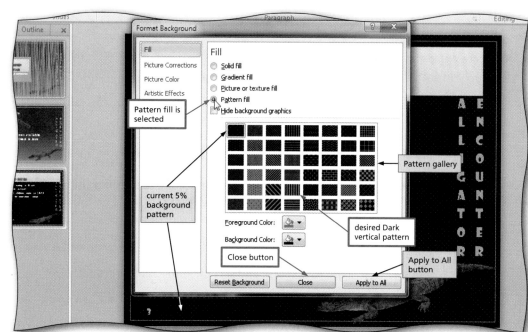

**Figure 8–75**

**2**

- Click the Dark vertical pattern (fourth color in fifth row) to apply this pattern to the Slide 3 background (Figure 8–76).

**Q&A** Can I apply this pattern to all the slides in the presentation?

Yes. You would click the Apply to All button in the Format Background dialog box.

**3**

- Click the Close button to close the Format Background dialog box.

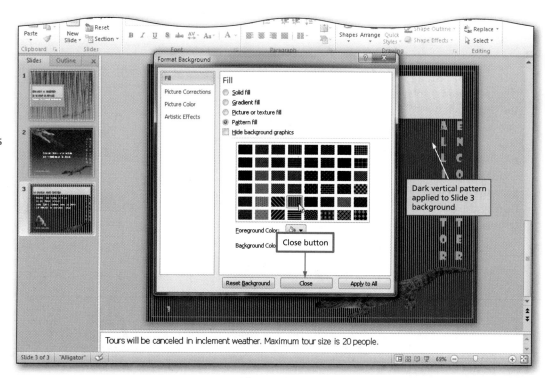

**Figure 8–76**

## To Add a Slide Transition

A final enhancement you will make in this presentation is to apply the Shred transition to all slides and then change the transition speed to 6.00 and the effect option to Particles Out. The following steps apply this transition and effect to the presentation.

**1** Apply the Shred transition in the Exciting category.

**2** Change the transition speed from 03.00 to 06.00.

**3** Change the Effect Option from Strips In to Particles Out.

**4** Apply these transitions to all slides in the presentation.

## To Change Document Properties

Before saving the presentation again, you want to add your name, class name, and some keywords as document properties. The following steps use the Document Information Panel to change document properties.

**1** Display the Document Information Panel and then type your name as the Author property.

**2** Type your course and section in the Subject property.

**3** Type `alligator, special events, safari` as the Keywords property.

**4** Close the Document Information Panel.

## To Print a Handout Using the Handout Master

The handout master you created has header and footer text using the Corbel font, a revised location for the footer placeholder, and the Alligator Body picture in the lower-right corner. The following steps print a handout using the handout master.

**1**
- Open the Backstage view and then display the Print gallery.

**2**
- Click the Full Page Slides button in the Settings area to display the gallery (Figure 8–77).

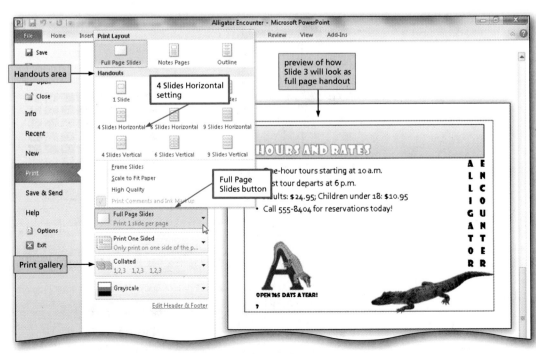

**Figure 8–77**

**3**
- Click 4 Slides Horizontal in the Handouts area.
- Click the Portrait Orientation button in the Settings area to display the Orientation gallery (Figure 8–78).

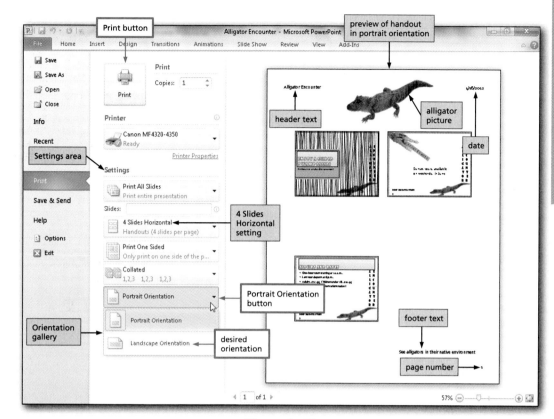

**Figure 8–78**

**4**
- Click Landscape Orientation to change the setting.
- Verify that 4 Slides Horizontal is selected as the option in the Settings area and that the preview of Page 1 shows the header text, date, footer text, page number, alligator picture, and three slides in landscape orientation.
- Click the Print button in the Print gallery to print the handout (Figure 8–79).

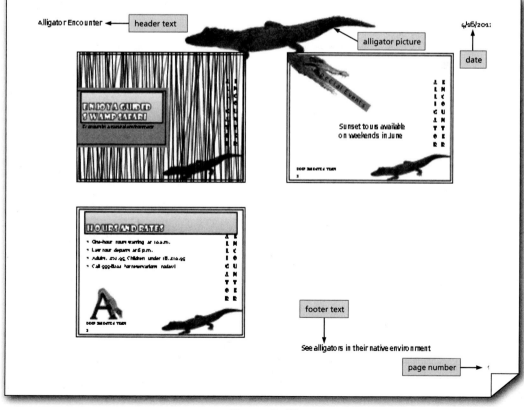

**Figure 8–79**

## To Print Speaker Notes Using the Notes Master

You also can print speaker notes while the Backstage view is displayed. The custom notes master you created has the same footer as the handout master, revised footer text using the Corbel font, the current date, and the resized Alligator Body picture in the lower-right corner. The following steps print notes pages using the notes master.

**1**
- With the Backstage view open, click the 4 Slides Horizontal button to display the gallery and then click Notes Pages in the Print Layout area.

- Click Landscape Orientation in the Settings area and then click Portrait Orientation in the gallery to change the setting.

- Verify that the page preview shows the header text, date, speaker notes, revised footer text, alligator picture, and page number in portrait orientation (Figure 8–80).

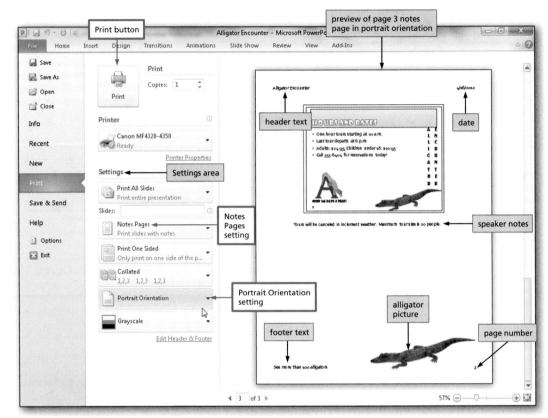

**Figure 8–80**

**2**
- Click the Previous Page and Next Page buttons to display previews of the other pages.
- Click the Print button in the Print gallery to print the notes (Figure 8–81).

**BTW**

**Certification**
The Microsoft Office Specialist (MOS) program provides an opportunity for you to obtain a valuable industry credential – proof that you have the PowerPoint 2010 skills required by employers. For more information, visit the PowerPoint 2010 Certification Web page (scsite.com/ppt2010/cert).

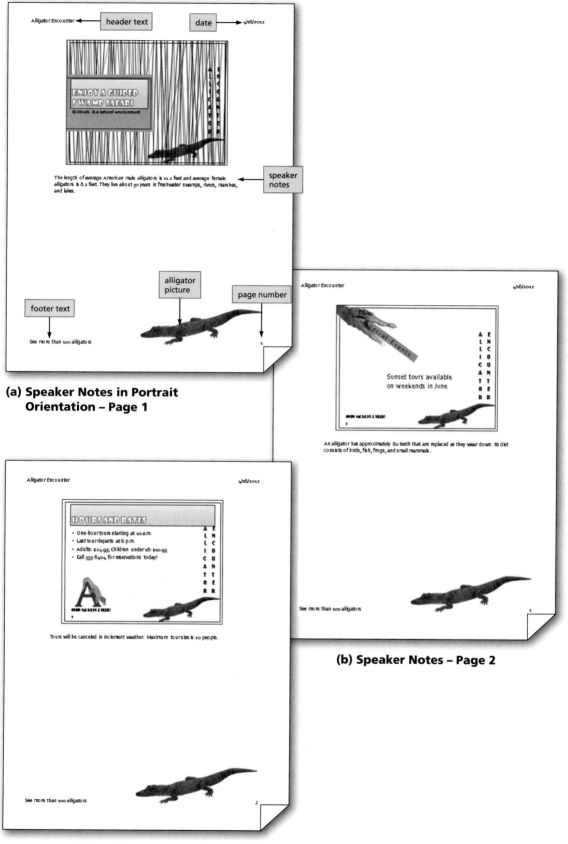

**(a) Speaker Notes in Portrait Orientation – Page 1**

**(b) Speaker Notes – Page 2**

**(c) Speaker Notes – Page 3**

**Figure 8–81**

## To Save and Quit PowerPoint

The presentation now is complete. You should save the slides and then quit PowerPoint.

**1** Save the Alligator Encounter presentation again with the same file name.

**2** Quit PowerPoint, closing all open documents.

# Chapter Summary

In this chapter you have learned how to customize master slide layouts by changing the slide and font themes, formatting the background and footers, and adding background graphics. You then inserted a placeholder, added and formatted text, applied a fill, and changed the internal margins. Also, you rotated a picture and a placeholder, displayed the background graphics, and renamed and deleted slide layouts. Then you customized the handouts and notes masters by adding a picture and changing the layout orientation. You then saved the slide master as a template, opened this template, added slide content, and printed a handout and speaker notes pages. The items listed below include all the new PowerPoint skills you have learned in this chapter.

1. Display a Slide Master (PPT 471)
2. Apply Slide and Font Themes to a Slide Master (PPT 472)
3. Customize a Theme Font (PPT 473)
4. Format a Slide Master Background and Apply a Quick Style (PPT 475)
5. Delete, Move, and Add Text to a Slide Master Footer (PPT 476)
6. Format Slide Master Footer Text (PPT 478)
7. Insert a Background Graphic into a Slide Master (PPT 479)
8. Insert a Placeholder into a Blank Layout (PPT 480)
9. Add and Format Placeholder Text (PPT 481)
10. Cut a Placeholder and Paste It into a Slide Master (PPT 484)
11. Change Character Spacing (PPT 486)
12. Apply a Fill to a Text Box and Increase Transparency (PPT 487)
13. Change a Text Box Internal Margin (PPT 488)
14. Rotate a Picture and a Text Box (PPT 489)
15. Hide and Unhide Background Graphics (PPT 490)
16. Rename a Slide Master and a Slide Layout (PPT 491)
17. Delete a Slide Layout (PPT 493)
18. Customize a Handout Using a Handout Master (PPT 496)
19. Customize a Notes Page Using a Notes Master (PPT 500)
20. Close Master View (PPT 502)
21. Save a Master as a Template (PPT 502)
22. Open a Template and Save a Presentation (PPT 503)
23. Apply a Fill Color to a Slide (PPT 507)
24. Apply a Pattern to a Slide (PPT 509)
25. Print a Handout Using the Handout Master (PPT 510)
26. Print Speaker Notes Using the Notes Master (PPT 512)

 If you have a SAM 2010 user profile, your instructor may have assigned an autogradable version of this assignment. If so, log into the SAM 2010 Web site at www.cengage.com/sam2010 to download the instruction and start files.

# Learn It Online

Test your knowledge of chapter content and key terms.

*Instructions:*  To complete the Learn It Online exercises, start your browser, click the Address bar, and then enter the Web address `scsite.com/ppt2010/learn`. When the Office 2010 Learn It Online page is displayed, click the link for the exercise you want to complete and then read the instructions.

### Chapter Reinforcement TF, MC, and SA

A series of true/false, multiple choice, and short answer questions that test your knowledge of the chapter content.

### Flash Cards

An interactive learning environment where you identify chapter key terms associated with displayed definitions.

### Practice Test

A series of multiple choice questions that test your knowledge of chapter content and key terms.

### Who Wants To Be a Computer Genius?

An interactive game that challenges your knowledge of chapter content in the style of a television quiz show.

### Wheel of Terms

An interactive game that challenges your knowledge of chapter key terms in the style of the television show *Wheel of Fortune*.

### Crossword Puzzle Challenge

A crossword puzzle that challenges your knowledge of key terms presented in the chapter.

# Apply Your Knowledge

Reinforce the skills and apply the concepts you learned in this chapter.

### Applying a Slide Theme to a Slide Master, Creating a New Theme Font, and Changing a Slide Master Background

*Note:*  To complete this assignment, you will be required to use the Data Files for Students. See the inside back cover of this book for instructions on downloading the Data Files for Students, or contact your instructor for information about accessing the required files.

*Instructions:*  Start PowerPoint. Open the presentation, Apply 8–1 Mathematics, located on the Data Files for Students.

The four slides in this presentation discuss the careers available to mathematics majors. The document you open is an unformatted presentation. You will apply a slide theme to a slide master, create a new theme font, and change the slide master background so the slides look like Figure 8–82.

*Perform the following tasks:*

1. Display the Slide Master view. Change the document theme to Angles, the colors to Civic, and then create a new Theme Font named Math using Bernard MT Condensed for the heading font and Microsoft Sans Serif for the body font, as shown in Figure 8–82a. Close Slide Master view.

2. On Slide 1, center the title text, change the size to 80 point, and then change the color to Red, Accent 1. Center the subtitle text, change the size to 48 point, and change the color to Blue-Gray, Text 2. Adjust the line break so that the word, CAREERS, is on the first line by itself. Resize the pictures and move them to the positions shown in Figure 8–82b. Adjust the color to Washout (Recolor area) on the bottom (abacus) picture.

*Continued >*

**Apply Your Knowledge** *continued*

3. On Slide 2, change the title text to 40 point and the color to Teal, Accent 3. Increase the size of the body text to 36 point and change the color to Dark Blue. Use the Format Painter to apply the same formatting changes to the title and body text on Slide 3. Increase the size of the clips on Slides 2 and 3 and move them to the locations shown in Figures 8–82c and 8–82d.

4. On Slide 4, change the layout to Picture with Caption. Insert the Math picture located on the Data Files for Students. Change the title text to 44 point and the color to Teal, Accent 3, and then move the text placeholder as shown in Figure 8–82e. Change the subtitle text to 28 point and the color to Dark Blue, and move the subtitle text placeholder to the location shown.

5. Change the arrow shape, as shown in Figure 8–82e, increase the font size to 36 point, change the text color to Yellow, and then bold this text. Apply the Intense Effect – Teal, Accent 3 Quick Style to the arrow, and then move the arrow to the location shown.

6. For all slides, change the transition to Cube and the duration to 03.00 seconds.

7. Change the document properties, as specified by your instructor. Save the presentation using the file name, Apply 8–1 Mathematics Careers. Submit the revised document in the format specified by your instructor.

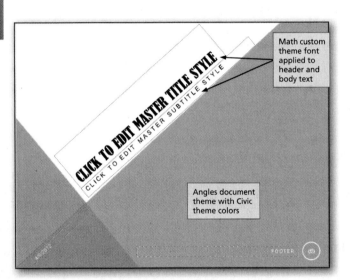

**(a) Slide Master Title Slide Layout**

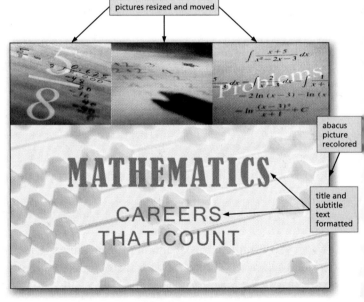

**(b) Slide 1**

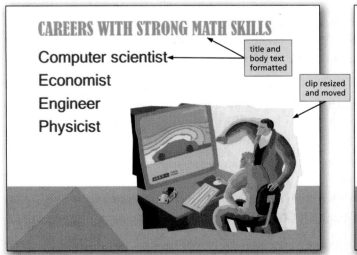

**(c) Slide 2**

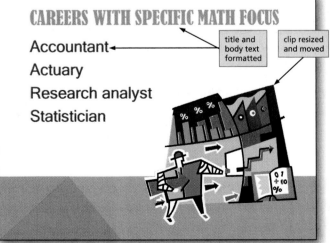

**(d) Slide 3**

**Figure 8–82**

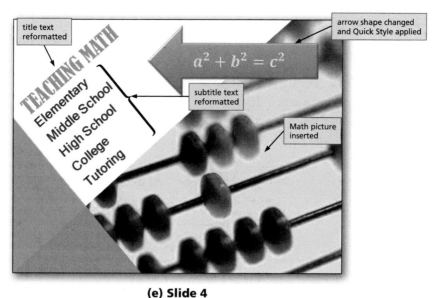

**(e) Slide 4**

**Figure 8–82 (Continued)**

# Extend Your Knowledge

Extend the skills you learned in this chapter and experiment with new skills. You may need to use Help to complete the assignment.

### Adding a Background Graphic to a Slide Master and Adjusting Footer Content and Placeholders

*Note:*   To complete this assignment, you will be required to use the Data Files for Students. See the inside back cover of this book for instructions on downloading the Data Files for Students, or contact your instructor for information about accessing the required files.

*Instructions:*   Start PowerPoint. Open the presentation, Extend 8–1 Bees, located on the Data Files for Students.
You will add a background graphic to a slide master; add footer slide numbers, date, and time; delete a footer placeholder; and move a footer placeholder, as shown in Figure 8–83.

*Perform the following tasks:*
1. Open Slide Master view and then select the Slide Master thumbnail. Add the slide number, date, and time to the footer placeholders. *Hint:* You may need to use Help to learn how to insert the time into the footer. Delete the center text placeholder in the footer area. Move the 'Date and time' footer placeholder to the upper-right area of the slide master. Right-align the 'Date and time' placeholder text, change the color to Black, and then bold this text, as shown in Figure 8–83a.

2. Add a background style by selecting Brass from the Preset colors in the Gradient fill area. Insert the Bees audio clip, located on the Data Files for Students, on the slide master, have it start automatically, and hide the sound icon during the show. You may need to use Help to learn how to insert the sound icon into the slide master. Close Slide Master view.

3. On the title slide, select the title text and change the font to Aharoni. Apply the Fill – White, Drop Shadow WordArt style to the title text, change the text fill color to Orange, the outline color to Black, and the outline line weight to 4.5 pt. Apply the Can Down text effect to the title, decrease the width of the title text to 7.5", and then move it to the location shown in Figure 8–83b.

4. Change the color of the subtitle text to Black and the font size to 44 point. Bold this text and then move the subtitle placeholder to the lower part of the slide.

5. On Slide 1, move the Beekeeper avatar picture to Slide 2. Increase the size of the bee clip and move it to the location shown in Figure 8–83b. Duplicate the bee clip by selecting it, holding the CTRL

*Continued >*

**Extend Your Knowledge** *continued*

key, and then moving the duplicate clip to the upper-right corner of the slide. Flip the second clip horizontally and move to the location shown. *Hint:* Select the bee clip and then select Rotate: Flip Horizontal (Picture Tools Format tab | Arrange group).

6. Open Slide Master view and select the Two Content Layout. Add the Honeycomb picture, located on the Data Files for Students, as a background graphic to this layout, and change the transparency to 65%, as shown in Figure 8–83c. Close Slide Master view.

7. Change the layout for Slide 2 to the Two Content Layout. Increase the size of the picture in the left placeholder, apply the Rotated White picture style, and then change the border color to Orange. Increase the size of the bulleted text to 28 point and then bold this text.

8. Change the title text font to Broadway and the font size to 54 point. Change the color of the text to Black.

9. Increase the size of the picture in the right placeholder, apply the Simple Frame, Black picture style, and then move the picture to the location shown. Increase the size of the Beekeeper avatar clip and move it to the location shown in Figure 8–83d.

10. Apply the Honeycomb transition to all slides and change the duration to 05.00 seconds.

11. Change the document properties, as specified by your instructor. Save the presentation using the file name, Extend 8–1 Beekeepers.

12. Submit the revised document in the format specified by your instructor.

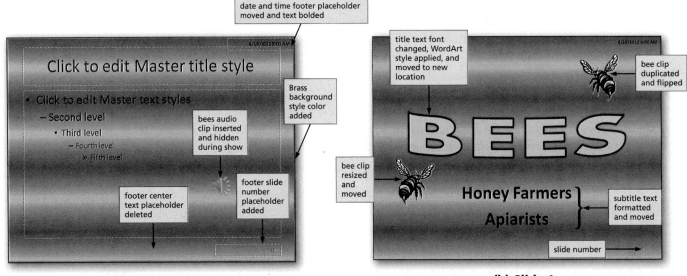

**(a) Slide Master**　　　　**(b) Slide 1**

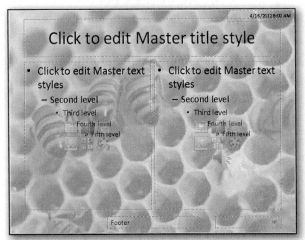

**(c) Slide Master Two Content Layout**

**(d) Slide 2**

**Figure 8–83**

## Make It Right

Analyze a presentation and correct all errors and/or improve the design.

### Changing a Font Theme and Background Style, Deleting a Placeholder and a Graphic, and Rotating a Placeholder on a Slide Master

*Note:* To complete this assignment, you will be required to use the Data Files for Students. See the inside back cover of this book for instructions on downloading the Data Files for Students, or contact your instructor for information about accessing the required files.

*Instructions:* Start PowerPoint. Open the presentation, Make It Right 8-1 Hang Gliding, located on the Data Files for Students.

Correct the formatting problems and errors in the presentation while keeping in mind the guidelines presented in this chapter.

*Perform the following tasks:*

1. Open Slide Master view, select the Office Theme Slide Master (Figure 8–84a), and delete the clip from the lower-right area of the slide. Change the font theme to Elemental. Also, delete the Date and time, Slide number, and Footer placeholders.

2. Select the Title Slide Layout (Figure 8–84b) and change the background style to the style of your choice. Increase the font size of the title text and then right-align this text. Rotate the subtitle text placeholder right 90 degrees and then move the placeholder under the title text placeholder. Delete the text placeholder in the upper-right corner of the Title Slide Layout, and also delete the three footer placeholders.

3. Select the Title and Content Layout, change the content placeholder left and right internal margins to 0.1", and change the top margin to 1.7". Close Slide Master view.

4. On Slide 1, change the layout to Title Slide. Delete the text and the text placeholder in the upper-right area of the slide. Change the title text font size to an appropriate size and insert a line break so it fits on two lines, bold this text, and then center it. Change the subtitle text font size and add line breaks so it fits on three lines, change the color, bold this text, and then center it. Increase the size of the picture and move the picture, the title text, and the subtitle text to the locations shown in Figure 8–84c.

5. On Slide 2 (Figure 8–84d), delete the first bulleted paragraph, bold the remainder of the text in the placeholder, and then move the placeholder downward. Insert a cloud shape, cut and paste the last bulleted paragraph into the cloud shape, increase the font size, and then move the shape to the upper-right area of the slide. Resize and move the title text placeholder so the title fits on one line above the cloud, increase the size of the font, bold the text, and then change the color.

6. Change the transition to Fly Through and the Effect Options to Out, and then change the duration to 3.00 for all slides.

7. Change the document properties, as specified by your instructor. Save the presentation using the file name, Make It Right 8-1 Hang Gliding School.

8. Submit the revised document in the format specified by your instructor.

*Continued >*

**Make It Right** *continued*

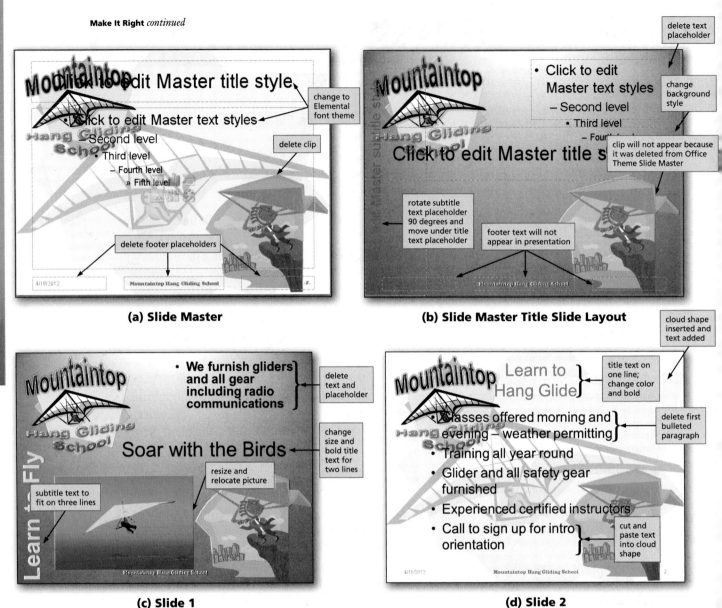

**Figure 8–84**

## In the Lab

Design and/or create a presentation using the guidelines, concepts, and skills presented in this chapter. Labs 1, 2, and 3 are listed in order of increasing difficulty.

### Lab 1: Formatting a Slide Master by Inserting a Placeholder, Applying a Fill, and Changing the Internal Margin

*Note:* To complete this assignment, you will be required to use the Data Files for Students. See the inside back cover of this book for instructions on downloading the Data Files for Students or contact your instructor for information about accessing the required files.

*Problem:* In your biology class, you learned that half of the world's animal species live in all four layers of rain forests. You decide to create a PowerPoint presentation to identify a few of these animal species and to give an example of which animals live in each rain forest layer. You create the slides shown in Figure 8–85 using files located on the Data Files for Students.

*Perform the following tasks:*

1. Open the presentation, Lab 8-1 Rain Forest, located on the Data Files for Students.

2. Open Slide Master view and select the Slide Master thumbnail. Apply the Austin document theme. On the Austin Slide Master, delete the slide number and date placeholders from the upper-right area of the slide, as shown in Figure 8–85a.

3. Insert a Picture placeholder in the left side of the Title Slide Layout. Adjust the size of the Picture placeholder so that it is approximately 6" × 4", as shown in Figure 8–85b. Close Slide Master view.

4. On Slide 1, select the layout, 1_Title Slide. Change the title text to `Rain Forest Animals` and then change the text font to 44-point bold, center the text, and then align the text in the middle of the placeholder. Increase the subtitle text font to 25 point, change the color to Black, Text 1, center the text, bold and italicize this text, and then align the text in the middle of the placeholder.

5. On Slide 1, insert the Waterfall picture located on the Data Files for Students in the Picture placeholder. Increase the size of the Frog picture and move it to the location shown in Figure 8–85c and then apply the Soft Edge Rectangle picture style to the picture.

6. Open Slide Master view. Select the Two Content Layout and then apply the Linear Down Gradient Fill to both content placeholders. Also, change the left internal margin to .5" in both content placeholders, as shown in Figure 8–85d. Close Slide Master view.

7. Apply the Two Content slide layout to Slides 2 and 3.

8. On Slides 2 and 3, bold and center the title text. Bold the text in both placeholders. Adjust the size of the pictures and move them to the locations shown in Figure 8–85e and Figure 8–85f. Apply the Rotated, White picture style to the snake picture and the Bevel Perspective style to the frog picture in Slide 2. Apply the Reflected Bevel, Black picture style to the gorilla picture and the Center Shadow Rectangle style to the toucan picture in Slide 3.

9. On Slide 4, change the title font to 40 point, bold this text, and then insert a line break after the word, Forests', to display the title text on two lines. Move the title text placeholder down slightly, as shown in Figure 8–85g.

10. Increase the size of the rain forest picture to 4.5" × 3.17" and move the picture to the left side of the slide. Add a 6 pt Orange border to the picture.

11. Increase the size of the SmartArt graphic to 4.5" × 5.5" and move the graphic to the right side of the slide. Apply the Colorful – Accent Colors and the Intense Effect SmartArt style to the graphic.

12. Apply the Ripple transition and change the duration to 04.00 seconds for all slides.

13. Change the document properties, as specified by your instructor. Save the presentation using the file name, Lab 8-1 Rain Forest Animals.

14. Submit the revised document in the format specified by your instructor.

*Continued >*

**In the Lab** *continued*

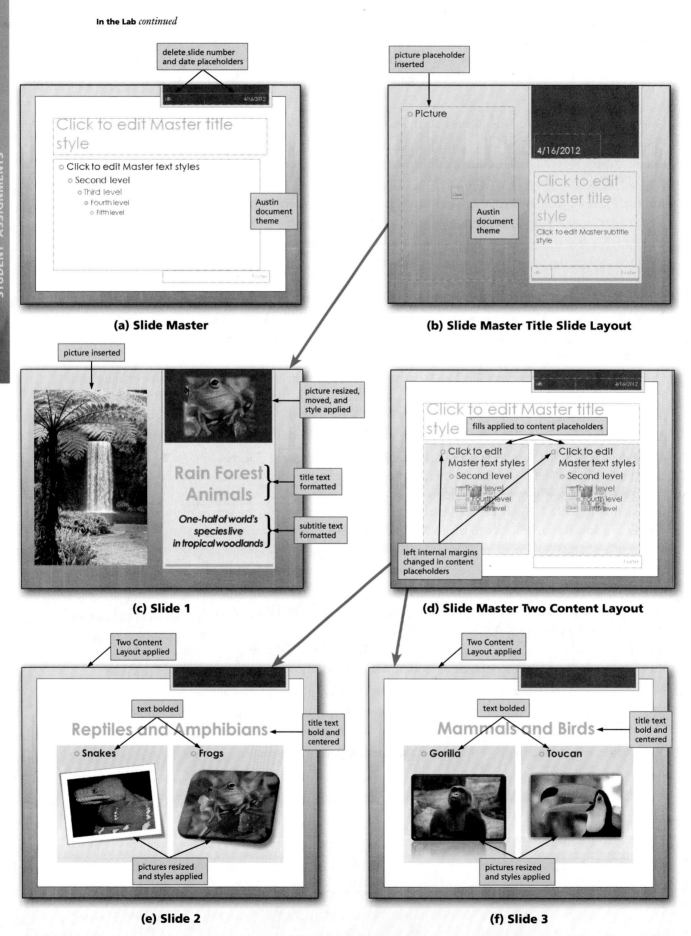

**Figure 8–85**

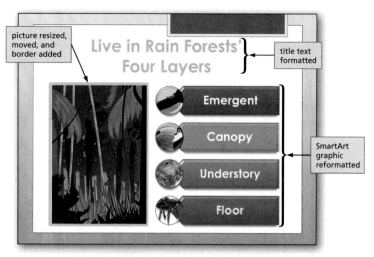

**(g) Slide 4**

**Figure 8–85 (Continued)**

# In the Lab

### Lab 2: Formatting and Renaming Slide Masters and Creating Handouts Using the Handout and Notes Masters

*Note:* To complete this assignment, you will be required to use the Data Files for Students. See the inside back cover of this book for instructions on downloading the Data Files for Students or contact your instructor for information about accessing the required files.

*Problem:* Many consumers grow and eat organic foods. Your garden club members have asked you to prepare a presentation about organic gardening for your next meeting. You create the slides shown in Figure 8–86 using files located on the Data Files for Students.

*Perform the following tasks:*

1. Open the presentation, Lab 8-2 Organic, located on the Data Files for Students.

2. Open Slide Master view. Select the Title and Content Layout, duplicate the title text placeholder, rotate it left 90 degrees, reduce the size to 1.25 × 7.5, and then move it to the left edge of the slide. Apply the Intense Effect – Olive Green, Accent 3 Quick Style.

3. Type ORGANIC in the rotated placeholder. Bold this text and then change the font to Cooper Black, the font size to 54 point, the character spacing to Very Loose, and the text direction to Stacked.

4. Apply Background Style 10 to the Title Slide, Title and Content, and Blank layouts. On the Title and Content Layout master, decrease the size of the title and the content placeholders by dragging the left sizing handles to the right until they are 7.67" wide, as shown in Figure 8–86a.

5. Change the Title and Content Layout name to Organic Title. Copy the rotated placeholder from the Organic Title layout to the Blank layout, as shown in Figure 8–86b.

6. Delete the Vertical Title and Text and the Title and Vertical Text layouts. Rename this slide master Organic. Close Slide Master view.

7. On Slide 1, change the title font to Cooper Black and the text color to Green. Increase the font size to 54 point and then bold this text. Increase the subtitle font size to 36 point, change the color to Purple, and then bold this text. Adjust the size of the subtitle text placeholder so that the text is displayed on two lines and then left-align this text. Insert a line break after the word, Plan, to display the subtitle text on two lines. Move the title and subtitle text placeholders to the locations shown in Figure 8–86c.

8. Resize and move the vegetable picture and then apply the Relaxed Perspective, White style to the picture, as shown in Figure 8–86c.

*Continued >*

**In the Lab** *continued*

9. On Slide 2, change the layout to Blank. Increase the size of the wheat picture so that it measures 7.5" × 8.74". Change the color to Orange, Accent color 6 Light, move the wheat picture so that it fills the slide, and then send this picture to the back. Increase the size of the second organic picture and move it to the location shown in Figure 8–86d. Insert a text box and type `In organic gardening, no synthetic fertilizers or pesticides are used.` Open

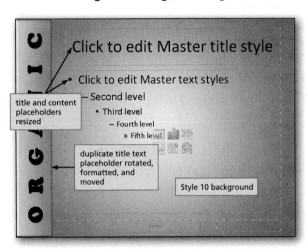

**(a) Slide Master Title and Content Layout**

**(b) Slide Master Blank Layout**

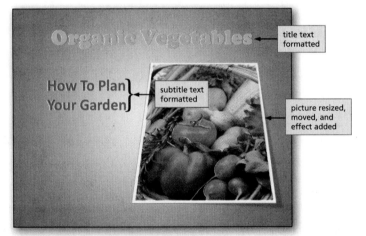

**(c) Slide 1**

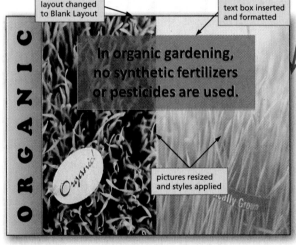

**(d) Slide 2**

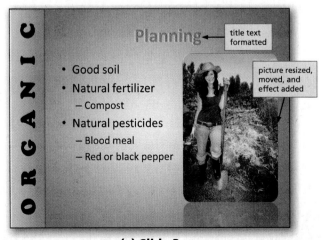

**(e) Slide 3**

**(f) Slide 4**

**Figure 8–86**

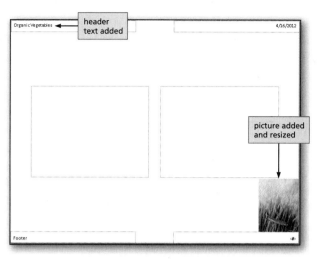

**(g) Handout Master**

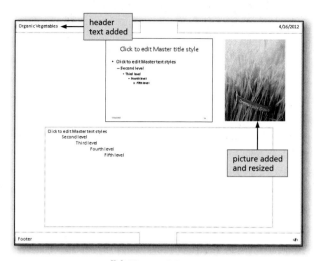

**(h) Notes Master**

**Figure 8–86 (Continued)**

the Format Shape dialog box and make sure the Wrap text in shape check box is checked. Change the left and right internal margins to 0.5" and the top and bottom internal margins to 0.25". Increase the size of the text to 40 point and then bold and center the text. Apply an Orange, Accent 6, Darker 25% solid fill color to the text box and change the transparency to 40%. If necessary, change the size of the text box so that the text is on three lines and then move it to the location shown in Figure 8–86d.

10. On Slide 3, change the title text font color to Orange, Accent 6, Darker 25%, change the font size to 48 point, and then bold this text. Increase the size of the picture, add the Reflected Rounded Rectangle picture style, and then move the picture to the location shown in Figure 8–86e.

11. On Slide 4, change the title text font color to Orange, Accent 6, Darker 25%, change the font size to 48 point, and then bold this text. Apply the Light downward diagonal pattern to this slide and change the foreground color to Orange, Accent 6. Increase the size of the picture, add the Beveled Oval, Black picture style, and then move the picture to the location shown in Figure 8–86f.

12. Apply the Cover transition and then change the duration to 03.00 seconds for all slides.

13. Open the handout master, change the orientation to landscape, and then change the Slides per page to 2 Slides. Type `Organic Vegetables` as the header text. Insert the Organic picture, change the size to 1.8" × 1.38", and then move it to the lower-right area of the handout master, as shown in Figure 8–86g.

14. Open the notes master and then type `Organic Vegetables` as the header text. Insert the Organic picture, change the size to 2.75" × 2.11", and then move it to the right side of the notes master, as shown in Figure 8–86h. Close the Slide Master view.

15. Change the document properties, as specified by your instructor. Save the presentation using the file name, Lab 8-2 Organic Vegetables.

16. Submit the revised document in the format specified by your instructor.

## In the Lab

### Lab 3: Adding and Formatting Placeholders, Adding a Graphic, Hiding Background Graphics on Individual Slides, and Saving a Slide Master as a Template

*Note:* To complete this assignment, you will be required to use the Data Files for Students. See the inside back cover of this book for instructions on downloading the Data Files for Students or contact your instructor for information about accessing the required files.

*Continued >*

**In the Lab** *continued*

*Problem:* You work for a home remodeling company. Your manager has decided to run monthly ads for his company in two local newspapers. Each newspaper will run a 10" × 8" ad that can be revised each month. Your manager plans to insert pictures of the remodeling jobs he has completed. He has asked you to set up a template so that he can insert a picture and change the text each month. He also has asked you to prepare the first month's ads. You create the slide master template shown in Figure 8–87a and then create the ads for the month, as shown in Figure 8–87.

*Perform the following tasks:*

1. Open the presentation, Lab 8-3 Handy Man, located on the Data Files for Students.

2. Select everything on the slide by using the Select All button (Home tab | Editing group), click the Copy button in the Clipboard group, and then open Slide Master view and paste it onto the Office Theme Slide Master. Decrease the width of the title text placeholder to 5.83". Add the Style 5 background style and change the theme font to Essential. Add the text, **Ad for month of:**, in the center footer placeholder and change the font color to Black, as shown in Figure 8–87a.

3. Hide the logo and text box background graphics on the Title Slide Layout only.

4. Select the Title and Content Layout, delete the content placeholder, and then insert a Picture placeholder. Resize the placeholder to 4.92" × 5.83" and then move it to the location shown in Figure 8–87b. Insert a text placeholder, resize it to 3.08" × 3", change the font size of the first level text to 24 point, delete the second-, third-, fourth-, and fifth-level text, and then position it on the right side of the slide below the logo and text box. Delete the footer placeholder. Rename this layout, Ad1.

5. Select the Two Content layout, delete the two content placeholders, and then insert a picture placeholder. Resize the placeholder to 3.17" × 4.33" and then move it to the location shown on the left side of Figure 8–87c. Duplicate this picture placeholder and move it to the right side of the slide below the logo and text box. Insert a text placeholder below the left picture placeholder, change the font size of the first level text to 24 point, and then delete the second-, third-, fourth,- and fifth-level text. Resize the placeholder to 1.5" × 4.33". Delete the footer placeholder. Rename this layout, Ad2.

6. Delete all the layouts in the slide master except for the Title Slide, Ad1, and Ad2 layouts. Close the Slide Master view and change the Slide 1 layout to Title Slide.

7. Save this slide master as a template and name it Lab 8-3 Handy Max.

8. Create a new presentation using the Lab 8-3 Handy Max template (Figure 8–87b). Save the presentation using the file name, Lab 8-3 Handy Max Ad1.

9. On Slide 1, type **Kitchens** in the title text placeholder, type **Southside Chronicle** in the subtitle text placeholder, and then type **April** after the text in the footer placeholder. Delete the logo and text box (Figure 8–87d).

10. Insert a new slide and select the Ad1 layout. On Slide 2 (Figure 8–87e), type **Kitchen Remodeling** in the title text placeholder and change the font color to Purple. Insert the picture, Kitchen, located on the Data Files for Students, in the picture placeholder. Insert the Flowchart: Punched Tape shape in the lower part of the picture, type **Does Your Kitchen Need an Update?**, and then apply the Intense Effect – Aqua, Accent 5 to the shape. Increase the size of the font to 24 point, change the font color to Yellow, and then bold this text.

11. In the text placeholder, type the text shown in Figure 8–87e. Bold this text. Add the White marble Shape Fill texture to the text placeholder.

12. Change the document properties, as specified by your instructor. Save the presentation again.

13. Create a new presentation by using the Lab 8-3 Handy Max template (Figure 8–87c). Save the presentation using the file name, Lab 8-3 Handy Max Ad2.

14. On Slide 1, type **Living/Family Rooms** in the title text placeholder, type **Northside Chronicle** in the subtitle text placeholder, and then type **April** after the text in the footer placeholder. Delete the logo and text box (Figure 8–87f).

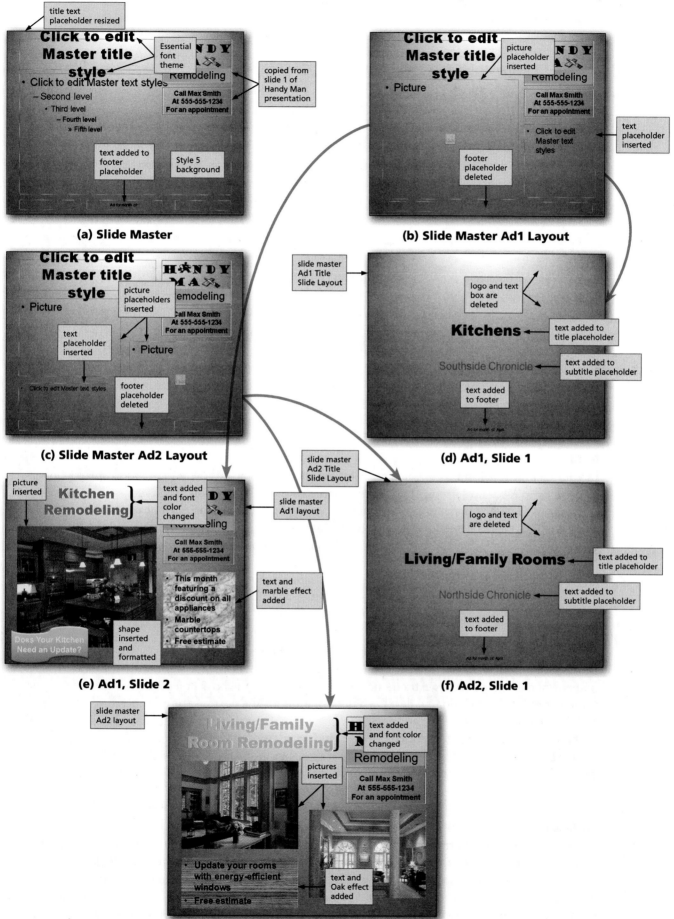

**(a) Slide Master**

**(b) Slide Master Ad1 Layout**

**(c) Slide Master Ad2 Layout**

**(d) Ad1, Slide 1**

**(e) Ad1, Slide 2**

**(f) Ad2, Slide 1**

**(g) Ad2, Slide 2**

**Figure 8–87**

*Continued >*

**In the Lab** *continued*

15. Insert a new slide and select Ad2 layout. On Slide 2 (Figure 8–87g), type `Living/Family Room Remodeling` in the title text placeholder and change the font color to Green. Insert the pictures Den and Family Room, located on the Data Files for Students, in the picture placeholders.

16. In the text placeholder, type the text shown in Figure 8–87g. Bold this text. Add the Oak Shape Fill texture to the text placeholder. *Note:* You may need to increase the size of the text placeholder.

17. Change the document properties, as specified by your instructor. Save the presentation again.

18. Submit the revised documents in the format specified by your instructor.

# Cases and Places

Apply your creative thinking and problem-solving skills to design and implement a solution.

*Note:* To complete these assignments, you may be required to use the Data Files for Students. See the inside back cover of this book for instructions on downloading the Data Files for Students, or contact your instructor for information about accessing the required files.

As you design the presentations, remember to use the 7 × 7 rule: a maximum of seven words on a line and a maximum of seven lines on one slide.

## 1: Designing and Creating a Presentation about Smart Phones

### Academic

In your technical writing class, you have been assigned the topic of how to purchase a smart phone. You decide to focus on selecting a wireless carrier and plan, deciding on a style, comparing battery life, determining memory and storage space, and checking out accessories. Your instructor gives you permission to make a PowerPoint presentation instead of writing a paper to explain this topic to the class. Apply at least three objectives found at the beginning of this chapter to develop the presentation, including creating a new font theme, rotating a placeholder, and changing text direction. Use pictures and diagrams from Office.com if they are appropriate for this topic. Be sure to check spelling.

## 2: Designing and Creating a Presentation about Neighborhood Trees

### Personal

Your community of 100 homes and townhomes is about three years old, and many residents have expressed a desire to add some trees to the public areas and parkways in front of their homes. Your homeowners' association has extra money in the budget, and the board members have asked you, as president of your association, to develop a presentation for the next meeting. You research the topic and decide on at least three or four kinds of trees. Use at least three objectives found at the beginning of this chapter to develop the presentation, including adding a picture or graphic of a tree as a slide master background. Use pictures from Office.com if they are appropriate for this topic or use your personal digital pictures. Be sure to check spelling.

## 3: Designing and Creating a Presentation about Your Computer Repair Business

### Professional

To help with expenses during your last year of school, you decide to put your skills to use and start a small computer repair business. Your slide show will be running on a kiosk in the school library. Apply at least three objectives found at the beginning of this chapter to develop the presentation, including changing the slide master background and adding a footer, date, and time. Use pictures and clips from Office.com if they are appropriate for this topic or use your personal digital pictures. Add a picture to the handout master and create handouts that will be copied and made available next to the kiosk. Be certain to check spelling.

# 9 | Modifying a Presentation Using Graphical Elements

## Objectives

You will have mastered the material in this chapter when you can:

- Change a text box outline color, weight, and style
- Set text box formatting as the default for new text boxes
- Apply a gradient, texture, pattern, and effects to a text box
- Convert WordArt to SmartArt
- Reorder SmartArt shapes
- Promote and demote SmartArt text

- Add and remove SmartArt shapes
- Convert a SmartArt graphic to text
- Customize the Ribbon
- Combine and subtract shapes
- Save the presentation as a picture presentation
- Create a handout by exporting files to Microsoft Word

# 9 | Modifying a Presentation Using Graphical Elements

## Introduction

PowerPoint's themes determine the default characteristics of slide objects. Colors, border weights and styles, fills, effects, and other formatting options give the slides a unique character. You can create your own designs for text boxes, shapes, lines, and other slide content, and then reuse these graphical objects throughout the presentation. Once you learn to format one type of object, such as a text box, you can use similar techniques to format other slide objects, such as SmartArt and shapes. One efficient way to create consistent graphical elements is to save your settings as the default. Then, when you insert the same objects later during the presentation design process, they will have the same characteristics as the initial element.

SmartArt graphics have individual layouts, styles, and color schemes. If one of these designs does not meet the specific needs of your slide content, you can modify the graphic by adding shapes, reordering the current shapes, and changing each element's size and location. You also can convert the SmartArt to text or to a shape if SmartArt is not the best method of conveying your ideas to an audience. PowerPoint's myriad formatting options allow you to tailor graphical elements to best fit your unique design needs.

## Project — Presentation with Customized Text Boxes, SmartArt, and Shapes

Hot air ballooning has fascinated flight enthusiasts for more than two centuries. The freedom of flying silently through scenic landscapes is a thrill that pilots and their passengers experience throughout the world.

Hot air balloon rides often are scheduled during the summer months. Morning and evening are preferred times to fly because the winds are light and the balloon altitude is easy to control. First-time passengers often are given a ground school lesson that includes a discussion of the balloon parts and flight dynamics. The presentation you create in this chapter (Figure 9–1) would be useful to show during the ground school lesson. All four slides are created by modifying a starting file that has a variety of content. The title slide (Figure 9–1a) contains a text box that is formatted with an outline style, a weight, and a color. These modifications are saved as the default settings for all other text boxes inserted into other slides. The second slide (Figure 9–1b) features a new colorful picture and a formatted text box. The text on Slide 3 (Figure 9–1c) is converted from WordArt to a SmartArt graphic. The layout, style, color, and shapes are changed and enhanced. The final slide (Figure 9–1d) has bulleted text converted from a SmartArt graphic; it also has a hot air balloon composed of formatted shapes. After the slides are created, you save the presentation as a picture presentation and export the file to Microsoft Word to create a handout (Figures 9–1e and 9–1f).

# Overview

As you read through this chapter, you will learn how to create the presentation and handout shown in Figure 9–1 below and on the following page by performing these general tasks:

- Format text boxes.
- Set formatting as default.
- Draw and insert shapes, lines, and arrows.
- Convert WordArt to SmartArt.
- Add and remove SmartArt shapes.
- Promote and demote bullet levels in SmartArt.
- Convert SmartArt to text.
- Customize the Ribbon.

**BTW**

**Vector Graphics**
Geometric shapes, lines, arrows, and action buttons are vector graphics, which are drawn using mathematical formulas. The size, color, line width, starting and ending points, and other formatting attributes are stored as numeric values and are recalculated when you resize or reformat each shape. Most clip art and video games also use vector graphics.

**(a) Slide 1**

**(b) Slide 2**

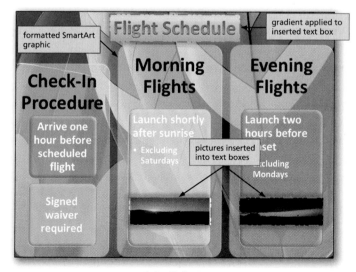

**(c) Slide 3**

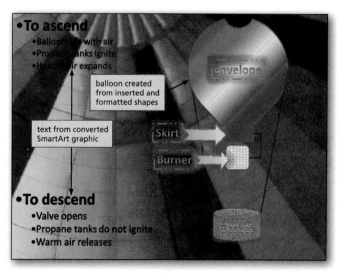

**(d) Slide 4**

**Figure 9–1**

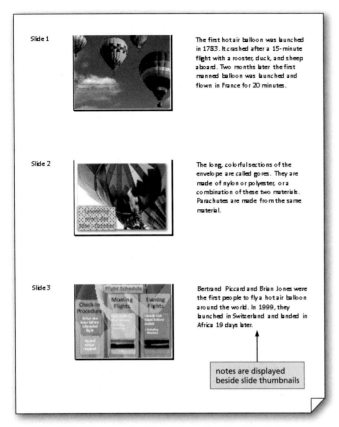

**(e) Microsoft Word Handout – Page 1**

**(f) Microsoft Word Handout – Page 2**

**Figure 9–1 (Continued)**

**Plan Ahead**

**General Project Guidelines**

When creating a PowerPoint presentation, the actions you perform and the decisions you make will affect the appearance and characteristics of the finished document. As you create a presentation with illustrations, such as the project shown in Figure 9–1 on the previous page and this page, you should follow these general guidelines:

1. **Choose colors wisely.** The appropriate use of color can add interest and help audience members retain information. Used inappropriately, however, mismatched colors will generate confusion and create an impression of unprofessionalism.

2. **Use keywords in SmartArt graphics.** The words you type into your SmartArt graphic can serve as a prompt of the key points you want to make in the presentation.

3. **Use politically correct language.** When you type words into text boxes, be mindful of the terms you are using to identify the images.

4. **Work with a buddy.** As you develop your slide content and then rehearse the presentation, ask a friend or work associate to assist you with various tasks.

When necessary, more specific details concerning the above guidelines are presented at appropriate points in the chapter. The chapter also will identify the actions performed and decisions made regarding these guidelines during the creation of the presentation shown in Figure 9–1.

## To Start PowerPoint and Save a File

If you are using a computer to step through the project in this chapter and you want your screens to match the figures in this book, you should change your computer's resolution to 1024 × 768. The following steps start PowerPoint and then save a file.

**1** Start PowerPoint. If necessary, maximize the PowerPoint window.

**2** Open the presentation, Balloons, located on the Data Files for Students.

**3** Save the presentation using the file name, Hot Air Balloons.

**Plan Ahead**

**Choose colors wisely.**
Color can create interest in the material on your slides, so you need to think about which colors best support the message you want to share with your audience. The color you add to text boxes signals that the viewer should pay attention to the contents. Orange, red, and yellow are considered warm colors and will be among the first colors your viewers perceive on your slide. Blue and green are considered cool colors, and they often blend into a background and are less obvious than the warm colors.

# Formatting Text Boxes

Text boxes can be formatted in a variety of ways to draw attention to slide content. You can apply formatting, such as fill color, gradient, texture, and pattern. You can add a picture; change the outline color, weight, and style; and then set margins and alignment. Once you determine the desired effects for a text box, you can save these settings as a default to achieve consistency and save time. Then, each time you insert another text box, the same settings will be applied.

In the following pages, you will perform these tasks on Slide 1:

1. Insert a text box into Slide 1.
2. Type text into the text box.
3. Change the text box outline color.
4. Change the text box outline weight.
5. Change the text box outline style.
6. Apply a glow effect to the text box.
7. Change the text box text to WordArt.
8. Increase the WordArt font size and center the paragraph in the text box.
9. Set the text box formatting as the default for new text boxes.

Once the text box formatting is complete on Slide 1, you then will perform these tasks on Slide 2:

1. Insert a text box and enter text.
2. Apply a pattern to the text box.
3. Change the text box pattern foreground and background colors.
4. Change the Slide 2 picture.

You also will perform these tasks on Slide 3:

1. Insert a text box and enter text.
2. Apply a gradient to the text box.
3. Align the text box in the center of the slide.

**BTW**

**The Ribbon and Screen Resolution** PowerPoint may change how the groups and buttons within the groups appear on the Ribbon, depending on the computer's screen resolution. Thus, your Ribbon may look different from the ones in this book if you are using a screen resolution other than 1024 × 768.

## To Insert a Text Box and Text

The default text box is displayed with the Calibri font and has no border, fill, or effects. To begin customizing the Hot Air Balloons presentation, you will insert a text box and then type the text that serves as the title to your presentation. The following steps insert a text box and enter text into the text box.

**1** Display the Insert tab, click the Text Box button (Insert tab | Text group), position the mouse pointer over the large cloud on Slide 1, and then click to insert the new text box.

**2** Type **Come Fly with Us** as the text box text (Figure 9–2).

**Note:** To help you locate screen elements that are referenced in the step instructions, such as buttons and commands, this book uses red boxes to point to these screen elements.

**Figure 9–2**

## To Change a Text Box Outline Weight

The first graphical change you will make to the text box is to increase the thickness of its border, which is called the outline. The weight, or thickness, of the text box border is measured in points. The following steps increase the outline weight.

- Click Format on the Ribbon to display the Drawing Tools Format tab.

- Click the Shape Outline button arrow (Drawing Tools Format tab | Shape Styles group) to display the Shape Outline gallery.

- Point to Weight in the Shape Outline gallery to display the Weight list (Figure 9–3).

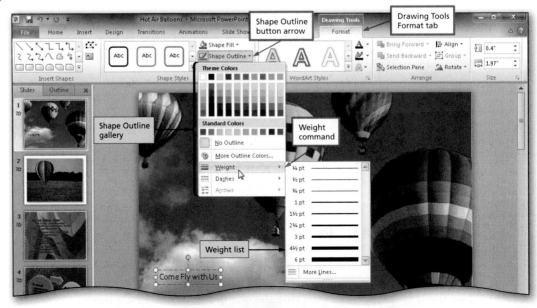

**Figure 9–3**

**2**

- Point to 3 pt to display a live preview of this outline line weight (Figure 9–4).

**Experiment**

- Point to various line weights on the Weight list and watch the border weights on the text box change.

**3**

- Click 3 pt to add an outline around the text box.

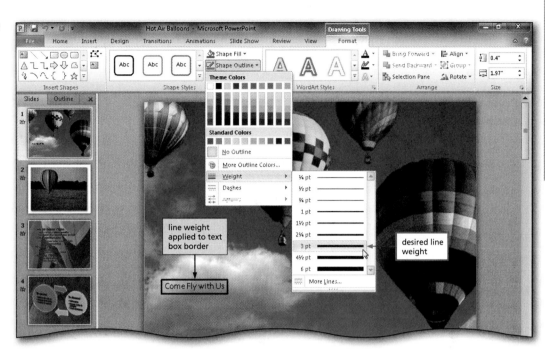

**Figure 9–4**

## To Change a Text Box Outline Color

The default outline color in the Office Theme is black. To coordinate with the colorful balloon picture and blue sky, you can change the outline color to a bright color. The following steps change the text box outline color.

**1**

- Click the Shape Outline button arrow (Drawing Tools Format tab | Shape Styles group) to display the Shape Outline gallery and then point to Blue in the Standard Colors area to display a live preview of that outline color on the text box (Figure 9–5).

**Experiment**

- Point to various colors in the Shape Outline gallery and watch the border colors on the text box change.

**2**

- Click Blue to change the text box border color.

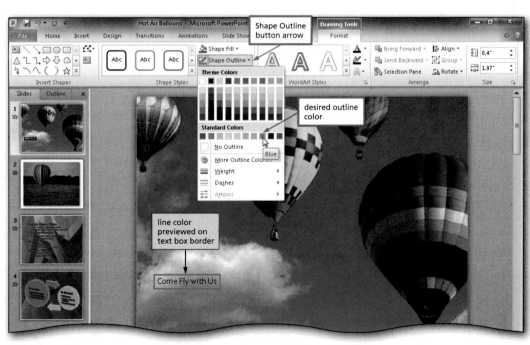

**Figure 9–5**

## To Change a Text Box Outline Style

The default outline style is a solid line. You can add interest by changing the style to dashes, dots, or a combination of dashes and dots. The following steps change the text box outline style.

- Click the Shape Outline button arrow (Drawing Tools Format tab | Shape Styles group) to display the Shape Outline gallery and then point to Dashes to display the Dashes list.

- Point to Long Dash Dot Dot to display a live preview of this outline style (Figure 9–6).

 **Experiment**

- Point to various styles in the Shape Outline gallery and watch the borders on the text box change.

- Click Long Dash Dot Dot to change the text box border style.

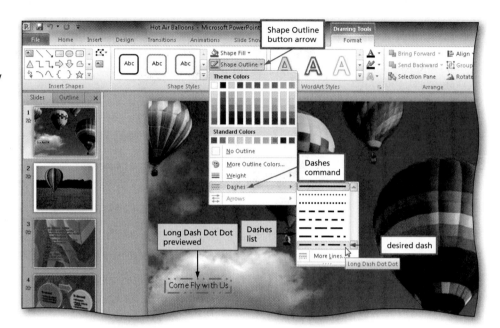

**Figure 9–6**

## To Apply an Effect to a Text Box

PowerPoint provides a variety of visual effects to add to the text box. They include shadow, glow, reflection, and 3-D rotation. The clouds in the Slide 1 background have uneven and transparent edges, so you can coordinate with this soft effect by adding a glow effect to the text box. The following steps apply an effect to the text box.

- Click the Shape Effects button (Drawing Tools Format tab | Shape Styles group) to display the Shape Effects gallery.

- Point to Glow to display the Glow gallery (Figure 9–7).

 **Experiment**

- Point to various effects in the Glow gallery and watch the glow edges change on the text box.

- Click the Blue, 18 pt glow, Accent color 1 (first color in fourth row) variation in the Glow Variations area to apply the glow effect.

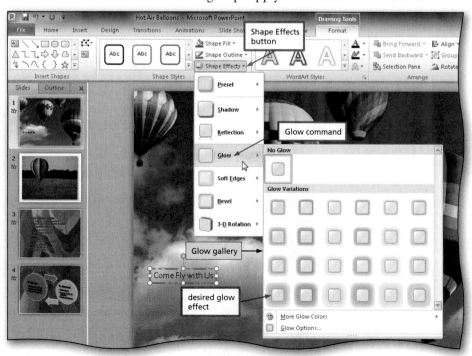

**Figure 9–7**

## To Format Text Box Text

The text box outline color, width, line style, and effect are set, so you now can choose a font and font size that complement the formatting changes. A WordArt style can add visual interest to the text box. The following steps change the text box text to WordArt, change the font size, and center the text in the text box.

**1** Select all the text box text, click the WordArt Styles More button (Drawing Tools Format tab | WordArt Styles group) to expand the gallery, and then click Gradient Fill – Orange, Accent 6, Inner Shadow (second letter A in fourth row) to apply this style.

**2** Increase the font size to 44 point.

**3** Center the text in the text box. If necessary, drag the text box to the location shown in Figure 9–8.

**Figure 9–8**

## To Set Text Box Formatting as the Default

The text box you inserted and formatted has a variety of visual elements that work well with the Hot Air Balloons picture and overall theme. For consistency, you can insert text boxes with the same formatting into other slides in the presentation. To save time and ensure all the formatting changes are applied, you can set the formatting of one text box as the default for all other text boxes you insert into the presentation. The following steps set the text box on Slide 1 as the default.

● Right-click the text box outline to display the shortcut menu (Figure 9–9).

**Figure 9–9**

● Click Set as Default Text Box on the shortcut menu to set the text box formatting as the default for any new text boxes.

**Q&A**

What should I do if the Set as Default Text Box command is not displayed on the shortcut menu?

Repeat Step 1 and be certain to click the text box border, not the interior of the box.

**Q&A**

Does setting the default text box affect all presentations or just the current one?

Only the current presentation is affected.

**BTW**

**Q&As**
For a complete list of the Q&As found in many of the step-by-step sequences in this book, visit the PowerPoint 2010 Q&A Web page (scsite.com/ppt2010/qa).

## To Insert a Formatted Text Box and Enter Text

Any new text boxes you insert will have the same formatting you applied to the Slide 1 text box. You want to emphasize to your presentation viewers that hot air balloon rides are offered daily from May through October, so a text box on Slide 2 is a good place to state this information. The following steps insert a formatted text box into Slide 2 and enter text.

① Display Slide 2, display the Insert tab, and then click the Text Box button.

② Insert the text box into the lower-left corner of the slide and then type `Launching` as the first line of the text box text.

③ Press SHIFT+ENTER to insert a line break and then type `every day` as the second text box line.

④ Press SHIFT+ENTER to insert a line break and then type `May - October` as the third text box line.

⑤ If necessary, drag the text box to the location shown in Figure 9–10.

**Figure 9–10**

## To Apply a Pattern to a Text Box

A pattern fill can call attention to a text box. PowerPoint provides a Pattern gallery, allowing you to change the appearance of the text box with a variety of horizontal and vertical lines, dots, dashes, and stripes. If desired, you can change the default fill foreground and background colors. The following steps apply a pattern to the Slide 2 text box and change the foreground and background colors.

**1**

- Right-click anywhere on the Slide 2 text box to display the shortcut menu.

- Click Format Shape on the shortcut menu to display the Format Shape dialog box. Drag the dialog box to the right so that you can view the text box (Figure 9–11).

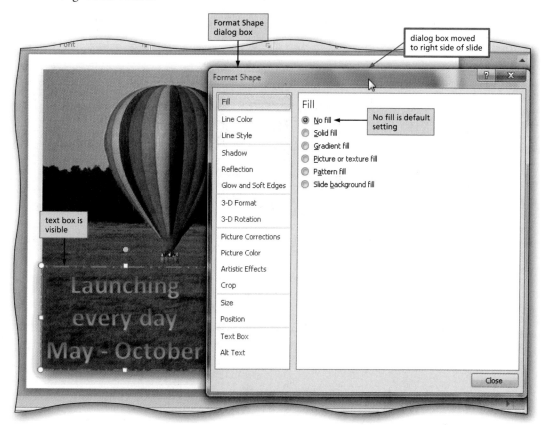

**Figure 9–11**

**2**

- Click Pattern fill (Format Shape dialog box) to display the Pattern gallery and the 5% pattern on the text box (Figure 9–12).

**Q&A**

Can I experiment with previewing the patterns on the text box?

No, the live preview function is not available.

**Figure 9–12**

**3**

- Click the Dotted diamond pattern (seventh color in third row) to apply this pattern to the Slide 2 text box.

**Q&A**

How can I delete a pattern if I decide not to apply one to my slide?

If you already have applied the pattern, click the Undo button on the Quick Access Toolbar.

- Click the Foreground Color button (Format Shape dialog box) to display a color gallery (Figure 9–13).

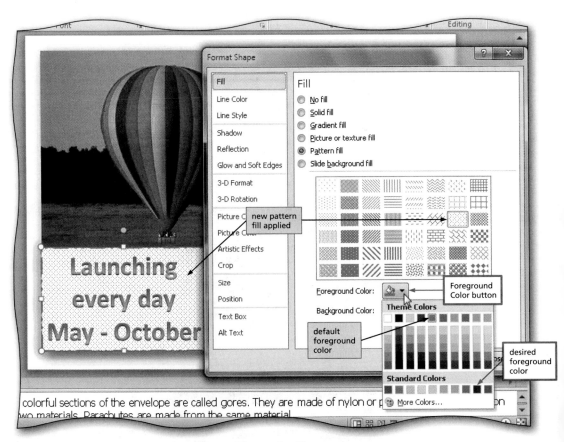

**Figure 9–13**

- Click Dark Blue (ninth color in Standard Colors row) to apply this color to the text box pattern and to display the Pattern gallery with the new foreground color.

- Click the Background Color button (Format Shape dialog box) to display a color gallery (Figure 9–14).

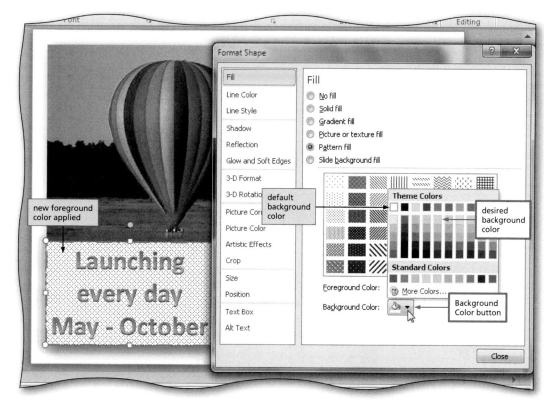

**Figure 9–14**

- Click Blue, Accent 1, Lighter 80% (fifth color in second Theme Colors row) to apply this color to the text box background and to display the Pattern gallery with the new background color (Figure 9–15).

- Click the Close button to close the Format Shape dialog box.

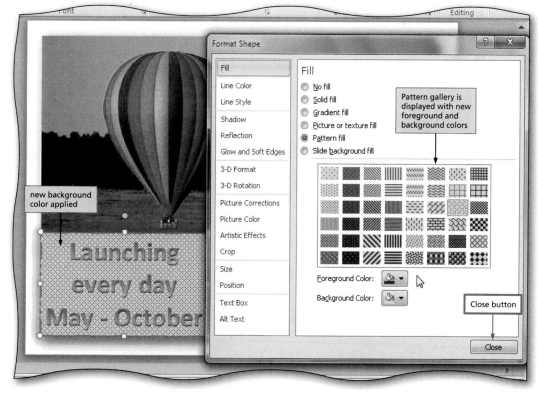

**Figure 9–15**

## To Apply a Gradient Fill to a Text Box

A gradient fill is another type of format you can apply to create interest in a slide element. It blends one color into another shade of the same color or another color. PowerPoint provides several preset gradients, or you can create your own custom color mix. The following steps insert a text box into Slide 3 and then apply a gradient fill.

**1**

- Display Slide 3, display the Insert tab, and then insert a text box near the top of the slide.

- Type **Flight Schedule** as the text box text, and if necessary, drag the text box to the location shown in Figure 9–16.

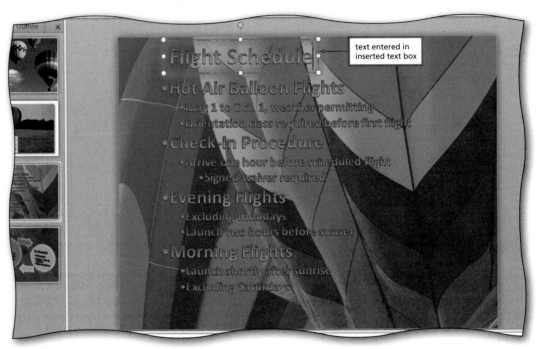

**Figure 9–16**

**2**

- Click the Drawing Tools Format tab and then click the Shape Fill button arrow (Drawing Tools Format tab | Shape Styles group) to display the Shape Fill gallery.

- Point to Gradient to display the Gradient gallery (Figure 9–17).

**Experiment**

- Point to various fills in the Gradient gallery and watch the interior of the text box change.

**3**

- Click the Linear Up (second variation in third row) variation in the Light Variations area to apply the gradient fill.

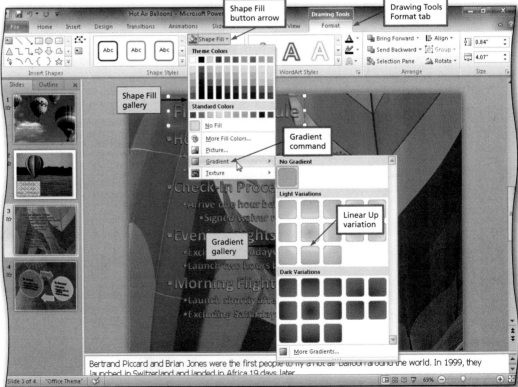

**Figure 9–17**

## To Center a Text Box

The text box on Slide 3 will serve as the title. You could attempt to center it horizontally on the slide and use the rulers to aid you in this process. A more efficient method of centering the text box between the left and right edges of the slide, however, is to use PowerPoint's align feature. You can align a slide element horizontally along the left or right sides or in the center of the slide, and you also can align an element vertically along the top, bottom, or middle of the slide. The following steps align the Slide 3 text box horizontally.

**1**

- With the Slide 3 text box selected, click the Align button (Drawing Tools Format tab | Arrange group) to display the Align menu (Figure 9–18).

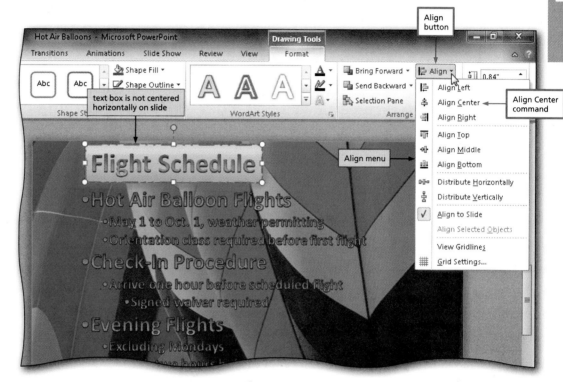

**Figure 9–18**

**2**

- Click Align Center to center the text box horizontally on the slide (Figure 9–19).

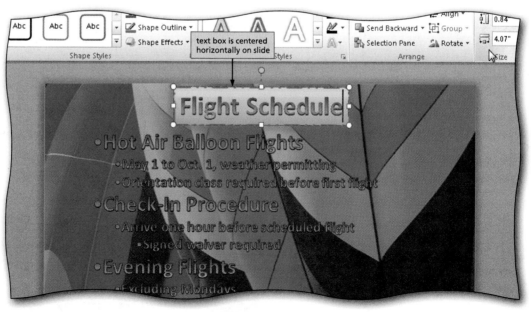

**Figure 9–19**

## To Change a Slide Picture

The picture on Slide 2 features a colorful balloon, but the brown grass that dominates the slide does not complement the formatted text box. A dramatic picture of a colorful balloon is located on the Data Files for Students. PowerPoint allows you to change a picture on a slide easily. The following steps change the Slide 2 picture.

**1**

- Display Slide 2, click anywhere on the picture except the text box to select the picture, and then click the Picture Tools Format tab (Figure 9–20).

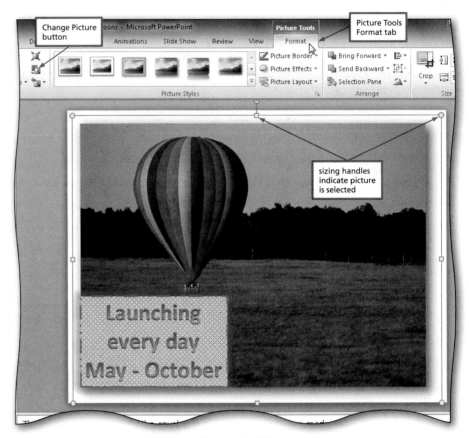

**Figure 9–20**

**2**

- Click the Change Picture button (Picture Tools Format tab | Adjust group) to display the Insert Picture dialog box.

- If necessary, select your USB flash drive in the list of available storage devices to display a list of files and folders on the selected USB flash drive and then navigate to the PowerPoint Chapter 09 folder.

- Click Balloon Burner to select the file name (Figure 9–21).

 What if the picture is not on a USB flash drive?

Use the same process, but select the drive containing the picture.

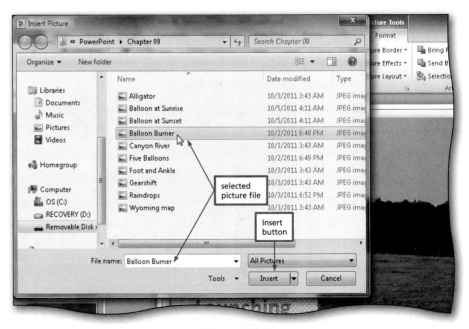

**Figure 9–21**

**3**

- Click the Insert button (Insert Picture dialog box) to change the Slide 2 picture (Figure 9–22).

**Q&A**

What if I do not want to use this picture?

Click the Undo button on the Quick Access Toolbar.

**Figure 9–22**

**Break Point:** If you wish to take a break, this is a good place to do so. Be sure to save the Hot Air Balloons file again and then you can quit PowerPoint. To resume at a later time, start PowerPoint, open the file called Hot Air Balloons, and continue following the steps from this location forward.

# Manipulating SmartArt

Every SmartArt layout has a unique design and graphical elements. The shapes maximize vertical and horizontal space for text and pictures. When your presentation calls for special design needs or additional shapes, you can change the defaults that specify where each SmartArt element is displayed. You can add, subtract, and reorder shapes; promote and demote text; make a single shape smaller or larger; and change the SmartArt fill, outline, and colors.

In the following pages, you will perform these tasks on Slide 3:

1. Convert WordArt paragraphs to a SmartArt Target List.
2. Reorder two shapes in the SmartArt layout.
3. Reorder two bulleted paragraphs in one shape.
4. Promote and demote bulleted paragraphs.
5. Change the SmartArt layout and style.
6. Resize the entire SmartArt layout and one shape within the layout.
7. Apply two pictures to SmartArt shapes.
8. Convert the SmartArt graphic to text.

**BTW**

**SmartArt in Handouts**
SmartArt diagrams are composed of individual vector graphics. Some presenters decide to include these diagrams in a handout but not as part of a presentation so that audience members can study the relationships among the shapes after the presentation has concluded.

<table>
<tr><td>Plan<br>Ahead</td><td>**Use keywords in SmartArt graphics.**<br>Most SmartArt shapes have very limited space for text. You must, therefore, carefully choose each word you are going to display in the graphic. The text you select can serve as keywords, or a speaking outline. If you glance at the SmartArt when you are presenting the slide show in front of an audience, each word should prompt you for the main point you are going to make. These keywords should jog your memory if you lose your train of thought or are interrupted.</td></tr>
</table>

## To Convert WordArt to SmartArt

The bulleted paragraphs on Slide 3 are formatted as WordArt. Although WordArt can add visual interest, using a graphical element such as SmartArt can be even more effective in helping the audience to grasp essential concepts. SmartArt diagrams are creative means to show processes, lists, cycles, and other relationships. PowerPoint suggests layouts that might fit the concept you are trying to present and then easily converts WordArt to SmartArt. The following steps convert WordArt to SmartArt.

**1**

- Display Slide 3, right-click anywhere in the WordArt bulleted list paragraphs to display the shortcut menu, and then point to Convert to SmartArt to display the SmartArt gallery.

 Does it matter where I place the cursor to right-click the WordArt?

No. As long as the cursor is placed in the WordArt text, you will be able to convert the paragraphs to SmartArt.

- Point to Target List in the gallery to display a live preview of that layout applied to the WordArt paragraphs (Figure 9–23).

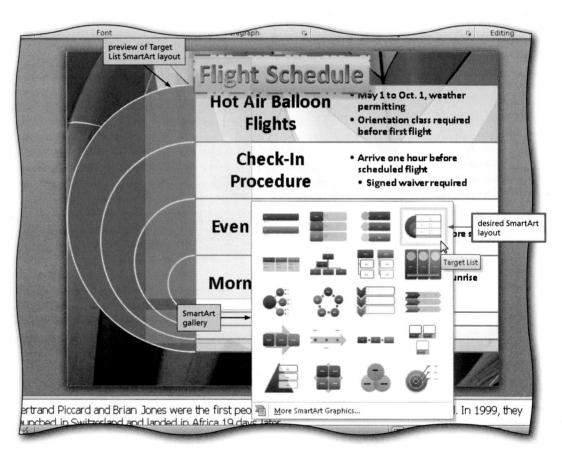

**Figure 9–23**

*Experiment*

- Point to various graphics in the SmartArt gallery and watch the layouts change.

**2**

- Click Target List in the SmartArt gallery to convert the WordArt to that layout.

Q&A How is the text arranged in the Target List layout?

The four first-level paragraphs are in the middle column of the graphic and have a larger font size than the eight bulleted second-level paragraphs.

## To Reorder SmartArt Shapes

Now that the SmartArt layout is created, you can modify the graphic. One change you can make is to change the order of the shapes. You decide that two items in the graphic should be displayed in a different order. First, the information regarding the morning flights should precede the details for the evening flights. Also, for consistency, you decide that the second bulleted paragraph in the morning and evening flight shapes should refer to the day of the week excluded from the schedule. Currently, the Excluding Mondays bulleted paragraph in the Evening Flights shape is the second item, and the Excluding Saturdays bulleted paragraph in the Morning Flights shape is the first item. PowerPoint provides tools to move shapes and paragraphs in a vertical layout up or down and the shapes and paragraphs in a horizontal layout right or left. The following steps reorder the Morning and Evening Flights shapes and the two bulleted paragraphs in the Evening Flights shape.

- Position the mouse pointer in the Morning Flights shape and then click to select it and the two bulleted paragraphs (Figure 9–24).

**Q&A** Why are both shapes selected?

The Morning Flights shape is a first-level paragraph, and the two bulleted second-level paragraphs are associated with it. When a first-level paragraph is selected, any related paragraphs also are selected with it.

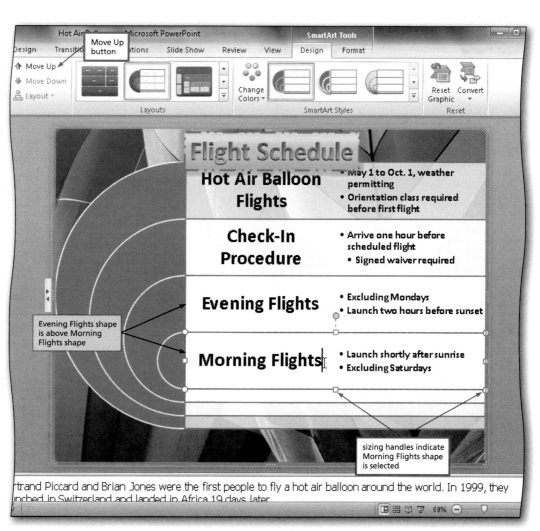

**Figure 9–24**

**Q&A** Why is the signed waiver bullet indented in the Check-In Procedure shape?

The original PowerPoint slide designer categorized this waiver as a subset of the one-hour preflight time paragraph. You now want to emphasize that this document is an important part of the check-in procedure and decide that it deserves equal prominence on the slide. You will, therefore, change this bulleted paragraph to the same level as the bullet above it in the next set of steps.

**2**

- With the SmartArt Tools Design tab displayed, click the Move Up button (SmartArt Tools Design tab | Create Graphic group) to reorder the Morning Flights shape above the Evening Flights shape.

- Position the mouse pointer in the bulleted paragraph, Excluding Mondays (Figure 9–25).

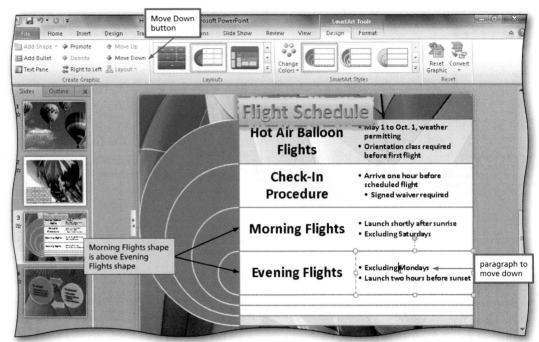

**Figure 9–25**

**3**

- Click the Move Down button (SmartArt Tools Design tab | Create Graphic group) to reorder the bulleted paragraph, Excluding Mondays, below the bulleted paragraph, Launch two hours before sunset.

## To Promote a SmartArt Bullet Level

PowerPoint provides tools that allow you to promote and demote bulleted text. These tools function in the same manner as the Increase List Level and Decrease List Level buttons that change the indents for bulleted text.

Another change you want to make on Slide 3 is to promote the bulleted paragraph, Signed waiver required, to the same level as the bullet above it, because this document is an important part of the check-in procedure. The following steps promote the second bullet in the Check-In Procedure shape.

- Position the mouse pointer in the bulleted paragraph, Signed waiver required (Figure 9–26).

- With the SmartArt Tools Design tab displayed, click the Promote button (SmartArt Tools Design tab | Create Graphic group) to decrease the indent of the bulleted paragraph.

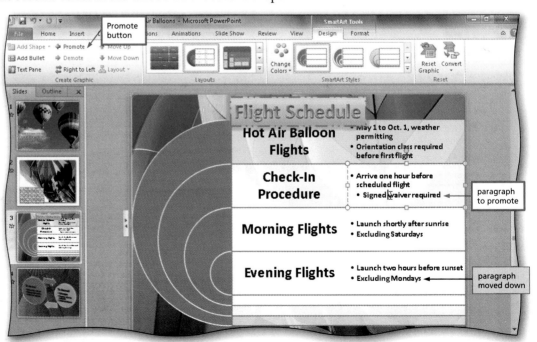

**Figure 9–26**

## To Demote a SmartArt Bullet Level

The two bulleted items in the Morning Flights and Evening Flights shapes both are second-level paragraphs. You decide that the two days that are excluded from the weekly schedule are not as important to emphasize as the launch times, so you want to demote those paragraphs. The following steps demote the second-level bulleted paragraphs.

- Position the mouse pointer in the bulleted paragraph, Excluding Saturdays (Figure 9–27).

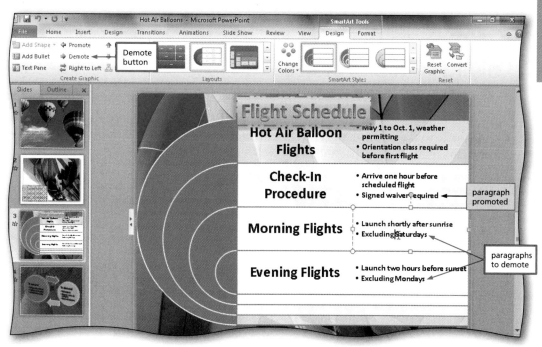

**Figure 9–27**

2

- With the SmartArt Tools Design tab displayed, click the Demote button (SmartArt Tools Design tab | Create Graphic group) to increase the indent of the bulleted paragraph.

- Position the mouse pointer in the bulleted paragraph, Excluding Mondays, and then click the Demote button to increase the indent of this paragraph (Figure 9–28).

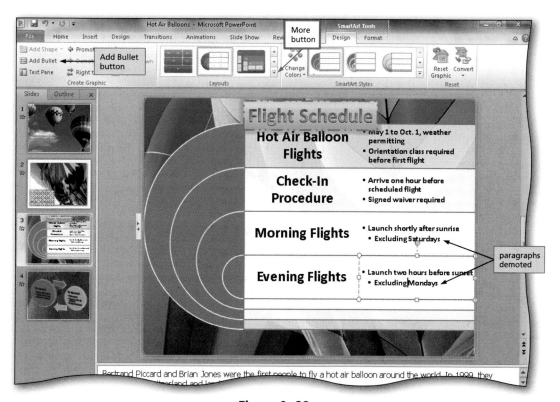

**Figure 9–28**

### To Add a SmartArt Bullet

If you need to add information to a SmartArt shape, you can create a new bulleted paragraph. This text would display below the last bulleted paragraph in the shape. If you wanted to add a SmartArt bullet, you would perform the following steps.

1. Select the SmartArt graphic shape where you want to insert the bulleted paragraph.
2. Click the Add Bullet button (SmartArt Tools Design tab | Create Graphic group) to insert a new bulleted paragraph below any bulleted text.

## To Change the SmartArt Layout

Once you begin formatting a SmartArt shape, you may decide that another layout better conveys the message you are communicating to an audience. PowerPoint allows you to change the layout easily. Any graphical changes that were made to the original SmartArt, such as moving shapes or promoting and demoting paragraphs, are applied to the new SmartArt layout. The following steps change the SmartArt layout.

- With the SmartArt Tools Design tab displaying, click the More button in the Layouts group to expand the Layouts gallery (Figure 9–29).

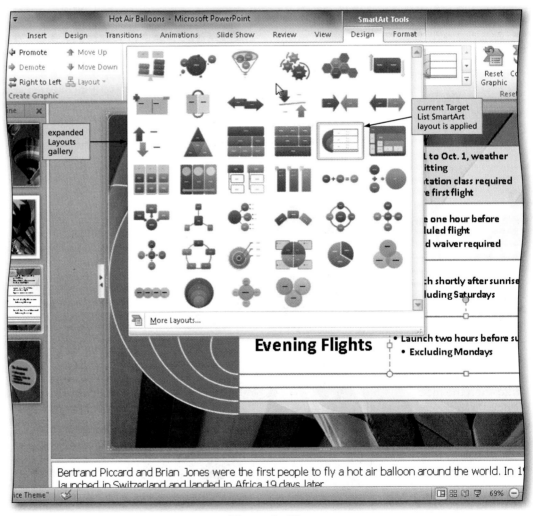

**Figure 9–29**

**2**

- Point to the Grouped List layout (first layout in fourth row) to display a live preview of this SmartArt layout (Figure 9–30).

 **Experiment**

- Point to various layouts in the gallery and watch the SmartArt layouts change.

**Q&A**

Are additional layouts available other than those displayed in the gallery?

Yes. Click More Layouts to display the Choose a SmartArt Graphic dialog box and then select another layout.

**3**

- Click Grouped List to change the layout.

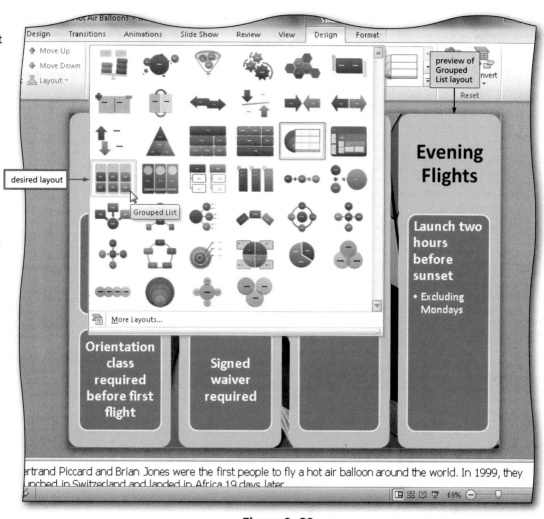

Figure 9–30

## To Remove a SmartArt Shape

Now that the new SmartArt layout is created, you can modify the graphic. One change you can make is to delete unnecessary elements. Slide 2 has similar information found in the first shape regarding the months when the flights are scheduled. In addition, the next slide you will create will have information about material covered in the orientation class. You can, therefore, delete the first shape to eliminate redundancy. The following steps remove a SmartArt shape.

**BTW**

**Line Spacing Measurements**

The lower part of each letter rests on an imaginary line called the baseline. The space between the baseline of one row of type and the baseline of the row beneath it is called line spacing. Typically, the line spacing is 120 percent of the font size. For example, if the font size is 10 point, the line spacing is 12 point so that two points of space are displayed between the lines.

- Click a light blue area of the left SmartArt shape, Hot Air Balloon Flights, to select it.

- Press and hold down the CTRL key and then click both rectangles, May 1 to Oct. 1, weather permitting and Orientation class required before first flight, to select all three shapes (Figure 9–31).

- Press the DELETE key to delete the entire left SmartArt shape.

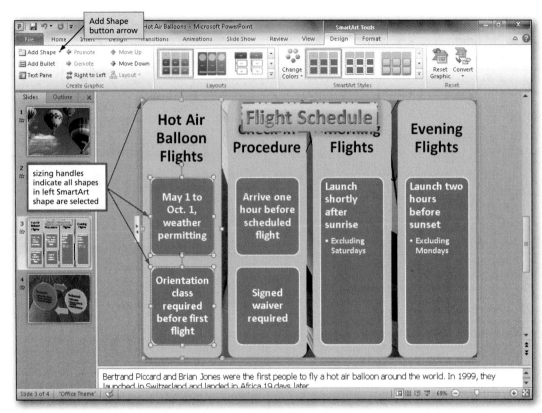

**Figure 9–31**

### TO ADD A SMARTART SHAPE

You may add a new SmartArt shape to the layout if you need to display additional information. PowerPoint gives you the option of adding this shape above or below a selected shape or to the left or the right side of the shape. If you wanted to add a SmartArt shape, you would perform the following steps.

1. Select a SmartArt graphic shape near where you want to insert another shape.
2. Click the Add Shape button arrow (SmartArt Tools Design tab | Create Graphic group) to display the Add Shape menu.
3. Click the desired location for the new shape, which would be after, before, above, or below the selected shape.

## To Resize a SmartArt Graphic by Entering an Exact Measurement

The SmartArt shape overlaps the Flight Schedule text box, so you can reduce the size of the shape. You can resize this slide element by dragging the sizing handles or by specifying exact measurements for the height and width. The following steps resize the SmartArt graphic by entering an exact measurement.

**1**

- Select the entire SmartArt graphic by clicking an outer edge of the graphic near the edge of the slide (Figure 9–32).

**Q&A**

How will I know the entire graphic is selected?

You will see the Text pane control and sizing handles around the outer edge of the SmartArt.

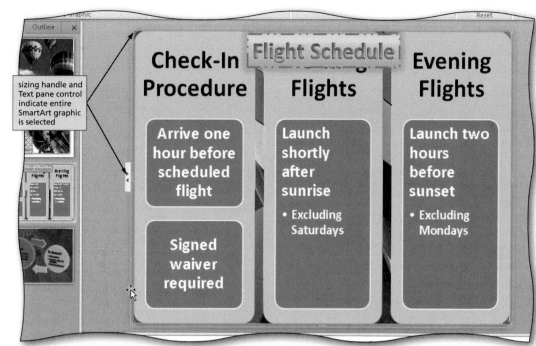

Figure 9–32

**2**

- Display the SmartArt Tools Format tab and then click the SmartArt Size button.

- Click the Shape Height down arrow repeatedly until 6.5" is displayed in the Height box (Figure 9–33).

**3**

- Drag the SmartArt graphic downward so its lower edge is aligned with the lower edge of the slide.

**Other Ways**

1. Right-click graphic, click Size and Position on shortcut menu, click Size tab (Layout dialog box), enter graphic height and width values in boxes, click OK button

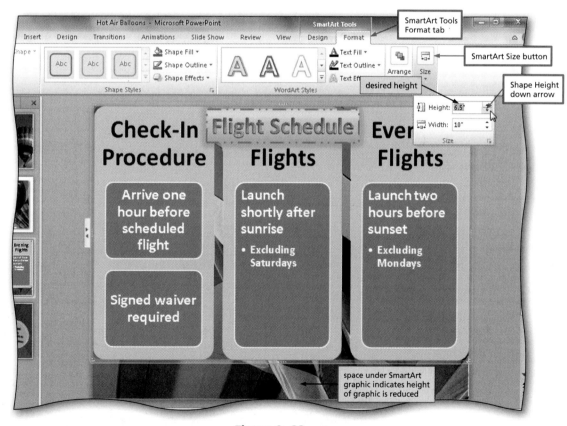

Figure 9–33

## To Resize a SmartArt Graphic Shape

The entire SmartArt shape and the text box now are the proper proportions to display together on the slide. In addition to changing the height and width of the SmartArt graphic, you also can change the height and width of one individual SmartArt shape in the graphic. You decide that you want to deemphasize the Check-In Procedure shape so that the Morning Flights and Evening Flights shapes are more prominent on the slide. The Check-In Procedure shape is composed of two parts: the outer light-blue shape and the inner medium-blue shape. Each shape must be sized individually. The following steps resize a SmartArt graphic shape.

**1**
- Click a light blue area of the left SmartArt shape, Check-In Procedure, to select it.

- With the SmartArt Tools Format tab displaying, click the Smaller button (SmartArt Tools Format tab | Shapes group) once to decrease the shape size (Figure 9–34).

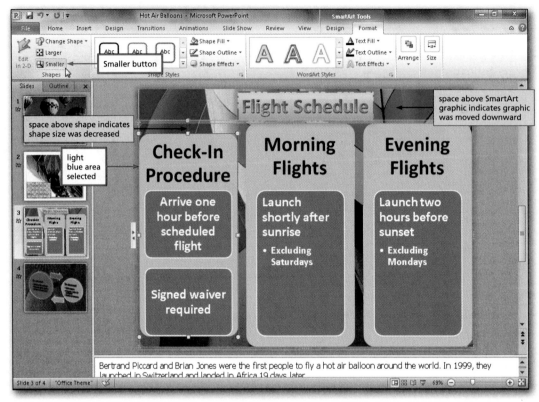

**Figure 9–34**

**2**
- Click the left shape, Arrive one hour before scheduled flight, to select it and then click the Smaller button two times (Figure 9–35).

**Q&A** Can I select both shapes in the Check-In Procedure shape and size them simultaneously?

No. Each shape must be sized independently.

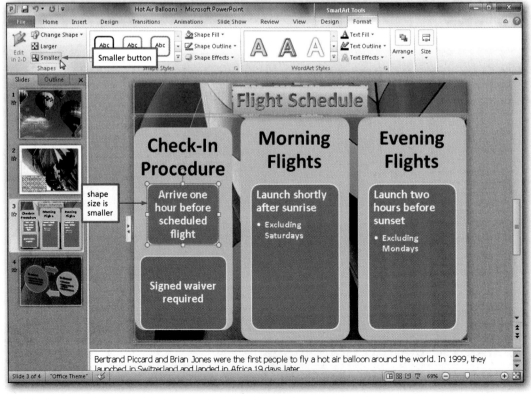

**Figure 9–35**

**3**

- Click the left shape, Signed waiver required, to select it and then click the Smaller button twice.

- Click a light blue area of the shape and then drag the shape downward so its lower edge is aligned with the lower edge of the slide.

- Drag the Arrive one hour before scheduled flight shape downward so that it displays as shown in Figure 9–36.

**Other Ways**

1. Right-click graphic, click Size and Position on shortcut menu, click Size tab (Layout dialog box), enter graphic height and width values in boxes, click OK button

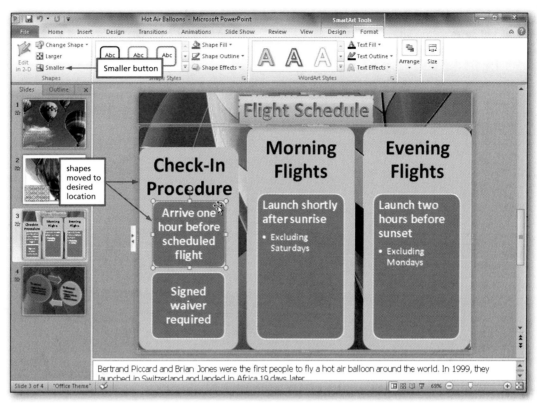

**Figure 9–36**

## To Apply a Picture to a Text Box

Sufficient space exists in the lower halves of the Morning Flights and Evening Flights shapes to insert a picture. For consistency with the slide title, you can insert a text box that has the default formatting and then add a picture. The following steps add a text box and then apply a picture into two SmartArt graphic shapes.

**1**

- Insert a text box below the bulleted paragraph, Excluding Saturdays, in the middle SmartArt shape.

- Click the Shape Fill button (Drawing Tools Format tab | Drawing group) to display the Shape Fill gallery (Figure 9–37).

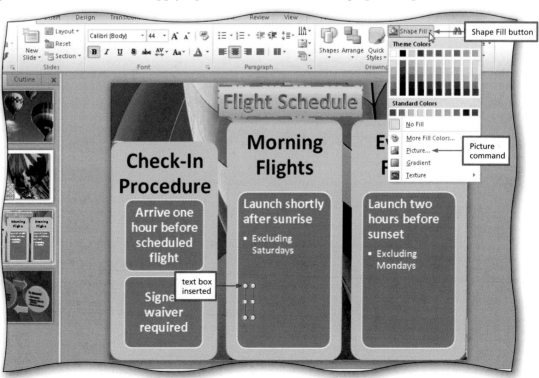

**Figure 9–37**

● Click Picture in the Shape Fill
gallery to display the Insert Picture
dialog box and then click Balloon
at Sunrise to select the file name
(Figure 9–38).

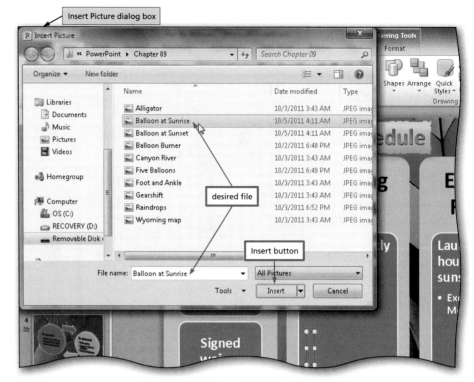

**Figure 9–38**

● Click the Insert button (Insert Picture
dialog box) to insert the picture into
the text box.

● Insert a text box below the bulleted
paragraph, Excluding Mondays, in
the right SmartArt shape, display
the Shape Fill gallery, and then
insert the picture, Balloon at Sunset.

● If necessary, drag the left and right
sizing handles of both boxes to
the outer edges of the medium-
blue shape and then use the Smart
Guides to align the two text boxes
horizontally (Figure 9–39).

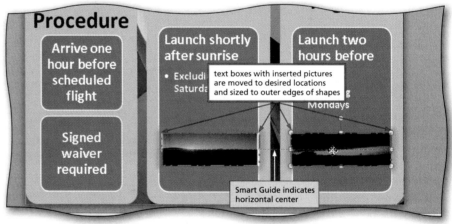

**Figure 9–39**

## To Add a SmartArt Style to the Graphic and Change the Color

To enhance the appearance of the rectangles in the Grouped List layout, you can
add a transparent three-dimensional style that allows some of the background to show
through the graphic. You also can add more colors. The following steps add the Powder
style and a Colorful range.

**1** Select the entire SmartArt graphic, display the SmartArt Tools Design tab, and then click
the More button in the SmartArt Styles group to expand the SmartArt Styles gallery.

**2** Click Powder in the 3-D area (first graphic in second row) to apply this style to the graphic.

**3** Click the Change Colors button (SmartArt Tools Design tab | SmartArt Styles group) to dis-
play the Change Colors gallery.

**4** Click Colorful Range – Accent Colors 5 to 6 (fifth graphic in Colorful row) to apply this
color variation to the graphic (Figure 9–40).

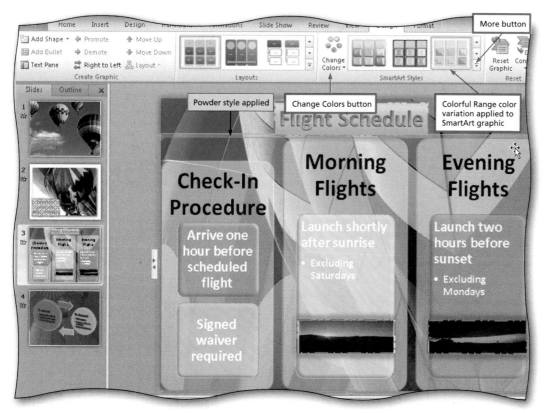

**Figure 9–40**

## To Convert a SmartArt Graphic to Text

Hot air balloon pilots must learn the techniques of ascending and descending, and the SmartArt shape on Slide 4 states the basic principles of how the pilot controls altitude. At times, you may decide that SmartArt is not the optimal method of presenting information to an audience and instead want to depict the same concept using text. PowerPoint allows you to remove the shapes and change the text in the graphic to a bulleted list. The following steps convert the SmartArt graphic to text.

**1**

- Display Slide 4 and then select the entire SmartArt graphic.

**Q&A**

If one of the SmartArt shapes is selected, how do I select the entire graphic?

Be certain to click the edge of the slide. You will see sizing handles and the Text pane control when the SmartArt graphic is selected.

- With the SmartArt Tools Design tab displaying, click the Convert button (SmartArt Tools Design tab | Reset group) to display the Convert menu (Figure 9–41).

**Figure 9–41**

**2**

- Click Convert to Text to display the SmartArt text as eight bulleted list paragraphs.

**Q&A**

Why would I want to convert the SmartArt graphic?

The bulleted list might be useful for instructional purposes. At times, audiences may prefer seeing instructions as paragraphs and not be distracted by the graphical SmartArt elements.

- Position the mouse pointer between the bullet character and the word, To, in the paragraph, To descend (Figure 9–42).

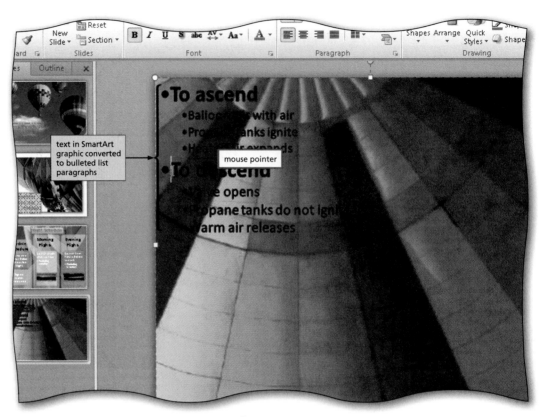

Figure 9–42

**3**

- Press the ENTER key six times to move the four paragraphs downward (Figure 9–43).

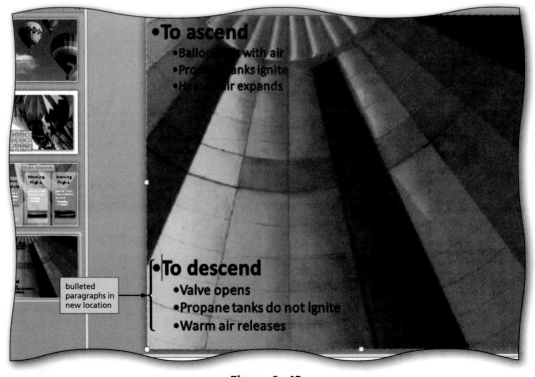

Figure 9–43

### To Convert a SmartArt Graphic to Shapes

An alternative to changing a graphic to text is changing a graphic to shapes. In this manner, a shape can be moved, resized, or deleted independently of any other shape in the SmartArt. If you wanted to convert a SmartArt graphic to shapes, you would perform the following steps.

1. Select the entire SmartArt graphic.
2. Click the Convert button (SmartArt Tools Design tab | Reset group) to display the Convert menu.
3. Click Convert to Shapes.

**Break Point:** If you wish to take a break, this is a good place to do so. Be sure to save the Hot Air Balloons file again and then you can quit PowerPoint. To resume at a later time, start PowerPoint, open the file called Hot Air Balloons, and continue following the steps from this location forward.

# Inserting and Modifying Shapes

Diagrams with labels often help audiences identify the parts of an object. Text boxes with clear, large type and an arrow pointing to a precise area of the object work well in showing relationships between components. The items in the Shapes gallery provide a variety of useful shapes you can insert into slides.

A hot air balloon has several components: They include the envelope, which is the colorful balloon that inflates; the skirt; the burner unit that releases heat into the envelope; and a basket to hold the pilot and the passengers. These parts can be depicted with a variety of items found in the Shapes gallery. At times, you may be unable to find a shape in the gallery that fits your specific needs. In those instances, you might find a similar shape and then alter it to your specifications.

## To Insert Shapes and an Arrow

You can draw four parts of the hot air balloon with shapes located in the Shapes gallery: Teardrop for the envelope, two rectangles for the skirt and the burner unit, and Flowchart: Magnetic Disk for the basket. In addition, the Notched Right Arrow shape can be inserted to serve as a leader line for labeling a hot air balloon part. The following steps insert four shapes and an arrow into Slide 4.

**1** With Slide 4 displaying, click the Shapes button (Home tab | Drawing group) to display the Shapes gallery and then click the Teardrop shape in the Basic Shapes area (fourth shape in second row).

**2** Position the mouse pointer near the top of the slide and then click to insert the Teardrop shape.

**3** Display the Shapes gallery and then click the Snip Same Side Corner Rectangle shape (fourth shape in Rectangles area).

**4** Position the mouse pointer below the Teardrop and then click to insert the Snip Same Side Corner Rectangle shape.

**5** Display the Shapes gallery, click the Rounded Rectangle shape (second shape in Rectangles area), and then insert this shape below the Snip Same Side Corner Rectangle shape.

**6** Display the Shapes gallery, click the Flowchart: Magnetic Disk shape in the Flowchart area (second shape in third row), and then insert this shape below the Rounded Rectangle shape.

**7** Use the Smart Guides to align the four shapes vertically.

**BTW**

**Using Metaphorical Shapes**
Use your imagination to use simple shapes and objects as metaphors. For example, a broken pencil can represent a stressful situation whereas a slice of cake can serve as imagery for a simple task. Make the shape large and bold, and use as few words as possible. Your audience should be able to understand and relate to the images without much explanation on the slides or from the speaker.

**8** Display the Shapes gallery, click the Notched Right Arrow shape in the Block Arrows area (sixth shape in second row), and then insert this shape in the middle of the slide (Figure 9–44).

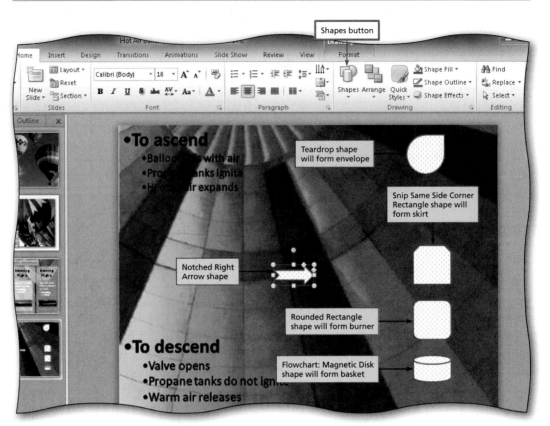

**Figure 9–44**

**BTW**

**Revising Your Presentation**
If you are going to present your slide show multiple times to a variety of audiences, consider the slides a work in progress. Each time you deliver your speech, you should be able to tweak the slides to clarify points, answer questions that arose during the presentation, and generate discussion. Revising a presentation is a positive step toward communicating your message clearly and powerfully.

## To Resize and Move a Shape

The five shapes on Slide 5 are the default sizes, and they need to be proportioned to reflect accurate hot air balloon dimensions. When you want to keep the resized shape proportions identical to the original shape, press the SHIFT key when clicking a sizing handle and then drag the mouse pointer inward or outward to decrease or increase the size. If you do not hold down the SHIFT key, you can elongate the height or the width to draw an object that is not identical to the shape shown in the Shapes gallery. If you want to alter the shape's proportions, drag one of the sizing handles inward or outward. The following steps resize the shapes and arrow.

**1** Select the Teardrop, press and hold down the SHIFT key, and then drag the lower-left corner sizing handle downward to the middle of the slide.

**2** Position the mouse pointer over the Teardrop rotation handle so that it changes to a Free Rotate pointer and then drag the mouse pointer clockwise so that the tip of the shape points to the lower edge of the slide.

**3** Select the Snip Same Side Corner Rectangle and then drag the middle sizing handle on the lower edge upward to the middle of the shape.

**4** Select the Rounded Rectangle, press and hold down the SHIFT key, and then drag a corner sizing handle inward.

**5** Select the Flowchart: Magnetic Disk, press and hold down the SHIFT key, and then drag a corner sizing handle outward.

**6** Select the Notched Right Arrow, press and hold down the SHIFT key, and then drag a corner sizing handle outward.

**7** Drag the shapes to the locations shown in Figure 9–45 using the Smart Guide to help you align the shapes vertically.

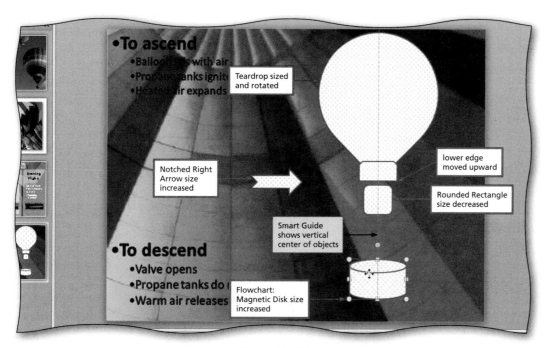

**Figure 9–45**

## To Apply a Fill to a Shape

The shapes on Slide 4 have a Light Green Divot fill. You can change the shape fill using the same types of fills you used for the text boxes in this presentation. For example, you can apply a gradient, pattern, texture, or picture. The method of applying these fill effects is similar to the steps you used to format text boxes. The following steps apply fills to the shapes.

**1**

- Select the Teardrop, click the Shape Fill button arrow (Drawing Tools Format tab | Drawing group) to display the Shape Fill gallery, and then point to Gradient to display the Gradient gallery (Figure 9–46).

🔍 **Experiment**

- Point to various gradients in the Gradient gallery and watch the interior of the Teardrop shape change.

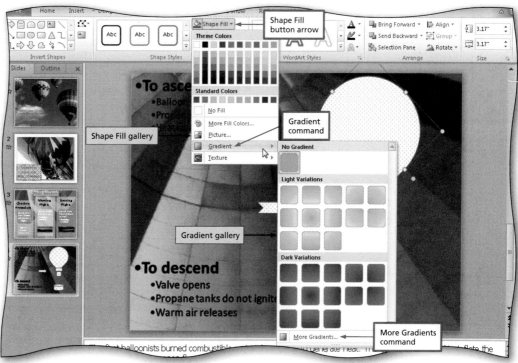

**Figure 9–46**

**2**

- Click More Gradients in the Gradient gallery to display the Format Shape dialog box. Drag the dialog box to the left so that you can view the balloon shapes.

- With the Fill pane displaying, click Gradient fill to expand the gradient options and then click the Preset colors button to display the Preset colors gallery (Figure 9–47).

Can I experiment with previewing the gradient colors?

No, the live preview feature is not available.

**3**

- Click Rainbow in the Preset colors gallery to apply the gradient fill to the Teardrop.

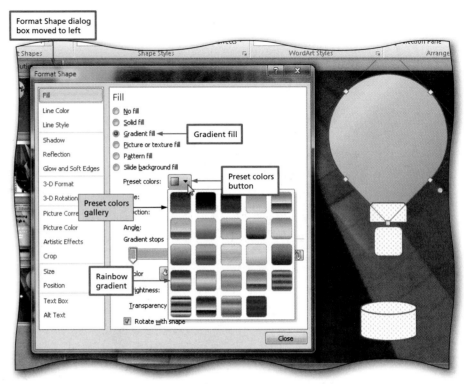

**Figure 9–47**

How can I delete a gradient fill if I decide not to apply one to the shape?

If you already have applied the pattern, you must click the Undo button on the Quick Access Toolbar.

**4**

- Select the Snip Same Side Corner Rectangle shape and then click Solid fill to display the Fill Color area.

- Click the Color button in the Fill Color area to display the Color palette (Figure 9–48).

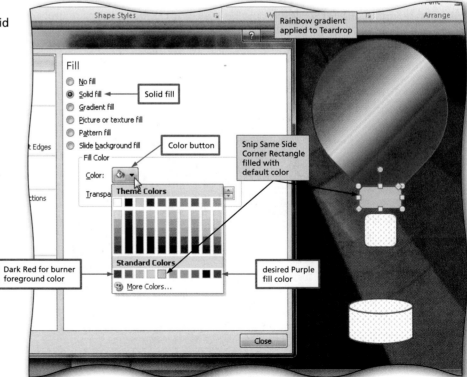

**Figure 9–48**

**5**

- Click Purple (last color in Standard Colors row) to apply the color to the shape.

- Select the Rounded Rectangle shape, click the Wave pattern (sixth color in second row) in the Pattern gallery, and then change the foreground color to Dark Red (first color in Standard Colors row) (Figure 9–49).

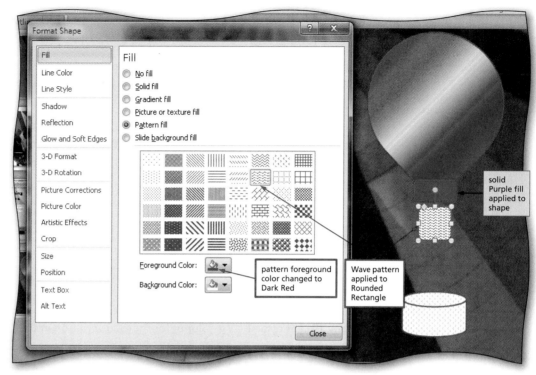

**Figure 9–49**

**6**

- Select the Flowchart: Magnetic Disk shape, click Picture or texture fill, and then click the Texture button to display the Texture gallery (Figure 9–50).

**7**

- Click Woven Mat (fourth texture in first row) to apply this texture to the shape.

- Click the Close button to close the Format Picture dialog box.

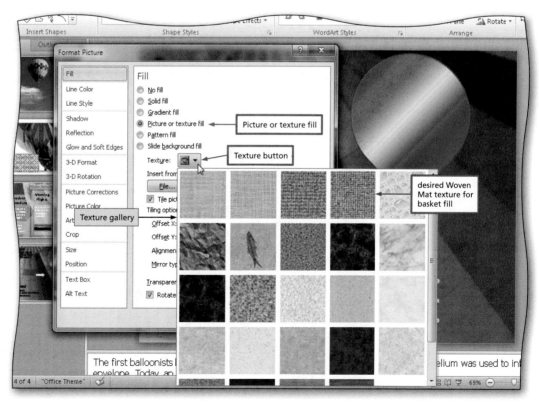

**Figure 9–50**

**Adding Contrast for Energy**

The samples in the Color palette columns range from light to dark. If you want your graphic to have a high level of energy, consider using colors at opposite ends of the columns to add a dramatic effect. The greater the contrast, the higher the energy. In contrast, if your goal is to give your graphic a peaceful feeling, use colors in the same row that have the same levels of intensity.

## To Change a Shape Fill and Outline and Apply Effects

Earlier in this project, you changed a text box outline color, weight, and style. You also applied a glow effect to a text box. You, similarly, can change the outline formatting and effects for a shape. For consistency, you can enhance the arrow by using the same formatting changes that you applied to the text box. The following steps change the arrow shape outline and apply an effect.

**1** Select the Notched Right Arrow, click the Shape Fill button (Drawing Tools Format tab | Shape Styles group), display the Gradient gallery, and then click Linear Right (first gradient in second row) in the Light Variations area.

**2** Click the Shape Outline button arrow (Drawing Tools Format tab | Shape Styles group), display the Weight gallery, and then click 3 pt.

**3** Display the Shape Outline gallery again and then click Blue in the Standard Colors area to change the shape border color.

**4** Display the Shape Outline gallery again, display the Dashes gallery, and then click Long Dash Dot Dot to change the border style.

**5** Display the Shape Effects gallery, display the Glow gallery, and then click the Blue, 18 pt glow, Accent color 1 (first color in fourth row) variation in the Glow Variations area to apply the glow effect (Figure 9–51).

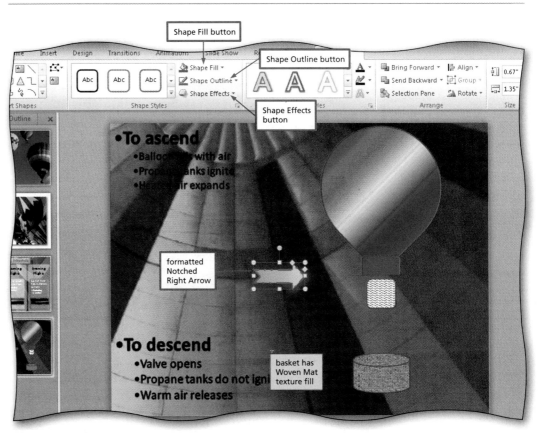

**Figure 9–51**

## To Set Shape Formatting as the Default

The Notched Right Arrow shape you inserted and formatted complements the default text box you inserted on the slides in the presentation. You will use this shape on several parts of Slide 4 to help identify parts of the hot air balloon. To save time and ensure all the formatting changes are applied, you can set the formatting of one shape as the default for all other shapes you insert into the presentation. The following steps set the arrow shape formatting on Slide 4 as the default.

**1**

- Right-click the Notched Right Arrow shape to display the shortcut menu (Figure 9–52).

**2**

- Click Set as Default Shape on the shortcut menu to set the shape formatting as the default for any new shapes.

**Figure 9–52**

## To Draw a Line

The shapes on Slide 4 help identify the parts of a hot air balloon. To complete the drawing, you need to connect the Teardrop, which represents the balloon's envelope, to the Flowchart: Magnetic Disk, which represents the basket. Line shapes are included in the Shapes gallery, and they include three straight lines, three straight elbow connectors, a Curve, a Freeform, and a Scribble line. The lines and connectors have zero, one, or two arrowheads. The following steps draw two straight lines without arrowheads and position these shapes on Slide 4.

**1**

- Display the Shapes gallery and then point to the Line shape (first shape in the Lines area) (Figure 9–53).

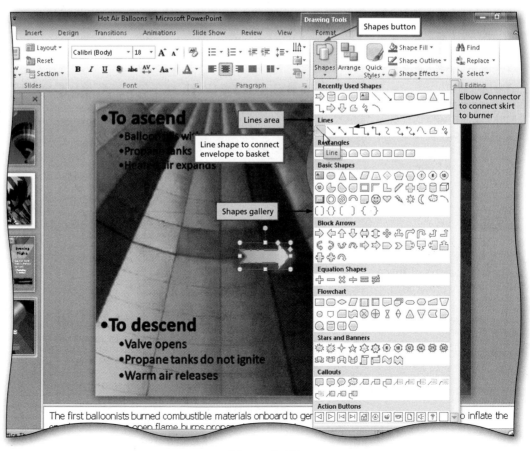

**Figure 9–53**

**2**
- Click the Line shape and then position the mouse pointer on the Teardrop to display the points (Figure 9–54).

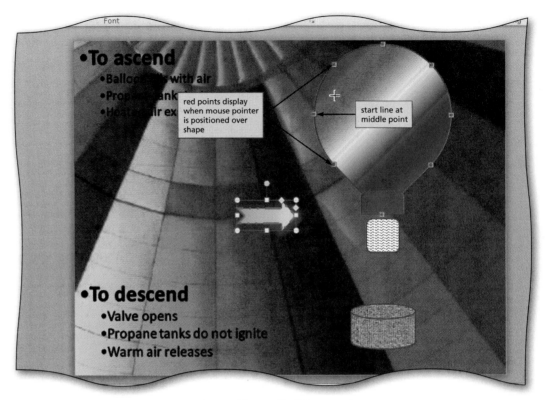

**Figure 9–54**

**Q&A**

What are the red squares on the perimeter of the Teardrop?

The squares are called points. Every shape is formed by a series of points connected with lines that are straight or curved. If desired, you can drag a point to alter the shape's form.

**3**
- Position the mouse pointer on the red point on the middle left side of the envelope (the Teardrop) and then click to insert one end of the line on this point.

- Drag the sizing handle at the other end of the line to the upper-left edge of the basket (the Flowchart: Magnetic Disk shape) (Figure 9–55).

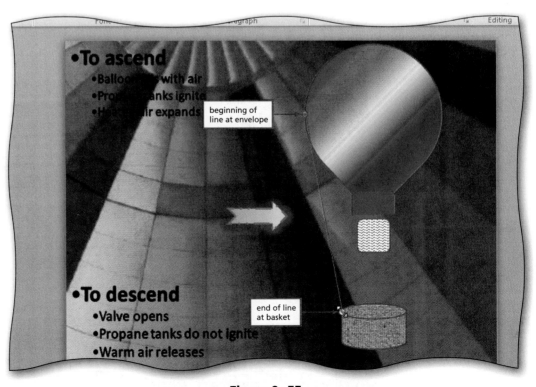

**Figure 9–55**

## To Change a Line Weight and Color

In this project, you changed a text box and shape outline color and weight. In a similar fashion, you can change line outline formatting. The line you drew on Slide 4 is thin, and the color does not display well against the colorful background. You can increase the line thickness and change its color to enhance the shape. The following steps change the line thickness and color.

- With the line selected, click the Shape Outline button (Drawing Tools Format tab | Drawing group) and then point to Weight to display the Weight gallery.

- Point to 2¼ pt to see a preview of that weight applied to the line (Figure 9–56).

 **Experiment**

- Point to various weights in the Weight gallery and watch the line thickness change.

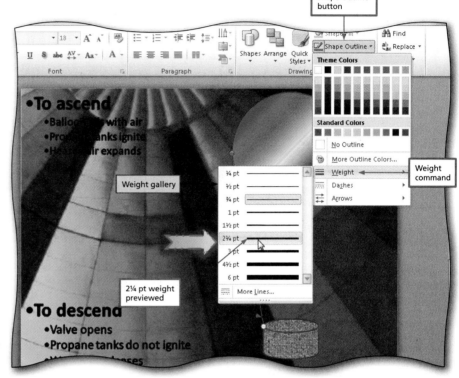

**Figure 9–56**

- Click 2¼ pt in the Weight gallery to apply that weight to the line.

- Click the Shape Outline button again and then point to Dark Blue (ninth color in Standard Colors area) to see a preview of that color applied to the line (Figure 9–57).

 **Experiment**

- Point to various colors in the Theme Colors gallery and watch the line color change.

- Click Dark Blue to apply that color to the line.

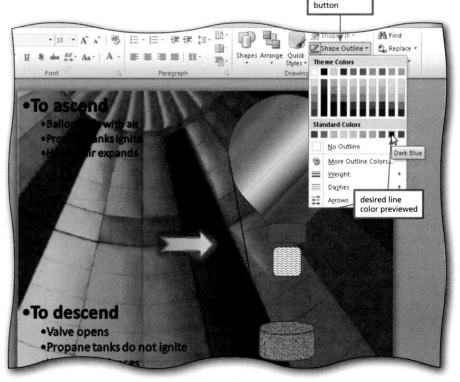

**Figure 9–57**

## To Set Line Formatting as the Default

The line you inserted and formatted will be used to complete the hot air balloon diagram. You can set these line attributes as the default for all other lines you will draw in the presentation. The following steps set the line shape on Slide 4 as the default.

- Right-click the line to display the shortcut menu (Figure 9–58).

- Click Set as Default Line on the shortcut menu to set the line formatting as the default for any new lines.

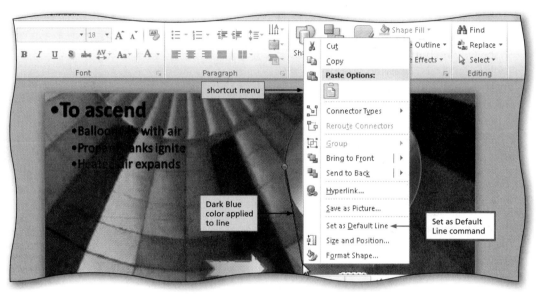

**Figure 9–58**

## To Draw Additional Lines

One more line is needed to connect the right side of the hot air balloon envelope to the right side of the basket. In addition, two lines are needed to connect the burner to the skirt. The following steps draw these lines.

- Display the Shapes gallery, select the Line shape, position the mouse pointer on the envelope, and then click the red point on the right side of the envelope to insert the line at this point.

- Drag the sizing handle at the other end of the line to the upper-right edge of the basket (Figure 9–59).

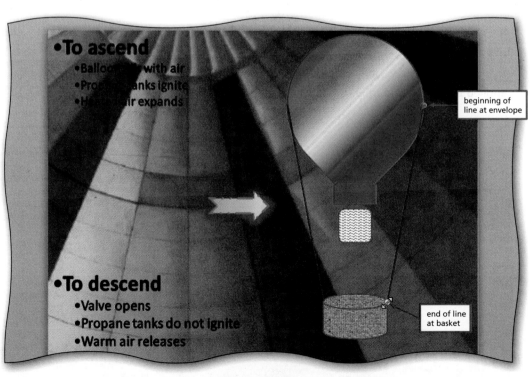

**Figure 9–59**

**2**

• Display the Shapes gallery and then point to the Elbow Connector (fourth line in the Lines area) (Figure 9–60).

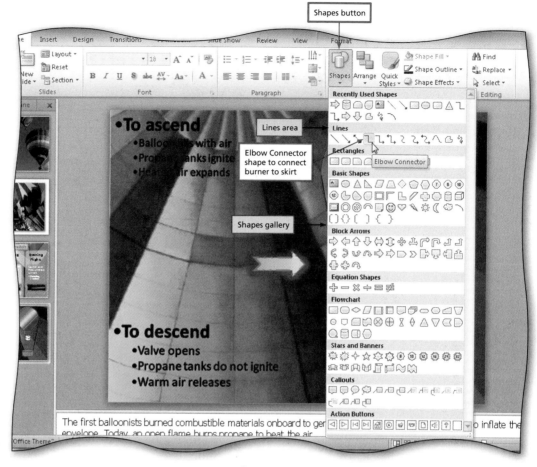

Figure 9–60

**3**

• Click the Elbow Connector, position the mouse pointer on the red point on the left side of the skirt (the Snip Same Side Corner Rectangle), and then click to insert one end of the line at this location.

• Drag the sizing handle at the other end of the line to the middle-left edge of the burner (the Rounded Rectangle) (Figure 9–61).

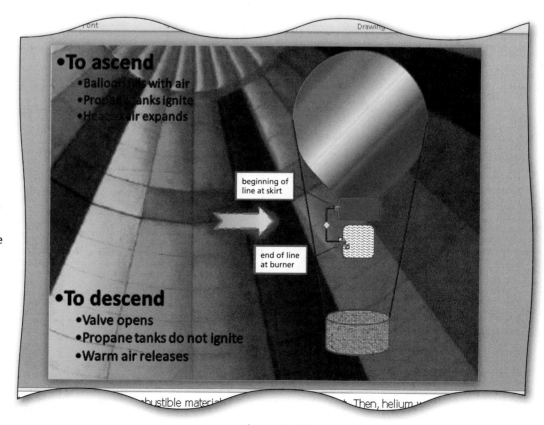

Figure 9–61

**4**

- Display the Shapes gallery, select the Elbow Connector, insert one end of the line on the red point on the right side of the skirt, and then drag the other end of the line to the middle-right edge of the burner (Figure 9–62).

**Figure 9–62**

## To Customize the Ribbon

Many commands available in PowerPoint are not included on any of the tabs on the Ribbon. You can, however, add such commands to the Ribbon or to the Quick Access Toolbar. One command combines shapes, and you could use it in this project to join all the shapes that form the hot air balloon. A second command subtracts shapes, so it would be useful to create a vent hole at the top of the balloon's envelope. The following steps customize the Ribbon by adding the Shape Combine and Shape Subtract commands to the Ribbon and then arranging their order in the group.

**1**

- With the Home tab displaying, open the Backstage view and then click Options to display the PowerPoint Options dialog box.

- Click Customize Ribbon in the left pane to display the Customize the Ribbon pane (Figure 9–63).

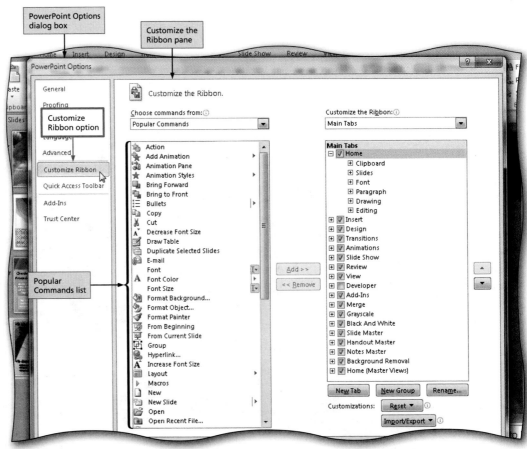

**Figure 9–63**

**2**

- Click the 'Choose commands from' box arrow to display the 'Choose commands from' list (Figure 9–64).

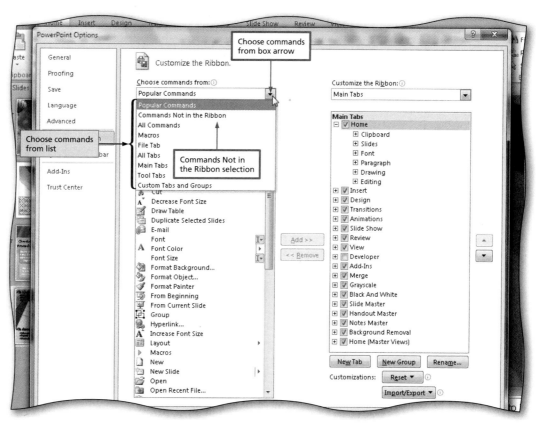

**Figure 9–64**

**3**

- Click Commands Not in the Ribbon in the 'Choose commands from' list to display a list of commands that do not display on the Ribbon (Figure 9–65).

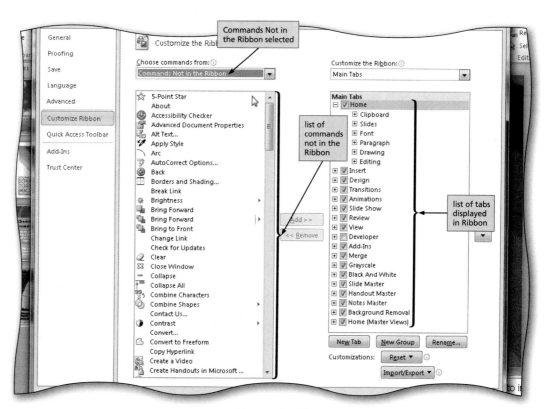

**Figure 9–65**

- Scroll to the bottom of the list and then click Shape Union to select this button.

- Click Drawing in the Main Tabs area to specify that the Shape Union button will be added in a new group between the Drawing and Editing groups on the Home tab (Figure 9–66).

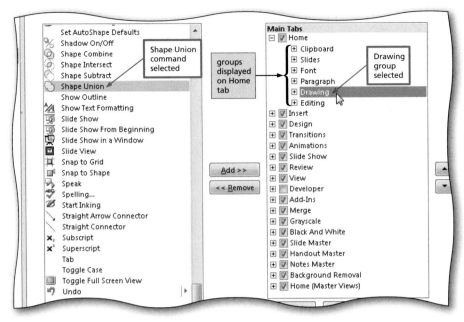

**Figure 9–66**

- Click the New Group button to create a new group.

- Click the Rename button and then type `Change Shape` as the new group name in the Display name text box (Rename dialog box) (Figure 9–67).

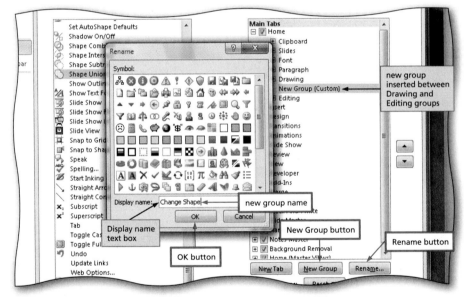

**Figure 9–67**

- Click the OK button (Rename dialog box) to rename the new group.

- Click the Add button to add the Shape Union button to the Change Shape group.

- Click Shape Subtract in the list of Commands Not in the Ribbon and then click the Add button to add the button to the Change Shape group (Figure 9–68).

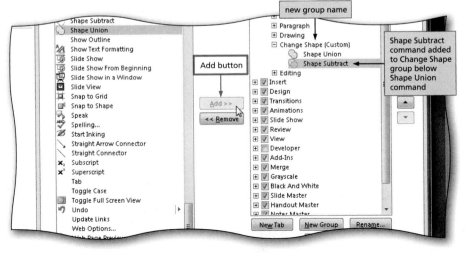

**Figure 9–68**

**7**

- Click the Move Up button (PowerPoint Options dialog box) to move the Shape Subtract button above the Shape Union button (Figure 9–69).

**8**

- Click the OK button to close the PowerPoint Options dialog box and display the two buttons in the new Change Shape group on the Home tab in the Ribbon.

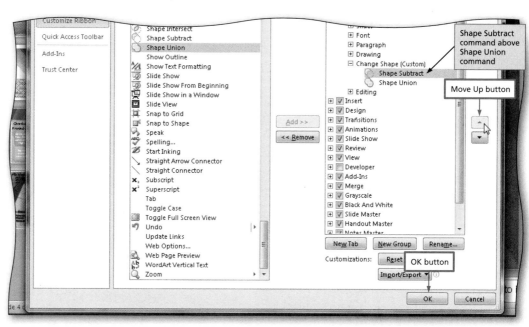

Figure 9–69

## To Subtract a Shape and Combine Shapes

The hot air balloon's envelope has a vent at the top to release air. You will add this vent to the Teardrop shape on Slide 4. One method of creating this vent is to overlap an Oval shape and the Teardrop shape and then use the Shape Subtract command you just added to the Ribbon to delete the overlapped portion. The following steps insert an Oval shape and then subtract this object.

**1**

- Display the Shapes gallery, select the Oval shape in the Basic Shapes area (second shape in first row), and then insert the shape on the top of the envelope (Teardrop).

- Use the Smart Guides to align the Oval shape vertically, as shown in Figure 9–70.

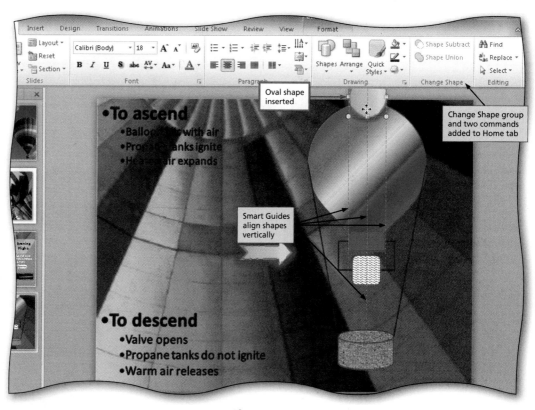

Figure 9–70

**2**

- Click the envelope to select it, press and hold down the CTRL key, and then click the oval to select both shapes (Figure 9–71).

**Q&A**

Do I need to select the shapes in this order?

Yes. When using the Shape Subtract command, you first select the shape that you want to keep and then click the shape that you want to delete.

**3**

- Click the Shape Subtract button (Home tab | Change Shape group) to delete the overlapped portion of the envelope.

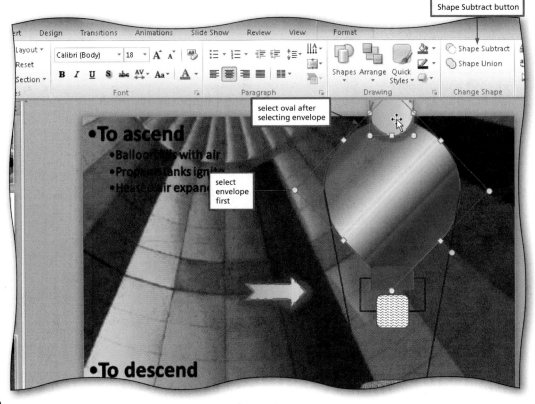

**Figure 9–71**

**4**

- Press and hold down the CTRL key and then click the skirt (Snip Same Side Corner Rectangle) to select it and the envelope (Figure 9–72).

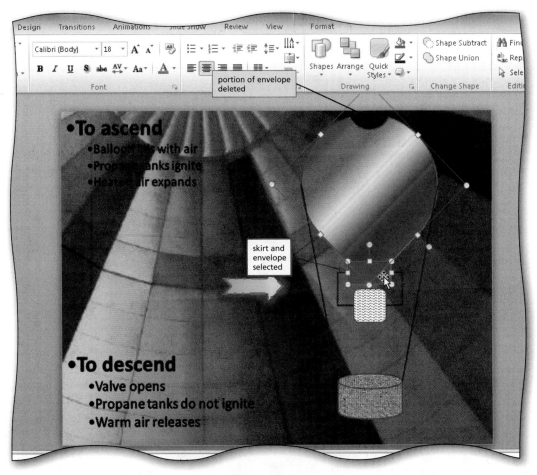

**Figure 9–72**

**5**

- Click the Shape Union button (Home tab | Change Shape group) to combine the hot air balloon envelope and skirt shapes (Figure 9–73).

- Press and hold down the CTRL key, click all the hot air balloon shapes to select the objects, and then click the Shape Union button to combine all the shapes.

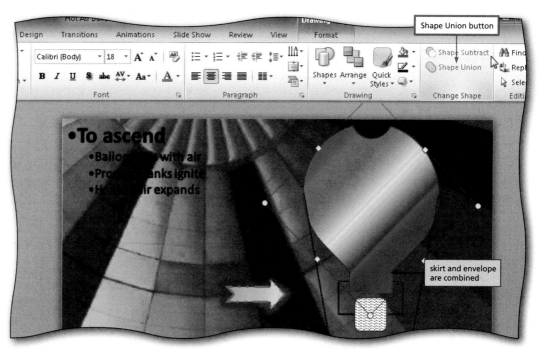

**Figure 9–73**

**Plan**
**Ahead**

**Use politically correct language.**
Many companies have strict policies in order to prevent harassment in the workplace. These guidelines are developed to protect employees from adverse treatment based on race, religion, national origin, gender, or other personal traits. Keep these policies in mind as you label components on your slides. For example, some females may be offended if you refer to an adult woman as a "girl," or an older athlete may resent being labeled as an "aging" rather than as a "veteran" player.

## To Label the Shapes

The final step in creating Slide 4 is to label the parts of the hot air balloon. The Notched Right Arrow shape and the text box are formatted as defaults, so the labeling process is easy to accomplish. The following steps insert text boxes and arrows into Slide 4 and then enter text in the text boxes.

**1** With Slide 4 displaying, insert a text box into the lower-right corner of the slide, type **Basket** in the text box, decrease the font size to 28 point, and move the text box to the middle of the basket.

**2** Insert a text box into the center of the slide, type **Envelope** in the text box, decrease the font size to 28 point, and move the text box to the middle of the envelope.

**3** Insert a text box into the center of the slide, type **Skirt** in the text box, decrease the font size to 28 point, and move the text box to the left side of the skirt and the left line.

**4** Insert a text box into the center of the slide, type **Burner** in the text box, decrease the font size to 28 point, and move the text box to the left side of the burner and the left line.

**5** Drag the Notched Right arrow between the Skirt text box and the hot air balloon skirt.

**BTW**

**Quick Reference**
For a table that lists how to complete the tasks covered in this book using the mouse, Ribbon, shortcut menu, and keyboard, see the Quick Reference Summary at the back of this book, or visit the PowerPoint 2010 Quick Reference Web page (scsite.com/ppt2010/qr).

**6** Insert a Notched Right arrow and drag it between the Burner text box and the hot air balloon burner.

**7** Press and hold down the SHIFT key, right-click the left elbow connector and the left line connecting the envelope to the basket, point to Send to Back, and then click Send to Back (Figure 9–74).

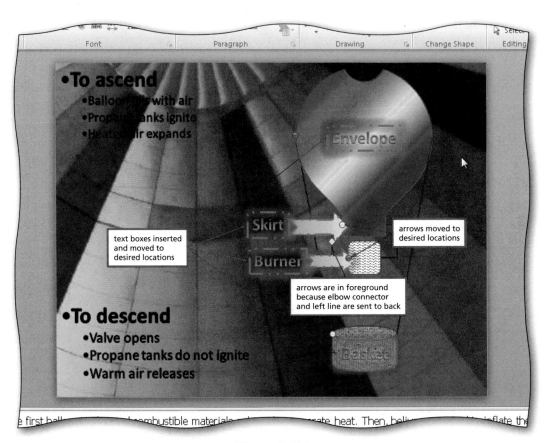

**Figure 9–74**

**Plan**
**Ahead**

**Work with a buddy.**
Although you may believe you create your best work when you work alone, research shows that the work product generally improves when two or more people work together on a creative task. A classmate or team member at work can assist you in many ways. For example, this person can help you gather research for your graphics and bulleted text or provide feedback on the slides' clarity and readability. As you rehearse, a buddy can time your talk and identify the times when the presentation lacks interest. If a buddy attends your actual presentation, he can give objective feedback on the components that worked and those that can use revision for the next time you present the material.

## To Save the Presentation as a Picture Presentation

If you are going to share your slides with other presenters and do not want them to alter the slide content, you can save each slide as a picture. When they run the slide show, each slide is one complete picture, so the text and shapes cannot be edited. You also can use an individual slide picture as a graphic on another slide or in another presentation. The following steps save a copy of the presentation as a picture presentation.

**1**

- Open the Backstage view, display the Save & Send tab, and then click Change File Type in the File Types area.

- Click PowerPoint Picture Presentation in the Presentation File Types area (Figure 9–75).

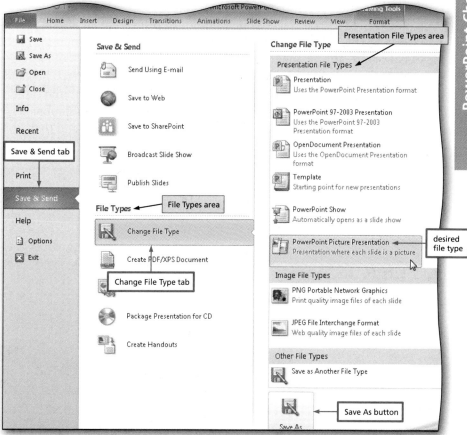

**Figure 9–75**

**2**

- Click the Save As button to display the Save As dialog box.

- Type **Balloon Picture Presentation** in the File name text box (Figure 9–76).

**3**

- Click the Save button (Save As dialog box) to save the presentation as a picture presentation.

- Click the OK button (Microsoft PowerPoint dialog box).

**Q&A**

Will the PowerPoint presentation and the PowerPoint Picture Presentation have the same file names?

Yes. PowerPoint creates a new picture presentation and also retains the slide show presentation with identical file names.

**Figure 9–76**

## To Create a Handout by Exporting a File to Microsoft Word

The handouts you create using Microsoft PowerPoint are useful to distribute to audiences. Each time you need to create these handouts, however, you need to open the file in PowerPoint and then print from the Backstage view. As an alternative, it might be convenient to save, or export, the file as a Microsoft Word document if you are going to be using Microsoft Word to type a script or lecture notes. The handout can have a variety of layouts; for example, the notes you type in the Notes pane can be displayed to the right of or beneath the slide thumbnails, blank lines can be displayed to the right of or beneath the slide thumbnails, or just an outline can be displayed. The following steps export the presentation to Microsoft Word and then create a handout.

- Open the Backstage view, display the Save & Send tab, and then click Create Handouts in the File Types area (Figure 9–77).

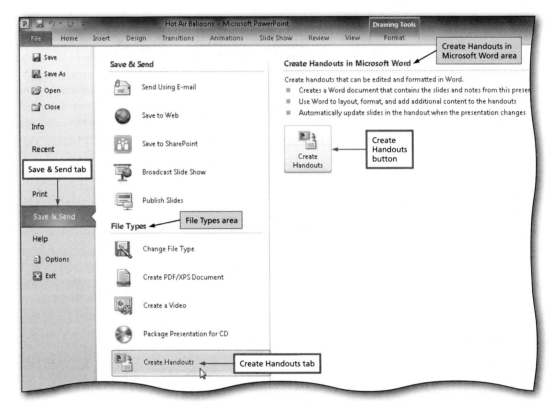

**Figure 9–77**

**2**
- Click Create Handouts in the Create Handouts in Microsoft Word area to display the Send to Microsoft Word dialog box (Figure 9–78).

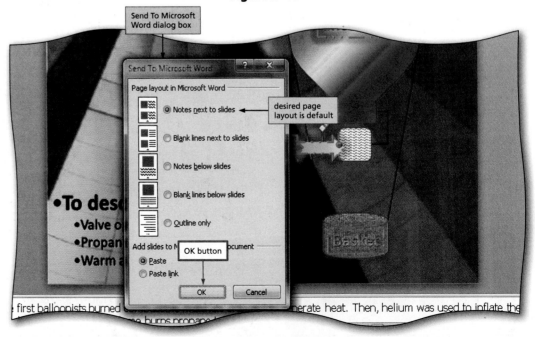

**Figure 9–78**

**③**

- Click the OK button to save the file with the default 'Notes next to slides' layout.

- If the handout does not display in a new Microsoft Word window, point to the Microsoft Word program button on the Windows taskbar to see a live preview of the handout (Figure 9–79).

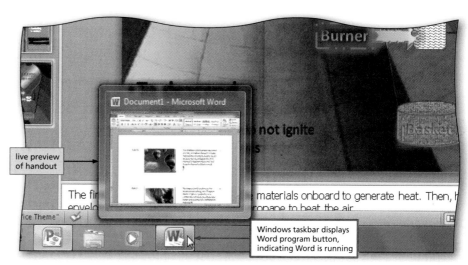

**Figure 9–79**

## To Reset the Ribbon

Your work with the PowerPoint presentation is complete. The following steps remove the Change Shape group and the Shape Combine and Shape Subtract commands from the Home tab.

**①** Display the Backstage view, click Options to display the PowerPoint Options dialog box, and then click Customize Ribbon in the left pane to display the Customize the Ribbon pane.

**②** Click the Reset button (PowerPoint Options dialog box) to display the Reset menu and then click Reset all customizations.

**③** Click the Yes button (Microsoft Office dialog box) to delete all customizations.

**④** Click the OK button (PowerPoint Options dialog box) to close it.

**Q&A**

Do I need to remove the group and commands from the Ribbon?

No. For consistency, the Ribbon is reset after the added group and commands are no longer needed. If you share a computer with others, you should reset the Ribbon.

## To Change Document Properties

Before saving the presentation again, you want to add your name, class name, and some keywords as document properties. The following steps use the Document Information Panel to change document properties.

**①** Display the Document Information Panel and then type your name as the Author property.

**②** Type your course and section in the Subject property.

**③** Type **hot air balloon, orientation, schedule** as the Keywords property.

**④** Close the Document Information Panel.

**BTW**

**Certification**
The Microsoft Office Specialist (MOS) program provides an opportunity for you to obtain a valuable industry credential – proof that you have the PowerPoint 2010 skills required by employers. For more information, visit the PowerPoint 2010 Certification Web page (scsite.com/ppt2010/cert).

## To Print, Save, and Quit PowerPoint

The presentation now is complete. You should print the slides, save the presentation, and then quit PowerPoint.

**1** Print the Hot Air Balloons presentation as a handout with two slides per page.

**2** Save the Hot Air Balloons presentation again with the same file name.

**3** Quit PowerPoint, closing all open documents.

# Chapter Summary

In this chapter you have learned how to modify a presentation using text boxes, SmartArt, and shapes. You customized a text box, set it as the default, and then inserted new text boxes and applied formatting, including a texture, gradient, and pattern. You also converted WordArt to SmartArt and then formatted the shapes and bulleted paragraphs. Then you created a diagram from shapes, which had gradients and patterns applied. Finally, you saved the presentation as a picture presentation and exported the file to Microsoft Word to create a handout. The items listed below include all the new PowerPoint skills you have learned in this chapter.

1. Change a Text Box Outline Weight (PPT 534)
2. Change a Text Box Outline Color (PPT 535)
3. Change a Text Box Outline Style (PPT 536)
4. Apply an Effect to a Text Box (PPT 536)
5. Set Text Box Formatting as the Default (PPT 537)
6. Apply a Pattern to a Text Box (PPT 539)
7. Apply a Gradient Fill to a Text Box (PPT 542)
8. Center a Text Box (PPT 543)
9. Change a Slide Picture (PPT 544)
10. Convert WordArt to SmartArt (PPT 546)
11. Reorder SmartArt Shapes (PPT 547)
12. Promote a SmartArt Bullet Level (PPT 548)
13. Demote a SmartArt Bullet Level (PPT 549)
14. Change the SmartArt Layout (PPT 550)
15. Remove a SmartArt Shape (PPT 551)
16. Resize a SmartArt Graphic by Entering an Exact Measurement (PPT 552)
17. Resize a SmartArt Graphic Shape (PPT 553)
18. Apply a Picture to a Text Box (PPT 555)
19. Convert a SmartArt Graphic to Text (PPT 557)
20. Apply a Fill to a Shape (PPT 561)
21. Set Shape Formatting as the Default (PPT 564)
22. Draw a Line (PPT 565)
23. Change a Line Weight and Color (PPT 567)
24. Set Line Formatting as the Default (PPT 568)
25. Draw Additional Lines (PPT 568)
26. Customize the Ribbon (PPT 570)
27. Subtract a Shape and Combine Shapes (PPT 573)
28. Save the Presentation as a Picture Presentation (PPT 576)
29. Create a Handout by Exporting a File to Microsoft Word (PPT 578)

If you have a SAM 2010 user profile, your instructor may have assigned an autogradable version of this assignment. If so, log into the SAM 2010 Web site at www.cengage.com/sam2010 to download the instruction and start files.

# Learn It Online

Test your knowledge of chapter content and key terms.

*Instructions:* To complete the Learn It Online exercises, start your browser, click the Address bar, and then enter the Web address `scsite.com/ppt2010/learn`. When the Office 2010 Learn It Online page is displayed, click the link for the exercise you want to complete and then read the instructions.

### Chapter Reinforcement TF, MC, and SA
A series of true/false, multiple choice, and short answer questions that test your knowledge of the chapter content.

### Flash Cards
An interactive learning environment where you identify chapter key terms associated with displayed definitions.

### Practice Test
A series of multiple choice questions that test your knowledge of chapter content and key terms.

### Who Wants To Be a Computer Genius?
An interactive game that challenges your knowledge of chapter content in the style of a television quiz show.

### Wheel of Terms
An interactive game that challenges your knowledge of chapter key terms in the style of the television show *Wheel of Fortune*.

### Crossword Puzzle Challenge
A crossword puzzle that challenges your knowledge of key terms presented in the chapter.

# Apply Your Knowledge

Reinforce the skills and apply the concepts you learned in this chapter.

### Formatting Text Boxes, Manipulating SmartArt, Adding and Reordering SmartArt Shapes, and Changing a Picture
*Note:* To complete this assignment, you will be required to use the Data Files for Students. See the inside back cover of this book for instructions on downloading the Data Files for Students, or contact your instructor for information about accessing the required files.

*Instructions:* Start PowerPoint. Open the presentation, Apply 9-1 Five Speed, located on the Data Files for Students.

The slides in this presentation give instructions for learning to drive a five-speed vehicle. The document you open is a partially formatted presentation. You will apply a gradient and a pattern to a text box and a shape, change the outline style of a text box, add and reorder SmartArt shapes, and change a picture so the slides look like Figure 9–80.

*Perform the following tasks:*
1. On Slide 1, change the gradient fill in the text box to From Center. Change the outline color of the text box to Dark Red, change the outline weight to 3 pt, and then change the outline style to Long Dash.

2. Change the picture in the lower-left corner of the slide to Gearshift, located on the Data Files for Students. Increase the picture size to 3.37" × 2.25" and move the picture to the lower-right corner of the slide, as shown in Figure 9–80a on the next page.

3. Start the audio clip on Slide 1 automatically and hide the icon during the show.

4. On Slide 2, insert a text box, type `Clutch` in the text box, increase the font size to 32 point, change the font color to White, center the text, and then bold this text. Apply a Black fill and then apply the Preset 5 effect to the text box. Set the current text box formatting as the default for new text boxes.

*Continued >*

**Apply Your Knowledge** *continued*

5. Insert three additional text boxes into Slide 2. Type **Brake** in one text box, type **Gas** in the second text box, and then type **5-Speed Setup** in the third text box. Decrease the font size of the third text box text to 20 point. Move the text boxes to the locations shown in Figure 9–80b.

6. Insert the Rectangle shape, apply the Dark vertical pattern, and then change the foreground color to Black. Set the shape outline to No Outline. Apply the Preset 5 effect to the shape and then set the shape as the default for future shapes. Change the size of this shape to 0.75" × 0.75" and move it below the Clutch text box.

7. Insert the Rectangle shape, change the size to 0.58" × 1.25", and then move this shape below the Brake text box. Insert another Rectangle shape, change the size to 0.92" × 0.5", and then move this shape below the Gas text box.

8. Use the Smart Guides to align the text boxes and shapes, as shown in Figure 9–80b. Copy the four text boxes and three shapes from Slide 2 to Slide 3 and Slide 4 and reposition if necessary, as shown in Figures 9–80c and 9–80d.

9. On Slide 2, add a shape before the first shape in the SmartArt graphic. Type **Check your pedals.** in the shape, change the font size to 20 point, and then bold this text.

10. On Slide 4, move the fifth shape in the SmartArt graphic (second shape in second row) so that it is the last shape, as shown in Figure 9–80d.

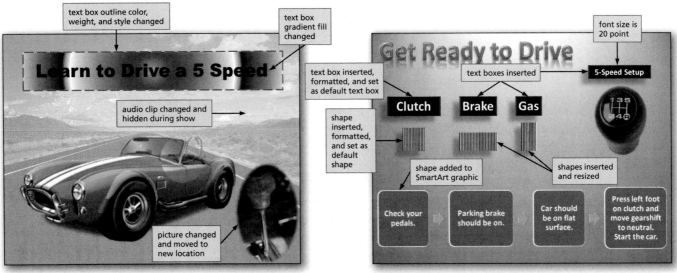

(a) Slide 1          (b) Slide 2

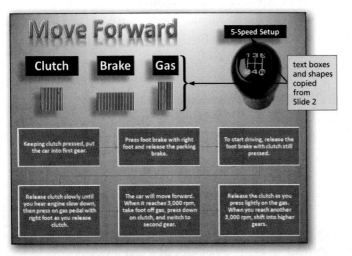

(c) Slide 3

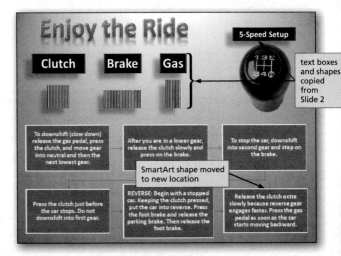

(d) Slide 4

**Figure 9–80**

11. Change the transition for all slides from Window to Zoom and then change the duration to 03.00 seconds.

12. Change the document properties, as specified by your instructor. Save the presentation using the file name, Apply 9-1 Drive a 5 Speed. Submit the revised document in the format specified by your instructor.

## Extend Your Knowledge

Extend the skills you learned in this chapter and experiment with new skills. You may need to use Help to complete the assignment.

### Applying a Texture and Changing the Outline Color of a Text Box, Demoting SmartArt Bullet Levels, and Inserting Arrows

*Note:* To complete this assignment, you will be required to use the Data Files for Students. See the inside back cover of this book for instructions on downloading the Data Files for Students, or contact your instructor for information about accessing the required files.

*Instructions:* Start PowerPoint. Open the presentation, Extend 9-1 Tango, located on the Data Files for Students. You will apply a texture and change the outline color of a text box, demote a SmartArt bullet level, and insert arrows, as shown in Figure 9–81 on the next page.

*Perform the following tasks:*

1. On Slide 1, insert a text box, type `Step by Step`, change the font to Arial, change the font size to 36 point, change the font color to White, and then bold this text. Apply a Purple mesh texture to the text box, add a 1½ pt outline, and then change the outline color to Orange. Set the current text box formatting as the default for new text boxes. Move the text box to the location shown in Figure 9–81a.

2. On Slide 2, insert a text box and type `Tango Styles` in the box. Center the text box on the slide, as shown in Figure 9–81b.

3. Remove the three white square shapes in the SmartArt graphic on Slide 2.

4. On Slide 3, insert a text box and type `Tango Attire` in the box. Center the text box on the slide horizontally, as shown in Figure 9–81c.

5. In the SmartArt graphic on Slide 3, demote the text `Gauchos, boots, and spurs` so that it is indented under the word, Men. With the SmartArt graphic still selected, click the Change Colors button (SmartArt Tools Design Tab | SmartArt Styles group) and then click Recolor Pictures in SmartArt Graphic to change the color of the pictures.

6. On Slide 4, insert a text box and type `Basic Steps` in the box. Center the text box on the slide horizontally, as shown in Figure 9–81d.

7. Change the pattern fill in the three right footprints on Slide 4 to Outlined diamond.

8. Insert an Arrow line shape (second shape in the Lines area) behind the number 1 circle, change the line weight to 2¼ pt, and then change the color to Red, as shown in Figure 9–81d. Set the current line formatting as the default. Click the end of the arrow and then rotate the shape upward.

9. Insert four more Arrow line shapes and move the shapes to the locations shown in Figure 9–81d. Send the arrows to the back so they are underneath the numbers.

10. Apply the Flip transition to all slides and change the duration to 02:50 seconds.

11. Change the document properties, as specified by your instructor. Save the presentation using the file name, Extend 9-1 Learn to Tango.

12. Submit the revised document in the format specified by your instructor.

*Continued >*

**Extend Your Knowledge** *continued*

**(a) Slide 1**

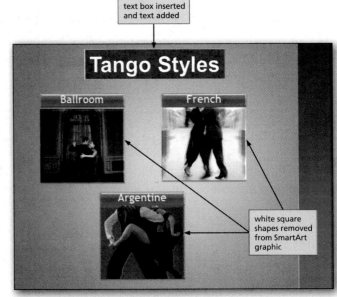

**(b) Slide 2**

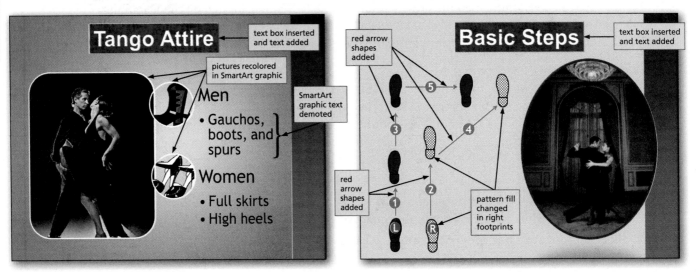

**(c) Slide 3**

**(d) Slide 4**

**Figure 9–81**

## Make It Right

Analyze a presentation and correct all errors and/or improve the design.

### Changing a Text Box Fill, Reordering SmartArt Shapes, and Changing a Picture

*Note:* To complete this assignment, you will be required to use the Data Files for Students. See the inside back cover of this book for instructions on downloading the Data Files for Students, or contact your instructor for information about accessing the required files.

*Instructions:* Start PowerPoint. Open the presentation, Make It Right 9-1 National Parks, located on the Data Files for Students.

Correct the formatting problems and errors in the presentation while keeping in mind the guidelines presented in this chapter.

*Perform the following tasks:*

1. On Slide 1 (Figure 9–82a), change the Ranked by Total Acreage text box fill to Linear Down Gradient and remove the outline. Increase the font size to 36 point, change the font color to Brown, Accent 2, and then adjust the size of the text box. Move the text box to the lower-right corner of the slide.

2. On Slide 2 (Figure 9–82b), change the acreage for the Grand Canyon from 2.4 to 1.2 and reorder the SmartArt shapes so that the Grand Canyon is listed in the tenth position below Everglades, Florida. Also, switch the layout of the graphic so that the acreage figures are on the right side of the SmartArt graphic. *Hint:* With the SmartArt graphic selected, select the Right to Left button (SmartArt Tools Design tab | Create Graphic group).

3. On Slide 3 (Figure 9–82c on the next page), correct the information to state that Wrangell-St. Elias is the largest National Park. Also, change the weight and color of the arrow shape to match the weight and color of the outline shape on the text box.

4. On Slide 4 (Figure 9–82d), change the Montana map picture to the Wyoming map picture, located on the Data Files for Students. Change the Wyoming picture style to Reflected Bevel, White.

5. On Slide 5 (Figure 9–82e), change the Iguana picture to the Alligator picture, located on the Data Files for Students. Remove the artistic effect from the Florida map picture.

6. On Slide 6 (Figure 9–82f), change the top river picture to the Canyon River picture, located on the Data Files for Students, and increase the size of the picture to 3.24" × 4.08". If necessary, bring the title text to the front of this picture.

7. For all slides, apply the Fly Through transition, change the Effect Option to Out, and change the duration to 02:50 seconds.

8. Change the document properties, as specified by your instructor. Save the presentation using the file name, Make It Right 9-1 Largest US National Parks.

9. Submit the revised document in the format specified by your instructor.

**(a) Slide 1**

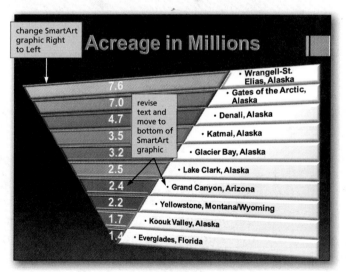

**(b) Slide 2**

**Figure 9–82**

*Continued >*

**Make It Right** *continued*

**(c) Slide 3**

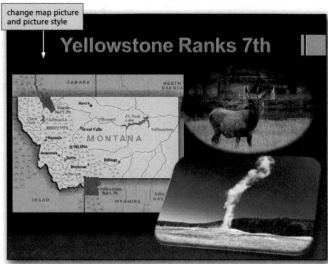

**(d) Slide 4**

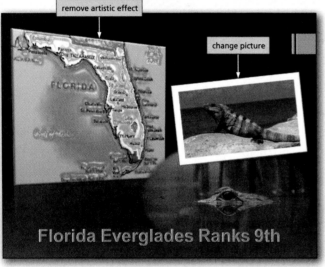

**(e) Slide 5**

**(f) Slide 6**

**Figure 9–82 (Continued)**

## In the Lab

Design and/or create a presentation using the guidelines, concepts, and skills presented in this chapter. Labs 1, 2, and 3 are listed in order of increasing difficulty.

### Lab 1: Applying a Picture to a Text Box, Converting SmartArt to Shapes, and Converting SmartArt to Text

*Note:* To complete this assignment, you will be required to use the Data Files for Students. See the inside back cover of this book for instructions on downloading the Data Files for Students or contact your instructor for information about accessing the required files.

*Problem:* Saving and using rain water can be a great way to conserve water. Whether you are watering your garden or washing your car, rain water is a great way to use one of our most valuable natural resources.

A rain barrel is an excellent way to catch rain and store it. Members of your garden club have been discussing building a rain barrel, and you decide to create a PowerPoint presentation to give some basic instructions. You create the slides shown in Figure 9–83 using files located on the Data Files for Students.

*Perform the following tasks:*

1. Open the presentation, Lab 9-1 Rain Barrel, located on the Data Files for Students.

2. On Slide 1, remove the background from the umbrella picture, increase the size, and move it to the lower-left corner of the slide, as shown in Figure 9–83a.

3. Insert a text box, type **CATCH THE RAIN** in the text box, change the font to Broadway, change the font color to White, and then center the text in the text box. Change the font size to 60 point for the words, Catch the, and 88 point for the word, Rain. Change the outline color to White, the outline weight to 3 pt, and then increase the size of the text box to 3.74" × 5". Apply the Raindrops picture to the text box and then move it to the position shown in Figure 9–83a.

4. Change the font size of the text in the text box located at the bottom of the slide to 36 point, change the font color to Dark Red, and then bold this text. Adjust the size of the text box so that the text fits on four lines, as shown in Figure 9–83a. Change the outline weight of the text box to 3 pt and then change the outline style to Round Dot.

5. On Slide 2, convert the SmartArt graphic at the top of the slide to shapes. Apply a Subtle Effect – Red, Accent 2 Quick Style effect to the three text shapes and change the font to Broadway, as shown in Figure 9–83b.

6. Apply the Water droplets texture to the Teardrop shape on the left side of Slide 2.

7. Convert the SmartArt graphic on the right side of Slide 2 to text. Increase the font size of the text to 34 point, change the font color to black, and then change the bullets to Checkmark Bullets. Change the size of the text box, apply the Water droplets texture, change the outline color of the text box to Red, and then change the outline weight to 3 pt. Move the text box to the location shown in Figure 9–83b.

8. Add the Style 7 background style to Slide 2.

9. Apply the Ripple transition and change the duration to 03.75 seconds for all slides.

10. Change the document properties, as specified by your instructor. Save the presentation using the file name, Lab 9-1 Catch the Rain.

11. Submit the revised document in the format specified by your instructor.

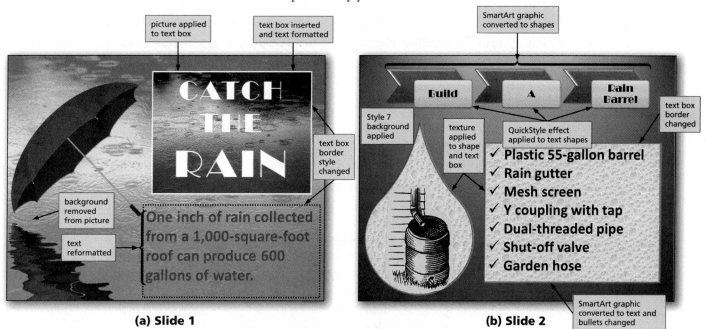

**(a) Slide 1**          **(b) Slide 2**

**Figure 9–83**

## In the Lab

### Lab 2: Inserting and Drawing Shapes, Creating a Handout by Exporting a File to Microsoft Word, and Saving a Presentation as a Picture Presentation

*Note:* To complete this assignment, you will be required to use the Data Files for Students. See the inside back cover of this book for instructions on downloading the Data Files for Students or contact your instructor for information about accessing the required files.

*Problem:* Your family is opening a cheese store in northern Wisconsin. The store will offer cheese from local farmers, imported cheese, and sausage. The store will also feature gift baskets and some small specialty items, such as homemade jams. You volunteered to put together a small advertising campaign for the new store, and you decide to create a PowerPoint presentation to share your ideas with the family. You will create an ad for the local newspaper and a sign to hang in the library and the village hall. You create the slides shown in Figure 9–84.

*Perform the following tasks:*

1. Open the presentation, Lab 9-2 Cheese Shop, located on the Data Files for Students.

2. On Slide 1, apply the Oak texture to the text box in the lower-left corner of the slide, and then remove the yellow outline on the text box. Move the text box to the left side of the yellow rectangle above the canopy in the cheese shop picture, as shown in Figure 9–84a.

3. Insert the Explosion 1 shape into the upper-left corner of the slide, type **Coming Soon**, and then increase the size of the shape to 2.5" × 3.12". Increase the font size to 28 point, change the font color to Black, and then bold this text. Change the shape fill color to Yellow, change the shape outline color to Olive Green, Accent 3, and then change the line weight to 3 pt.

4. On Slide 2, insert a text box and type **The Grate Cheese Store Products** in the box. Change the font to Bernard MT Condensed and increase the font size to 36 point. Apply the Small grid pattern fill to the text box and change the foreground color to Yellow. Move the text box to the area shown in Figure 9–84b and center the text box horizontally on the slide.

5. Convert the WordArt text on Slide 2 to the Vertical Bracket List SmartArt graphic. Change the size of the SmartArt graphic to 6.53" × 7.83", change the color to Transparent Gradient Range – Accent 6, and then apply the Sunset Scene SmartArt style. Move the Sausage shape up so that it is above the Gift Baskets shape. Demote the two paragraphs, Swiss and Cheddar, in the first shape so they are indented below the word, Imported. Center the SmartArt graphic horizontally on the slide.

6. On Slide 3, create the baseboard by inserting the Rectangle shape, increasing the size of the shape to 1.17" × 10", applying a White fill, changing the outline color to Black, and changing the outline weight to 2¼ pt. Send the baseboard shape backward until it is behind the mouse and Cloud Callout shape, and move it to the area shown in Figure 9–84c. Also, insert the Flowchart: Delay shape, increase the size to 1.42" × 1.15", and then Rotate Left 90° (Drawing Tools Format tab | Arrange group). Apply the Subtle Effect – Black, Dark 1 Shape QuickStyle to the shape. Move the shape to the position shown in Figure 9–84c. Duplicate this shape, move it slightly to the right, and then apply a Black fill, as shown in Figure 9–84c.

7. Create the cheese for Slide 3 by customizing the Ribbon and adding the Shape Subtract command in a new group named Cheese. Insert a slide with the Blank layout. Insert the Right Triangle shape, change the size of the shape to 2.5" × 3.5", apply a Yellow fill, and then change the outline weight to No Line. Apply the Preset 9 effect to the shape. Insert the Oval shape, change the size of the shape to .5" × .5", and then duplicate this shape two times. Insert another Oval shape, change the size of the shape to .75" × .75", and duplicate this shape two times. Move the six oval shapes on the Right Triangle shape, as shown in Figure 9–84d.

8. Select the Right Triangle shape, hold down the CTRL key, select the six oval shapes, and then click the Shape Subtract button on the Ribbon. Copy the cheese shape to the cloud shape on Slide 3. Delete Slide 4.

9. Reset the Ribbon. Change the document properties, as specified by your instructor. Save the presentation using the file name, Lab 9-2 The Grate Cheese Shop.

10. Save the presentation as a picture presentation using the file name, Lab 9-2 Cheese Shop Picture Presentation. Open the picture presentation, display Slide 3, change the size of the picture to 1.7" × 2.35", and then copy the picture to the Clipboard. Close the Lab 9-2 Cheese Shop Picture Presentation file without saving. Paste the picture on Slide 1 in the file, Lab 9-2 The Grate Cheese Shop. Move the picture to the right side of the yellow rectangle in the cheese store clip, as shown in Figure 9–84a.

11. Type **Ad for The Chronicle.** in the Slide 1 Notes pane. Type **Sign for the library.** in the Slide 2 Notes pane. Type **Sign for Small Business News bulletin board at the library.** in the Slide 3 Notes pane.

12. Create a handout in Microsoft Word using the 'Notes next to slides' page layout, as shown in Figure 9–84e on the next page.

13. Submit the revised document in the format specified by your instructor.

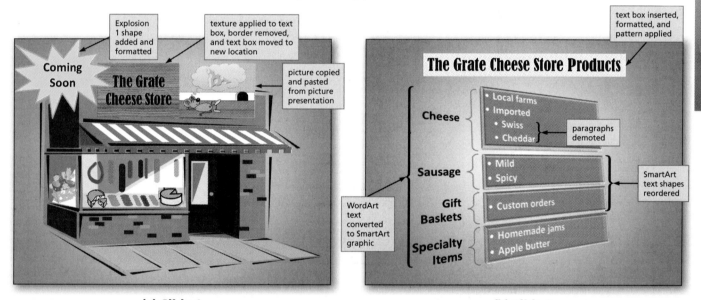

**(a) Slide 1**

**(b) Slide 2**

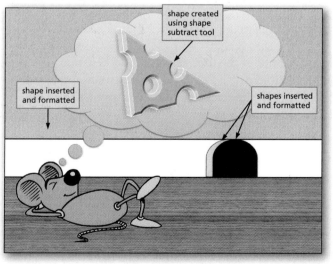

**(c) Slide 3**

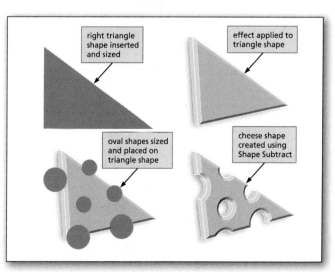

**(d) Cheese Diagram**

**Figure 9–84**

*Continued >*

**In the Lab** *continued*

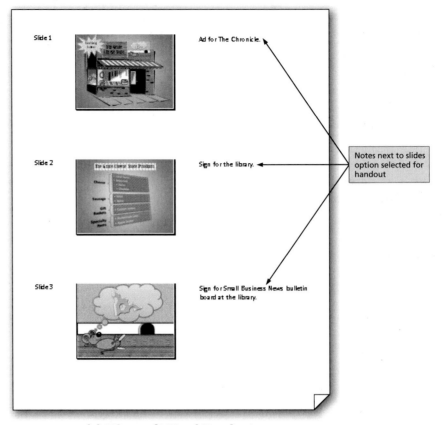

**(e) Microsoft Word Handout**

**Figure 9–84 (Continued)**

## In the Lab

### Lab 3: Changing a SmartArt Layout, Sizing SmartArt Shapes, Formatting Text Boxes, and Inserting Arrow Shapes

*Note:* To complete this assignment, you will be required to use the Data Files for Students. See the inside back cover of this book for instructions on downloading the Data Files for Students or contact your instructor for information about accessing the required files.

*Problem:* Your anatomy class is studying the bone structure of the foot and ankle. To help you memorize and learn the names of the bones, you decide to create a PowerPoint presentation that will be a study guide now and also will be a valuable tool later in the semester when you give a short talk about this subject to your classmates. You create the presentation shown in Figure 9–85.

*Perform the following tasks:*
1. Open the presentation, Lab 9-3 Foot and Ankle, located on the Data Files for Students. Change the built-in font style to Office Classic 2. On Slide 1, insert the Rectangle shape, change the size to 7.5" × 3.75", apply a Black fill, and then move the shape to the left side of the slide, as shown in Figure 9–85a.
2. Change the SmartArt layout on Slide 1 to Vertical Process. Change the size of the SmartArt graphic to 7" × 3.98" and move it on top of the black rectangle shape. Bring the graphic to the front. Change the font size to 28 point and then bold this text. Change the size of each SmartArt shape to 0.84" × 3.08". Change the colors to Colorful Range – Accent Colors 5 to 6 and the style to Inset, and then change the font color to Black.
3. On Slide 1, insert a text box and type **Anatomy of the Foot and Ankle** in the text box. Change the font size to 44 point, center the text in the text box, and then bold this text. Use line

breaks to display the text in the text box in five lines, as shown in Figure 9–85a. Apply the Dotted grid pattern fill to the text box, change the foreground color to Light Green, and then change the background color to Yellow. Apply the Preset 4 effect to the text box, change the outline color of the text box to Green, and then change the outline weight to 4½ pt. Move the text box to the location shown in Figure 9–85a. Apply the Style 9 background to the slide.

4. Display Slide 2 and then change the picture to Foot and Ankle, located on the Data Files for Students.

5. Customize the Ribbon by adding a group called Foot to the Home tab and then adding the Shape Union command to this new group.

6. To create arrow callouts, insert the Rectangle shape, change the size to 0.53" × 2.09", and then remove the outline. Insert the Chevron shape (from the Block Arrows area), remove the outline, and then duplicate the shape. Overlap the chevrons at each end of the rectangle, select the rectangle, select the two chevron shapes so that the three shapes are selected, and then click Shape Union on the Home tab to create the arrow callout shown in Figure 9–85b. Change the shape fill color to Aqua, Accent 5, apply a Preset 4 effect to the arrow shape, and then change the transparency to 30%. Type **Fibula** in the arrow shape, change the font size to 24 point, and then bold this text. Set the arrow as a default shape.

7. Duplicate the Fibula arrow callout three times. Type **Tibia** in the second arrow callout and change the color to Green. Type **Talus** in the third arrow callout and change the color to Olive Green, Accent 3. Type **Malleolus** in the fourth arrow callout and change the color to Light Green. Move these four arrows to the locations shown in Figure 9–85b.

8. On Slide 2, insert the Down Arrow Callout from the Block Arrows area and type **Metatarsals** in the shape, change the color of the shape to Yellow, increase the size of the shape, and then move it to the location shown in Figure 9–85b. Insert the Down Arrow Callout, type **Phalanges** in the shape, change the color to Orange, Accent 6, increase the size of the shape, and then move it to the location shown in Figure 9–85b.

9. Insert the Oval shape into Slide 2 and change the size to 1.38" × 2.42". Change the color of the shape fill to Yellow, change the transparency to 70%, add an outline and change the color to Black, and then change the outline weight to 2¼ pt. Move this shape to the location shown. Duplicate this oval shape and change the size to 1.08" × 2.25". Change the color of the shape fill to Orange, Accent 6 and move this shape to the location shown in Figure 9–85b.

10. Apply Background Style 9 to Slide 2.

11. Apply the Cube transition and change the duration to 03.00 seconds for all slides.

12. Reset the Ribbon. Change the document properties, as specified by your instructor. Save the presentation using the file name, Lab 9-3 Anatomy of Foot and Ankle.

13. Submit the revised document in the format specified by your instructor.

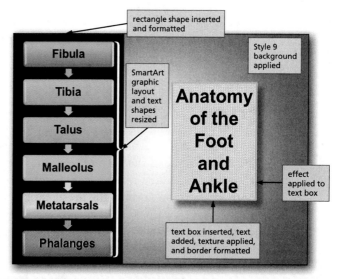

(a) Slide 1

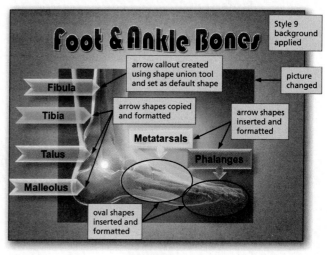

(b) Slide 2

**Figure 9–85**

# Cases and Places

Apply your creative thinking and problem-solving skills to design and implement a solution.

*Note:* To complete these assignments, you may be required to use the Data Files for Students. See the inside back cover of this book for instructions on downloading the Data Files for Students, or contact your instructor for information about accessing the required files.

As you design the presentations, remember to use the 7 × 7 rule: a maximum of seven words on a line and a maximum of seven lines on one slide.

## 1: Designing and Creating a Presentation about Communication Devices for People with Special Needs

**Academic**

As an education major, you are researching communication devices that assist people with special needs. One of your relatives is visually impaired and has shown you some of the gadgets he uses, such as a voice-command television, computer, and printer. He uses a scanner to copy and then play back the contents of his mail and other documents in a computer program. He also has a modified mouse and a braille keyboard for his computer. You decide to do a PowerPoint presentation to explain the devices your family member uses and to list other devices you find in your research. Apply at least three objectives found at the beginning of this chapter to develop the presentation, including applying borders and effects to text boxes and adding or removing SmartArt shapes. Use pictures and diagrams from Office.com if they are appropriate for this topic. Be sure to check spelling.

## 2: Designing and Creating a Presentation about Soccer

**Personal**

You have been playing soccer for many years and, in addition to playing, are coaching an adult soccer team. You decide to create a PowerPoint presentation to explain some of the soccer rules to new team members. Some of the current team members have difficulty understanding what off sides means, so you will explain that in the presentation as well. Apply at least three objectives found at the beginning of this chapter to develop the presentation, including using shapes to show a diagram of the soccer field and players' positions. You can also include a SmartArt graphic and change the layout and size of the shapes to list some of the rules. Use pictures and diagrams from Office.com if they are appropriate for this topic. Be sure to check spelling.

## 3: Designing and Creating a Presentation about School Funding

**Professional**

You are a member of the board of directors of the ABC Charter School. After several years of financial crisis at the school, a very large sum of money was donated to the school. Members of the board and the managers of the school are meeting to decide how this money will be used. The director of the school has received many ideas from faculty, staff members, students, and parents. He has shared these ideas with you and asks you to prepare a PowerPoint presentation for the upcoming meeting. Some of the ideas submitted are: updating the computer lab, expanding the library, building a greenhouse next to the science lab, hiring an additional art teacher, expanding the music program to include a band or an orchestra, and starting a competitive basketball program for boys and girls. You may have a few ideas of your own to share. The presentation should include applying pictures, textures, or patterns to text boxes and a Microsoft Word handout to be distributed at the meeting. Use pictures from Office.com if they are appropriate for this topic or use your personal digital pictures. Be sure to check spelling.

# 10 | Developing a Presentation with Content from Outside Sources

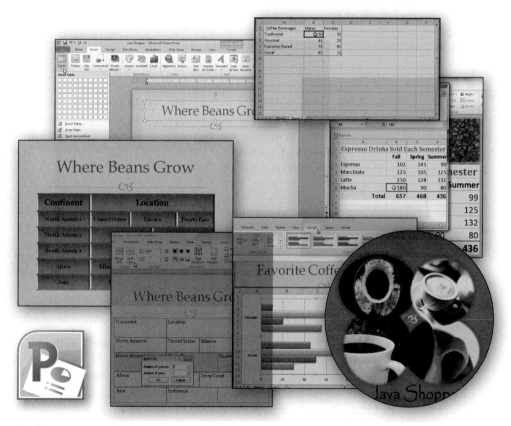

## Objectives

You will have mastered the material in this chapter when you can:

- Insert an object from a file
- Draw and format a table
- Resize, split, distribute, and arrange table columns and rows
- Embed and edit a file
- Apply effects and borders to chart elements
- Add a hyperlink to a chart element

- Change a chart type
- Switch chart rows and columns
- Edit chart data
- Use chart labels, axes, gridlines, and backgrounds
- Apply a Quick Style to a chart
- Arrange chart elements
- Create a hyperlink to a PDF

# 10 | Developing a Presentation with Content from Outside Sources

## Introduction

**BTW**

**Using Charts and Tables**
Charts and tables can be outstanding tools to give meaning to the figures and facts you want to emphasize in your presentation and to help audiences understand abstract concepts and the relationships between sets of data. Overloading your slides with data may confuse your audience and defeat the purpose of these graphical elements. Present only one main idea in a chart or table.

Adding visuals to a presentation could help audience members remember the important facts you want to share. Researchers have found that adding such graphics as tables, charts, graphs, and maps increases retention by more than 50 percent. The audience also believes that speakers who include visuals in their presentations are more qualified and believable than speakers who do not have accompanying visuals. In addition, studies have shown that meeting times are reduced and decisions are reached more quickly when group members have seen visuals that help them reach a consensus.

PowerPoint has many features that allow you to insert visuals and then modify them directly on the slide. For example, you can embed a Microsoft Word document and then edit its text or replace its graphics. You can link an Excel worksheet with a PowerPoint slide so that when numbers are modified in the worksheet, the corresponding numbers on the PowerPoint slide also are updated. These tools help you work productively and generate slides with graphics that help your audience comprehend and remember your message.

## Project — Presentation with Embedded Files and Formatted Charts and Table

**BTW**

**Coffee Preferences**
More than one-half of adults consume at least one cup of coffee each day, according to the National Coffee Association. One-third of this group prefers an elaborate drink made with milk, and another one-third favors black coffee or espresso. A 16-ounce cup of name-brand coffee has approximately 330 mg of caffeine, which is the same amount of caffeine found in seven 12-ounce cans of diet cola.

More than one-half of adults drink at least one coffee beverage daily. Gourmet coffee drinks, such as espresso-based and milk-based beverages, are gaining popularity and now account for approximately 40 percent of the coffee consumed. Consumers patronize chain and independent coffeehouses to relax, chat with friends, or browse the Internet. The locally owned coffee shops on or near college campuses often provide an outstanding venue to study and complete homework assignments.

The presentation you create in this chapter (Figure 10–1) would be useful to show to the Java Shoppe owners who are deciding what types of drinks to offer at their new campus location. You begin Slide 1 (Figure 10–1a) by inserting a flyer with graphics and text (Figure 10–1b). You then learn that the name of the shop will change from Java Stop to Java Shoppe, so you edit the name directly on the slide. The second slide (Figure 10–1c) includes a chart that you draw and enhance using PowerPoint's tools and graphical features. You insert the table on Slide 3 (Figure 10–1d on page 596) from a Microsoft Excel worksheet (Figure 10–1e) that contains the results of a year long student survey. Students who drink espresso-based beverages were asked to indicate which beverage they preferred. When you learn that some of the surveys were not included in the table, you edit several of the numbers, and then Microsoft Excel updates the totals automatically. The last slide (Figure 10–1f) features a Microsoft Excel chart (Figure 10–1g) that you insert and then enhance. If you click the chart when running the presentation, a hyperlinked Adobe Acrobat file (Figure 10–1h) displays.

## Overview

As you read through this chapter, you will learn how to create the presentation shown in Figure 10–1 on this page and the next by performing these general tasks:

- Insert a graphic from a file.
- Insert a Microsoft Excel worksheet.
- Link and embed a file.
- Edit a linked object and an embedded file.
- Format chart elements.
- Arrange chart elements.
- Draw and modify a table.
- Create a hyperlink to a PDF document.

**BTW**

**First Impressions**
The first slide in your presentation sets the tone of your entire presentation. Before you say one word, your audience sees what you have projected on the screen and forms a first impression of whether the speech is going to be interesting, professional, and relevant. Take care in designing an opening slide that meets the audience's expectations and generates interest in the remainder of the presentation.

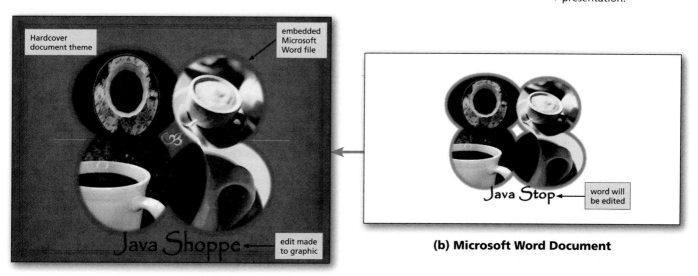

**(a) Slide 1 (Title Slide)**

**(b) Microsoft Word Document**

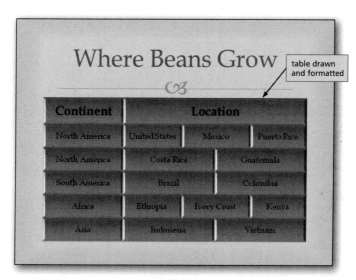

**(c) Slide 2**

**Figure 10–1**

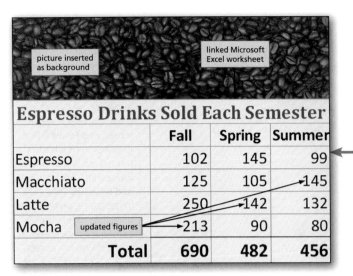

**(d) Slide 3**

**(e) Original Microsoft Excel Worksheet**

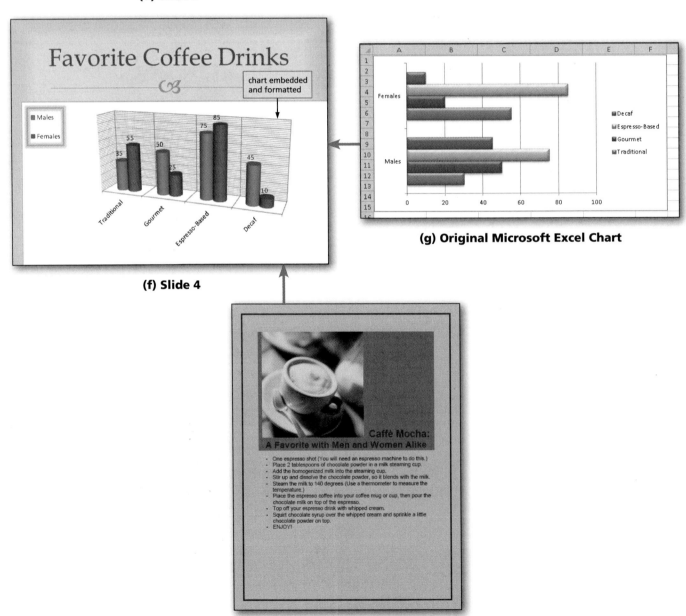

**(f) Slide 4**

**(g) Original Microsoft Excel Chart**

**(h) Hyperlinked Adobe Acrobat Document**

**Figure 10–1 (Continued)**

Plan
Ahead

**General Project Guidelines**

When creating a PowerPoint presentation, the actions you perform and the decisions you make will affect the appearance and characteristics of the finished document. As you create a presentation with illustrations, such as the project shown in Figure 10–1 on pages PPT 595 to PPT 596, you should follow these general guidelines:

1. **Use powerful words to accompany the text on your slides.** The slides are meant to enhance your talk by clarifying main points and calling attention to key ideas. Your speech should use words that explain and substantiate your visuals.

2. **Develop tables that are clear and meaningful.** Tables are extremely useful vehicles for presenting complex relationships. Their design plays an important part of successfully conveying the information to the audience.

3. **Use appropriate colors when formatting graphics you want people to remember.** Numerous studies have shown that appropriate graphics help audiences comprehend and remember the information presented during a speech. Color has been shown to increase retention by as much as 80 percent. When choosing colors for your graphics, use hues that fit the tone and objective of your message.

When necessary, more specific details concerning the above guidelines are presented at appropriate points in the chapter. The chapter also will identify the actions performed and decisions made regarding these guidelines during the creation of the presentation shown in Figure 10–1.

## To Start PowerPoint and Save a File

If you are using a computer to step through the project in this chapter and you want your screens to match the figures in this book, you should change your computer's resolution to 1024 × 768. The following steps start PowerPoint and then save a file.

**1** Start PowerPoint. If necessary, maximize the PowerPoint window.

**2** Apply the Hardcover document theme.

**3** Save the presentation using the file name, Java Shoppe.

Plan
Ahead

**Use powerful words to accompany the text on your slides.**

Carefully plan the speech that coordinates with the slides in your presentation. Use examples that substantiate the objects on the slides, and use familiar, precise words and terms that enlighten the audience. Do not include obvious material as filler because audience members will reach the conclusion that you are wasting their time with meaningless information that they do not need to know.

# Inserting Graphics or Other Objects from a File

PowerPoint allows you to insert many types of objects into a presentation. You can insert clips, pictures, video and audio files, and symbols, and you also can copy and paste or drag and drop objects from one slide to another. At times you may want to insert content created with other Microsoft Office programs, such as a Word flyer, an Excel table or graph, a Paint graphic, or a document created with another Microsoft Windows-based application. The original document is called the **source**, and the new document that

**BTW**

**The Ribbon and Screen Resolution**
PowerPoint may change how the groups and buttons within the groups appear on the Ribbon, depending on the computer's screen resolution. Thus, your Ribbon may look different from the ones in this book if you are using a screen resolution other than 1024 × 768.

**BTW**

**Q&As**
For a complete list of the Q&As found in many of the step-by-step sequences in this book, visit the PowerPoint 2010 Q&A Web page (scsite.com/ppt2010/qa).

contains this object is called the **destination**. When you want to copy a source document object, such as a Word flyer, to a destination document, such as your PowerPoint slide, you can use one of three techniques.

- **Embedding** — An **embedded object** becomes part of the destination slide, but you edit and modify the contents using the source program's commands and features. In this project, for example, you will embed a Word document and then edit the text using Microsoft Word without leaving PowerPoint. In addition, you will embed an Excel chart and then modify the object using Microsoft Excel while Slide 4 is displayed. The embedded file is static, meaning that any changes you make to the object in PowerPoint will be reflected only on the destination PowerPoint slide and not in the original source file.

- **Linking** — Similar to an embedded object, a **linked object** also is created in another application and is stored in the **source file**, the original file in which the object was created. The linked object maintains a connection to its source and does not become part of the destination slide. Instead, a connection, or link, made between the source and destination objects gives the appearance that the objects are independent. In reality, the two objects work together so that when one is edited, the other is updated. If the original object is changed, the linked object on the slide also changes. In this project, for example, you will link a Microsoft Excel table and then edit the data using Excel. As the numbers in the table change, the numbers in the linked table on the PowerPoint slide also are updated to reflect those changes. Likewise, if you change data to the linked table in your PowerPoint slide, that data will change in the Excel source document.

- **Copying and pasting** — An object that you copy from a source document and then paste in a destination document becomes part of the destination program. Any edits that you make are done using the destination software. For example, if you copy a picture from a Word document, paste it into your slide, and then recolor or remove the background, those changes are made using PowerPoint's commands and do not affect the source object.

The first two techniques described above are termed **object linking and embedding** (**OLE**, pronounced o-lay). This means of sharing material developed in various sources and then updating the files within a destination program is useful when you deliver presentations frequently that display current data that changes constantly. For example, your PowerPoint presentation may contain a chart reflecting current student registration statistics for the upcoming semester, or you may include a table with election tallies for Student Government Association candidates.

## To Insert a File with Graphics and Text

The first object you will add to your presentation is a graphical flyer created in Microsoft Word. This flyer contains artwork and text developed as part of an advertising campaign for the new coffee shop on campus, and you desire to use this document in your slide show to promote this business. The following steps insert a Microsoft Word file with a graphic and text.

**1**

- Click Insert on the Ribbon and then click the Insert Object button (Insert tab | Text group) to display the Insert Object dialog box (Figure 10–2).

What is the difference between the Create new and the 'Create from file' options?

The Create new option opens an application and allows you to develop an original object. In contrast, the 'Create from file' option prompts you to locate a file that already is created and saved so you can modify the object using the program that was used to create it.

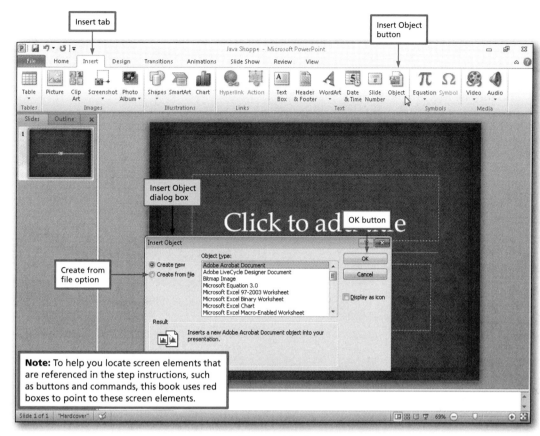

**Figure 10–2**

**2**

- Click 'Create from file' (Insert Object dialog box) to display the File text box.

- Click the Browse button and then navigate to the PowerPoint Chapter 10 folder.

- Click Java Stop Flyer to select the Microsoft Word file (Figure 10–3).

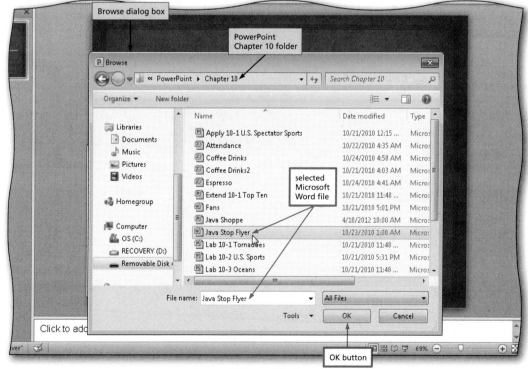

**Figure 10–3**

**3**

- Click the OK button (Browse dialog box) to insert the file name into the File text box (Insert Object dialog box) (Figure 10–4).

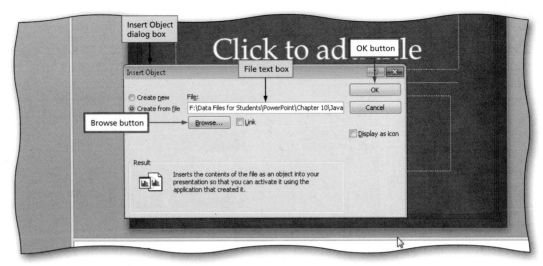

**Figure 10–4**

**4**

- Click the OK button (Insert Object dialog box) to display the Java Stop Flyer contents on Slide 1.

**Q&A** Why did several seconds pass before this flyer was displayed on the slide?

PowerPoint takes more time to insert embedded and linked inserted objects than it takes to perform an ordinary cut-and-paste or copy-and-paste action. You must be patient while PowerPoint is inserting the object.

- Position the object in the center of the slide so that the decorative design on the title slide is displayed in the middle of the four ovals in the object (Figure 10–5).

**Figure 10–5**

**Q&A** Does PowerPoint take more time to position embedded objects than copied objects?

Yes, you must be patient while PowerPoint responds to your mouse or arrow key movements.

**Q&A** How can I center the object precisely over the decorative object?

Drag the object so that it is near the decoration and then use the ARROW keys to move the object in small increments.

## To Edit an Embedded File

The flyer provides an excellent graphic and text to use on Slide 1, but the business has changed its name since the document was created. You want to change the word, Stop, to the word, Shoppe. PowerPoint allows you to edit an embedded file easily by opening the source program, which in this case is Microsoft Word. The following steps edit the Microsoft Word text.

**1**

- Double-click the embedded coffee object to start the Microsoft Word program and open the document on Slide 1 (Figure 10–6).

**Q&A**

Why are the horizontal and vertical rulers displayed in my Word document but not in the Word document shown in Figure 10–6?

Your Microsoft Word setting to show the rulers is checked.

**Figure 10–6**

**2**

- Double-click the word, Stop, to select it and then type **Shoppe** as the replacement text (Figure 10–7).

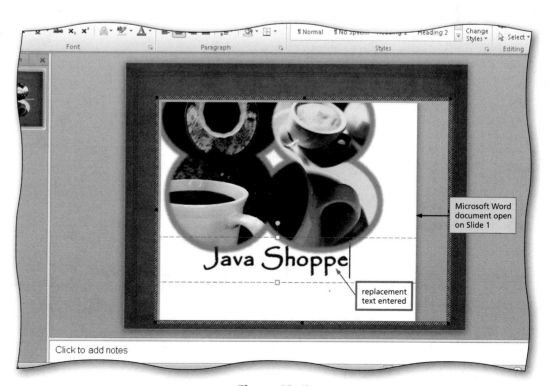

**Figure 10–7**

**3**

- Click outside the Word document to close Microsoft Word and display the edited flyer object on Slide 1.

- If necessary, position the object as shown in Figure 10–8.

edited flyer object on Slide 1

**Figure 10–8**

**Other Ways**

1. Right-click Word object, point to Document Object on shortcut menu, click Edit

**BTW**

**Customizing Table Formatting**
The variety of table styles in the Quick Styles gallery presents several options to give a table a professional and colorful design and format. You, however, may desire to customize the layout by adding or modifying borders, the background color, or the font. To clear a style from a table, display the Table Tools Design tab, click the More button in the Table Styles group, and then click Clear Table.

# Drawing and Adjusting a Table

Tables are useful graphical elements to present data organized in descriptive rows and columns. Each cell created from the intersection of a row and column has a unique location name and contains numeric or textual data that you can edit.

In the following pages, you will perform these tasks on Slide 2:

1. Draw a table.
2. Draw table rows.
3. Draw table columns.
4. Erase a table line.
5. Split a table column and row.
6. Add shading to a table.
7. Add a gradient fill to a table.
8. Add a cell bevel.
9. Distribute table rows.
10. Resize table columns and rows.
11. Center the table.

**Plan Ahead**

**Develop tables that are clear and meaningful.**
Use a table to present complex material, but be certain the information makes useful comparisons. Tables generally are used to show relationships between sets of data. For example, they may show prices for grades of gasoline in three states, the number of in-state and out-of-state students who have applied for admission to various college programs, or the rushing and passing records among quarterbacks in a particular league. The units of measurement, such as dollars, specific majors, or yards, should be expressed clearly on the slides. The data in the rows and columns should be aligned uniformly. Also, the table labels should be meaningful and easily read.

## To Draw a Table

PowerPoint allows you to insert a table in several ways. You can click the Table button on the Insert tab and either click the Insert Table command or drag your mouse pointer to specify the number of rows and columns you need. You also can click the Insert Table button in a content placeholder. Another method that allows flexibility is to use the mouse pointer as a pencil to draw the outer edges and then add the columns and rows. The following steps draw a table on Slide 2.

- Insert a new slide with the Title Only layout. Type **Where Beans Grow** as the title text.

- Display the View tab and then click the Ruler check box (View tab | Show group) to display the horizontal and vertical rulers.

- Display the Insert tab and then click the Table button (Insert tab | Tables group) to display the Table gallery (Figure 10–9).

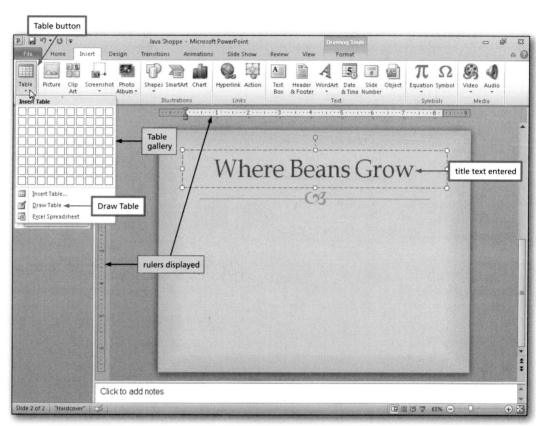

**Figure 10–9**

- Click Draw Table and then position the mouse pointer, which has the shape of a pencil, in the upper-left area below the slide title.

**Q&A**

If I decide I do not want to draw a table, how can I change the mouse pointer to the block arrow?

Press the ESC key.

- Drag the pencil pointer to the lower-right corner of the slide to draw the outer edges of the table (Figure 10–10).

**Figure 10–10**

• Release the mouse button to create the table frame.

**Q&A** Must my table be the same size or be positioned in the same location shown in the figure?

No. You will resize and reposition the table later in this project.

## To Draw Table Rows

Once you draw the four sides of the table, you then can use the mouse pointer as a pencil to draw lines for the columns and rows in the positions where you desire them to display. You could, therefore, draw columns having different widths and rows that are spaced in irregular heights. The following steps draw four lines to create five table rows.

• Position the pencil pointer inside the table approximately 1" from the top table edge (Figure 10–11).

**Q&A** How can I get my pencil pointer to reappear if it no longer is displaying?

Click the Draw Table button (Table Tools Design tab | Draw Borders group).

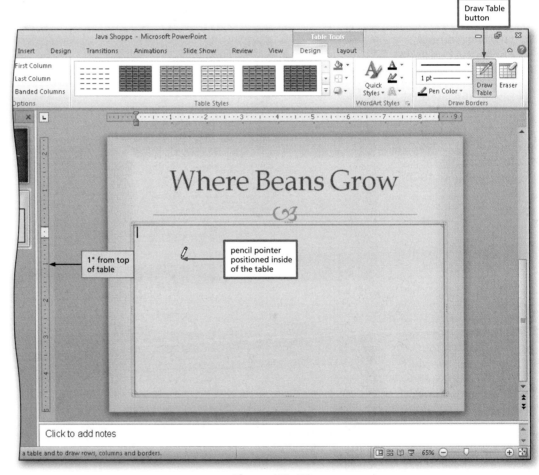

**Figure 10–11**

**2**

- Drag the pencil pointer to the right to draw a horizontal line across the entire table and divide the table into two cells (Figure 10–12), then release the mouse button.

**Q&A**  Should I drag the pencil pointer to the right edge of the table?

No. PowerPoint will draw a complete line when you begin to move the pencil pointer in one direction.

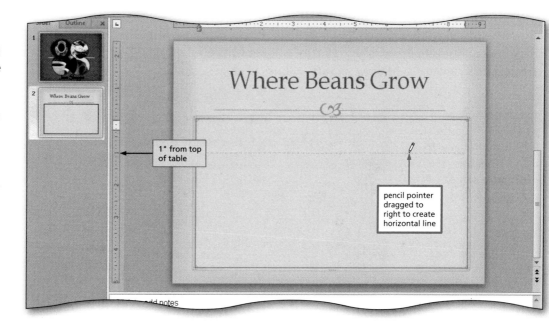

**Figure 10–12**

**Q&A**  If I drew the line in the incorrect location, how can I erase it?

Press the ESC key or click the Eraser button (Table Tools Design tab | Draw Borders group) and then click the line.

**3**

- Draw three additional horizontal lines, as shown in Figure 10–13, and then release the mouse pointer.

**Q&A**  Do I need to align the lines in the precise positions shown?

No. You will create evenly spaced rows later in this project.

**Figure 10–13**

## To Draw Table Columns

The pencil pointer is useful to draw table columns with varying widths. The two major categories in the table are continents and countries. The countries column will be subdivided to show the countries where coffee beans are grown. The following steps draw six vertical lines to create columns.

**1**

- Position the pencil pointer inside the table approximately 2.5" from the left table edge (Figure 10–14).

**Q&A** Can I change the line color?

Yes. Click the Pen Color button (Table Tools Design tab | Draw Borders group) and then select a different color.

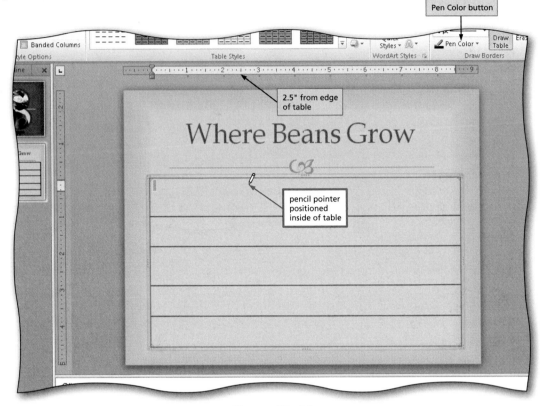

**Figure 10–14**

**2**

- Drag the pencil pointer down through all the horizontal lines to draw a vertical line that divides the table into 10 cells.

- Position the pencil pointer inside the second cell in the second row approximately 4.5" from the left table edge, as shown in Figure 10–15.

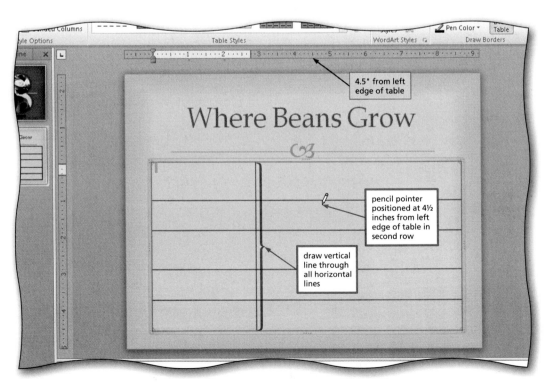

**Figure 10–15**

**3**

- Drag the pencil pointer down slightly to draw a vertical line in only that cell (Figure 10–16) and then release the mouse button.

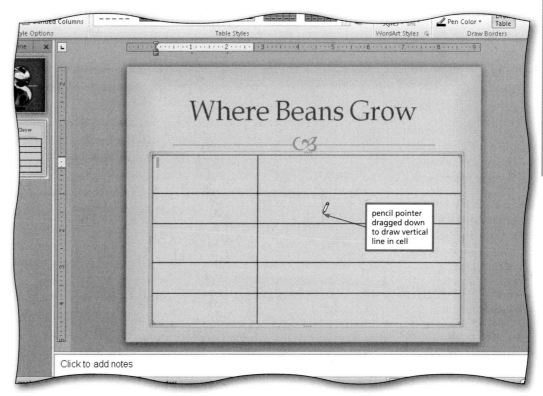

**Figure 10–16**

**4**

- Draw four additional vertical lines, as shown in Figure 10–17, and then release the mouse button.

**Q&A**

Are vertical and horizontal lines the only types of lines I can draw?

No. You also can draw a diagonal line from one corner of a cell to another corner.

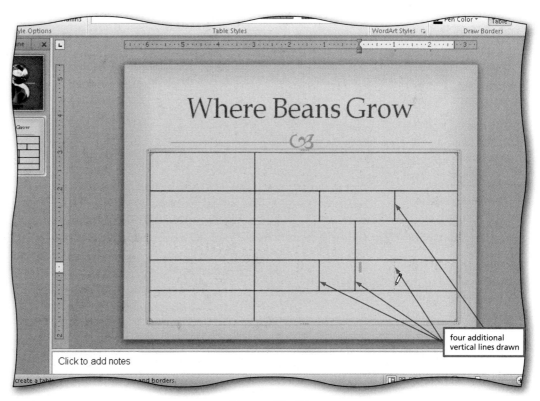

**Figure 10–17**

## To Erase a Table Line

Because the number of countries is different for each continent, the number of cells in each row varies. The eraser pointer is useful to delete unnecessary column lines. The fourth row in the table should be identical to the second row and have four cells. PowerPoint supplies an eraser tool that allows you to delete vertical and horizontal lines in a table. The following steps use the eraser to delete one vertical line in a row.

- Click the Table Eraser button (Table Tools Design tab | Draw Borders group).

- Position the mouse pointer, which has the shape of an eraser, over the third line in the fourth row (Figure 10–18).

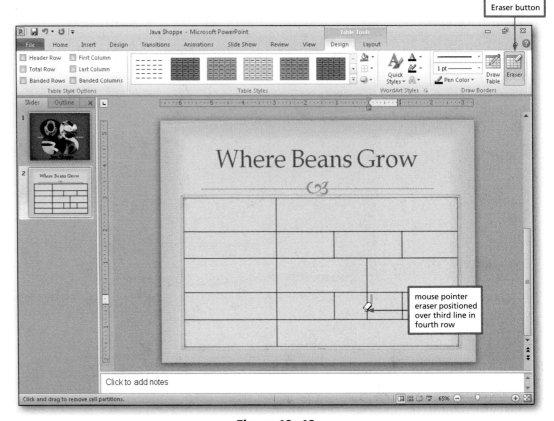

**Figure 10–18**

- Click the vertical line to erase it (Figure 10–19).

- Press the ESC key to change the mouse pointer to the block arrow.

- If necessary, drag the edges of the cells so the cell widths are similar to those in the figure.

- Display the View tab and then click the Ruler check box (View tab | Show group) to hide the horizontal and vertical rulers.

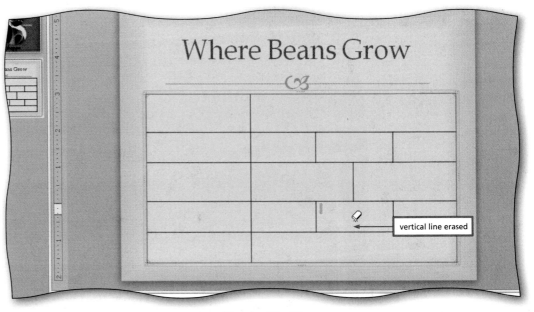

**Figure 10–19**

## To Enter Data in a Table

Coffee beans are grown in several countries throughout the world. The table you created will list the continent names on the left side of each row and the location names on the right side. The first row will label the two parts of the table. To place data in a cell, you click the cell and then type text. The following steps enter data in the cells of the empty table.

**1** Position the mouse pointer in the upper-left cell of the table, type `Continent` in the cell, and then press the TAB key to advance the insertion point to the next cell.

**2** Type `Location` in the upper-right cell and then press the TAB key to advance the insertion point to the first cell in the second row.

**3** Type `North America` and then press the TAB key to advance the insertion point to the next cell. Type `United States` and then press the TAB key to advance the insertion point to the next cell. Type `Mexico` and then press the TAB key to advance the insertion point to the next cell. Type `Puerto Rico` and then press the TAB key to advance the insertion point to the first column of the third row.

**4** In the third row, type `North America` in the first column, `Costa Rica` in the second column, and `Guatemala` in the third column. Press the TAB key to advance the insertion point to the first column of the fourth row.

**5** In the fourth row, type `Africa` in the first column, `Ethiopia` in the second column, `Ivory Coast` in the third column, and `Kenya` in the fourth column. Press the TAB key to advance the insertion point to the first column of the fifth row.

**6** In the fifth row, type `Asia` in the first column and `Indonesia` in the second column (Figure 10–20).

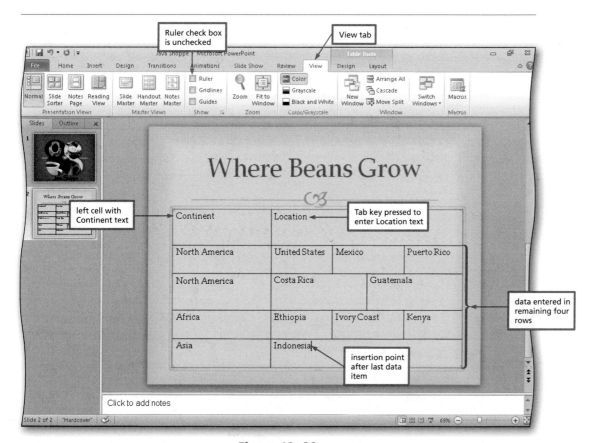

**Figure 10–20**

## To Split a Table Column and Row

The Asia row in the table identifies Indonesia as the only location growing coffee beans. Your research indicates that the Vietnamese also grow coffee plants, so you need to add that location to the right side of the last row. The layout of this row should be identical to the second North America row. In addition, you learn that coffee also is grown in Brazil and Colombia, which are located in South America. You easily can create additional table columns and rows by dividing current cells and rows. The following steps split a column and a row.

**1**

- With the mouse pointer positioned in the Indonesia cell, click the Table Tools Layout tab to display the Table Tools Layout Ribbon and then click the Split Cells button (Table Tools Layout tab | Merge group) to display the Split Cells dialog box (Figure 10–21).

**Q&A**

Are the default numbers in the dialog box always 2 columns and 1 row?

Yes, but you can increase the numbers if you need to divide the cell into more than two halves or need to create two or more rows within one cell.

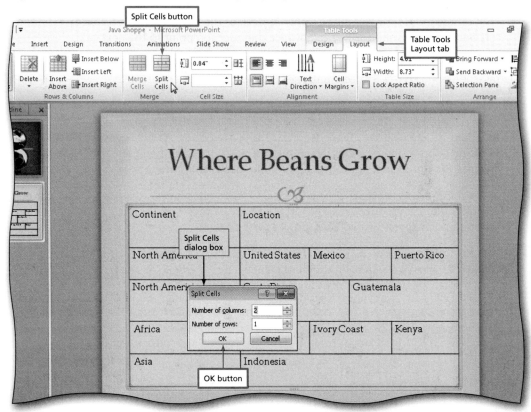

**Figure 10–21**

**2**

- Click the OK button (Split Cells dialog box) to create a third cell in the Asia row.

- Position the mouse pointer in the second North America cell.

- Click the Select button (Table Tools Layout tab | Table group) to display the Select menu (Figure 10–22).

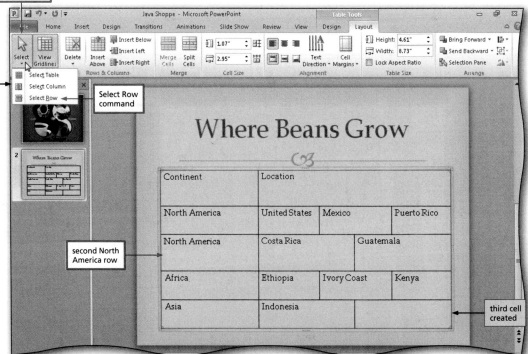

**Figure 10–22**

**3**

- Click Select Row in the Select menu to select the second North America row.

- With the Table Tools Layout tab displaying, click the Split Cells button (Table Tools Layout tab | Merge group) to display the Split Cells dialog box (Figure 10–23).

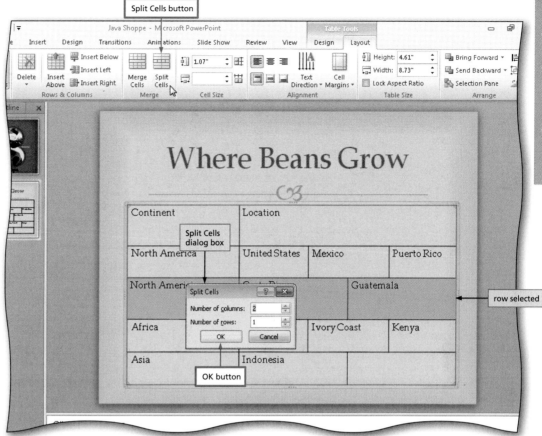

**Figure 10–23**

**4**

- Click the 'Number of columns' box down arrow one time to decrease the number of columns to 1.

- Click the 'Number of rows' box up arrow one time to increase the number of rows to 2 (Figure 10–24).

**Q&A**

How many rows and columns can I create by splitting the cells?

The maximum number varies depending upon the width and height of the selected cell.

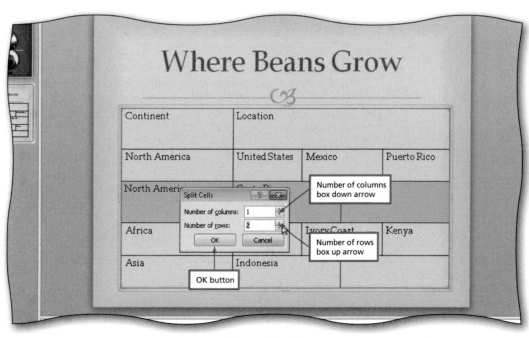

**Figure 10–24**

**5**

- Click the OK button (Split Cells dialog box) to create a row below the second North America row.

**Other Ways**

1. Right-click table, click Split Cells on shortcut menu, enter number of columns and rows, click OK button

## To Enter Additional Data in a Table

With the additional row and column added to the table, you now can add the South America data in the inserted row and also add the location, Vietnam, to the new cell in the Asia row. The following steps enter data in the new cells.

**1** If necessary, position the mouse pointer in the first cell of the fourth row and then type **South America** in the cell. Press the TAB key to advance the insertion point to the adjacent right column cell and then type **Brazil** and **Colombia** in the cells in this row.

**2** Press the DOWN ARROW key two times to position the mouse pointer in the new cell in the Asia row and then type **Vietnam** in the cell (Figure 10–25).

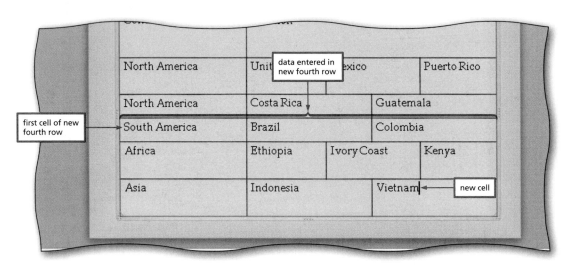

**Figure 10–25**

**Plan Ahead**

**Use appropriate colors when formatting graphics you want people to remember.** Studies have shown that men and women differ slightly in their recall of graphics formatted with various colors. Men remembered objects colored with shades of violet, dark blue, olive green, and yellow. Women recalled objects they had seen with dark blue, olive green, yellow, and red hues.

## To Add Shading to a Table

You can format the table in several ways to make it more visually appealing. By adding shading, you can color the background. The following steps add shading to the table.

**1**

• Click the Select button (Table Tools Layout tab | Table group) to display the Select menu (Figure 10–26).

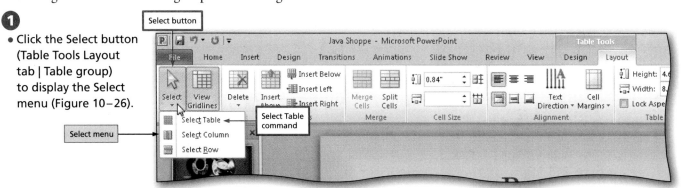

**Figure 10–26**

- Click Select Table in the Select menu to select the entire table.

- Click the Table Tools Design tab and then click the Shading button arrow (Table Tools Design tab | Table Styles group) to display the Shading gallery.

- Point to Olive Green, Accent 6 (rightmost color in first Theme Colors row) in the Shading gallery to display a live preview of that color applied to the table in the slide (Figure 10–27).

 **Experiment**

- Point to various colors in the Shading gallery and watch the background of the table change.

**3**

- Click Olive Green, Accent 6 in the Shading gallery to apply the selected color to the table.

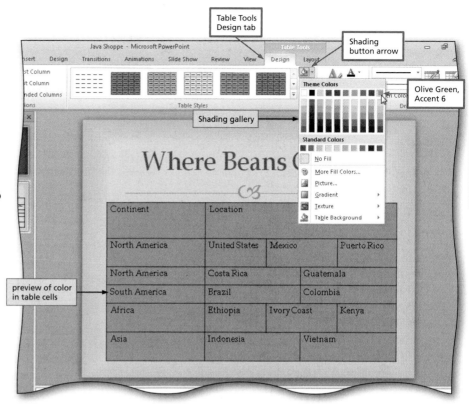

**Figure 10–27**

## To Add a Gradient Fill to a Table

Another enhancement you can make to the table is to add a gradient fill so that one shade of the olive green color gradually progresses to another shade of the same color. The following steps add a gradient fill to the table.

**1**

- With the table still selected, click the Shading button arrow (Table Tools Design tab | Table Styles group) again to display the Shading menu.

- Point to Gradient to display the Gradient gallery and then point to Linear Down in the Dark Variations area (second gradient in first row) to display a live preview of that gradient applied to the table in the slide (Figure 10–28).

 **Experiment**

- Point to various gradients in the Gradient gallery and watch the background of the table change.

**2**

- Click Linear Down in the Shading gallery to apply the selected gradient to the table.

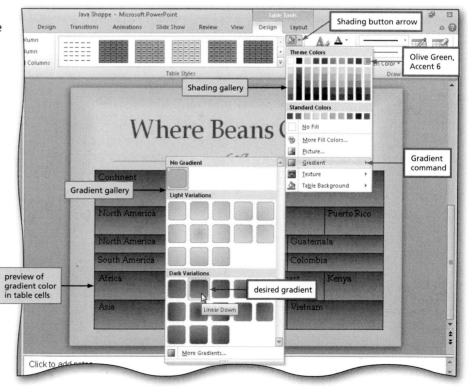

**Figure 10–28**

## To Add a Cell Bevel

Bevels modify the cell edges to give a 3-D effect. Some bevels give the appearance that the cell is protruding from the table, while others give the effect that the cell is depressed into the table. The following steps add a bevel to the table cells.

- With the table still selected, click the Effects button (Table Tools Design tab | Table Styles group) to display the Effects menu.

- Point to Cell Bevel on the Effects menu to display the Cell Bevel gallery.

- Point to Art Deco (rightmost bevel in last row) to display a live preview of that bevel applied to the table in the slide (Figure 10–29).

 **Experiment**

- Point to various bevel effects in the Bevel gallery and watch the table cells change.

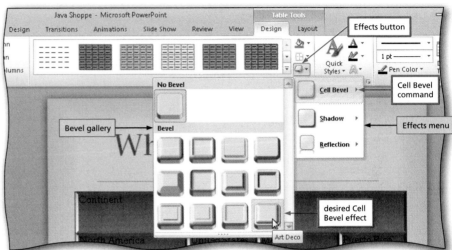

**Figure 10–29**

- Click Art Deco in the Bevel gallery to apply the selected bevel effect to the table.

## To Distribute Table Rows

The horizontal lines you drew are not spaced equidistant from each other. At times you may desire the row heights to vary. In the Slide 2 table, however, you desire the heights of the rows to be uniform. To make each selected row the same height, you distribute the desired rows. The following steps distribute table rows.

- With the table still selected, display the Table Tools Layout tab and then select the cells in the second, third, fourth, fifth, and sixth rows (Figure 10–30).

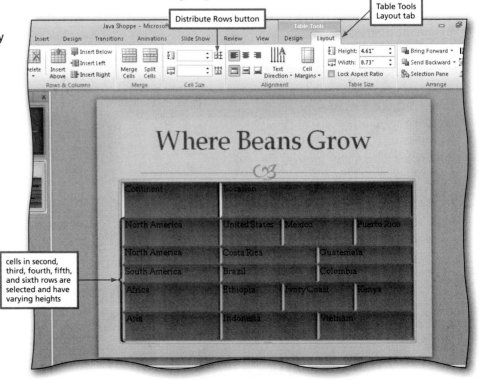

**Figure 10–30**

**2**

- Click the Distribute Rows button (Table Tools Layout tab | Cell Size group) to equally space the five continent rows vertically (Figure 10–31).

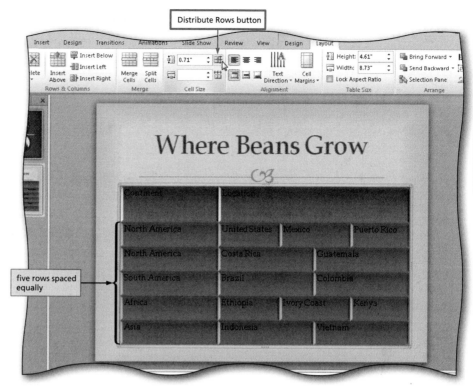

Figure 10–31

## To Resize Table Columns and Rows

The first table row should have a taller height than the rows beneath it because it signifies the two table categories. In addition, the continents portion of the table should be narrower than the countries portion because it has fewer words and only one cell per row. The following steps resize the table columns and rows.

**1**

- With the Table Tools Layout tab displaying, position the insertion point in the Continent cell in the first row.

- Click the Table Row Height box down arrow (Table Tools Layout tab | Cell Size group) as needed to reduce the height to 0.8" (Figure 10–32).

Figure 10–32

● Click the Table
Column Width box
down arrow (Table
Tools Layout tab | Cell
Size group) as needed
until the cell width is
2.5" (Figure 10–33).

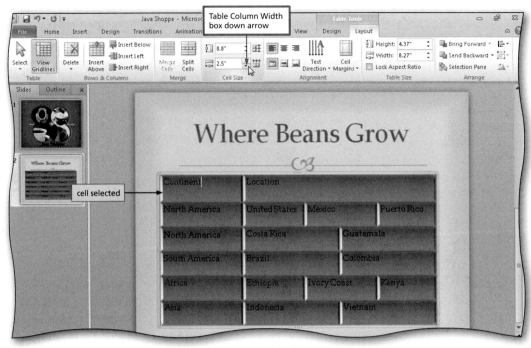

**Figure 10–33**

## To Align Data in Cells

The next step is to change the alignment of the data in all the table cells. In addition to aligning text horizontally in a cell (left, center, or right), you can align it vertically within a cell (top, middle, or bottom). The following steps center data in the table both horizontally and vertically.

**1** Select all the table cells and then click the Center button (Table Tools Layout tab | Alignment group) to center the text horizontally in the cells.

**2** Click the Center Vertically button (Table Tools Layout tab | Alignment group) to center the contents of the cells vertically (Figure 10–34).

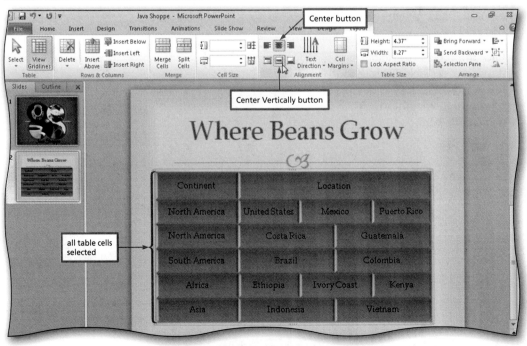

**Figure 10–34**

## To Center the Table

The table should be positioned an equal distance between the left and right slide edges. To center the table, you align it in the middle of the slide. The following steps center the table horizontally.

**1**

- With the insertion point in the table, click the Align button (Table Tools Layout tab | Arrange group) to display the Align menu (Figure 10–35).

**2**

- Click Align Center on the Align menu, so PowerPoint adjusts the position of the table evenly between the left and right sides of the slide. If necessary, adjust the table vertically on the slide, so that it is displayed below the decorative slide background element.

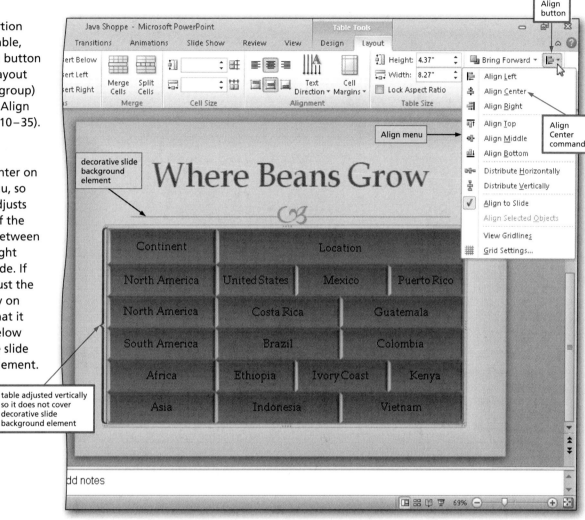

**Figure 10–35**

## To Format Table Data

The final table enhancement is to bold and increase the font size of the text in the first row. The following steps bold the text in the first row and then increase the font size.

**1** Select the first row, display the Home tab, and then click the Bold button to bold the text.

**2** Increase the font size to 28 point (Figure 10–36).

**BTW**

**Positioning a Table**
At times you might desire to place a table, text box, shape, or other element in a precise location on the slide. To specify a position, right-click the object, click Format Object or Format Shape on the shortcut menu, click Position in the left pane of the Format Object or Format Shape dialog box, and then enter the precise measurements of the horizontal and vertical distances from either the top-left corner or the center of the slide.

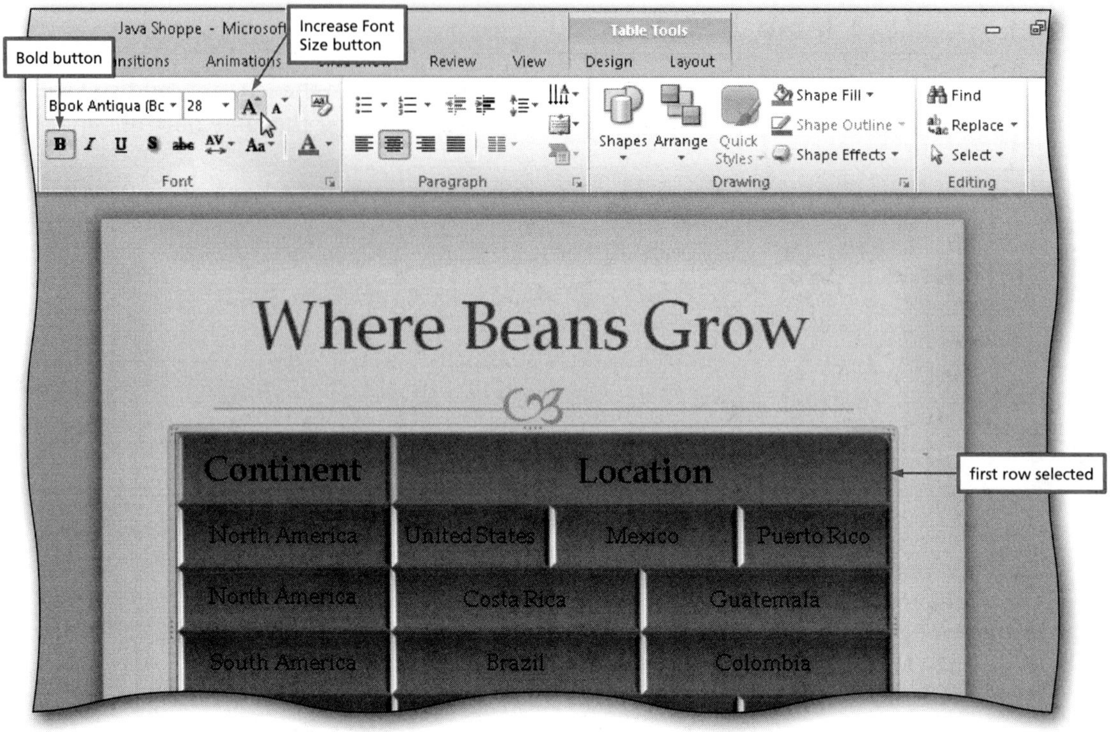


**Figure 10–36**

**Break Point:** If you wish to take a break, this is a good place to do so. Be sure to save the Java Shoppe file again and then you can quit PowerPoint. To resume at a later time, start PowerPoint, open the file called Java Shoppe, and continue following the steps from this location forward.

**BTW**

**File Sizes**
Files with embedded objects typically have larger file sizes than those with linked objects because the source data is stored in the presentation. In order to keep file sizes manageable, Microsoft recommends inserting a linked object rather than an embedded object when the source file is large or complex.

# Inserting a Linked Spreadsheet

Linked files maintain a connection between the source file and the destination file. When you select the **Link check box** in the Insert Object dialog box, the object is inserted as a linked object instead of an embedded object. Your PowerPoint presentation stores a representation of the original file and information about its location. If you later move or delete the source file, the link is broken, and the object will not be available. Consequently, if you make a presentation on a computer other than the one on which the presentation was created, and the presentation contains linked objects, be certain to include a copy of the source files. The source files must be stored in the exact location as originally specified when you linked them to your presentation.

PowerPoint associates a linked file with a specific application, which PowerPoint bases on the file extension. For example, if you select a source file with the file extension **.docx**, PowerPoint recognizes the file as a Microsoft Word file. Additionally, if you select a source file with the file extension **.xlsx**, PowerPoint recognizes the file as a Microsoft Excel file.

In the following pages, you will insert a linked Excel worksheet, align it on the slide, and then edit three cells.

## To Insert a Linked Excel Worksheet

An Excel worksheet contains a table with tallies of the number of students expressing a preference for a particular espresso drink. You can insert this object and specify that it is linked from the PowerPoint slide to the Excel worksheet so that any edits made to specific cells are reflected in both the source and destination files. The following steps insert and link the Microsoft Excel worksheet.

**1**

- Insert a new slide with the Blank layout.

- Insert the Coffee Beans picture from your USB flash drive as a background for the new slide (Figure 10–37).

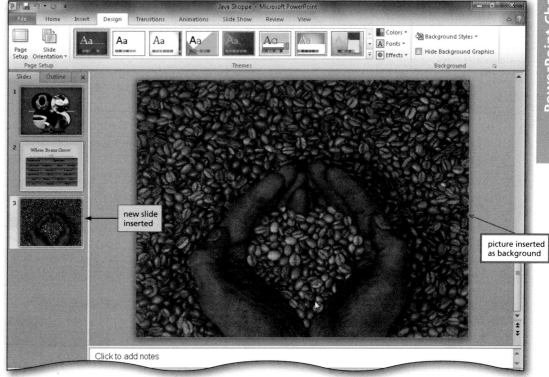

**Figure 10–37**

**2**

- Click Insert on the Ribbon and then click the Insert Object button (Insert tab | Text group) to display the Insert Object dialog box.

- Click 'Create from file' (Insert Object dialog box) to display the File text box (Figure 10–38).

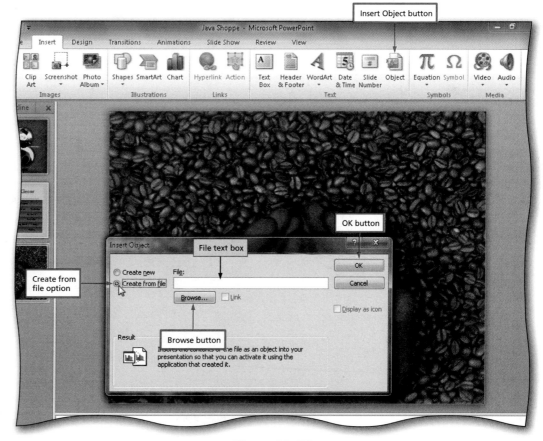

**Figure 10–38**

● Click the Browse button, navigate to the PowerPoint Chapter 10 folder, and then click Espresso to select the file name (Figure 10–39).

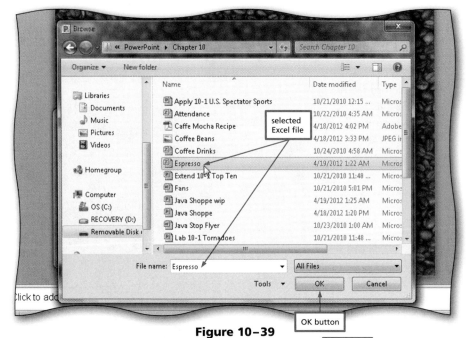

**Figure 10–39**

● Click the OK button (Browse dialog box) to insert the file name into the File text box (Insert Object dialog box).

● Click the Link check box (Insert Object dialog box) to place a check mark in it (Figure 10–40).

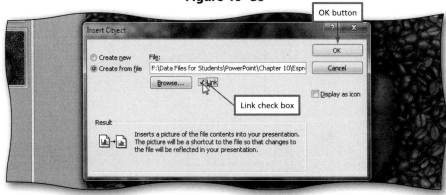

**Figure 10–40**

● Click the OK button (Insert Object dialog box) to insert the Espresso Excel worksheet into Slide 3.

● Display the Drawing Tools Format tab and then click the Shape Height box up arrow repeatedly to change the worksheet height to 5" (Figure 10–41).

**Q&A** Why did the worksheet width change when I changed the height measurement?

The worksheet's width and height stay in proportion to each other, so when you change one dimension, the other dimension changes accordingly.

**Figure 10–41**

## To Align a Worksheet

PowerPoint inserts the table on Slide 3 in a location that is not visually appealing. You can drag the table to a location, but you also can have PowerPoint precisely align the object horizontally in the left, center, or right areas of the slide, and vertically in the top, middle, or bottom of the slide. The following steps align the table horizontally and vertically on Slide 3.

**1**

- With the Drawing Tools Format tab displaying, click the Align button (Drawing Tools Format tab | Arrange group) to display the Align menu (Figure 10–42).

**Figure 10–42**

**2**

- Click Align Center on the Align menu to position the worksheet evenly between the left and right edges of the slide.

- Click the Align button again to display the Align menu and then click Align Bottom to position the worksheet at the lower edge of the slide (Figure 10–43).

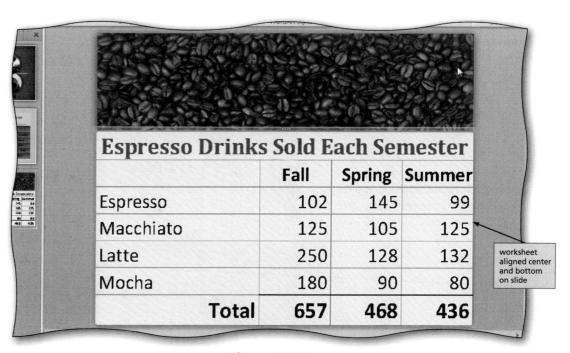

**Figure 10–43**

# To Edit a Linked Worksheet

Each table or worksheet cell is identified by a unique address, or **cell reference**, representing the intersection of a column and row. The column letter is first and is followed by the row number. For example, cell B6 is located at the intersection of the second column, B, and the sixth row. Three cells need updating in the worksheet to reflect additional survey results. When the numbers in the cell change, the totals at the bottom of each column change to reflect the updated sum of each column. The following steps edit cells in the linked table.

**1**
- Double-click the table to open Microsoft Excel and display the worksheet.

- Click the Mocha cell for the Fall semester to make cell B6 the active cell (Figure 10–44).

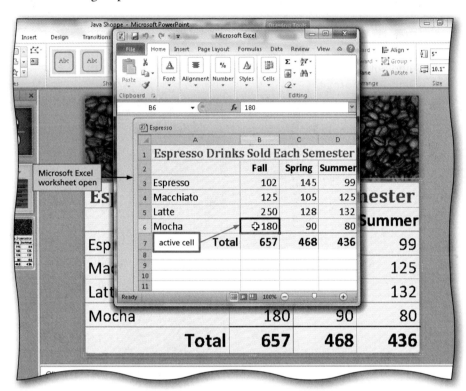

**Figure 10–44**

**2**
- Type 213 as the replacement number and then press the ENTER key to recalculate the Fall total.

- Click the Latte cell for the Spring semester, type 142 as the replacement number, and then press the ENTER key to recalculate the Spring total.

- Click the Macchiato cell for the Summer semester, type 145 as the replacement number, and then press the ENTER key to recalculate the Summer total (Figure 10–45).

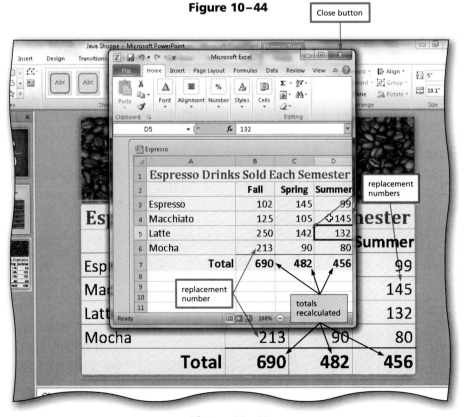

**Figure 10–45**

**3**

- Click the Close button in the upper-right corner of the Microsoft Excel window to quit Excel (Figure 10–46).

- Click the Save button (Microsoft Excel dialog box) to save your edited numbers in the worksheet and to display the updated table in Slide 3.

Figure 10–46

**Break Point:** If you wish to take a break, this is a good place to do so. Be sure to save the Java Shoppe file again and then you can quit PowerPoint. To resume at a later time, start PowerPoint, open the file called Java Shoppe, and continue following the steps from this location forward. Note: PowerPoint will prompt you to update the Excel file that you modified.

# Inserting and Modifying an Embedded Excel Chart

The Microsoft Word file you inserted into Slide 1 is an embedded object. You edited the business name using the Microsoft Word source program, but the change is stored only on the PowerPoint slide, not the original Word document. You, likewise, will insert and then modify a Microsoft Excel chart on Slide 4. This object will be embedded, so any changes you make to the layout, legend, or background will be reflected in the destination object on the slide.

In the following pages, you will perform these tasks on Slide 4:

1. Insert a chart from a file.
2. Align the chart.
3. Switch rows and columns.
4. Change a chart type.
5. Apply a Quick Style.
6. Format a legend.
7. Display chart labels.
8. Hide an axis.
9. Display gridlines.
10. Format the background.
11. Edit data.
12. Add a hyperlink.

**BTW**

**Using Excel within PowerPoint**
The Microsoft Excel chart you insert in this project is located on the Data Files for Students. When you want to create your own chart, you can open Excel from within PowerPoint, enter data, and then create a chart. The chart becomes an embedded Excel object, so you later can modify the worksheet or use Excel's formatting tools to enhance the chart. To open Excel within PowerPoint, display the Insert tab, click the Table button (Insert tab | Tables group), and then click Excel Spreadsheet.

## To Insert a Chart from a File

The chart you want to insert into your slide show was created in Microsoft Excel. The file consists of two sheets: one for the chart and another for the numbers used to create the chart. The chart is on Sheet 1. The following steps insert a chart from Sheet 1 of the Microsoft Excel file.

- Insert a new slide with the Title Only layout. Type **Favorite Coffee Drinks** as the title text.

- Click Insert on the Ribbon and then click the Insert Object button (Insert tab | Text group) to display the Insert Object dialog box (Figure 10–47).

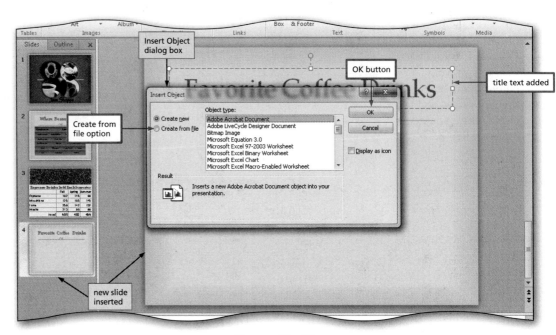

**Figure 10–47**

- Click 'Create from file' (Insert Object dialog box) to display the File text box.

- Click the Browse button, navigate to the PowerPoint Chapter 10 folder, and then click Coffee Drinks to select the Excel file name (Figure 10–48).

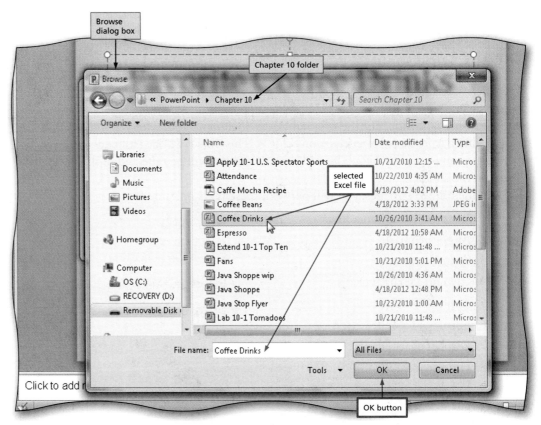

**Figure 10–48**

**③**

- Click the OK button (Browse dialog box) to display the File text box and then click the OK button (Insert Object dialog box) to insert an Excel chart into Slide 4.

- Display the Drawing Tools Format tab and then click the Shape Height box up arrow repeatedly to change the worksheet height to 5" (Figure 10–49).

**Q&A**

Why did the chart width change when I changed the height measurement?

The chart's width and height stay in proportion to each other, so when you change one dimension, the other dimension changes accordingly.

---

**Other Ways**

1. Right-click Excel chart, click Copy, exit Microsoft Excel, click Paste button arrow (Home tab | Clipboard group), click Use Destination Theme & Embed Excel Workbook

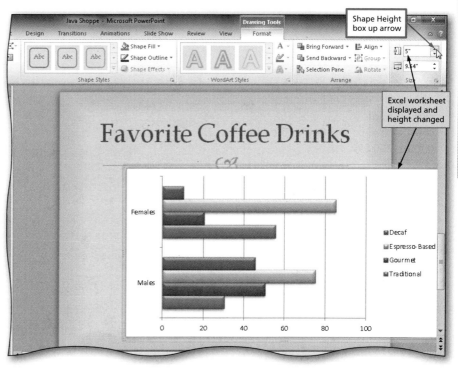

**Figure 10–49**

---

## To Align a Chart

You aligned the table on Slide 3 horizontally and vertically. You, likewise, want to align the chart on Slide 3 so that it is displayed in an appropriate location on the slide. Although you can drag the chart on the slide, you also can use PowerPoint commands to align the object horizontally in the left, center, or right areas of the slide, and vertically in the top, middle, or bottom of the slide. The following steps align the chart horizontally and vertically on Slide 4.

**①**

- With the Drawing Tools Format tab displaying, click the Align button (Drawing Tools Format tab | Arrange group) to display the Align menu (Figure 10–50).

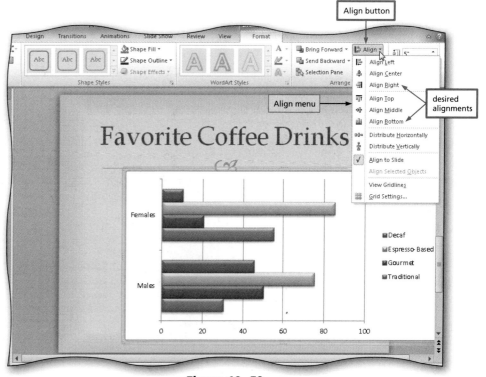

**Figure 10–50**

• Click Align Right on the Align menu to position the chart along the right edge of the slide.

• Click the Align button again to display the Align menu and then click Align Bottom to position the chart at the lower edge of the slide (Figure 10–51).

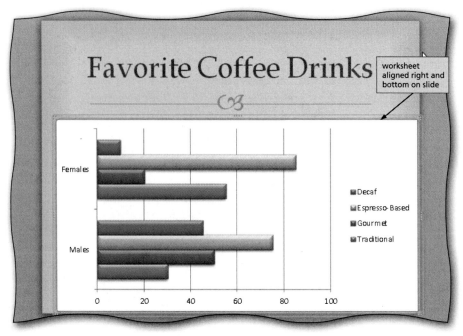

**Figure 10–51**

## To Switch Rows and Columns in a Chart

Excel created the chart on Slide 4 (Sheet 1 in the Excel file) based on the values in the worksheet on Sheet 2 of the Excel file. The scale is based on the values in the **y-axis**, which also is called the **vertical axis** or **value axis**. The titles along the **x-axis**, also referred to as the **horizontal axis** or **category axis**, are derived from the top row of the Slide 2 worksheet and are displayed above the bottom edge of the chart. Each bar in the chart has a specific color to represent one of the four coffee drinks preferred by males and females. You can switch the data in the chart so that a male and female bar is displayed for each of the four coffee drinks. The following steps switch the rows and columns in the chart.

• Double-click the Slide 4 chart to start the Microsoft Excel program and open the document.

• Click the plot area to select it and then display the Chart Tools Design tab on the Ribbon (Figure 10–52).

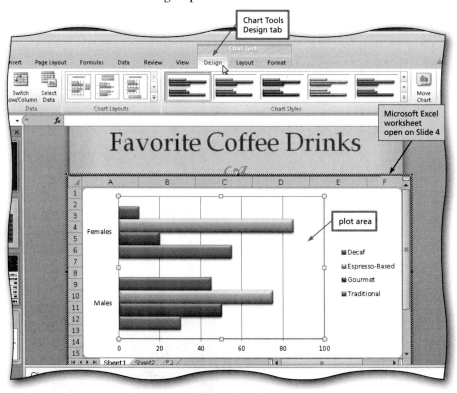

**Figure 10–52**

**2**

- Click the Switch Row/Column button (Chart Tools Design tab | Data group) to swap the data charted on the x-axis with the data on the y-axis (Figure 10–53).

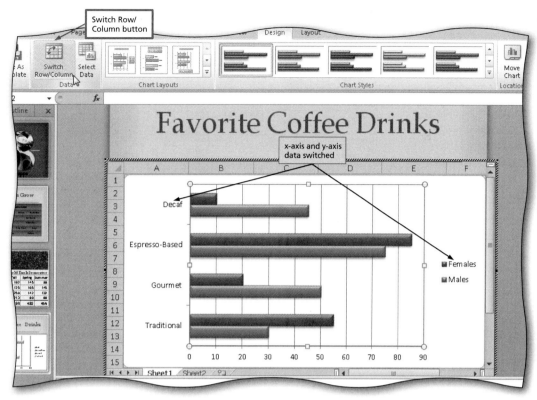

**Figure 10–53**

## To Change a Chart Type

The bar chart represents data horizontally for each of the four coffee drinks. You can change the chart appearance by selecting another type in the Insert Chart dialog box. The sample charts are divided into a variety of categories, including bar, column, and pie. The cylinder type that you want to use in the presentation is located in the Column area. The following steps change the chart to a Clustered Cylinder chart type.

**1**

- Click the Change Chart Type button (Chart Tools Design tab | Type group) to display the Change Chart Type dialog box (Figure 10–54).

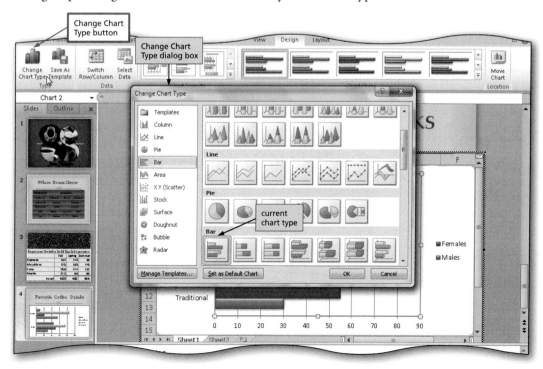

**Figure 10–54**

- Scroll up and then click the Clustered Cylinder chart type (first chart in second row) in the Column area to select this chart type (Figure 10–55).

**Q&A**

Is a preview available?

No live preview is available when using the Change Chart Type dialog box.

- Click the OK button (Change Chart Type dialog box) to change the chart in the selection rectangle to Clustered Cylinder.

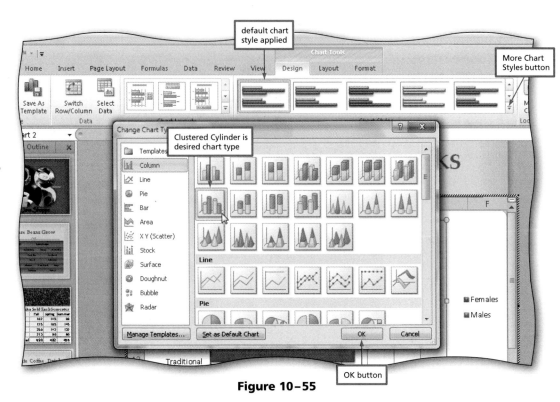

**Figure 10–55**

## To Apply a Quick Style to a Chart

You can modify the chart's appearance easily by selecting one of the 36 styles available in the Chart Styles gallery. These styles have a variety of colors and backgrounds and display in both 2-D and 3-D. The following steps apply a Quick Style to the chart.

- Click the More button in the Chart Styles gallery (Chart Tools Design tab | Chart Styles group) to expand the gallery (Figure 10–56).

- Click Style 34 in the Chart Styles gallery (second style in fifth row) to apply the chart style to the chart.

**Q&A**

Does the Chart Styles gallery have a live preview feature?

No. This feature is not available.

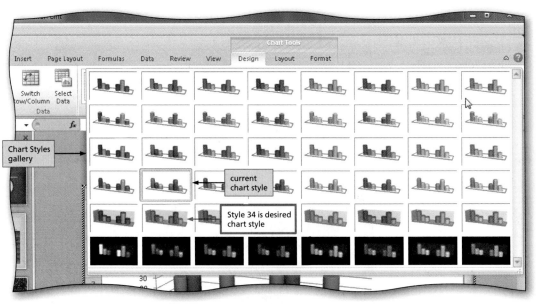

**Figure 10–56**

## To Format a Chart Legend

The legend on the right side of the chart identifies the colors assigned to each of the cylinders. You can modify the default legend in a variety of ways, including moving its location, changing the fill and outline, adding an effect, and changing the font. The following steps format the legend.

**1**
- Display the Chart Tools Layout tab and then click the Legend button (Chart Tools Layout tab | Labels group) to display the Legend menu (Figure 10–57).

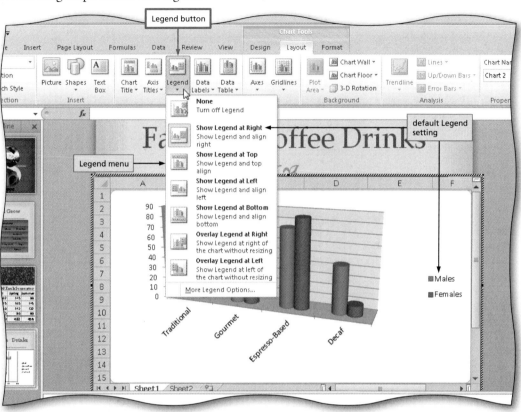

**Figure 10–57**

**2**
- Click Show Legend at Left to display the legend on the left side of the selection rectangle.

**Q&A** Is a live preview available?

No, this feature is not offered.

- Click the Legend button again to display the Legend menu (Figure 10–58).

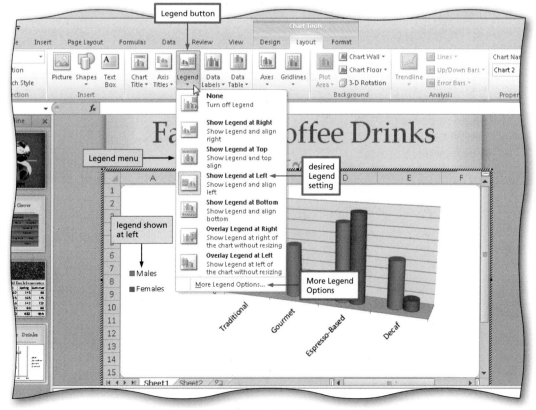

**Figure 10–58**

**3**

- Click More Legend Options to display the Format Legend dialog box.

- Click Border Color in the left panel to display the Border Color pane, click Solid line to expand the line options, and then click the Color button to display the Color gallery (Figure 10–59).

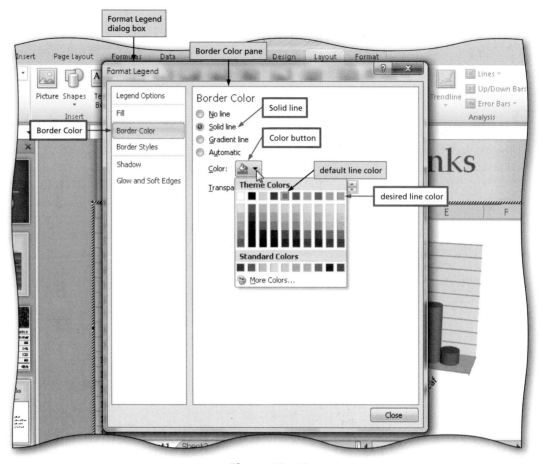

**Figure 10–59**

**4**

- Click Orange, Accent 6 (rightmost color in first Theme Colors row) to change the line color.

- Click Border Styles in the left panel to display the Border Styles pane and then click the Width box up arrow repeatedly until 2 pt is displayed in the Width box (Figure 10–60).

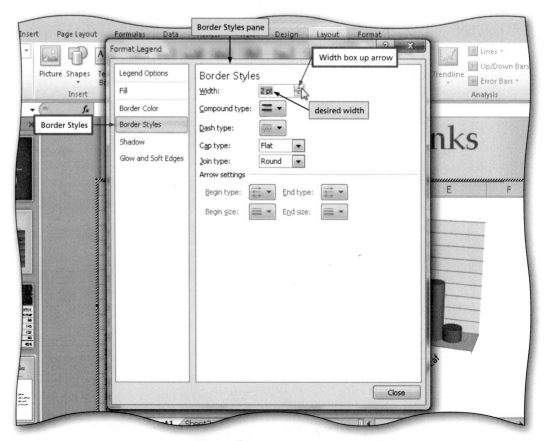

**Figure 10–60**

**5**

- Click Glow and Soft Edges in the left pane to display the Glow and Soft Edges pane and then click the Presets button in the Glow area to display the Glow gallery (Figure 10–61).

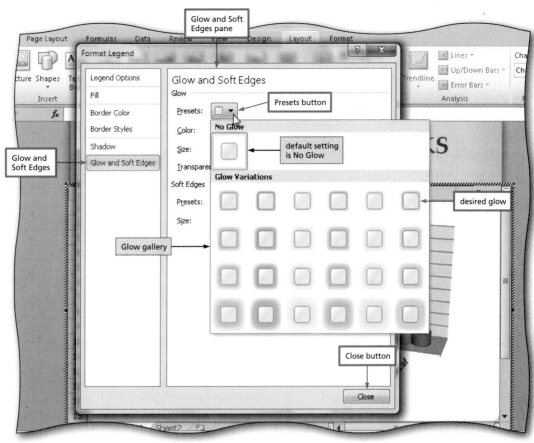

**Figure 10–61**

**6**

- Click Orange, 5 pt glow, Accent color 6 (last variation in first row) to select this Glow preset.
- Click the Close button (Format Legend dialog box) to apply the formatting changes to the legend.

**7**

- Drag the legend to the upper-left corner of the selection rectangle and then drag the lower sizing handle downward to increase the size of the legend, as shown in Figure 10–62.

**Other Ways**

1. Right-click legend, click Format Legend on shortcut menu

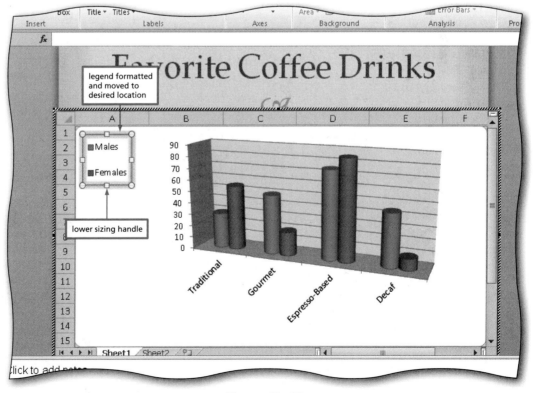

**Figure 10–62**

## To Display Chart Labels

To increase readability, you can display the exact value of each cylinder in the chart. These values are linked to the values in the worksheet that was used to create the original chart. They update automatically when you change the data in the worksheet cells. If desired, you can change the labels' appearance and style. The following steps display the chart labels.

- Click the Data Labels button (Chart Tools Layout tab | Labels group) to display the Data Labels menu (Figure 10–63).

- Click Show to turn on the data labels above each chart cylinder.

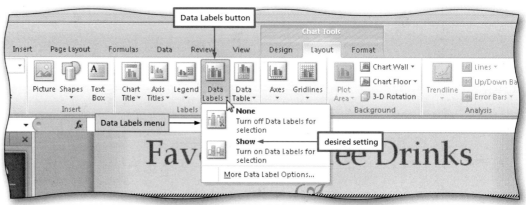

**Figure 10–63**

## To Hide a Chart Axis

The chart labels you just added display the totals for male and female coffee drinkers' preferences. The same information is displayed in the vertical axis on the left side of the chart. To eliminate this duplication, you can choose not to display the y-axis. The following steps hide a chart axis.

- Click the Axes button (Chart Tools Layout tab | Axes group) to display the Axes menu, point to Primary Vertical Axis on the Axis menu, and then point to None on the Primary Vertical Axis menu (Figure 10–64).

- Click None to hide the vertical axis on the left side of the chart.

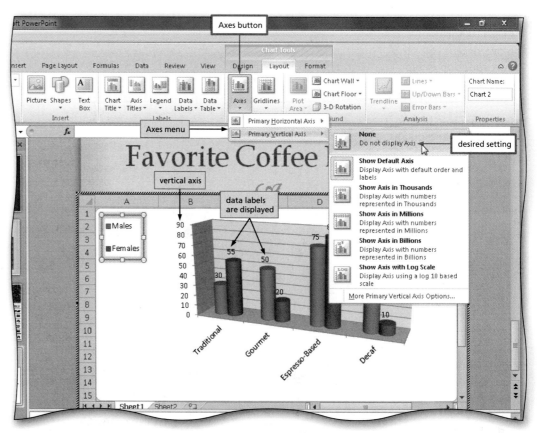

**Figure 10–64**

## To Display Chart Gridlines

Horizontal and vertical gridlines can display on a chart to help viewers identify the values represented by each bar. The gridlines align with the horizontal and vertical axes and extend across the plot area from left to right or top to bottom. The following steps display both horizontal and vertical gridlines.

**1**

• Click the Gridlines button (Chart Tools Layout tab | Axes group) to display the Gridlines menu, point to Primary Horizontal Gridlines on the Gridlines menu, and then point to Major & Minor Gridlines on the Primary Horizontal Gridlines menu (Figure 10–65).

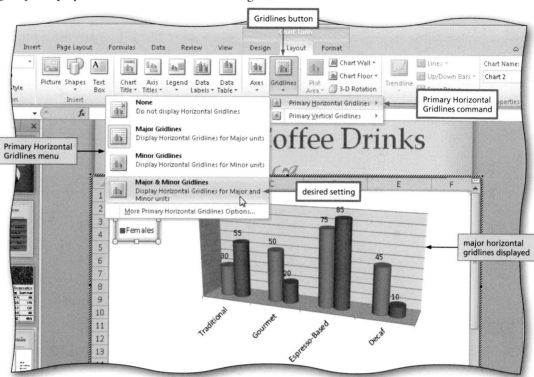

**Figure 10–65**

**2**

• Click Major & Minor Gridlines to display both types of gridline units on the left and rear sides of the chart.

• Click the Gridlines button again to display the Gridlines menu, point to Primary Vertical Gridlines on the Gridlines menu, and then point to Major Gridlines on the Primary Vertical Gridlines menu (Figure 10–66).

**3**

• Click Major Gridlines to display vertical gridline units on the rear side of the chart.

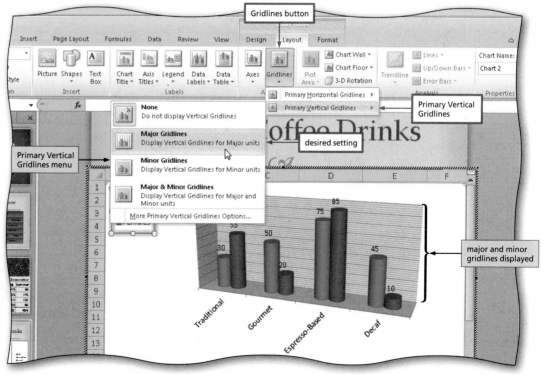

**Figure 10–66**

 How would I hide gridlines if I did not want them to display?

Click the Gridlines button, point to either Primary Horizontal Gridlines or Primary Vertical Gridlines, and then click None.

## To Format a Chart Background

The area behind the chart cylinders is called the **chart wall**, and the area below the cylinders is called the **chart floor**. Both of these chart elements are considered part of the chart background. You can modify the wall and floor in a variety of ways, including clearing all background elements. The following steps clear the chart wall and chart floor fill.

**1**

- Click the Chart Wall button (Chart Tools Layout tab | Background group) to display the Chart Wall menu (Figure 10–67).

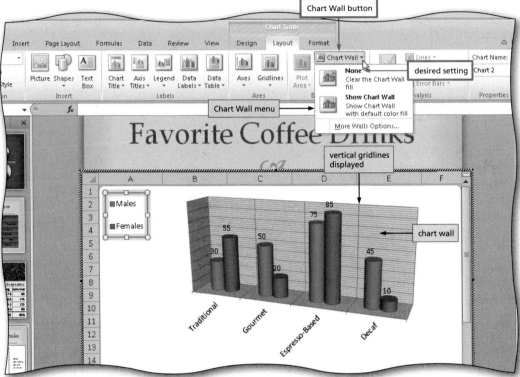

**Figure 10–67**

**2**

- Click None on the Chart Wall menu to clear the chart wall fill.

- Click the Chart Floor button (Chart Tools Layout tab | Background group) to display the Chart Floor menu (Figure 10–68).

**3**

- Click None on the Chart Floor menu to clear the chart floor fill.

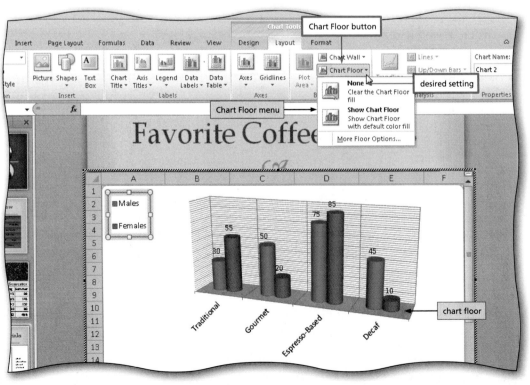

**Figure 10–68**

## To Edit Data in a Chart

The data in Sheet 2 of the worksheet is used to create the chart on Slide 1. If you edit this data, the corresponding cylinders in the chart change height to reflect new numbers. The chart is an embedded object, so when you double-click this object to open it, Microsoft Excel opens within PowerPoint. When you modify the data and close the worksheet, the chart will reflect the changes. The original file stored on your Data Disk for Students, however, will not change. The following steps edit three cells in the worksheet.

**1**

- Click the Sheet 2 tab to display the worksheet.

- Click the Traditional cell for Males to make cell B2 the active cell (Figure 10–69).

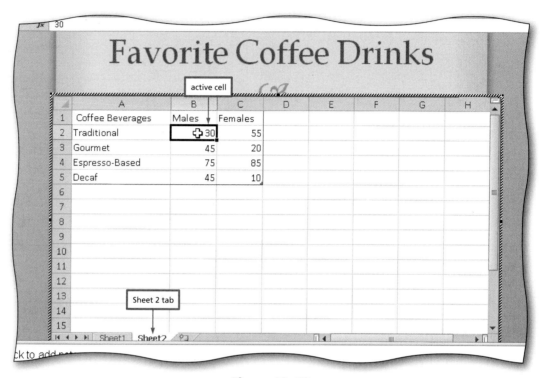

**Figure 10–69**

**2**

- Type 35 as the replacement number and then press the DOWN ARROW key to make cell B3 (Males Gourmet) the active cell.

- Type 50 as the replacement number and then press the RIGHT ARROW key to make cell C3 (Females Gourmet) the active cell.

- Type 25 as the replacement number (Figure 10–70).

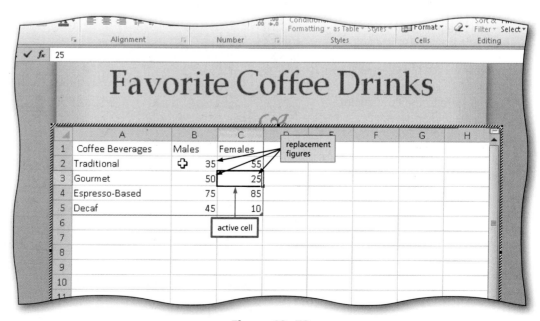

**Figure 10–70**

- Click the Sheet 1 tab to display the updated chart (Figure 10–71).

- Click outside the selection rectangle to close Microsoft Excel and display the formatted and edited chart on Slide 4.

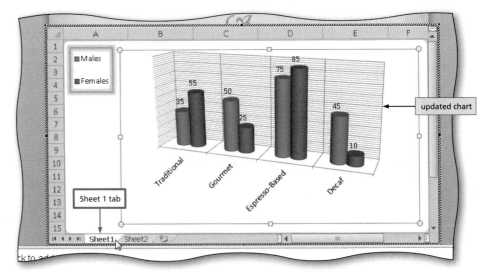

**Figure 10–71**

## To Add a Hyperlink to a Chart

A hyperlink connects one element on a slide to another slide, presentation, picture, file, Web page, or e-mail address. Presenters use hyperlinks to display these elements to an audience. In this Java Shoppe presentation, you will create a hyperlink from the chart on Slide 4 to an Adobe Acrobat PDF document giving the recipe for a specific coffee drink. When you click the chart during a slide show, Adobe Acrobat starts and then opens this PDF. The following steps hyperlink the chart to an Adobe Acrobat document.

- With the table selected, display the Insert tab and then click the Hyperlink button (Insert tab | Links group) to display the Insert Hyperlink dialog box.

- If necessary, click the Existing File or Web Page button in the Link to area.

- If necessary, click the Current Folder button in the Look in area and then navigate to the PowerPoint Chapter 10 folder.

- Click Caffe Mocha Recipe to select this file as the hyperlink (Figure 10–72).

- Click the OK button (Insert Hyperlink dialog box) to insert the hyperlink.

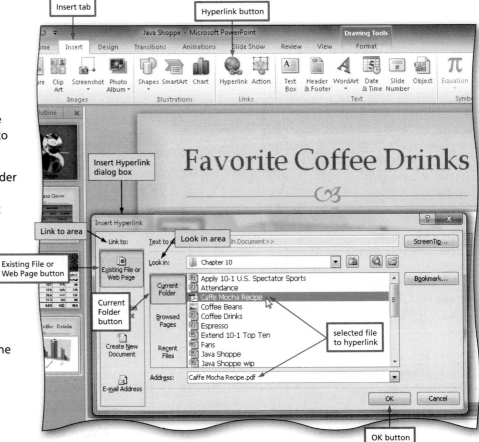

**Figure 10–72**

## To Add a Transition between Slides

A final enhancement you will make in this presentation is to apply a transition, change the effect option, and change the transition speed. The following steps apply this transition to the presentation.

**1** Apply the Flip transition in the Exciting category to all slides.

**2** Change the effect option to Left.

**3** Change the transition speed from 1.20 to 3.00 seconds.

## To Change Document Properties

Before saving the presentation again, you want to add your name, class name, and some keywords as document properties. The following steps use the Document Information Panel to change document properties.

**1** Display the Document Information Panel and then type your name as the Author property.

**2** Type your course and section in the Subject property.

**3** Type `coffee drinks, java shoppe, coffee beans` as the Keywords property.

**4** Close the Document Information Panel.

**BTW**

**Quick Reference**
For a table that lists how to complete the tasks covered in this book using the mouse, Ribbon, shortcut menu, and keyboard, see the Quick Reference Summary at the back of this book, or visit the PowerPoint 2010 Quick Reference Web page (scsite.com/ppt2010/qr).

## To Run, Print, Save, and Quit PowerPoint

The presentation now is complete. You should run the presentation, view the hyperlinked file, print the slides, save the presentation, and then quit PowerPoint.

**1** Run the Java Shoppe presentation. When Slide 4 is displayed, click the chart to display the Caffe Mocha Recipe document as the hyperlinked file.

**2** Click the Close button in the upper-right corner of the Adobe Acrobat window to quit the program and return to Slide 4. End the slide show.

**3** Print the Java Shoppe presentation as a handout with two slides per page (Figure 10–73 on the next page).

**4** Save the Java Shoppe presentation again with the same file name.

**5** Quit PowerPoint, closing all open documents.

**BTW**

**Certification**
The Microsoft Office Specialist (MOS) program provides an opportunity for you to obtain a valuable industry credential — proof that you have the PowerPoint 2010 skills required by employers. For more information, visit the PowerPoint 2010 Certification Web page (scsite.com/ppt2010/cert).

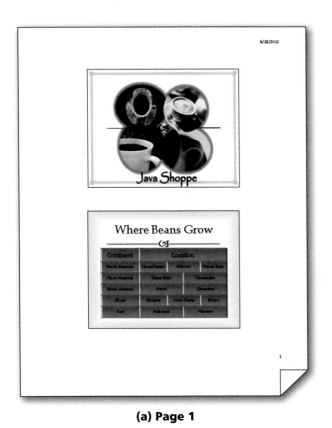

**(a) Page 1**

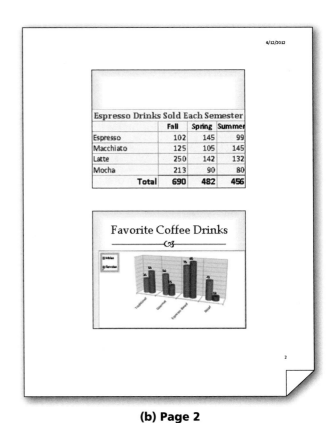

**(b) Page 2**

**Figure 10–73**

## Chapter Summary

In this chapter you have learned how to develop a presentation using information you inserted from a Microsoft Word flyer and Microsoft Excel table and chart. These documents were either embedded or linked, and you edited each of them to update words or numbers. You also drew a table and enhanced this object by changing the chart type, background, gridlines, and legend. Finally, you hyperlinked an Adobe Acrobat file to the chart. The items listed below include all the new PowerPoint skills you have learned in this chapter.

1. Insert a File with Graphics and Text (PPT 598)
2. Edit an Embedded File (PPT 601)
3. Draw a Table (PPT 603)
4. Draw Table Rows (PPT 604)
5. Draw Table Columns (PPT 606)
6. Erase a Table Line (PPT 608)
7. Split a Table Column and Row (PPT 610)
8. Add Shading to a Table (PPT 612)
9. Add a Gradient Fill to a Table (PPT 613)
10. Add a Cell Bevel (PPT 614)
11. Distribute Table Rows (PPT 614)
12. Resize Table Columns and Rows (PPT 615)
13. Center the Table (PPT 617)
14. Insert a Linked Excel Worksheet (PPT 618)
15. Align a Worksheet (PPT 621)
16. Edit a Linked Worksheet (PPT 622)
17. Insert a Chart from a File (PPT 624)
18. Align a Chart (PPT 625)
19. Switch Rows and Columns in a Chart (PPT 626)
20. Change a Chart Type (PPT 627)
21. Apply a Quick Style to a Chart (PPT 628)
22. Format a Chart Legend (PPT 629)
23. Display Chart Labels (PPT 632)
24. Hide a Chart Axis (PPT 632)
25. Display Chart Gridlines (PPT 633)
26. Format a Chart Background (PPT 634)
27. Edit Data in a Chart (PPT 635)
28. Add a Hyperlink to a Chart (PPT 636)

If you have a SAM 2010 user profile, your instructor may have assigned an autogradable version of this assignment. If so, log into the SAM 2010 Web site at www.cengage.com/sam2010 to download the instruction and start files.

# Learn It Online

Test your knowledge of chapter content and key terms.

*Instructions:*   To complete the Learn It Online exercises, start your browser, click the Address bar, and then enter the Web address **scsite.com/ppt2010/learn**. When the Office 2010 Learn It Online page is displayed, click the link for the exercise you want to complete and then read the instructions.

### Chapter Reinforcement TF, MC, and SA
A series of true/false, multiple choice, and short answer questions that test your knowledge of the chapter content.

### Flash Cards
An interactive learning environment where you identify chapter key terms associated with displayed definitions.

### Practice Test
A series of multiple choice questions that test your knowledge of chapter content and key terms.

### Who Wants To Be a Computer Genius?
An interactive game that challenges your knowledge of chapter content in the style of a television quiz show.

### Wheel of Terms
An interactive game that challenges your knowledge of chapter key terms in the style of the television show *Wheel of Fortune*.

### Crossword Puzzle Challenge
A crossword puzzle that challenges your knowledge of key terms presented in the chapter.

# Apply Your Knowledge

Reinforce the skills and apply the concepts you learned in this chapter.

### Embedding and Editing an Excel Chart, and Inserting Graphics from a Word Document

*Note:*   To complete this assignment, you will be required to use the Data Files for Students. See the inside back cover of this book for instructions on downloading the Data Files for Students, or contact your instructor for information about accessing the required files.

*Instructions:*   Start PowerPoint. Open the presentation, Apply 10-1 U.S. Spectator Sports, located on the Data Files for Students.

The slides in this presentation provide data about the total attendance for popular U.S. spectator sports. The document you open is a partially formatted presentation. You will insert an Excel chart, edit the chart, and insert a graphic from a Word document so the slides look like the ones shown in Figure 10–74 on the next page.

*Perform the following tasks:*
1. You will not make any changes to Slide 1 (Figure 10–74b). Open the Attendance Excel workbook (Figure 10–74a), located on the Data Files for Students. Copy the Total Attendance bar chart to the Clipboard.
2. On Slide 2, delete the title placeholder and then paste the bar chart into the content placeholder using the Use Destination Theme & Embed Workbook pasting option. Close the Excel workbook.
3. Using the Chart Tools Design tab, apply Chart Style 26 to the chart. Using the Chart Tools Format tab, apply the Gradient fill – Olive Green, Accent 4, Reflection WordArt Style to the chart title. Resize the chart and center it on the slide, as shown in Figure 10–74c.

*Continued >*

STUDENT ASSIGNMENTS

**Apply Your Knowledge** *continued*

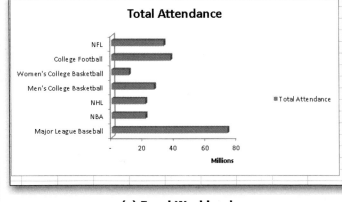

(a) Excel Workbook

(b) Slide 1

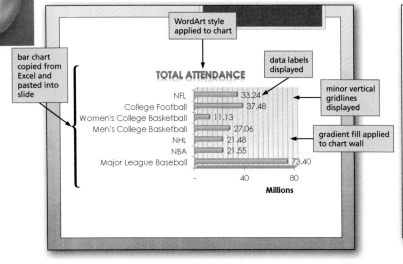

(c) Slide 2

(d) Fans Word Document

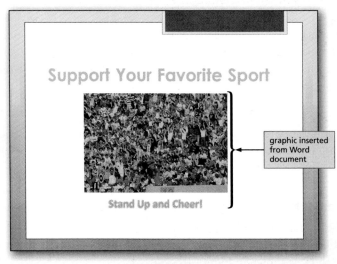

(e) Slide 3

**Figure 10–74**

4. Using the Chart Tools Layout tab, change the Legend label option to None for the chart. For the Primary Vertical Gridlines, display the minor gridlines. Display the data labels for the chart. Apply the Linear Gradient fill to the chart wall.

5. On Slide 3, use the Create from file option of the Insert Object dialog box to insert a graphic from the Fans Word document (Figure 10–74d). Resize the graphic and move it to the location shown in Figure 10–74e.

6. Apply the Cube transition in the Exciting group to all slides and then change the duration to 02.50 seconds.

7. Change the document properties, as specified by your instructor. Save the presentation using the file name, Apply 10-1 U.S. Spectator Sports Attendance. Submit the revised document in the format specified by your instructor.

## Extend Your Knowledge

Extend the skills you learned in this chapter and experiment with new skills. You may need to use Help to complete the assignment.

### Drawing and Formatting a Table

*Note:* To complete this assignment, you will be required to use the Data Files for Students. See the inside back cover of this book for instructions on downloading the Data Files for Students, or contact your instructor for information about accessing the required files.

*Instructions:* Start PowerPoint. Open the presentation, Extend 10-1 Top Ten, located on the Data Files for Students. You will draw and format a table, copy the table to another slide, and complete the tables, as shown in Figure 10–75.

*Perform the following tasks:*

1. You will not make any changes to Slide 1 (Figure 10–75a).

**(a) Slide 1**

**Figure 10–75**

*Continued >*

**Extend Your Knowledge** *continued*

2. Display Slide 2 and then click the Table button. Click the Draw Table button and then draw the shape of the table shown in Figure 10–75b. Change the line weight to 3 pt and the pen color to Orange, Accent 2 (Table Tools Design tab | Draw Borders group). Click the Draw Table button and then click the four main borders of the table to apply the new border settings. (*Hint:* Click each border on its inside edge.) Add four columns and six rows, similar to those shown in Figure 10–75b. If necessary, adjust the size of column 1 to look like Figure 10–75b. Select columns 2, 3, and 4, and then click Distribute Columns (Table Tools Layout tab | Cell Size group). Select all the rows and then click Distribute Rows.

3. Apply an Ice Blue, Background 2 Shading to all the cells, as shown in Figure 10–75b.

4. On Slide 2, use Table 10–1 to enter the headings and data for the top five cities. Align the text of all cells to center vertically. Center the first row and then change the font size to 20 and the font color to White. Center the first column and then change the font size to 20 and the font color to White. Center the last column. Change the font for all cells to Calibri. For all cells except the first row and first column, center the text, and bold the text in the cells.

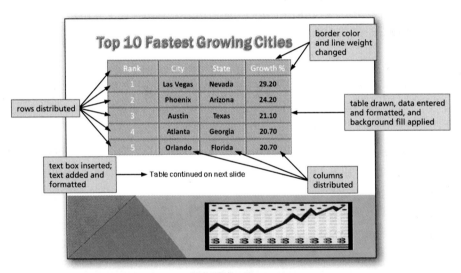

**(b) Slide 2**

**Figure 10–75 (Continued)**

| Table 10–1 Top 10 Fastest Growing Cities | | | |
|---|---|---|---|
| **Rank** | **City** | **State** | **Growth %** |
| 1 | Las Vegas | Nevada | 29.20 |
| 2 | Phoenix | Arizona | 24.20 |
| 3 | Austin | Texas | 21.10 |
| 4 | Atlanta | Georgia | 20.70 |
| 5 | Orlando | Florida | 20.70 |
| 6 | Charlotte | North Carolina | 19.00 |
| 7 | Houston | Texas | 17.50 |
| 8 | Dallas | Texas | 16.30 |
| 9 | Sacramento | California | 15.00 |
| 10 | Jacksonville | Florida | 13.80 |

5. Insert a text box below the table and type `Table continued on next slide` in the box. Center the text, bold it, and then move the text box to the location shown in Figure 10–75b. Copy the table and the text box from Slide 2 to Slide 3.

6. On Slide 3, replace the data in the table with the bottom five cities' data shown in Table 10–1. If necessary, adjust size of columns so the table appears as shown. Replace the text in the text box with `Table continued from previous slide` and move the text box above the table, as shown in Figure 10–75c.

7. Change the transition from Push to Clock in the Exciting area and change the duration to 03:00 seconds.

8. Change the document properties, as specified by your instructor. Save the presentation using the file name, Extend 10-1 Top Ten U.S. Cities.

9. Submit the revised document in the format specified by your instructor.

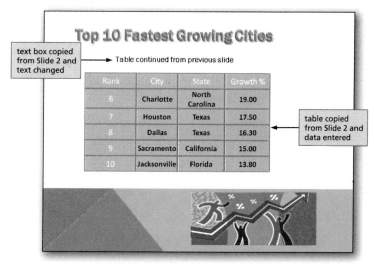

**(c) Slide 3**

**Figure 10–75 (Continued)**

# Make It Right

Analyze a presentation and correct all errors and/or improve the design.

### Changing a Chart and Editing a Table

*Note:* To complete this assignment, you will be required to use the Data Files for Students. See the inside back cover of this book for instructions on downloading the Data Files for Students, or contact your instructor for information about accessing the required files.

*Instructions:* Start PowerPoint. Open the presentation, Make It Right 10-1 U.S. Longest Rivers, located on the Data Files for Students.

Correct the formatting problems and errors in the presentation while keeping in mind the guidelines presented in this chapter.

*Continued >*

**Make It Right** *continued*

*Perform the following tasks:*

1. You will not make any changes to Slide 1 (Figure 10–76a). On Slide 2 (Figure 10–76b), select the second column. Split the column into two columns using the Split Cells button. Select rows 2–10 in column 2. Using the Format Painter, copy the formatting to rows 2–10 in column 3. Enter the data from Table 10–2 in the second column. If necessary, adjust the size of the table. Distribute the columns so that each column has the same width. Add an Offset Diagonal Top Left shadow effect to the table. *Hint:* Click the Effects button (Table Tools Design tab | Table Styles group). Change the size of the Blur shadow to 7 pt.

**(a) Slide 1**

**Figure 10–76**

| Table 10–2 Longest Rivers Data |
|---|
| **Runs Along** |
| 10 states |
| 5 states |
| 1 state |
| 3 states |
| 2 states |
| 3 states |
| 2 states |
| 2 states |
| 3 states |
| 5 states |

2. On Slide 3 (Figure 10–76c), change the chart type of the line chart to the Clustered Horizontal Cylinder bar chart. Switch the row and column data for the chart. Apply the Style 34 chart style to the chart. Select the chart legend, click the Shape Outline button arrow, and then apply a light blue (seventh in Standard Colors row) border around the legend.

3. For all slides, apply the Ripple transition, change the Effect Option to From Bottom-Left, and then change the duration to 02:50 seconds.

4. Change the document properties, as specified by your instructor. Save the presentation using the file name, Make It Right 10-1 U.S. Longest Rivers in Miles.

5. Submit the revised document in the format specified by your instructor.

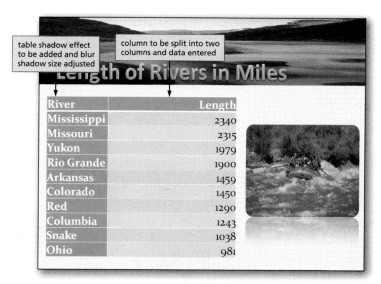

**(b) Slide 2**

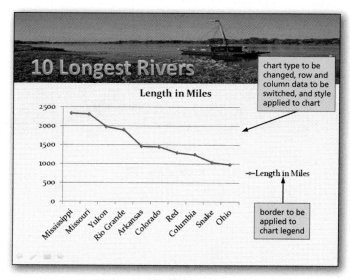

**(c) Slide 3**

**Figure 10–76 (Continued)**

## In the Lab

Design and/or create a presentation using the guidelines, concepts, and skills presented in this chapter. Labs 1, 2, and 3 are listed in order of increasing difficulty.

### Lab 1: Linking a Chart from a File, Embedding a File, and Editing an Embedded File

*Note:* To complete this assignment, you will be required to use the Data Files for Students. See the inside back cover of this book for instructions on downloading the Data Files for Students or contact your instructor for information about accessing the required files.

*Problem:* You are doing a report on tornadoes for a class project. You have acquired data on the top five states with the most tornadoes as well as the top five states with the most severe tornadoes. Using this data, you create the slides shown in Figure 10–77.

*Perform the following tasks:*
1. Open the presentation, Lab 10-1 Tornadoes, located on the Data Files for Students. You will not make any changes to Slide 1 (Figure 10–77a).

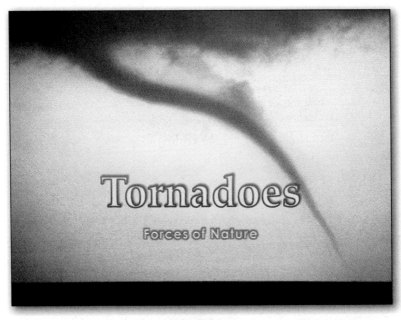

**(a) Slide 1**

**Figure 10–77**

2. Open the Severe Tornadoes Excel workbook located on the Data Files for Students (Figure 10–77b). Copy the chart to the Clipboard. On Slide 2 (Figure 10–77c), select the content placeholder and then paste the chart, keeping the source formatting and linking it. In the Severe Tornadoes Excel workbook, change the average number of storms for Oklahoma to **17.** Save and close the Excel workbook. If necessary, adjust the size of the chart and move it to the location shown in Figure 10–77c.

3. Select the chart title on Slide 2. Click the Hyperlink button (Insert tab | Links group), enter the following URL as the address, and then click the OK button: `http://www.nssl.noaa` `.gov/edu/safety/tornadoguide.html`

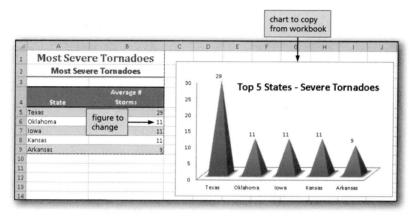

**(b) Severe Tornadoes Excel Workbook**

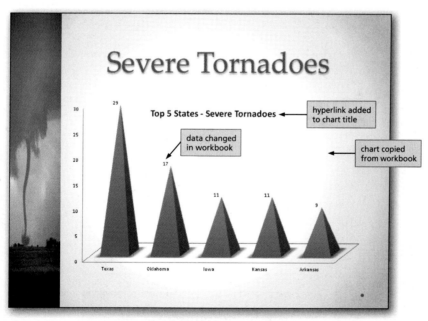

**(c) Slide 2**

**Figure 10–77 (Continued)**

*Continued >*

**In the Lab** *continued*

4. On Slide 3, select the content placeholder and then embed the Tornadoes Excel workbook (Figure 10–77d), located on the Data Files for Students. Edit the Violent Storms column in the embedded file by entering **29** for Texas, **7** for Oklahoma, **17** for Florida, **11** for Kansas, and **7** for Nebraska, then click outside the worksheet (Figure 10–77e).

5. Apply the Vortex transition and change the duration to 03:00 seconds for all slides.

6. Change the document properties, as specified by your instructor. Save the presentation using the file name, Lab 10-1 Tornadoes – Forces of Nature.

7. Submit the revised document in the format specified by your instructor.

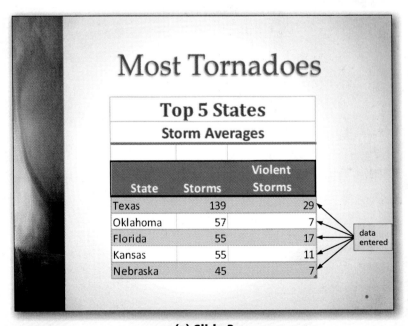

**(d) Tornadoes Excel Workbook**

**(e) Slide 3**

**Figure 10–77 (Continued)**

## In the Lab

### Lab 2: Linking and Editing a File, Changing a Chart Type, and Inserting a Graphic from a File

*Note:*  To complete this assignment, you will be required to use the Data Files for Students. See the inside back cover of this book for instructions on downloading the Data Files for Students or contact your instructor for information about accessing the required files.

*Problem:*  Sports have been a part of society since at least 4000 BC and are played throughout the world. You have gathered data about 10 popular sports in the United States for males and females who are seven years of age and older. You decide to create a presentation to display the results you have found. You create the slides shown in Figure 10–78 using files located on the Data Files for Students.

*Perform the following tasks:*
1. Open the presentation, Lab 10-2 U.S. Sports, located on the Data Files for Students. You will not make any changes to Slide 1 (Figure 10–78a).
2. On Slide 2, select the content placeholder and then insert the Excel workbook (Figure 10–78b on the next page) by linking to the Popular Sports workbook, located on the Data Files for Students.

**(a) Slide 1**

**Figure 10–78**

*Continued >*

**In the Lab** *continued*

3. Edit the Popular Sports workbook. Change the walking female percentage to **38%**. Change the bicycling male percentage to **25%**. Change the golfing male percentage to **18%**. Save and close the workbook. The percentages in the table should now match those shown in Figure 10–78c. If they do not match, right-click the table and then click Update Link on the shortcut menu. If necessary, adjust the size of the table and move it to the location shown in Figure 10–78c.

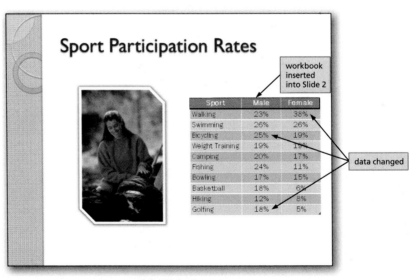

(b) **Popular Sports Excel Workbook**

(c) **Slide 2**

**Figure 10–78 (Continued)**

4. On Slide 3, change the chart type of the column chart to Clustered Bar in 3-D. Change the chart layout to Layout 7. Show Major horizontal and, if necessary, Major & Minor vertical gridlines. Change the vertical axis title to `Sport Activity` and the horizontal axis title to `Participation Rate`. Put a black border around the legend. The chart should appear as shown in Figure 10–78d.

5. On Slide 4, select the content placeholder and insert the graphic from the Reasons Word document. If necessary, adjust the size of the graphic and move it to the location shown in Figure 10–78e.

6. Apply the Shape transition and change the duration to 02.25 seconds for all slides.

7. Change the document properties, as specified by your instructor. Save the presentation using the file name, Lab 10-2 Most Popular U.S. Sports Activities.

8. Submit the revised document in the format specified by your instructor.

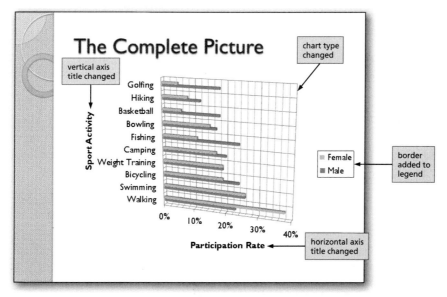

**(d) Slide 3**

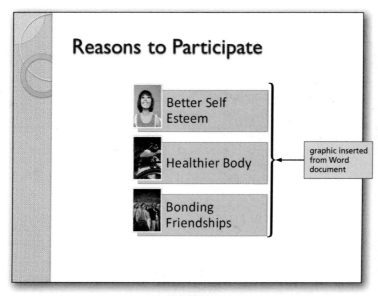

**(e) Slide 4**

**Figure 10–78 (Continued)**

## In the Lab

### Lab 3: Drawing and Formatting a Table, Inserting and Formatting a Bar Chart, and Inserting an Excel Spreadsheet

*Note:* To complete this assignment, you will be required to use the Data Files for Students. See the inside back cover of this book for instructions on downloading the Data Files for Students or contact your instructor for information about accessing the required files.

*Problem:* As part of your work-study program for an aquatic park, you are tasked with creating a presentation about the world's oceans and seas. You have collected data on the relative sizes of the oceans and seas and will use them in your presentation. You create the presentation shown in Figure 10–79.

*Perform the following tasks:*

1. Open the presentation, Lab 10-3 Oceans, located on the Data Files for Students. You will not make any changes to Slide 1 (Figure 10–79a).

2. On Slide 2 (Figure 10–79b), delete the content placeholder using the Cut button and then draw a table that has two columns and 10 rows. Select all the rows and then distribute the rows (Table Tools Layout tab | Cell Size group). Enter the data for rows 2–10, using the data from the first nine rows of Table 10–3. Right-align the text in the second column. Erase the divider between the cells in the first row. Enter **Area in Square Miles** in the first row, center this text, bold it, and then designate it as the header row. Apply the Light Style 2 - Accent 1 table style to the table. If necessary, adjust the size of the table, as shown in Figure 10–79b.

3. Insert a text box below the table and then type **Continued on next slide** in the box. Center the text and then move the text box to the location shown.

**(a) Slide 1**

**Figure 10–79**

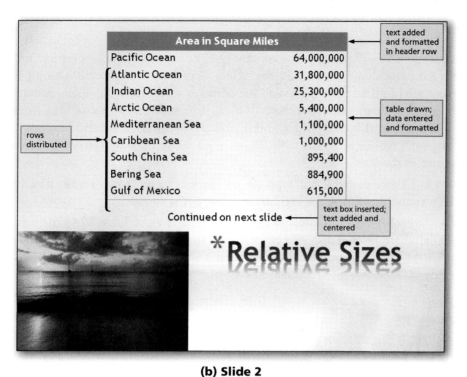

**(b) Slide 2**

**Figure 10–79 (Continued)**

| Table 10–3 Table Data for Slides 2 and 3 | |
|---|---|
| Pacific Ocean | 64,000,000 |
| Atlantic Ocean | 31,800,000 |
| Indian Ocean | 25,300,000 |
| Arctic Ocean | 5,400,000 |
| Mediterranean Sea | 1,100,000 |
| Caribbean Sea | 1,000,000 |
| South China Sea | 895,400 |
| Bering Sea | 884,900 |
| Gulf of Mexico | 615,000 |
| Okhotsk Sea | 613,800 |
| East China Sea | 482,300 |
| Hudson Bay | 475,800 |
| Japan Sea | 389,100 |
| Andaman Sea | 308,100 |
| North Sea | 222,100 |
| Red Sea | 169,100 |
| Baltic Sea | 163,000 |

*Continued >*

**In the Lab** *continued*

4. On Slide 3 (Figure 10–79c), delete the content placeholder using the Cut button and then draw a table that has two columns and nine rows. Select all the rows, and click Distribute Rows (Table Tools Layout tab | Cell Size group). Using the remaining data from Table 10–3, enter the data for rows 2–9. Erase the divider between the cells in the first row. Enter `Area in Square Miles` in the first row, center this text, bold it, and then designate it as the header row. Apply the Light Style 2 – Accent 1 table style to the table. Right-align the second column. Position and size the table as shown in the figure.

5. Insert a text box above the table and type `Continued from previous slide` in the box. Center the text and then move the text box to the location shown.

6. On Slide 4 (Figure 10–79d), use the data in the first five rows of Table 10–3 to create a Clustered Bar in 3-D bar chart. Do not display a chart title or legend. Display the major horizontal gridlines and remove the primary vertical axis title. Apply the Style 27 chart style to the chart. Apply the Gradient Fill – Green, Accent 4, Reflection WordArt Style to the vertical axis labels.

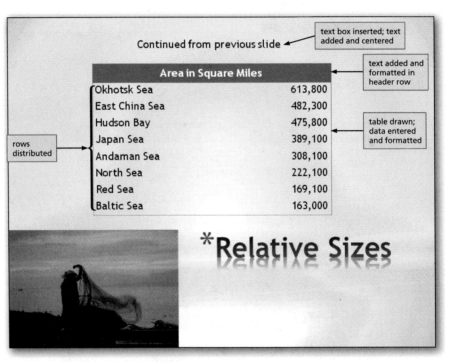

**(c) Slide 3**

**Figure 10–79 (Continued)**

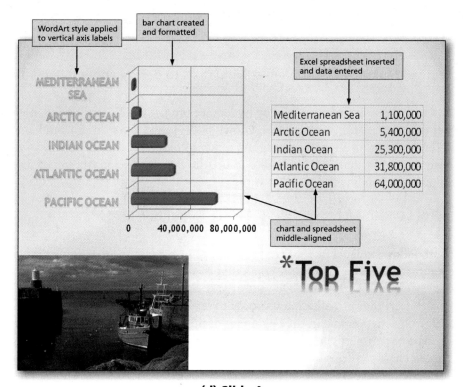

**(d) Slide 4**

**Figure 10–79 (Continued)**

7. Insert an Excel spreadsheet on Slide 4 and enter the five largest ocean names and square mileage data, as shown in the figure. Select the bar chart and spreadsheet and middle-align them on the slide as shown in the figure.

8. Apply the Doors transition and change the duration to 02.75 seconds for all slides.

9. Change the document properties, as specified by your instructor. Save the presentation using the file name, Lab 10-3 Oceans and Seas.

10. Submit the revised document in the format specified by your instructor.

# Cases and Places

Apply your creative thinking and problem-solving skills to design and implement a solution.

*Note:*   To complete these assignments, you may be required to use the Data Files for Students. See the inside back cover of this book for instructions on downloading the Data Files for Students, or contact your instructor for information about accessing the required files.

As you design the presentations, remember to use the 7 × 7 rule: a maximum of seven words on a line and a maximum of seven lines on one slide.

## 1: Designing and Creating a Presentation about Studying Abroad

**Academic**

While talking with fellow students in your study group, you have learned that some of them have chosen to study abroad. Researching online, you found that the most popular countries where U.S. students study are Mexico (7%), France (8%), Italy (9%), Spain (9%), and Great Britain (24%). You decide to create a PowerPoint presentation to present your findings at your next study group meeting. Apply at least three objectives found at the beginning of this chapter to develop the presentation, including using chart backgrounds and adding hyperlinks to chart elements. You can hyperlink the country labels in the chart to Web sites about each country. Use pictures and diagrams from Office.com if they are appropriate for this topic. Be sure to check spelling.

## 2: Designing and Creating a Presentation about Why People Travel

**Personal**

You enjoy traveling, and you have been curious about the purpose people have for traveling in general. You have researched and found that, according to surveys done by the U.S. Travel Data Center and Nation Travel Survey, the reasons reported for trips have been ranked in terms of millions of trips per year. Pleasure is responsible for 434 million trips, business or conventions for 220 million trips, and other reasons for 34 million trips. You decide to create a PowerPoint presentation to explain the reasons to your family members, who have been asking about why people travel. Apply at least three objectives found at the beginning of this chapter to develop the presentation, including drawing a table and arranging table columns and rows. You can also include a chart displaying the number of times you have traveled over the past five years (3, 7, 5, 9, and 6 trips, respectively). Use pictures and diagrams from Office.com if they are appropriate for this topic or use your personal digital pictures. Be sure to check spelling.

## 3: Designing and Creating a Presentation about Recycled Tires

**Professional**

You are employed as a customer service representative at a local tire store. Customers often ask you about recycling their old tires. You explain that instead of being taken to a landfill, more than 50 million worn tires each year are processed into tire crumb, which is a granulated product used to manufacture footwear, playground equipment, trash cans, and asphalt. To better explain the benefits of tire recycling, you will prepare a presentation that explains the uses of recycled rubber. Apply at least three objectives found at the beginning of this chapter to develop the presentation, and include a chart showing recycled tire components and a table with the countries that produce natural rubber. Use pictures from Office. com if they are appropriate for this topic or use your personal digital pictures. Be sure to check spelling.

# 11 | Organizing Slides and Creating a Photo Album

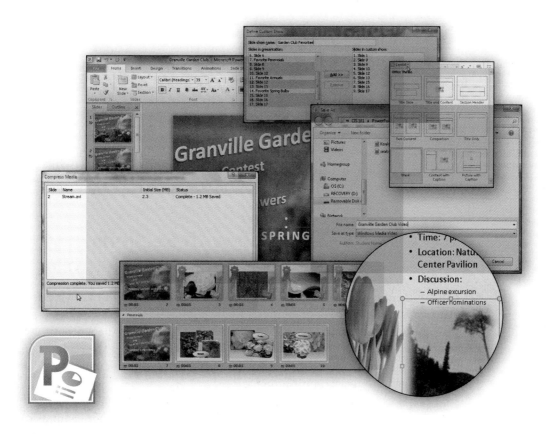

## Objectives

You will have mastered the material in this chapter when you can:

- Create a section break
- Rename a section
- Reorder a section
- Create a custom slide show
- Set up a custom size
- Create a photo album
- Reorder pictures in a photo album
- Adjust the quality of pictures in a photo album

- Add captions to pictures in a photo album
- Use the Research task pane to look up information
- Change slide orientation
- Copy and compress a video file
- E-mail a presentation
- Create a video from a presentation

# 11 | Organizing Slides and Creating a Photo Album

## Introduction

**BTW**

**Using Photographs**
The adage, "A picture is worth a thousand words," is relevant when PowerPoint slides are displayed to an audience. One picture can evoke emotions and create a connection between the speaker and the listeners. A carefully selected image with an engaging message conveys a message that your audience will remember long after the presentation has ended.

Sharing photographs and videos has become a part of our everyday lives. We often use digital cameras and visit online social media Web sites to share our adventures, special occasions, and business activities. The presentations can be organized into sections so that particular slides are shown to specific audiences. For example, one large presentation created for freshmen orientation can be divided into one section for registration, another for financial aid, and a third for campus activities, and each section would be shown to different audiences.

In addition, PowerPoint's ability to create a photo album allows you to organize and distribute your pictures by adding interesting layouts, vibrant backgrounds, and meaningful captions. These photo albums can be e-mailed, published to a Web site, or turned into a video to distribute to friends and business associates, who do not need PowerPoint installed on their computers to view your file.

## Project — Presentation with Sections and a Photo Album

**BTW**

**Gardening Benefits Health**
Gardening as a hobby improves physical and mental health. Planting, weeding, and digging in the garden give a cardiovascular workout that can burn up to 600 calories per hour. These activities also increase endurance, strength, and flexibility. In addition, working in a garden can reduce stress, especially if plants with soothing scents and colors are grown.

Gardening is a hobby that provides relaxation, satisfaction, and beautification to millions of people in a wide variety of climates. Many communities have organized gardening clubs where members share advice and show photographs of their beautiful yards and flower beds. The Granville Garden Club officers are planning their annual spring meeting where they will announce the winners of the photo contest and display pictures of members' gardening accomplishments.

The presentation you create in this chapter (Figure 11–1) will be shown at the spring meeting. You divide the slide show into sections for the photo contest winners (Figure 11–1a), the members' favorite perennials, favorite annuals, and favorite spring bulbs. You then create a photo album, add members' pictures and make adjustments to brightness and contrast, and add captions (Figures 11–1b and 11–1c). You also create a second photo album with black-and-white images (Figure 11–1d). In addition, you create two slides with a custom size to use as a marketing tool to promote the annual meeting and insert a video file on one of the slides (Figure 11–1e). You then e-mail the meeting announcement file to a member and also convert another file to a video so that members who do not have PowerPoint installed on their computers can view the photo contest winners' pictures in the presentation.

(a) **Photo Contest Section Slide**

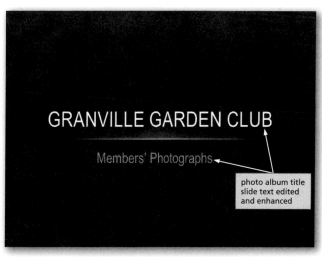

(b) **Photo Album Title Slide**

(c) **Photo Album Slide**

(d) **Black-and-White Photo Album Slide**

(e) **Custom Size Slide**

**Figure 11–1**

**BTW**

**Designing Postcards**
Marketing personnel have found that a postcard is an effective means of sending information to a specific audience. The customary 6″ × 4″ size is large enough to support eye-catching images yet small enough to get the message into the readers' hands. Designers recommend using two-thirds of the postcard for a graphic and one-third for text.

# Overview

As you read through this chapter, you will learn how to create the presentation shown in Figure 11–1 on page PPT 659 by performing these general tasks:

- Create and organize sections.
- Create a custom slide show.
- Start a photo album and add color and black-and-white photos.
- Enhance photo album elements.
- Perform research.
- Specify a custom slide size.
- Copy and compress a video file.
- Create a video from a presentation.

**Plan Ahead**

> **General Project Guidelines**
>
> When creating a PowerPoint presentation, the actions you perform and the decisions you make will affect the appearance and characteristics of the finished document. As you create a presentation with illustrations, such as the project shown in Figure 11–1 on page PPT 659, you should follow these general guidelines:
>
> 1. **Use photographs with sharp focus and contrast.** The adage, "A picture is worth a thousand words," is relevant in a PowerPoint presentation. When your audience can see a visual representation of the concept you are describing during your talk, they are apt to understand and comprehend your message. Be certain your pictures are sharp and clear.
>
> 2. **Use hyperlinks to show slides with landscape and portrait orientations.** All slides in one presentation must be displayed in either landscape or portrait orientation. If you want to have variety in your slide show or have pictures or graphics that display best in one orientation, consider using hyperlinks to mix the two orientations during your presentation.
>
> 3. **Rehearse, rehearse, rehearse.** Outstanding slides lose their value when the presenter is unprepared to speak. Always keep in mind that the visual aspects are meant to supplement a speaker's verbal message. Practice your presentation before different types of audiences to solicit feedback, and use their comments to improve your speaking style.
>
> When necessary, more specific details concerning the above guidelines are presented at appropriate points in the chapter. The chapter also will identify the actions performed and decisions made regarding these guidelines during the creation of the presentation shown in Figure 11–1.

## To Start PowerPoint and Save a File

If you are using a computer to step through the project in this chapter and you want your screens to match the figures in this book, you should change your computer's resolution to 1024 × 768. The following steps start PowerPoint and then save a file.

**1** Start PowerPoint. If necessary, maximize the PowerPoint window.

**2** Open the presentation, Garden Club, located on the Data Files for Students.

**3** Save the presentation using the file name, Granville Garden Club.

# Creating Sections and a Custom Slide Show

Quality PowerPoint presentations are tailored toward specific audiences, and experienced presenters adapt the slides to meet the listeners' needs and expectations. Speakers can develop one slide show and then modify the content each time they deliver the presentation. In the Granville Garden Club slide show, for example, a speaker may decide to place the slides that announce the photo contest winners at the end of the presentation to build suspense. Or, these slides can appear at the beginning of the presentation to generate discussion.

You can divide the slides into **sections** to help organize the slides. These sections serve the same function as dividers in a notebook or tabs in a manual: They help the user find required information and move material in a new sequence. In PowerPoint, you can create sections, give them unique names, and then move slides into each section. You then can move one entire section to another part of the slide show or delete the section if it no longer is needed. Each section can be displayed or printed individually.

A **custom show** is an independent set of slides to show to a specific audience. These slides can be in a different order than in the original presentation. For example, you may desire to show a title slide, the last nine slides, and then Slides 2, 5, and 8, in that order. One PowerPoint file can have several custom shows to adapt to specific audiences.

## To Insert Slides with a Section Layout

You can help your audience understand the organization of your slide show if you have one slide announcing the content of each section. One of PowerPoint's layouts is named Section Header, and it is similar to the Title Slide layout because it has a title and a subtitle placeholder. Your presentation will have four sections: photo contest winners, favorite annuals, favorite perennials, and favorite spring bulbs. To ensure consistency and save time, you can create one slide with a Section Header layout and then duplicate and modify it for each section. The following steps insert the four section slides.

**1**

- With Slide 1 selected and the Home tab displaying, click the New Slide button arrow (Home tab | Slides group) to display the Office Theme gallery (Figure 11–2).

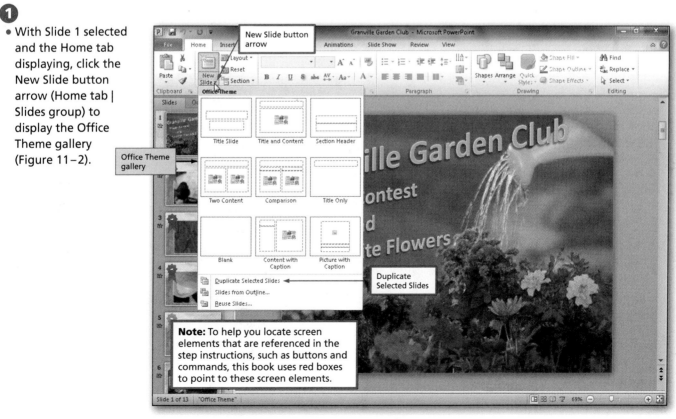

**Figure 11–2**

**2**

- Click Duplicate Selected Slides in the Office Theme gallery to create a new Slide 2 that is a duplicate of Slide 1.

- Click the Slide Layout button (Home tab | Slides group) to display the Office Theme layout gallery (Figure 11–3).

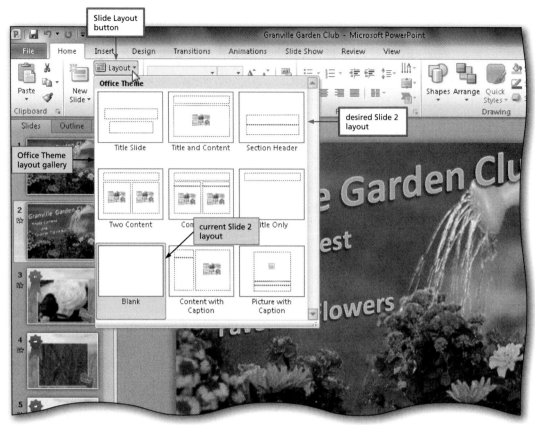

**Figure 11–3**

**3**

- Click the Section Header layout to apply that layout to the new Slide 2 (Figure 11–4).

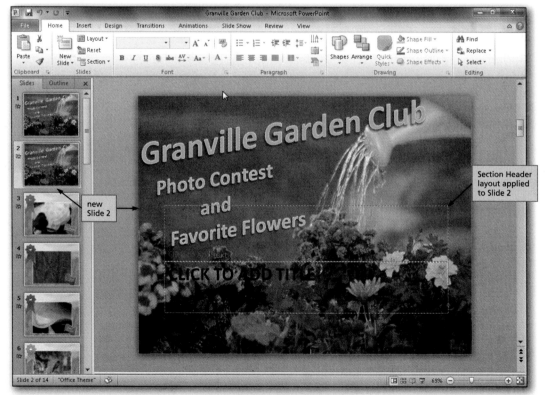

**Figure 11–4**

**Other Ways**

1. Right-click Slide 1, click Duplicate Slide on shortcut menu

## To Apply an Artistic Effect and Add a Title

The slide with the Section Header layout should have characteristics similar to the title slide to give the presentation continuity. One method of slightly altering the title slide is to apply an artistic effect that shows some of the slide's distinctive traits. The following steps apply an artistic effect to the new slide.

**1** With Slide 2 displaying, select the picture, and then display the Picture Tools Format tab.

**2** Click the Artistic Effects button (Picture Tools Format tab | Adjust group) to display the Artistic Effects gallery.

**3** Click Blur (last effect in second row) to apply this effect to the Slide 2 picture.

**4** Click in the title text placeholder and then type `Photo Contest Winners` as the title text.

**5** Change the title text font color to Yellow (fourth color in Standard Colors row) and then click the Character Spacing button (Home tab | Font group) and change the character spacing to Very Loose (Figure 11–5).

**Figure 11–5**

**BTW**

**The Ribbon and Screen Resolution**
PowerPoint may change how the groups and buttons within the groups appear on the Ribbon, depending on the computer's screen resolution. Thus, your Ribbon may look different from the ones in this book if you are using a screen resolution other than 1024 × 768.

**BTW**

**Q&As**
For a complete list of the Q&As found in many of the step-by-step sequences in this book, visit the PowerPoint 2010 Q&A Web page (scsite. com/ppt2010/qa).

## To Duplicate and Edit the Section Slides

Slide 2 is formatted appropriately to display at the beginning of the photo contest section of the slide show. A similar slide should display at the beginning of the favorite annuals, favorite perennials, and favorite spring bulbs sections. The following steps duplicate Slide 2 and edit the title text.

**1** With Slide 2 selected and the Home tab displaying, click the New Slide button arrow and then click Duplicate Selected Slides.

**2** Repeat Step 1 twice to insert two additional duplicate slides.

**3** Display Slide 3, select the title text, and then type `Favorite Annuals` in the title text placeholder.

**4** Display Slide 4, select the title text, and then type `Favorite Perennials` in the title text placeholder.

**5** Display Slide 5, select the title text, and then type `Favorite Spring Bulbs` in the title text placeholder (Figure 11–6).

**Figure 11–6**

## To Arrange Slides in Slide Sorter View

The four slides with a Section Header layout currently are displayed after the title slide. They are followed by 12 slides grouped into four categories, each of which has a distinct background. The photo contest winners' slides have a pastel sky and field, the annuals have a tan field background, the perennials have a green background, and the spring bulbs have a pink background. One of the four section slides you formatted should be positioned at the beginning of each category. When the presentation has only a few slides, you easily can drag and drop the slide thumbnails in the Slides pane. Your Granville Garden Club presentation, however, has 13 slides. To easily arrange the slides, you can change to Slide Sorter view and drag and drop the thumbnails into their desired locations. The following steps arrange the slides in Slide Sorter view.

**1**

- Click the Slide Sorter view button to display the slides in Slide Sorter view and then click the Slide 3 thumbnail (Favorite Annuals) to select it.

- Drag the Zoom slider to the left to change the zoom percentage to 60% so that all the slides are displayed (Figure 11–7).

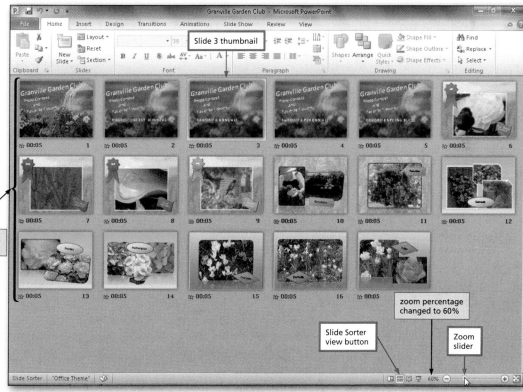

**Figure 11–7**

**2**

- Drag the Slide 3 thumbnail between the Slide 9 and Slide 10 thumbnails so that a vertical bar is displayed in the desired location for Slide 3 (Figure 11–8).

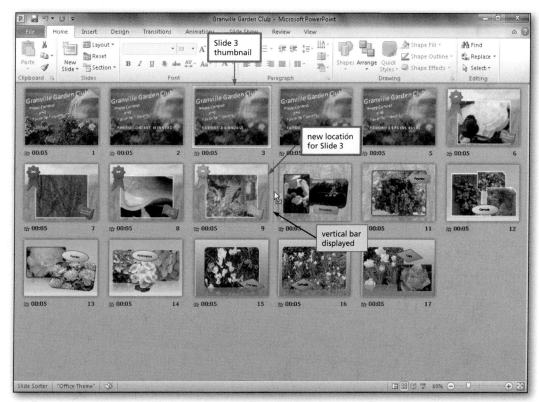

**Figure 11–8**

- Release the mouse button to display the Slide 3 thumbnail in a new location as Slide 9.

- Select the new Slide 3 (Favorite Perennials) and drag it between Slide 11 and Slide 12.

- Select the new Slide 3 (Favorite Spring Bulbs) and drag it between Slide 14 and Slide 15 (Figure 11–9).

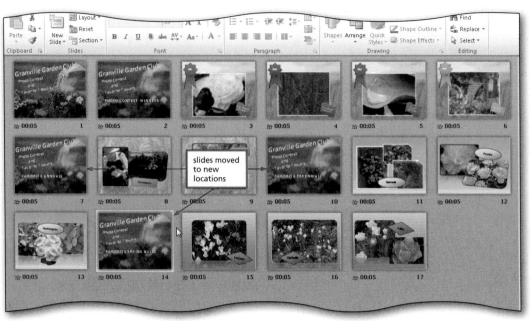

**Figure 11–9**

## To Create a Section Break

The slides in the presentation are divided into four categories: photo contest winners, annuals, perennials, and spring bulbs. At times, you may want to display slides from one particular category or move this particular group to another part of the presentation. You can create a section break to organize slides into a particular group. The following steps create five sections in the presentation.

- In Slide Sorter view, position the mouse pointer between Slide 1 and Slide 2 and then click once to display the vertical bar (Figure 11–10).

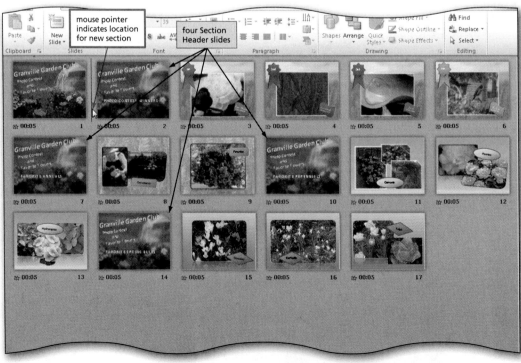

**Figure 11–10**

**2**

- With the Home tab displaying, click the Section button (Home tab | Slides group) to display the Section menu (Figure 11–11).

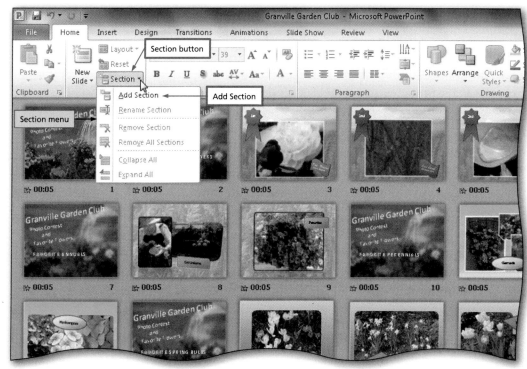

**Figure 11–11**

**3**

- Click Add Section in the menu to create a section.

- Scroll up to verify that the new section is named Default Section and consists of Slide 1.

**Q&A** Why is a section name shown as Untitled Section instead of Default Section?

If you place the mouse pointer before Slide 1, the section is named Untitled Section; if you place the mouse pointer between Slides 1 and 2, then it is named Default Section.

- Position the mouse pointer between Slide 6 and Slide 7, which is the start of the slides with annuals, and then click once to display the vertical bar (Figure 11–12).

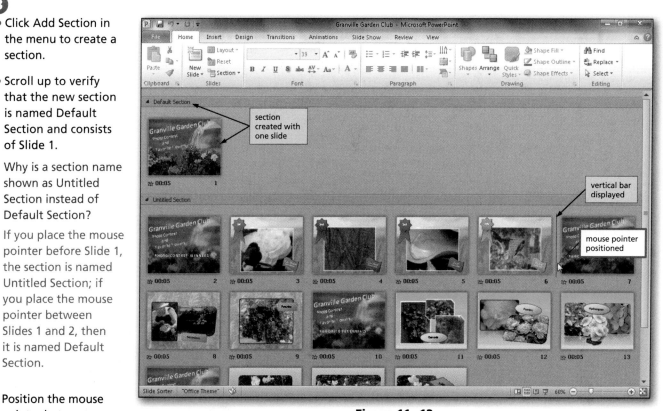

**Figure 11–12**

**4**

- Click the Section button (Home tab | Slides group) to display the Section menu and then click Add Section in the menu to create a section with the name, Untitled Section.

- Position the mouse pointer between Slide 9 and Slide 10, which is the start of the slides with perennials (Figure 11–13).

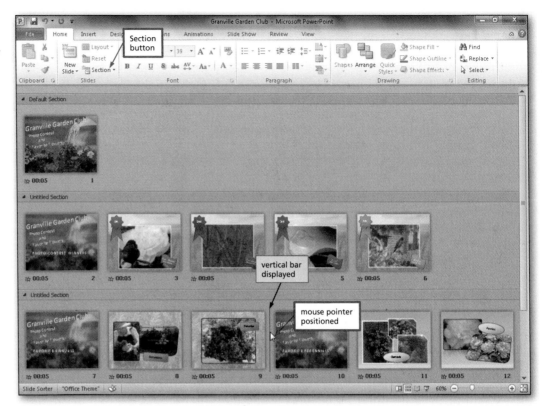

**Figure 11–13**

**5**

- Click the Section button and then click Add Section in the menu to create a section with the name, Untitled Section.

- Scroll down to display the final slides in the presentation, position the mouse pointer between Slide 13 and Slide 14, and then create a section (Figure 11–14).

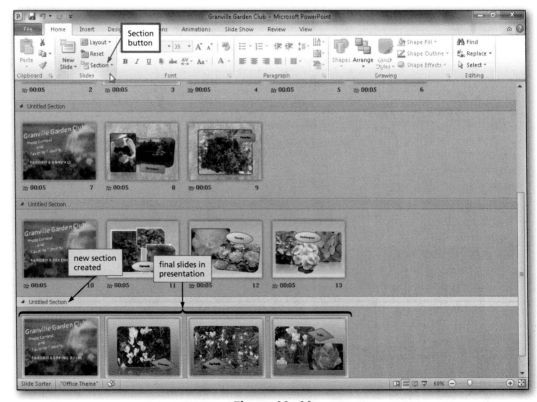

**Figure 11–14**

## To Rename a Section

The default section names, Untitled and Default, do not identify the content of the slides in the group. You can give each section a unique name to easily categorize the slides. The following steps rename each of the five sections in the presentation.

**1**

- With the last section featuring the spring bulbs selected and the Home tab displaying, click the Section button (Home tab | Slides group) to display the Section menu (Figure 11–15).

**Q&A**

If the spring bulbs section is not highlighted, how can I select it?

Click the divider between the sections. You will know the section is selected when the divider is gold.

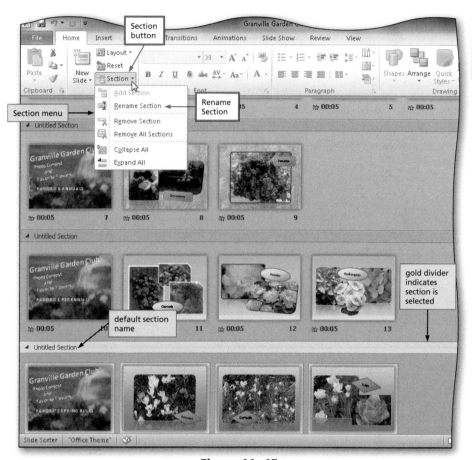

**Figure 11–15**

**2**

- Click Rename Section in the menu to display the Rename Section dialog box.

- Type **Spring Bulbs** in the Section name text box (Figure 11–16).

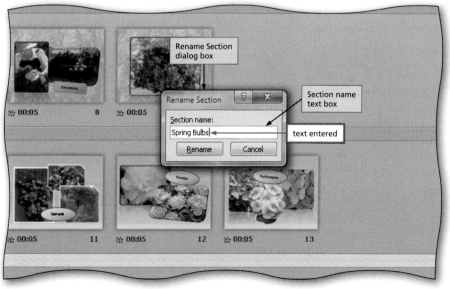

**Figure 11–16**

- Click the Rename button (Rename Section dialog box) to change the section name.

- Click the divider for the perennials section (Slide 10 through Slide 13) to select it and then click the Section button (Home tab | Slides group) to display the Section menu (Figure 11–17).

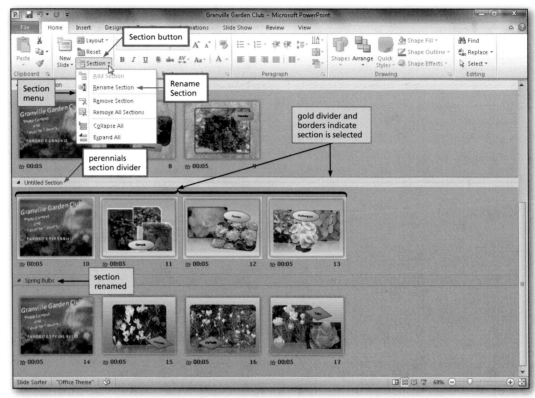

**Figure 11–17**

❹

- Click Rename Section to display the Rename Section dialog box, type **Perennials** in the Section name text box, and then click the Rename button to change the section name.

- Select the divider for the annuals section (Slide 7 through Slide 9), display the Rename Section dialog box, type **Annuals** as the new section name, and then click the Rename button (Figure 11–18).

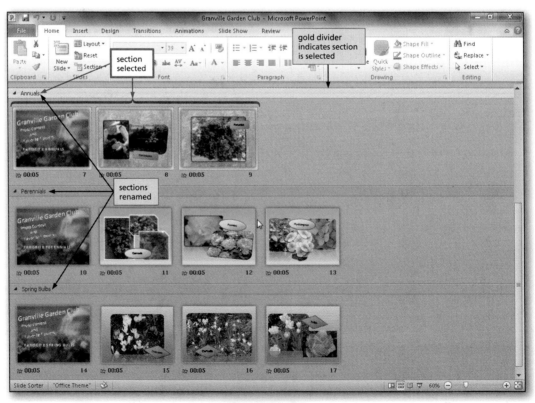

**Figure 11–18**

**5**

- Scroll up to display the first two sections, select the divider for the photo contest winners slides (Slide 2 through Slide 6), display the Rename Section dialog box, type **Photo Contest Winners** as the new section name, and then click the Rename button.

- Select the divider for Slide 1, display the Rename Section dialog box, type **Garden Club Title** as the new section name, and then click the Rename button (Figure 11–19).

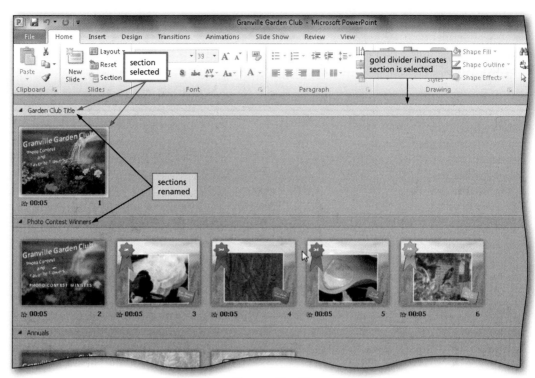

**Figure 11–19**

**Other Ways**

1. Right-click section divider, click Rename Section on shortcut menu

## To Collapse and Reorder Sections

When slides are organized into sections, it is easy to change the order in which the sections display. Garden Club members have expressed much more interest this year in perennials than annuals, so you want to change the order of these two sets of slides in your presentation. Because your presentation consists of multiple sections, you can collapse the sections so that only the section titles are displayed. You then can reorder the sections and expand the sections. The following steps collapse the sections, reorder the annual and perennial sections, and expand the sections.

**1**

- With the first section featuring the Garden Club Title selected and the Home tab displaying, click the Section button (Home tab | Slides group) to display the Section menu (Figure 11–20).

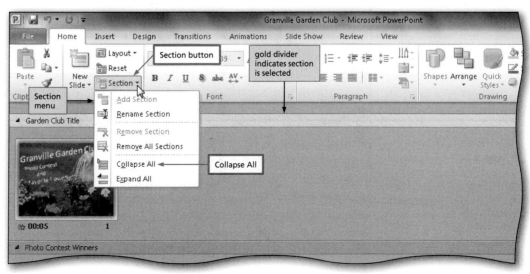

**Figure 11–20**

**2**

- Click Collapse All in the Section menu to display only the section names.

- Click the Perennials section name to select it and then drag the section upward between the Photo Contest Winners and Annuals sections (Figure 11–21).

**Q&A** How do I know when I am dragging the section name if the slides will be positioned in the desired location?

A vertical bar indicates where the slides in the section will move.

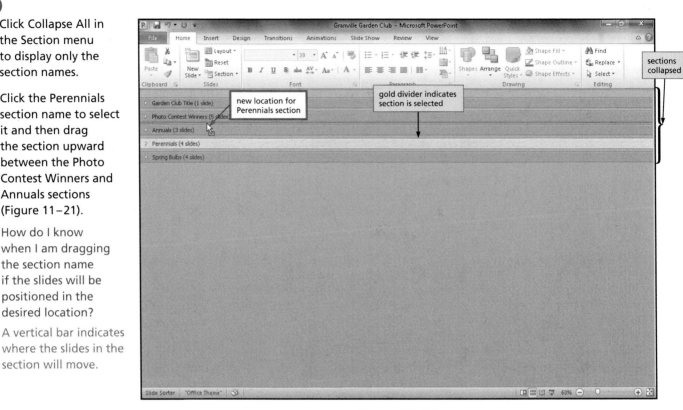

**Figure 11–21**

**3**

- Release the mouse button to move the Perennials section between the Photo Contest Winners and Annuals sections.

- Click the Section button (Home tab | Slides group) to display the Section menu (Figure 11–22).

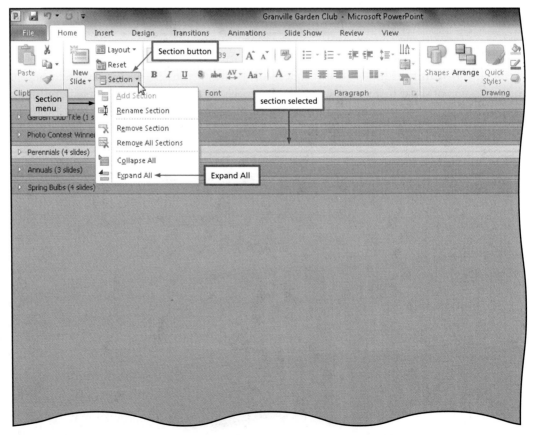

**Figure 11–22**

**4**

• Click Expand All in the Section menu to display all the slides in their corresponding sections (Figure 11–23).

**5**

• Run the presentation to display all the slides in the desired order.

**Figure 11–23**

**To Show a Presentation with Manual Timing**

The Granville Garden Club slides are set to display for specified times. If you desire to override the automatic timings and advance the slides manually, you would perform the following steps.

1. Display the Slide Show tab and then click the Set Up Slide Show button (Slide Show tab | Set Up group) to display the Set Up Show dialog box.

2. Click Manually in the Advance slides area (Set Up Show dialog box) and then click the OK button.

**Break Point:** If you wish to take a break, this is a good place to do so. Be sure to save the Granville Garden Club file again and then you can quit PowerPoint. To resume at a later time, start PowerPoint, open the file called Granville Garden Club, and continue following the steps from this location forward.

## To Create a Custom Slide Show

Many presenters deliver their speeches in front of targeted audiences. For example, the director of human resources may present one set of slides for new employees, another set for potential retirees, and a third for managers concerned with new regulations and legislation. Slides for all these files may be contained in one file, and the presenter can elect to show particular slides to accompany specific speeches. PowerPoint allows you to create a **custom show** that displays only selected slides. The following steps create a custom show.

**1**

- Click the Normal view button to display the slides in Normal view and then display the Slide Show tab.

- Click the Custom Slide Show button (Slide Show tab | Start Slide Show group) to display the Custom Slide Show list (Figure 11–24).

**Figure 11–24**

**2**

- Click Custom Shows to open the Custom Shows dialog box (Figure 11–25).

**Figure 11–25**

**3**

- Click the New button (Custom Shows dialog box) to display the Define Custom Show dialog box.

- Click Slide 1 in the 'Slides in presentation' area to select this slide (Figure 11–26).

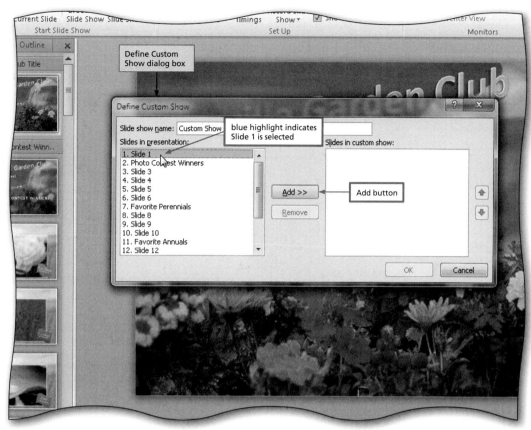

**Figure 11–26**

**4**

- Click the Add button (Define Custom Show dialog box) to add this slide to the 'Slides in custom show' area.

- Scroll down, press and hold down the CTRL key, and then click Slide 8, Slide 9, Slide 10, Slide 12, Slide 13, Slide 15, Slide 16, and Slide 17 in the 'Slides in presentation' area.

- Click the Add button (Define Custom Show dialog box) to add these slides to the 'Slides in custom show' area (Figure 11–27).

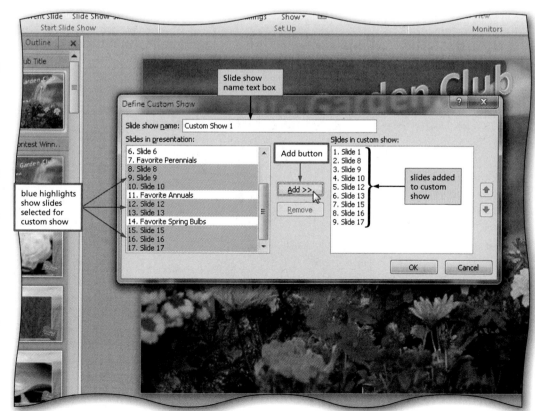

**Figure 11–27**

**5**

• Select the text in the 'Slide show name' text box (Define Custom Show dialog box) and then type **Garden Club Favorites** as the new name (Figure 11–28).

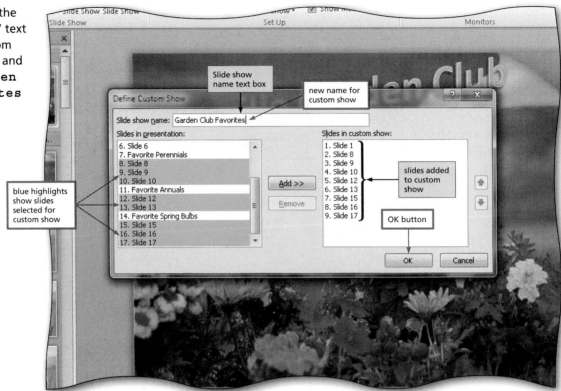

**Figure 11–28**

 **6**

• Click the OK button (Define Custom Show dialog box) to create the new Garden Club Favorites custom show and display the Custom Shows dialog box (Figure 11–29).

**7**

• Click the Close button (Custom Shows dialog box) to close the dialog box.

**Figure 11–29**

## To Open and Edit a Custom Slide Show

A PowerPoint file may have several custom slide shows. You can elect to display one of them at any time depending upon the particular needs of your audience. If you need to reorder the slides, you can change the sequence easily. The following steps open a custom show and edit the slide sequence.

**1**

- With the Slide Show tab displaying, click the Custom Slide Show button (Slide Show tab | Start Slide Show group) to display the Custom Slide Show list (Figure 11–30).

**Q&A** Why does Garden Club Favorites display in the Custom Slide Show list?

The names of any custom shows will be displayed in the list. If desired, you could click this custom show name to run the slide show and display the selected slides.

**Figure 11–30**

**2**

- Click Custom Shows to display the Custom Shows dialog box (Figure 11–31).

**Figure 11–31**

**3**

- With the Garden Club Favorites custom show selected in the Custom shows area, click the Edit button (Custom Shows dialog box) to display the Define Custom Show dialog box.

- Click Slide 15 in the 'Slides in custom show' area to select it (Figure 11–32).

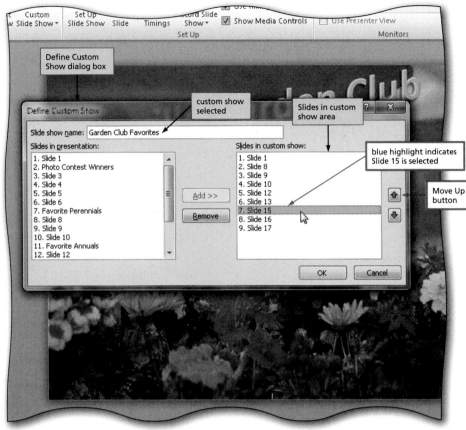

**Figure 11–32**

**4**

- Click the Move Up button five times to move Slide 15 below Slide 1 as the second slide in the custom show (Figure 11–33).

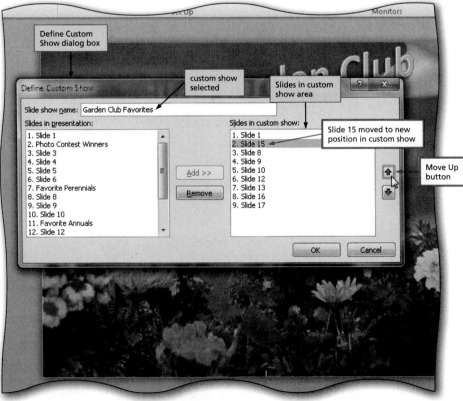

**Figure 11–33**

**5**

- Click Slide 16 in the 'Slides in custom show' area to select it and then click the Move Up button five times to move Slide 16 below Slide 15 as the third slide in the custom show.

- Click Slide 17 in the 'Slides in custom show' area to select it and then click the Move Up button seven times to move Slide 17 below Slide 1 as the second slide in the custom show (Figure 11–34).

**Q&A** Can I move the slides so they display later in the custom show?

Yes. Select the slide you want to reorder and then click the Move Down button.

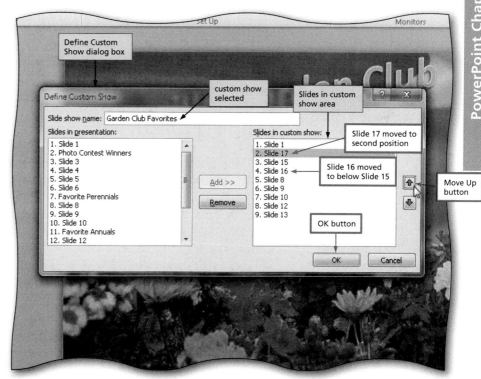

**Figure 11–34**

**6**

- Click the OK button (Define Custom Show dialog box) to create the revised Garden Club Favorites custom show and display the Custom Shows dialog box (Figure 11–35).

**7**

- Click the Show button (Custom Shows dialog box) to run the Garden Club Favorites custom show.

- When all the slides have displayed, press the ESC button to end the custom show.

- Save the Granville Garden Club file. Do not close this file.

**Figure 11–35**

**Break Point:** If you wish to take a break, this is a good place to do so. You can quit PowerPoint now. To resume at a later time, start PowerPoint, open the file called Granville Garden Club, and continue following the steps from this location forward.

Plan
Ahead

**Use photographs with sharp focus and contrast.**
Clear, sharp pictures provide details that draw an audience into your presentation. High-quality photographs impress your audience and state that you have an eye for detail and take pride in your work. When your slides are projected on a large screen, any imperfection is magnified, so you must take care to select photographs that are in focus and have high contrast.

**BTW**

**Hyperlinking Custom Shows**
You can hyperlink to a custom show with slides relating to a specific topic in your presentation. Click the Hyperlink button (Insert tab | Links group), click the Place in This Document button, and then select the custom show in the 'Select a place in this document' list.

# Creating a Photo Album

A PowerPoint **photo album** is a presentation that contains pictures to share with friends and business colleagues. It can contain a theme, a vibrant background, custom captions, a specific layout, frames around pictures, and text boxes. You can enhance the quality of the pictures by increasing or decreasing brightness and contrast, and you also can rotate the pictures in 90-degree increments. You also can change color pictures to display in black and white.

You can share your photo album in a variety of ways. You can, for example, e-mail the file, publish it to the Web, or print the pictures as handouts.

## To Start a Photo Album and Add Pictures

Once you have gathered files of digital pictures, you can begin building a photo album. You initially create the album and then later enhance its appearance. The following steps start a photo album and add pictures.

**1**

• Display the Insert tab and then click the New Photo Album button, which is displayed on the Ribbon as the Photo Album button (Insert tab | Images group), to display the Photo Album dialog box (Figure 11–36).

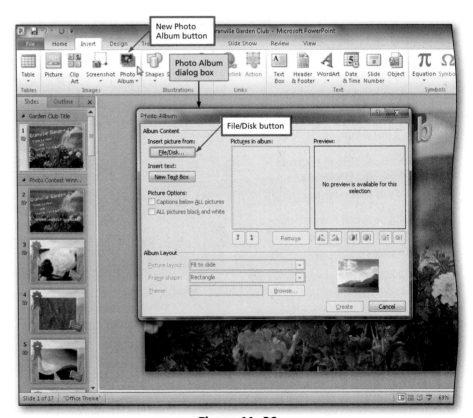

**Figure 11–36**

• Click the File/Disk button to display the Insert New Pictures dialog box.

• If necessary, double-click your USB flash drive in the list of available storage devices to display a list of files and folders on the selected USB flash drive and then navigate to the PowerPoint Chapter 11 folder (Figure 11–37).

**Figure 11–37**

❸

• Click the Views button arrow on the toolbar (Insert New Pictures dialog box) to display the view settings (Figure 11–38).

**Figure 11–38**

**4**

- Click List in the view settings to change the view setting and display only the picture file names.

- Click Border to select the file name, press and hold down the CTRL key, and then click Early Spring, Garden Wall, Purple Glory, Rock Garden and Greenery, Rock Garden, Spring Time, and Summer Time to select additional files to insert (Figure 11–39).

**Q&A**

If I mistakenly select a file name, how can I remove the selection?

Click the file name again.

**5**

- Click the Insert button (Insert New Pictures dialog box) to add the pictures to the album.

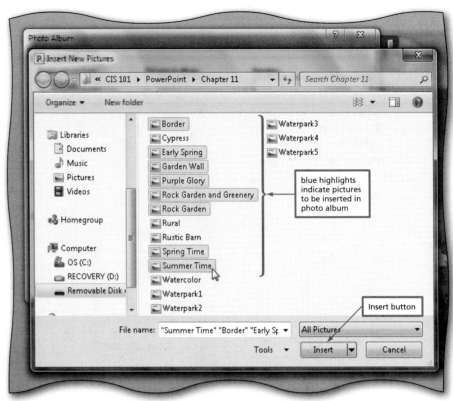

**Figure 11–39**

## To Reorder Pictures in a Photo Album

PowerPoint inserted the pictures in alphabetical order, which may not be the desired sequence for your album. You easily can change the order of the pictures in the same manner that you change the slide order in a custom show. The following steps reorder the photo album pictures.

**1**

- Click the second picture, Early Spring, to select it (Figure 11–40).

**2**

- Click the Move Down button four times to move the Early Spring photo downward between the Rock Garden and Spring Time photos so that it now is picture 6 in the album.

- Select the third picture, Purple Glory, and then click the Move Up button one time to move this picture upward between the Border and Garden Wall photos so that it now is the second picture.

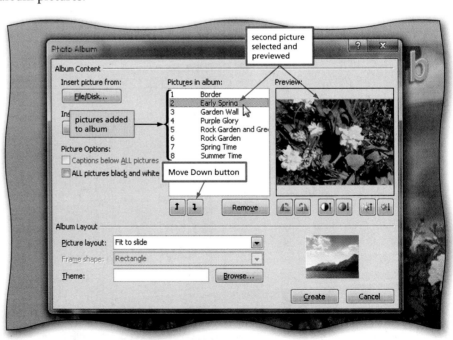

**Figure 11–40**

# To Adjust the Rotation of a Photo Album Image

Digital images have either a portrait (vertical) or landscape (horizontal) orientation. If a picture is displayed in your album with the wrong orientation, you can rotate the image in 90-degree increments to the left or the right. The following steps rotate a photo album picture.

**1**

• Click the third picture, Garden Wall, to select it and display a preview (Figure 11–41).

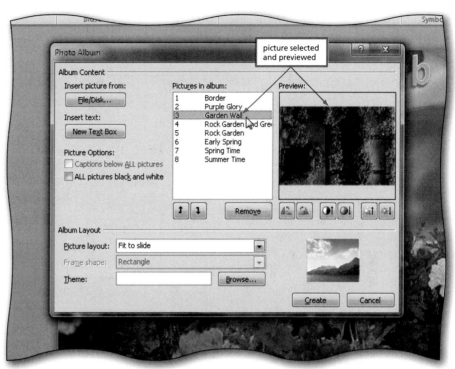

**Figure 11–41**

**2**

• Click the Rotate Left 90° button (Photo Album dialog box) to turn the picture to the left (Figure 11–42).

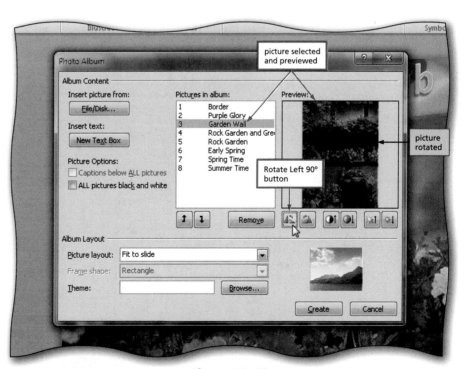

**Figure 11–42**

## To Adjust the Contrast of a Photo Album Image

A picture you insert may need correcting to enhance its visual appeal. You can adjust the difference between the darkest and lightest areas of the picture by increasing or decreasing the contrast. The following steps adjust the contrast of a photo album picture.

- Click the fifth picture, Rock Garden, to select it and display a preview (Figure 11–43).

- Click the Increase Contrast button (Photo Album dialog box) six times to change the contrast of this picture.

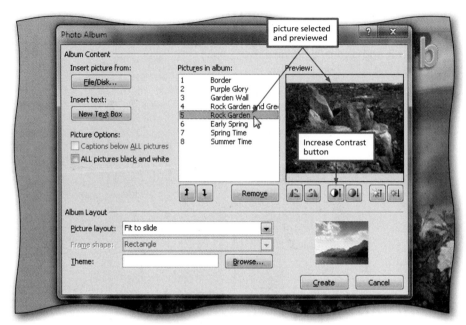

**Figure 11–43**

## To Adjust the Brightness of a Photo Album Image

If a picture in the photo album is too light or too dark, you can adjust its brightness to enhance its appearance. The following step adjusts the contrast of a photo album picture.

- With the Rock Garden picture selected, click the Decrease Brightness button (Photo Album dialog box) four times to darken the picture (Figure 11–44).

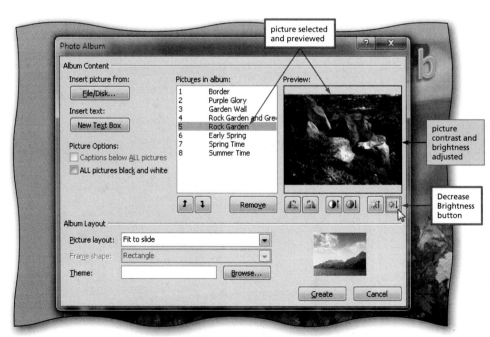

**Figure 11–44**

## To Change a Photo Album Layout

PowerPoint inserts each photo album picture so that it fills, or fits, one entire slide. You can modify this layout to display two or four pictures on a slide, display a title, or add white space between the image and the slide edges. You also can add a white or black border around the perimeter of each picture. The following steps change an album layout.

**1**

• With the Photo Album dialog box displayed, click the Picture layout box arrow in the Album Layout area (Photo Album dialog box) to display the Picture layout list (Figure 11–45).

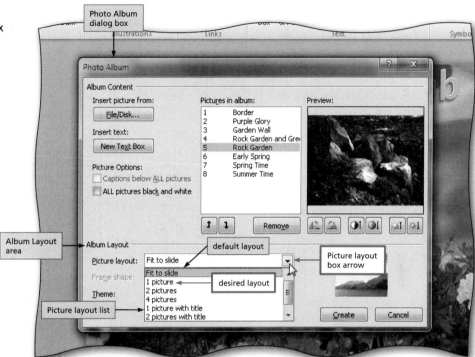

**Figure 11–45**

**2**

• Click 1 picture in the Picture layout list to change the layout so that one picture is displayed on each slide and a rectangular border is displayed around each picture.

• Click the Frame shape box arrow in the Album Layout area (Photo Album dialog box) to display the Frame shape list (Figure 11–46).

**3**

• Click Simple Frame, Black in the Frame shape list to add a black border around the picture.

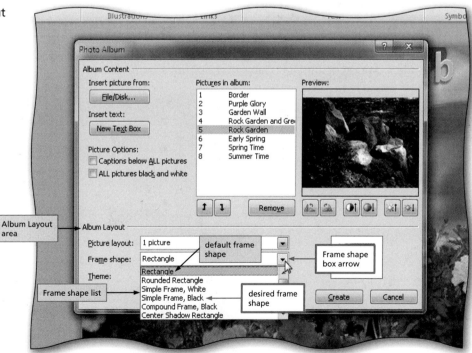

**Figure 11–46**

## To Add a Photo Album Theme

The themes that are used to design a presentation also are available to add to a photo album. These themes determine the colors and fonts that complement each other and increase the visual appeal of the slides. The following steps add a theme to the photo album.

**1**

- Click the Browse button in the Album Layout area (Photo Album dialog box) to display the Choose Theme dialog box.

- Scroll down and then click Horizon in the theme list to select this theme (Figure 11–47).

**2**

- Click the Select button (Choose Theme dialog box) to apply this theme to the presentation.

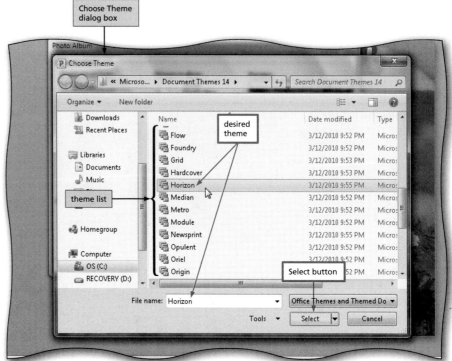

**Figure 11–47**

## To Add Captions below All Pictures

If you desire a caption below each picture, you can request PowerPoint add this feature to the slides. The file name is displayed as the caption text, but you can edit and add effects to this text. The following step selects the picture option to add a caption below all pictures in the photo album.

**1**

- In the Picture Options area (Photo Album dialog box), click the 'Captions below ALL pictures' check box to add a check mark (Figure 11–48).

**Figure 11–48**

## To Create a Photo Album

Once you have determined the picture sequence, layout, and frame shape, you are ready to make the photo album. The following step creates the photo album.

**1**

- Click the Create button (Photo Album dialog box) to close the dialog box and create a photo album with a title page and eight pictures (Figure 11–49).

**Q&A**

Why does a particular name display below the Photo Album title?

PowerPoint displays the user name that was entered when the program was installed. To see this name, display the Backstage view, click Options to display the PowerPoint Options dialog box, and then view or change the name entered in the User name text box in the Personalize your copy of Microsoft Office area.

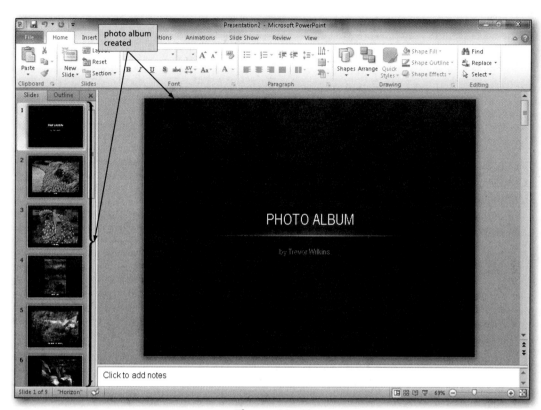

**Figure 11–49**

## To Edit a Photo Album

Once you review the photo album PowerPoint creates, you can modify the contents by adding and deleting pictures, changing the layout and borders, and adding transitions. The following steps edit the photo album by changing the border color and adding a text box on a new slide.

**1**

- Display the Insert tab and then click the New Photo Album button arrow (Insert tab | Images group) to display the Photo Album menu (Figure 11–50).

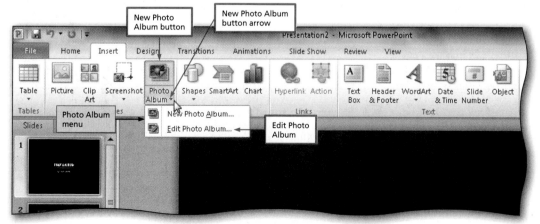

**Figure 11–50**

**2**

- Click Edit Photo Album in the menu to display the Edit Photo Album dialog box.

- Click the Frame shape box arrow to display the Frame shape list and then click Simple Frame, White in the list to change the border color from black to white.

- Click the New Text Box button (Edit Photo Album dialog box) to insert a new slide as Slide 9 in the album with the name, Text Box.

- Click the Move Up button eight times to move this picture upward as the first picture in the slide show (Figure 11–51).

**Q&A**

Can I insert a text box on one slide that already has a picture?

Yes. Click the Text Box button (Insert tab | Text group) and then click the slide where you want to insert the text box. You then can arrange the text box and picture on the slide.

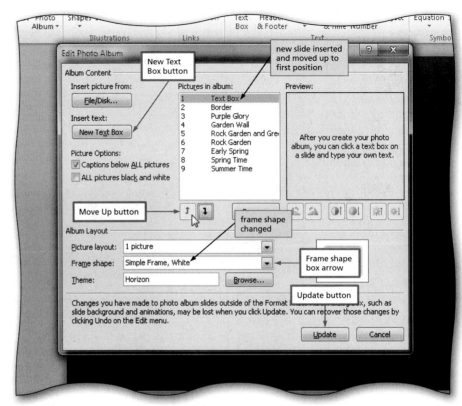

**Figure 11–51**

**3**

- Click the Update button (Edit Photo Album dialog box) to make the changes to the photo album.

- Apply the Glitter transition and then change the duration to 5 seconds for all slides.

---

**BTW**

**Linking Files**
If you link one file in landscape orientation to another in portrait orientation, you can give the impression that you have mixed the orientations. It is suggested you save both presentations in one folder so that the links will remain connected if you move or copy the folder.

## To Insert and Format Text in a Photo Album

PowerPoint inserts text into the slides, such as the file name for captions and the user name associated with the Microsoft Office installation as the subtitle text on the title slide. You can revise and format this text by changing the font, font size, color, and any other font styles and effects. The following steps edit text in the photo album.

**1** With Slide 1 displaying, select the title text, Photo Album, and then type `Granville Garden Club` as the replacement text.

**2** Select the subtitle text and then type `Members' Photographs` as the replacement text.

**3** Increase the font size of the title text to 48 point and the subtitle text to 32 point.

**4** Display Slide 2, select the words, Text Box, and then type `The Granville Garden Club is celebrating its 10`[th] `year of community beautification.` as the replacement text.

**5** Press the ENTER key two times and then type, `These photographs reflect our members' tremendous gardening talents.` as the second paragraph.

**6** Display Slide 3, select the caption text, and then type `Colorful flowers make attractive borders.` as the new caption.

**7** Display Slide 7, select the caption text, and then type `Boulders create an interesting garden focal point.` as the new caption.

**8** Display Slide 1 and then run the slide show.

## To Change Document Properties and Save the Photo Album Presentation

Before saving the photo album presentation, you want to add your name, class name, and some keywords as document properties. The following steps use the Document Information Panel to change document properties and then save the document.

**1** Display the Document Information Panel and then type your name as the Author property.

**2** Type your course and section in the Subject property.

**3** Type `garden club, photo contest, annuals, perennials, bulbs` as the Keywords property.

**4** Close the Document Information Panel.

**5** Save the presentation with the file name, Granville Photo Album (Figure 11–52).

**BTW**

**Resetting Placeholders**
You can reset all customization changes to the preset options. Click the Reset button (Home tab | Slides group) or right-click the slide or thumbnail and then click Reset Slide on the shortcut menu. To retain custom formatting changes and move the placeholders to their original locations, right-click the slide or thumbnail and then click the Layout button (Home tab | Slides group) and reapply the active layout from the Layout gallery.

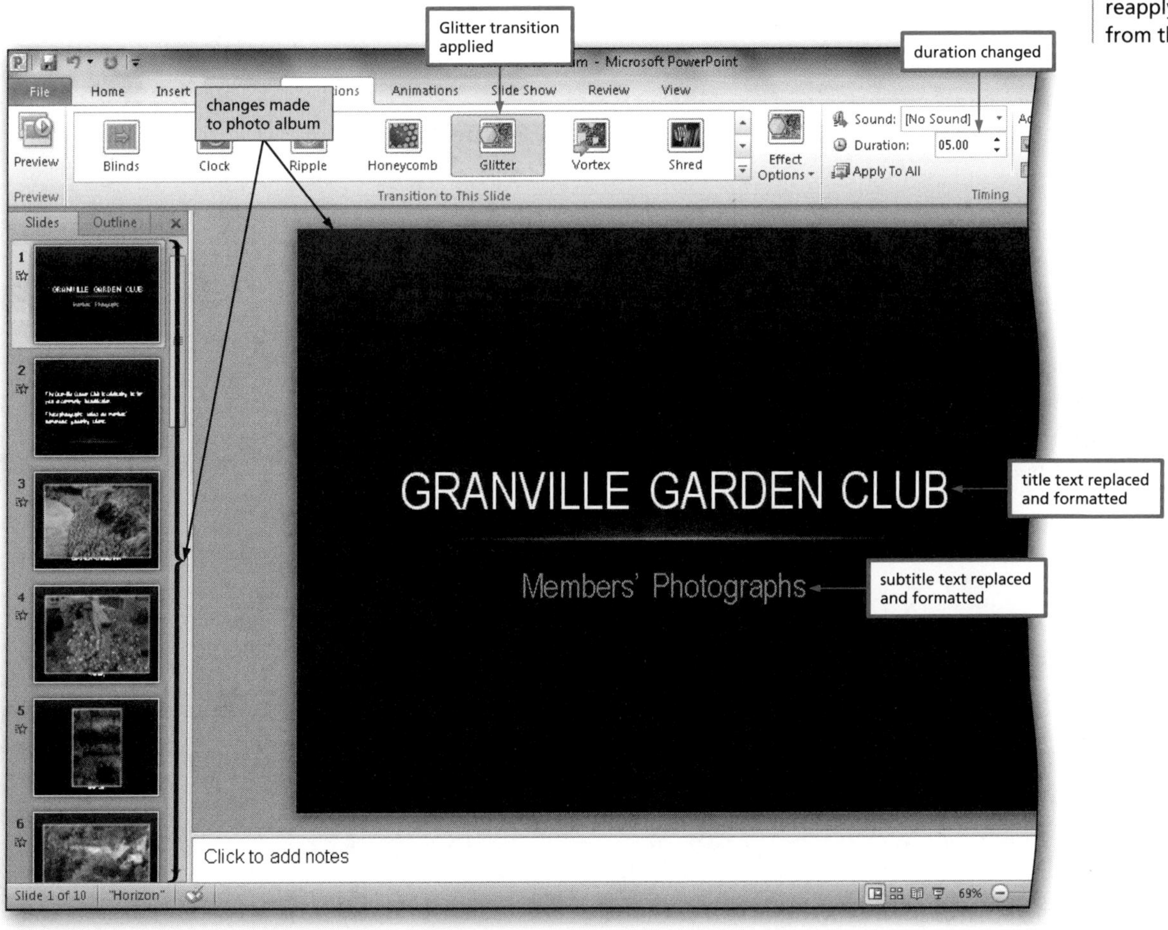

**Figure 11–52**

## To Create Black-and-White Images in a Photo Album

Black-and-white pictures often generate interest and give a unique version of the color photographs. The series of shades ranging from black to white, or grayscale, provide a different perspective on our world. The following steps edit a photo album to use black-and-white images.

**1**

• Display the Insert tab, click the New Photo Album button arrow and then click Edit Photo Album.

• Click the 'ALL pictures black and white' check box to add a check mark (Figure 11–53).

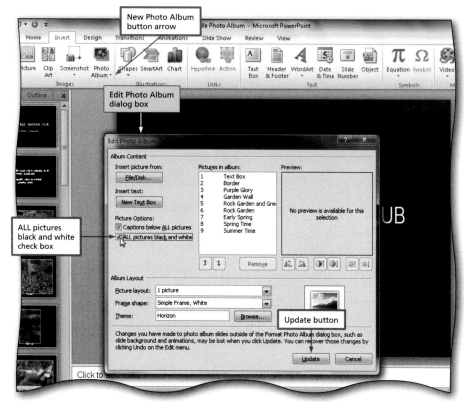

**Figure 11–53**

**2**

• Click the Update button (Edit Photo Album dialog box) to change the photographs from color to black-and-white images on the slides.

• Run the slide show.

• Save the presentation with the file name, Granville Photo Album Black and White.

• Print the presentation as a handout with two slides per page (Figure 11–54).

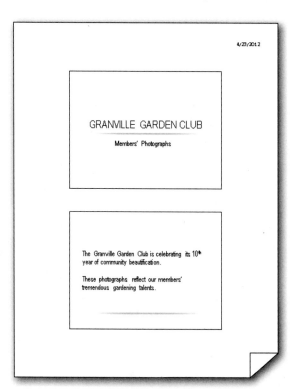

**(a) Handout Page 1**

**Figure 11–54**

(b) Handout Page 2

(c) Handout Page 3

(d) Handout Page 4

(e) Handout Page 5

**Figure 11–54 (Continued)**

## To Close a Presentation

The second photo album with the black-and-white pictures is complete. The following step closes the Granville Photo Album Black and White file.

 With the Backstage view open, click Close to close the open Granville Photo Album Black and White file without quitting PowerPoint.

## To Use the Research Pane to Find Information

You can search for information regarding a wide variety of topics using PowerPoint's reference materials. A commonly used research tool is the thesaurus to find synonyms for words on your slides or in the Notes pane. The Research task pane also includes a dictionary, encyclopedia, and translation services. In addition, if you are connected to the Web, it provides a search engine and other useful Web sites.

Assume you desire to learn about geraniums, which are featured on Slide 12 in the Granville Garden Club presentation. The following steps use the Research task pane to locate Web sites that provide information about this particular flower.

- If necessary, open the Granville Garden Club presentation.

- Display the Review tab and then click the Research button (Review tab | Proofing group) to display the Research task pane (Figure 11–55).

**Q&A**

Why does my Research task pane look different?

Your computer's settings and Microsoft's Web site search settings determine the way your Research task pane is displayed.

**Figure 11–55**

**2**

- Type `geranium` in the Search for text box and then click the Start searching button to perform an Internet search for Web sites with information about this search term (Figure 11–56).

**Q&A** What is Bing?

It is the name of Microsoft's search engine, which is a program that locates Web sites, Web pages, images, videos, news, maps, and other information related to a specific topic.

**Q&A** What should I do if I see the message, No results were found, instead of a list of search results?

If a 'Get updates to your services' icon is displayed at the bottom of the Research pane, click it, follow instructions to update your services, and then repeat your search.

**Figure 11–56**

**3**

- Click the Search for box arrow in the Research task pane to display a list of search locations (Figure 11–57).

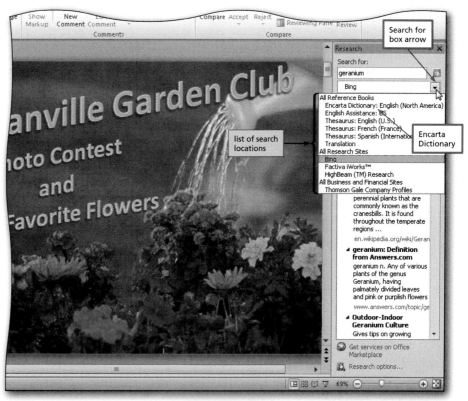

**Figure 11–57**

**4**
- Click Encarta Dictionary in the list to display information about a geranium (Figure 11–58).

**5**
- Click the Close button in the Research task pane.

**Figure 11–58**

**BTW**

**Turn Off Slide Timings**
If you recorded narration with slide timings, you might decide to play the comments for your audience but want to advance the slides manually. PowerPoint gives you the option to turn slide timings off and then turn them back on without having to recreate them. Click the Set Up Slide Show button (Slide Show tab | Set Up group) and then click Manually in the Advance slides area (Set Up Show dialog box). To turn the slide timings back on, click 'Using timings, if present' in the Advance slides area (Set Up Show dialog box).

### TO RECORD NARRATION

In some situations, you may want your viewers to hear recorded narration that accompanies slides. If your topic is flowers grown by local gardeners, you may want to hear their voices describe the plants that are displayed on slides. You can record narration separately and then add this file to the slide. You also can record narration while the slide show is running. To record this narration, you would perform the following steps.

1. Display the Slide Show tab and then click the Record Slide Show button arrow (Slide Show tab | Set Up group).

2. Click Start Recording from Beginning if you want to begin with the first slide or click Start Recording from Current Slide if you want to begin with the slide that is displaying on your screen.

3. Click the Narrations and laser pointer check box (Record Slide Show dialog box) and, if appropriate, click the Slide and animation timings check box (Record Slide Show dialog box) to select or remove the check mark.

4. Click the Start Recording button (Record Slide Show dialog box).

5. When you have finished speaking, right-click the slide and then click End Show on the shortcut menu.

### To Preview Narration

Once you have recorded narration, you can play the audio to review the sound. To preview this narration, you would perform the following steps.

1. In Normal view, click the sound icon on the slide.
2. Display the Audio Tools Playback tab and then click the Play button (Audio Tools Playback tab | Preview group).

### To Show a Presentation with or without Narration

If you have recorded narration to accompany your slides, you can choose whether to include this narration when you run your slide show. You would perform the following steps to run the slide show either with or without narration.

1. Display the Slide Show tab and then click the Set Up Slide Show button (Slide Show tab | Set Up group) to display the Set Up Show dialog box.
2. If you do not want the narration to play, click the 'Show without narration' check box in the Show options area (Set Up Show dialog box) and then click the OK button.
3. If you have chosen to show the presentation without narration and then desire to allow audience members to hear this recording, click the 'Show without narration' check box in the Show options area (Set Up Show dialog box) to uncheck this option and then click the OK button.

**BTW**

**Golden Rectangle Proportion**
Research has determined that people prefer reading a sheet of paper that is approximately the size of their head. This ideal size has the proportion, called the golden rectangle, which is one-and-one-half times longer than its width.

**Break Point:** If you wish to take a break, this is a good place to do so. You can quit PowerPoint now. To resume at a later time, start PowerPoint, open the file called Granville Garden Club, and continue following the steps from this location forward.

## Sharing and Distributing a Presentation

Many people design PowerPoint presentations to accompany a speech given in front of an audience, and they also develop the slide shows to share with family, work associates, and friends in a variety of ways. For example, they can print a slide on thick paper and send the document through the mail. They also can e-mail the file or create a video to upload to a Web site or view on a computer. Video files can become quite large in file size, so PowerPoint allows you to reduce the size by compressing the file.

**Use hyperlinks to show slides with landscape and portrait orientations.**
When you are creating your presentation, you have the option to display all your slides in either the default landscape orientation or in portrait orientation. You may, however, desire to have slides with both orientations during a single presentation. Using hyperlinks is one solution to mixing the orientations. Apply a hyperlink to an object on the last slide in one orientation and then hyperlink to another presentation with slides in the other orientation. If you desire to hyperlink to one particular slide in a second presentation, click the Bookmark button in the Insert Hyperlink dialog box and then select the title of the slide you want to use as your link. Once you have displayed the desired slides in the second presentation, create another hyperlink from that presentation back to a slide in your original presentation.

**Plan Ahead**

## To Change the Slide Orientation

By default, PowerPoint displays slides in landscape orientation, where the width dimension is greater than the height dimension. You can change this setting to specify that the slides display in portrait orientation, so the height dimension is greater than the width dimension. The portrait orientation is useful to display tall objects, people who are standing, or faces. The following steps change the slide orientation.

- Open the presentation, Spring Meeting, located on the Data Files for Students.

- Display the Design tab and then click the Slide Orientation button (Design tab | Page Setup group) to display the Slide Orientation gallery (Figure 11–59).

**2**
- Click Portrait to change the slide orientation from landscape to portrait.

**Figure 11–59**

## To Set Up a Custom Size

To announce the Granville Garden Club's spring meeting and encourage members to attend, you want to mail postcards to the members' homes. To simplify the process, you can create a PowerPoint slide that is the precise measurement of a postcard, print the card on heavy paper stock, and mail the card to club members. You can specify that your PowerPoint slides are a precise dimension. The following steps change the slide size to a custom size.

**1**
- With the Design tab displaying, click the Page Setup button (Design tab | Page Setup group) to display the Page Setup dialog box.

- Click the 'Slides sized for' box arrow to display the size list (Figure 11–60).

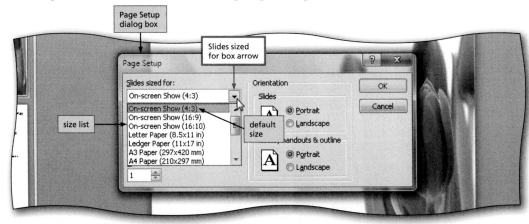

**Figure 11–60**

**2**

- Scroll down and then click Custom in the size list.

- Click the Width down arrow repeatedly until 5 is displayed in the Width text box.

- Click the Height down arrow repeatedly until 7 is displayed in the Height text box (Figure 11–61).

 **Q&A**

Can I type the width and height measurements in the text boxes instead of clicking the down arrows repeatedly?

Yes. You also can click and hold down the mouse button instead of repeatedly clicking the arrows until the desired dimensions are displayed.

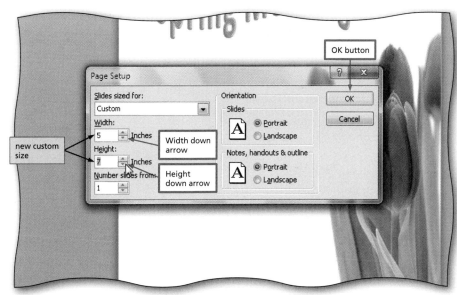

**Figure 11–61**

**3**

- Click the OK button (Page Setup dialog box) to apply the custom sizes and close the dialog box.

## To Display Multiple Presentation Windows Simultaneously

When you are reviewing elements of several presentations, it often is efficient and convenient to open both presentations and display them simultaneously on the screen. The following steps display three open presentations simultaneously.

**1**

- Open the presentation, Alpine Beauty, located on the Data Files for Students and then display the View tab (Figure 11–62).

**Figure 11–62**

**2**

- Click the Cascade button (View tab | Window group) to display the three open presentations – Alpine Beauty, Spring Meeting, and Granville Garden Club – from the upper-left to the lower-right corners of the screen.

**Q&A**

What is the difference between the Cascade button and the Arrange All button?

When you click the Cascade button, the open windows display overlapped, or stacked, on each other. Clicking the Arrange All button tiles all the open windows side by side on the screen. Each window may display narrower than in normal view so that all the open windows are visible simultaneously.

- If necessary, click the Alpine Beauty presentation title bar to display that presentation in the front of the screen (Figure 11–63).

**Q&A**

The Alpine Beauty title bar is not visible on my screen. Can I move the presentation windows so that it is visible?

Yes. You can drag the presentation title bars to arrange the windows.

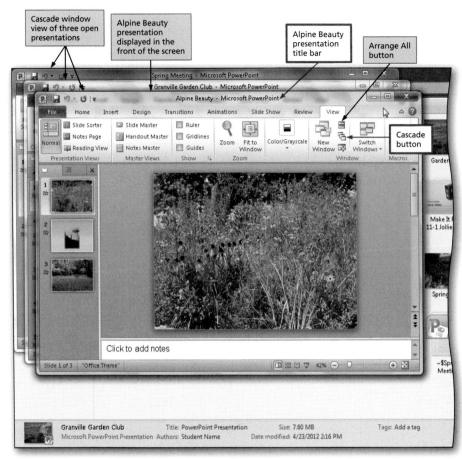

**Figure 11–63**

## To Copy a Video File

Slide 2 in the Alpine Beauty presentation contains a video clip of a stream that you want to insert at the bottom of Slide 2 in the Spring Meeting file. With multiple presentations open simultaneously on your screen, you can view all the slides quickly and decide which elements of one presentation you desire to copy to another. The following steps copy the video file from Slide 2 of the Alpine Beauty presentation to Slide 2 of the Spring Meeting presentation.

**1**

- Click the Slide 2 thumbnail of the Alpine Beauty presentation to display that slide.

- Right-click the video image in the center of the slide to select it and to display the shortcut menu (Figure 11–64).

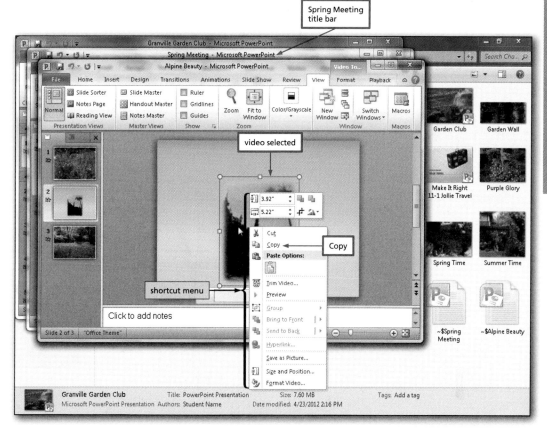

**Figure 11–64**

**2**

- Click Copy on the shortcut menu.

- Click the Spring Meeting presentation title bar to display that presentation in the front of the screen.

- If necessary, click the Slide 2 thumbnail of the Spring Meeting presentation to display that slide.

- Right-click the slide to display the shortcut menu and then point to the Use Destination Theme Paste Option button to display a preview of the video clip on that slide (Figure 11–65).

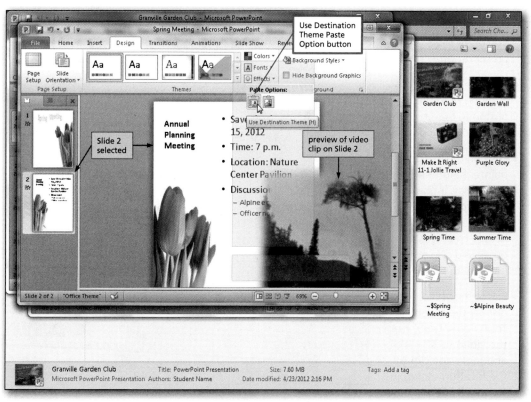

**Figure 11–65**

- Click the Use Destination Theme Paste Option button to insert the video into the slide.

- If necessary, drag the Spring Meeting title bar downward so the Alpine Beauty title bar is visible (Figure 11–66).

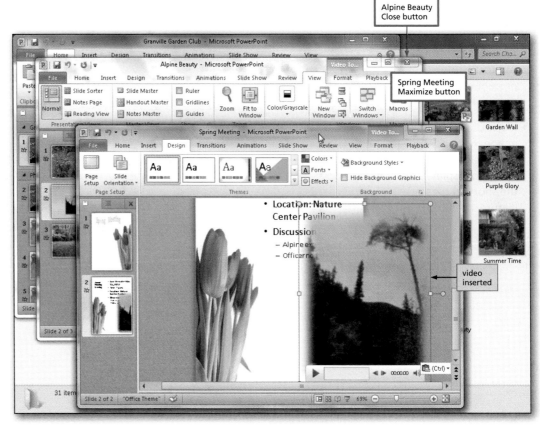

**Figure 11–66**

④

- Click the Alpine Beauty Close button to close that presentation.

- Click the Spring Meeting Maximize button to maximize the PowerPoint window.

- Position the mouse pointer before the word, May, in the first paragraph and then press the SHIFT+ENTER keys to create a line break and display the entire date on one line.

- Select the video, display the Video Tools Format tab, size the video to 3" × 4", and move the clip to the location shown in Figure 11–67.

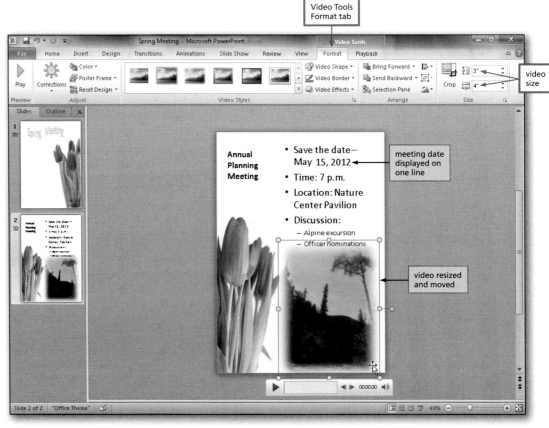

**Figure 11–67**

## To Compress a Video File

The file size of videos can be quite large. This size can pose a problem if you desire to e-mail a presentation or if the space on a storage device is small. PowerPoint includes a feature that will compress your file to reduce its size. You can specify one of three compression qualities: Presentation, Internet, or Low. In this project, you are going to e-mail the Spring Meeting file, so you desire to keep the file size as small as possible without sacrificing too much resolution quality. The following steps compress the video file.

**1**

• With the video clip selected on Slide 2, display the Backstage view and then click the Compress Media button (Info tab | Media Size and Performance area) to display the Media Size and Performance menu (Figure 11–68).

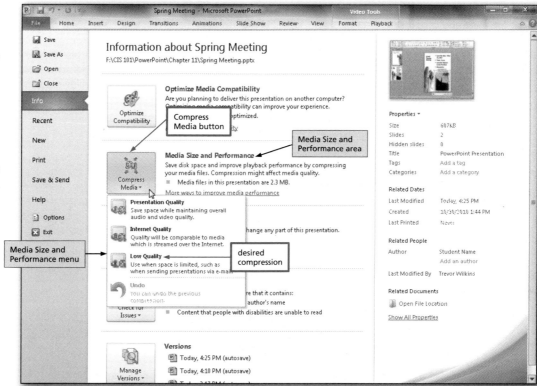

**Figure 11–68**

**2**

• Click Low Quality to display the Compress Media dialog box and compress the file (Figure 11–69).

**3**

• Click the Close button (Compress Media dialog box) to return to the Backstage view.

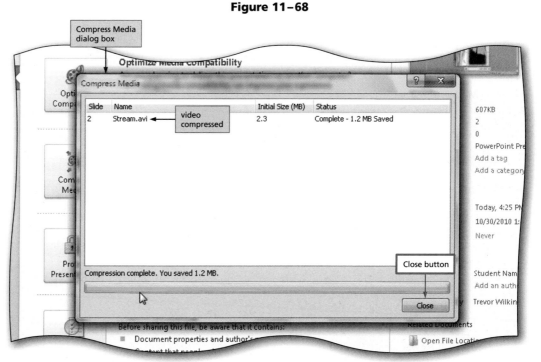

**Figure 11–69**

## To E-Mail a Slide Show from within PowerPoint

Presenters often e-mail their presentations to friends and colleagues to solicit feedback and share their work. PowerPoint offers a convenient method of e-mailing a presentation directly within PowerPoint. The following steps e-mail the slide show.

**1**

- With the Backstage view displaying, display the Save & Send tab (Figure 11–70).

**Figure 11–70**

**2**

- Click the Send as Attachment button in the Send Using E-mail area to open the Spring Meeting. pptx – Message (HTML) window in Microsoft Outlook (Figure 11–71).

**Q&A**

Must I use Microsoft Outlook to send this e-mail message?

No, you do not have to have Outlook installed; however, you should have an e-mail program installed in Windows to send the e-mail. If you don't use Outlook, you could install Windows Live Mail or another e-mail program. An e-mail program must be installed for the step to work.

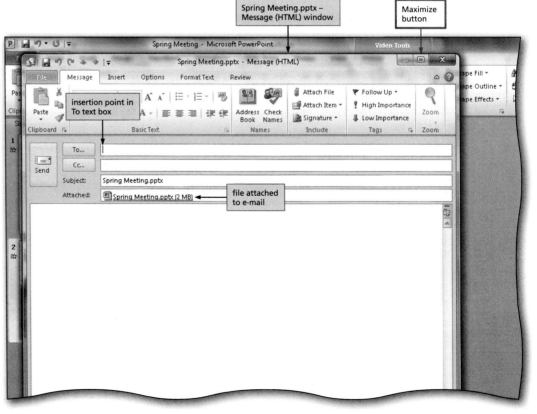

**Figure 11–71**

**3**

- If necessary, click the Maximize button in the Spring Meeting. pptx – Message (HTML) window to maximize the window.

- With the insertion point in the To text box, type **rose. stewart@ hotmail.com** (with no spaces) to enter the e-mail address of the recipient.

- Click to position the insertion point in the Subject text box, select the file name that is displaying, and then type **Upcoming Meeting** as the subject.

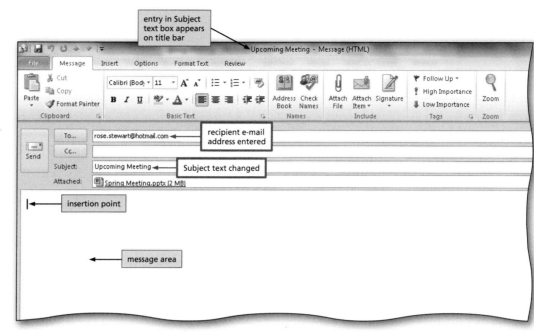

**Figure 11–72**

- Press the TAB key two times to move the insertion point into the message area (Figure 11–72).

**4**

- Type **Ms. Stewart,** as the greeting line.

- Press the ENTER key to move the insertion point to the beginning of the next line.

- Type **The announcement for our upcoming Spring Meeting is attached. I hope you will be able to join us.** to enter the message text.

- Press the ENTER key twice to insert a blank line and move the insertion point to the beginning of the next line. Type **Trevor Wilkins** as the signature line (Figure 11–73).

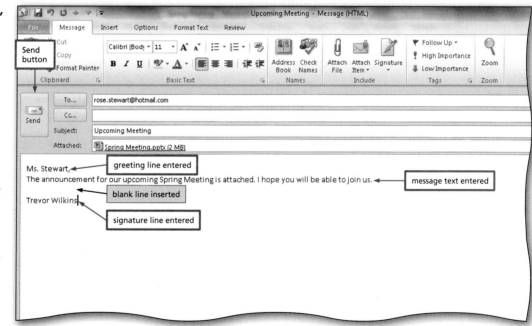

**Figure 11–73**

**Q&A** May I type my own name instead of Trevor's name?

Yes. You may desire to have your name on the title slide, or your instructor may request that you substitute your name or provide other identifying information.

## To Send an E-Mail Message

The message to Rose Stewart is created and ready to be sent. The following step sends the completed e-mail message and attached presentation to Rose Stewart.

**1** Click the Send button in the message header to send the e-mail message and to close the message window.

**BTW**

**E-Mail Subject Text**
Use meaningful words in the Subject text box to help your mail recipient identify your e-mail message. Unsolicited e-mail messages, called spam, account for more than 92 percent of all e-mail messages, according to one research study.

## To Run the Presentation, Change Document Properties, and Save the Presentation

When you run the Spring Meeting presentation, the video will play automatically because the file had that setting in the Alpine Beauty presentation. Before saving the presentation, you want to add your name, class name, and some keywords as document properties. The following steps run the slide show, use the Document Information Panel to change document properties, and then save the document.

**1** Display Slide 1 and then run the presentation.

**2** Display the Document Information Panel and then type your name as the Author property.

**3** Type your course and section in the Subject property.

**4** Type `annual spring meeting, alpine excursion, officers nominations` as the Keywords property.

**5** Close the Document Information Panel.

**6** Save the presentation with the file name, Spring Meeting Mailer.

**7** Display the Backstage view and then click Close to close the Spring Meeting Mailer file without quitting PowerPoint.

**Plan Ahead**

**Rehearse, rehearse, rehearse.**
Speakers should spend as much time practicing their presentations as they do preparing their PowerPoint slides. Frequently, however, they use the majority of their preparation time designing and tweaking the slides. Audience members expect to see a presenter who is prepared, confident, and enthusiastic. Practicing the presentation helps convey this image. As you rehearse, focus on a strong introduction that grasps the audience's attention and previews the main points of your talk. You have only one chance to make a good first impression, so begin the speech by establishing eye contact with audience members in various parts of the room. Resist the urge to stare at the slides projected on the screen. Your audience came to your presentation to hear you speak, and rehearsing will help you deliver a high-quality talk that exceeds their expectations.

### To Broadcast a Slide Show

PowerPoint's broadcast slide show feature allows you to share your presentation remotely with anyone having an Internet connection. As you display your slides, they see a synchronized view of your slide show in their Web browser, even if they do not have PowerPoint installed on their computers. To broadcast your presentation, you would perform the following steps.

1. Click the Broadcast Slide Show button (Slide Show tab | Start Slide Show group).

2. Ensure that PowerPoint Broadcast Service is selected in the Broadcast Service area and then click the Start Broadcast button (Broadcast Slide Show dialog box).

3. Enter your Windows Live ID e-mail address and password (Connecting to pptbroadcast.officeapps.live.com dialog box) and then click the OK button.

PowerPoint connects to the PowerPoint broadcast service, prepares the broadcast, and then provides a link that you can share with a maximum of 50 remote users. When these people visit the Web site and you start the slide show, they view your presentation with any annotations you make. When you have displayed the last slide, click the End Broadcast button below the Ribbon.

## To Create a Video

Watching video files is a common activity with the advent of easy-to-use recording devices and Web sites that host these files. You can convert your PowerPoint presentation to a video file and upload it to a Web site or share the file with people who do not have PowerPoint installed on their computers. The following steps create a video of the Granville Garden Club presentation.

**1**

- Display the Granville Garden Club file and, if necessary, click the Maximize button in the title bar to maximize the window.

- Display the Backstage view and then display the Save & Send tab.

- Click the Create a Video tab in the File Types area to display the Create a Video area (Figure 11–74).

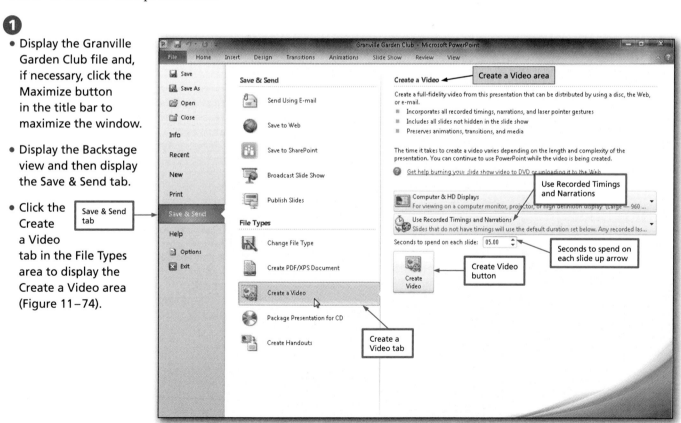

**Figure 11–74**

- Click Use Recorded Timings and Narrations in the Create a Video area to display the Use Recorded Timings and Narrations menu (Figure 11–75).

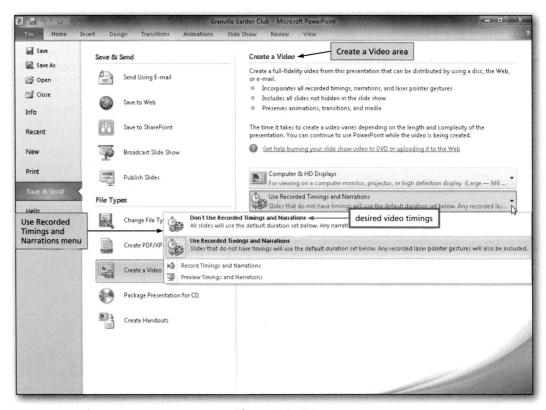

**Figure 11–75**

- Click Don't Use Recorded Timings and Narrations to select that option.

- Click the 'Seconds to spend on each slide' up arrow five times to increase the time to 10 seconds (Figure 11–76).

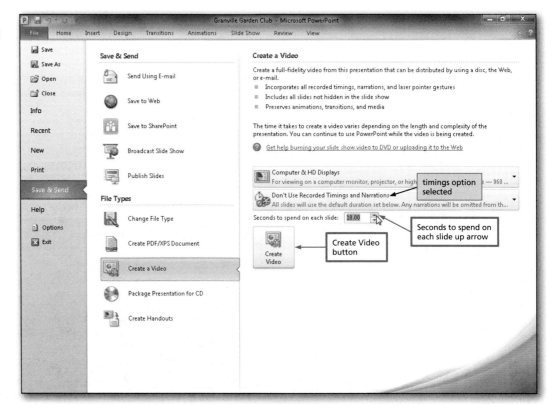

**Figure 11–76**

**4**
- Click the Create Video button to open the Save As dialog box.

- Change the video file name to Granville Garden Club Video (Figure 11–77).

**5**
- Click the Save button (Save As dialog box) to begin creating the Granville Garden Club Video file.

**Q&A**

Does PowerPoint use a long period of time to create the video?

Yes. It may take several minutes to export the presentation to a video. Windows Media Player will display an error message stating that the file is in use if you attempt to open the video file while it is being created.

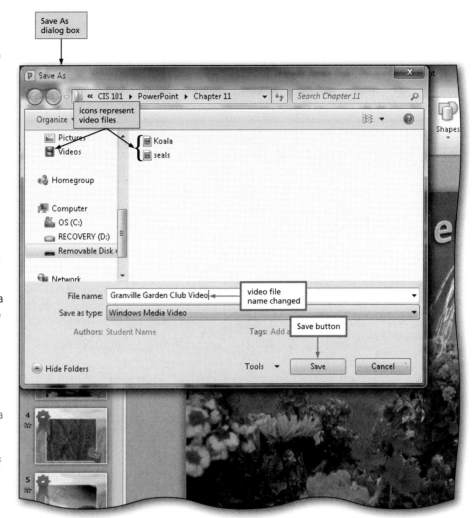

**Figure 11–77**

## To Change Document Properties and Save the Presentation

Before saving the presentation, you want to add your name, class name, and some keywords as document properties. The following steps use the Document Information Panel to change document properties and then save the document.

**1** Display the Document Information Panel and then type your name as the Author property.

**2** Type your course and section in the Subject property.

**3** Type **photo contest, perennials, annuals, bulbs** as the Keywords property.

**4** Close the Document Information Panel.

**5** Save the presentation again.

**BTW**

**Quick Reference**
For a table that lists how to complete the tasks covered in this book using the mouse, Ribbon, shortcut menu, and keyboard, see the Quick Reference Summary at the back of this book, or visit the PowerPoint 2010 Quick Reference Web page (scsite.com/ppt2010/qr).

**BTW**

**Certification**
The Microsoft Office Specialist (MOS) program provides an opportunity for you to obtain a valuable industry credential – proof that you have the PowerPoint 2010 skills required by employers. For more information, visit the PowerPoint 2010 Certification Web page (scsite.com/ ppt2010/cert).

### To Use Presenter View

Experienced speakers often deliver a presentation using two monitors: one to display their speaker notes privately, and a second to display the slides and project them on a large screen for the audience to view. PowerPoint's **Presenter view** supports the use of two monitors connected to one computer so they can view the slide currently being projected while viewing the slide thumbnails, reading their speaker notes, viewing the elapsed time, lightening or darkening the audience's screen, or customizing the presentation by skipping the next slide or reviewing a slide previously displayed. A computer must support the use of multiple monitors and must be configured to use this feature. To use Presenter view, you would perform the following steps.

1. Display the Slide Show tab and then click the Use Presenter View check box (Slide Show tab | Monitors group) to select it to display the Display Settings dialog box.

2. On the Monitor tab, click the icon that represents the monitor you desire to use for your private use and then click the 'This is my main monitor' check box to select it.

3. Click the icon that represents the second monitor that your audience will view, click the 'Extend my Windows Desktop onto this monitor' check box to select it, and then click the OK button.

4. Ensure that the audience's monitor icon is displayed in the Show On list (Slide Show tab | Monitors group).

5. Click the Set Up Slide Show button (Slide Show tab | Set Up group) to display the Set Up Show dialog box.

6. Select the desired options and then click the OK button (Set Up Show dialog box).

7. Run the slide show.

## To Run and Print the Presentation

The presentation now is complete. You should run the slide show, print handouts, and then quit PowerPoint.

**1** Run the slide show.

**2** Print the presentation as a handout with six horizontal slides per page (Figure 11–78).

**3** Quit PowerPoint, closing all open documents.

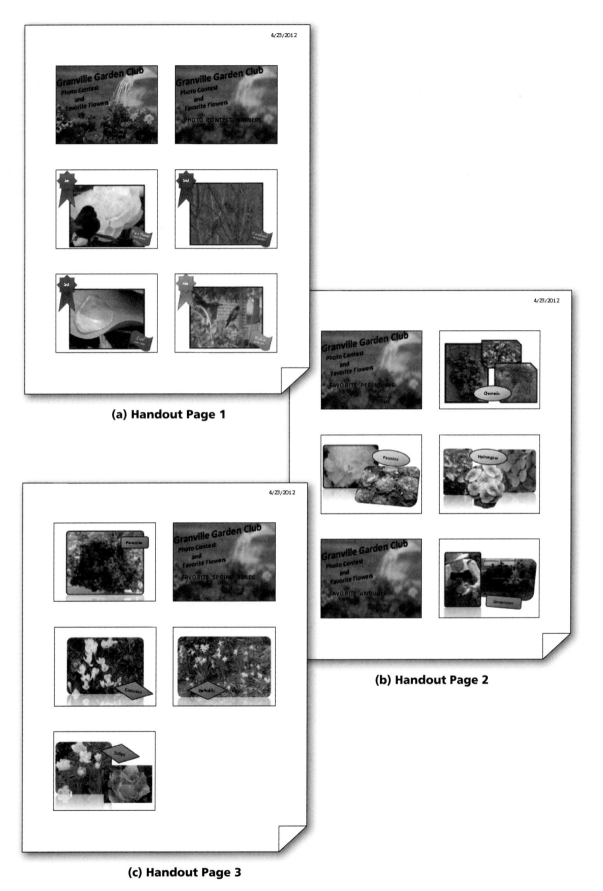

**(a) Handout Page 1**

**(b) Handout Page 2**

**(c) Handout Page 3**

**Figure 11–78**

# Chapter Summary

In this chapter you have learned how to organize a presentation into sections and then rename and move entire sections in the file. You then created a photo album, added and organized pictures, selected a theme and layout, adjusted a picture's contrast and brightness, and edited captions. You also changed the images to black and white in a separate photo album. Then, you specified a custom size and modified two slides by changing the slide orientation to portrait and inserting and compressing a video file. You then e-mailed the file and converted another file to video. The items listed below include all the new PowerPoint skills you have learned in this chapter.

1. Insert Slides with a Section Layout (PPT 661)
2. Arrange Slides in Slide Sorter View (PPT 664)
3. Create a Section Break (PPT 666)
4. Rename a Section (PPT 669)
5. Collapse and Reorder Sections (PPT 671)
6. Create a Custom Slide Show (PPT 674)
7. Open and Edit a Custom Slide Show (PPT 677)
8. Start a Photo Album and Add Pictures (PPT 680)
9. Reorder Pictures in a Photo Album (PPT 682)
10. Adjust the Rotation of a Photo Album Image (PPT 683)
11. Adjust the Contrast of a Photo Album Image (PPT 684)
12. Adjust the Brightness of a Photo Album Image (PPT 684)
13. Change a Photo Album Layout (PPT 685)
14. Add a Photo Album Theme (PPT 686)
15. Add Captions below All Pictures (PPT 686)
16. Create a Photo Album (PPT 687)
17. Edit a Photo Album (PPT 687)
18. Create Black-and-White Images in a Photo Album (PPT 690)
19. Use the Research Pane to Find Information (PPT 692)
20. Change the Slide Orientation (PPT 696)
21. Set Up a Custom Size (PPT 696)
22. Display Multiple Presentation Windows Simultaneously (PPT 697)
23. Copy a Video File (PPT 698)
24. Compress a Video File (PPT 701)
25. E-Mail a Slide Show from within PowerPoint (PPT 702)
26. Create a Video (PPT 705)

 If you have a SAM 2010 user profile, your instructor may have assigned an autogradable version of this assignment. If so, log into the SAM 2010 Web site at www.cengage.com/sam2010 to download the instruction and start files.

## Learn It Online

**Test your knowledge of chapter content and key terms.**

*Instructions:* To complete the Learn It Online exercises, start your browser, click the Address bar, and then enter the Web address **scsite.com/ppt2010/learn**. When the Office 2010 Learn It Online page is displayed, click the link for the exercise you want to complete and then read the instructions.

**Chapter Reinforcement TF, MC, and SA**
A series of true/false, multiple choice, and short answer questions that test your knowledge of the chapter content.

**Flash Cards**
An interactive learning environment where you identify chapter key terms associated with displayed definitions.

**Practice Test**
A series of multiple choice questions that test your knowledge of chapter content and key terms.

**Who Wants To Be a Computer Genius?**
An interactive game that challenges your knowledge of chapter content in the style of a television quiz show.

**Wheel of Terms**
An interactive game that challenges your knowledge of chapter key terms in the style of the television show *Wheel of Fortune*.

**Crossword Puzzle Challenge**
A crossword puzzle that challenges your knowledge of key terms presented in the chapter.

# Apply Your Knowledge

Reinforce the skills and apply the concepts you learned in this chapter.

## Creating and Reordering Sections and Creating Custom Slide Shows

*Note:* To complete this assignment, you will be required to use the Data Files for Students. See the inside back cover of this book for instructions on downloading the Data Files for Students, or contact your instructor for information about accessing the required files.

*Instructions:* Start PowerPoint. Open the presentation, Apply 11-1 Hantel Lodge, located on the Data Files for Students.

The slides in this presentation provide data about the activities available at the Hantel Lodge. The document you open is a partially formatted presentation. You will insert section breaks, reorder and rename sections, change the slide orientation, and create two custom slide shows so that the presentation matches the one shown in Figure 11–79.

*Perform the following tasks:*

1. You will not make any changes to Slide 1 (Figure 11–79a). Select Slide 2 and add a section break. Select the section divider and rename the section `Ski`.

2. Select Slide 4 and add a section break. Select the section divider and rename the section `Snowboard`.

3. Select the Default Section divider (before Slide 1) and rename the section `Hantel Lodge`.

4. Reorder the sections by moving the Snowboard section before the Ski section. The slides should now appear in the order shown in Figures 11–79b through 11–79e on the next page.

5. Change the slide orientation of the presentation to Portrait.

6. Create a custom slide show called Skiing. Include only Slides 1, 4, and 5 in the custom slide show.

7. Create a second custom slide show called Snowboarding. Include only Slides 1, 2, and 3 in this custom slide show.

8. Change the document properties, as specified by your instructor. Save the presentation using the file name, Apply 11-1 Hantel Lodge Activities. Submit the revised document in the format specified by your instructor.

slide orientation changed to Portrait

# Hantel Lodge

Popular Activities

**(a) Slide 1**
**Figure 11–79**

*Continued >*

**Apply Your Knowledge** *continued*

**(b) Slide 2**

**(c) Slide 3**

**(d) Slide 4**

**(e) Slide 5**

**Figure 11–79 (Continued)**

# Extend Your Knowledge

Extend the skills you learned in this chapter and experiment with new skills. You may need to use Help to complete the assignment.

### Formatting Sections and Broadcasting a Presentation

*Note:* To complete this assignment, you will be required to use the Data Files for Students. See the inside back cover of this book for instructions on downloading the Data Files for Students, or contact your instructor for information about accessing the required files.

*Instructions:* Start PowerPoint. Open the presentation, Extend 11-1 Fun Festival, located on the Data Files for Students. You will add and format sections to create the presentation shown in Figure 11–80. You will then broadcast your presentation.

*Perform the following tasks:*

1. You will not make any changes to Slide 1 (Figure 11–80a).
2. Select Slide 2. Add a section break and rename it `Seasonal`. Select Slide 4. Add a section break and rename it `Special Occasion`.
3. Select the Seasonal section and then change the transition from Checkerboard to Reveal to this section only, and change the duration to 02.00 seconds. Select the Special Occasion section and then change the transition from Checkerboard to Random Bars to this section only, and change the duration to 02.50 seconds. Change the document properties, as specified by your instructor. Save the presentation as Extend 11-1 Fun Festival Party Supplies. The slides should appear as shown in Figures 11–80a through 11–80e on this page and pages PPT 714 to PPT 715.
4. Broadcast the slide show to your instructor and to two classmates.
5. Submit the document in the format specified by your instructor.

**(a) Slide 1**
**Figure 11–80**

*Continued >*

**Extend Your Knowledge** *continued*

**(b) Slide 2**

**(c) Slide 3**

**Figure 11–80 (Continued)**

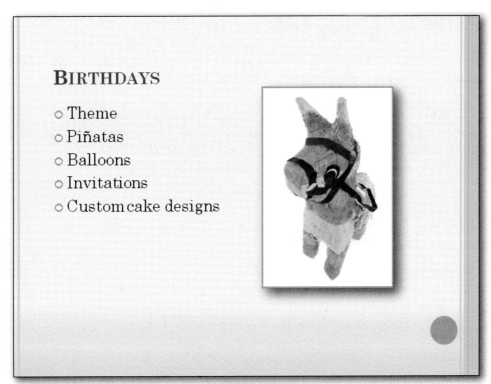

**(d) Slide 4**

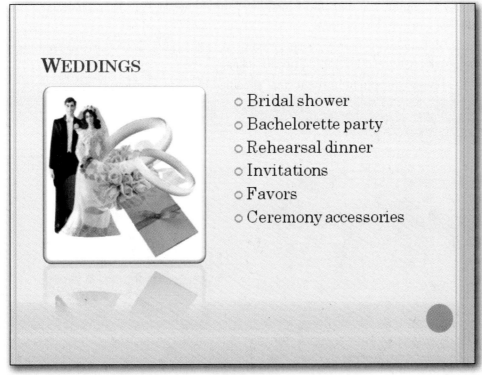

**(e) Slide 5**

**Figure 11–80 (Continued)**

## Make It Right

Analyze a presentation and correct all errors and/or improve the design.

### Selecting a Custom Size, Modifying Sections, and Proofing a Presentation

*Note:* To complete this assignment, you will be required to use the Data Files for Students. See the inside back cover of this book for instructions on downloading the Data Files for Students, or contact your instructor for information about accessing the required files.

*Instructions:* Start PowerPoint. Open the presentation, Make It Right 11-1 Jollie Travel, located on the Data Files for Students.

Correct the formatting problems and errors in the presentation while keeping in mind the guidelines presented in this chapter.

*Perform the following tasks:*

1. Change the size of the slides to a custom width of 11" and a height of 8".

2. Display the slides in Slide Sorter view (Figure 11–81a). Select the Travel section and rename the section **Jollie Travel**. Select the Untitled Section and rename the section **Hawaii**. Select the Alaska section and move it before the Hawaii section. The Alaskan Getaway slide should now appear before the two Hawaiian Getaway slides.

3. On Slide 4 (Figure 11–81b), use the Research proofing tool to look up the word, Hello, in Hawaiian. (*Hint:* Type **Hello in Hawaiian** in the research search box.) Enter the Hawaiian word in row 2, column 2 of the table. Look up the phrase, Thank You, in Hawaiian. Enter the Hawaiian word in row 3, column 2 of the table. Finally, look up the word, Family, in Hawaiian. Enter the Hawaiian word in row 4, column 2.

4. Change the document properties, as specified by your instructor. Save the presentation using the file name, Make It Right 11-1 Jollie Travel Packages.

5. Submit the revised document in the format specified by your instructor.

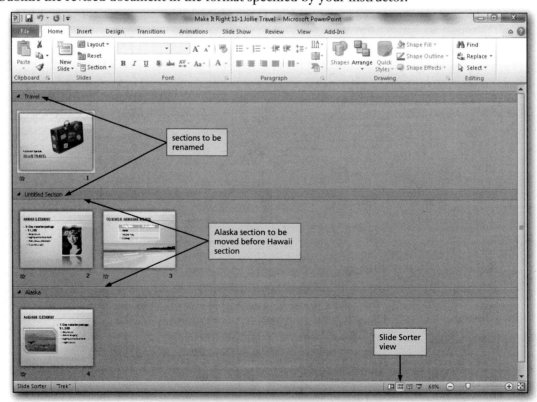

**(a) Presentation in Slide Sorter View**

**Figure 11–81**

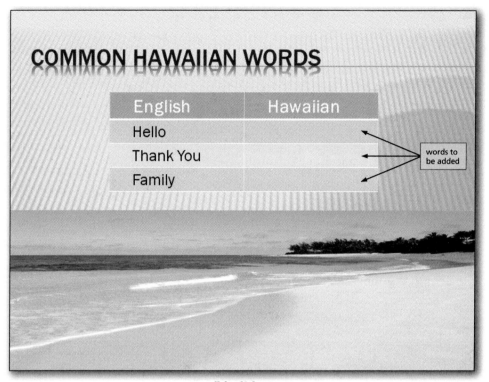

**(b) Slide 4**
**Figure 11–81 (Continued)**

## In the Lab

Design and/or create a presentation using the guidelines, concepts, and skills presented in this chapter. Labs 1, 2, and 3 are listed in order of increasing difficulty.

### Lab 1: Working with Multiple Presentation Windows Simultaneously, Setting Manual Timing, Compressing Media Files, and E-Mailing a Presentation

*Note:*   To complete this assignment, you will be required to use the Data Files for Students. See the inside back cover of this book for instructions on downloading the Data Files for Students or contact your instructor for information about accessing the required files.

*Problem:*   You are volunteering for a local zoo and decide to enhance a presentation for a grade school class by adding videos of horses, koalas, and seals in the wild. One of the videos is in a separate presentation. You create the slides shown in Figure 11–82 on pages PPT 718 through PPT 720.

*Perform the following tasks:*
1. Open the presentation, Lab 11-1 Animals, located on the Data Files for Students. You will not make any changes to Slide 1 (Figure 11–82a).
2. Open the Horses presentation located on the Data Files for Students and then cascade the two open document windows on the screen. Select Slide 2 (Figure 11–82b) of the Horses presentation. Copy the video clip from Slide 2 and paste it into the right content placeholder of Slide 2 of the Lab 11-1 Animals presentation (Figure 11–82c). In the Lab 11-1 Animals presentation, change the video to Start Automatically. Close the Horses presentation. Maximize the Lab 11-1 Animals presentation.

*Continued >*

**In the Lab** *continued*

3. On Slide 3, insert the Koala video, located on the Data Files for Students, in the left content placeholder. Apply the Metal Rounded Rectangle video style to the video clip and change the video to Start Automatically. The slide should appear as shown in Figure 11–82d.

4. On Slide 4, insert the Seals video, located on the Data Files for Students, in the right content placeholder. Apply the Metal Rounded Rectangle video style to the video clip and change the video to Start Automatically. The slide should appear as shown in Figure 11–82e.

5. Set up the slide show to advance slides manually.

6. Change the document properties, as specified by your instructor. Save the presentation using the file name, Lab 11-1 Animals Presentation.

7. Compress the media files in the presentation to Low Quality. Save the presentation using the file name, Lab 11-1 Animals Presentation – E-mail.

8. E-mail the Lab 11-1 Animals Presentation – E-mail to your instructor.

9. Submit the Lab 11-1 Animals Presentation in the format specified by your instructor.

**(a) Slide 1**

**Figure 11–82**

**(b) Slide 2 Horses Presentation**

**(c) Slide 2 Animals Presentation**

**Figure 11–82 (Continued)**

*Continued >*

**In the Lab** *continued*

(d) Slide 3

(e) Slide 4

**Figure 11–82 (Continued)**

# In the Lab

## Lab 2: Creating a Photo Album, Adding Captions, Reordering Pictures, Adjusting Rotation of Images, and Recording from the Current Slide

*Note:* To complete this assignment, you will be required to use the Data Files for Students. See the inside back cover of this book for instructions on downloading the Data Files for Students or contact your instructor for information about accessing the required files.

*Problem:* You work part time at a water park and have been asked to create a presentation for an upcoming advertising campaign. You decide to put together a photo album using photos from the park and create the slides shown in Figure 11–83 on pages PPT 722 to PPT 724 using files located on the Data Files for Students.

*Instructions Part 1:* Start PowerPoint.
*Perform the following tasks:*
 1. Insert a new photo album.
 2. Insert the Waterpark1, Waterpark2, Waterpark3, Waterpark4, and Waterpark5 pictures located on the Data Files for Students. Do not create the album until you are asked to do so.
 3. Select the Waterpark2 picture in the album and move it above the Waterpark1 picture. Rotate the picture counterclockwise.
 4. Select the Waterpark5 picture in the album and rotate the picture clockwise.
 5. Change the Picture layout to '1 picture with title.' Select the 'Captions below All pictures' picture option.
 6. Select the Executive theme for the photo album. Create the photo album.
 7. On Slide 1, change the title to `SlideNPlay Waterpark`. The slide should appear as shown in Figure 11–83a.
 8. On Slide 2, change the caption to `Mega Slides`. The slide should appear as shown in Figure 11–83b.
 9. On Slide 3, change the caption to `Speed Races`. The slide should appear as shown in Figure 11–83c.
 10. On Slide 4, change the caption to `Pick Your Path`. The slide should appear as shown in Figure 11–83d.
 11. On Slide 5, change the caption to `Survey the Ruins`. The slide should appear as shown in Figure 11–83e.
 12. On Slide 6, change the caption to `See You Later`. The slide should appear as shown in Figure 11–83f.
 13. Apply the Gallery transition and change the duration to 02.50 seconds for all slides
 14. Change the document properties, as specified by your instructor. Save the presentation using the file name, Lab 11-2 SlideNPlay Waterpark.
 15. Submit the document in the format specified by your instructor.

*Instructions Part 2:* If necessary, open the file called Lab 11-2 SlideNPlay Waterpark.
*Perform the following tasks:*
 1. Select Slide 4. Record the slide show from the current slide. *Note:* The following steps contain narration that you will read while progressing through the slides. For Slide 4, read the following narration: `"We offer great rides for you and your family to enjoy all day long, ranging from this downhill water slide"`
 2. Advance to Slide 5, read the following narration: `"to this slide through ancient ruins, where you will slide past images of previous civilizations until you exit into our wading pool."`
 3. Advance to Slide 6, and read the following narration: `"Above all else, we want you to have fun in our park and come back to visit us again all season long."`
 4. Stop the presentation so that the recording session ends.

*Continued >*

**In the Lab** *continued*

5. Display Slide 1 and then run the slide show to view the presentation and to hear the narration you just recorded.

6. Save the presentation using the file name, Lab 11-2 SlideNPlay Waterpark – Narration.

7. Submit the revised document in the format specified by your instructor.

**(a) Slide 1**

**(b) Slide 2**

**Figure 11–83**

Speed Races ← caption changed

**(c) Slide 3**

Pick Your Path ← caption changed

**(d) Slide 4**

**Figure 11–83 (Continued)**

*Continued >*

**In the Lab** *continued*

**(e) Slide 5**

**(f) Slide 6**

**Figure 11–83 (Continued)**

## In the Lab

**Lab 3: Creating a Black-and-White Photo Album, Adjusting Images, Inserting Text, Using Presenter View, and Recording from the Beginning of a Slide Show**

*Note:* To complete this assignment, you will be required to use the Data Files for Students. See the inside back cover of this book for instructions on downloading the Data Files for Students or contact your instructor for information about accessing the required files.

*Problem:* As part of your volunteer work at a local museum, you are tasked with creating a presentation featuring some of the local artists whose works are on display. You have collected the necessary pictures and will include them in your presentation. As an added artistic effect, you decide to present them all in black and white. You create the presentation shown in Figure 11–84 on pages PPT 726 to PPT 727.

*Instructions Part 1:* Start PowerPoint.
*Perform the following tasks:*

1. Insert a new photo album.

2. Insert the Rural, Cypress, Watercolor, and Rustic Barn pictures located on the Data Files for Students, in that order. Do not create the album until you are asked to do so.

3. Select the 'All pictures black and white' picture option, the 1 picture layout, and the Simple Frame, White Frame shape.

4. Select the Cypress picture in the album and increase the brightness of the picture four times.

5. Select the Rustic Barn picture in the album and decrease the contrast of the picture two times.

6. Select the Paper theme for the photo album. Create the photo album.

7. On Slide 1, change the title to **W. L. Surr Gallery**. Use your name in place of Student Name.

8. On Slide 5 (Figure 11–84e), insert a text box below the picture. Center the text box. Enter the text, **Come See Our Exhibit!** in the text box. Change the font size to 28 pt. Apply the Fill – Olive Green, Text 1, Inner Shadow WordArt style (third style in second row) to this text.

9. Apply the Shape transition and change the duration to 02.00 seconds for all slides.

10. Set up the presentation to run in Presenter view. The slides should appear as shown in Figures 11–84a through 11–84e.

11. Change the document properties, as specified by your instructor. Save the presentation using the file name, Lab 11-3 Surr Gallery.

12. Submit the document in the format specified by your instructor.

*Instructions Part 2:* If necessary, open the file called Lab 11-3 Surr Gallery.
*Perform the following tasks:*

1. Select Slide 1. Record the slide show from the beginning. *Note:* The following steps contain narration that you will read while progressing through the slides. For this slide, read the following narration: **"Welcome to the W.L. Surr Gallery's exhibit of local artwork."**

2. Advance to Slide 2 and read the following narration: **"This submission is from an artist who was visiting a rural area up north and was inspired to create this painting."**

3. Advance to Slide 3 and read the following narration: **"From the ocean side, the next artist found a lone cypress tree and decided to share its beauty with us."**

4. Advance to Slide 4 and read the following narration: **"This next landscape captures an old West scene using water colors to bring out the landscape."**

*Continued >*

**In the Lab** *continued*

5. Advance to Slide 5 and read the following narration: **"Finally, this rustic barn exudes that old-time comfort feeling. Please come visit our exhibit to see these and even more works by local artists."**

6. Stop the presentation so that the recording session ends.

7. Run the slide show from beginning to see the slide show and play the narration you just recorded.

8. Save the presentation using the file name, Lab 11-3 Surr Gallery – Narration.

9. Save the presentation as a video using the file name, Lab 11-3 Surr Gallery – Video.

10. Submit the revised document and the video in the format specified by your instructor.

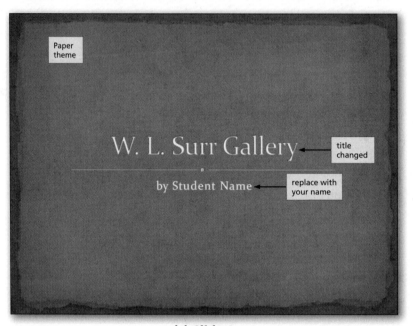

**(a) Slide 1**

**(b) Slide 2**

**Figure 11–84**

**(c) Slide 3**

**(d) Slide 4**

**(e) Slide 5**

**Figure 11–84 (Continued)**

# Cases and Places

Apply your creative thinking and problem-solving skills to design and implement a solution.

*Note:* To complete these assignments, you may be required to use the Data Files for Students. See the inside back cover of this book for instructions on downloading the Data Files for Students, or contact your instructor for information about accessing the required files.

As you design the presentations, remember to use the 7 × 7 rule: a maximum of seven words on a line and a maximum of seven lines on one slide.

## 1: Designing and Creating a Presentation about Club Activities

**Academic**

While working with fellow students in your student club, you have been given photos of different activities your club has sponsored. You have pictures from the last bowling night (Bowling1.jpg and Bowling2.jpg), marathon (Marathon1.jpg and Marathon2.jpg), and Mardi Gras mask building party (Party Mask.jpg). You decide to create a PowerPoint photo album presentation using the photos to display at a future club meeting. Apply at least three objectives found at the beginning of this chapter to develop the presentation, including adding captions to pictures and inserting text in a photo album. Use the pictures located on the Data Files for Students or other pictures and diagrams from Office.com if they are appropriate for this topic. Be sure to check spelling.

## 2: Designing and Creating a Presentation about Youth Summer Camp

**Personal**

You are volunteering for a local youth club summer camp this upcoming summer. You have been asked to create a PowerPoint presentation to illustrate various camp activities using pictures from last year's camp. Apply at least three objectives found at the beginning of this chapter to develop the presentation, including creating one section for each activity and adding a caption to each picture. You also can include narration describing how much fun each activity can provide. Use your personal digital pictures or pictures and diagrams from Office.com if they are appropriate for this topic. Be sure to check spelling.

## 3: Designing and Creating a Presentation about Conference Meeting Rooms

**Professional**

Your company is researching meeting rooms for an upcoming conference. You decide to create a photo album of the available meeting rooms so the committee can select the appropriate rooms. The conference will have lab sessions, guest speakers, and hands-on demonstrations. Apply at least three objectives found at the beginning of this chapter to develop the presentation, and include captions and text in the photo album to describe the functionality of each room. Use pictures from Office.com if they are appropriate for this topic or use your personal digital pictures. Be sure to check spelling.

# NOTES

# NOTES

# NOTES

# NOTES

# Appendix A
# Project Planning Guidelines

## Using Project Planning Guidelines

The process of communicating specific information to others is a learned, rational skill. Computers and software, especially Microsoft Office 2010, can help you develop ideas and present detailed information to a particular audience.

Using Microsoft Office 2010, you can create projects such as Word documents, PowerPoint presentations, Excel spreadsheets, and Access databases. Productivity software such as Microsoft Office 2010 minimizes much of the laborious work of drafting and revising projects. Some communicators handwrite ideas in notebooks, others compose directly on the computer, and others have developed unique strategies that work for their own particular thinking and writing styles.

No matter what method you use to plan a project, follow specific guidelines to arrive at a final product that presents information correctly and effectively (Figure A–1). Use some aspects of these guidelines every time you undertake a project, and others as needed in specific instances. For example, in determining content for a project, you may decide that a chart communicates trends more effectively than a paragraph of text. If so, you would create this graphical element and insert it in an Excel spreadsheet, a Word document, or a PowerPoint slide.

## Determine the Project's Purpose

Begin by clearly defining why you are undertaking this assignment. For example, you may want to track monetary donations collected for your club's fund-raising drive. Alternatively, you may be urging students to vote for a particular candidate in the next election. Once you clearly understand the purpose of your task, begin to draft ideas of how best to communicate this information.

## Analyze Your Audience

Learn about the people who will read, analyze, or view your work. Where are they employed? What are their educational backgrounds? What are their expectations? What questions do they have?

---

**PROJECT PLANNING GUIDELINES**

**1. DETERMINE THE PROJECT'S PURPOSE**
*Why are you undertaking the project?*

**2. ANALYZE YOUR AUDIENCE**
*Who are the people who will use your work?*

**3. GATHER POSSIBLE CONTENT**
*What information exists, and in what forms?*

**4. DETERMINE WHAT CONTENT TO PRESENT TO YOUR AUDIENCE**
*What information will best communicate the project's purpose to your audience?*

**Figure A–1**

Design experts suggest drawing a mental picture of these people or finding photos of people who fit this profile so that you can develop a project with the audience in mind.

By knowing your audience members, you can tailor a project to meet their interests and needs. You will not present them with information they already possess, and you will not omit the information they need to know.

Example: Your assignment is to raise the profile of your college's nursing program in the community. How much do they know about your college and the nursing curriculum? What are the admission requirements? How many of the applicants admitted complete the program? What percent pass the state board exams?

## Gather Possible Content

Rarely are you in a position to develop all the material for a project. Typically, you would begin by gathering existing information that may reside in spreadsheets or databases. Web sites, pamphlets, magazine and newspaper articles, and books could provide insights of how others have approached your topic. Personal interviews often provide perspectives not available by any other means. Consider video and audio clips as potential sources for material that might complement or support the factual data you uncover.

## Determine What Content to Present to Your Audience

Experienced designers recommend writing three or four major ideas you want an audience member to remember after reading or viewing your project. It also is helpful to envision your project's endpoint, the key fact you wish to emphasize. All project elements should lead to this ending point.

As you make content decisions, you also need to think about other factors. Presentation of the project content is an important consideration. For example, will your brochure be printed on thick, colored paper or posted on the Web? Will your PowerPoint presentation be viewed in a classroom with excellent lighting and a bright projector, or will it be viewed on a notebook computer monitor? Determine relevant time factors, such as the length of time to develop the project, how long readers will spend reviewing your project, or the amount of time allocated for your speaking engagement. Your project will need to accommodate all of these constraints.

Decide whether a graph, photo, or artistic element can express or emphasize a particular concept. The right hemisphere of the brain processes images by attaching an emotion to them, so audience members are more apt to recall these graphics long term rather than just reading text.

As you select content, be mindful of the order in which you plan to present information. Readers and audience members generally remember the first and last pieces of information they see and hear, so you should place the most important information at the top or bottom of the page.

## Summary

When creating a project, it is beneficial to follow some basic guidelines from the outset. By taking some time at the beginning of the process to determine the project's purpose, analyze the audience, gather possible content, and determine what content to present to the audience, you can produce a project that is informative, relevant, and effective.

## Appendix B

# Publishing Office 2010 Web Pages Online

With Office 2010 programs, you use the Save As command in the Backstage view to save a Web page to a Web site, network location, or FTP site. **File Transfer Protocol (FTP)** is an Internet standard that allows computers to exchange files with other computers on the Internet.

You should contact your network system administrator or technical support staff at your Internet access provider to determine if their Web server supports Web folders, FTP, or both, and to obtain necessary permissions to access the Web server.

## Using an Office Program to Publish Office 2010 Web Pages

When publishing online, someone first must assign the necessary permissions for you to publish the Web page. If you are granted access to publish online, you must obtain the Web address of the Web server, a user name, and possibly a password that allows you to connect to the Web server. The steps in this appendix assume that you have access to an online location to which you can publish a Web page.

### TO CONNECT TO AN ONLINE LOCATION

To publish a Web page online, you first must connect to the online location. To connect to an online location using Windows 7, you would perform the following steps.

1. Click the Start button on the Windows 7 taskbar to display the Start menu.
2. Click Computer in the right pane of the Start menu to open the Computer window.
3. Click the 'Map network drive' button on the toolbar to display the Map Network Drive dialog box. (If the 'Map network drive' button is not visible on the toolbar, click the 'Display additional commands' button on the toolbar and then click 'Map network drive' in the list to display the Map Network Drive dialog box.)
4. Click the 'Connect to a Web site that you can use to store your documents and pictures' link (Map Network Drive dialog box) to start the Add Network Location wizard.
5. Click the Next button (Add Network Location dialog box).
6. Click 'Choose a custom network location' and then click the Next button.
7. Type the Internet or network address specified by your network or system administrator in the text box and then click the Next button.
8. Click 'Log on anonymously' to deselect the check box, type your user name in the User name text box, and then click the Next button.
9. If necessary, enter the name you want to assign to this online location and then click the Next button.

10. Click to deselect the Open this network location when I click Finish check box, and then click the Finish button.

11. Click the Cancel button to close the Map Network Drive dialog box.

12. Close the Computer window.

### TO SAVE A WEB PAGE TO AN ONLINE LOCATION

The online location now can be accessed easily from Windows programs, including Microsoft Office programs. After creating a Microsoft Office file you wish to save as a Web page, you must save the file to the online location to which you connected in the previous steps. To save a Microsoft Word document as a Web page, for example, and publish it to the online location, you would perform the following steps.

1. Click File on the Ribbon to display the Backstage view and then click Save As in the Backstage view to display the Save As dialog box.

2. Type the Web page file name in the File name text box (Save As dialog box). Do not press the ENTER key because you do not want to close the dialog box at this time.

3. Click the 'Save as type' box arrow and then click Web Page to select the Web Page format.

4. If necessary, scroll to display the name of the online location in the navigation pane.

5. Double-click the online location name in the navigation pane to select that location as the new save location and display its contents in the right pane.

6. If a dialog box appears prompting you for a user name and password, type the user name and password in the respective text boxes and then click the Log On button.

7. Click the Save button (Save As dialog box).

The Web page now has been published online. To view the Web page using a Web browser, contact your network or system administrator for the Web address you should use to connect to the Web page.

## Appendix C

# Saving to the Web Using Windows Live SkyDrive

## Introduction

**Windows Live SkyDrive**, also referred to as **SkyDrive**, is a free service that allows users to save files to the Web, such as documents, spreadsheets, databases, presentations, videos, and photos. Using SkyDrive, you also can save files in folders, providing for greater organization. You then can retrieve those files from any computer connected to the Internet. Some Office 2010 programs including Word, PowerPoint, and Excel can save files directly to an Internet location such as SkyDrive. SkyDrive also facilitates collaboration by allowing users to share files with other SkyDrive users (Figure C–1).

**Figure C–1**

Note: An Internet connection is required to perform the steps in this appendix.

## To Save a File to Windows Live SkyDrive

You can save files directly to SkyDrive from within Word, PowerPoint, and Excel using the Backstage view. The following steps save an open PowerPoint presentation (Xanada Investment Corp, in this case) to SkyDrive. These steps require you to have a Windows Live account. Contact your instructor if you do not have a Windows Live account.

**1**

- Start PowerPoint and then open a document you want to save to the Web (in this case, the Xanada Investment Corp presentation).

- Click File on the Ribbon to display the Backstage view (Figure C–2).

**Figure C–2**

**2**

- Click the Save & Send tab to display the Save & Send gallery (Figure C–3).

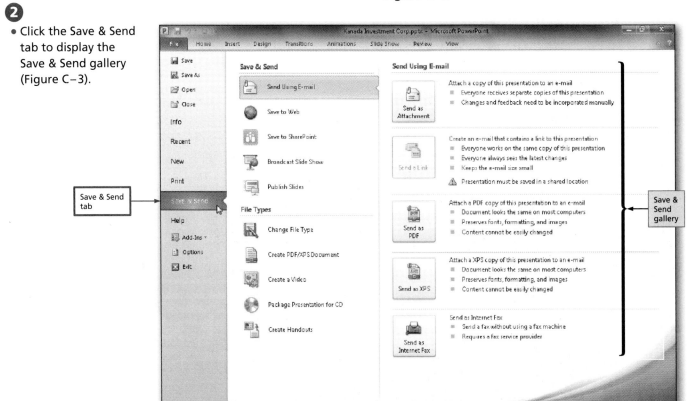

**Figure C–3**

**3**

- Click Save to Web in the Save & Send gallery to display information about saving a file to the Web (Figure C–4).

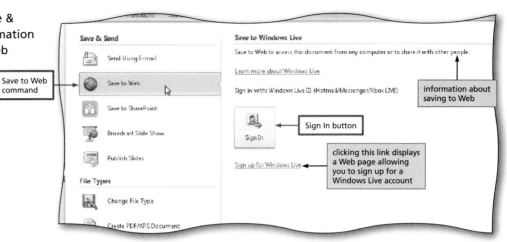

**Figure C–4**

**4**

- Click the Sign In button to display a Windows Live login dialog box that requests your e-mail address and password (Figure C–5).

 What if the Sign In button does not appear?

If you already are signed into Windows Live, the Sign In button will not be displayed. Instead, the contents of your Windows Live SkyDrive will be displayed. If you already are signed into Windows Live, proceed to Step 6.

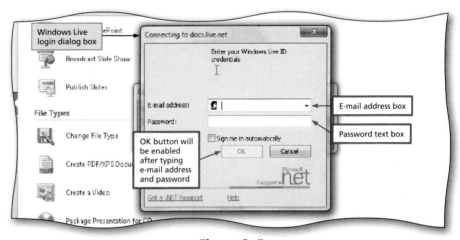

**Figure C–5**

**5**

- Enter your Windows Live e-mail address in the E-mail address box (Windows Live login dialog box).

- Enter your Windows Live password in the Password text box.

- Click the OK button to sign into Windows Live and display the contents of your Windows Live SkyDrive in right pane of the Save & Send gallery.

- If necessary, click the My Documents folder to set the save location for the document (Figure C–6).

 What if the My Documents folder does not exist?

Click another folder to select it as the save location. Record the name of this folder so that you can locate and retrieve the file later in this appendix.

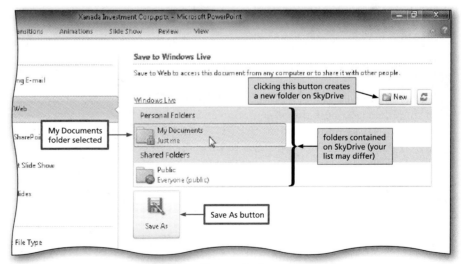

**Figure C–6**

 What is the difference between the personal folders and the shared folders?

Personal folders are private and are not shared with anyone. Shared folders can be viewed by SkyDrive users to whom you have assigned the necessary permissions.

● Click the Save As button in the right pane of the Save & Send gallery to contact the SkyDrive server (which may take some time, depending on the speed of your Internet connection) and then display the Save As dialog box (Figure C–7).

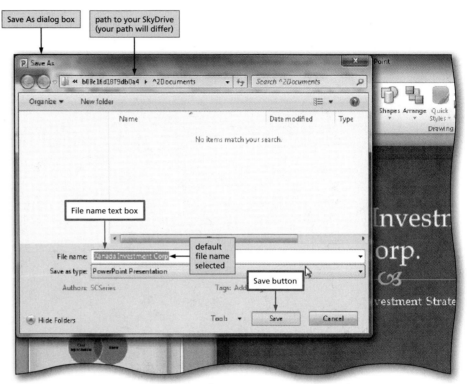

**Figure C–7**

● Type **Xanada Investment Web** in the File name text box to enter the file name and then click the Save button (Save As dialog box) to save the file to Windows Live SkyDrive (Figure C–8).

**Q&A**

Is it necessary to rename the file?

It is good practice to rename the file. If you download the file from SkyDrive to your computer, having a different file name will preserve the original file.

**Figure C–8**

● If you have one PowerPoint presentation open, click the Close button on the right side of the title bar to close the presentation and quit PowerPoint; or if you have multiple PowerPoint presentations open, click File on the Ribbon to open the Backstage view and then click Exit in the Backstage view to close all open presentations and quit PowerPoint.

## Web Apps

Microsoft has created a scaled-down, Web-based version of its Microsoft Office suite, called **Microsoft Office Web Apps,** or **Web Apps**. Web Apps contains Web-based versions of Word, PowerPoint, Excel, and OneNote that can be used to view and edit files that are saved to SkyDrive. Web Apps allows users to continue working with their files even while they are not using a computer with Microsoft Office installed. In addition to working with files located on SkyDrive, Web Apps also enables users to create new Word documents, PowerPoint presentations, Excel spreadsheets, and OneNote notebooks. After returning to a computer with the Microsoft Office suite, some users choose to download files from SkyDrive and edit them using the associated Microsoft Office program.

## To Open a File from Windows Live SkyDrive

Files saved to SkyDrive can be opened from a Web browser using any computer with an Internet connection. The following steps open the Xanada Investment Web file using a Web browser.

**1**

- Click the Internet Explorer program button pinned on the Windows 7 taskbar to start Internet Explorer.

- Type **skydrive.live.com** in the Address bar and then press the ENTER key to display a SkyDrive Web page requesting you sign in to your Windows Live account (Figure C–9).

**Q&A** Why does the Web address change after I enter it in the Address bar?

The Web address changes because you are being redirected to sign into Windows Live before you can access SkyDrive.

**Q&A** Can I open the file from Microsoft PowerPoint instead of using the Web browser?

If you are opening the file on the same computer from which you saved it to the SkyDrive, click File on the Ribbon to open the Backstage view. Click the Recent tab and then click the desired file name (Xanada Investment Web, in this case) in the Recent Presentations list, or click Open and then navigate to the location of the saved file (for a detailed example of this procedure, refer to the Office 2010 and Windows 7 chapter at the beginning of this book).

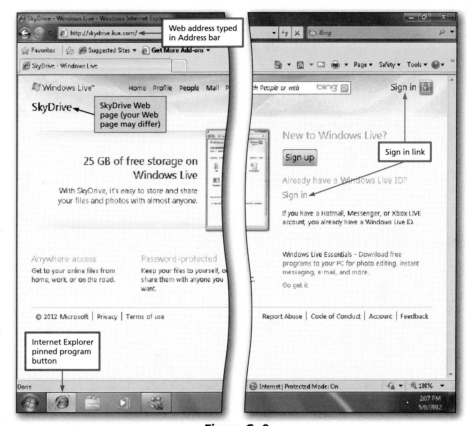

**Figure C–9**

**2**

- Click the Sign in link to display the Windows Live ID and Password text boxes (Figure C–10).

**Q&A** Why can I not locate the Sign in link?

If your computer remembers your Windows Live sign in credentials from a previous session, your e-mail address already may be displayed on the SkyDrive Web page. In this case, point to your e-mail address to display the Sign in button, click the Sign in button, and then proceed to Step 3. If you cannot locate your e-mail address or Sign in link, click the Sign in with a different Windows Live ID link and then proceed to Step 3.

**Figure C–10**

- If necessary, enter your Windows Live ID and password in the appropriate text boxes and then click the Sign in button to sign into Windows Live and display the contents of your SkyDrive (Figure C–11).

**Q&A**

What do the icons beside the folders mean?

The lock icon indicates that the folder is private and is accessible only to you. The people icon signifies a folder that can be shared with SkyDrive users to whom you have assigned the necessary permissions. The globe icon denotes a folder accessible to anyone on the Internet.

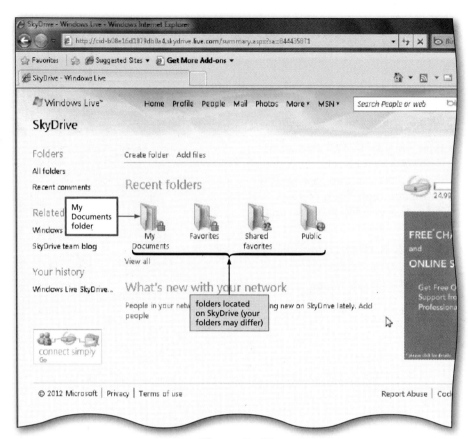

**Figure C–11**

**4**

- Click the My Documents folder, or the folder containing the file you wish to open, to select the folder and display its contents (Figure C–12).

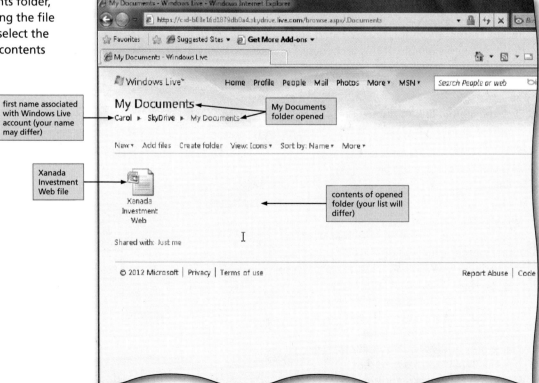

**Figure C–12**

**5**

- Click the Xanada Investment Web file to select the file and display information about it (Figure C–13).

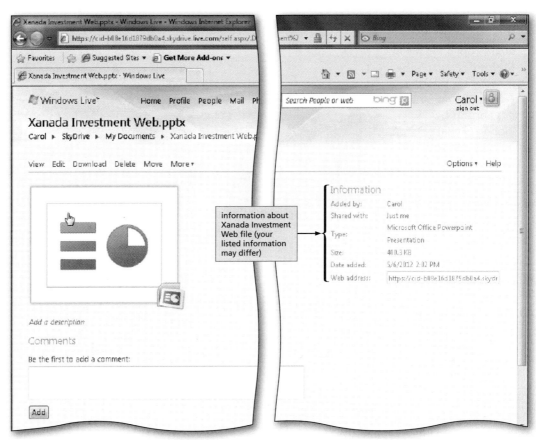

**Figure C–13**

**6**

- Click the Download link to display the File Download dialog box (Figure C–14).

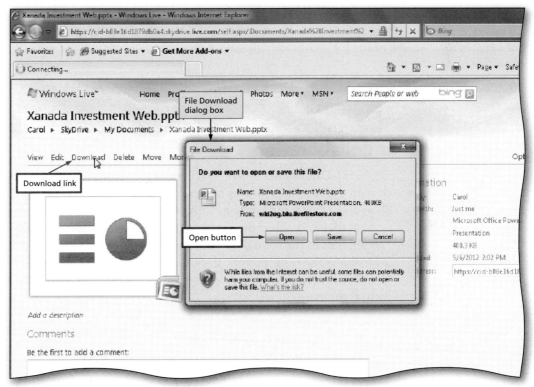

**Figure C–14**

- Click the Open button (File Download dialog box) to open the file in Microsoft PowerPoint. If necessary, click the Enable Editing button if it appears below the Ribbon so that you can edit the presentation in PowerPoint (Figure C–15).

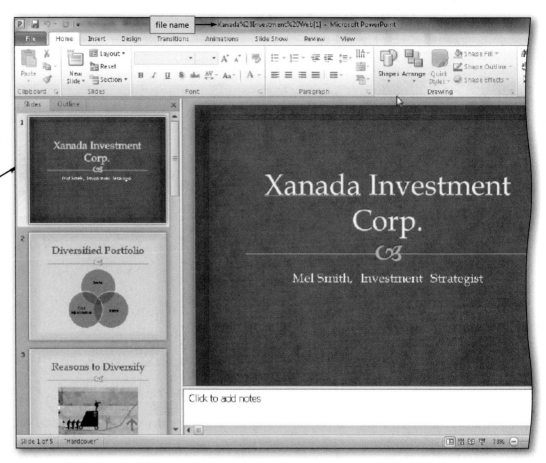

**Figure C–15**

**Q&A**

What if I want to save the file on my computer's hard disk?

Refer to the Office 2010 and Windows 7 chapter at the beginning of this book.

**Q&A**

Why does the file name on the title bar look different from the file name I typed when saving the document?

Because you are opening the file directly from SkyDrive without first saving it to your computer, the file name may differ slightly. For example, spaces may be replaced with "%20" and a number in parentheses at the end of the file name may indicate you are opening a copy of the original file that is stored online.

## Collaboration

In today's workplace, it is common to work with others on projects. Collaborating with the members of your team often requires sharing files. It also can involve multiple people editing and working with a certain set of files simultaneously. Placing files on SkyDrive in a public or shared folder enables others to view or modify the files. The members of the team then can view and edit the files simultaneously using Web Apps, enabling the team to work from one set of files. Collaboration using Web Apps not only enables multiple people to work together, it also can reduce the amount of time required to complete a project.

# Index

# Quick Reference Summary

## Microsoft PowerPoint 2010 Quick Reference Summary

| Task | Page Number | Mouse | Ribbon | Shortcut Menu | Keyboard Shortcut |
|---|---|---|---|---|---|
| **Action Button, Copy** | PPT 348 | | Copy button (Home tab \| Clipboard group) | Copy | CTRL+C |
| **Action Button, Edit Setting** | PPT 349 | | Action button (Insert tab \| Links group) | | |
| **Action Button, Insert** | PPT 344 | | Shapes button (Insert tab \| Illustrations group), Action Buttons area | | |
| **Animated GIF (Movie), Insert** | PPT 174 | | Picture button (Insert tab \| Images group) | | |
| **Animation, Add after Existing Effect** | PPT 413, 414 | | Add Animation button (Animations tab \| Advanced Animation group) | | |
| **Animation, Associate Sound with** | PPT 430 | | Add sound to slide, click sound icon, Play button (Animations tab \| Animation group), With Previous | | |
| **Animation, Change Direction** | PPT 412 | | Effect Options button (Animations tab \| Animation group) | | |
| **Animation, Change Order** | PPT 420 | | Animation Pane button (Animations tab \| Advanced Animation group) | | |
| **Animation, Dim Text After** | PPT 440 | | Animation Pane button (Animations tab \| Advanced Animation group), Animation Order list arrow, Effect Options, After animation list arrow | | |
| **Animation, Modify Timing** | PPT 416 | | Start Animation Timing button arrow (Animations tab \| Timing group) | | |
| **Animation, Preview Sequence** | PPT 416 | | Preview button (Animations tab \| Preview group) | | |
| **Animation Painter, Use to Copy Animations** | PPT 433 | | Animation Painter button (Animations tab \| Advanced Animation group) | | |
| **Audio File, Insert** | PPT 167 | | Insert Audio button (Insert tab \| Media group) | | |

| Task | Page Number | Mouse | Ribbon | Shortcut Menu | Keyboard Shortcut |
|------|-------------|-------|--------|---------------|-------------------|
| **Audio Options, Add** | PPT 170 | | Audio options check boxes (Audio Tools Playback tab \| Audio Options group) | | |
| **Broadcast Presentation** | PPT 705 | | Broadcast Slide Show button (Slide Show tab \| Start Slide Show group), Start Broadcast button (Broadcast Slide Show dialog box) | | |
| **Bullet, Format Color** | PPT 379 | | Bullets button arrow (Home tab \| Paragraph group), Bullets and Numbering, Color button | Bullets, Bullets and Numbering | |
| **Bullet, Format Size** | PPT 377 | | Bullets button arrow (Home tab \| Paragraph group), Bullets and Numbering, Size box | Bullets, Bullets and Numbering | |
| **Bullet Character, Change to Number** | PPT 380 | | Numbering button arrow (Home tab \| Paragraph group) | Bullets, Bullets and Numbering | |
| **Bullet Character, Change to Picture** | PPT 372 | | Bullets button arrow (Home tab \| Paragraph group), Bullets and Numbering, Picture button (Bullets and Numbering dialog box) | | |
| **Bullet Character, Change to Symbol** | PPT 375 | | Bullets button arrow (Home tab \| Paragraph group), Bullets and Numbering, Customize button (Bullets and Numbering dialog box) | | |
| **Bullet Characters, Remove** | PPT 382 | | Bullets button arrow (Home tab \| Paragraph group), None | Bullets, None | |
| **Character Spacing, Change** | PPT 486 | | Character Spacing button (Home tab \| Font group); Font Dialog Box Launcher (Home tab \| Font Group), Character Spacing tab | | |
| **Chart, Align** | PPT 625 | | Align button (Drawing Tools Format tab \| Arrange group) or (Chart Tools Format tab \| Arrange group) | | |
| **Chart, Animate** | PPT 437 | | More button (Animations tab \| Animation group) | | |
| **Chart, Apply Quick Style** | PPT 628 | | More button (Chart Tools Design tab \| Chart Styles group) | | |
| **Chart, Apply Style** | PPT 223 | | More button (Chart Tools Design tab \| Chart Styles group) | | |
| **Chart, Change Layout** | PPT 226 | | More button (Chart Tools Design tab \| Chart Layouts group) | | |
| **Chart, Change Type** | PPT 627 | | Change Chart Type button (Chart Tools Design tab \| Type group) | | |
| **Chart, Display Gridlines** | PPT 633 | | Gridlines button (Chart Tools Layout tab \| Axes group) | | |
| **Chart, Display Labels** | PPT 632 | | Data Labels button (Chart Tools Layout tab \| Labels group) | | |

**Microsoft PowerPoint 2010 Quick Reference Summary** *(continued)*

| Task | Page Number | Mouse | Ribbon | Shortcut Menu | Keyboard Shortcut |
|------|-------------|-------|--------|---------------|-------------------|
| **Chart, Format Background** | PPT 634 | | Chart Wall button (Chart Tools Layout tab \| Background group) | | |
| **Chart, Format Legend** | PPT 629 | | Legend button (Chart Tools Layout tab \| Labels group) | Format Legend | |
| **Chart, Hide Axis** | PPT 632 | | Axes button (Chart Tools Layout tab \| Axes group), Primary Vertical Axis or Primary Horizontal Axis, None | | |
| **Chart, Insert** | PPT 220 | Insert Chart button in content placeholder | Chart button (Insert tab \| Illustrations group) | | |
| **Chart, Insert from Excel** | PPT 624 | | Insert Object button (Insert tab \| Text group), Create from file, browse to file with chart | Copy chart in Microsoft Excel, exit Microsoft Excel, Paste button arrow (Home tab \| Clipboard group), Use Destination Theme & Embed Workbook | |
| **Chart, Resize** | PPT 228 | Drag sizing handle to desired location | | | |
| **Chart, Rotate** | PPT 230 | | Format Selection button (Chart Tools Format tab \| Current Selection group) | | |
| **Chart, Separate a Pie Slice** | PPT 229 | Select slice and drag | | | |
| **Chart, Switch Rows and Columns** | PPT 626 | | Switch Row/Column button (Chart Tools Design tab \| Data group) | | |
| **Chart Shape, Change Outline Color** | PPT 226 | | Shape Outline button arrow (Chart Tools Format tab \| Shape Styles group) | | |
| **Chart Shape, Change Outline Weight** | PPT 224 | | Shape Outline button arrow (Chart Tools Format tab \| Shape Styles group), Weight | | |
| **Clip Art, Insert** | PPT 27 | Clip Art button in content placeholder | Clip Art button (Insert tab \| Images group) | | |
| **Clip Art, Photo, or Shape, Move** | PPT 36 | Drag | | | ARROW KEYS move selected image in small increments |
| **Clip Art, Regroup** | PPT 162 | | Group button (Drawing Tools Format tab \| Arrange group), Regroup | Group, Regroup | |
| **Clip Art, Ungroup** | PPT 157 | | Group button (Picture Tools Format tab \| Arrange group), Ungroup | Group, Ungroup | |
| **Clip Object, Recolor** | PPT 158 | | Shape Fill button (Drawing Tools Format tab \| Shape Styles group) | Format Shape, Solid fill option button, Color button (Format Shape dialog box) | |
| **Columns, Adjust Spacing** | PPT 369 | | Columns button (Home tab \| Paragraph group), More Columns, Spacing box | | |

**Microsoft PowerPoint 2010 Quick Reference Summary** *(continued)*

| Task | Page Number | Mouse | Ribbon | Shortcut Menu | Keyboard Shortcut |
|------|-------------|-------|--------|---------------|-------------------|
| **Columns, Create in a Placeholder** | PPT 367 | | Columns button (Home tab \| Paragraph group) | | |
| **Comment, Delete** | PPT 274 | | Delete Comment button (Review tab \| Comments group) | | |
| **Comment, Edit** | PPT 282 | | Edit Comment button (Review tab \| Comments group) | | |
| **Comment, Insert** | PPT 281 | | New Comment button (Review tab \| Comments group) | | |
| **Comments, Print** | PPT 271 | | Page Layout button (File tab \| Print tab), check 'Print Comments and Ink Markup' box | | CTRL+P |
| **Copy** | PPT 108, 155, 348 | | Copy button (Home tab \| Clipboard group) | Copy | CTRL+C |
| **Credits, Create** | PPT 442 | | More button (Animations tab \| Animation group), More Entrance Effects, Credits | | |
| **Custom Slide Show, Create** | PPT 674 | | In Normal view, Custom Slide Show button (Slide Show tab \| Start Slide Show group), Custom Shows, New | | |
| **Custom Slide Show, Edit** | PPT 677 | | In Normal view, Custom Slide Show button (Slide Show tab \| Start Slide Show group), Custom Shows, select show, Edit | | |
| **Digital Signature, Create and Add** | PPT 309 | | Protect Presentation button (File tab \| Info tab), Add a Digital Signature | | |
| **Document Inspector, Start** | PPT 303 | | Check for Issues button (File tab \| Info tab), Inspect Document | | |
| **Document Properties, Change** | PPT 46 | | Properties button (File tab \| Info tab) | | |
| **Document Theme, Change Color** | PPT 81 | | Colors button (Design tab \| Themes group) | | |
| **Document Theme, Choose** | PPT 5 | | More button (Design tab \| Themes group) | | |
| **Embedded File, Edit** | PPT 601 | Double-click embedded object to open source program | | Document Object, Edit | |
| **File with Graphics and Text, Insert** | PPT 598 | | Insert Object button (Insert tab \| Text group), Create from file | | |
| **Fill Color, Apply to Slide** | PPT 507 | | Background Styles button (Design tab \| Background group), Format Background, Fill pane | Format Background, Fill pane | |
| **Fill Color, Set Transparency** | PPT 507 | | Background Styles button (Design tab \| Background group), Format Background, Fill pane, Transparency slider | Format Background, Fill pane, Transparency slider | |
| **Font, Change** | PPT 102 | Font box arrow on Mini toolbar | Font box arrow (Home tab \| Font group) | Font, Font tab (Font dialog box) | CTRL+SHIFT+F |

**Microsoft PowerPoint 2010 Quick Reference Summary** *(continued)*

| Task | Page Number | Mouse | Ribbon | Shortcut Menu | Keyboard Shortcut |
|------|-------------|-------|--------|---------------|-------------------|
| **Font, Change Color** | PPT 13 | Font Color button or Font Color button arrow on Mini toolbar | Font Color button or Font Color button arrow (Home tab \| Font group) | Font, Font tab (Font dialog box) | CTRL+SHIFT+F |
| **Font Size, Decrease** | PPT 104 | Decrease Font Size button or Font Size box arrow on Mini toolbar | Decrease Font Size button or Font Size box arrow (Home tab \| Font group) | | CTRL+SHIFT+< |
| **Font Size, Increase** | PPT 11 | Increase Font Size button or Font Size box arrow on Mini toolbar | Increase Font Size button or Font Size box arrow (Home tab \| Font group) | | CTRL+SHIFT+> |
| **Footer, Add** | PPT 289, 476 | | Header & Footer button (Insert tab \| Text group) | | |
| **Format Painter** | PPT 105 | Format Painter button on Mini toolbar | Format Painter button (Home tab \| Clipboard group) | | |
| **Guides, Display** | PPT 357 | | Guides check box (View tab \| Show group) | Grid and Guides, 'Display drawing guides on screen' check box | ALT+F9 |
| **Handout, Create by Exporting File to Microsoft Word** | PPT 578 | | Create Handouts button (File tab \| Save & Send tab) | | |
| **Handout, Print** | PPT 184, 510 | | Print button (File tab \| Print tab) | | |
| **Handout Master, Use** | PPT 496, 510 | | Handout Master button (View tab \| Master Views group) | | |
| **Header, Add** | PPT 289 | | Header & Footer button (Insert tab \| Text group) | | |
| **Hyperlink, Add** | PPT 339, 341, 636 | | Hyperlink button (Insert tab \| Links group) | Hyperlink | CTRL+K |
| **Hyperlink to Another PowerPoint File** | PPT 350 | | Action button (Insert tab \| Links group), Hyperlink to list arrow, Other PowerPoint Presentation | | |
| **Hyperlink to a Word File** | PPT 353 | | Action button (Insert tab \| Links group), Hyperlink to list arrow, Other File | | |
| **Line, Change Weight or Color** | PPT 567 | | Shape Outline button (Drawing Tools Format tab \| Shape Styles group), Weight or choose color | | |
| **Line, Draw** | PPT 565 | | More button (Drawing Tools Format tab \| Insert Shapes group), click desired Line shape | | |
| **Line, Set Formatting as Default** | PPT 568 | | | Set as Default Line | |
| **Line Break, Enter** | PPT 371 | | | | SHIFT+ENTER |
| **Line Spacing, Change** | PPT 367 | | Line Spacing button (Home tab \| Paragraph group) | Paragraph | |
| **Linked File, Insert** | PPT 618 | | Insert Object button (Insert tab \| Text group), Create from file, Link check box | | |
| **Linked Worksheet, Edit** | PPT 622 | Double-click linked object to open source program | | | |
| **List, Animate** | PPT 439 | | More button (Animations tab \| Animation group) | | |

**Microsoft PowerPoint 2010 Quick Reference Summary** *(continued)*

| Task | Page Number | Mouse | Ribbon | Shortcut Menu | Keyboard Shortcut |
|---|---|---|---|---|---|
| **List Level, Decrease** | PPT 18 | Decrease List Level button on Mini toolbar | Decrease List Level button (Home tab \| Paragraph group) | | SHIFT+TAB or ALT+SHIFT+LEFT ARROW |
| **List Level, Increase** | PPT 17 | Increase List Level button on Mini toolbar | Increase List Level button (Home tab \| Paragraph group) | | TAB or ALT+SHIFT+RIGHT ARROW |
| **Manual Timing, Show Presentation with** | PPT 673 | | Set Up Slide Show button (Slide Show tab \| Set Up group), Manually (Set Up Show dialog box) | | |
| **Master View** | PPT 471 | | Slide Master button (View tab \| Master Views group) | | |
| **Merge a Presentation** | PPT 270 | | Compare button (Review tab \| Compare group) | | |
| **Narration, Record** | PPT 694 | | Record Slide Show button arrow (Slide Show tab \| Set Up group), Start Recording from Beginning or Start Recording from Current Slide, Narrations and laser pointer check box (Record Slide Show dialog box), Start Recording button (Record Slide Show dialog box), End Show | | |
| **Next Slide** | PPT 25 | Next Slide button on vertical scroll bar or next slide thumbnail on Slides tab | | | PAGE DOWN |
| **Normal View** | PPT 153 | Normal view button at lower-right PowerPoint window | Normal View button (View tab \| Presentation Views group) | | |
| **Notes Master, Use** | PPT 500, 512 | | View Notes Master button (View tab \| Master Views group) | | |
| **Numbered List, Format** | PPT 382 | | Numbering button arrow (Home tab \| Paragraph group), Bullets and Numbering | Numbering, Bullets and Numbering | |
| **Open Presentation** | PPT 50 | | Open (File tab) | | CTRL+O |
| **Outline, Open as Presentation** | PPT 335 | | Open (File tab), File Type arrow, All Outlines, select Word file, Open button | | |
| **Password, Set** | PPT 305 | | Protect Presentation button (File tab \| Info tab), Encrypt with Password | | |
| **Paste** | PPT 109 | | Paste button (Home tab \| Clipboard group) | Paste | CTRL+V |
| **Pattern Fill, Apply to Slide** | PPT 509 | | Background Styles button (Design tab \| Background group), Format Background, Fill pane, Pattern fill | Format Background, Fill pane, Pattern fill | |
| **Photo, Insert** | PPT 32, 83 | Insert Picture from File button in content placeholder or Insert Clip Art button in content placeholder | Picture button or Clip Art button (Insert tab \| Images group) | | |

**Microsoft PowerPoint 2010 Quick Reference Summary** *(continued)*

| Task | Page Number | Mouse | Ribbon | Shortcut Menu | Keyboard Shortcut |
|------|-------------|-------|--------|---------------|-------------------|
| **Photo Album, Add Captions Below All Pictures** | PPT 686 | | New Photo Album button arrow (Insert tab \| Images group), Captions below ALL pictures check box (Photo Album dialog box) | | |
| **Photo Album, Add Theme** | PPT 686 | | New Photo Album button arrow (Insert tab \| Images group), Browse button in Album Layout area (Photo Album dialog box) | | |
| **Photo Album, Change Layout** | PPT 685 | | New Photo Album button arrow (Insert tab \| Images group), Picture layout box arrow (Photo Album dialog box) | | |
| **Photo Album, Create** | PPT 687 | | New Photo Album button arrow (Insert tab \| Images group), Create button (Photo Album dialog box) | | |
| **Photo Album, Create Black-and-White Images** | PPT 690 | | New Photo Album button arrow (Insert tab \| Images group), ALL pictures black and white check box (Photo Album dialog box), Update | | |
| **Photo Album, Edit** | PPT 687 | | New Photo Album button arrow (Insert tab \| Images group), Edit Photo Album | | |
| **Photo Album, Reorder Pictures** | PPT 682 | | New Photo Album button arrow (Insert tab \| Images group), Move Up or Move Down button (Photo Album dialog box) | | |
| **Photo Album, Start and Add Pictures** | PPT 680 | | New Photo Album button (Insert tab \| Images group) | | |
| **Photo Album Image, Adjust Brightness** | PPT 684 | | New Photo Album button arrow (Insert tab \| Images group), Increase Brightness or Decrease Brightness button (Photo Album dialog box) | | |
| **Photo Album Image, Adjust Contrast** | PPT 684 | | New Photo Album button arrow (Insert tab \| Images group), Increase Contrast or Decrease Contrast button (Photo Album dialog box) | | |
| **Photo Album Image, Adjust Rotation** | PPT 683 | | New Photo Album button arrow (Insert tab \| Images group), Rotate Left 90° or Rotate Right 90° button (Photo Album dialog box) | | |
| **Picture, Add an Artistic Effect** | PPT 145 | | Artistic Effects button (Picture Tools Format tab \| Adjust group) | Format Picture, Artistic Effects (Format Picture dialog box) | |

## Microsoft PowerPoint 2010 Quick Reference Summary *(continued)*

| Task | Page Number | Mouse | Ribbon | Shortcut Menu | Keyboard Shortcut |
|------|-------------|-------|--------|---------------|-------------------|
| Picture, Add Border | PPT 91 | | Picture border button (Picture Tools Format tab \| Picture Styles group) | | |
| Picture, Animate | PPT 411, 414, 415, 425 | | Select picture, choose animation in Animation gallery (Animations tab \| Animation group) | | |
| Picture, Change | PPT 544 | | Change Picture button (Picture Tools Format tab \| Adjust group), select new picture file | | |
| Picture, Clear Formatting | PPT 291 | | Reset Picture button (Picture Tools Format tab \| Adjust group) | | |
| Picture, Compress | PPT 410 | | Compress Pictures button (Picture Tools Format tab \| Adjust group) | | |
| Picture, Correct | PPT 87 | | Corrections button (Picture Tools Format tab \| Adjust group) | Format Picture, Picture Corrections (Format Picture dialog box) | |
| Picture, Crop | PPT 409 | | Crop button (Picture Tools Format tab \| Size group), drag cropping handles | | |
| Picture, Recolor | PPT 143 | | Color button (Picture Tools Format tab \| Adjust group) | Format Picture, Picture Color (Format Picture dialog box) | |
| Picture, Remove Background | PPT 405, 407 | | Remove Background button (Picture Tools Format tab \| Adjust group) | | |
| Picture, Rotate | PPT 489 | Drag rotation handle | | | |
| Picture Border, Change Color | PPT 92 | | Picture Border button (Picture Tools Format tab \| Picture Styles group) | | |
| Picture Effects, Apply | PPT 89 | | Picture Effects button (Picture Tools Format tab \| Picture Styles group) | Format Picture | |
| Picture Presentation, Save as | PPT 576 | | Change File Type (File tab \| Save & Send tab), PowerPoint Picture Presentation | | |
| Picture Style, Apply | PPT 87 | | More button (Picture Tools Format tab \| Picture Styles group) | | |
| Pictures, Align | PPT 360, 362 | | Align button (Picture Tools Format tab \| Arrange group) | | |
| Placeholder, Delete | PPT 149 | | | | Select placeholder, DELETE |
| Placeholder, Move | PPT 148 | Drag | | | |
| Placeholder, Resize | PPT 148 | Drag sizing handles | | | |
| Presentation, Check for Compatibility | PPT 301 | | Check for Issues button, (File tab \| Info tab), Check Compatibility | | |

## Microsoft PowerPoint 2010 Quick Reference Summary *(continued)*

| Task | Page Number | Mouse | Ribbon | Shortcut Menu | Keyboard Shortcut |
|---|---|---|---|---|---|
| Presentation, Create Self-Running | PPT 447 | | Set Up Slide Show button (Slide Show tab \| Set Up group), 'Browsed at a kiosk (full screen)' option | | |
| Presentation, Display Multiple Windows Simultaneously | PPT 697 | | With multiple presentations open, Cascade button or Arrange All button (View tab \| Window group) | | |
| Presentation, Mark as Final | PPT 308 | | Protect Presentation button, (File tab \| Info tab), Mark as Final | | |
| Presentation, Package for CD or DVD | PPT 297 | | Package Presentation for CD (File tab \| Send & Save tab), Package Presentation for CD button | | |
| Presentation, Print | PPT 51, 184, 271 | | Print button (File tab \| Print tab) | | CTRL+P |
| Presentation Change, Accept | PPT 276 | | Accept Change button (Review tab \| Compare group) | | |
| Presentation Change, Reject | PPT 278, 280 | | Reject Change button (Review tab \| Compare group) | | |
| Presentation Changes, End Review | PPT 283 | | End Review button (Review tab \| Compare group) | | |
| Presentation Changes, Review | PPT 273 | | Reviewing Pane button (Review tab \| Compare group) | | |
| Presenter View, Use | PPT 708 | | Use Presenter View check box (Slide Show tab \| Monitors group), icon on Monitor tab, 'This is my main monitor' check box, icon that represents second monitor, 'Extend my Windows Desktop onto this monitor' check box, Set Up Slide Show button (Slide Show tab \| Set Up group) | | |
| Previous Slide | PPT 26 | Previous Slide button on vertical scroll bar or click previous slide thumbnail on Slides tab | | | PAGE UP |
| Quit PowerPoint | PPT 50 | Close button on title bar | Exit (File tab) | Right-click Microsoft PowerPoint button on taskbar, click Close window | ALT+F4 |
| Reading View | PPT 154 | Reading view button at lower-right PowerPoint window | Reading View button (View tab \| Presentation Views group) | | |
| Research Pane, Use to Find Information | PPT 692 | | Research button (Review tab \| Proofing group) | | Press ALT and click word to research |

**Microsoft PowerPoint 2010 Quick Reference Summary** *(continued)*

| Task | Page Number | Mouse | Ribbon | Shortcut Menu | Keyboard Shortcut |
|---|---|---|---|---|---|
| **Resize** | PPT 33, 93, 148 | Drag sizing handles | Enter height and width values (Picture Tools Format tab \| Size group or Drawing Tools Format tab \| Size group) | Format Picture or Format Shape, Size tab, or enter height and width in Shape Height and Shape Width boxes | |
| **Ribbon, Customize** | PPT 570 | | Options (File tab), Customize Ribbon (PowerPoint Options dialog box) | | |
| **Ribbon, Reset** | PPT 579 | | Options (File tab), Customize Ribbon, Reset button (PowerPoint Options dialog box) | | |
| **Rulers, Display** | PPT 359 | | Ruler check box (View tab \| Show group) | Ruler | |
| **Save a Presentation** | PPT 14, 295, 297, 300 | Save button on Quick Access Toolbar | Save or Save As (File tab) | | CTRL+S or F12 |
| **Save a Slide as an Image** | PPT 296 | | Change File Type (File tab, Save & Send tab), JPEG File Interchange Format, Save As button | | |
| **Save as a PowerPoint Show** | PPT 295 | | Change File Type (File tab \| Save & Send tab), PowerPoint Show, Save As button | | |
| **Save in a Previous Format** | PPT 300 | | Change File Type (File tab \| Save & Send tab), PowerPoint 97-2003 Presentation, Save As button | | |
| **Screen Clipping, Use** | PPT 288 | | Screenshot button (Insert tab \| Images group), Screen Clipping command | | |
| **Section, Create Break** | PPT 666 | Click mouse where section break desired, then follow Ribbon steps | In Slide Sorter view, Section button (Home tab \| Slides group), Add Section | | |
| **Section, Rename** | PPT 669 | | Section button (Home tab \| Slides group), Rename Section | Rename Section | |
| **Sections, Collapse or Expand** | PPT 671 | | Section button (Home tab \| Slides group), Collapse All or Expand All | Collapse All or Expand All | |
| **Sections, Reorder** | PPT 682 | Drag section name | | Move Section Up or Move Section Down | |
| **Shape, Apply Fill** | PPT 561 | | Shape Fill button (Drawing Tools Format tab \| Shape Styles group) or Shape Fill button (Home tab \| Drawing group) | Format Shape, Fill pane | |
| **Shape, Apply Style** | PPT 110 | | More button or Format Shape Dialog Box Launcher in Shapes Style gallery (Drawing Tools Format tab \| Shape Styles group) | Format Shape | |

**Microsoft PowerPoint 2010 Quick Reference Summary** *(continued)*

| Task | Page Number | Mouse | Ribbon | Shortcut Menu | Keyboard Shortcut |
|---|---|---|---|---|---|
| **Shape, Change Fill Color** | PPT 347 | | Shape Fill button arrow (Drawing Tools Format tab \| Shape Styles group) | | |
| **Shape, Insert** | PPT 106 | | Shapes button (Home tab \| Drawing group), More button (Drawing Tools Format tab \| Insert Shapes group) | | |
| **Shape Fill, Increase Transparency** | PPT 487 | | Drawing Dialog Box Launcher (Home tab \| Drawing group), Fill Pane, Transparency slider (Format Shape dialog box) | | |
| **Shape Formatting, Set as Default** | PPT 564 | | | Set as Default Shape | |
| **Slide, Add** | PPT 14 | | New Slide button (Home tab \| Slides group) | | CTRL+M |
| **Slide, Arrange** | PPT 39 | Drag slide in Slides tab or Outline tab to new position, or in Slide Sorter view drag to new position | | | |
| **Slide, Delete** | PPT 152 | | | Delete Slide | DELETE |
| **Slide, Duplicate** | PPT 38 | | New Slide button arrow (Home tab \| Slides group), Duplicate Selected Slides | Duplicate Slide | |
| **Slide, Format Background** | PPT 95 | | Background Styles button (Design tab \| Background group) | Format Background | |
| **Slide, Hide** | PPT 363 | | Hide Slide button (Slide Show tab \| Set Up group) | Hide Slide (Slide Sorter view or thumbnail on Slides tab) | |
| **Slide, Insert Picture as Background** | PPT 97 | | Background Styles button (Design tab \| Background group) | Format Background, Picture or texture fill, Insert from File (Format Background dialog box) | |
| **Slide, Reuse from an Existing Presentation** | PPT 285 | | New Slide button arrow (Home tab \| Slides group), Reuse Slides command | | |
| **Slide, Select Layout** | PPT 21 | | Layout button or New Slide button arrow (Home tab \| Slides group) | | |
| **Slide, Set Size** | PPT 292 | | Page Setup button (Design tab \| Page Setup group), 'Slides sized for' box arrow | | |
| **Slide, Set Up Custom Size** | PPT 696 | | Page Setup button (Design tab \| Page Setup group), 'Slides sized for' box arrow, Custom | | |
| **Slide Layout, Delete** | PPT 493 | | Delete button (Home tab \| Slides group) (must be in Slide Master view) | Delete Layout | DELETE |
| **Slide Master, Apply Slide and Font Themes** | PPT 472 | | Themes button (Slide Master tab \| Edit Theme group) | | |

## Microsoft PowerPoint 2010 Quick Reference Summary *(continued)*

| Task | Page Number | Mouse | Ribbon | Shortcut Menu | Keyboard Shortcut |
|------|-------------|-------|--------|---------------|-------------------|
| **Slide Master, Display** | PPT 471 | | Slide Master button (View tab \| Master Views group) | | |
| **Slide Master, Format Background and Apply a Quick Style** | PPT 475 | | Background Styles button (Slide Master tab \| Background group) | | |
| **Slide Master, Hide and Unhide Background Graphics** | PPT 490 | | Hide/Unhide Background Graphics check box (Slide Master tab \| Background group) | | |
| **Slide Master, Insert a Background Graphic** | PPT 479 | | Insert Picture button (Insert tab \| Images group) | | |
| **Slide Master, Insert Placeholder** | PPT 480, 484 | | Insert Placeholder button (Slide Master tab \| Master Layout group) | | |
| **Slide Master and Slide Layout, Rename** | PPT 491 | | Rename button (Slide Master tab \| Edit Master group) | | |
| **Slide Number, Insert** | PPT 182 | | Insert Slide Number button (Insert tab \| Text group) or Header & Footer button (Insert tab \| Text group), Slide number check box | | |
| **Slide Objects, Rename** | PPT 422 | | Select button (Home tab \| Editing group), Selection Pane | | |
| **Slide Orientation, Change** | PPT 696 | | Slide Orientation button (Design tab \| Page Setup group) | | |
| **Slide Show, Adjust Timings Manually** | PPT 446 | | Select slide and set timing (Transitions tab \| Timing group) | | |
| **Slide Show, Draw on Slides During Show** | PPT 313 | | Pointer button, Pen (Slide Show toolbar), drag mouse to draw | | |
| **Slide Show, E-mail from within PowerPoint** | PPT 702 | | Send Using E-mail (File tab \| Save & Send tab), Send as Attachment button | | |
| **Slide Show, End** | PPT 49 | Click black ending slide | | End Show | ESC or HYPHEN |
| **Slide Show, Highlight Items During Show** | PPT 312 | | Pointer button, Highlighter (Slide Show toolbar), drag mouse to highlight | | |
| **Slide Show, Rehearse Timings** | PPT 444 | | Rehearse Timings button (Slide Show tab \| Set Up group) | | |
| **Slide Show, Set Resolution** | PPT 294 | | Resolution box arrow (Slide Show tab \| Monitors group) | | |
| **Slide Show View** | PPT 47 | Slide Show view button at lower-right PowerPoint window | From Beginning button (Slide Show tab \| Start Slide Show group) | | F5 |
| **Slide Sorter View** | PPT 153, 664 | Slide Sorter view button at lower-right PowerPoint window | Slide Sorter button (View tab \| Presentation Views group) | | |
| **Slides, Insert with a Section Layout** | PPT 661 | | Slide Layout button (Home tab \| Slides group), Section Header layout | | |
| **SmartArt, Change Layout** | PPT 550 | | More button (SmartArt Tools Design tab \| Layouts group) | | |

**Microsoft PowerPoint 2010 Quick Reference Summary** *(continued)*

| Task | Page Number | Mouse | Ribbon | Shortcut Menu | Keyboard Shortcut |
|------|-------------|-------|--------|---------------|-------------------|
| **SmartArt, Convert to Text or Shapes** | PPT 557, 559 | | Convert button (SmartArt Tools Design tab \| Reset group) | | |
| **SmartArt, Remove Shape** | PPT 551 | | | | Select shape, DELETE |
| **SmartArt, Resize Graphic Shape** | PPT 554 | | Smaller or Larger button (SmartArt Tools Format tab \| Shapes group) | Size and Position, Size tab | |
| **SmartArt Bullet Level, Promote or Demote** | PPT 548, 549 | | Promote button or Demote button (SmartArt Tools Design tab \| Create Graphic group) | | |
| **SmartArt Graphic, Add Text** | PPT 208 | | Text Pane button (SmartArt Tools Design tab \| Create Graphic group) | | See Table 4–2, PPT 207 |
| **SmartArt Graphic, Animate** | PPT 435, 436 | | More button (Animations tab \| Animation group) | | |
| **SmartArt Graphic, Apply Style** | PPT 210 | | More button (SmartArt Tools Design tab \| SmartArt Styles group) | | |
| **SmartArt Graphic, Change Color** | PPT 211 | | Change Colors button (SmartArt Tools Design tab \| SmartArt Styles group) | | |
| **SmartArt Graphic, Insert** | PPT 206 | | SmartArt button (Insert tab \| Illustrations group) | | |
| **SmartArt Graphic, Insert Picture** | PPT 209 | Insert Picture from File button in picture placeholder | | | |
| **SmartArt Graphic, Resize** | PPT 212, 553 | Drag sizing handle to desired location | Shape width and Shape height boxes (SmartArt Tools Format tab \| Size group) | Size and Position, Size tab | |
| **SmartArt Shapes, Reorder** | PPT 547 | | Move Up or Move Down button (SmartArt Tools Design tab \| Create Graphic group) | | |
| **Speaker Notes, Add** | PPT 179 | In Normal view, click Notes pane and type notes | | | |
| **Speaker Notes, Print** | PPT 187, 512 | | Page Layout button (File tab \| Print tab), Notes Pages | | |
| **Spelling, Check** | PPT 181 | | Spelling button (Review tab \| Proofing group) | Spelling (or click correct word on shortcut menu) | F7 |
| **Stacking Order, Change** | PPT 146 | | Bring Forward or Send Backward button (Picture Tools Format tab \| Arrange group) | Send to Back or Bring to Front | |
| **Symbol, Insert** | PPT 233 | | Symbol button (Insert tab \| Symbols group) | | |
| **Synonym, Find and Insert** | PPT 178 | | Thesaurus button (Review tab \| Proofing group) | Synonyms | SHIFT+F7 |
| **Table, Add Borders** | PPT 238 | | Border button arrow (Table Tools Design tab \| Table Styles group) | | |
| **Table, Add Cell Effects** | PPT 614 | | Effects button (Table Tools Design tab \| Table Styles group) | | |
| **Table, Add Effect** | PPT 238 | | Effects button (Table Tools Design tab \| Table Styles group) | | |

**Microsoft PowerPoint 2010 Quick Reference Summary** *(continued)*

| Task | Page Number | Mouse | Ribbon | Shortcut Menu | Keyboard Shortcut |
|------|-------------|-------|--------|---------------|-------------------|
| Table, Add Gradient Fill | PPT 613 | | Shading button arrow (Table Tools Design tab \| Table Styles group), Gradient | | |
| Table, Add Shading | PPT 612 | | Shading button arrow (Table Tools Design tab \| Table Styles group) | | |
| Table, Align | PPT 617 | | Align button (Table Tools Layout tab \| Arrange group) | | |
| Table, Apply Style | PPT 236 | | More button (Table Tools Design tab \| Table Styles group) | | |
| Table, Distribute Rows | PPT 614 | | Distribute Rows button (Table Tools Layout tab \| Cell Size group) | | |
| Table, Draw | PPT 603 | | Table button (Insert tab \| Tables group), Draw Table, drag pencil pointer | | |
| Table, Insert | PPT 232 | Insert Table button in content placeholder | Table button (Insert tab \| Tables group) | | |
| Table, Merge Cells | PPT 242 | | Merge Cells button (Table Tools Layout tab \| Merge group) | Merge Cells | |
| Table, Resize | PPT 240 | Drag sizing handle to desired location | Height and Width boxes (Table Tools Layout tab \| Table Size group) | | |
| Table, Resize Columns and Rows | PPT 615 | Drag column or row borders | Table Row Height or Table Column Width arrows (Table Tools Layout tab \| Cell Size group) | | |
| Table, Split Columns or Rows | PPT 610 | | Split Cells button (Table Tools Layout tab \| Merge group) | Split Cells | |
| Table Cell, Add Image | PPT 241 | | | Format Shape, Picture or texture fill | |
| Table Cell, Center Text Vertically | PPT 245 | | Center Vertically button (Table Tools Layout tab \| Alignment group) | Format Shape, Text Box, Vertical alignment arrow | |
| Table Cell, Change Text Direction | PPT 244 | | Text Direction button (Table Tools Layout tab \| Alignment group) | Format Shape, Text Box, Text direction arrow | |
| Table Line, Erase | PPT 608 | | Table Eraser button (Table Tools Design tab \| Draw Borders group), click line to erase | | |
| Table Rows and Columns, Draw | PPT 604, 606 | | Draw Table button (Table Tools Design tab \| Draw Borders group), drag pencil pointer | | |
| Template, Save a Master As | PPT 502 | | Change File type (File tab \| Save & Send tab), Template, Save As button | | |
| Text, Add Shadow | PPT 103 | | Text Shadow button (Home tab \| Font group) | | |
| Text, Align Horizontally | PPT 150 | Align Text buttons on Mini toolbar | Align Text buttons (Home tab \| Paragraph group) | Paragraph, Alignment box (Paragraph dialog box) | CTRL+R (right), CTRL+L (left), CTRL+E (center) |